# THEORY OF COMPUTATION

VIVEK KULKARNI
*Chief Architect*
*Persistent Systems Limited*
*Pune*

OXFORD
UNIVERSITY PRESS

Oxford University Press is a department of the University of Oxford. It furthers the University's objective of excellence in research, scholarship, and education by publishing worldwide. Oxford is a registered trademark of Oxford University Press in the UK and in certain other countries

Published in India by
Oxford University Press
Ground Floor, 2/11, Ansari Road, Daryaganj, New Delhi, 110 002, India



First published in 2013
Eighth impression 2019



ISBN-13: 978-0-19-808458-7
ISBN-10: 0-19-808458-7

Typeset in TimesLT-Std
by Ideal Publishing Solutions, Delhi
Printed in India by Repro India Ltd., Surat

*To,*
*The unknown source*
*of positive energy*
*that we call*
***God***

What is common among
*infinity* in mathematics,
*halting problem* in computer science, and
*God* in religion?

# Preface

A model of computation or an automaton is the mathematical abstraction of a solution. Any problem that can be solved by computers can be solved using a computational model. The theory of computation deals with how efficiently problems can be solved using such computational models. It is imperative for engineers to understand what is computable, and if it is computable, how it can be implemented on a machine. It is also important for them to understand how to design languages so as to write instructions that a computer can understand (formal languages), and also to design computing machines that can perform complex computations.

*Theory of Computation* entails three major theories—automata theory, computability theory (often termed Turing theory), and complexity theory. These three theories together are regarded as the *modern theory of computation*. Computability theory encompasses Turing machines, Markov algorithms, and Post machines. Finite automata, pushdown automata, grammars, etc., are discussed as part of automata theory. These are simpler models of computation that are useful for restricted applications and are limited in power unlike the Turing model. Today, Turing theory plays a fundamental role in the existence of stored- program computers (Von Neumann computers) and in the evolution of programming languages. A key feature of the Turing theory is that it does not rely on any external assumption and is therefore complete in itself. Complexity theory entails identifying and classifying problems on the basis of resource requirement (mostly, time to run and space) for their solutions.

This subject is the backbone of a number of areas in computer engineering—compiler construction, language processing, and operating system design—among many others. Nowadays, it is even used in the field of image processing for symbolic pattern recognition. The subject also has its roots in different programming paradigms such as procedural programming, object-oriented programming, and functional programming.

## ABOUT THE BOOK

***Theory of Computation*** is designed as a textbook for students pursuing undergraduate courses in computer science and engineering, and information technology. It can also be used as a reference for postgraduate courses in computer science and engineering. The emphasis of the book is on concepts such as automata theory, regular expressions, grammars, and Turing theory. This is further supported by working examples that provide knowledge about the practical applications of each.

The book also deals with theory related to the practical aspects of computations—problem solvability, program verification, and algorithmic solutions. It is assumed that the reader has some exposure to the concepts of data structures and algorithms. The book contains plenty of objective type questions and review questions for practice. An attempt has been made to deal with the complex concepts therein from an engineer's perspective.

## HOW TO USE THIS BOOK

It is presumed that the readers of the book have basic knowledge of algorithms and programming. The first three chapters are introductory and provide proper logical sequencing. Engineering graduates are introduced to programming much before they undergo the course on Theory of Computation. Keeping this in mind, Chapter 4 on Turing machines has been included before the other topics. A Turing machine is equivalent in computational power to any modern high-level programming language. Hence, students can easily pick up the concept of designing Turing machines as they are already trained to write algorithms. The chapter on finite state machines (which have minimal computational power) comes before the discussion on Turing machines (which are capable of computing any computable function) to provide better understanding of the limits of computability. Instructors who agree with this may follow the chapters in the order given in the book.

However, instructors who may want to use the course material in the conventional style may skip Chapter 4 after completing Chapters 1–3 and instead follow it up with Chapters 5–7, after which the remaining chapters can be taken up in the original sequence given in the book.

## KEY FEATURES

- The language has been kept simple throughout the textbook to help the reader understand complex mathematical concepts in an easy manner.
- Each procedure in the text is given in algorithmic form so that the reader can learn the concepts in any programming language.
- Each algorithm is simulated in detail for the reader to understand its working for all possible sets of input conditions. The emphasis is on solving the problem to the fullest, rather than for only a specific input condition.
- Several illustrations are provided in each chapter to support the text.
- Each chapter contains a good number of solved examples that help the reader in understanding the mechanics behind a particular concept.
- Numerous objective type questions are included, along with answers, at the end of each chapter, to help readers validate their understanding of key concepts.
- Specially designed review questions and exercises are provided towards the end of each chapter for practising various computations and their applications.
- The appendices include implementation details and C source codes for all key algorithms discussed in the book and five model question papers to help students prepare for their university examinations.
- All the end-chapter questions are annotated according to *Bloom's taxonomy* as Remember (R), Understand (U), Apply (A), Analyse (L), Evaluate (E), and Create (C), to indicate different levels of learning. This will help the readers test their level of understanding and enhance their problem-solving capabilities.

## ONLINE RESOURCES

The companion website of the book http://oupinheonline.com/book/kulkarni-theory-computation/9780198084587 contains the following online resources to aid the faculty and students using this book:

*For faculty*

- Chapter-wise PowerPoint slides
- Solutions manual containing answers to all the end-chapter review questions

*For students*

- Complete source codes for all the programs provided in the book
- Solutions to model test papers given in Appendix B

## ORGANIZATION OF THE BOOK

The book is divided into eleven chapters and two appendices. The following is a brief description of each of them:

*Chapter 1* covers the basic concepts of theoretical computer science such as alphabets, symbols, sets, relations, and languages, which are the prerequisites for the rest of the book.

*Chapter 2* gives details about finite state machines (FSMs), their capabilities, construction, applications, and related algorithms. It also details the finite automata (FA) concepts—deterministic finite automata (DFA), non-deterministic finite automata (NFA), and their inter-conversions.

*Chapter 3* discusses regular languages and their representation using regular expressions. It also elaborates on the relation between regular sets and FA, and the mechanics of constructing FA from a given regular expression and vice-versa. The chapter also talks about the applications of regular expressions and regular languages.

*Chapter 4* is devoted to the study of Turing machines (TMs). It explains how the algorithmic solutions for different types of problems can be obtained. This would otherwise be impossible using finite state machines. It also throws light on unsolvable and undecidable problems. It examines the concept of a universal Turing machine (UTM), which laid the foundation for the world's first digital computer.

*Chapter 5* comprises concepts related to the hierarchy of grammars and especially those related to context-free grammars (CFG). It gives detailed information on how to simplify a given grammar and the applications of CFG. The chapter also sets the relation between regular grammar, regular expressions, and finite automata.

*Chapter 6* takes a practical approach to dealing with pushdown automata (PDA). It helps in finding algorithmic solutions to problems that are solvable using a single stack. The chapter also throws light on the relation between CFG and PDA.

*Chapter 7* encompasses the use of grammars in compilers and language processors. It deals with LR grammars and the applications of this class of deterministic grammars in constructing SLR parsers, canonical-LR parsers, and LALR parsers.

*Chapter 8* provides details on obtaining algorithmic solutions using the Post machine (PM). It also comments on the relative powers of FA, PDA, PM, and TM.

*Chapter 9* explains the concept of undecidable problems related to TM and CFG. It emphasizes the limited computation ability of a computer due to the halting problem.

*Chapter 10* helps us comprehend the concepts related to algorithm complexity measures and their notations, and the classification of different types of problems as P, NP, NP-hard, and NP-complete.

*Chapter 11* aids in the understanding of production systems, Markov algorithm, and labelled Markov algorithm—a computational model different from TM.

*Appendix A* includes implementations of the key algorithms related to regular languages discussed in this text. It will help the reader apply the concepts learnt throughout the book.

*Appendix B* includes five model question papers. Their solutions are available at www.oupinheonline.com. This will help students prepare and practise for their end-semester examinations.

## ACKNOWLEDGEMENTS

I would like to thank all my well-wishers, students, and family members who encouraged me, directly or indirectly, during the course of writing this book. I appreciate the efforts put in by the editorial staff at Oxford University Press, India, whose support throughout the development of this book helped in making it more comprehensive. My special thanks to all the reviewers for their constructive criticism and valuable suggestions.

My honest gratitude towards the *gurus*—Alan Turing, David Gries, Bertrand Meyer, Edger Dijkstra, Luca Cardelli, Donald Knuth, John Hopcroft, Jeffrey Ullman, and Alfred Aho—for being lighthouses in guiding me in my journey in the sea of computer science.

Any comments or suggestions that can be incorporated in future editions of this book may be sent to me at vivek_kulkarni@yahoo.com.

**Vivek Kulkarni**

# Features of the Book

### Program Codes

Numerous program codes in C along with algorithms and their descriptions are provided to illustrate the implementation of the concepts learnt in the book.

```
void infix_to_postfix(char* input_string, char* output_string)
{
      int check_priority(char c);
      int i = 0, j = 0;
      char c;
      while (input_string[i] != '\0')
      {
            switch (input_string[i])
            {
                  case 'a' :
```

### Examples

Nearly 200 solved examples are provided in the text. These examples are supported with algorithms followed by simulation for all possible input conditions.

**Example 4.1** Consider an SFM for a TM with the following:

$$I = \{0, 1, b\!\!/\}$$
$$S = \{\alpha, \beta, \gamma = \text{halt}\}$$
$$D = \{L, R, N\}$$

The SFM is given in Table 4.3.

Find the purpose of the aforementioned TM, provided the initial TM is as given in Fig. 4.2.

### Production Systems

A separate chapter on production systems covering concepts such as Post–Markov–Thue (PMT) production system, Post canonical system, and Post normal form, etc., is provided in the book.

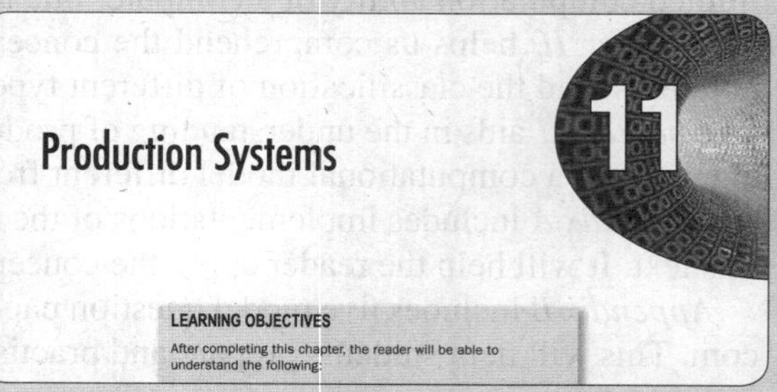

11
Production Systems
LEARNING OBJECTIVES
After completing this chapter, the reader will be able to understand the following:


### Notes

The text is supported by plenty of notes. These notes provide additional information related to the topic under discussion.

*Note*: We could use a simpler algorithm as well, whic
blank character $b\!\!/$; the remaining number of 0's gives t
destroy the input parameter, and hence we do not use

## Objective Questions

Over 100 objective type questions are given to help readers assess their theoretical knowledge. Answers to these questions are provided at the end of every chapter.

**Objective Questions**

(L) 6.1 If $L$ is a language generated by the grammar $S \rightarrow 0S0 \mid 00$, which of the following statements is true?

(a) It is possible tc construct a DPDA that accepts the lang:age $L$.

(b) It is not possible to construct a DPDA

## Review Questions

More than 250 review questions, provided at the end of every chapter, test the reader's understanding of the concepts.

**Review Questions**

(A) 6.1 Convert the given FA, $M = \{(q_0, q_1, q_2), (0, 1), \delta, (q_0), (q_2)\}$ into its equivalent PDA; the transition function $\delta$ for $M$ is defined as

| | 0 | 1 |
|---|---|---|
| $q_0$ | $q_0$ | $q_1$ |
| $q_1$ | $q_1$ | $q_2$ |
| $q_2$ | $q_2$ | $q_2$ |

## Appendices

Appendices containing C codes provide practical implementations of the concepts learnt in the book while model test papers are included for students to practise and test their understanding.

**Implementations**

**Model Question Papers**

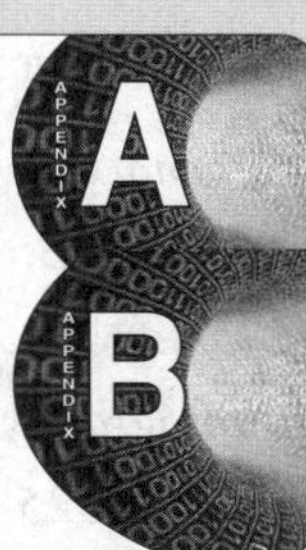


End-chapter exercises throughout the book are graded according to Bloom's taxonomy. The questions have been annotated based on different levels of testing—Remember (R), Understand (U), Apply (A), Analyse (L), Evaluate (E), and Create (C). This will help students check and enhance their problem-solving and analysing capabilities.

# Brief Contents

# Detailed Contents

# Preliminaries

**LEARNING OBJECTIVES**

After completing this chapter, the reader will be able to understand the following:

- Basic concepts, namely, symbols, alphabets, strings, and language
- Preliminaries related to set theory, relations, and set operations
- Closure properties of relations
- Basics of graph theory and properties
- Formal versus natural languages
- Introduction to mathematical induction

## 1.1 INTRODUCTION

Mathematical preliminaries, such as set theory, different operations on sets, relations, and graphs, and principle of mathematical induction, play an important role in efficiently grasping the concepts of theory of computation. The aim of this chapter is to acquaint the reader with all such necessary concepts and serve as a quick reference guide.

## 1.2 BASIC CONCEPTS

Let us start with the discussion of a few basic elements that are required for defining the mathematical abstraction of computation, which will be dealt with in more detail later in this book.

### 1.2.1 Symbol

A symbol is an abstract or user-defined entity. It is analogous to a *point* in geometry, and cannot be formally defined. For example, letters, digits, or any other characters that one wishes to consider as a part of the language that is being designed, are said to be symbols. It is the basic unit (or constituent) of any language.

### 1.2.2 Alphabet

An alphabet is a finite set of symbols. It is denoted by $\Sigma$.

For example:

$$D = \{0, 1, 2, \ldots, 9\}$$
$$X = \{+, -, *, /, \%\}$$
$$Y = \{a, b, D, \$, @\}$$

A 'finite set' has finite—bounded or limited—number of elements. For example, set $D$ given here consists of numbers 0 to 9, which is 10 elements; similarly, set $X$ and set $Y$ have five elements each.

Here, sets $D$, $X$, and $Y$ are all alphabets. Note that alphabet $Y$ contains heterogeneous (not of the same type) entities.

In natural languages such as English, we call each character (or symbol) an alphabet. However, in computer science, a slightly different nomenclature is followed: Here, a finite set of all symbols is known as an alphabet.

As the symbols are user-defined, one can decide any alphabet set of his/her choice and define a language over it. Just as English and French might have similar symbols, but Marathi and Japanese have altogether different symbols, programming (or formal) languages, such as C, C++, Java, and C#, might have differences in their respective set of symbols. Therefore, it is up to the language designer or programmer to choose suitable symbols.

### 1.2.3 String (or Word)

A string (or word) is defined as a finite sequence of symbols over a given alphabet. Here, the phrase 'over a given alphabet' implies that all the symbols of a string should come from the same alphabet set. One cannot expect a Marathi symbol appended with a Japanese symbol to make a word. A string must contain symbols from one given alphabet set in order to be meaningful.

We can formulate strings by appending a finite number of symbols from one given alphabet set into finite sequences. The set of all strings over a given alphabet is defined as a language. Strings can be composed into statements (or sentences) as per the grammar rules defined for a given language. Conventionally, strings are denoted by small case letters, such as $x$, $y$, $z$, $u$, $v$, or $w$.

The *prefix* of a string is any number of leading symbols of the string. For example, if string $x = abc$, then, the prefixes of $x$ are $\{\epsilon, a, ab, abc\}$; where, $\epsilon$ (epsilon) is an empty string with length zero, that is, $|\epsilon| = 0$. Any prefix other than the string itself is called a *proper prefix*. In this example, the three prefixes, that is, $\epsilon$, $a$, and $ab$ are proper prefixes of string $abc$.

The *suffix* of a string is any number of trailing symbols of the string. In this example, suffixes of string $x$ are $\{\epsilon, c, bc, abc\}$. Any suffix other than the string itself is called a *proper suffix*. Here, $\epsilon$, $c$, and $bc$ are proper suffixes of string $abc$.

If $w$ and $x$ are two strings, then $wx$ is called the *concatenation* of these two strings.

## 1.3 SETS

A set is defined as a collection of well-defined and distinct objects. These objects, or entities, are called the *members* (or *elements*) of the set.

For example, consider a set $A$ such that:

$$A = \{1, 2, 3\}$$

Here, 1, 2, and 3 are members of set $A$. The symbol $\in$ is used to indicate a member of a set. For example, '$1 \in A$' means '1 is a member of $A$'.

Similarly, we use the symbol $\notin$ to indicate that an element is not a member of a set. For example, '$4 \notin A$' means '4 is not a member of $A$'.

Any two sets $A$ and $B$ are considered equivalent if and only if they have precisely the same elements. For example, consider set $B = \{1, 2, 3\}$. We can see that set $A$ also contains the same elements as in set $B$; hence, they are equivalent.

Sets can be finite or infinite. For example, sets $A$ and $B$ have finite numbers of elements, and are hence, *finite* sets. However, consider a set of all integers $I = \{\ldots, -2, -1, 0, 1, 2, \ldots\}$; we can see that it is an unbounded set, containing infinite elements. Therefore, set $I$ is an *infinite* set.

### 1.3.1 Operations

There are many operations that are typically performed over sets, namely, union, intersection, difference, concatenation, and closure. Let us learn about each of them in detail.

#### *Set Union*

The union of two sets is defined as:

$$A \cup B = \{x \mid x \in A \text{ or } x \in B)$$

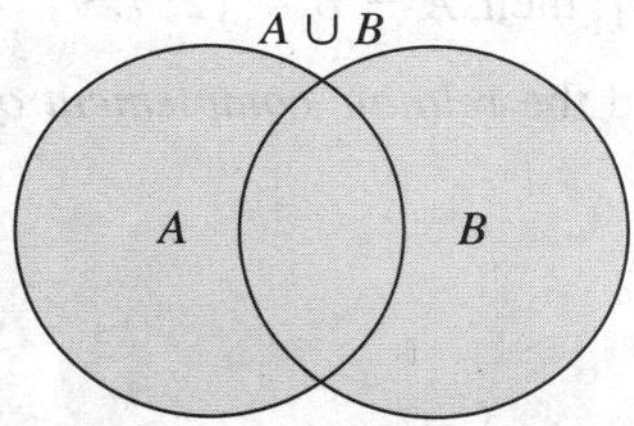


**Figure 1.1** Venn diagram for $A \cup B$

A union of two sets includes elements from both the sets. If a given element exists in both the sets, then it appears only once in their union—this operation is analogous to the Boolean OR operation. Any element in the union of two sets $A$ and $B$ is an element of either $A$ or $B$, or both. The Venn diagram for the union operation is shown in Fig. 1.1. The grey area in the figure represents the result of the union.

> ***Note***: Venn diagrams are used to represent logical relations among sets diagrammatically. A Venn diagram is constructed with a collection of simple closed curves drawn in a plane, each representing a set.

For example:

If $A = \{1, 2, 3\}$ and $B = \{1, 3, 4, 6\}$, then, $A \cup B = \{1, 2, 3, 4, 6\}$.

Note that although the elements 1 and 3 are members of both the sets $A$ and $B$, they appear only once in in the set $A \cup B$.

#### *Set Intersection*

The intersection of two sets is defined as:

$$A \cap B = \{x \mid x \in A \text{ and } x \in B)$$

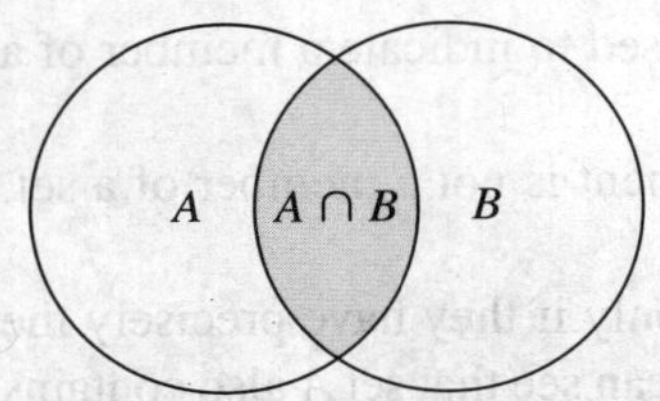


Figure 1.2 Venn diagram for $A \cap B$

An intersection is essentially the set of elements that exist in both the sets—this operation is analogous to the Boolean 'AND' operation; any element in the intersection of two sets $A$ and $B$ is an element of set $A$ as well as set $B$. The Venn diagram in Fig. 1.2 shows the intersection operation. The grey area in the figure represents the result of the intersection.

For example:

If $A = \{1, 2, 3\}$ and $B = \{1, 3, 4, 6\}$, then, $A \cap B = \{1, 3\}$.

### *Set Difference*

The difference of two sets is defined as:

$$A - B = \{x \mid x \in A \text{ and } x \notin B\}$$

or $$A - B = A - (A \cap B)$$

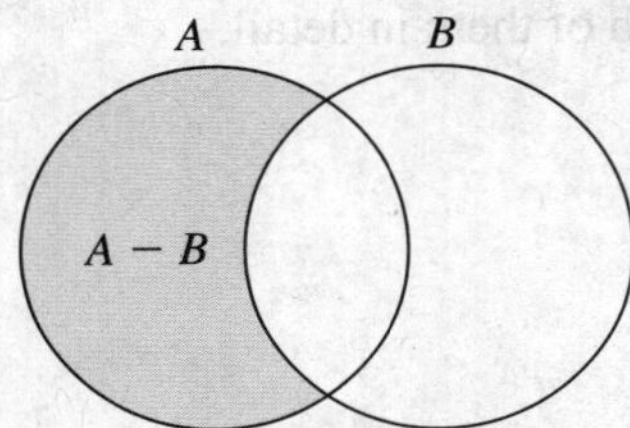


Figure 1.3 Venn diagram for $A - B$

Hence, the difference set $(A - B)$ includes those elements in set $A$ that are not present in set $B$. The Venn diagram in Fig. 1.3 represents the difference operation $(A - B)$. The grey area in the figure represents the result of the operation.

For example:

If $A = \{1, 2, 3, 7, 9\}$ and $B = \{1, 3, 4, 6\}$, then, $A - B = \{2, 7, 9\}$.

The set difference $(A - B)$ is also called the *relative complement of* B *in* A.

### *Cartesian Product*

The Cartesian product of two sets is defined as:

$$A \times B = \{(a, b) \mid a \in A \text{ and } b \in B, \forall a \,\&\, \forall b\}$$

It defines the association of every element of set $A$ with each element of set $B$.

For example:

$$\{1, 2\} \times \{\text{red, blue}\} = \{(1, \text{red}), (1, \text{blue}), (2, \text{red}), (2, \text{blue})\}$$
$$\{a, b\} \times \{a, b\} = \{(a, a), (a, b), (b, a), (b, b)\}$$

In the Cartesian product $(A \times B)$, each pair of the form $(a, b)$ is called an *ordered pair*, because there is an ordering imposed on how to formulate the pair; the first symbol comes from set $A$, while the second comes from set $B$. An ordered pair is also referred to as a *tuple*.

### *Subset*

If every member of set $A$ is a member of set $B$, then set $A$ is said to be a *subset* of set $B$.

We write this as $A \subseteq B$

Here, set $B$ is said to be the *superset* of set $A$.

For example: $\{1, 4\} \subseteq \{1, 2, 3, 4, 5\}$

Sets $A$ and $B$ are said to be equal if they have the same members.

This means, $A = B$, iff (if and only if) $A \subseteq B$ and $B \subseteq A$; that is, both are subsets of each other.

If $A$ is a subset of $B$, but not equal to $B$, then $A$ is said to be a *proper subset* of $B$, which is written as:

$A \not\subseteq B$ or $A \subset B$ (note the difference between $\subseteq$ and $\not\subseteq$ or $\subset$).

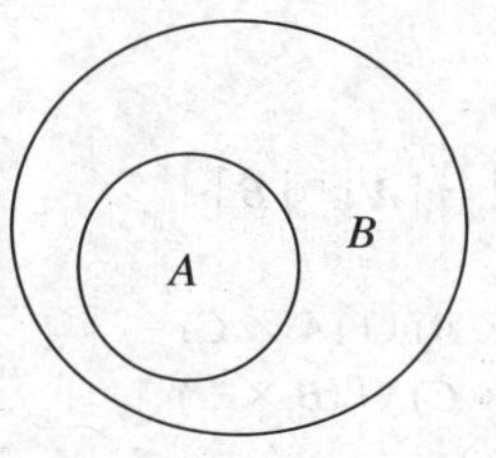


**Figure 1.4** Venn diagram for $A \not\subseteq B$ (proper subset)

In other words, if $A \subseteq B$, and $A \neq B$, that is, if every member of $A$ is present in $B$, and there is at least one member in $B$ that is not present in $A$, then $A$ is said to be a proper subset of $B$.

For example, the set $\{1, 4\}$ is a proper subset of the set $\{1, 2, 3, 4, 5\}$. Hence we can write:

$$\{1, 4\} \not\subseteq \{1, 2, 3, 4, 5\}$$

The Venn diagram in Fig. 1.4 represents a proper subset.

> ***Note:*** The empty set $\phi$ is a subset of every set, and every set is a subset of itself. For example, let us consider a set $A$. Then,
>
> $\phi \subseteq A$
> $A \subseteq A$

### *Power Set*

The power set of a set $A$ is the set of all subsets of $A$, including itself, and the empty set, $\phi$. It is denoted by $2^A$.

For example, if $A = \{0, 1, 2\}$,
then, $2^A = \{\phi, \{0\}, \{1\}, \{2\}, \{0, 1\}, \{0, 2\}, \{1, 2\}, \{0, 1, 2\}\}$

We see that $A$ in this example has 3 elements, while $2^A$ has $2^3 = 8$ elements. In short, if we denote the number of elements in $A$ as '$|A|$', then number of elements in $2^A$ is:

$$|2^A| = 2^{|A|}$$

In general, the power set of a finite set with $n$ elements has $2^n$ elements.

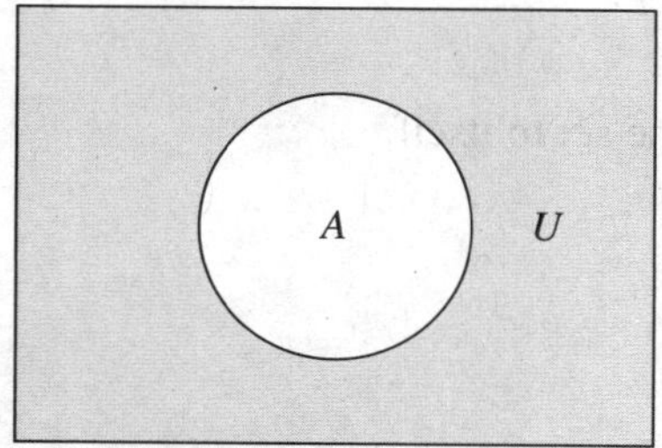


**Figure 1.5** Venn diagram for $A'$ (Complement of $A$)

### *Complement of a Set*

A set that encompasses all possible sets that can exist is called a *universal set*, and is denoted by $U$.

The complement of any set $A$ is defined as:

$$A' = U - A$$

Figure 1.5 shows a diagrammatic representation of the universal set $U$; the grey area denotes $A'$.

***Note***: Some important observations:

- $A \cup B = B \cup A$
- $(A \cup B) \cup C = A \cup (B \cup C)$
- $A \subseteq (A \cup B)$
- $A \cup A = A$
- $A \cup \phi = A$
- $A \cap B = B \cap A$
- $(A \cap B) \cap C = A \cap (B \cap C)$
- $(A \cap B) \subseteq A$
- $A \cap A = A$
- $A \cap \phi = \phi$
- $A \cap A' = \phi$
- $A \cup A' = U$
- $A - A = \phi$
- $U' = \phi$
- $\phi' = U$
- $A - B = A \cap B'$
- $|A \times B| = |B \times A| = |A| * |B|$
- $(A \times \phi) = \phi$
- $A \times (B \cup C) = (A \times B) \cup (A \times C)$
- $(A \cup B) \times C = (A \times C) \cup (B \times C)$

### Set Concatenation

Concatenation of two sets $A$ and $B$ is defined as:

$$A \cdot B = AB = \{x \mid x = ab, \forall a \in A \text{ and } \forall b \in B\}$$

This means that every string from set $A$ is concatenated with each string in set $B$.

For example, if $A = \{000, 111\}$, and $B = \{101, 010\}$,
then, $AB = \{000101, 000010, 111101, 111010\}$

Note that

1. $AB \neq BA$
   For these example sets,
   $BA = \{101000, 101111, 010000, 010111\}$
2. $A(BC) = (AB)C$, where, A, B, and C are sets.

### Set Closure

Closure of a set is defined as:

$$S^* = S^0 \cup S^1 \cup S^2 \ldots,$$

where, $S^0 = \{\epsilon\}$,
and $S^i = S^{i-1} \cdot S$; for $i > 0$.

Closure of a set is thus a repetitive concatenation of the set to itself.
For example:
If $S = \{01, 11\}$, then, from the definition:

$$S^0 = \{\epsilon\}$$
$$S^1 = S^0 \cdot S = \{\epsilon\} \cdot \{01, 11\} = \{01, 11\}$$
$$S^2 = S^1 \cdot S = \{01, 11\} \cdot \{01, 11\} = \{0101, 0111, 1101, 1111\}$$

$$
\begin{aligned}
S^3 &= S^2 \cdot S \\
&= \{0101, 0111, 1101, 1111\} \cdot \{01, 11\} \\
&= \{010101, 010111, 011101, 011111, 110101, 110111, 111101, 111111\}
\end{aligned}
$$

Thus, we have:

$$
\begin{aligned}
S^* &= S^0 \cup S^1 \cup S^2 \cup S^3 \cup \ldots \\
&= \{\epsilon, 01, 11, 0101, 0111, 1101, 1111, 010101, 010111, \ldots\}
\end{aligned}
$$

Similarly, if $S = \{0, 1\}$,
then, $S^* = \{\epsilon, 0, 1, 00, 01, 10, 11, 000, \ldots\}$.

> ***Note***: $S^*$ essentially records all possible combinations of the strings from set $S$. By definition, $S^*$ is an infinite set, even if the original set $S$ is finite.

### 1.3.2 Cardinality

Cardinality of a set is defined as the number of elements in the set. If $A$ is any set, then its cardinality is denoted as '$|A|$'.

1. Two sets $S_1$ and $S_2$ are said to have the same cardinality if there is one-to-one mapping of the elements of $S_1$ onto $S_2$. One-to-one mapping among the sets is defined if one element of a given set is associated with at most one element of the other set. Refer to Section 1.4 for more details.
2. For finite sets, if '$S_1$' is a proper subset of $S_2$, then $S_1$ and $S_2$ have different cardinalities. In fact, $|S_1| < |S_2|$.
3. Statement 2 is not always true for infinite sets. For example:

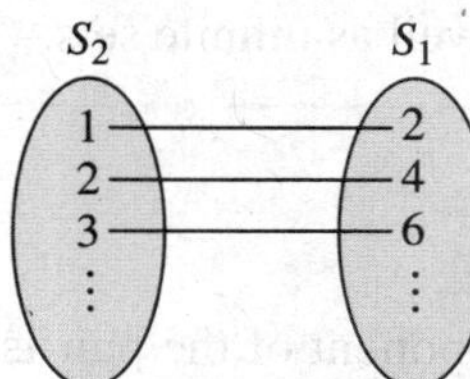

**Figure 1.6** Subset having same cardinality

$S_1 \Rightarrow$ set of positive even integers, that is, $S_1 = \{2, 4, 6, 8, \ldots\}$
$S_2 \Rightarrow$ set of all positive integers, that is, $S_2 = \{1, 2, 3, 4, 5, 6, 7, \ldots\}$

We observe that $S_1$ is a proper subset of $S_2$. However, they have the same cardinality, because there exists one-to-one and onto mapping of positive even integers and all positive integers (refer to Fig. 1.6). As we can observe, every element of $S_2$ is mapped to exactly one element of $S_1$ (one-to-one) and all the elements of $S_1$ are mapped to at least one element of $S_2$ (onto).

### 1.3.3 Countable and Uncountable Sets

Countability is the property which signifies the existence of a successor. For instance, given any integer $i$, one can always find its successor $i + 1$.

Finite sets are always countable. Likewise, infinite sets that can be placed in one-to-one correspondence with the set of natural numbers, $N = \{1, 2, 3, 4, 5, \ldots\}$, are said to be *countably infinite*, *countable*, or *enumerable*. For example, sets $S_1$ and $S_2$ in Fig. 1.6 are countably infinite.

Some infinite sets are *uncountable*. For example, let us consider the set of real numbers $R$:

One cannot find the successor for any given real number. This is because, between any two real numbers there is an infinite number of other real numbers.

Hence the set $R$ is an infinite set, which is uncountable.

**Example 1.1** Show that if set $S$ is uncountable and set $T$ is countable, then '$(S - T)$' is uncountable.

***Solution*** Let us consider the set $S$ as a set of real numbers, $R$, which is an uncountable set, and $T$ as the set of all integers, $I$, which is a countable set. As we know, all whole integers are included in the set of real numbers; hence, $I \subseteq R$.

If we consider the set $(R - I)$, only the whole integers will be removed from the set $R$; this means, $(R - I)$ still consists of all real numbers, except the whole integers. Hence, the property of the real numbers that between any two real numbers there are infinite real numbers still holds true, and the ability to find the successor is missing even with $(R - I)$.

Hence, $(R - I)$ still remains uncountable.

Therefore, if $S$ is uncountable and $T$ is countable, then $(S - T)$ is uncountable.

**Example 1.2** Show that any subset of a countable set is countable.

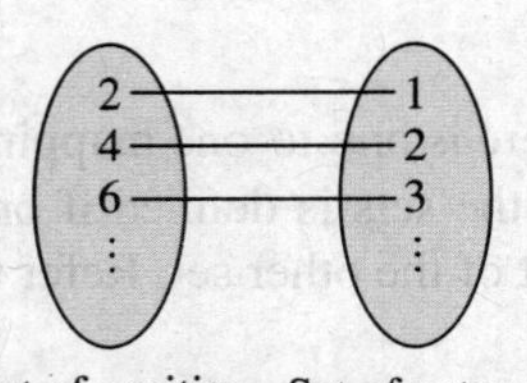


**Figure 1.7** Subset of a countable set is countable

***Solution*** It is known that any finite set is countable; and any subset of a finite set is also finite, and hence, countable.

We also need to prove the same for the countably infinite sets.

Let us consider the set of natural numbers, which is countably infinite. Let us consider its subset as the set of all positive even integers, which is also infinite.

As the set of all positive even integers can be placed in one-to-one correspondence with the set of natural numbers (refer to Fig. 1.7), it is also countably infinite.

Hence, the given statement is proved, for finite as well as infinite sets.

## 1.4 RELATIONS

A relation is a set of ordered pairs (or tuples), where the first component of the pair is from the set called the *domain*, and the second component is from the set called the *range* (or *co-domain*). In a relation, if the domain and range are the same set $S$, then we say that the relation is *on* set $S$ (refer to Fig. 1.8).

A *binary relation* can be defined as follows:

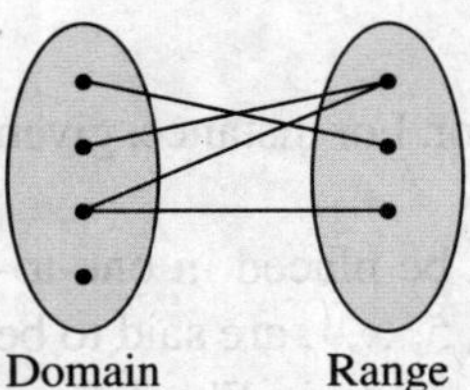


**Figure 1.8** Relation

$$_AR_B = \{(a, b) \mid a \in A \text{ and } b \in B\},$$

where, set $A$ is the domain set, and set $B$ is the range set.

For example, the relation in Fig. 1.7 can be listed as:

$$R = \{(2, 1), (4, 2), (6, 3), ...\}$$

***Note***: In this section, we will discuss binary relations. There is a more generic form of relations, which is known as n*-ary relations* or *finitary relations*.

Note that a relation is directional, and the order of $A$ and $B$ is important: this means that ${}_AR_B \neq {}_BR_A$.

If $R$ is a relation and $(a, b)$ is an ordered pair in $R$, then we write it as: ${}_aR_b$.
Every relation is a subset of the Cartesian product of domain and range sets:

$${}_AR_B \subseteq (A \times B)$$

A relation may encompass four types of associations: 'one-to-one', 'one-to-many', 'many-to-one', and 'many-to-many'. Figure 1.9 depicts these different associations pictorially.

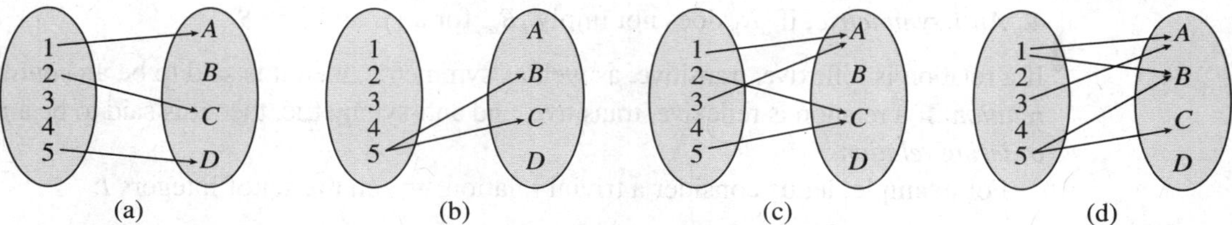


**Figure 1.9** Types of associations in a relation (a) One-to-one (b) One-to-many (c) Many-to-one (d) Many-to-many

The associations, one-to-one (Fig. 1.9a) and many-to-one (Fig. 1.9c), are referred to as *functions*, as they yield a single value from the range (or output) set. Domain and range can thus be respectively envisioned as *input* and *output* in terms of programming nomenclature. Most of the programming languages define functions, which have a single return value of some return type. For example, refer to the following function that returns the balance for a bank account.

```
Integer getBalance (String bankAccNumber);
```

Here, the set of all bank account numbers is a domain, while the integer amount that it returns is the range.

The associations, one-to-many (Fig. 1.9b) and many-to-many (Fig. 1.9d), are sometimes referred to as multi-valued functions, or set-valued functions. For example, every real number greater than zero has two square roots—the square roots of 4, for instance, are $\{+2, -2\}$.

If every member of the range set is associated with at least one element of the domain set, then the relation is considered as an *onto* relation; otherwise it is considered as an *into* relation. For any machine (or program) to be predictable (or deterministic), it is required to know what input (domain) generates what output. In other words, every machine (or program) needs to be an onto relation. We observe that none of the associations in Fig. 1.9 are onto relations—they are all into relations. Figure 1.10 depicts

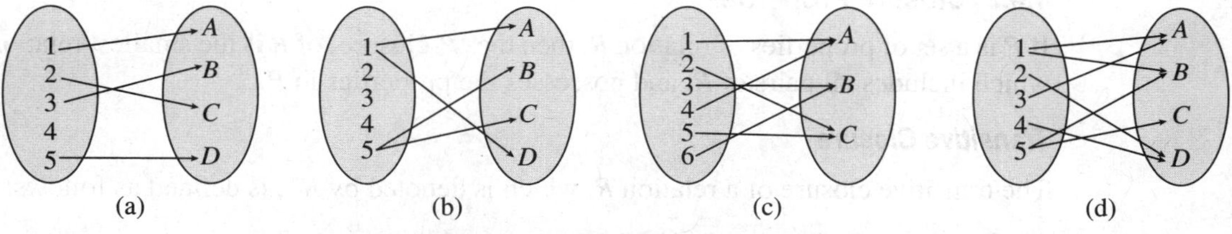


**Figure 1.10** Onto relations (a) One-to-one and onto (b) One-to-many and onto (c) Many-to-one and onto (d) Many-to-many and onto

onto relations; we observe that for every association in the figure, every member of the range set is associated with at least one input (domain) element.

### 1.4.1 Properties

If $R$ is a relation on set $S$ (domain and range is the same set $S$), then it is said to be:

1. *Reflexive*, if ${}_aR_a$ exists for all $a$ in $S$
2. *Transitive*, if ${}_aR_b$ and ${}_bR_c$ imply ${}_aR_c$, for all $a$, $b$, and $c$ in $S$
3. *Symmetric*, if ${}_aR_b$ implies ${}_bR_a$, for all $a$ and $b$ in $S$
4. *Anti-symmetric*, if ${}_aR_b$ does not imply ${}_bR_a$, for all $a$ and $b$ in $S$

If a relation is reflexive, transitive, as well as symmetric, then it is said to be an *equivalence relation*. If a relation is reflexive, transitive, and anti-symmetric, then it is said to be a *partial ordering relation*.

For example, let us consider a trivial relation '=' on the set of integers $I$:

1. It is reflexive because, $a = a, \forall a \in I$
2. It is transitive because, if $a = b$ and $b = c$, then $a = c, \forall a, \forall b, \forall c \in I$
3. It is symmetric because, if $a = b$ then $b = a, \forall a, \forall b \in I$

Therefore, it is an equivalence relation.

An equivalence relation on a set $S$ divides it into disjoint equivalence classes; the elements of each class (subset) have similar properties. This is the reason behind the origin of the concept of a class in object-oriented languages. For example, if we consider the operation to find: the 'remainder after dividing any decimal number by 3', we can distribute the digits {0, 1, 2, ..., 9} into three equivalent classes, namely, {0, 3, 6, 9}, {1, 4, 7}, and {2, 5, 8}, that are associated with the remainders 0, 1, and 2 respectively when divided by 3.

In case of partial ordering relations, anti-symmetry imposes some ordering on the set elements. For example, a partial ordering relation '<=' on the set of integers $I$, imposes ordering of the type:

$$\ldots <= -2 <= -1 <= 0 <= +1 <= +2 <= +3 <= \ldots$$

> ***Note***: '<' is actually a *total ordering* relation. It means that every two set elements are related to each other. Partial ordering is a more generic class, whereas total ordering is a specialization of the same. Binary tree is an example of a partial ordering relation, which means not every two nodes in the tree are related.

### 1.4.2 Closure Properties

If $P$ is a set of properties of relation $R$, then the '$P$-closure' of $R$ is the smallest relation $R_1$, which includes all pairs of $R$, and possesses the properties in $P$.

#### *Transitive Closure*

The transitive closure of a relation $R$, which is denoted by $R^+$, is defined as follows:

1. If $(a, b) \in R$, then $(a, b)$ is in $R^+$
2. If $(a, b) \in R^+$ and $(b, c) \in R^+$, then $(a, c)$ is in $R^+$

For example, let $S = \{1, 2, 3\}$, and $R$ is a relation on $S$, such that $R = \{(1, 2), (2, 2), (2, 3)\}$

Then, $R^+ = \{(1, 2), (2, 2), (2, 3), (1, 3)\}$

We can see that as (1, 2) and (2, 3) are the members of $R^+$, (1, 3) is also added.

### *Reflexive and Transitive Closure*

Reflexive and transitive closure of a relation $R$, which is denoted by $R^*$, is defined as follows:

$$R^* = R^+ \cup \{(a, a) \mid \forall a \in S\}, \text{ where } R \text{ is a relation defined over set } S.$$

For example, for the set $S$ and relation $R$:

$$R^* = \{(1, 1), (1, 2), (1, 3), (2, 2), (2, 3), (3, 3)\}$$

Here, (1, 1) and (3, 3) are added in addition to $R^+$, while (2, 2) is already a member.

### *Symmetric Closure*

Symmetric closure of a relation $R$ is defined as follows:

If $(a, b) \in R$, then $(a, b)$ and $(b, a)$ are in the symmetric closure of $R$.

Thus, symmetric closure of $R = R \cup \{(b, a) \mid (a, b) \in R\}$

In other words, symmetric closure of $R$ is the union of $R$ with its inverse relation, $R^{-1}$.
For example, let us consider relation, $R = \{(1, 2), (2, 2), (2, 3)\}$ over set $S = \{1, 2, 3\}$,
Then, symmetric closure of $R = \{(1, 2), (2, 2), (2, 3), (2, 1), (3, 2)\}$.

---

**Example 1.3** Find the transitive closure and symmetric closure of the relation:

$$R = \{(1, 2), (2, 3), (3, 4), (5, 4)\}$$

***Solution*** Transitive closure $R^+ = \{(1, 2), (2, 3), (3, 4), (5, 4), (1, 3), (2, 4), (1, 4)\}$

As (1, 2) and (2, 3) are members of $R^+$, (1, 3) is added. Similarly since (2, 3) and (3, 4) are members of $R^+$, (2, 4) is added; and since (1, 2) and (2, 4) are members of $R^+$, (1, 4) is added.

Symmetric closure of $R = \{(1, 2), (2, 3), (3, 4), (5, 4), (2, 1), (3, 2), (4, 3), (4, 5)\}$

Since (1, 2) is a member of $R$, (2, 1) is added. Similarly, (3, 2), (4, 3), and (4, 5) are also added in the symmetric closure of $R$.

---

## 1.5 GRAPHS

A graph is formally defined by a tuple:

$$G = (V, E)$$

where, $V$ = Finite set of vertices or nodes,
and $E = \{(v_1, v_2) \mid v_1, v_2 \in V\}$, that is, finite set of edges connecting the vertices.

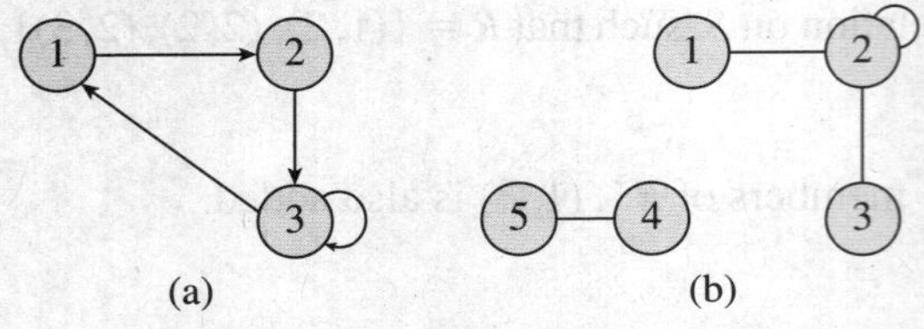


**Figure 1.11** Graphs (a) Undirected (b) Digraph

The set of edges $E$ is essentially a relation on set $V$, where the domain and range is the same set, that is, $V$. It is not always necessary that all the vertices need to be connected to some other vertex. One vertex can also be connected with many vertices, including itself. If every vertex in a graph is connected with every other vertex, then the graph is termed as a *completely connected* graph.

Graphs are generally denoted using a pictorial representation. They can be either directed or undirected (refer to Fig. 1.11).

For example, let us consider the graph $G$ in Fig. 1.11(a):

$$V = \{1, 2, 3, 4, 5\}$$
$$E = \{(1, 2), (2, 2), (2, 3), (4, 5)\}$$

The graph in Fig. 1.11(a) is undirected, as the edges have no directions. Two vertices are said to be *adjacent* if they are connected by an edge. The edges, which are just a pair of vertices and not ordered pairs, record only the adjacency in case of undirected graph.

One can also write set $E$ as:

$$E = \{(2, 1), (2, 2), (3, 2), (5, 4)\}$$

Since the graph is undirected, the order of vertices does not matter.

We observe that the graph in Fig. 1.11(a) is divided into two disjoint subsets of vertices based on the adjacency, $\{1, 2, 3\}$ and $\{4, 5\}$. Such a graph is called a *disjoint graph.*

A finite sequence of vertices, '$v_1, v_2, \ldots, v_k$', $k \geq 1$, such that there is an edge $(v_i, v_{i+1})$ for each $i$, $1 \leq i < k$, is called a *path*. The length of such a path is '$k - 1$', which denotes the number of edges on the path.

If $v_1 = v_k$, then the path is said to be cyclic, or a *cycle*. It is also referred to as a *self-loop* for the particular node.

If a path is not cyclic, then it is called a *linear path*. A linear path of $n$ nodes always consists of '$n - 1$' edges. For example, if we consider the linear path '$1 - 2 - 3$' in Fig. 1.11(a), we observe that ignoring the loop on node 2, the path consists of only 2 edges, namely, (1, 2) and (2, 3); and the number of nodes is three, namely, 1, 2, and 3.

### 1.5.1 Directed Graph (or Digraph)

A digraph is denoted by:

$$G = (V, E)$$

where, $V$: Finite set of vertices, and $E$: Finite set of *ordered pairs* of vertices called *arcs.*

An arc $(v_1, v_2)$ from vertex $v_1$ to vertex $v_2$ is denoted by: '$v_1 \rightarrow v_2$'; here, $v_1$ is called the *predecessor* of $v_2$, and $v_2$ is called the *successor* of $v_1$.

For example, let us refer to Fig. 1.11(b). For the graph given in the figure, we have:

$$V = \{1, 2, 3\}$$
$$E = \{(1, 2), (2, 3), (3, 3), (3, 1)\}$$

The order of vertices is important in a directed graph. The ordered pair (1, 2) denotes the edge from the node labelled '1' to the node labelled '2', and not vice versa.

> ***Note***: A graph can be defined as a relation over a set of vertices. It is not merely a diagram, but a visualization of the underlying relation.

### 1.5.2 Tree

A tree is a digraph with the following properties:

1. There exists one vertex called the *root* vertex that does not have a predecessor and from which there is a path to every other vertex in the graph.
2. Each vertex other than the root has exactly one predecessor; the immediate predecessor of a node is called the *parent node*.
3. The successors of each vertex are ordered from the left; the immediate successor of a node is called the *child node*,

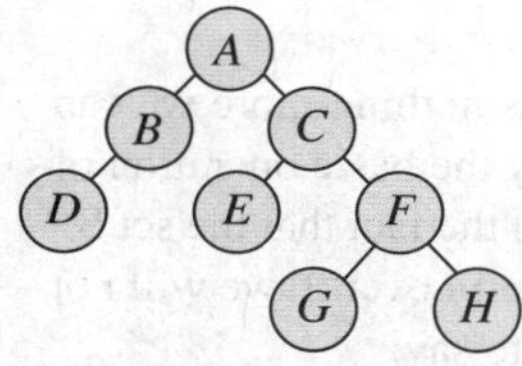

**Figure 1.12** A tree

Figure 1.12 shows an example tree, whose root vertex is *A*. Nodes *B*, *C*, and *F* are the interior vertices (or *intermediate nodes*), and *D*, *E*, *G*, *H* are the *leaf nodes* or *leaves*—these are nodes that do not have any successors. Node *C* is the parent of nodes *E* and *F*, while *E* and *F* are the child nodes of *C*. Further, node *C* is the *ancestor* of nodes *G* and *H*, as the path from *C* leads to *G* or *H*, while *G* and *H* are said to be the *descendants* of *C*. Similarly, *A* is the ancestor of *D*, and *D* is the descendant of *A*.

An ancestor is not generally the immediate parent, but could be the parent of either a parent or his/her parent, and so on. This might involve many levels, with the only condition that the path from the ancestor should lead to its descendants.

> ***Note***: Though a tree is a digraph, the edges in Fig. 1.12 are not drawn as arcs. This is because, in case of a tree, it is assumed that the edges are directed from parent to the children and not vice versa. They may or may not be shown by an arrow.

## 1.6 LANGUAGES

A language is defined as a set of strings comprising symbols from one alphabet.

Note that the null set $\phi$ and the set consisting of empty string, that is, $\{\epsilon\}$, are also considered as languages.

The set of all strings over a fixed alphabet $\Sigma$ is a language, and is denoted by $\Sigma^*$.

For example:

Let $\Sigma = \{a\}$; then,
$\Sigma^* = \{\epsilon, a, aa, aaa, \ldots\}$.

Similarly, let $\Sigma = \{0, 1\}$; then,

$$\Sigma^* = \{\epsilon, 0, 1, 00, 01, 10, 11, 000, \ldots\}$$

These are all possible combinations of 0's and 1's.

From the language $\Sigma^*$, if we exclude $\epsilon$, the empty word, the remaining set is a language denoted by $\Sigma^+$.

Thus, $\Sigma^+ = \{0, 1, 00, 01, 10, 11, 000, \ldots\}$

For any given alphabet $\Sigma$, any subset of $\Sigma^*$ is a language; hence, $\Sigma^*$ is considered as a universal language over $\Sigma$, as it includes all possible strings over $\Sigma$.

**Theorem 1.1**

For any alphabet $\Sigma$,

$$\Sigma^* = \Sigma^{**}$$

*Proof*

We know that language $\Sigma^*$ over an alphabet $\Sigma$ is the set of all possible strings of symbols from $\Sigma$.

Now, $\Sigma^{**} = (\Sigma^*)^*$ = Set of all possible combinations of strings of symbols over $\Sigma^*$.

Therefore, in turn, $\Sigma^{**}$ is the set of all possible string combinations of symbols from $\Sigma$.

Therefore, $\Sigma^* = \Sigma^{**}$

***Note***: As we have already included all possible strings from $\Sigma$, there is nothing more we can add. Hence, $\Sigma^*$ is pronounced as $\Sigma$-closure. All strings are obtained by the basic operation of concatenation of symbols to one another. The term *closure* comes from the fact that the set S* is closed, and no matter how many more concatenations we might perform over it, we will not get any additional strings than those in $\Sigma^*$. We can extend this further to say:

$\Sigma^* = \Sigma^{**} = \Sigma^{***} = \Sigma^{****}$, and so on.

### 1.6.1 Formal Language

The language we have defined is the minimal form of formal language. The word *formal* refers to the fact that all the rules for the language are explicitly stated in terms of the possible strings of symbols that can occur, and the valid sentence forms. In other words, semantics (or the meaning) of any statement in a formal language is directed by the *syntax* (or *grammar*, or *form*) of the statement.

A formal language is considered as symbols on paper and not as expressions of ideas as in 'natural languages' like English. In natural languages, a single statement might mean different things when ultered differently and in different situations. However, in formal languages, any statement always has the same meanings, as directed by the syntax.

All programming languages are formal languages. The term formal used here emphasises that the form of the strings of symbols has more importance than anything else.

## 1.7 MATHEMATICAL INDUCTION

Mathematical induction is a method of mathematical proof typically used to demonstrate that a given statement, $S(n)$ is true for all values of $n = 1, 2, 3, 4, \ldots$

**Principle** Let $S(n)$ denote the statement to be proved involving variable $n$, and let us suppose:

1. $S(1)$ is true;
2. If $S(k)$ is true for $n = k$, and '$S(k + 1)$' is also true, then, $S(n)$ is true for all values of $n$.

A statement is proved using induction by showing that the first statement in the infinite sequence of statements is true, and then proving that if any one statement in the infinite sequence of statements is true, then so is the next one. This is based on the successor relationship among the infinite sequence of statements.

The following steps are involved in inductive proof:

***Induction basis*** This step tests if the statement, $S(n)$ holds true when $n$ is equal to its lowest possible value. Usually, $n = 0$ or $n = 1$.

***Induction hypothesis (or inductive hypothesis)*** In this step, it is assumed that $S(n)$ is true for some value of $n$, that is, for $n = k$.

***Inductive step*** This step tests if the statement also holds when $n = k + 1$. If the step is true for $n = k + 1$, then it is true for all values of $n$.

---

**Example 1.4** Prove that for all natural numbers $n$, $1 + 3 + 5 + \cdots + (2n - 1) = n^2$

***Solution*** Let us prove the statement using mathematical induction.

*Induction basis:* Let us first prove the statement for $n = 1$, which is the lowest possible value for $n$. Substituting $n = 1$, we get $1 = 1^2$, which is true.

*Inductive hypothesis:* Let us assume that this statement is true for some positive integer $k$, that is, for $n = k$. That means, the following statement is assumed to be true:

$$1 + 3 + 5 + \cdots + (2k - 1) = k^2$$

*Inductive step:* Now we need to prove the statement for $n = k + 1$. From the inductive hypothesis, we have:

$$1 + 3 + 5 + \cdots + (2k - 1) = k^2$$

Therefore, if $n = k + 1$, we have:

$$\begin{aligned}
&[1 + 3 + 5 + \cdots + (2k - 1)] + [2(k + 1) - 1] \\
&= k^2 + [2(k + 1) - 1] \\
&= k^2 + (2k + 2 - 1) \\
&= k^2 + 2k + 1 \\
&= (k + 1)^2
\end{aligned}$$

Thus, the given statement is true for $n = k + 1$ as well; so, by the principle of mathematical induction, we conclude that it is true for all $n = 1, 2, 3, \ldots$

**Example 1.5** Prove that for all natural numbers $n$, $1 + 2 + 3 + \cdots + n = n(n + 1) / 2$

***Solution*** Let us prove the statement using mathematical induction:

*Induction basis:* Let us first prove the statement for $n = 1$, which is the lowest possible value for $n$. Substituting $n = 1$, we get $1 = 1(1 + 1) / 2 = 1(2) / 2 = 1$; hence it is true for $n = 1$.

*Inductive hypothesis:* Let us assume that this statement is true for some positive integer $k$, that is, $n = k$. This means, the following statement is assumed to be true:

$$1 + 2 + 3 + \ldots + k = k(k + 1) / 2$$

*Inductive step:* Now we need to prove the statement for $n = k + 1$. From the inductive hypothesis, we have:

$$1 + 2 + 3 + \ldots + k = k(k + 1) / 2$$

Therefore, for $n = k + 1$, we have:

$$\begin{aligned} & 1 + 2 + 3 + \cdots + k + k + 1 \\ &= [k(k + 1) / 2] + (k + 1) \\ &= [k(k + 1) / 2] + 2(k + 1) / 2 \\ &= (k + 1)(k + 2) / 2 \\ &= (k + 1)[(k + 1) + 1] / 2 \end{aligned}$$

Thus, the given statement is true for $n = k + 1$ as well; so, by the principle of mathematical induction, we conclude that it is true for all $n = 1, 2, 3, \ldots$

## SUMMARY

A *symbol* is an abstract or a user-defined entity. It is analogous to a *point* in geometry, and cannot be formally defined. For example, letters, digits, or any other characters that one wishes to consider as a part of the language that is being designed, are said to be symbols. It is the basic unit (or constituent) of any language.

An 'alphabet' is a finite set of symbols. It is denoted by $\Sigma$. For example, $D = \{0, 1, 2, \ldots, 9\}$. As the symbols are user defined, one can decide any alphabet set of his/her choice and define a language over it.

A *string* or *word* is defined as a finite sequence of symbols over a given alphabet. Here, the phrase, 'over a given alphabet', means that all the symbols of a word should come from the same alphabet set. A string must contain the symbols from only one given alphabet in order to be meaningful. We can formulate words by appending a finite number of symbols from one given alphabet set into finite sequences.

The *prefix* of a string includes any number of leading symbols of the string. For example, if string $x = abc$, then the prefixes of $x$ are: $\epsilon$, $a$, $ab$, and $abc$. The prefix of a string, other than the string itself, is called *proper prefix*. In this example, the three prefixes $\{\epsilon, a, ab\}$ are proper prefixes of $abc$.

The *suffix* of a string is any number of trailing symbols of the string. For this example, suffixes of string $x$ are: $\epsilon$, $c$, $bc$, and $abc$. The suffix of a string, other than itself, is called *proper suffix*. In this example: $\epsilon$, $c$, and $bc$ are proper suffixes of string $abc$.

If $w$ and $x$ are two strings, then $wx$ is called the *concatenation* of these two strings.

A *set* is a collection of well-defined and distinct objects. These objects or entities in the set are called the *members* (or *elements*) of the set.

Typical operations on sets include: union, intersection, difference, and complement. Other operations include concatenation and closure.

If every member of set $A$ is a member of set $B$, then $A$ is said to be a *subset* of $B$; and $B$ is called the *superset* of $A$.

The *power set* of a set $A$ is the set of all subsets of $A$, including $A$ itself and the empty set $\phi$. It is written as $2^A$.

The *Cartesian product* of two sets is defined as:

$A \times B = \{(a, b) \mid a \in A \text{ and } b \in B, \forall a \;\&\; \forall b\}$

It defines the association of every element of set $A$ with each element of set $B$.

For example:

$\{1, 2\} \times \{\text{red, blue}\} = \{(1, \text{red}), (1, \text{blue}), (2, \text{red}), (2, \text{blue})\}$

*Cardinality* of a set is defined as the number of elements in the set. If $A$ is any set, then its cardinality is denoted by $|A|$.

Countability is the property which signifies the existence of a successor. For example, given any integer $i$ one can always find its successor, as '$i + 1$'. Finite sets are always countable. Infinite sets that can be placed in one-to-one correspondence with the set of natural numbers, $N = \{1, 2, 3, 4, 5, \ldots\}$, are said to be *countably infinite*, or just *countable* or *enumerable*.

Some infinite sets are uncountable. For example, the set of real numbers $R$ is infinite and uncountable, as one cannot find the successor for any given real number. This is because between any two real numbers, there are infinite numbers of other real numbers. Hence, the set of real numbers in uncountable.

A *relation* is a set of ordered pairs (or tuples), where the first component of the pair is from the set called the *domain*, and the second component is from the set called the *range* (or *co-domain*). In a relation, if the domain and range are the same set S, then we say that the relation is *on* set S.

A *binary relation* is defined as:

${}_AR_B = \{(a, b) \mid a \in A \text{ and } b \in B\}$,

where, set $A$ is the domain set and set $B$ is the range set.

Every relation is a subset of the Cartesian product of the domain and range set:

${}_AR_B \subseteq (A \times B)$

A relation can encompass four types of associations: one-to-one, one-to-many, many-to-one, and many-to-many. The domain and range can be respectively visualized as *input* and *output*, in terms of programming nomenclature.

If $R$ is a relation on set $S$ (domain and range is the same set $S$), it is said to be:

1. *Reflexive*, if ${}_aR_a$ exists for all $a$ in $S$
2. *Transitive*, if ${}_aR_b$ and ${}_bR_c$ imply ${}_aR_c$, for all $a$, $b$, and $c$ in $S$
3. *Symmetric*, if ${}_aR_b$ implies ${}_bR_a$, for all $a$ and $b$ in $S$
4. *Anti-symmetric*, if ${}_aR_b$ does not imply ${}_bR_a$, for all $a$ and $b$ in $S$

If a relation is reflexive, transitive, as well as symmetric, then it is said to be an *equivalence relation*. If a relation is reflexive, transitive, and anti-symmetric, then it is called a *partial ordering relation*.

*Transitive closure of a relation R*, that is, $R^+$, is defined as:

1. If $(a, b) \in R$, then $(a, b)$ is in $R^+$
2. If $(a, b) \in R^+$ and $(b, c) \in R^+$, then $(a, c)$ is in $R^+$

*Reflexive and Transitive closure of a relation R*, that is, $R^*$, is defined as:

$R^* = R^+ \cup \{(a, a) \mid \forall a \in S\}$ where $R$ is a relation defined over set $S$.

*Symmetric closure of a relation R* is defined as:

If $(a, b) \in R$, then $(a, b)$ and $(b, a)$ are in the symmetric closure of $R$

Thus, symmetric closure of $R = R \cup \{(b, a) \mid (a, b) \in R\}$. In other words, the symmetric closure of $R$ is the union of $R$ with its inverse relation, $R^{-1}$.

A 'graph' is formally defined by a tuple:

$G = (V, E)$

where, $V$ = Finite set of vertices or nodes

$E = \{(v_1, v_2) \mid v_1, v_2 \in V\}$, that is, finite set of edges connecting the vertices.

In case of a directed graph (or digraph), set $E$ is a finite set of ordered pairs of vertices called *arcs*. An arc ($v_1$, $v_2$) from vertex $v_1$ to vertex $v_2$ is denoted by, '$v_1 \rightarrow v_2$'; here, $v_1$ is called the *predecessor* of $v_2$, and $v_2$ is called the *successor* of $v_1$.

A graph is defined as a relation over the set of vertices. It is not merely a diagram, but a visualization of the underlying relation.

A *tree* is a digraph having the following properties:

1. There exists one vertex called the *root* vertex that does not have a predecessor and from which, there is a path to every other vertex in the graph.
2. Each vertex other than the root has exactly one predecessor.
3. The successors of each vertex are ordered from the left.

A *language* is defined as a set of strings of symbols from one alphabet. The null set $\phi$ and the set consisting of empty string, that is, $\{\epsilon\}$, are also languages.

The set of all strings over a fixed alphabet $\Sigma$ is a language, and is denoted by $\Sigma^*$.

For example:

Let $\Sigma = \{a\}$; then,

$\Sigma^* = \{\epsilon, a, aa, aaa, ...\}$

For any given alphabet $\Sigma$, any subset of $\Sigma^*$ is a language. Hence, $\Sigma^*$ is considered as a universal language over $\Sigma$, as it includes all possible strings over $\Sigma$.

*Mathematical induction* is a method of mathematical proof, typically used to demonstrate that a given statement, $S(n)$ is true for all values of $n = 1, 2, 3, 4, ...$

The principle of mathematical induction involves the following steps:

1. Test whether the statement is true for $n = 1$. If $S(1)$ is true, then we proceed to the next step.
2. Assume that the statement is true for some value of $n$, that is, for $n = k$. This means, we assume $S(k)$ is true.
3. Test whether the statement is true for '$n = k + 1$'. If $S(k + 1)$ is true, it means that the statement is true for all values of $n$.

## EXERCISES

This section lists a few unsolved problems, to help the readers understand the topic better and practise examples related to the preliminaries.

### Objective Questions

(U) 1.1 A relation $R$ is defined on the set of integers as $_xR_y$ if f$(x + y)$ is even. Which of the following statements is true?

(a) $R$ is not an equivalence relation.
(b) $R$ is an equivalence relation having one equivalence class.
(c) $R$ is an equivalence relation having two equivalence classes.
(d) $R$ is an equivalence relation having three equivalence classes.

(U) 1.2 If $A$ and $B$ are sets, then which of the following statements is false?

(a) $(A \cup B) \cup C = A \cup (B \cup C)$
(b) $A \subseteq (A \cup B)$
(c) $(A \cap B) \cap C = A \cap (B \cap C)$
(d) $(A \cup B) \times C \neq (A \times C) \cup (B \times C)$

(U) 1.3 The less than relation '$<$' on real numbers is:

(a) A partial ordering relation since it is asymmetric and reflexive
(b) A partial ordering relation since it is anti-symmetric and reflexive
(c) Not a partial ordering relation since it is not asymmetric and not reflexive
(c) Not a partial ordering relation since it is not asymmetric and is reflexive
(e) None of these

Remember (R), Understand (U), Apply (A), Analyse (L), Evaluate (E), and Create (C)

Ⓤ 1.4 Which of the following statements is true for the relation $R = A \times B$, where $A = \{0\}$, and $B = \{1, 2, 3\}$?

S1: $R$ is reflexive

S2: $R$ is transitive

S3: $R$ is symmetric

S4: $R$ is anti-symmetric

(a) S1 and S2
(b) S1 only
(c) S2 only
(d) S2 and S3
(e) S4 only
(f) S3 only
(g) None of these
(h) All of these

Ⓤ 1.5 State whether the following statement is true or false:

'A tree is a partial ordering relation.'

Ⓡ 1.6 If $R$ is a relation, then $R^*$ means ______________.

## Review Questions

Ⓡ 1.1 Define the following and give suitable examples.

(a) Cardinality of a set
(b) Closure of a set
(c) Alphabet
(d) Symbol
(e) Language
(f) Word

Ⓐ 1.2 If $R = \{(a, b), (b, c), (c, a)\}$ is a relation over $\{a, b, c\}$, find $R^+$ and $R^*$.

Ⓛ 1.3 Differentiate between natural and formal languages.

Ⓐ 1.4 Find the transitive closure and the symmetric closure of the relation:

$$R = \{(1, 2), (2, 3), (3, 4), (5, 4)\}$$

Ⓐ 1.5 Show that 'the set of real numbers $R$ is not countable'.

Ⓤ 1.6 Let $L$ be a language. It is clear from its definition that $L^+ \subseteq L^*$. Under what circumstances are they equal?

Ⓤ 1.7 Show that if $S$ uncountable and $T$ is countable, then $S - T$ is uncountable.

Ⓤ 1.8 Show that any equivalence relation $R$ on a set $S$ partitions $S$ into disjoint equivalent classes.

Ⓐ 1.9 Find the transitive closure and reflexive and transitive closure for the following relation set:

$$R = \{(a, b), (a, c), (c, d), (a, a), (b, a)\}$$

Ⓐ 1.10 For the sets $A = \{a, b, c, d\}$ and $B = \{c, d, e\}$, find the following:

(a) $A - B$
(b) $A \times B$
(c) $2^B$ (power set)

**Answers to Objective Questions**

1.1. (c) 1.2. (d) 1.3. (b) 1.4. (e) 1.5. True 1.6. reflexive and transitive closure of $R$

# 2 Finite State Machines

## LEARNING OBJECTIVES

After completing this chapter, the reader will be able to understand the following:

- Concept and notations of finite state machine (FSM)
- Formalism of FSM as finite automata (FA)
- FA as language acceptor (or recognizer)
- Deterministic finite automata (DFA) and non-deterministic finite automata (NFA)
- Equivalence of NFA and DFA
- DFA minimization
- NFA with $\epsilon$-transitions
- Equivalence of NFA with $\epsilon$-transitions, NFA, and DFA
- Moore and Mealy machines and their equivalence
- Moore's algorithm for FSM equivalence
- Properties and limitations of FSM
- Two-way finite automata

## 2.1 INTRODUCTION

The term finite state machine (FSM) is used for all such programs that have a finite number of functions, but do not have any memory for storing the intermediate results. It is a simple and primitive computational model, which has many applications, but limited power due to lack of memory.

The term 'machine' is used throughout this book to refer to predictable programs, whose behaviour can be understood without executing them. The term 'state' is typically used for different functions that are constituents of a program. A 'program', here, is defined as a collection of unique functions, each one performing an atomic and unique task. A program is said to be completely executed when the task of each function is performed one by one, in order, until the last.

### 2.1.1 Concept of Basic Machine

As we know, every machine ideally takes an input and produces an output. A basic machine recognizes an input from an input set, *I*, and produces an output from an output set, *O*, where *I* and *O* are finite sets. This definition is more like an abstraction of any machine or program: Here, we are not interested in what is happening inside the machine, that is, *how* the output is produced by the machine; we are only interested in *what* output it is producing. Effectively, such abstraction of machine behaviour is more like representing the machine as a mapping function between the input and the output sets, showing the output that is generated after providing a certain input.

A basic machine can be viewed as a function, which maps the input set, *I*, to the output set, *O*. This function is known as a machine function (MAF); it is expected to be an 'onto' relation:

$$\text{MAF}: I \rightarrow O$$

Let us look at a few examples of a basic machine:

1. All logic gates, such as AND, and OR, can be viewed as basic machines. For example, let us consider the AND gate where,

   $I = \{(0, 0), (0, 1), (1, 0), (1, 1)\}$
   $O = \{0, 1\}$

   Table 2.1 shows the MAF for the aforementioned AND gate.

   **Table 2.1** MAF for AND gate

| *I* | (0, 0) | (0, 1) | (1, 0) | (1, 1) |
|---|---|---|---|---|
| *O* | 0 | 0 | 0 | 1 |

   Here, we observe that the input is a combination of multiple input symbols. Such a machine is also called a 'combinational machine'.
2. A decimal-to-binary converter can be treated as a basic machine having the following inputs and outputs:

   $I = \{0, 1, 2, \ldots\}$
   $O = \{000, 001, 010, \ldots\}$

3. A weighing machine that we normally see at railway stations or bus stands is also a good example of a basic machine. Here the output is the weight ticket, which is obtained after inserting a coin:

   $I = \{\text{coin}\}$
   $O = \{\text{printed weight ticket}\}$

4. Electrical appliances, such as electric fans, are basic machines with regulator positions as the input set, and the speed in revolutions per minute (rpm) as the output set:

   $I = \{\text{pos1, pos2, pos3, pos4, pos5}\}$
   $O = \{\text{speed A, speed B, speed C, speed D, speed E}\}$

In all the aforementioned examples, we see that there is an in input, which, after going into the machine, gives a particular output. Thus, ignoring the internal details and concerning only with inputs and outputs, every machine can be viewed as a basic machine. A basic machine performs only a table look-up from a finite-sized table called the MAF table. This table has neither memory nor internal states.

It is impossible to create a virtual table that can store infinite word sets in a tabular form. Let us consider a basic machine that produces output in the form of 'yes' or 'no' to check whether a given word is from a given infinite language. This is possible only with the help of a machine having internal states; on reading the input, the machine selects a particular path from the initial state to reach the final state, and produces a valid output. Such a machine has a finite number of internal states, and is called an FSM.

## 2.2 FINITE STATE MACHINE

In case of an FSM, unlike for a basic machine, we are concerned with the machine (or program) behaviour, especially, regarding *what* internal states the machine has, and *how* each state behaves on receiving different intermediate inputs.

An FSM is represented by a pair of functions, namely:

Machine function: MAF: $I \times S \rightarrow O$
State transition function: STF: $I \times S \rightarrow S$

where, $S$: Finite set of internal states of the machine
$I$: Finite set of input symbols (or input alphabet)
$O$: Finite set of output symbols (or output alphabet)

If we know the current state of the machine and the current input symbol, the MAF tells us the (intermediate) output; and the STF indicates the next state of the machine. Both these functions collectively define an FSM. The behaviour of such a machine can be completely determined (or predicted) provided its initial state and the input are known.

### 2.2.1 Examples

Let us try to understand the concept through a few simple examples:

---

**Example 2.1** Construct a binary adder as a finite state machine.

***Solution*** We need to construct two tables, namely MAF and STF, to represent the working of a binary adder.

The input, being in binary form, consists of two symbols, either 0, or 1. For a binary adder, the input set, $I$, is a combination of the two input symbols, that is, a pair of input symbols, as shown here:

$$I = \{(0, 0), (0, 1), (1, 0), (1, 1)\}$$

A finite set of states, S, is defined as:

$$S = \{\text{carry, no carry}\}.$$

Initially, the machine is always in the 'no carry' state; and at any given time, the machine may be in one of the two states, that is, 'carry' or 'no carry', depending on the result of the previous addition.

Let us consider a situation in which the current state of the machine is 'carry' and the current input is '(0, 0)'. Then the output will be 0 + 0 + 1 (carry) = 1, and the machine moves to the next state, which will be a 'no carry' state. Similarly, if the current state of the machine is 'no carry' and the input is '(1, 1)', then the output will be 1 + 1 + 0 (no carry) = 0. The machine again moves to the next state, that is, the 'carry' state.

Thus, the addition of the two input symbols at any given point depends not only on the current input, but also on the current state of the machine. For example, '(0 + 0)' is not always 0; it can also be 1, if the machine is in the 'carry' state, as we have already seen.

The MAF and STF for the binary adder are shown in Table 2.2.

**Table 2.2** MAF and STF for binary adder (a) MAF: $I \times S \rightarrow O$ (b) STF: $I \times S \rightarrow S$

| $I$ \ $S$ | Carry | No carry |
|---|---|---|
| (0, 0) | 1 | 0 |
| (0, 1) | 0 | 1 |
| (1, 0) | 0 | 1 |
| (1, 1) | 1 | 0 |

(a) (Outputs)

| $I$ \ $S$ | Carry | No carry |
|---|---|---|
| (0, 0) | No carry | No carry |
| (0, 1) | carry | No carry |
| (1, 0) | carry | No carry |
| (1, 1) | carry | carry |

(b) (Next states)

Let us simulate the working of the binary adder that we have designed for adding two numbers: 1011 and 1111. The initial state will always be 'no carry' when we begin the addition. The simulation is shown in Fig. 2.1.

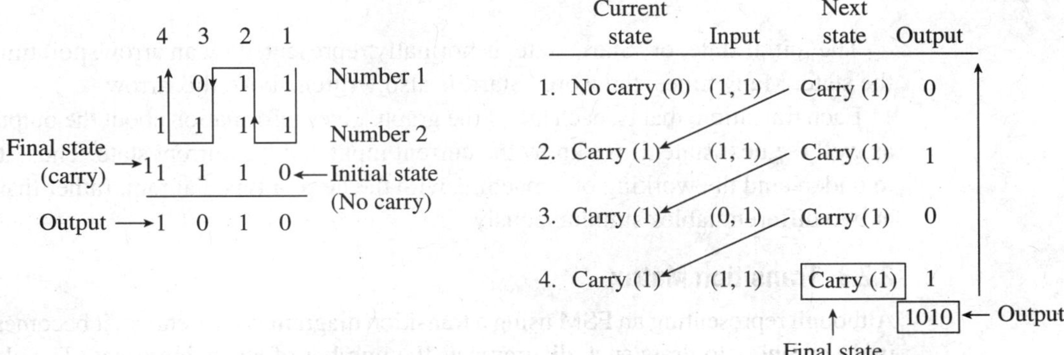


**Figure 2.1** Binary adder simulation for input '1011 + 1111'

The two input binary numbers considered for simulation in Fig. 2.1 are 1011 and 1111. The first pair of input symbols is (1, 1), which is obtained from the least significant bits (right-most bits) of both the binary input numbers. 'No carry' is the initial state, or the beginning state. Upon reading the input (1, 1), the FSM makes a transition from 'no carry' state to 'carry' state, and generates an intermediate output, 0. Then, it reads the next pairs of digits—(1, 1), (0, 1), and (1, 1)—and transits at every stage, generating some intermediate output. Thus, the addition of the two input binary numbers yields the output '1010' with carry. Figure 2.1 explains each step in detail.

A more convenient representation of the FSM is possible using a transition diagram instead of state tables.

### 2.2.2 Transition Diagram (or Transition Graph)

A transition diagram, also known as transition graph, is a directed graph (or digraph), whose vertices correspond to the states of an FSM and the directed edges correspond to the transitions from one state to another on reading the input symbol, which is written above the directed edge.

Sometimes, the input symbol is also followed by a punctuation character, such as '/' or '→', followed by the output symbol. For example, '(0, 0) → 1'; this can also be written as '(0, 0) / 1'. Figure 2.2 shows the transition graph for the binary adder constructed in Example 2.1.

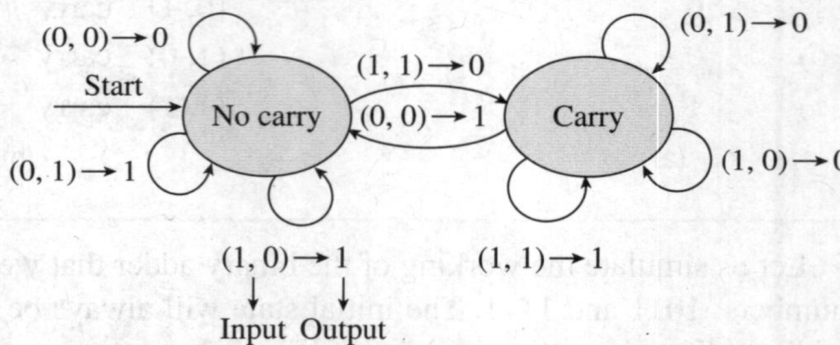


**Figure 2.2** Transition graph (TG) for binary adder

The initial state, or 'Start' state, is normally represented by an arrow, pointing towards the state. Many times, the word 'Start' is also written above this arrow.

Each transition, that is, each arc of the graph, gives information about the output symbol as well the next state, if we know the current input and the current state. Thus, it is easier to understand the working of a machine with the help of this diagram, rather than looking at two different tables simultaneously.

### 2.2.3 Transition Matrix

Although representing an FSM using a transition diagram is convenient, it becomes increasingly complex to draw such diagrams as the number of states increases. The alternative, in such cases, is to use a transition matrix.

A transition matrix has its rows and columns labelled by the states from the set, $S$. Along the intersection of the $i$th row and the $j$th column in the matrix, there is an input symbol from the input set, $I$, that causes the transition from the current state $S_i$ to the next new state $S_j$, followed by a punctuation, '/', and the output symbol from the output set, $O$.

In order to represent a transition from state $S_i$ to $S_j$ for more than one input symbol, the 'logical OR' symbol, that is, the '∨' symbol, is used; and if there is no transition from state $S_i$ to state $S_j$, then the symbol, '–', is placed for that entry in the matrix.

The transition matrix for the binary adder in Example 2.1 is shown in Table 2.3.

**Table 2.3** Transition matrix for binary adder

| Current state \ Next state | No carry | Carry |
|---|---|---|
| No carry | (0, 1)/1 ∨ (0, 0)/0 ∨ (1, 0)/1 | (1, 1)/0 |
| Carry | (0, 0)/1 | (0, 1)/ 0 ∨ (1, 0)/0 ∨ (1, 1)/1 |

---

**Example 2.2** Design an FSM for a divisibility-by-3 tester for decimal numbers.

***Solution*** Decimal numbers are base-10 numerals containing digits from 0 to 9. Hence, the input set, $I$, is:

$$I = \{0, 1, 2, 3, 4, 5, 6, 7, 8, 9\}$$

From this set, digits 0, 3, 6, and 9 are of same type, that is, they are all divisible by 3. Similarly, digits 1, 4, and 7 generate remainder 1, when divided by 3; and digits 2, 5, and 8 generate remainder 2 when divided by 3.

Based on this similarity, we can group the digits together, and the resultant set of inputs will effectively consist of only three different classes of inputs:

$$I = \{(0, 3, 6, 9), (1, 4, 7), (2, 5, 8)\}$$

Let us consider the possible outputs: If the number is divisible by 3, the output is '1', which means yes, it is divisible; and if the number is not divisible by 3, then the output is '0', which implies no, it is not divisible.

Hence, the output set is:

$$O = \{0, 1\}$$

When we divide a number by 3, it is possible to get three different remainder values: 0, 1, and 2. If we get 0 as the remainder, then the decimal number is divisible by 3, and the machine produces output 1 (yes, it is divisible); and if the remainder is either 1 or 2, the machine produces output 0 (no, it is not divisible).

Depending on these remainder values, we can have three different states for the machine:

$$S = \{S_0, S_1, S_2\}$$

where, $S_0$: Zero-remainder state
$S_1$: One-remainder state
$S_2$: Two-remainder state

The state tables for the divisibility-by-3 tester are shown in Table 2.4.

**Table 2.4** State tables for the divisibility-by-3 tester (a) MAF: $I \times S \rightarrow O$ (b) STF: $I \times S \rightarrow S$

| $S$ \ $I$ | (0, 3, 6, 9) | (1, 4, 7) | (2, 5, 8) |
|---|---|---|---|
| $S_0$ | 1 | 0 | 0 |
| $S_1$ | 0 | 0 | 1 |
| $S_2$ | 0 | 1 | 0 |

(a)

| $S$ \ $I$ | (0, 3, 6, 9) | (1, 4, 7) | (2, 5, 8) |
|---|---|---|---|
| $S_0$ | $S_0$ | $S_1$ | $S_2$ |
| $S_1$ | $S_1$ | $S_2$ | $S_0$ |
| $S_2$ | $S_2$ | $S_0$ | $S_1$ |

(b)

At every step in the division of any multi-digit decimal input, the remainder from the previous division step is concatenated to the next input digit to form the number to be considered for division in the next step. For example, if the machine is in state $S_1$, that is, one-remainder state, and the input is (1, 4, 7)—that is, either 1, or 4, or 7—then the next step considers for division either '11', or '14', or '17', respectively. Now, if we divide these numbers by 3, we get remainder 2. Hence, the machine moves from state $S_1$ to state $S_2$ with output '0'. This output indicates that the number '11', '14', or '17', as the case may be, is not divisible by 3.

Similarly, if the machine is in state $S_2$, and the input is (1, 4, 7), then the numbers formed are respectively '21', '24', or '27', which are divisible by 3. Therefore, the machine moves to zero-remainder state, that is, state $S_0$, with output '1', meaning that the number is divisible by 3. The transition diagram for the machine is shown in Fig. 2.3.

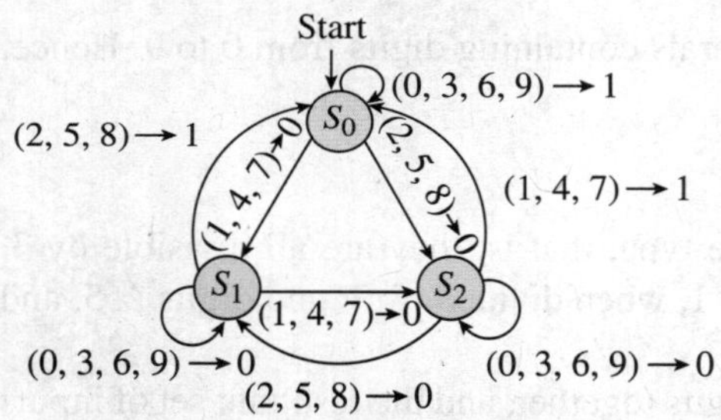


**Figure 2.3** Transition graph (TG) for divisibility-by-3 tester

We see that $S_0$—the zero-remainder state—is the initial state. The final state could be either $S_0$, $S_1$, or $S_2$, depending on the input number.

Now, let us simulate the working of the machine that we have designed on two arbitrary numbers, '112' and '1416', as shown in Fig. 2.4.

| Current state | Input | Next state | Output |
|---|---|---|---|
| $S_0$ | 1 | $S_1$ | 0 |
| $S_1$ | 1 | $S_2$ | 0 |
| $S_2$ | 2 | $S_1$ (Final state) | 1 (Output (non-divisible)) |

| Current state | Input | Next state | Output |
|---|---|---|---|
| $S_0$ | 1 | $S_1$ | 0 |
| $S_1$ | 4 | $S_2$ | 0 |
| $S_2$ | 1 | $S_0$ | 1 |
| $S_0$ | 6 | $S_0$ (Final state) | 1 (Output (divisible)) |

**Figure 2.4** Divisiblity-by-3 tester simulation for input numbers '112' and '1416'

The transition matrix for the divisibility-by-3 tester is shown in Table 2.5.

**Table 2.5** Transition matrix for divisibility-by-3 tester

| Current state \ Next state | $S_0$ | $S_1$ | $S_2$ |
|---|---|---|---|
| $S_0$ | 0/1 V 3/1 V 6/1 V 9/1 | 1/0 V 4/0 V 7/0 | 2/0 V 5/0 V 8/0 |
| $S_1$ | 2/1 V 5/1 V 8/1 | 0/0 V 3/0 V 6/0 | 1/0 V 4/0 V 7/0 |
| $S_2$ | 1/1 V 4/1 V 7/1 | 2/0 V 5/0 V 8/0 | 0/0 V 3/0 V 6/0 V 9/0 |

---

**Example 2.3** Design an FSM for divisibility-by-5 tester for decimal numbers.

***Solution*** We can use an approach similar to the one in Example 2.2. In this case, it is possible to have five different remainder values: 0, 1, 2, 3, and 4, as we are dividing by 5. If we do not want to know whether machine is in state $S_1$, $S_2$, $S_3$, or $S_4$ after reading the input number, that is, if we do not want to know about the exact value of the remainder, but only want an answer in the form of 'yes' (it is divisible), or 'no' (it is not divisible), then we require only two states:

$$S = \{q_0\,(\text{divisible}),\ q_1\,(\text{not divisible})\}$$

We know that if any decimal number ends in 0 or 5, then it is divisible by 5; else it is not divisible by 5. Depending on this fact, we can group the input digits into two categories: (0, 5) and (1, 2, 3, 4, 6, 7, 8, 9) Therefore, the input set, $I$, and the state set, $S$, are:

$$I = \{(0, 5), (1, 2, 3, 4, 6, 7, 8, 9)\}$$
$$S = \{q_0, q_1\}$$

In this example, we are not interested in the different remainder values. Hence, when the remainder is either 1, 2, 3, or 4, that is, when the number is not divisible by 5, the machine will lie in state $q_1$; and if the remainder is 0, that is, the number is divisible by 5, then it will lie in state $q_0$. However, the initial state of the machine is always $q_0$.

The STF and MAF tables for the divisibility-by-5 tester are shown in Table 2.6.

**Table 2.6** STF and MAF tables for the divisibility-by-5 tester (a) MAF: $I \times S \rightarrow 0$ (b) STF: $I \times S \rightarrow S$

| S \ I | (0, 5) | (1, 2, 3, 4, 6, 7, 8, 9) |
|---|---|---|
| $q_0$ | 1 | 0 |
| $q_1$ | 1 | 0 |

(a)

| S \ I | (0, 5) | (1, 2, 3, 4, 6, 7, 8, 9) |
|---|---|---|
| $q_0$ | $q_0$ | $q_1$ |
| $q_1$ | $q_0$ | $q_1$ |

(b)

The transition diagram is shown in Fig. 2.5.

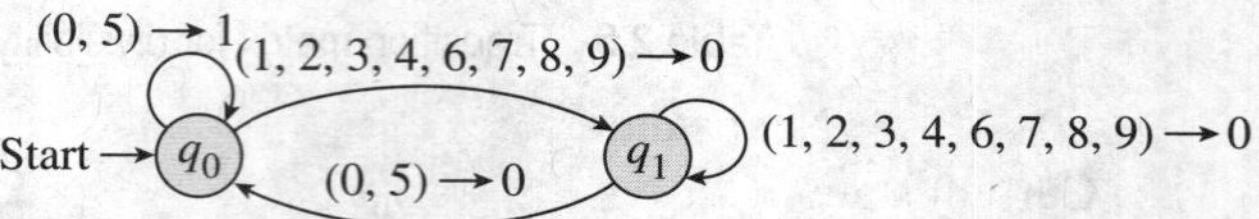


**Figure 2.5** Transition diagram for divisibility-by-5 tester

The transition matrix for the same is shown in Table 2.7.

**Table 2.7** Transition matrix for divisibility-by-5 tester

| Current state \ Next state | $q_0$ | $q_1$ |
|---|---|---|
| $q_0$ | (0, 5)/1 | (1, 2, 3, 4, 6, 7, 8, 9)/0 |
| $q_1$ | (0, 5)/1 | (1, 2, 3, 4, 6, 7, 8, 9)/0 |

**Example 2.4** Design an FSM for divisibility-by-2 tester for unary numbers.

***Solution*** Unary numbers use a single letter or digit to represent a number. For example, decimal number 5 can be represented in unary form as '11111', or 'aaaaa', or 'bbbbb', or '00000', and so on, depending on what letter or digit we choose to represent.

Let us consider the case: $\Sigma = \{a\}$, which means that we choose the letter '*a*' to represent the numbers. Hence, the set of all non-zero positive integers over $\Sigma$ can be represented as {a, aa, aaa, aaaa, …}.

Now, if we divide a number by 2, the possible remainder values are 0, which means it is divisible; or 1, which means it is not divisible by 2. Therefore, the set of states can be represented as:

$$S = \{p \text{ (divisible)}, q \text{ (non-divisible)}\}$$

As we are going to represent unary numbers using symbol 'a', the set of input symbols is:

$$I = \{a\}$$

Further, as discussed in the previous examples, the set of output symbols is:

$$O = \{0 \text{ (not divisible)}, 1 \text{ (divisible)}\}$$

The STF and MAF tables for the divisibility-by-2 tester for unary numbers are shown in Table 2.8.

**Table 2.8** STF and MAF tables for the divisibility-by-2 tester (a) MAF: $I \times S \rightarrow O$ (b) STF: $I \times S \rightarrow S$

| *S* \ *I* | *a* |
|---|---|
| *p* | 0 |
| *q* | 1 |

(a)

| *S* \ *I* | *a* |
|---|---|
| *p* | *q* |
| *q* | *p* |

(b)

The initial state of the machine is *p*, which is the zero-remainder state. If we get one '*a*', the machine moves from state *p* to state *q*, that is, the one-remainder state. Next, in state *q*, if it gets one more '*a*', then the number becomes 2, which is divisible by 2. Therefore, the machine moves to state $p$, and gives the output as 1.

The transition diagram for this machine is shown in Fig. 2.6, and the transition matrix is shown in Table 2.9.

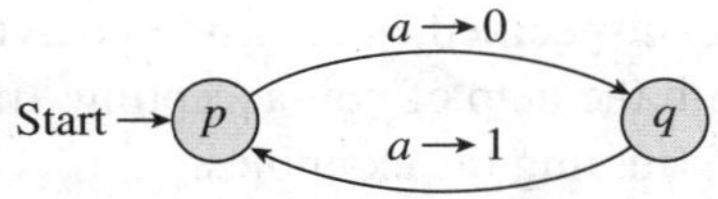


**Figure 2.6** Transition diagram for divisibility-by-2 tester for unary numbers

**Table 2.9** Transition matrix for divisibility-by-2 tester for unary numbers

| Current state \ Next state | $p$ | $q$ |
|---|---|---|
| $p$ | — | $a/0$ |
| $q$ | $a/1$ | — |

## 2.3 FINITE AUTOMATA

Finite automaton (FA) is the mathematical model (or formalism) of an FSM. Mathematical models of machines are the abstractions and simplifications of how certain machines actually work. They help us understand specific properties of these machines. An FA portrays the FSM as a language acceptor. The formal definition of an FA is as follows:

### *Formal Definition*

FA is denoted by a five-tuple:

$$M = (Q, \Sigma, \delta, q_0, F)$$

where,

$Q$: Finite set of states
$\Sigma$: Finite input alphabet
$q_0$: Initial state of FA, $q_0 \in Q$
$F$: Set of final states, $F \subseteq Q$
$\delta$: STF that maps $Q \times \Sigma$ to $Q$, i.e., $\delta: Q \times \Sigma \rightarrow Q$

The aforementioned definition of the transition function, $\delta$, is for deterministic FA, or DFA. The transition function for non-deterministic FA, or NFA, is different and is discussed later in this chapter.

As the definition is formalized, we only need to get familiar with the standard names or symbols that are used. A few notational differences between FA and FSM that we can identify are: $Q$ is analogous to state set, $S$; $\Sigma$ is analogous to input set, I; and the state transition function, '$\delta: Q \times \Sigma \rightarrow Q$', is analogous to 'STF: $I \times S \rightarrow S$'.

We observe that the formal definition for FA does not include output set, $O$; therefore, this formalism may be called FA without output. We further observe that FA, instead, has final states that can be reached only when the input is acceptable (or valid).

Any subset of $Q$ can be marked as the set of final states, $F$, depending on the solution. Upon reading the entire input string, if the machine resides in any of the final states, then the input string is considered to be 'accepted' by the machine. On the other hand, if the machine resides in any of the non-final states, then the input read is considered to be 'rejected' by the machine. Conceptually, this is equivalent to generating the output 'true' if valid and 'false' if otherwise—more like a Boolean function. Thus, FA acts as an input acceptor or rejecter.

Usually, in the transition graph of the problem solution, rejection is not explicitly shown: The paths in the transition graph, which are unspecified, are considered as rejection paths. At times, these can be explicitly shown with the help of non-accepting 'trap states'. This will be dealt with in greater detail while discussing the examples.

In case of DFA, neither for state $q$ in $Q$, nor for the input symbol '$a$' in $\Sigma$, does '$\delta(q, a)$' contain more than one element. Thus, the transition would be of the form:

$$\delta(q, a) = p$$

where, $p$ is the unique next state in $Q$, to which the machine makes the transition ($p$ may or may not be equal to $q$). This means that if the DFA is in state $q$ and reads a symbol '$a$', then it moves to the unique next state '$p$'.

For example, let us consider the FA:

$$M = (\{q_0, q_1, q_2, q_3\}, \{0, 1\}, \delta, q_0, \{q_0\})$$

Here, $q_0$ is the initial state as well as the final state. Hence, the set of all states, $Q$, is:

$$Q = \{q_0, q_1, q_2, q_3\}$$

The set of input symbols, or input alphabet, is:

$$\Sigma = \{0, 1\}$$

The transition function, $\delta$, will be as shown in Table 2.10.

The aforementioned FA is the automata that accepts all strings containing even number of 0's and even number of 1's over the input alphabet, $\Sigma = \{0, 1\}$.

**Table 2.10** Example state transition table ($\delta$: $Q \times \Sigma \rightarrow Q$)

| $Q$ \ $\Sigma$ | 0 | 1 |
|---|---|---|
| $q_0$ | $q_2$ | $q_1$ |
| $q_1$ | $q_3$ | $q_0$ |
| $q_2$ | $q_0$ | $q_3$ |
| $q_3$ | $q_1$ | $q_2$ |

### 2.3.1 Transition Graph

The transition graph for FA is almost the same as that for FSM, as we have seen earlier in Section 2.2.2. The only difference is that in case of FA, we need to represent the final states differently, and we do not have any output symbols. The final states are represented by two concentric circles, instead of a single circle that is used to represent the normal (or non-final) states.

The transition diagram for FA, whose transition table is shown in Table 2.10, is shown in Fig. 2.7.

We observe that the transitions, that is, the directed edges in the graph are labelled only using the input symbols, as there are no output symbols to be considered. Here, $q_0$ is the initial state and is represented by an arrow, which has the string 'start' associated with it. Besides, $q_0$ is also the final state, so it is

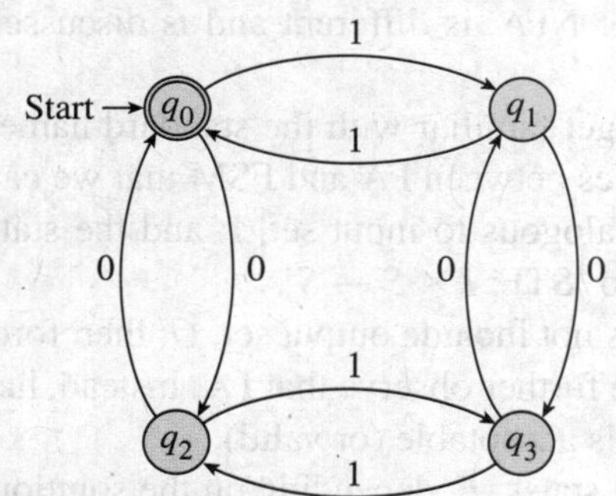

**Figure 2.7** Transition graph for the example FA

indicated by two concentric circles; we observe that $q_1$, $q_2$, and $q_3$ are non-final states, and are hence represented by single circles (refer to 'notation (1)' in Fig. 2.8).

There is a slightly different notation that is used at times for representing the transition graph for an FA. The additional notation—notation (2)—for each representation is shown in Fig. 2.8.

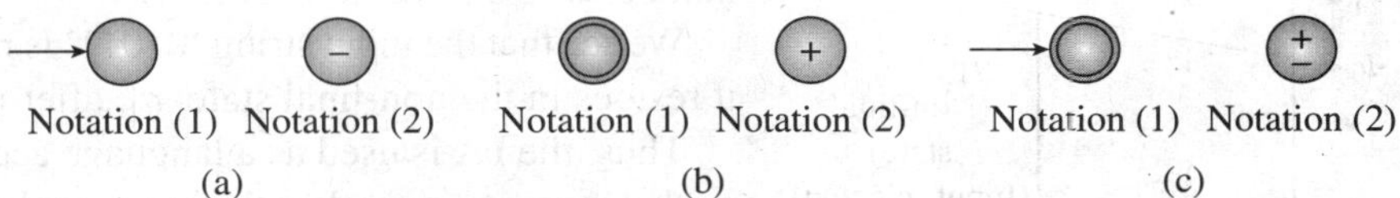


**Figure 2.8** Some additional notations for transition graph of FA (a) Initial state (b) Final state (c) If initial and final states are same

This figure explains the different types of notations used to denote the initial and final states. According to notation (2) in Fig. 2.8(a), the initial state can be denoted by a symbol, '−' (minus sign), inside the state circle, whereas according to notation (1), it is represented by an arrow pointing to the state circle along with the string 'start' attached to it. The final state is denoted by a symbol, '+' (plus sign), inside a state circle according to notation (2) in Fig. 2.8(b), whereas according to notation (1), it is represented by two concentric circles. If initial state is also a final state, then we write a '±' sign inside the state circle in notation (2) in Fig. 2.8(c), while according to notation (1), this is represented by an arrow pointing towards two concentric circles.

### 2.3.2 Functions

The example FA in Fig. 2.7 accepts only the strings over $\Sigma = \{0, 1\}$ that contain even number of 0's and even number of 1's. All these acceptable strings can be aggregated into an infinite set or language $L$ defined as:

$L = \{$set of all strings over $\Sigma = \{0, 1\}$ containing even number of 0's and even number of 1's$\}$

A conclusion that can be drawn from the aforementioned finding is that though the language $L$ is infinite, we can construct a machine (FA) that can accept any string from the language $L$ and reject any other string which is not part of the language $L$.

| Current state | Current input symbol | Next state |
|---|---|---|
| (Initial) $q_0$ | 0 | $q_2$ |
| $q_2$ | 0 | $q_0$ |
| $q_0$ | 1 | $q_1$ |
| $q_1$ | 1 | $q_0$ (Final) (Accepted the input) |

**Figure 2.9** Example FA accepting the input '0011'

In other words, the FA constructed for a given language checks the validity of the strings from the language. It checks whether the input string is a part of the language or not. If the input string is part of the language, the FA accepts it by making a transition to the final state after reading the string. Otherwise, it resides in one of the non-final states, indicating that it has rejected the string.

Let us simulate the working of the FA represented in Fig. 2.7 for the input string '0011' (refer to Fig. 2.9).

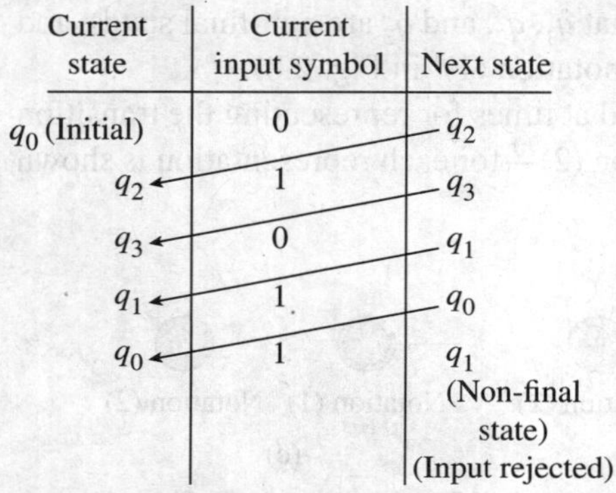

Current state
Current input symbol
Next state
$q_0$ (Initial)
0
$q_2$
$q_2$
1
$q_3$
$q_3$
0
$q_1$
$q_1$
1
$q_0$
$q_0$
1
$q_1$
(Non-final state)
(Input rejected)


**Figure 2.10** Example FA rejecting the input '01011'

Input string '0011' contains even number of 0's as well as even number of 1's. Hence, the input string is accepted by the FA, which is indicated by the final state, $q_0$, in which the machine resides after reading the string '0011'.

Let us now simulate the working of FA for the input '01011'; we see that this is not a valid string as it does not contain even number of 1's (refer to Fig. 2.10).

We see that the input string '01011' is rejected by the FA as it resides in the non-final state, $q_1$, after reading the string.

Thus, the FA is used as a language acceptor. It only relies on the transitions based on the input symbols, and these transitions are based on the input patterns only. Hence, the FA can accept an infinite language as well.

### 2.3.3 Acceptance of a String

A string '$x$' is said to be accepted by an FA given by:

$$M = (Q, \Sigma, \delta, q_0, F),$$
$$\text{if } \delta(q_0, x) = p,$$

for some $p \in F$ (i.e., $p$ is a member of $F$)

As we know, $\delta$ is a state transition function that maps $Q \times \Sigma$ to $Q$. Thus, each individual transition can be denoted by:

$$\delta(q_0, a_1) = q_1$$

where, '$q_0$' is the current state, '$a_1$' is the current input symbol, and '$q_1$' is the next state.

Similarly, we can have another transition represented as:

$$\delta(q_1, a_2) = q_2$$

We may combine these two as:

$$\delta(q_0, a_1 a_2) = \delta(\delta(q_0, a_1), a_2) = \delta(q_1, a_2) = q_2$$

This means that if the current state is $q_0$, then after reading string '$a_1\ a_2$', the state reached is $q_2$.

Similarly, the definition, '$\delta(q_0, x) = p$' means that after reading string '$x$' symbol by symbol (one symbol at a time), the machine reaches state $p$. If this state $p$ is a final state, that is, if $p$ is a member of the set $F$, then '$x$' is accepted by the automata $M$; else if $p \notin F$, then it is rejected by $M$.

### 2.3.4 Acceptance of a Language

A language is a set of strings over some alphabet. If there is a language L such that:

$$L = \{x \mid \delta(q_0, x) = p, \text{ for some } p \in F\},$$

then it is said to be accepted by the FA, *M*, and is denoted by *L*(*M*). In such a case the language accepted by automata *M* is also called a 'regular set' or 'regular language'.

If all the strings '*x*' of a language are accepted by an FA, then the language is said to be accepted by the FA, that is, for every string '*x*', $\delta$ ($q_0$, *x*) makes the FA move to the final state, after reading all symbols in '*x*'.

### 2.3.5 Some Examples of FA as Acceptor

In this section, let us look at some examples, where FA acts as an acceptor or recognizer.

---

**Example 2.5** Design an FA that reads strings made up of the letters in the word 'CHARIOT' and recognizes those strings that contain the word 'CAT' as a substring.

***Solution*** Here the alphabet $\Sigma$ consists of seven symbols:

$$\Sigma = \{C, H, A, R, I, O, T\}$$

We need to consider all possible strings made up of these seven symbols and design an FA, which would recognize only those which contain 'CAT' as a substring. In turn, we can say that the FA we are going to design would make a transition to the final state only if the input string contains 'CAT' as a substring.

The working of the FA will be as follows:

If the FA reads the symbol 'C' while in the start state, that is, $q_0$, then it makes a transition to state $q_1$; otherwise remains in the same state. Now in state $q_1$, if the FA reads symbol 'A', then it makes a transition to another state, that is, state $q_2$. Similarly, in $q_2$, if FA reads symbol 'T', then it makes a transition to $q_3$, which is the final state.

Essentially, states $q_1$, $q_2$, and $q_3$ respectively indicate that the substrings 'C', 'CA', and 'CAT' have been read.

Figure 2.11 shows the transition graph for the recognizer FA. The FA that is constructed here is actually a sequence detector program, while the sequence it is trying to detect is 'CAT'.

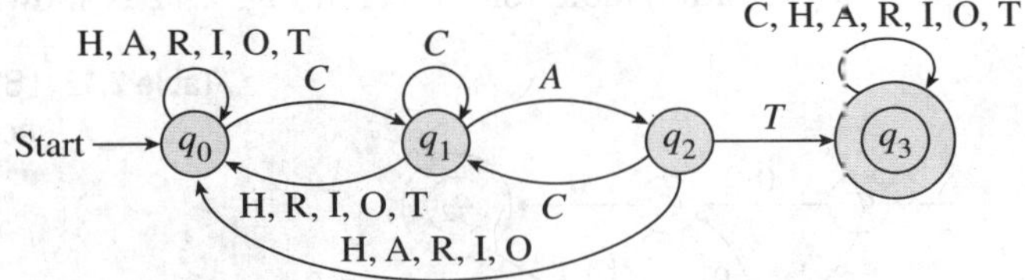


**Figure 2.11** Recognizer FA as a sequence detector

We observe that the state $q_0$ is the start (or initial) state, and $q_3$ is the final state. If the FA reads any symbol from $\Sigma$ while in $q_3$ (final state), it does not make a transition to any other state as it has already recognized the substring 'CAT' by then.

The state transition table for the FA is shown in Table 2.11.

**Table 2.11** State transition table for recognizer FA

| $Q$ \ $\Sigma$ | $C$ | $H$ | $A$ | $R$ | $I$ | $O$ | $T$ |
|---|---|---|---|---|---|---|---|
| $q_0$ | $q_1$ | $q_0$ | $q_0$ | $q_0$ | $q_0$ | $q_0$ | $q_0$ |
| $q_1$ | $q_1$ | $q_0$ | $q_2$ | $q_0$ | $q_0$ | $q_0$ | $q_0$ |
| $q_2$ | $q_1$ | $q_0$ | $q_0$ | $q_0$ | $q_0$ | $q_0$ | $q_3$ |
| $q_3$ | $q_3$ | $q_3$ | $q_3$ | $q_3$ | $q_3$ | $q_3$ | $q_3$ |

**Example 2.6** Design an FA that reads strings made up of {0, 1} and accepts only those strings which end in either '00' or '11'.

***Solution*** Here, the alphabet $\Sigma$ is given as:

$$\Sigma = \{0, 1\}$$

We need to construct an FA that is capable of reading all possible strings over $\Sigma$, but accepts only those strings which end in '00' or '11'. This is yet another example of a sequence detector (refer Fig. 2.12).

The FA has two final states: One that accepts strings ending with '00', that is, state $q_2$, and the other that accepts strings ending with '11', that is, state $q_4$.

In Fig. 2.12, states $q_1$ and $q_2$ respectively indicate that the substrings '0' and '00' have been read. Similarly, states $q_3$ and $q_4$ respectively indicate that the substrings '1' and '11' have been read. The self-loop in state $q_2$ on symbol '0' indicates that any string that ends in three or more 0's anyway ends with two 0's; thus, once two 0's have been read, more 0's does not change the acceptance criteria—that the string should end in '00'. Similarly, one can explain the self-loop on state $q_4$ on symbol '1'.

The states $q_1$ and $q_2$, upon reading '1' transit to state $q_3$, indicating that one '1' has been read. Similarly, states $q_3$ and $q_4$ transit to state $q_1$ upon reading the '0', indicating that the string ends with '0'. If $q_1$ reads one more '0', then it transits to the final state $q_2$, indicating that the sequence ends with '00'.

The state transition table for the FA in Fig. 2.12 is shown in Table 2.12.

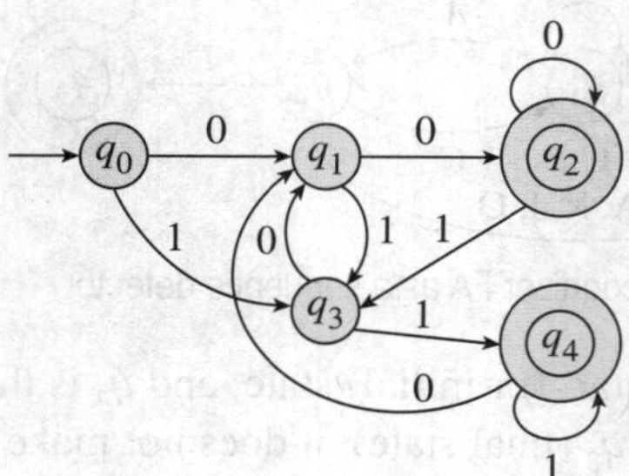


**Figure 2.12** FA accepting strings which end in either '00' or '11'

**Table 2.12** State transition table for acceptor FA

| $Q$ \ $\Sigma$ | 0 | 1 |
|---|---|---|
| $q_0$ | $q_1$ | $q_3$ |
| $q_1$ | $q_2$ | $q_3$ |
| $q_2$ | $q_2$ | $q_3$ |
| $q_3$ | $q_1$ | $q_4$ |
| $q_4$ | $q_1$ | $q_4$ |

Let us trace the FA for input, '111'. The sequence of states starting with the initial (start) state $q_0$ will be: $q_0 \rightarrow q_3 \rightarrow q_4 \rightarrow q_4$. Thus, the last state in the sequence is $q_4$, which is a final state, and hence, the input '111' is accepted by the FA.

Now, let us trace the input, '0110', starting with the start state $q_0$. On input '0', the FA makes a transition from state $q_0$ to state $q_1$. On reading the next symbol, that is, '1', it changes to state $q_3$. Similarly, for the third symbol, that is, '1', it switches from state $q_3$ to state $q_4$. Though $q_4$ is a final state, there is one more symbol, that is, '0', that needs to be read; and which is the last symbol of the string '0110'. On reading the last symbol, the FA makes a transition from state $q_4$ to state $q_1$. Thus, the sequence of states for the input string '0110' is: $q_0 \rightarrow q_1 \rightarrow q_3 \rightarrow q_4 \rightarrow q_1$. As $q_1$ is a non-final state, and is the last state of the sequence after reading the input string '0110', the string is not accepted (that is, it is rejected) by the FA.

### 2.3.6 FA as Finite Control

The FA can be visualized as a finite control with the input string written on a tape, and each tape cell containing one symbol from the string; let '$' denote the end of the string.

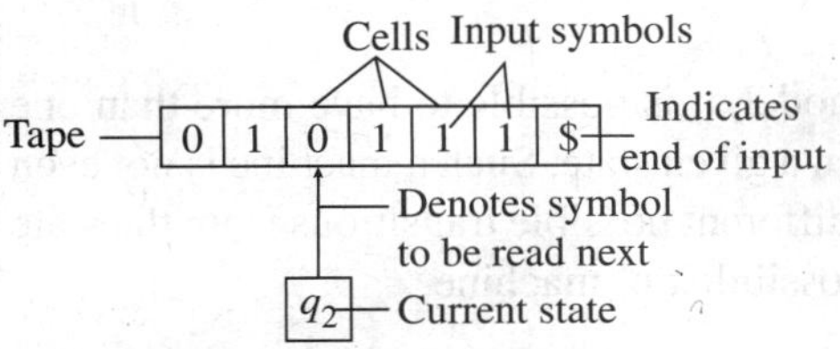


**Figure 2.13** Finite control representation of FA

A pointer or head points to a cell on the tape from which the next symbol will be read. The head is labelled by the state label that represents the current state of the machine (refer to Fig. 2.13).

The FA reads symbols one by one from a finite tape, whose end of string is indicated by 'S'. Let us say the FA in Fig. 2.12 resides in state $q_2$ at a given instance, and is about to read the symbol '0' from the tape cell. After reading the symbol, the FA's head will point to the next adjacent cell on the right-hand side, and will transit to the next state (which may or may not be the same as the current state). This means that after reading the current symbol in the cell, the head always moves to the right to read the next symbol. If it reads '$' (indicating the end of input), and at this stage, if the FA is in the final state, then the input string is accepted, otherwise it is rejected.

**Theorem 2.1**

Every FA can be represented using a transition graph (TG), but not every TG satisfies the definition of an FA.

*Proof*

Consider the transition graph consisting of only one node as shown in Fig. 2.14(a).

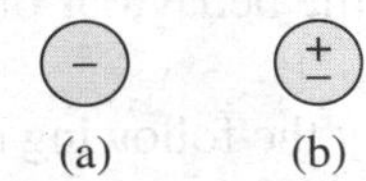


**Figure 2.14** Transition graph and FA (a) TG (b) FA

Figure 2.14(a) represents a TG that accepts no string—not even an empty string ($\epsilon$) of zero length—as there is no final state. This is because, in order to be able to accept anything, the FA must have a final state. Hence, the TG in Fig. 2.14(a) cannot be called an FA.

Now, Fig. 2.14(b) represents an FA, which accepts only the empty string, that is, $\epsilon$, because its initial and final states are same—there is only one state. We also observe from the figure that there is no other transition. Therefore, Fig. 2.14(b) represents the TG for an FA accepting only $\epsilon$ string.

Hence, the theorem is proved.

## 2.4 DETERMINISTIC FINITE AUTOMATA

We have already mentioned about the deterministic finite automata (DFA) in Section 2.3. An FA is said to be deterministic if for every state there is a unique input symbol, which takes the state to the required next unique state. This means that given a state $S_j$, the same input symbol does not cause the FA to move into more than one state—there is always a unique next state for an input symbol (read, for any state transition. Refer to Fig. 2.15).

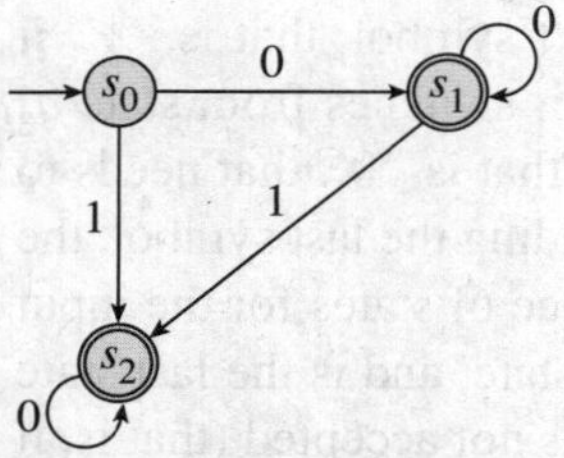

**Figure 2.15** Example DFA

Figure 2.15 shows that from state $S_0$, there is only one transition on reading symbol '0' and symbol '1'. Similarly, for states $S_1$ and $S_2$, there are unique transitions on reading symbols '0' and '1'. No state exists from which there is more than one transition for the same input symbol. Therefore, the example FA, represented using Fig. 2.14, is a DFA.

We now see that all the examples we have seen before (i.e., Figures 2.7, 2.11, and 2.12) are DFAs.

## 2.5 NON-DETERMINISTIC FINITE AUTOMATA

In a non-deterministic finite automata (NFA) model, it is possible to have more than one transition on reading the same input symbol from a given state. Such a machine is not even probabilistic, as no weights are assigned to the different possible transitions from the state for the same symbol; this is also known as a 'possibilistic' machine.

An NFA is denoted by the five-tuple notation:

$$M = (Q, \Sigma, \delta, q_0, F)$$

where, $Q$, $\Sigma$, $q_0$, and $F$ have their usual meanings.

The only change is the state transition function, $\delta$, that maps from $Q \times \Sigma$ to $2^Q$:

$$\delta : Q \times \Sigma \rightarrow 2^Q$$

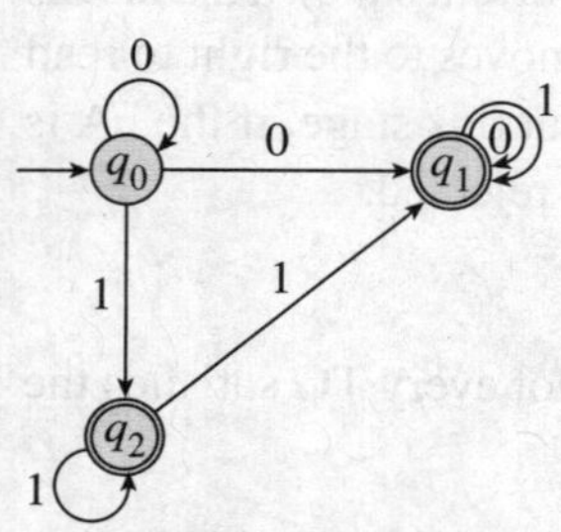

**Figure 2.16** Example NFA

For an example, refer to Fig. 2.16. The FA shown in the figure is an NFA. We observe that from state $q_0$, on reading the input symbol '0', there are two different transitions: first to state $q_0$, and the other to state $q_1$. There is no unique next state for the transition on symbol '0' from state $q_0$. This means that state $q_0$, on reading symbol '0', can go to either $q_1$ or to itself, that is, '$q_0$'. Hence, it is possibilistic; and so, the behaviour of the NFA, cannot be predicted.

The transitions can be represented by the following equation:

$$\delta\,(q_0, 0) = \{q_0, q_1\}$$

**Table 2.13** State transition function, $\delta$, for NFA in Fig. 2.16

| $Q$ \ $\Sigma$ | 0 | 1 |
|---|---|---|
| $q_0$ | $\{q_0, q_1\}$ | $q_2$ |
| $q_1$ | $q_1$ | $q_1$ |
| $q_2$ | $\phi$ | $\{q_1, q_2\}$ |

We observe from Table 2.13 that even from state $q_2$ there are two different transitions on reading the same input symbol '1', and it is not possible to determine the next state. Therefore, this is called a non-deterministic FA or NFA.

For the example NFA in Fig. 2.16, set of states $Q$ is $\{q_0, q_1, q_2\}$. Hence, the power set of $Q$, that is, the set of all possible subsets of $Q$ can be expressed as:

$$2^Q = \{\phi, \{q_0\}, \{q_1\}, \{q_2\}, \{q_0, q_1\}, \{q_0, q_2\}, \{q_1, q_2\}, \{q_0, q_1, q_2\}\}$$

where, '$\phi$' is an empty set, as we know.

We observe that $\delta(q_0, 0) = \{q_0, q_1\}$

where, $\{q_0, q_1\}$ is a member of $2^Q$.

Now, it is clear why the state transition function for an NFA is:

$$\delta : Q \times \Sigma \rightarrow 2^Q$$

Similarly, $\delta(q_2, 1) = \{q_1, q_2\}$, which is also a member of $2^Q$.

## 2.6 EQUIVALENCE OF NFA AND DFA

The NFA and DFA are equivalent to each other; in other words, for every NFA, there exists an equivalent DFA accepting the same set of words (or language). Therefore, the capabilities of an NFA and its equivalent DFA are the same. Hence, NFA and DFA have equal powers.

Let us consider a simple example shown in Fig. 2.17.

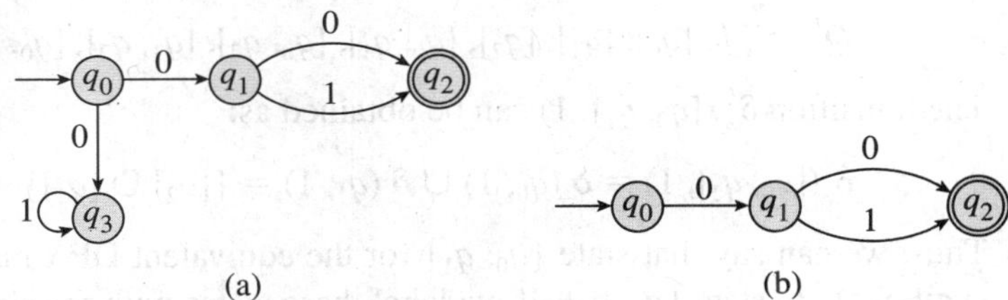


**Figure 2.17** NFA vs DFA (a) Example NFA (b) Equivalent DFA

Figure 2.17(a) shows an example NFA, with two different transitions from state $q_0$ on reading symbol '0'. The string is said to be accepted only if, after reading that string, the machine resides in one of the final states. Therefore, only two strings, '00' and '01' are accepted by the NFA in Fig. 2.17(a). The second path, on reading symbol '0' from state $q_0$, does not reach the final state anyway.

Thus, the language accepted by the NFA in Fig. 2.17(a) is:

$$L_1 = \{00, 01\}$$

Now, the DFA in Fig. 2.17(b) accepts the language:

$$L_2 = \{00, 01\}$$

We observe that $L_1 = L_2$.

Therefore, the NFA and DFA in Fig. 2.17 are equivalent to each other, and accept the same language $\{00, 01\}$. Therefore, their power is same.

Let us now study some methods for converting an NFA to its equivalent DFA.

### 2.6.1 NFA to DFA Conversion (Method I)

As we know, an NFA can be represented by a five-tuple:

$$M = (Q, \Sigma, \delta, q_0, F)$$

where,

$$\delta = Q \times \Sigma \rightarrow 2^Q$$

The main difference between NFA and DFA is the state transition function, $\delta$. The entries in the state transition table for NFA are sets, instead of singular entries as in DFA.

Hence, while converting an NFA into its equivalent DFA, let us consider $Q' = 2^Q$, as the set of states for the resulting DFA.

Then, the state function for the DFA will be:

$$\delta' : Q' \times \Sigma \rightarrow Q'$$

This means that every combination of states can be considered as a new state, and can be given a new label.

For example, for the DFA equivalent to the example NFA in Fig. 2.16, we consider $\{q_2\}$, $\{q_0, q_1\}$, $\{q_0, q_2\}$ as three different states: Let us label them as $p_0$, $p_1$, and $p_2$, respectively.

The transitions from these states can be obtained by combining the transitions for the constituent states. Thus, $Q'$ can be represented as:

$$Q' = \{\phi, [q_0], [q_1], [q_2], [q_0, q_1], [q_0, q_2], [q_1, q_2], [q_0, q_1, q_2]\}$$

The transition $\delta'$ $([q_0, q_1], 1)$ can be obtained as:

$$\delta'([q_0, q_1], 1) = \delta\ (q_0, 1) \cup \delta\ (q_1, 1) = \{[q_2] \cup [q_1]\} = \{q_1, q_2\}$$

Thus, we can say that state $\{q_0, q_1\}$ for the equivalent DFA makes transition on reading symbol '1' to state $\{q_1, q_2\}$. If we label these states with the singular labels, as discussed earlier, the equivalent DFA will contain the unique next states for each symbol on which the transition is made.

A combination of states is considered as a final state for the resultant DFA, if at least one of the states constituting the combination is a final state for the given NFA. The initial state remains unchanged for the resultant DFA.

Let us study some examples to explore this further.

---

**Example 2.7** Convert the NFA: $M = [\{q_0, q_1\}, \{0, 1\}, \delta, q_0, \{q_1\}]$, where $\delta$ is as shown in Table 2.14, to its equivalent DFA.

***Solution*** For the given NFA, $Q = \{q_0, q_1\}$, $\Sigma = \{0, 1\}$, $F = \{q_1\}$, and initial state is $q_0$. Let us denote the resultant DFA as:

$$M' = \{Q', \Sigma, \delta', [q_0], F'\}$$

where,

$\Sigma = \{0, 1\}$ and the initial state, $q_0$, are the same as that of the given NFA—the entry point cannot be changed if the language accepted is required to be same for equivalence.

**Table 2.14** State transition table for example NFA

| Q \ Σ | 0 | 1 |
|---|---|---|
| $q_0$ | $\{q_0, q_1\}$ | $\{q_1\}$ |
| $q_1$ | $\phi$ | $\{q_0, q_1\}$ |

The power set of $Q$ is given by:

$$2^Q = \{\phi, [q_0], [q_1], [q_0, q_1]\}$$

As per the method discussed, the finite set of states for the resultant (and equivalent) DFA, that is, $Q'$ can be written as:

$$Q' = \{[q_0], [q_1], [q_0, q_1]\}$$

We see that $\phi$, is excluded, as it does not denote any state of the given NFA, and hence, is irrelevant.

Now, we need to find the state transition function for the DFA:

$$\delta' : Q' \times \Sigma \rightarrow Q'$$

This means that we need to find all the transitions from every state in $Q'$ on reading both the input symbols '0' and '1'.

From Table 2.14, which shows the state table of the given NFA, we have:

$$\delta'([q_0], 0) = [q_0, q_1]$$
$$\delta'([q_0], 1) = [q_1]$$

$$\delta'([q_1], 0) = \phi \quad \text{(this means no transition)}$$
$$\delta'([q_1], 1) = [q_0, q_1]$$

Now, there is one more state remaining, to determine the transitions, that is, for $[q_0, q_1]$:

$$\delta'([q_0, q_1], 0) = [\delta(q_0, 0) \cup \delta(q_1, 0)] = [\{q_0, q_1\} \cup \phi] = [q_0, q_1]$$
$$\delta'([q_0, q_1], 1) = [\delta(q_0, 1) \cup \delta(q_1, 1)] = [\{q_1\} \cup \{q_0, q_1\}] = [\{q_0, q_1\}] = [q_0, q_1]$$

**Table 2.15** State transition table for resultant DFA

| Q' \ Σ | 0 | 1 |
|---|---|---|
| $[q_0]$ | $[q_0, q_1]$ | $[q_1]$ |
| $[q_1]$ | – | $[q_0, q_1]$ |
| $[q_0, q_1]$ | $[q_0, q_1]$ | $[q_0, q_1]$ |

Using the aforementioned information, the state transition table for resultant DFA is written as shown in Table 2.15.

The transition diagram for the resultant equivalent DFA can be drawn as shown in Fig. 2.18(a).

As $q_0$ is the initial state of the given NFA, $\{q_0\}$ is the initial state of the resultant DFA. Similarly, '$q_1$' is the final state for the given NFA;

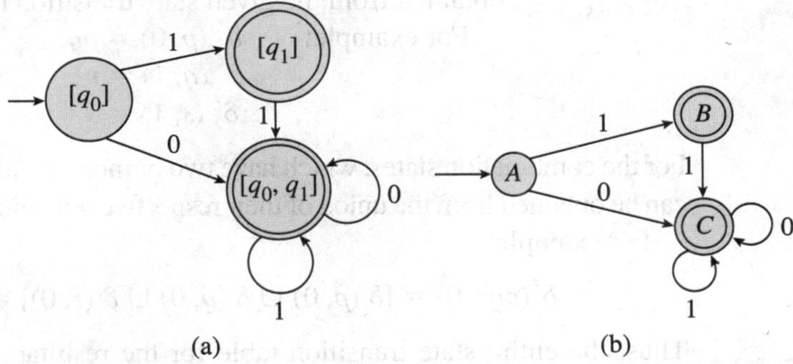


**Figure 2.18** DFA equivalent to the NFA in Table 2.14 (a) Equivalent DFA (b) Equivalent DFA after relabelling

hence, for the resultant DFA, we need to consider all such states, which contain $q_1$ as one of the constituents of the final states.

Therefore, $F' = \{q_1, [q_0, q_1]\}$

The machine necessarily should only have one initial state. However, it can have multiple final states.

Let us now change the labels of the states for the DFA as:

$$A: [q_0];\ B: [q_1];\ \text{and}\ C: [q_0, q_1]$$

Then, the DFA can be redrawn as shown in Fig. 2.18(b). For this DFA after relabelling, we have:

$Q' = \{A, B, C\}$,
$\Sigma = \{0, 1\}$,
initial state $= A$, and
$F' = \{B, C\}$

Likewise, the state transition function, $\delta'$, for the equivalent DFA can now be rewritten as shown in Table 2.16.

**Table 2.16** DFA state transition table

| $Q'$ \ $\Sigma$ | 0 | 1 |
|---|---|---|
| $A$ | $C$ | $B$ |
| $B$ | – | $C$ |
| $C$ | $C$ | $C$ |

---

**Example 2.8** Convert the NFA $[\{p, q, r, s\}, \{0, 1\}, \delta, p, \{s\}]$ to its equivalent DFA, where the state transition function, $\delta$, is as shown in Table. 2.17.

***Solution*** For the resultant DFA, $\Sigma = \{0, 1\}$, the initial state is also $p$, and

$$Q' = \{p, q, r, s, pq, pr, ps, qr, qs, rs, pqr, pqs, prs, qrs, pqrs\}$$

Note that we have excluded $\phi$ (null set) from $2^Q$. All the states having '$s$' as one of the constituents are the final states for the resultant DFA, because '$s$' is the final state for the given NFA. Therefore, the set of final states for the resultant DFA is given by:

$$F' = \{s, ps, qs, rs, pqs, prs, qrs, pqrs\}$$

**Table 2.17** State transition table for example NFA

| $Q$ \ $\Sigma$ | 0 | 1 |
|---|---|---|
| $p$ | $p, q$ | $p$ |
| $q$ | $r$ | $r$ |
| $r$ | $s$ | – |
| $s$ | $s$ | $s$ |

We can relabel the states from $Q'$ by numbers from 1 to 15, in sequence.

For the states $p$, $q$, $r$, and $s$, the state transition function, $\delta'$, can be directly obtained from the given state transition table in Table 2.17.

For example; $\delta'(p, 0) = pq$
$\delta'(q, 1) = r$
$\delta'(s, 1) = s$

For the combination states, which have two or more symbols together representing a state, $\delta'$ can be obtained from the union of their respective transitions in the NFA state transition table.

For example:

$$\delta'(pqr, 0) = [\delta(p, 0) \cup \delta(q, 0) \cup \delta(r, 0)] = [\{p, q\} \cup \{r\} \cup \{s\}] = [pqrs]$$

Thus, the entire state transition table for the resultant DFA is as shown in Table 2.18. Observe that along with the normal state symbol, the new labels are also shown in the brackets. The symbol, '*', indicates the final states.

**Table 2.18** State transition table for resultant DFA

| Q′ | | Σ 0 | 1 |
|---|---|---|---|
| (1) | *p* | *pq* (5) | *p* (1) |
| (2) | *q* | *r* (3) | *r* (3) |
| (3) | *r* | *s* (4) | – |
| *(4) | *s* | *s* (4) | *s* (4) |
| (5) | *pq* | *pqr* (11) | *pr* (6) |
| (6) | *pr* | *pqs* (12) | *p* (1) |
| *(7) | *ps* | *pqs* (12) | *ps* (7) |
| (8) | *qr* | *rs* (10) | *r* (3) |
| *(9) | *qs* | *rs* (10) | *rs* (10) |
| *(10) | *rs* | *s* (4) | *s* (4) |
| (11) | *pqr* | *pqrs* (15) | *pr* (6) |
| *(12) | *pqs* | *pqrs* (15) | *prs* (13) |
| *(13) | *prs* | *pqs* (12) | *ps* (7) |
| *(14) | *qrs* | *rs* (10) | *rs* (10) |
| *(15) | *pqrs* | *pqrs* (15) | *prs* (13) |

↑
New labels

'*': Final states

## 2.6.2 DFA Minimization

The DFA thus obtained can be minimized. In order to minimize the DFA, one needs to identify the equivalent states.

### *Equivalent States*

Two or more states are said to be equivalent states if they undergo the same transitions on reading the same input symbol (true for all the transitions) and are of the same type, that is, either final states or non-final. This means that all these states move to the same next state after reading the same input symbol. Furthermore, they all are of the same type—either final or non-final). Hence, if one or more states have the same transitions, but they are of different types—that is, one is a final transition and the other, a non-final transition—they are not considered as equivalent states.

The equivalent states are used to minimize the DFA: If there is more than one state that is equivalent, we can remove all the equivalent states but one. The one state thus kept replaces all other equivalent states in the DFA. However, there are certain rules that we need to follow.

### DFA Minimization Rules

For reducing equivalent states to a single state, one should follow the following rules:

1. We can replace one non-final state by its equivalent non-final state only.
2. We can replace one final state by its equivalent final state only.
3. We *cannot* replace the initial state by any other state.
4. We *cannot* replace one final state by a non-final state, or one non-final state by a final state.
5. Replacing state *A* by state *B* means deleting all entries related to state *A*, that is, all the transitions for state *A* from the state transition table. Furthermore, wherever we find any transition where '*A*' is the next state; we replace it by state *B*; and state *A* can be deleted from the set of states *Q* for the DFA.
6. After minimizing the DFA applying all the aforementioned five steps, if we find any more equivalent states as a result of the reduction, we repeat the same five steps again; else we stop.

For example, in Table 2.18, the states *rs* (10) and *s* (4) both transit to state *s* (4) on reading input '0'; as well as on reading input '1'. This means that they have the same transition on reading both the input symbols. Moreover, they are both final states. Therefore, these two states are equivalent.

Similarly, *prs* (13) is equivalent to *ps* (7); *qrs* (14) is equivalent to *qs* (9); and *pqrs* (15) is equivalent to *pqs* (12).

Therefore, we can replace:

| | | |
|---|---|---|
| *rs* (10) | by | *s* (4) |
| *prs* (13) | by | *ps* (7) |
| *qrs* (14) | by | *qs* (9) |
| *pqrs* (15) | by | *pqs* (12) |

After these replacements, and now using only the new labels (i.e., numbers only) the reduced transition table for the resultant DFA is as shown in Table 2.19. The symbol '*' represents the final states; and the black circle '•' indicates the modified entries due to replacements.

**Table 2.19** Minimized state transition table

| $Q'$ \ $\Sigma$ | 0 | 1 |
|---|---|---|
| 1 | 5 | 1 |
| 2 | 3 | 3 |
| 3 | 4 | – |
| *4 | 4 | 4 |
| 5 | 11 | 6 |
| 6 | 12 | 1 |
| *7 | 12 | 7 |
| 8 | 4 • | 3 |
| *9 | 4 • | 4 • |
| 11 | 12 • | 6 |
| *12 | 12 • | 7 • |

'*': Final states
'•': Modified entries due to replacement

We now observe from Table 2.19 that state 4 and state 9 are equivalent, and both are final. Similarly, states 7 and 12 are both equivalent and final; this indicates that further reduction is possible. Hence, replacing state 9 by 4; and state 12 by 7, we get a further minimized table, as shown in Table 2.20.

We see that no further minimization of Table 2.20 is possible. Therefore, we can now draw the transition graph for the resultant DFA, as shown in Fig. 2.19(a).

We observe from Fig. 2.19(a) that it is a disconnected graph having two parts: Part I contains one initial and one final state, and part II contains only final state, but no initial state.

As we know, the working of a machine always starts from an initial state; hence, we can directly exclude part II from the transition graph. Therefore, part I of the graph is the final DFA. We can again change the state labels using symbols 'A' to 'E', and the final DFA can be drawn as shown in Fig. 2.19(b).

**Table 2.20** Further minimization of the state transition table

| $Q'$ \ Σ | 0 | 1 |
|---|---|---|
| 1 | 5 | 1 |
| 2 | 3 | 3 |
| 3 | 4 | – |
| *4 | 4 | 4 |
| 5 | 11 | 6 |
| 6 | 7 • | 1 |
| *7 | 7 • | 7 |
| 8 | 4 | 3 |
| 11 | 7 • | 6 |

'*': Final states
'•': Modified entries due to replacement

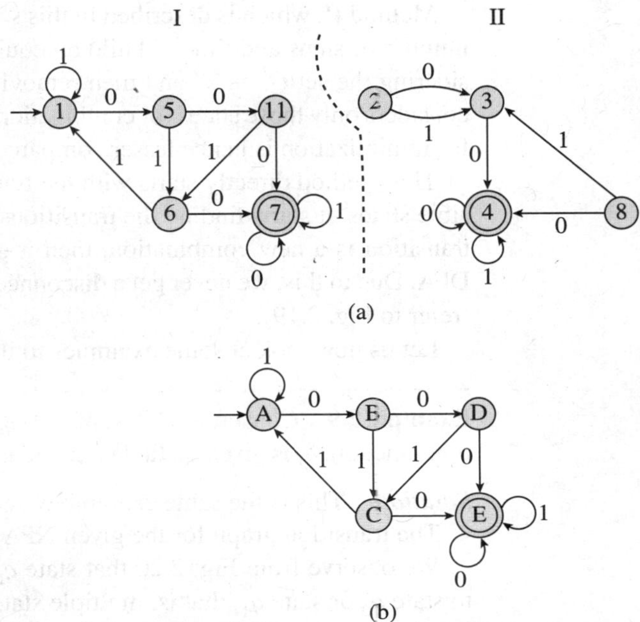


**Figure 2.19** Transition graph for the minimized DFA (a) TG for DFA drawn from Table 2.20 (b) Final minimized DFA

### *Unreachable States*

A state is said to be an 'unreachable state' if it cannot be reached from the initial state on reading any input symbol. These unreachable states do not take part in string acceptance, and hence must be removed in order to minimize the DFA; they are like pieces of dead code that never get executed in any run of a computer program. For example, the states labelled 2, 3, 4, and 8 in Fig. 2.19(a) are unreachable states; they make a disconnected graph, as discussed earlier. Hence, these states along with their transitions are removed in order to minimize the DFA.

### *Dead (or Trap) States*

Dead states (or trap states) are those non-final (or non-accepting) states whose transitions for every input symbol terminate on them. This means that these states have no outgoing transitions, except to themselves. These are called trap states because once entered, there is no escape (as in the hang state of a computer program). Moreover, any transition to a dead state becomes undefined. Just as the unreachable states, these dead states and transitions that are incident on these dead states must be removed in order to minimize the DFA. For example, refer to the dead state $q_3$ in Fig. 2.17(a).

## 2.6.3 NFA to DFA Conversion (Method II)

In method I, we considered all possible subsets of $Q$ (i.e., $2^Q$) as the possible states for the resultant DFA. Later, however, we had to remove many of the state combinations during the minimization process.

Method II, which is described in this section, is much easier and direct—it takes lesser number of steps and time to build an equivalent DFA using this method. Instead of considering the set $Q' = 2^Q$ and then removing the states that are not required, this method considers only those states (or combinations of states) that are required. The effort required for minimization is hence lesser compared to the previous method.

This method directly starts with the transition diagram. Instead of considering all possible states, it starts finding the transitions, one state at a time. If the next state of a given transition is a new combination, then it gets added to the set of states for the resultant DFA. Due to this, we never get a disconnected transition graph as we obtained in method I (refer to Fig. 2.19).

Let us now look at some examples to illustrate this method.

---

**Example 2.9** Convert the NFA: $M = [\{q_0, q_1\}, \{0, 1\}, \delta, q_0, \{q_1\}]$ where, the state transition function, $\delta$, is given in Table 2.21, to its equivalent DFA.

***Solution*** This is the same example we considered earlier (refer to Example 2.7).

The transition graph for the given NFA is as shown in the Fig. 2.20.

We observe from Fig. 2.20 that state $q_0$, on reading input '0', makes transition either to state $q_0$ or state $q_1$, that is, multiple states. This means that for the equivalent resultant DFA, we need the combination state $[q_0\ q_1]$. Let us therefore create a new state with label '$q_0\ q_1$' as shown in Fig. 2.21(a). As this new state contains the label $q_1$, which is the final state for the given NFA, we mark this state as the final state for the resultant DFA, as shown—with double concentric circles—in Fig. 2.21(a).

**Table 2.21** State transition table for example NFA

| $Q$ \ $\Sigma$ | 0 | 1 |
|---|---|---|
| $q_0$ | $\{q_0, q_1\}$ | $\{q_1\}$ |
| $q_1$ | $\phi$ | $\{q_0, q_1\}$ |

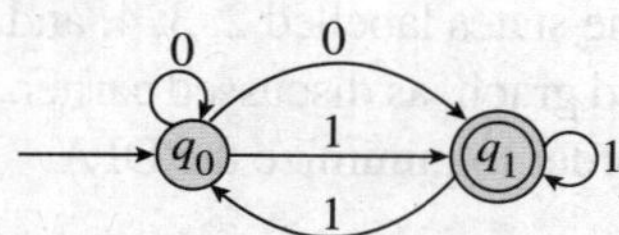


**Figure 2.20** TG for example NFA given in Table 2.21

State $q_0$ on reading input '1' goes to only '$q_1$', therefore, we add one more state to the resultant DFA labelled '$q_1$', which is also a final state (refer to Fig. 2.21b).

Since there is no transition from state $q_1$ on reading input '0' for the given NFA, therefore, no transition from state $q_1$ is labelled with a '0'. However, state $q_1$, on reading input '1', goes either to state $q_0$ or state $q_1$; therefore, we show a transition from state $q_1$ to state $q_0\ q_1$. Since, state $q_0\ q_1$ already exists as a part of the resultant DFA, we do not need to create a new state (refer to Fig. 2.21c).

Now, there is only one state $q_0\ q_1$ for which the transitions need to be realized:

$$\begin{aligned}\delta'(q_0\ q_1, 0) &= \delta(q_0, 0) \cup \delta(q_1, 0)\\ &= \{q_0, q_1\} \cup \phi\\ &= q_0\ q_1\end{aligned}$$

Similarly,

$$\begin{aligned}\delta'(q_0\ q_1, 1) &= \delta(q_0, 1) \cup (q_1, 1)\\ &= \{q_1\} \cup \{q_0, q_1\}\\ &= q_0\ q_1\end{aligned}$$

Figure 2.21(d) shows these two transitions, which are self loops.

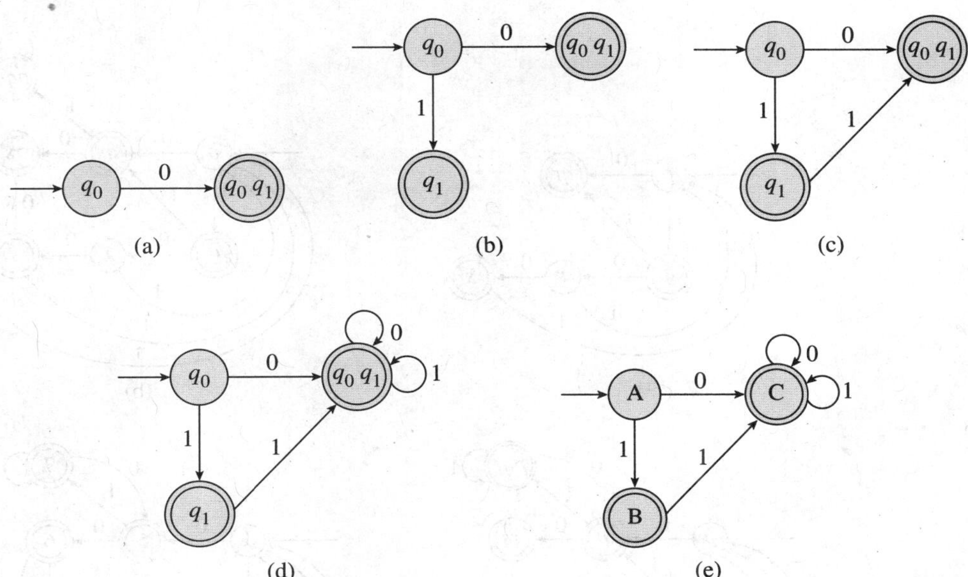


**Figure 2.21** DFA construction from the given NFA (a) Step 1 (b) Step 2 (c) Step 3 (d) Step 4 (e) Final DFA

Since, there is no state remaining to be considered for finding the transitions, Fig. 2.21(d) could be the final DFA. However, according to our convention, we change the labels for the states so as to make them singular labels: We label state $q_0$ as 'A'; state $q_1$ as 'B'; and state $q_0\ q_1$ as C. Thus, we draw the transition graph for the final DFA, as shown in Fig. 2.21(e).

We observe that this DFA is exactly the same as that we have obtained by applying the first method—refer to Fig. 2.18(b). The state transition table will also be the same as Table 2.16.

For the aforementioned example, we see that the complexity of both the methods is the same, as there are only three state combinations to work with, and all are required combinations.

Let us now look at some non-trivial examples to illustrate that method II is more efficient than method I.

---

**Example 2.10** Construct DFA equivalent to NFA: $M = [\{p, q, r, s\}, \{0, 1\}, \delta, p, \{q, s\}]$ where, $\delta$ is given in Table 2.22.

**Table 2.22** State transition table for example NFA

| Q \ Σ | 0 | 1 |
|---|---|---|
| $p$ | $q, r$ | $q$ |
| $q$ | $r$ | $q, r$ |
| $r$ | $s$ | $p$ |
| $s$ | — | $p$ |

***Solution*** The transitions from the states $p$, $q$, $r$, and $s$ for the resultant DFA can be obtained directly from Table 2.22, which are:

$\delta'(p, 0) = qr$ (new state required) $\quad \delta'(p, 1) = q$
$\delta'(q, 0) = r \quad \delta'(q, 1) = qr$
$\delta'(r, 0) = s \quad \delta'(r, 1) = p$
$\delta'(s, 0) = \phi \quad \delta'(s, 1) = p$

where, $\delta'$ is the state transition function for the equivalent DFA.

These transitions are reflected in Fig. 2.12(a), with five states $p$, $q$, $r$, $s$, and $qr$, of which $q$, $s$, and $qr$ are the final states because for the given

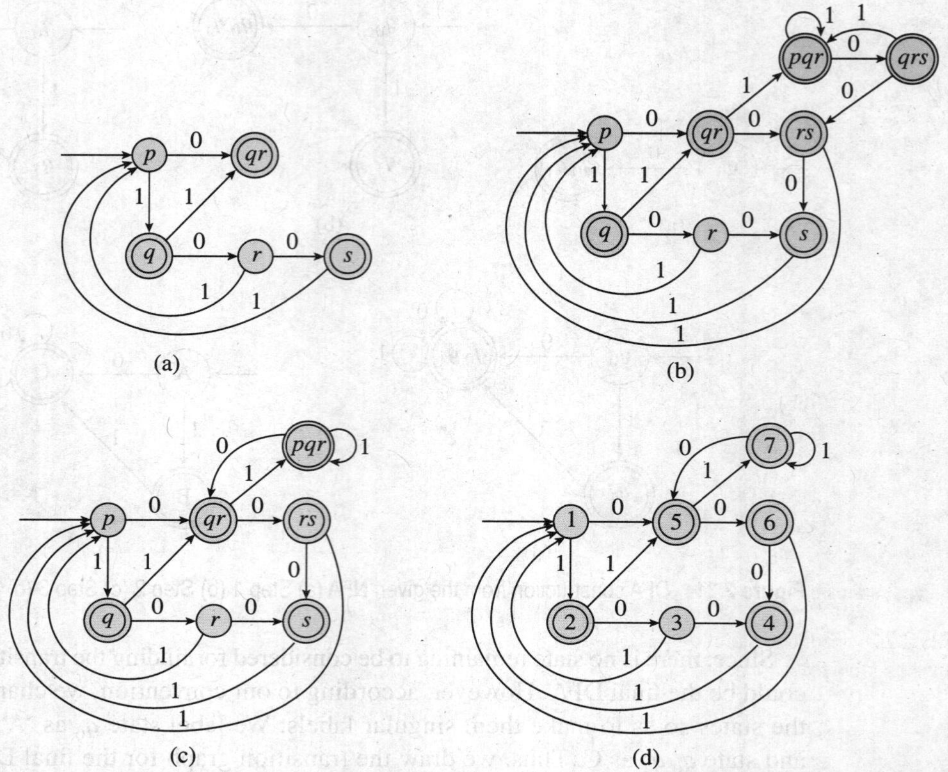


**Figure 2.22** NFA to DFA conversion steps (a) Step 1 (b) Step 2 (c) DFA (without relabelling) (d) Final DFA

NFA, $F = \{q, s\}$. Hence, for the resultant DFA, we mark those states as final, which contain either $q$, $s$, or both the symbols.

The initial state will be same as that of the given NFA, that is, $p$—refer to Fig. 2.22(a).

Now, we have finished with transitions from states $p$, $q$, $r$, and $s$. However, there is one new state $qr$ that we need to introduce as per the method, and find the transitions from the same:

$$\delta'(qr, 0) = \delta(q, 0) \cup \delta(r, 0)$$
$$= \{r\} \cup \{s\}$$
$$= rs \quad \text{(new state)}$$

Similarly,

$$\delta'(qr, 1) = \delta(q, 1) \cup \delta(r, 1)$$
$$= \{q, r\} \cup \{p\}$$
$$= pqr \quad \text{(new state)}$$

Thus, we must add two new states, $rs$ and $pqr$, and both are final states. Let us now find transitions for both these states:

$$\delta'(rs, 0) = \delta(r, 0) \cup \delta(s, 0) = \{s\} \cup \phi$$
$$= s \quad \text{(already existing state)}$$

$$\delta'(rs, 1) = \delta(r, 1) \cup \delta(s, 1) = \{p\} \cup \{p\}$$
$$= p \quad \text{(already existing state)}$$
$$\delta'(pqr, 0) = \delta(p, 0) \cup \delta(q, 0) \cup \delta(r, 0) = \{q, r\} \cup \{r\} \cup \{s\}$$
$$= qrs \quad \text{(new state)}$$
$$\delta'(pqr, 1) = \delta(p, 1) \cup \delta(q, 1) \cup \delta(r, 1) = \{q\} \cup \{q, r\} \cup \{p\}$$
$$= pqr \quad \text{(already added state)}$$

**Table 2.23** State transition table for resultant DFA

| $Q'$ \ $\Sigma$ | 0 | 1 |
|---|---|---|
| $p$ | $qr$ | $q$ |
| $*q$ | $r$ | $qr$ |
| $r$ | $s$ | $p$ |
| $*s$ | – | $p$ |
| $*qr$ | $rs$ | $pqr$ |
| $*rs$ | $s$ | $p$ |
| $*pqr$ | $qrs$ | $pqr$ |
| $*qrs$ | $rs$ | $pqr$ |

'*': Final states

We now have a new state, *qrs*, which is a final state, and we need to find the transitions from that state:

$$\delta'(qrs, 0) = \delta(q, 0) \cup \delta(r, 0) \cup \delta(s, 0)$$
$$= \{r\} \cup \{s\} \cup \phi$$
$$= rs \quad \text{(already added state)}$$
$$\delta'(qrs, 1) = \delta(q, 1) \cup \delta(r, 1) \cup \delta(s, 1)$$
$$= \{q, r\} \cup \{p\} \cup \{p\}$$
$$= pqr \quad \text{(already added state)}$$

The state transition table for the resultant DFA is as shown in Table 2.23.

Now, there is no new state remaining to be added, or to find the transitions form. Hence, the transition graph now can be drawn as in Fig. 2.22(b). We observe from the figure that we have considered only eight states, whereas using method I, we would have 15 states to begin with. Further, this method can never generate a disconnected graph, unlike in method I. In this way, we save on the time that is consumed to find out the transitions for unnecessary states.

Let us now draw the state transition table using the TG shown in Fig. 2.22(b), and check if it can be reduced further.

We observe from Table 2.23 that states '*r*' and '*rs*' have the same transitions on the same input symbols; but '*r*' is a non-final state, while '*rs*' is a final state. Therefore, we cannot replace '*rs*' by '*r*', or vice versa.

However, we can replace state *qrs* by state *qr*, as these are equivalent states. The modified state transition table can be redrawn as in Table 2.24, after replacing '*qrs*' by '*qr*'.

**Table 2.24** Reduced state transition table for resultant DFA

| $Q'$ \ $\Sigma$ | 0 | 1 |
|---|---|---|
| $p$ | $qr$ | $q$ |
| $*q$ | $r$ | $qr$ |
| $r$ | $s$ | $p$ |
| $*s$ | – | $p$ |
| $*qr$ | $rs$ | $pqr$ |
| $*rs$ | $s$ | $p$ |
| $*pqr$ | $qr$ | $pqr$ |

As Table 2.24 cannot be reduced further, we now draw the TG as shown in Fig. 2.22(c). After changing the state labels, we can further redraw it as in Fig. 2.22(d), which is the final equivalent DFA.

## 2.7 NFA WITH $\epsilon$-TRANSITIONS

NFA with $\epsilon$-transitions is an NFA that includes transitions on the empty input symbol, that is, '$\epsilon$' (epsilon). This is also called an NFA with $\epsilon$-moves.

### *Formal Definition*

NFA with $\epsilon$-moves is denoted by a 5-tuple:

$$M = (Q, \Sigma, \delta, q_0, F)$$

where,

$Q$: Finite set of states
$\Sigma$: Finite input alphabet
$q_0$: Initial state contained in $Q$
$F$: Set of final states $\subseteq Q$
$\delta$: State function mapping $Q \times (\Sigma \cup \{\epsilon\})$ to $2^Q$
i.e., $\delta: Q \times (\Sigma \cup \{\epsilon\}) \rightarrow 2^Q$

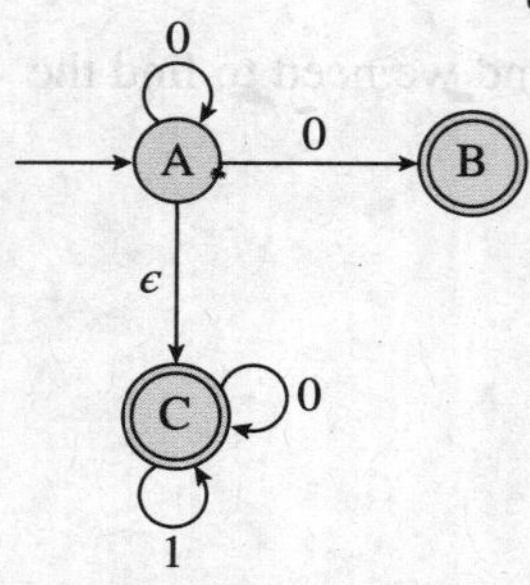

**Figure 2.23** Example NFA with ε-transitions

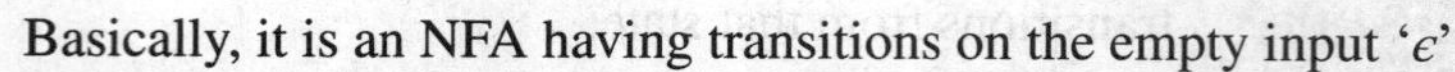
Basically, it is an NFA having transitions on the empty input 'ε'.

For example, let us refer to Fig. 2.23, which shows one ε-transition from state A to state C.

The term ε-transition means a transition on an empty input; it is actually a path whose length is zero. In the aforementioned example, we can say that the distance between state $A$ and state $C$ is zero—reading 'ε' is as good as reading no input symbol. Figure 2.24 shows another example NFA with ε-transitions.

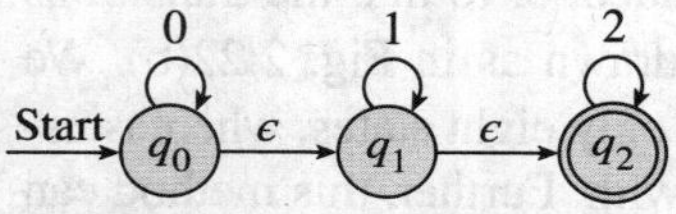

**Figure 2.24** Example NFA with ε-transitions

We observe from Fig. 2.24 that there are two ε-transitions: One from state $q_0$ to state $q_1$, and another from state $q_1$ to state $q_2$. We also see that from every state there is a unique transition on the same symbol. Then, the question may arise: Why is this FA considered an NFA? The answer to this question is that any FA with ε-moves is always an NFA. A DFA can never have ε-moves.

There is one more reason, which is explained as follows:

From Fig. 2.24, we can write:

$$\delta(q_0, 0) = q_0$$
$$\delta(q_0, \epsilon) = q_1 \quad (2.1)$$

Therefore, $\delta(q_0, 0\epsilon) = \delta(\delta(q_0, 0), \epsilon)$
$= \delta(q_0, \epsilon)$
$= q_1$

Here, '0ε' means zero concatenated with an empty string, that is, only '0'. Therefore,

$$\delta(q_0, 0\epsilon) = \delta(q_0, 0)$$
$$= q_0 \quad (2.2)$$

From Eqs (2.1) and (2.2), we can write,

$$\delta(q_0, 0) = \{q_0, q_1\}$$

Similarly,

$$\delta(q_1, 1) = \{q_1, q_2\}$$

Thus, on a single symbol, from state $q_0$, the FA has two different transitions. The same thing holds for state $q_1$ as well. Therefore, the diagram must be an NFA (obviously, with ε-moves).

### 2.7.1 Significance of NFA with $\epsilon$-Transitions

Now, let us try to address the question: Why would we need NFA with $\epsilon$-moves?

If we want to construct an FA, which accepts the language:

$L$ = Set of strings with zero or more number of 0's, followed by zero or more number of 1's, followed by zero or more number of 2's

It becomes very difficult and may even seem impossible to directly draw an NFA or DFA from the aforementioned language description. However, we may observe that the NFA with $\epsilon$-moves in Fig. 2.24 accepts exactly the same language described here. Hence, it becomes very easy to draw an NFA with $\epsilon$-moves from the language description, with the help of $\epsilon$-transitions.

Now, let us check whether the NFA accepts the string '$\epsilon$', that is, with zero number of 0's, followed by zero number of 1's, followed by zero number of 2's.

Let us start with the initial state:

$$\delta(q_0, \epsilon) = q_1$$
$$\delta(q_1, \epsilon) = q_2$$

Therefore, $\delta(q_0, \epsilon\epsilon) = q_2$

Here, '$\epsilon\epsilon$' is nothing but '$\epsilon$';

hence, $\delta(q_0, \epsilon) = q_2$ (final state)

We see that starting from the initial state, $q_0$, and reading string $\epsilon$, the machine reaches the final state $q_2$; hence, the machines accepts '$\epsilon$'.

Let us now check the acceptance of '002'—two number of 0's, followed by zero number of 1's, followed by one number of 2's:

$$\delta(q_0, 0) = q_0$$
$$\delta(q_0, 0) = q_0$$
$$\delta(q_0, \epsilon) = q_1$$
$$\delta(q_1, \epsilon) = q_2$$
$$\delta(q_2, 2) = q_2 \text{ (final state)}$$

Therefore, $\delta(q_0, 00\epsilon\epsilon 2) = q_2$

i.e., $\delta(q_0, 002) = q_2$

This means that '002' is a valid string, as $q_2$ is the final state, which is reached upon reading the input string '002'.

Thus, we see that NFA with $\epsilon$-moves helps us split complex language acceptance problems into smaller ones. The solutions to these problems can then be integrated with the help of $\epsilon$-transitions.

For example, in Fig. 2.24, state $q_0$ accepts inputs consisting of zero or more number of '0's; state $q_1$ accepts inputs with zero or more number of '1's; and state $q_2$ accepts zero or more number of '2's. Hence, the original language $L$ now is formed by sequencing these three parts, so as to make one follow the other.

### 2.7.2 State Transition Table for NFA with $\epsilon$-Transitions

The state transition table for an NFA with $\epsilon$-moves (or transitions) is similar to that of an NFA or DFA. The only difference is that along with the columns labelled by input symbols from $\Sigma$, there is an additional column labelled '$\epsilon$'.

This is in line with the transition function defined earlier:

$$\delta : Q \times (\Sigma \cup \{\epsilon\}) \rightarrow 2^Q$$

The state transition table for the NFA with $\epsilon$-moves in Fig. 2.24 is as shown in Table 2.25.

**Table 2.25** State transition table for NFA with $\epsilon$-moves in Fig. 2.24

| $Q$ \ $\Sigma \cup \{\epsilon\}$ | 0 | 1 | 2 | $\epsilon$ |
|---|---|---|---|---|
| $q_0$ | $\{q_0\}$ | $\phi$ | $\phi$ | $\{q_1\}$ |
| $q_1$ | $\phi$ | $\{q_1\}$ | $\phi$ | $\{q_2\}$ |
| $q_2$ | $\phi$ | $\phi$ | $\{q_2\}$ | $\phi$ |

Hence, a transition for NFA with $\epsilon$-moves can be described as:

$\delta\ (q, a) =$ set of all states $p$ such that there is a transition labelled $a$ from state $q$ to state $p$, where $a$ is either $\epsilon$ or $a \subseteq \Sigma$

### 2.7.3 $\epsilon$-Closure of a State

The set of all states $p$, such that there is a path from state $q$ to state $p$ labelled '$\epsilon$', is known as $\epsilon$-closure ($q$). In other words, it is the set of all the states having distance zero from state $q$. It is pronounced as 'epsilon closure of $q$'.

For example, let us consider the NFA with $\epsilon$-moves in Fig. 2.24:

$$\epsilon\text{-closure } (q_0) = \{q_0, q_1, q_2\}$$

Here, '$q_0$' is also added to the set because every state is at distance zero from itself.

Similarly, $\epsilon$-closure ($q_1$) = $\{q_1, q_2\}$, and $\epsilon$-closure ($q_2$) = $\{q_2\}$.

We use a separate denotation, $\hat{\delta}$, to represent the $\epsilon$-closure of a state. It is defined as:

$$\hat{\delta}(q_0, \epsilon) = \epsilon\text{-closure } (q_0) = \{q_0, q_1, q_1\}$$

## 2.8 EQUIVALENCE OF NFA AND NFA WITH $\epsilon$-TRANSITIONS

Let us consider an NFA with $\epsilon$-moves, which is given by:

$$M_1 = (Q, \Sigma, \delta, q_0, F)$$

where, $\delta : Q \times (\Sigma \cup \{\epsilon\}) \rightarrow 2^Q$

This can be converted to an NFA without $\epsilon$-moves, as follows:

$$M_2 = (Q, \Sigma, \delta', q_0, F')$$

where, $\delta' : Q \times \Sigma \rightarrow 2^Q$

We observe here that $Q$, $\Sigma$, and the initial state $q_0$ are the same in $M_1$ and $M_2$, but the set of final states, $F$ and $F'$, might not be same.

Likewise, the state transition function, $\delta'$, for the required NFA is given as:

$$\delta'(q, a) = \epsilon\text{-closure}\ (\delta(\hat{\delta}(q, \epsilon), a)) \tag{2.1}$$

where, $\hat{\delta}(q, \epsilon) = \epsilon$-closure $(q)$

Let us look at an example to illustrate this conversion method.

---

**Example 2.11** Convert the NFA with $\epsilon$-moves in Fig. 2.24 to its equivalent NFA without $\epsilon$-moves, accepting the same language.

***Solution*** Using the definition of $\epsilon$-closure, we have:

$$\begin{aligned}
&\epsilon\text{-closure}\ (q_0) = \{q_0, q_1, q_2\}\\
&\epsilon\text{-closure}\ (q_1) = \{q_1, q_2\}\\
&\epsilon\text{-closure}\ (q_2) = \{q_2\}
\end{aligned}$$

We observe that '$q_2$' is a member of $\epsilon$-closure $(q_0)$, which means that '$q_2$' is at zero distance from '$q_0$'. Similarly, '$q_2$' is at distance zero from '$q_1$' as well. Note that '$q_2$' is the only final state for given NFA with $\epsilon$-moves:

$$F = \{q_2\}$$

From, this observation, the set of final states for the resultant equivalent NFA without $\epsilon$-moves is given by:

$$F' = \{q_0, q_1, q_2\}$$

Now, let us find the state transition function, $\delta'$, for the resultant NFA. This can be obtained with the help of the rule in Eq. (2.1):

$$\begin{aligned}
\delta'\ (q_0, 0) &= \epsilon\text{-closure}\ (\delta\ (\hat{\delta}\ (q_0, \epsilon), 0))\\
&= \epsilon\text{-closure}\ (\delta\ (\{q_0, q_1, q_2\}, 0))\\
&= \epsilon\text{-closure}\ (\delta\ (q_0, 0) \cup \delta\ (q_1, 0) \cup \delta\ (q_2, 0))\\
&= \epsilon\text{-closure}\ (\{q_0\} \cup \phi \cup \phi)\\
&= \epsilon\text{-closure}\ (q_0)\\
&= \{q_0, q_1, q_2\}
\end{aligned}$$

$$\begin{aligned}
\delta'\ (q_0, 1) &= \epsilon\text{-closure}\ (\delta\ (\hat{\delta}\ (q_0, \epsilon), 1))\\
&= \epsilon\text{-closure}\ (\delta\ (\{q_0, q_1, q_2\}, 1))\\
&= \epsilon\text{-closure}\ \{\delta\ (q_0, 1) \cup \delta\ (q_1, 1) \cup \delta\ (q_2, 1)\\
&= \epsilon\text{-closure}\ (\phi \cup \{q_1\} \cup \phi)\\
&= \epsilon\text{-closure}\ (q_1)\\
&= \{q_1, q_2\}
\end{aligned}$$

$$\begin{aligned}
\delta'\ (q_0, 2) &= \epsilon\text{-closure}\ (\delta\ (\hat{\delta}\ (q_0, \epsilon), 2))\\
&= \epsilon\text{-closure}\ (\delta\ (\{q_0, q_1, q_2\}, 2))\\
&= \epsilon\text{-closure}\ (\delta\ (q_0, 2) \cup \delta\ (q_1, 2) \cup \delta\ (q_2, 2))
\end{aligned}$$

$$= \epsilon\text{-closure } (\phi \cup \phi \cup \{q_2\})$$
$$= \epsilon\text{-closure } (q_2)$$
$$= \{q_2\}$$

$$\delta' (q_1, 0) = \epsilon\text{-closure } (\delta (\hat{\delta} (q_1, \epsilon), 0))$$
$$= \epsilon\text{-closure } (\delta (\{q_1, q_2\}, 0))$$
$$= \epsilon\text{-closure } (\delta (q_1, 0) \cup \delta (q_2, 0))$$
$$= \epsilon\text{-closure } (\phi \in \phi)$$
$$= \epsilon\text{-closure } (\phi)$$
$$= \phi$$

Similarly, we can obtain:

$$\delta' (q_1, 1) = \{q_1, q_2\}$$
$$\delta' (q_1, 2) = \{q_2\}$$
$$\delta' (q_2, 0) = \phi$$
$$\delta' (q_2, 1) = \phi$$
$$\delta' (q_2, 2) = \{q_2\}$$

**Table 2.26** State transition table for NFA without $\epsilon$-transitions

| $Q$ \ $\Sigma$ | 0 | 1 | 2 |
|---|---|---|---|
| $q_0$ | $\{q_0, q_1, q_2\}$ | $\{q_1, q_2\}$ | $\{q_2\}$ |
| $q_1$ | $\phi$ | $\{q_1, q_2\}$ | $\{q_2\}$ |
| $q_2$ | $\phi$ | $\phi$ | $\{q_2\}$ |

From the aforementioned transitions, we construct the state transition table for the resultant NFA without $\epsilon$-transitions as shown in Table 2.26.

The resultant NFA without $\epsilon$-moves can be represented by a TG shown in Fig. 2.25(a).

We observe that there is a transition from state $q_0$ to state $q_1$, labelled '0, 1', meaning that there are two transitions from state $q_0$ to state $q_1$; one on reading input symbol '0', and the other on reading input symbol '1'. Here they are combined for simplicity. For a more specific diagram, refer to Fig. 2.25(b), where all transitions are shown separately.

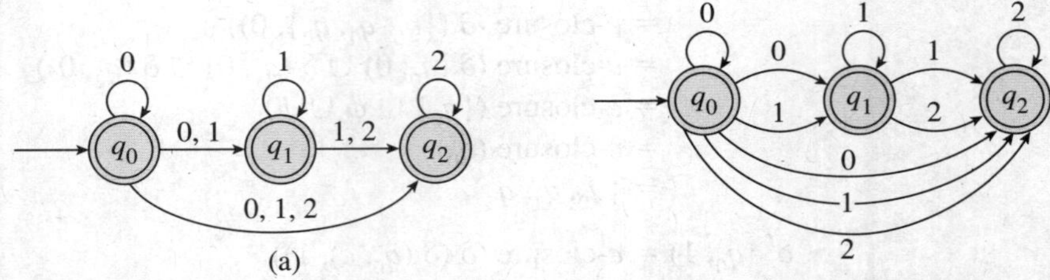


**Figure 2.25** NFA without $\epsilon$-moves (a) Resultant NFA without $\epsilon$-moves (b) NFA without $\epsilon$-moves (all transitions separately shown)

As we have already discussed, '$q_2$' is a final state here because it is also a final state for the given NFA with $\epsilon$-moves. In addition, '$q_0$' also becomes a final state for the resultant NFA without $\epsilon$-moves, because $\epsilon$-closure ($q_0$) contains '$q_2$', which is the final state of given NFA with $\epsilon$-moves. For the same reason, '$q_1$' is also a final state now for the resultant NFA without $\epsilon$-moves.

## 2.9 EQUIVALENCE OF DFA AND NFA WITH $\epsilon$-TRANSITIONS

There are two different approaches (or methods) for constructing a DFA from a given NFA with $\epsilon$-moves, namely:

1. Indirect conversion method
2. Direct conversion method

The direct method takes lesser number of steps to obtain the equivalent DFA and hence, it is faster than the indirect method.

### 2.9.1 Indirect Conversion Method

This method consists of two different sub-parts:

1. Construct the NFA without $\epsilon$-moves from the given NFA with $\epsilon$-moves; and
2. Construct an equivalent DFA from this newly-constructed NFA without $\epsilon$-moves, using either of the two methods discussed in Section 2.6.

Let us look at an example to demonstrate the indirect conversion method.

---

**Example 2.12** Construct an equivalent DFA for the NFA with $\epsilon$-moves shown in Fig. 2.24.

***Solution*** For the given NFA with $\epsilon$-moves in Fig. 2.24, we have already constructed an equivalent NFA without $\epsilon$-moves in Fig. 2.25.

For converting this NFA without $\epsilon$-moves in Fig, 2.25 to its equivalent DFA, let us use conversion method II (refer to Section 2.6.3).

From Table 2.26, which is the state transition table for the NFA in Fig. 2.25, we can directly write the state transition function, $\delta_1$, for the resultant DFA:

$$\delta_1 (q_0, 0) = q_0\, q_1\, q_2 \quad \text{(new state)}$$
$$\delta_1 (q_0, 1) = q_1\, q_2 \quad \text{(new state)}$$
$$\delta_1 (q_0, 2) = q_2 \quad \text{(already existing state)}$$
$$\delta_1 (q_1, 1) = \phi$$
$$\delta_1 (q_1, 1) = q_1\, q_2$$
$$\delta_1 (q_1, 2) = q_2$$
$$\delta_1(q_2, 0) = \phi$$
$$\delta_1 (q_2, 1) = \phi$$
$$\delta_1 (q_2, 2) = q_2$$

These transitions are shown in Fig. 2.26(a); here, transitions from the states '$q_0\, q_1\, q_2$' and '$q_1\, q_2$' are unprocessed.

The new states '$q_1\, q_2$' and '$q_0\, q_1\, q_2$' are also final states, because '$q_0$', '$q_1$', and '$q_2$' are the final states of the original NFA.

Now,

$$\delta_1 (q_1, q_2, 0) = \delta' (q_1, 0) \cup \delta' (q_2, 0) = \phi \cup \phi$$
$$= \phi$$

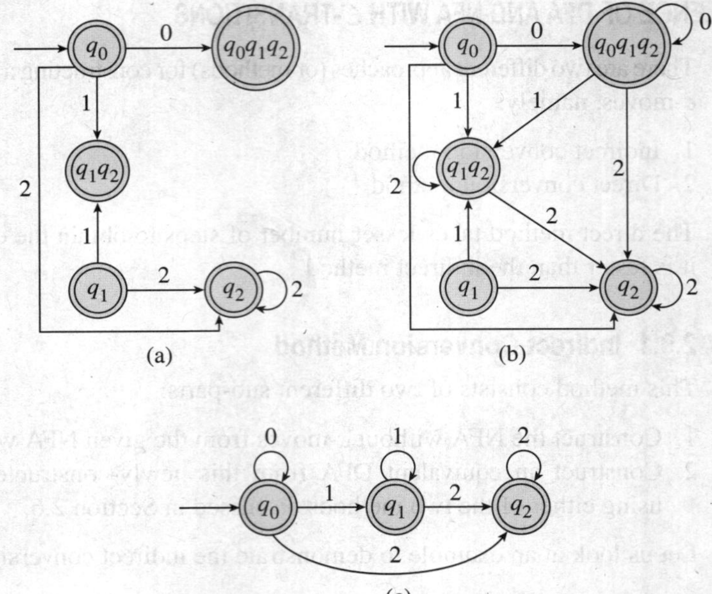


**Figure 2.26** Construction of DFA from the given NFA (a) Step 1 (b) Step 2 (all transitions shown, no state unprocessed) (c) Final DFA

$$\begin{aligned}
\delta_1(q_1\, q_2, 1) &= \delta'(q_1, 1) \cup \delta'(q_2, 1) = \{q_1, q_2\} \cup \phi \\
&= q_1\, q_2 \text{ (already existing state)}
\end{aligned}$$

$$\begin{aligned}
\delta_1(q_1\, q_2, 2) &= \delta'(q_1, 2) \cup \delta'(q_2, 2) \\
&= \{q_2\} \cup \{q_2\} \\
&= q_2 \text{ (already existing state)}
\end{aligned}$$

$$\begin{aligned}
\delta_1(q_0\, q_1\, q_2, 0) &= \delta'(q_0, 0) \cup \delta'(q_1, 0) \cup \delta'(q_2, 0) \\
&= \{q_0, q_1, q_2\} \cup \phi \cup \phi \\
&= q_0\, q_1\, q_2 \text{ (already existing state)}
\end{aligned}$$

$$\begin{aligned}
\delta_1(q_0\, q_1\, q_2, 1) &= \delta'(q_0, 1) \cup \delta'(q_1, 1) \cup \delta'(q_2, 1) \\
&= \{q_1, q_2\} \cup \{q_1, q_2\} \cup \phi \\
&= q_1\, q_2 \text{ (already existing state)}
\end{aligned}$$

$$\begin{aligned}
\delta_1(q_0\, q_1\, q_2, 2) &= \delta'(q_0, 2) \cup \delta'(q_1, 2) \cup \delta'(q_2, 2) \\
&= \{q_2\} \cup \{q_2\} \cup \{q_2\} \\
&= q_2 \text{ (already existing state)}
\end{aligned}$$

Since we are now left with no new state, the modified state transition diagram for the equivalent DFA, with all the states and their respective transitions, can be drawn as shown in Fig. 2.26(b). The state transition table for the same is as shown in Table 2.27.

From the table, we observe that we can replace state '$q_0\, q_1\, q_2$' by state '$q_0$', and state '$q_1\, q_2$' by '$q_1$' as these are equivalent states. We now have the minimized state transition table as shown in Table 2.28. The TG for this can be drawn as in Fig. 2.26 (c).

**Table 2.27** State transition table for the equivalent DFA

| $Q'$ \ $\Sigma$ | 0 | 1 | 2 |
|---|---|---|---|
| $*q_0$ | $q_0q_1q_2$ | $q_1q_2$ | $q_2$ |
| $*q_1$ | – | $q_1q_2$ | $q_2$ |
| $*q_2$ | – | – | $q_2$ |
| $*q_1q_2$ | – | $q_1q_2$ | $q_2$ |
| $*q_0q_1q_2$ | $q_0q_1q_2$ | $q_1q_2$ | $q_2$ |

'*': Final states

**Table 2.28** Reduced state transition table for the DFA

| $Q'$ \ $\Sigma$ | 0 | 1 | 2 |
|---|---|---|---|
| $*q_0$ | $q_0$ • | $q_1$ • | $q_2$ |
| $*q_1$ | – | $q_1$ • | $q_2$ |
| $*q_2$ | – | – | $q_2$ |

'*': Final states
'•': Modified entries

## 2.9.2 Direct Conversion Method

In this approach, we directly begin with the initial state, and go on adding states as and when required to the diagram, till we come to the stage when there exists no state without having the transitions specified. Here, each state label consists of two parts: The first part is the state label, and the other part is a combination of all the state symbols, which are reachable from the given state.

States that are reachable for a given state $p$ are the states, which are at zero distance from the state $p$, that is, all such states '$q$', to which there are paths from the state $p$ labelled as '$\epsilon$', excluding the state $p$ itself.

**Example 2.13** Consider the NFA with $\epsilon$-moves shown in Fig. 2.24. Construct the DFA equivalent to it using direct approach.

***Solution*** Let us begin with the start state $q_0$ of the given NFA with $\epsilon$-moves. We create a new state as a part of the resultant DFA; the first part of the label is '$q_0$', and the second part includes all the reachable states of state $q_0$, that is, '$q_1$, $q_2$', as shown in Fig. 2.27(a).

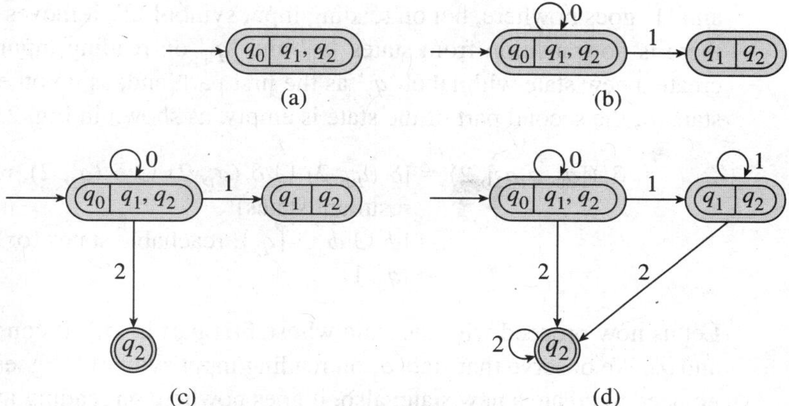


**Figure 2.27** DFA construction from NFA with $\epsilon$-moves (a) Step 1 (b) Step 2 (c) Step 3 (d) DFA

Since state $q_2$, which is a final state for the given NFA with $\epsilon$-moves, is reachable from state $q_0$; we mark this new state as a final state.

We now proceed to find the transitions from this new state:

Let us create new states if we find any new combination for the next state. From Table 2.25, which represents the state transition function, $\delta$, for the NFA with $\epsilon$-moves in Fig. 2.25, we can directly write the state function, $\delta_1$, for the resultant DFA.

We observe that in the given NFA with $\epsilon$-moves, state $q_0$ on reading the input symbol '0' goes to itself. We now proceed with the next symbol in the same state label, that is, '$q_1$'. State $q_1$ on reading input symbol '0' goes nowhere. Similarly, the other part of the label, that is, state $q_2$ also does not have any transition on reading input symbol '0'. Hence, the next state is the same state; so we add the self loop on symbol '0'. This can be explained with the help of the following equation:

$$\begin{aligned}\delta_1([q_0, q_1q_2], 0) &= [\delta(q_0, 0) \cup \delta(q_1, 0) \cup \delta(q_2, 0), \text{reachable states from the resultant states}]\\ &= [\{q_0\} \cup \phi \cup \phi, \text{reachable states for } q_0]\\ &= [q_0, q_1q_2]\end{aligned}$$

There are no transitions from state $q_0$ on reading input symbols '1' and '2': state $q_1$ on reading input symbol '1' goes to state $q_1$; state $q_2$ has no transition on reading input symbol '1'. Therefore, we create a new state with first part of the label as $q_1$, and the second part as all reachable states from '$q_1$', that is, state $q_2$. Hence, we mark this state also as a final state, as state $q_2$ is reachable from state $q_1$. The current stage of the TG is reflected in Fig. 2.27(b).

$$\begin{aligned}\delta_1([q_0, q_1q_2], 1) &= [\delta(q_0, 1) \cup \delta(q_1, 1) \cup \delta(q_2, 1), \text{reachable states from the resultant states}]\\ &= [\phi \cup \{q_1\} \cup \phi, \text{reachable states for } q_1]\\ &= [q_1, q_2]\end{aligned}$$

Now, we proceed with the next symbol in state $q_0$: state $q_2$ on reading input symbols '0' and '1' goes nowhere, but on reading input symbol '2', it moves to state $q_2$. Furthermore, there is no transition from states '$q_0$' and '$q_1$' on reading input symbol '2'. Hence, we create a new state with label '$q_2$' as the first part, and, as no other state is reachable from state $q_2$, the second part of the state is empty, as shown in Fig. 2.27(c).

$$\begin{aligned}\delta_1([q_0, q_1q_2], 2) &= [\delta(q_0, 2) \cup \delta(q_1, 2) \cup \delta(q_2, 2), \text{reachable states from the resultant states}]\\ &= [\phi \cup \phi \cup \{q_2\}, \text{reachable states for } q_2]\\ &= [q_2, ]\end{aligned}$$

Let us now proceed with the state whose first part is '$q_1$'. It consists of two symbols—$q_1$ and $q_2$. We observe that state $q_1$ on reading input symbol '1' goes to itself; hence, there is no need to create a new state; also, it goes nowhere on reading input symbols '0' and '2'. Likewise, the next state, $q_2$, transits to nowhere on reading input symbols '0' and '1', but on reading '2', it goes to state $q_2$ which is already created.

Therefore, we have:

$$\begin{aligned}\delta_1([q_1, q_2], 1) &= [\delta(q_1, 1) \cup \delta(q_2, 1), \text{reachable states}]\\ &= [\{q_1\} \cup \phi, \text{reachable states for } q_1]\\ &= [q_1, q_2]\\ \delta_1([q_1, q_2], 2) &= [\delta(q_1, 2) \cup \delta(q_2, 2), \text{reachable states}]\\ &= [\phi \cup \{q_2\}, \text{reachable states for } q_2]\\ &= [q_2, ]\end{aligned}$$

Finally, the only remaining state is $q_2$, which on reading input symbol '2', goes to itself. This ends the process of finding new states and transitions. This stage of the DFA is reflected in Fig. 2.27(d).

Let us compare this DFA with the DFA in Fig. 2.26(c). We observe that it is the same DFA. Hence,

$$\begin{aligned}\delta_1([q_2, ], 2) &= [\delta(q_2, 2), \text{reachable states}]\\ &= [\{q_2\}, \text{reachable states for } q_2]\\ &= [q_2, ]\end{aligned}$$

---

## 2.10 FINITE AUTOMATA WITH OUTPUT

As we know, FA is the mathematical model of FSM, and is defined by a five-tuple: $(Q, \Sigma, \delta, q_0, F)$, which does not include information regarding the output. After reading a string, if the FA resides in a final state, the string is considered as 'accepted' by the FA; otherwise, it is 'rejected'. Since FA is the language acceptor (or recognizer), it can generate only these two outcomes—more like a Boolean function.

The definition of FA we have studied so far includes the limited power of FSM as language acceptor. We can now formalize the definition of FSM with output and machine function (MAF) as well. There are two different types (or visualizations) of the FSM that generate output, namely:

1. Moore machine
2. Mealy machine

In this section, we are going to study the formalism around these two different FSM types.

### 2.10.1 Moore Machine

A Moore machine is a machine with finite number of states, and for which the output symbol at any given time depends only upon the current state of the machine (and not on the input symbol read).

#### *Formal Definition*

A Moore machine is a six-tuple that is defined as follows:

$$M = (Q, \Sigma, \Delta, \delta, \lambda, q_0)$$

where,

$Q$: Finite set of states
$\Sigma$: Finite input alphabet
$\Delta$: An output alphabet
$\delta$: State transition function (STF); $\delta: Q \times \Sigma \rightarrow Q$
$\lambda$: Machine function (MAF); $\lambda: Q \rightarrow \Delta$
$q_0$: Initial state of the machine

Thus, for a Moore machine, an output symbol is associated with each state. When the machine is in a particular state, it generates the output, irrespective of the input that caused the transition.

Let us look at an example to illustrate this machine.

---

**Example 2.14** Construct a Moore machine to find out the residue-modulo-3 for binary numbers.

***Solution*** If $i$ is a binary number, and if we write '0' after $i$ then, its value becomes $2i$. For example, consider a binary number:

$i = 1$ (value = 1)

If we write '0' after $i$, then we have:

$i.0 = 10$ (value $= 2 \times 1$)

As another example, let us we consider:

$i = 100$ (value = 4)

Then, $i.0 = 1000$ (value $= 8 = 2 \times 4$)

Similarly, if we write '1' after $i$, where $i$ is any binary number, its value becomes '$2i + 1$'. For example, consider the binary number:

$i = 1$ (value = 1)

Then, $i.1 = 11$ (value $= 3 = 2 \times 1 + 1$)

As another example, let us consider:

$i = 100$ (value = 4)

$i.1 = 1001$ (value $= 9 = 2 \times 4 + 1$)

As we are constructing a machine to determine the remainder (or residue) when we divide any binary number by 3, the different remainder values that we can have are: 0, 1, and 2.

In Table 2.29, let us consider a case in which the remainder from the previous result is 2—that is, 10 in binary form. Now, if we write 0 after it, it becomes 4—that is, 100 in binary form. When we divide this by 3, the remainder will be 1. In the division process, we read the input from left to right, one digit at a time. The digit we read is divided by the divisor (in this example, the divisor is 3). The next digit is then concatenated to the remainder of

**Table 2.29** Different remainder values

| Remainder value ($R$) | 0 | 1 | 2 |
|---|---|---|---|
| When we write '0' after ($R$) and divide by 3, remainder = $2R \bmod 3$ | 0 | 2 | 1 |
| When we write '1' after ($R$) and divide by 3, remainder = $(2R + 1) \bmod 3$ | 1 | 0 | 2 |

**Table 2.30** Machine function for Moore machine, $\lambda : Q \rightarrow \Delta$

| State $Q$ | $q_0$ | $q_1$ | $q_2$ |
|---|---|---|---|
| Output $\Delta$ | 0 | 1 | 2 |

this division to form the next number to be divided. We continue this process till all the digits in the input string are exhausted. We are going to use the same in our computations.

As we are interested in constructing a Moore machine for which the output depends only on the current state of the machine, we can associate the three different remainder values with three different states: remainder 0 with state $q_0$, remainder 1 with state $q_1$, and remainder 2 with state $q_2$, as described in the MAF shown in Table 2.30.

Now, Table 2.31 shows the state transition table for the required Moore machine. This is same as Table 2.29 depicting formal notation.

We observe that Table 2.31 is an exact reflection of Table 2.29 that we prepared earlier. The transition graph for this can be drawn as in Fig. 2.28. In the diagram, along with every state vertex, there is a symbol written below, which is an output symbol associated with that state.

**Table 2.31** State transition table for Moore machine

| $Q$ \ $\Sigma$ | 0 | 1 |
|---|---|---|
| $q_0$ | $q_0$ | $q_1$ |
| $q_1$ | $q_2$ | $q_0$ |
| $q_2$ | $q_1$ | $q_2$ |

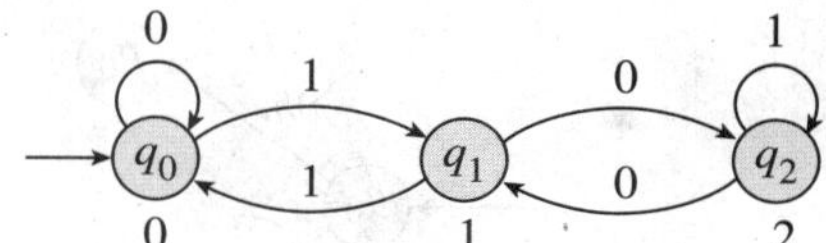


**Figure 2.28** TG for Moore machine

## 2.10.2 Mealy Machine

A Mealy machine is a machine with finite number of states, and for which the output symbol at any given time is a function of (i.e., it depends on) the current input symbol as well as the current state of the machine.

***Formal Definition***

A Mealy machine is denoted by a six-tuple:

$$M = (Q, \Sigma, \Delta, \delta, \lambda, q_0)$$

where,

$Q$: Finite set of states
$\Sigma$: Finite input alphabet

$\Delta$: Finite output alphabet
$\delta$: State transition function (STF); $\delta: Q \times \Sigma \to Q$
$\lambda$: Machine function (MAF); $\lambda: Q \times \Sigma \to \Delta$
$q_0$: Initial state of the machine

Thus, for this type of machine, the output depends on both current state and the current input symbol. We may recall that this is the same FSM that we have discussed in the beginning of this topic, that is, Section 2.2. All the examples we have seen earlier in the section are Mealy machines.

---

**Example 2.15** Design a Mealy machine that accepts the language consisting of strings from $\Sigma^*$, where $\Sigma = \{0, 1\}$, and ending with double '0's or double '1's.

***Solution*** Let us assume that the output alphabet, $\Delta = \{y, n\}$, indicating whether the input string is accepted or not: *y*—that is, yes—will be the output if the string is accepted, and *n*—that is, no—will be the output if the string is not accepted by the machine.

Let us assume that the initial state of the machine is '$q_0$'. From state $q_0$ there will be two transitions: one on reading input symbol '0', and the other on reading input symbol '1', as $\Sigma = \{0, 1\}$.

On reading input symbol '0', the machine makes the transition to some other state, say '$p_0$', which looks for a second consecutive zero to get double '0's. Similarly, on reading input symbol '1', the machine transits to another state, say '$p_1$', which looks for a second consecutive one to get double '1's. The situation is represented in Fig. 2.29(a).

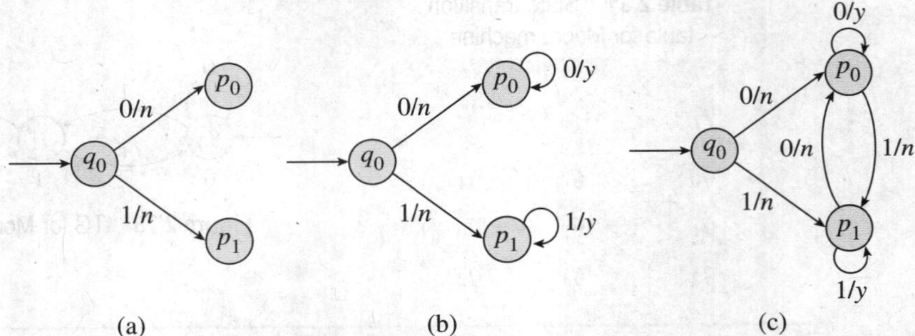


**Figure 2.29** Construction of Mealy machine (a) Step 1 (b) Step 2 (c) Final Mealy machine

In state $p_0$ if the machine reads '0', it remains in the same state and produces output '*y*', as consecutively two 0's have been read. It continues to remain in the same state on reading more 0's, because the string may be of the form '0000'—any number of '0's more than two '0's always end in at least two '0's. Similarly, in state $p_1$ if machine reads '1', it transits to the same state with output '*y*', indicating it has read double '1's. This state is reflected in Fig. 2.29(b).

Now, in state $p_0$, if the machine reads symbol '1', it makes a transition to state $p_1$, which checks for a second consecutive '1'. Next, in state $p_1$, if the machine reads '0', it transits to state $p_0$ which looks for a second consecutive '0'. The output in both these cases is '*n*', as the second consecutive letter is yet to be read.

Here ends the process of finding transitions on both '0' and '1' from every state of the machine. Figure 2.29(c) shows the final Mealy machine that complies with the given requirements.

---

**Example 2.16** Design a Mealy machine for incrementing the value of any binary number by one. The output should also be a binary number, whose value is one more than the number given.

***Solution*** In order to obtain the 2's complement of a binary number, we first take the 1's complement and add '1' to it.

For example, let 1011 be the given binary number. Then we calculate the 2's complement as follows:

1011 – given binary number
0100 – 1's complement
+ 1 – add one
0101 – 2's complement

We use a similar method to design a machine that will add '1' to a given binary number.

We will revise the aforementioned method, as shown here:

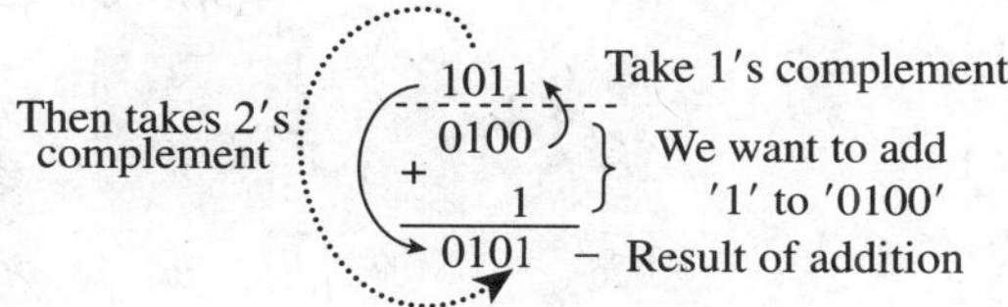


Thus, in order to add '1' to any binary number, we find the 1's complement of the given number and then find the 2's complement of the 1's complement that we have obtained.

In other words, given a number, the output should be the incremented result of adding '1' to the given number. For example:

0100 – Given number
0101 – Incremented result

Instead of first finding the 1's complement and then the 2's complement, we can adopt a simple direct approach, by following the simple steps given here:

1. Read bit by bit from the least significant bit (LSB) of the given binary number. This is more like reading the input string in the reverse order, that is, from right to left.
2. Keep on replacing the 1's by 0's, till we reach the first 0 (from the right).
3. Replace this first 0 by 1.
4. After this first 0, keep the remaining bits as they are.

In our example:

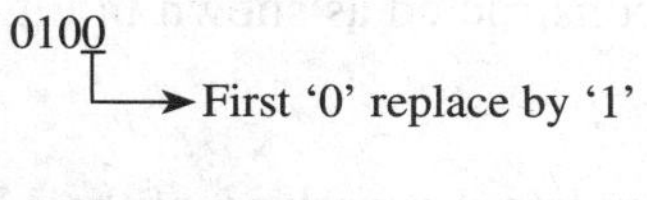

In our design, there will be two states:

$$Q = \{q_0, q_1\}$$

State $q_0$ is the initial state, which is associated with replacing all 1's by 0's till it reaches the first 0. After reaching the first 0, while reading from right to left, the machine replaces it by 1 and moves to the next state $q_1$. State $q_1$ on reading '0' generates output 0, and on reading '1', generates output 1. It thus ensures that the remaining bits are not changed.

Figure 2.30 depicts the final Mealy machine. For this machine, as we know:

**Figure 2.30** Mealy machine to increment value of a binary number by '1'

$$Q = \{q_0, q_1\}$$
$$\Sigma = \{0, 1\}$$
$$\Delta = \{0, 1\}$$

Tables 2.32(a) and 2.32(b) respectively represent the state transition function, $\delta$, and the machine function, $\lambda$.

**Table 2.32** STF and MAF (a) $\delta : Q \times \Sigma \rightarrow Q$
(b) $\lambda : Q \times \Sigma \rightarrow \Delta$

(a)

| Q \ Σ | 0 | 1 |
|---|---|---|
| $q_0$ | $q_1$ | $q_0$ |
| $q_1$ | $q_1$ | $q_1$ |

(b)

| Q \ Σ | 0 | 1 |
|---|---|---|
| $q_0$ | 1 | 0 |
| $q_1$ | 0 | 1 |

**Example 2.17** Design a Mealy machine to find the 2's complement of a given binary number.

***Solution*** Let us have a simple algorithm similar to that of the previous example:

1. Read bit by bit from LSB (right to left, in the reverse order).
2. Keep the bits unchanged till you reach the first '1' from the right side; do not replace this first '1' by '0'. That remains unchanged as well.
3. The remaining bits are to be changed from 0 to 1, and from 1 to 0.

The design here again requires two states:

$$Q = \{q_0, q_1\}$$

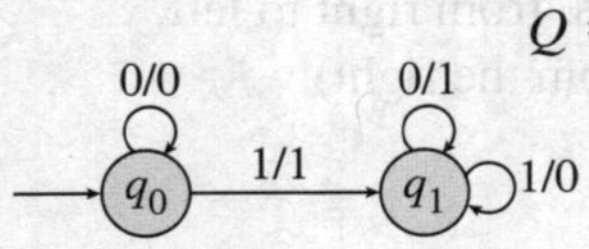

**Figure 2.31** Mealy machine to find 2's complement of a binary number

The initial state, $q_0$ reads all the 0's (from right to left) without replacing them, till it reaches the first '1'. Upon reading the first '1', it makes a transition to state $q_1$. In this state, the machine replaces each '0' that is read, by 1, and every '1' that is read, by 0. The Mealy machine can be constructed as shown in Fig. 2.31.

***Simulation***

Let us now simulate the working of the Mealy machine in Fig. 2.31 on an input binary number, '1010' (shown in Fig. 2.32). Note that the machine reads the input string from right to left, one bit at a time.

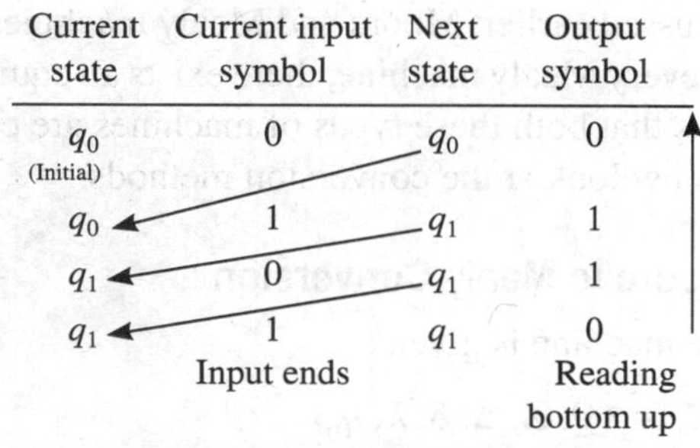

Current state
Current input symbol
Next state
Output symbol
$q_0$
(Initial)
0
$q_0$
0
$q_0$
1
$q_1$
1
$q_1$
0
$q_1$
1
$q_1$
1
$q_1$
0
Input ends
Reading bottom up


**Figure 2.32** Simulation of Mealy machine

The output can be obtained by reading from bottom to top as we are considering the input in the reverse order, that is, right to left. The output will be '0110'. Hence, '0110' is the 2's complement of '1010'.

Let us check the validity of the answer that we have obtained, by our usual method:

| | | |
|---|---|---|
| | 1010 | – number given |
| | 0101 | – 1's complement |
| + | 1 | – add 1 |
| | 0110 | – 2's complement |

Hence, the answer obtained is correct.

### 2.10.3 Finite State Transducer

A finite state transducer (FST) is an FSM with output tape. As we know, an ordinary FSM has only an input tape from where the input symbols are read.

As we know, Moore and Mealy machines generate output for every input that is read—every transition yields some output symbol. In a way, these machines generate the output string upon reading the input string or sequence. Let us assume that these machines can write the output symbols one at each transition onto an output tape that stores the output string generated. Such machines are called finite state transducers—a transducer translates (or transduces) the input string into an output string.

We observe that examples such as finding the residue-modulo-3 do not require the intermediate outputs to be stored. Since only the final remainder value is of importance, there is no need to store the intermediate outcomes. However, let us consider examples such as obtaining 1's or 2's complement of a binary number, or incrementing a binary number by one. These examples require to store the output somewhere, such as, the output tape.

Essentially, Moore and Mealy machines can be implemented as FSTs if the example at hand must store the output sequence upon reading the input sequence, one symbol at a time.

## 2.11 EQUIVALENCE OF MOORE AND MEALY MACHINES

In the previous sections, we have seen the equivalence of NFA with DFA, as well as with $\epsilon$-moves. Similarly, converting a Moore machine to its equivalent Mealy is also possible.

As discussed earlier, Moore and Mealy machines are two different visualizations of an FSM. For every Mealy machine, there exists an equivalent Moore machine, and vice versa. This means that both these types of machines are equivalent to one another.

Let us now look at the conversion methods.

### 2.11.1 Moore to Mealy Conversion

If a Moore machine is given as:

$$M_1 = (Q, \Sigma, \Delta, \delta, \lambda, q_0)$$

then, its equivalent Mealy machine is:

$$M_2 = (Q, \Sigma, \Delta, \delta, \lambda', q_0)$$

where, $\lambda' (q, a) = \lambda (\delta (q, a))$

$\forall (q \subset Q \text{ and } \forall a \subset \Sigma)$

In case of a Moore machine, the output only depends on the machine's state. On the other hand, in case of a Mealy machine, it depends on the machine's state as well as the input symbol read. Hence, the only difference between the two is the machine function, $\lambda$.

The aforementioned rule stated, that is, $\lambda' (q, a) = \lambda (\delta (q, a))$, associates the output of the next state, that is, $\lambda (\delta (q, a))$ with the transition for the resultant Mealy machine, that is, $\lambda' (q, a)$.

---

**Example 2.18** Consider a Moore machine that we have already designed (refer to Fig. 2.28) for finding residue-mod-3 for any binary number, redrawn as Fig. 2.33(a). Convert this Moore machine to its equivalent Mealy machine.

***Solution*** Consider the Moore machine in Fig. 2.33(a).

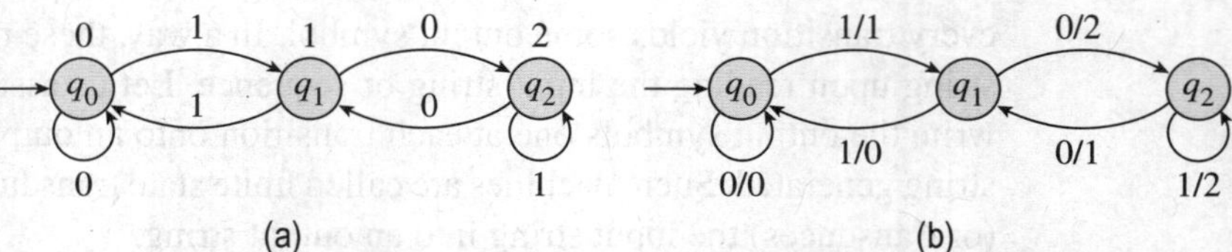


**Figure 2.33** Moore to Mealy Conversion (a) Moore machine (b) Equivalent Mealy machine

**Table 2.33** State transition function, $\delta : Q \times \Sigma \rightarrow Q$

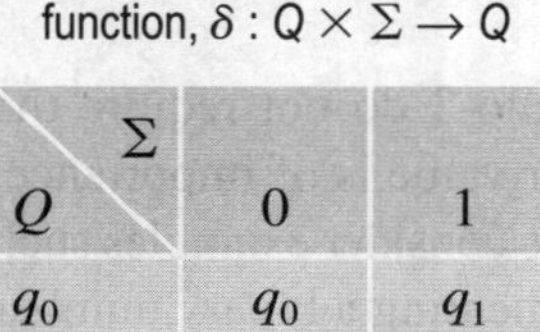

| $Q$ \ $\Sigma$ | 0 | 1 |
|---|---|---|
| $q_0$ | $q_0$ | $q_1$ |
| $q_1$ | $q_2$ | $q_0$ |
| $q_2$ | $q_1$ | $q_2$ |

The state transition function, $\delta$, for this Moore machine is as shown in Table 2.33.

Similarly, the machine function, $\lambda$, is as shown in the Table 2.34.

We need to convert this Moore machine to its equivalent Mealy machine using the state transition function, $\delta$, shown in Table 2.33. For this we only need to compute the changed $\lambda'$, that is, the machine function.

**Table 2.34** Machine function, $\lambda : Q \rightarrow \Delta$

| $Q$ | $q_0$ | $q_1$ | $q_2$ |
|---|---|---|---|
| $\Delta$ | 0 | 1 | 2 |

As per the conversion rule:

$$\lambda' (q, a) = \lambda (\delta (q, a))$$

We may write:

$$\lambda'(q_0, 0) = \lambda(\delta(q_0, 0)) = \lambda(q_0) = 0$$
$$\lambda'(q_0, 1) = \lambda(\delta(q_0, 1)) = \lambda(q_1) = 1$$
$$\lambda'(q_1, 0) = \lambda(\delta(q_1, 0)) = \lambda(q_2) = 2$$
$$\lambda'(q_1, 1) = \lambda(\delta(q_1, 1)) = \lambda(q_0) = 0$$
$$\lambda'(q_2, 0) = \lambda(\delta(q_2, 0)) = \lambda(q_1) = 1$$
$$\lambda'(q_2, 1) = \lambda(\delta(q_2, 1)) = \lambda(q_2) = 2$$

**Table 2.35** MAF ($\lambda'$: Q $\times$ $\Sigma \to \Delta$) for the equivalent Mealy machine

| Q \ $\Sigma$ | 0 | 1 |
|---|---|---|
| $q_0$ | 0 | 1 |
| $q_1$ | 2 | 0 |
| $q_2$ | 1 | 2 |

From this information, we can now create a table for the MAF of the equivalent Mealy machine as shown in Table 2.35; and the TG for the equivalent Mealy machine can be drawn as shown in Fig. 2.33(b).

Here, the output is associated with the transition, that is, it depends on the state making the transition, as well as on the input that causes the transition.

***Note***: Let us consider both Moore and Mealy machines shown in Fig. 2.33 for the input sequence (or string) '1010' of length, $n = 4$.

After simulation, the output sequence for the Moore machine is:

$$\Rightarrow q_0 \xrightarrow{1} q_1 \xrightarrow{0} q_2 \xrightarrow{1} q_2 \xrightarrow{0} q_1$$

0 1 2 2 1

Output sequence

Length of the output sequence for Moore machine $= 5 = (n + 1)$

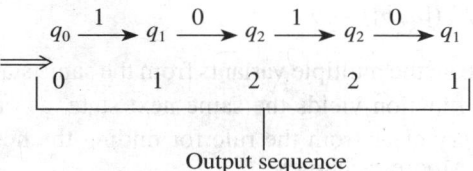

Now, let us observe the the output sequence for the Mealy machine after simulation, which is as follows:

$$q_0 \xrightarrow{1} q_1 \xrightarrow{0} q_2 \xrightarrow{1} q_2 \xrightarrow{0} q_1$$

1 2 2 1

Output sequence

The length of the output sequence for Mealy machine $= 4 = n$.

Thus, for the Moore machine, the output sequence contains one symbol more than the symbols in the input sequence, while the output sequence for the Mealy machine contains exactly the same number of symbols as in the input sequence. The additional output is generated by the Moore machine as soon as it enters the initial state, even before any input symbol is read and hence, is insignificant.

### 2.11.2 Mealy to Moore Conversion

Let us consider a given Mealy machine:

$$M_1 = (Q, \Sigma, \Delta, \delta, \lambda, q_0)$$

Then its equivalent Moore machine is:

$$M_2 = ([Q \times \Delta], \Sigma, \Delta, \delta', \lambda', [q_0, b_0])$$

where, '$b_0$' is an arbitrarily selected member of $\Delta$

$$\delta'([q, b], a) = [\delta(q, a), \lambda(q, a)]$$
$$\lambda'([q, b]) = b$$

This conversion is slightly non-trivial. As we cannot determine the output symbol that the equivalent Moore machine holds in each state; we end up creating all possible combinations of the state symbols and the output symbols, $Q \times \Delta$. It is almost like creating multiple variants of the same state that only differ in the associated output symbol.

Each state label, thus, has two symbols: one that is a state symbol and the other its associated output symbol. Hence, in order to find the new machine function, $\lambda'$, for the resultant Moore machine, it simply needs to return the associated output symbol:

$$\lambda'([q, b]) = b$$

As we create the multiple variants from the same state that differ only in the output symbol, the state function yields the same next state, as one cannot change the state behaviour. This is very clear from the rule for finding the new state transition function, $\delta'$, for the resultant Moore machine:

$$\delta'([q, b], a) = [\delta(q, a), \lambda(q, a)]$$

We see that the output symbol, $b$, has no role to play in determining the next state. This means that all the state variants obtained by associating the different output symbols—$[q, b_1]$, $[q, b_2]$, etc.—make transitions to the same next state.

Another important thing is to decide the initial state for the resultant Moore machine. Now, there exist multiple variants for the initial state, which could be of the form: $[q_0, b_i]$, $[q_0, b_j]$, ..., $[q_0, b_n]$, etc., as there are multiple output symbols. As per the rule, any state $[q_0, b_0]$ can be considered as an initial state, where $b_0$ is an arbitrarily selected member of $\Delta$. The output symbol that is associated with the initial state is irrelevant here, as it gets generated even before any input symbol is read and is hence, insignificant.

---

**Example 2.19** Consider the Mealy machine that we have designed to accept strings ending with '00' or '11' as in Fig. 2.29(c), which is redrawn in Fig. 2.34(a). The state transition tables for this machine are shown in Table 2.36. Construct the equivalent Moore machine.

**Table 2.36** State transition tables for Mealy machine in Fig. 2.34(a) (a) $\delta: Q \times \Sigma \rightarrow Q$ (b) $\lambda: Q \times \Sigma \rightarrow \Delta$

| $Q$ \ $\Sigma$ | 0 | 1 |
|---|---|---|
| $q_0$ | $p_0$ | $p_1$ |
| $p_0$ | $p_0$ | $p_1$ |
| $p_1$ | $p_0$ | $p_1$ |

(a)

| $Q$ \ $\Sigma$ | 0 | 1 |
|---|---|---|
| $q_0$ | $n$ | $n$ |
| $p_0$ | $y$ | $n$ |
| $p_1$ | $n$ | $y$ |

(b)

***Solution*** According to the conversion rule, the resultant Moore machine consists of:

$$Q' = [Q \times \Delta] = \{[q_0, n], [q_0, y], [p_0, n], [p_0, y], [p_1, n], [p_1, y]\}$$

Similarly, $\delta'$ and $\lambda'$ can be determined, as follows:

1. $\delta'([q_0, n], 0) = [\delta(q_0, 0), \lambda(q_0, 0)] = [p_0, n]$
   $\delta'([q_0, n], 1) = [\delta(q_0, 1), \lambda(q_0, 1)] = [p_1, n]$
   $\lambda'([q_0, n]) = n$
2. $\delta'([q_0, y], 0) = [\delta(q_0, 0), \lambda(q_0, 0)] = [p_0, n]$
   $\delta'([q_0, y], 1) = [\delta(q_0, 1), \lambda(q_0, 1)] = [p_1, n]$
   $\lambda'([q_0, y]) = y$
3. $\delta'([p_0, n], 0) = [\delta(p_0, 0), \lambda(p_0, 0)] = [p_0, y]$
   $\delta'([p_0, n], 1) = [\delta(p_0, 1), \lambda(p_0, 1)] = [p_1, n]$
   $\lambda'([p_0, n]) = n$

Similarly,

4. $\delta'([p_0, y], 0) = [p_0, y]$
   $\delta'([p_0, y], 1) = [p_1, n]$
   $\lambda'([p_0, y]) = y$
5. $\delta'([p_1, n], 0) = [\delta(p_1, 0), \lambda(p_1, 0)] = [p_0, n]$
   $\delta'([p_1, n], 1) = [\delta(p_1, 1), \lambda(p_1, 1)] = [p_1, y]$
   $\lambda'([p_1, n]) = n$

Similarly,

6. $\delta'([p_1, y], 0) = [p_0, n]$
   $\delta'([p_1, y], 1) = [p_1, y]$
   $\lambda'([p_1, y]) = y$

The transition graph for the equivalent Moore machine is as shown in Fig. 2.34(b).

Note that states, $[q_0, n]$ and $[q_0, y]$, have the same transitions or behaviour. Similarly, $[p_0, n]$ and $[p_0, y]$ as well as $[p_1, n]$ and $[p_1, y]$ have the same behaviour, except that these states generate different outputs.

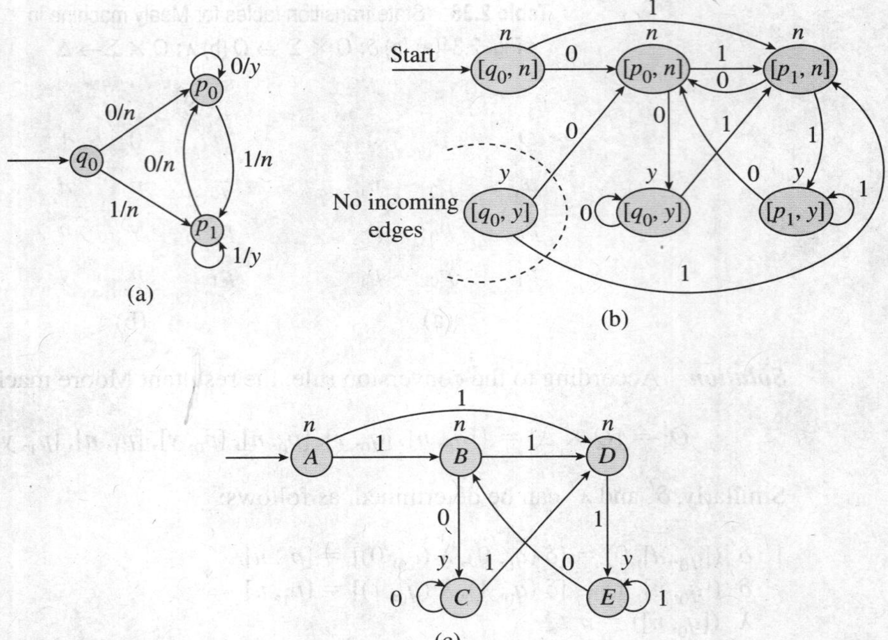


**Figure 2.34** Mealy to Moore conversion (a) Mealy machine (b) Equivalent Moore machine (c) Minimized Moore machine after relabelling

We may relabel the states as we wish. Note that the state $[q_0, n]$ has been arbitrarily selected as the initial state, from among $[q_0, n]$ and $[q_0, y]$. We can remove state $[q_0, y]$, as there are no incoming edges to this state. After removing this state and relabelling the remaining states, we get the final Moore machine as shown in Fig. 2.34(c).

### 2.11.3 Additional Examples on Moore and Mealy Machines

Let us examine some more examples on Moore and Mealy machines and their inter-conversion.

**Example 2.20** Construct Mealy and Moore machines for the following:

For input from, $\Sigma^*$, where $\Sigma = (0, 1)$, if the input ends in '101', the output should be '$x$'; if the input ends in '*110*', output should be '$y$'; otherwise, output should be '$z$'.

***Solution*** This is a simple sequence detector design problem. Let us start with the construction of the Mealy machine:

Consider the first string pattern '101', and draw a minimal diagram as shown in Fig. 2.35(a). We can modify this diagram to accept '110' as shown in Fig. 2.35(b). The remaining possible transitions are as shown in Fig. 2.35(c). The STF and MAF for this Mealy machine are as shown in Table 2.37.

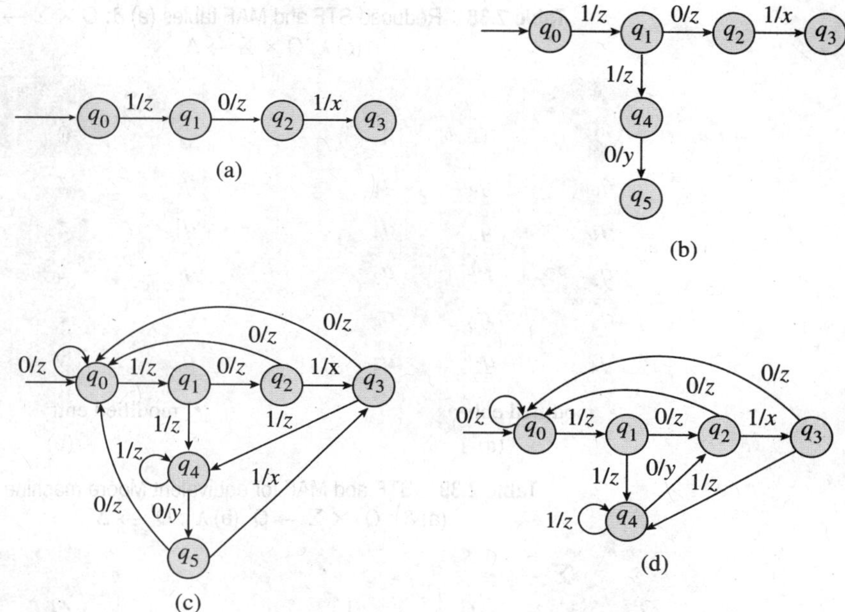


**Figure 2.35** Construction of Mealy machine (a) Step 1 (b) Step 2 (c) Step 3 (d) Mealy machines

**Table 2.37** STF and MAF for Mealy machine in Figure 2.34(c) (a) $\delta : Q \times \Sigma \rightarrow Q$ (b) $\lambda : Q \times \Sigma \rightarrow \Delta$

| $Q$ \ $\Sigma$ | 0 | 1 |
|---|---|---|
| $q_0$ | $q_0$ | $q_1$ |
| $q_1$ | $q_2$ | $q_4$ |
| $q_2$ | $q_0$ | $q_3$ |
| $q_3$ | $q_0$ | $q_4$ |
| $q_4$ | $q_5$ | $q_4$ |
| $q_5$ | $q_0$ | $q_3$ |

(a)

| $Q$ \ $\Sigma$ | 0 | 1 |
|---|---|---|
| $q_0$ | $z$ | $z$ |
| $q_1$ | $z$ | $z$ |
| $q_2$ | $z$ | $x$ |
| $q_3$ | $z$ | $z$ |
| $q_4$ | $y$ | $z$ |
| $q_5$ | $z$ | $x$ |

(b)

We observe that states $q_2$ and $q_5$ are equivalent; therefore, we replace $q_5$ by $q_2$. The reduced STF and MAF tables are obtained as in Table 2.38.

The reduced Mealy machine transition graph is as shown in Fig. 2.35(d). The STF and MAF tables for the equivalent Moore machine can be obtained by using the conversion method (refer to Table 2.39). Out of the states, $[q_0, x]$, $[q_0, y]$, and $[q_0, z]$, any one can be considered as the initial state, and the other two can be omitted in order to get the final answer.

**Table 2.38** Reduced STF and MAF tables (a) $\delta: Q \times \Sigma \to Q$ (b) $\lambda: Q \times \Sigma \to \Delta$

| $Q$ \ $\Sigma$ | 0 | 1 |
|---|---|---|
| $q_0$ | $q_0$ | $q_1$ |
| $q_1$ | $q_2$ | $q_4$ |
| $q_2$ | $q_0$ | $q_3$ |
| $q_3$ | $q_0$ | $q_4$ |
| $q_4$ | $q_2$• | $q_4$ |

'•' modified entry

(a)

| $Q$ \ $\Sigma$ | 0 | 1 |
|---|---|---|
| $q_0$ | $z$ | $z$ |
| $q_1$ | $z$ | $z$ |
| $q_2$ | $z$ | $x$ |
| $q_3$ | $z$ | $z$ |
| $q_4$ | $y$ | $z$ |

'•' modified entry

(b)

**Table 2.39** STF and MAF for equivalent Moore machine (a) $\delta': Q' \times \Sigma \to Q'$ (b) $\lambda': Q' \to \Delta$

| $Q'$ \ $\Sigma$ | 0 | 1 |
|---|---|---|
| $[q_0, x]$ | $[q_0, z]$ | $[q_1, z]$ |
| $[q_0, y]$ | $[q_0, z]$ | $[q_1, z]$ |
| $[q_0, z]$ | $[q_0, z]$ | $[q_1, z]$ |
| $[q_1, x]$ | $[q_2, z]$ | $[q_4, z]$ |
| $[q_1, y]$ | $[q_2, z]$ | $[q_4, z]$ |
| $[q_1, z]$ | $[q_2, z]$ | $[q_4, z]$ |
| $[q_2, x]$ | $[q_0, z]$ | $[q_3, x]$ |
| $[q_2, y]$ | $[q_0, z]$ | $[q_3, x]$ |
| $[q_2, z]$ | $[q_0, z]$ | $[q_3, x]$ |
| $[q_3, x]$ | $[q_0, z]$ | $[q_4, z]$ |
| $[q_3, y]$ | $[q_0, z]$ | $[q_4, z]$ |
| $[q_3, z]$ | $[q_0, z]$ | $[q_4, z]$ |
| $[q_4, x]$ | $[q_2, y]$ | $[q_4, z]$ |
| $[q_4, y]$ | $[q_2, y]$ | $[q_4, z]$ |
| $[q_4, z]$ | $[q_2, y]$ | $[q_4, z]$ |

(a)

| $Q$ | $\Delta$ |
|---|---|
| $[q_0, x]$ | $x$ |
| $[q_0, y]$ | $y$ |
| $[q_0, z]$ | $z$ |
| $[q_1, x]$ | $x$ |
| $[q_1, y]$ | $y$ |
| $[q_1, z]$ | $z$ |
| $[q_2, x]$ | $x$ |
| $[q_2, y]$ | $y$ |
| $[q_2, z]$ | $z$ |
| $[q_3, x]$ | $x$ |
| $[q_3, y]$ | $y$ |
| $[q_3, z]$ | $z$ |
| $[q_4, x]$ | $x$ |
| $[q_4, y]$ | $y$ |
| $[q_0, z]$ | $z$ |

(b)

**Example 2.21** Construct Mealy and Moore machines for the following:

For the input from $\Sigma^*$, where $\Sigma = \{0, 1, 2\}$, print the residue-modulo-5 of the input treated as a ternary (base 3, with digits 0, 1, and 2) number.

***Solution*** Let us first look at some properties of ternary numbers:

1. If $i$ is a ternary number, and if we write 0 after it, then its value becomes $3i$.

   For example, $1.0 = 1 \times 3^1 + 0 \times 3^0$
   $= 3 + 0$
   $= 3$
   $= 3 \times 1$

   Similarly, $2.0 = 2 \times 3^1 + 0 \times 3^0 = 6 = 3 \times 2$

2. If $i$ is a ternary number, and if we write 1 after it, then its value becomes '$3i + 1$'.

   For example, $1.1 = 1 \times 3^1 + 1 \times 3^0 = 3 + 1 = 3 \times 1 + 1$
   $2.1 = 2 \times 3^1 + 1 \times 3^0 = 6 + 1 = 3 \times 2 + 1$

3. If $i$ is a ternary number, and if we write 2 after it, then its value becomes '$3i + 2$'.

   For example, $1.2 = 1 \times 3^1 + 2 \times 3^0 = 3 + 2 = 3 \times 1 + 2$
   $2.2 = 2 \times 3^1 + 2 \times 3^0 = 6 + 2 = 3 \times 2 + 2$

As we are dividing a ternary number by 5, we can have five different values for the remainders; namely, 0, 1, 2, 3, and 4. These are the five outputs that the machine generates. The remainder values are expressed in decimal (base 10) number format as usual.

**Table 2.40** MAF ($\lambda : Q \rightarrow \Delta$) for the Moore machine

| $Q$ | $q_0$ | $q_1$ | $q_2$ | $q_3$ | $q_4$ |
|---|---|---|---|---|---|
| $\Delta$ | 0 | 1 | 2 | 3 | 4 |

It is easier to construct a Moore machine in which each output is associated with a unique state. This means, depending on the value of the remainder to be printed, there are five different states for the Moore machine:

$$Q = \{q_0, q_1, q_2, q_3, q_4\}$$

The machine function is as depicted in the Table 2.40.

Depending on the remainder in the previous state, if the next digit is 0, 1, or 2, then, the next remainder value can be obtained as shown in Table 2.41.

**Table 2.41** Different remainders

| Remainder ($R$) | 0 | 1 | 2 | 3 | 4 |
|---|---|---|---|---|---|
| After writing 0 after $R$ ($3R$ mod 5) | 0 | 3 | 1 | 4 | 2 |
| After writing 1 after $R$ ($3R + 1$) mod 5 | 1 | 4 | 2 | 0 | 3 |
| After writing 2 after $R$ ($3R + 2$) mod 5 | 2 | 0 | 3 | 1 | 4 |

If the current remainder is: $R = 3$, and if the next digit is 0, then:

$$3.0 \text{ (ternary)} = 3 \times 3 = 9 \text{ (decimal)}$$

If we divide 9 by 5, the remainder is 4.

Similarly, if $R = 1$, and if 2 is the next digit, then,

$$1.2 \text{ (ternary)} = 3 \times 1 + 2 = 5 \text{ (decimal)}$$

If we divide 5 by 5, the remainder is 0.

Table 2.41 can be directly converted into the state transition table as shown in Table 2.42. Each column in Table 2.41 is analogous to a row in Table 2.42.

Using the MAF (Table 2.40) and the STF (Table 2.42), we can draw TG for the Moore machine as shown in Fig. 2.36.

**Table 2.42** STF ($\delta : Q \times \Sigma \rightarrow Q$) for Moore machine

| $Q$ \ $\Sigma$ | 0 | 1 | 2 |
|---|---|---|---|
| $q_0$ | $q_0$ | $q_1$ | $q_2$ |
| $q_1$ | $q_3$ | $q_4$ | $q_0$ |
| $q_2$ | $q_1$ | $q_2$ | $q_3$ |
| $q_3$ | $q_4$ | $q_0$ | $q_1$ |
| $q_4$ | $q_2$ | $q_3$ | $q_4$ |

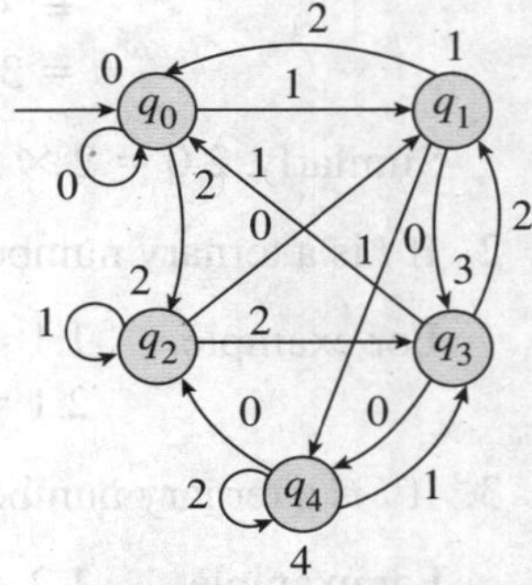

**Figure 2.36** Moore machine

Now, the equivalent Mealy machine can be obtained using the conversion rule. The state function, $\delta$, for the resultant Mealy machine is the same as in Table 2.42; and the revised machine function, $\lambda'$, can be obtained using the rule:

$$\lambda'(q, a) = \lambda(\delta(q, a))$$

Using the aforementioned rule, the machine function for the Mealy machine can be written as shown in the Table 2.43.

Using the STF (Table 2.42) and MAF (Table 2.43), the transition graph for the equivalent Mealy machine can be drawn as shown in Fig. 2.37.

**Table 2.43** MAF ($\lambda' : Q \times \Sigma \rightarrow \Delta$) for equivalent Mealy machine

| $Q$ \ $\Sigma$ | 0 | 1 | 2 |
|---|---|---|---|
| $q_0$ | 0 | 1 | 2 |
| $q_1$ | 3 | 4 | 0 |
| $q_2$ | 1 | 2 | 3 |
| $q_3$ | 4 | 0 | 1 |
| $q_4$ | 2 | 3 | 4 |

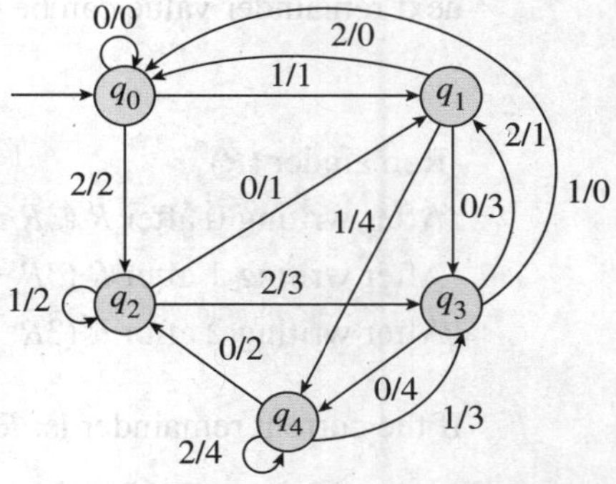

**Figure 2.37** Equivalent Mealy machine

---

**Example 2.22** Design a Moore machine that will read sequences made up of letters *A*, *E*, *I*, *O*, *U* and will give an output having the same sequences, except that in those cases where an '*I*' directly follows an '*E*', it will be changed to '*U*'.

***Solution*** This is again a simple sequence detector problem. Let us first design the Mealy machine, which we can then convert to its equivalent Moore machine.

The constraint here is that if '*I*' directly follows '*E*' in any string over $\Sigma = \{A, E, I, O, U\}$, it must be replaced with '*U*'; the rest of the symbols remain as they are.

Step 1 in Fig. 2.38 takes care of identifying the special case, where '*I*' directly follows '*E*' in any string over $\Sigma = \{A, E, I, O, U\}$.

State $q_0$, on reading input symbol '*E*' moves to a new state $q_1$ just to remember that '*E*' has been read. Now, in state $q_1$ if '*I*' is the current symbol read, that means, it is the symbol that directly follows the previous symbol '*E*'; hence, it needs to be replaced with '*U*' as shown in Fig. 2.38(a). State $q_1$, on reading symbol '*E*' retains the same state, as the next symbol could be 'I'—a string might contain the pattern '...*EEI*...'; hence the self loop from state $q_1$ on reading symbol '*E*'.

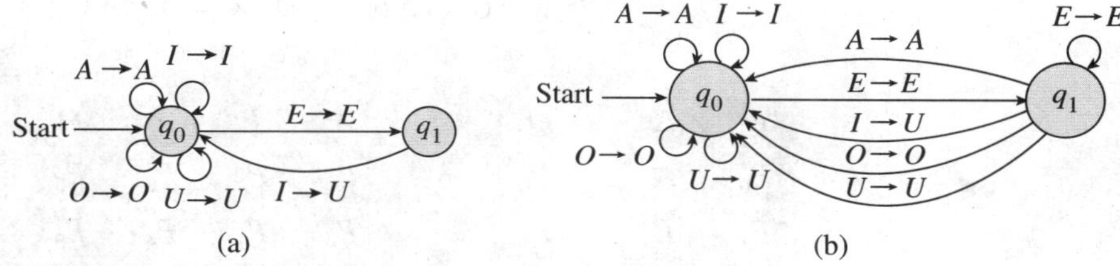


**Figure 2.38** Mealy machine as a sequence detector (a) Step 1 (b) Step 2

Figure 2.38(b) gives the complete Mealy machine. It keeps the rest of the symbols as they are. We now need to convert this Mealy machine to its equivalent Moore machine.

As we know, the states of the equivalent Moore machine can be obtained as $[Q \times \Delta]$, where $Q$ is the set of states and $\Delta$ is the output set of the Mealy machine. Thus, the STF and MAF for the equivalent Moore machine can be obtained as shown in Table 2.44.

**Table 2.44** STF and MAF for the equivalent Moore machine (a) $\lambda' : Q' \times \Delta$ (b) $\delta' : Q' \times \rightarrow O'$

| $Q$ | $\Delta$ |
|---|---|
| $[q_0, A]$ | $A$ |
| $[q_0, E]$ | $E$ |
| $[q_0, I]$ | $I$ |
| $[q_0, O]$ | $O$ |
| $[q_0, U]$ | $U$ |
| $[q_1, A]$ | $A$ |
| $[q_1, E]$ | $E$ |
| $[q_1, I]$ | $I$ |
| $[q_1, O]$ | $O$ |
| $[q_1, U]$ | $U$ |

(a)

| $Q'$ \ $\Sigma$ | $A$ | $E$ | $I$ | $O$ | $U$ |
|---|---|---|---|---|---|
| $[q_0, A]$ | $[q_0, A]$ | $[q_1, E]$ | $[q_0, I]$ | $[q_0, O]$ | $[q_0, U]$ |
| $[q_0, E]$ | $[q_0, A]$ | $[q_1, E]$ | $[q_0, I]$ | $[q_0, O]$ | $[q_0, U]$ |
| $[q_0, I]$ | $[q_0, A]$ | $[q_1, E]$ | $[q_0, I]$ | $[q_0, O]$ | $[q_0, U]$ |
| $[q_0, O]$ | $[q_0, A]$ | $[q_1, E]$ | $[q_0, I]$ | $[q_0, O]$ | $[q_0, U]$ |
| $[q_0, U]$ | $[q_0, A]$ | $[q_1, E]$ | $[q_0, I]$ | $[q_0, O]$ | $[q_0, U]$ |
| $[q_1, A]$ | $[q_0, A]$ | $[q_1, E]$ | $[q_0, U]$ | $[q_0, O]$ | $[q_0, U]$ |
| $[q_1, E]$ | $[q_0, A]$ | $[q_1, E]$ | $[q_0, U]$ | $[q_0, O]$ | $[q_0, U]$ |
| $[q_1, I]$ | $[q_0, A]$ | $[q_1, E]$ | $[q_0, U]$ | $[q_0, O]$ | $[q_0, U]$ |
| $[q_1, O]$ | $[q_0, A]$ | $[q_1, E]$ | $[q_0, U]$ | $[q_0, O]$ | $[q_0, U]$ |
| $[q_1, U]$ | $[q_0, A]$ | $[q_1, E]$ | $[q_0, U]$ | $[q_0, O]$ | $[q_0, U]$ |

(b)

In Table 2.44(b), if we consider $[q_0, A]$ as an initial state, the states, which can be included in the minimized Moore machine, are: $[q_0, A]$, $[q_1, E]$, $[q_0, I]$, $[q_0, O]$, and $[q_0, U]$. No transition from the initial state will ever reach any other state. It is clear from Table 2.44(b) that these are the only five states that are the next states for all the transitions.

Let us now relabel the states as:

$$[q_0, A] \equiv P_0 \qquad [q_1, E] \equiv P_1$$
$$[q_0, I] \equiv P_2 \qquad [q_0, O] \equiv P_3$$
$$[q_0, U] \equiv P_4$$

The reduced STF and MAF tables of the equivalent Moore machine are as shown in Table 2.45.

**Table 2.45** Reduced STFs and MAFs for the equivalent Moore machine (a) $\lambda'' : Q'' \rightarrow \Delta$ (b) $\delta'' : Q'' \times \rightarrow Q''$

| $Q$ | $\Delta$ |
|---|---|
| $P_0$ | $A$ |
| $P_1$ | $E$ |
| $P_2$ | $I$ |
| $P_3$ | $O$ |
| $P_4$ | $U$ |

(a)

| $Q''$ \ $\Sigma$ | $A$ | $E$ | $I$ | $O$ | $U$ |
|---|---|---|---|---|---|
| $P_0$ | $P_0$ | $P_1$ | $P_2$ | $P_3$ | $P_4$ |
| $P_1$ | $P_0$ | $P_1$ | $P_4$ | $P_3$ | $P_4$ |
| $P_2$ | $P_0$ | $P_1$ | $P_2$ | $P_3$ | $P_4$ |
| $P_3$ | $P_0$ | $P_1$ | $P_2$ | $P_3$ | $P_4$ |
| $P_4$ | $P_0$ | $P_1$ | $P_2$ | $P_3$ | $P_4$ |

(b)

Table 2.45(a) gives the machine function and Table 2.45(b) gives the state transition function for the equivalent Moore machine.

---

**Example 2.23** Consider the Moore machine described by the state transition table given in Table 2.46. Construct the corresponding Mealy machine.

**Table 2.46** State transition table for a Moore machine

| Current state | Next state | | Output |
|---|---|---|---|
| | $a = 0$ | $a = 1$ | |
| $q_1$ | $q_1$ | $q_2$ | 0 |
| $q_2$ | $q_1$ | $q_3$ | 0 |
| $q_3$ | $q_1$ | $q_3$ | 1 |

**Table 2.47** State transition table for the equivalent Mealy machine

| $Q$ \ $\Sigma$ | 0 | 1 |
|---|---|---|
| $q_1$ | $q_1$ | $q_2$ |
| $q_2$ | $q_1$ | $q_3$ |
| $q_3$ | $q_1$ | $q_3$ |

***Solution*** As we know, while obtaining the equivalent Mealy machine, the state transition function, $\delta$, remains the same, as shown in Table 2.47.

The machine function (or the output function) of the equivalent Mealy machine is given by:

$$\lambda'(q, a) = \lambda(\delta(q, a))$$

Applying this rule, we get:

$$\lambda'(q_1, 0) = \lambda(\delta(q_1, 0)) = \lambda(q_1) = 0$$

Similarly, $\lambda'(q_1, 1) = 0$

The complete machine function for the equivalent Mealy machine is as shown in Table 2.48.

The transition graph for the equivalent Mealy machine is as shown in Fig. 2.39.

**Table 2.48** Machine function ($\lambda$) for the equivalent Mealy machine

| $Q$ \ $\Sigma$ | 0 | 1 |
|---|---|---|
| $q_1$ | 0 | 0 |
| $q_2$ | 0 | 1 |
| $q_3$ | 0 | 1 |

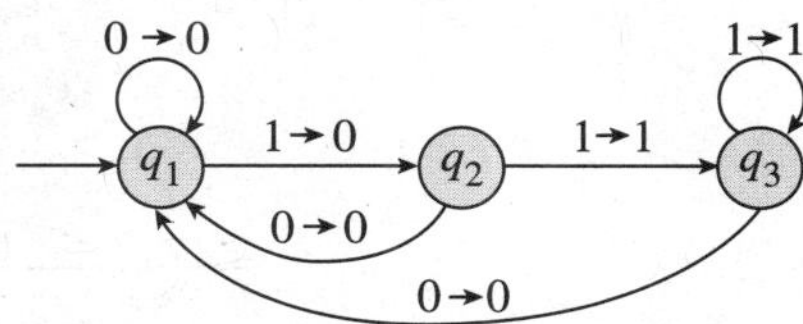


**Figure 2.39** TG for the equivalent Mealy machine

## 2.12 FSM EQUIVALENCE

Two FSM's, $M$ and $M'$, are said to be equivalent, if for each state $S_j$ in $M$, there corresponds at least one state $S_j'$ in $M'$, such that $S_j'$ is equivalent to $S_j$; and if, for each $S_j'$ in $M'$, there corresponds at least one $S_j$ in $M$, such that $S_j$ is equivalent to $S_j'$. We have already learnt about state equivalence earlier in Section 2.6.2.1. In simple terms, this means that two FSMs are equivalent if they accept the same language.

### 2.12.1 Moore's Algorithm

The Moore's algorithm for FSM equivalence is one of the decision algorithms for regular sets. The language accepted by any FSM is called a regular language, or a regular set.

***Algorithm***

If $M$ and $M'$ are two FSM's over $\Sigma$, where $|\Sigma| = n$ ('$n$' is the number of input signals); then, apply the following steps to check the equivalence of $M$ and $M'$:

1. Construct a comparison table consisting of $(n + 1)$ columns. In column 1, list all ordered pairs of vertices of the form $(v, v')$, where $v \subset M$, and $v' \subset M'$.
   In column 2, list all pairs of the form $(v_a, v_a')$, if there is a transition labelled a $\subset \Sigma$ leading from $v$ to $v_a$ and from $v'$ to $v_a'$.
   In column 3, list all pairs of the form $(v_b, v_b')$, if there is a transition labelled $b \subset \Sigma$ leading from $v$ to $v_b$ and from $v'$ to $v_b'$. Repeat this for all '$n$' symbols from $\Sigma$.
2. If the pair $(v_a, v_a')$, has not occurred previously in column 1, place it in the column 1 and repeat step 1 for that pair.
   Repeat step 2 for each pair, $(v_b, v_b')$, $(v_c, v_c')$, and so on.

3. If in the table, suppose a pair $(v, v')$ is reached in which, $v$ is the final vertex (or final state) of $M$, and $v'$ is a non-final vertex of $M'$; or vice-versa, then stop and declare that the two FSMs, $M$ and $M'$, are not equivalent.
Otherwise, stop when there are no more new pairs in columns 2, 3, ..., $n$ that do not occur in column 1. In this case, the two FSM's $M$ and $M'$ are equivalent.

---

**Example 2.24** Two FSMs, $M$ and $M'$, are given in Fig. 2.40. Check the equivalence of the two FSMs by applying Moore's algorithm.

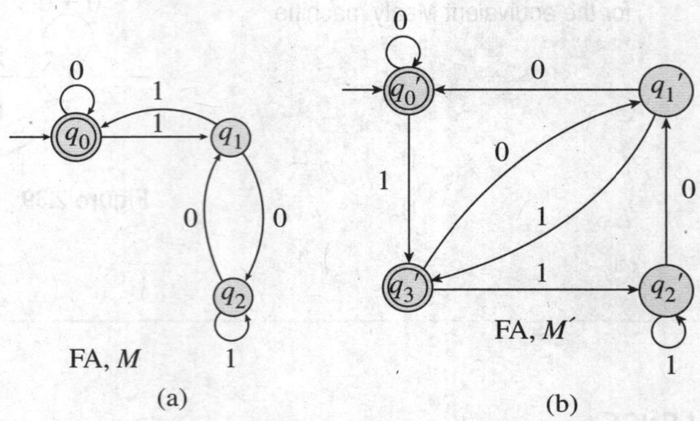


**Figure 2.40** Example FSMs (a) FSM M (b) FSM M′

***Solution*** For the given FSMs,

$$\Sigma = \{0, 1\}$$

Hence, $|\Sigma| = n = 2$

**Table 2.49** Comparison table for FSMs in Fig. 2.45

| $(v, v')$ | $(v_0, v_0')$ | $(v_1, v_1')$ |
|---|---|---|
| $(q_0, q_0')$ | $(q_0, q_0')$ | $(q_1, q_3')$ |
| $(q_1, q_3')$ | $(q_2, q_1')$ | $(q_0, q_2')$ |

As per the algorithm, we must create $(n + 1) = 2 + 1 = 3$ columns labelled $(v, v')$, $(v_0, v_0')$, and $(v_1, v_1')$. Table 2.49 shows the comparison between $M$ and $M'$.

We begin with the pair of initial states $(q_0, q_0')$. State $(q_0, q_0')$, on reading input symbol '0', goes to state $(q_0, q_0')$, where both $q_0$ and $q_0'$ are final states; and on reading input symbol '1', it goes to $(q_1, q_3')$, where both $q_1$ and $q_3'$ are non-final states.

Therefore, we can proceed to the next step: we observe that $(q_0, q_0')$ is already there in column 1, but $(q_1, q_3')$ is not there. Therefore, we place it in column 1 and repeat the procedure. State $(q_1, q_3')$, on reading input symbol '0', goes to state $(q_2, q_1')$—here, both $q_2$ and $q_1$ are non-final states; and on reading input symbol '1', it goes to state $(q_0, q_2')$—here, $q_0$ is the final state in $M$, while $q_2'$ is a non-final state in $M'$; therefore, we stop here and declare that the given FSMs, $M$ and $M'$, are non-equivalent.

---

**Example 2.25** For the two FSMs given in Fig. 2.41, check the equivalence using Moore's algorithm.

***Solution*** For the given FSMs,

$$\Sigma = \{0, 1\}$$

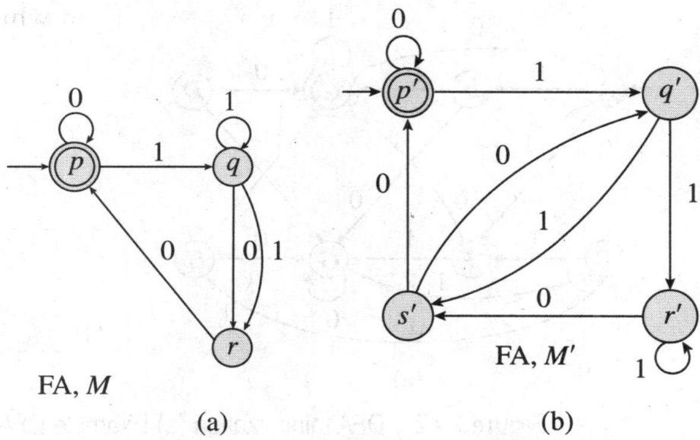


**Figure 2.41** Example FSMs (a) FSM $M$ (b) FSM $M'$

Hence, $|\Sigma| = n = 2$

Therefore, we need to create $(n + 1) = 3$ columns labelled $(v, v')$, $(v_0, v_0')$, and $(v_1, v_1')$. The comparison between the two FSMs, $M$ and $M'$, can be made as in Table 2.50.

**Table 2.50** Comparison table for FSMs in Fig. 2.46

| $(v, v')$ | $(v_0, v_0')$ | $(v_1, v_1')$ |
|---|---|---|
| $(p, p')$ | $(p, p')$ | $(q, q')$ |
| $(q, q')$ | $(r, s')$ | $(q, r')$ |
| $(r, s')$ | $(p, p')$ | $(q, q')$ |
| $(q, r')$ | $(r, s')$ | $(q, r')$ |

We begin with both the initial states $(p, p')$, which yield a new pair, $(q, q')$, for the transition on reading input symbol '1'. Placing $(q, q')$ in column 1 and finding the transitions for input symbols '0' and '1', we see that the next states are: $(r, s')$ and $(q, r')$—both new pairs.

Let us first consider $(r, s')$, and place it is column 1, which yields pairs $(p, p')$ and $(q, q')$ for transition on reading input symbols '0' and '1' respectively—these are already there in column 1.

Therefore, we consider the only remaining new pair, $(q, r')$, and place it in column 1. Neither of the transitions from $(q, r')$ yield any new pair. Hence, there is no other new pair to process; so, we stop, and declare that the FSMs, $M$ and $M'$, in Fig. 2.46 are equivalent.

## 2.13 DFA MINIMIZATION (ANOTHER APPROACH)

The previous technique that we have seen in Section 2.6.2 uses the notion of equivalent states to reduce the state transition table. The only problem it has is that it requires more number of reduction iterations, which might be repetitive reduction. For instance, in Example 2.8, we have seen that while converting NFA to DFA (refer to Section 2.6.2.2), we had to make two reduction iterations over the transition table.

The technique that we are now going to see in this section is systematic, and finds all the equivalent states in a single step. Therefore, in one step we get a reduced or minimized DFA. This approach gives the same result, but is more efficient in terms of time.

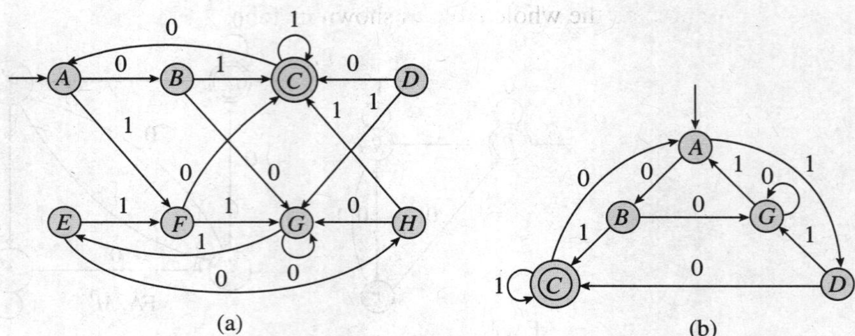


**Figure 2.42** DFA minimization (a) Example DFA (b) Minimized DFA

**Table 2.51** State transition table for the DFA in Fig. 2.47(a)

| Q \ Σ | 0 | 1 |
|---|---|---|
| *A* | *B* | *F* |
| *B* | *G* | *C* |
| *C* | *A* | *C* |
| *D* | *C* | *G* |
| *E* | *H* | *F* |
| *F* | *C* | *G* |
| *G* | *G* | *E* |
| *H* | *G* | *C* |

**Table 2.52** Finding equivalent states

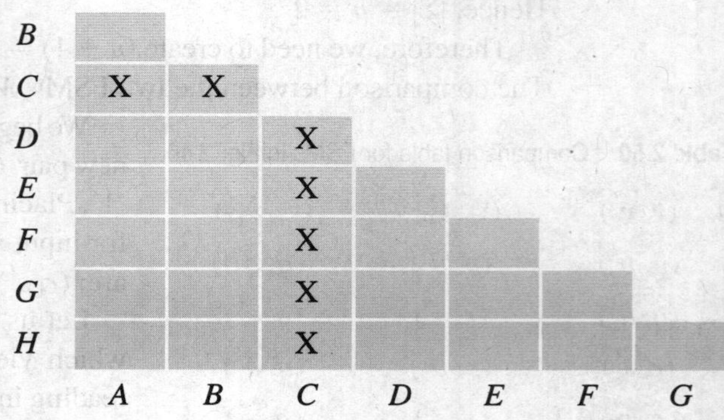

| | A | B | C | D | E | F | G |
|---|---|---|---|---|---|---|---|
| *B* | | | | | | | |
| *C* | X | X | | | | | |
| *D* | | | X | | | | |
| *E* | | | X | | | | |
| *F* | | | X | | | | |
| *G* | | | X | | | | |
| *H* | | | X | | | | |

Let us consider the DFA in Fig. 2.42(a). We want to minimize this DFA. The state transition table for this DFA is as shown in Table 2.51.

First draw a table as shown in Table 2.52 and put an 'X' (cross) for all combinations of final and non-final states. Here, consider combinations of '*C*' (final state) with all other states.

Now, start with the last column, that is, with combination (*G*, *H*).

$\delta(G, 0) = G \quad \delta(G, 1) = E$

and $\qquad\qquad\qquad\qquad\qquad\qquad (E, C)$

$\delta(H, 0) = G \quad \delta(H, 1) = C$

For pair (*E*, *C*), there is already an 'X' marked in the table, which means that these two states are non-equivalent. Therefore, we put 'X' for the pair (*G*, *H*).

We prepare the whole table as shown in Table 2.53.

**Table 2.53** Finding equivalent states

| | | | | | | | |
|---|---|---|---|---|---|---|---|
| *B* | X | | | | | | |
| *C* | X | X | | | | | |
| *D* | X | X | X | | | | |
| *E* | | X | X | X | | | |
| *F* | X | X | X | | X | | |
| *G* | X | X | X | X | X | X | |
| *H* | X | | X | X | X | X | X |
| | *A* | *B* | *C* | *D* | *E* | *F* | *G* |

Now, for combination $(D, F)$,

$$\delta(D, 0) = \delta(F, 0) = C$$
$$\delta(D, 1) = \delta(F, 1) = G$$

As both transitions are equal, we do not put an 'X' for the pair $(D, F)$—they are equivalent.

Similarly for $(B, H)$,

$$\delta(B, 0) = \delta(H, 0) = G$$
$$\delta(B, 1) = \delta(H, 1) = C$$

Therefore, *B* and *H* are equivalent. Hence, we do not put an 'X' for the pair $(B, H)$.

Now, let us observe the combination $(A, E)$:

$\delta(A, 0) = B$, $\delta(E, 0) = H$ — $(B, H)$ is an equivalent state combination

Similarly, $\delta(A, 1) = \delta(E, 1) = F$

Therefore, states *A* and *E* are equivalent. Hence, we do not place an 'X' for the pair $(A, E)$.

Thus, in one step, we have all pairs of equivalent states. Now we can reduce the STF Table 2.51 as shown in Table 2.54.

The minimized DFA can now be drawn as in Fig. 2.47(b).

**Table 2.54** Reduced state transition table

| *Q* \ Σ | 0 | 1 |
|---|---|---|
| *A* | *B* | *D*• |
| *B* | *G* | *C* |
| *C* | *A* | *C* |
| *D* | *C* | *G* |
| *G* | *G* | *A*• |

'•': Modified entries due to replacement of states

## 2.14 PROPERTIES AND LIMITATIONS OF FSM

Listed here are a few important properties and limitations of an FSM:

**Periodicity** A limitation of an FSM is that it does not have the capacity to arbitrarily remember large amounts of information. Since it has only a fixed number of states, the length of a sequence that it can remember is limited.

Moreover, we have seen a finite control representation of the FSM, where the read head always moves one position to the right after reading an input symbol (refer to Section 2.3.6). The head can never move in the reverse direction. Therefore, the FSM cannot retrieve what it has read previously, before coming to the current position on the tape; and since it cannot retrieve anything that is read earlier, it cannot remember them. This also means that the FSM eventually will always repeat a state or produce a periodic sequence of states.

**State determination** Since the initial state of an FSM and the input sequence given to it determines the output sequence, it is always possible to discover the unknown state in which the FSM resides at a particular instance.

**Impossibility of multiplication** As we have seen, an FSM cannot remember arbitrarily long sequences. We know that during multiplication operation, it is required to remember two full sequences corresponding to the multiplier and the multiplicand. Moreover, while multiplying, it is also required to store the partial sums that are obtained during the intermediate stages. Therefore, no FSM can multiply, given any two arbitrarily long numbers. This is because, essentially, an FSM does not have any memory.

**Impossibility of palindrome recognition** No FSM can recognize a palindrome string, because it does not have the capability to remember all the symbols it reads until the half-way point of input sequence. Hence, it cannot match them in reverse order, with the symbols in second half of the sequence. This is true even if we assume that the given FSM can recognize the mid-point of the sequence, which is also actually impossible.

**Impossibility to check if parentheses are well-formed** The aforementioned reason holds here also. As an FSM has no capability to remember the earlier input symbols that it reads, it cannot compare with the remaining input symbols to check for well-formed parentheses. This is an impossible task for any FSM.

In order to accomplish all these complex jobs, we require a more capable and powerful machine, which is has a finite number of states, but unlimited memory to remember arbitrarily long sequences. Further, its head should be able to move to the left as well as to the right, that is, in both directions, so that it can read whatever it has stored on its tape. In other words, it should have a capability to retrieve whatever is stored in the memory.

Since the FSM lacks the ability to store, we can say that an FSM is a program without variables and without assignment statement.

## 2.15 ADDITIONAL FSM EXAMPLES

Let us now look at some more examples of FSM.

---

**Example 2.26** Construct an NFA that accepts any positive number of occurrences of various strings from the following language L:

$$L = \{x \mid x \text{ is made up of } \{a, b\}, \text{ and } x \text{ ends with '}aab\text{'}\}$$

***Solution*** This is a typical sequence detector problem that we have earlier solved in the context of Mealy machines. Let us construct an NFA, which moves to a final state if

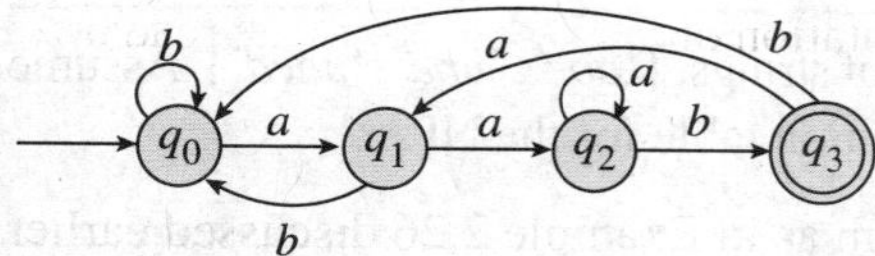


**Figure 2.43** NFA as a sequence detector

the string matching the expected pattern is found; otherwise it moves to a non-final state. Figure 2.42 shows an NFA that works as a detector for the given sequence.

We observe from Fig. 2.43 that state $q_0$ loops on reading input symbol '$b$' till it receives the input symbol '$a$'. State $q_1$ proceeds to $q_2$ on reading input symbol '$a$', but goes back to state $q_0$ on reading input symbol '$b$'—as the sequence of choice '$aab$' needs to begin with two '$a$'s.

Observe that state $q_2$ loops on input symbol '$a$', as it has already seen two consecutive '$a$'s; any more '$a$'s is not a problem, as we are waiting for a '$b$' after that—any string of the form '$aa...aaaaab$' anyway ends in '$aab$'.

State $q_3$ is the final state and can be reached upon reading the string that ends in '$aab$'. In state $q_3$, if there is another input symbol '$a$', it means that the string does not end in '$aab$'; hence, it jumps to state $q_1$, on reading symbol '$a$'. Similarly, state $q_3$ goes back to state $q_0$ upon reading symbol '$b$', as the string does not end in '$aab$'—it ends in '$aab\underline{b}$'.

***Note***: We may notice that Figure 2.42 is actually a DFA. Every DFA is, in a way, a specialization of the NFA. The converse may not be true, though.

**Example 2.27** Convert the Mealy machine in Fig. 2.44 to its equivalent Moore machine.

***Solution*** We begin with four state labels, using $Q' = [Q \times \Delta]$, for the equivalent Moore machine that we want to construct.

$$Q' = \{[S_0, 0], [S_0, 1], [S_1, 0], [S_1, 1]\}$$

**Figure 2.44** Example Mealy machine

Hence, we have:

$$\delta'([S_0, 0], a) = [\delta(S_0, a), \lambda(S_0, 0)]$$
$$= [S_1, 0]$$
$$= \delta'([S_0, 1], a)$$

Similarly, the transitions for the remaining states are obtained. The STF and MAF tables for the equivalent Moore machine are shown in Table 2.55.

**Table 2.55** STF and MAF tables for the equivalent Moore machine

| STF ($\delta'$) | | |
|---|---|---|
| $Q'$ \ $\Sigma$ | $a$ | $b$ |
| $[S_0, 0]$ | $[S_1, 0]$ | $[S_0, 0]$ |
| $[S_0, 1]$ | $[S_1, 0]$ | $[S_0, 0]$ |
| $[S_1, 0]$ | $[S_1, 1]$ | $[S_0, 1]$ |
| $[S_1, 1]$ | $[S_1, 1]$ | $[S_0, 1]$ |

| MAF ($\lambda'$) | |
|---|---|
| $Q'$ \ $\Sigma$ | $\Delta$ |
| $[S_0, 0]$ | 0 |
| $[S_0, 1]$ | 1 |
| $[S_1, 0]$ | 0 |
| $[S_1, 1]$ | 1 |

**Example 2.28** Design an NFA to recognize the set of strings, {'*abc*', '*abd*', '*aacd*'}. Assume that the input alphabet is $\{a, b, c, d\}$. Give the transition table for the NFA.

***Solution*** This is also a sequence detector problem as in Example 2.26 discussed earlier in this section.

The difference between Example 2.26 and this example is that this FA, as in Fig. 2.45, is designed to accepted only the designated three strings, {'*abc*', '*abd*', '*aacd*'}; while the NFA in Example 2.26 accepts all strings that end in a specified substring, the NFA in Fig. 2.45 accepts only the finite set of strings.

The state transition table for the NFA can be drawn as shown in Table 2.56.

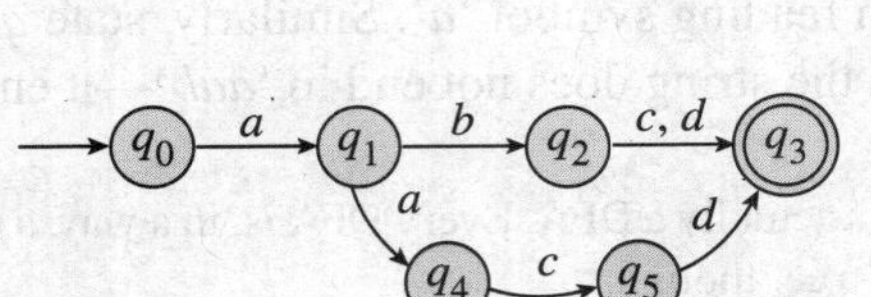


Figure 2.45 NFA accepting the given set of strings

Table 2.56 State transition table for the NFA

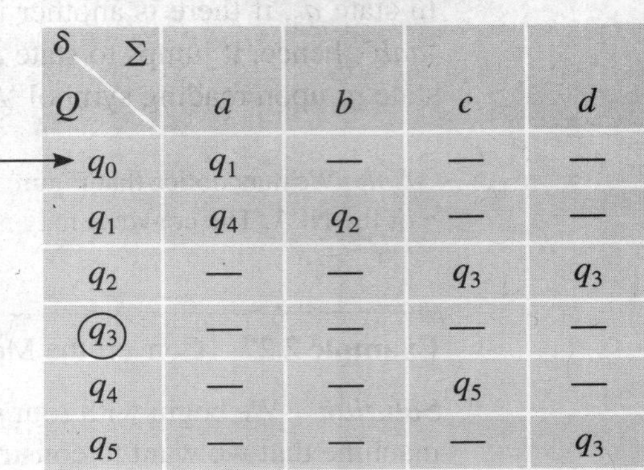

| $\delta$ / $Q$ \ $\Sigma$ | $a$ | $b$ | $c$ | $d$ |
|---|---|---|---|---|
| → $q_0$ | $q_1$ | — | — | — |
| $q_1$ | $q_4$ | $q_2$ | — | — |
| $q_2$ | — | — | $q_3$ | $q_3$ |
| ($q_3$) | — | — | — | — |
| $q_4$ | — | — | $q_5$ | — |
| $q_5$ | — | — | — | $q_3$ |

**Example 2.29** Construct the NFA/DFA for the following languages:

(a) $L = \{x \mid \Sigma = \{a, b, c\}$; '$x$' contains exactly one '$b$' immediately following '$c$'}
(b) $L = \{x \mid \Sigma = \{0, 1\}$; '$x$' starts with '1' and $|x|$ is divisible by 3}
(c) $L = \{x \mid \Sigma = \{a, b\}$; '$x$' contains any number of '$a$'s followed by at least one '$b$'}

***Solution***

(a) This is a sequence detector, where each string can contain exactly one '*b*' immediately following '*c*'. This means that the required machine must detect the substring '*cb*'. Figure 2.46 provides the solution—a DFA that detects substring '*cb*'.

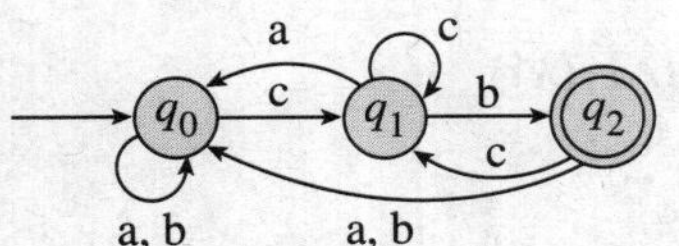


Figure 2.46 DFA that detects substring '*cb*'

(b) This is also a sequence detector problem, where each string should start with '1', and the length of the string (i.e., $|x|$) should be divisible by 3. As the string should start with '1', its length cannot be zero. Therefore, the minimum length of the string is 3, though zero is also divisible by 3.

If we begin with strings having length 3 (as this is the minimum length of the string), the allowed strings are: '100', '101', '110', '111'. For strings having length greater than 4, one can have any combination of 0's or 1's, with lengths in multiples of 3. The DFA that provides the solution is shown in Fig. 2.47.

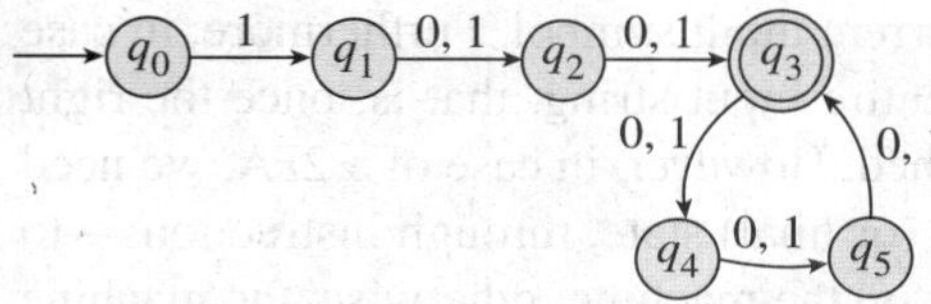


Figure 2.47 DFA that detects sequence required in Example (b)

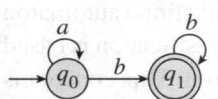

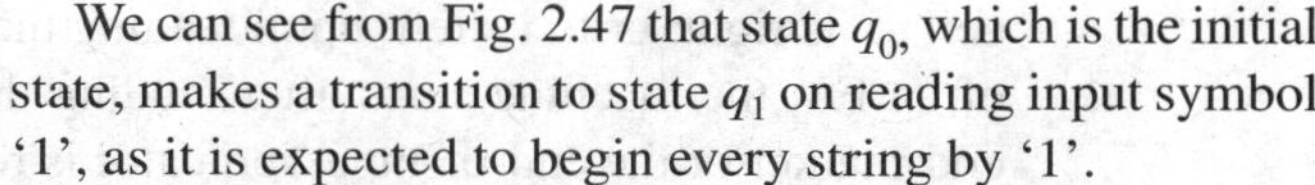

We can see from Fig. 2.47 that state $q_0$, which is the initial state, makes a transition to state $q_1$ on reading input symbol '1', as it is expected to begin every string by '1'.

States $q_1$ and $q_2$ helps in recognizing the four combinations: '100', '101', '110', '111'. State $q_3$ is reached upon reading any of these 4 strings.

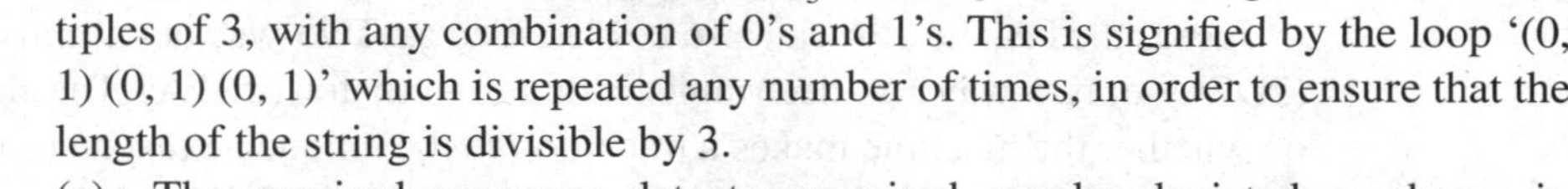

Beyond state $q_3$, the length of the string must be in multiples of 3, with any combination of 0's and 1's. This is signified by the loop '(0, 1) (0, 1) (0, 1)' which is repeated any number of times, in order to ensure that the length of the string is divisible by 3.

Figure 2.48 DFA that detects sequence in Example (c)

(c) The required sequence detector required can be depicted as shown in Fig. 2.48.

We observe that there is a loop labelled '*a*' over the state $q_0$, which represents any number of a's, that is, zero or more number of a's. On reading one '*b*', the DFA reaches the final state $q_1$. This state has a loop on '*b*' in order to cater to more number of *b*'s, as required.

## 2.16 TWO-WAY FINITE AUTOMATON

Two-way finite automaton (2FA) is similar to the FA that we have studied so far, except that these can read the input in either direction—left-to-right, or right-to-left. As we know, FA can read the input only from left-to-right (refer to Section 2.3.6 for details). The 2FA machines have a read head that can move in any direction from the current position, either left or right.

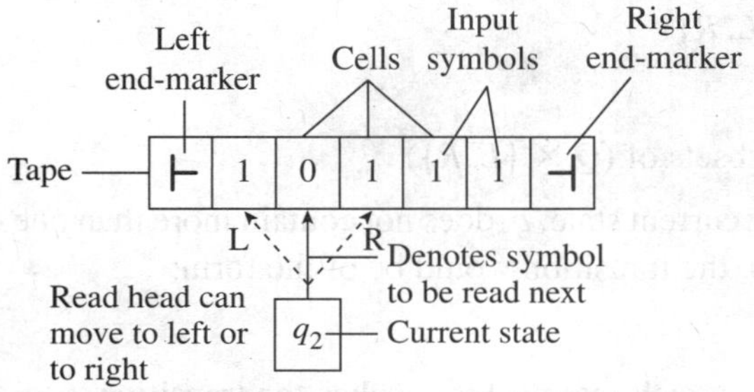


Figure 2.49 Finite control representation for 2FA

Though 2FA sounds to be more powerful than the normal single-way FA, its power is equivalent to that of the FA. The 2FA can accept only the regular sets as does the FA.

Finite control representation for 2FA is shown in Fig. 2.49.

Initially, the 2FA starts with the read head pointing to the cell containing the left end-marker. At any given point in time, the 2FA is in any state, say $q_i$, and makes a transition to some next state upon reading the current symbol on the tape cell. Moreover, unlike the FA, which can move only to one cell on the right, a 2FA can move to one cell left as well, after reading the current input symbol. The left and the right end-markers are the tape bounds, and at any given point in time, the read head cannot move beyond these two bounds. The input tape is thus finite just as that of the FA.

Since the 2FA head can move in any direction—either left or right—unlike the FA, there are certain differences in the 2FA formalism as well. For example, in case of an FA, the transition function only records the next state; while in the case of a 2FA, we need to record the direction (left or right) as well, in order to indicate whether it will point to the cell to its right, or to its left, upon reading the current input symbol. Furthermore, in case of an FA, the machine stops after reading the entire input string, that is, once the right end-marker or the end-of-input indicator is reached. However, in case of a 2FA, we need to explicitly make the machine move to the halt (or final) state, through instructions—to either 'accept halt' or 'reject halt'—in order to stop the machine; otherwise, the machine will keep on reading the input tape from left to right and right to left. This change is again because of the fact that the read head of a 2FA can move in any direction on the input tape.

Just as the FA, the 2FA can also be classified as: Two-way deterministic finite automaton (2DFA), or two-way non-deterministic finite automaton (2NFA). The classification is based on whether the machine makes a transition to the unique next state or not. This concept is same as that of the FA. Let us now formally define the 2FA.

### *Formal Definition*

A 2FA is formally denoted by an eight-tuple (or octuple):

$$M = (Q\ \Sigma, \vdash, \dashv, \delta, q_0, q_A, q_R)$$

where,

$Q$: Finite set of states
$\Sigma$: Finite input alphabet
$q_0$: Initial state of FA, $q_0 \in Q$
$q_A$: Accept halt (final) state of 2FA, $q_A \in Q$
$q_R$: Reject halt (final) state of 2FA, $q_R \in Q$
$\vdash$: Left end-marker symbol; $\vdash \notin \Sigma$
$\dashv$: Right end-marker symbol; $\dashv \notin \Sigma$

The '$\delta$' function for 2DFA is given by:

$$\delta : Q \times (\Sigma \cup \{\vdash, \dashv\}) \rightarrow (Q \times \{L, R\})$$

The '$\delta$' function for 2NFA is given by:

$$\delta : Q \times (\Sigma \cup \{\vdash, \dashv\}) \rightarrow \text{finite subsets of } (Q \times \{L, R\})$$

Thus, in case of the 2DFA, $\delta(q, a)$, for any current state, $q$, does not contain more than one element, upon reading a symbol '$a$'. Thus, the transition would be of the form:

$$\delta(q, a) = (p, d)$$

where, '$p$' is the unique next state in $Q$ to which the machine makes the transition—'$p$' may or may not be equal to '$q$'—and '$d$' is a direction, which is a member of $\{L, R\}$.

This means that the 2DFA reads a symbol '$a$', which is either an input symbol or an end-marker, and makes a transition to a unique next state. Then it moves one position to the right or to the left onto the input tape, of course not exceeding the bounds.

In case of a 2NFA consider the following transition:

$$\delta(q, a) = \{(p_1, d_1), (p_2, d_2), \ldots, (p_m, d_m)\}$$

where, '$q$', '$p_1$', '$p_2$', ..., '$p_m$' are states from $Q$; '$a$' is any input symbol in $(\Sigma \cup \{\vdash, \dashv\})$; and '$d_1$', '$d_2$', ..., '$d_m$' are directions from the set $\{L, R\}$.

The interpretation of this transition is that the 2NFA in state $q$, reads symbol '$a$', and possibly makes a transition to any state '$p_i$'. Then it moves one position onto the tape, either towards right or to the left of the current position. The 2NFA hence, is considered as an unpredictable (non-deterministic or possibilistic) machine, as it can perform any of the possible transitions while executing, though the current machine state and the current input symbol being read are the same.

---

**Example 2.30** Construct a 2DFA that accepts the following regular set:

$L = \{z \in \{a, b\}^* \mid$ number of $a$'s is a multiple of 3 and number of $b$'s is an even number$\}$

***Solution*** Every string '$z$' of the language consists of symbols '$a$' and '$b$', such that the number of $a$'s in '$z$' is a multiple of 3 and the number of $b$'s in '$z$' is an even number.

As per convention, the 2DFA starts reading from the left end-marker. We know that it can read from left to right as well as from right to left, and also that it can read the symbols again that have been read earlier. Let us use this fact to check both the expected conditions on the number of $a$'s and '$b$'s.

While moving from left to right, the 2DFA keeps track only of the number of $a$'s, and ignores all '$b$'s; and while moving from right to left, the 2DFA keeps track only of the number of $b$'s and ignores all $a$'s. Thus, as per the design consideration, the 2DFA checks one condition while moving in one direction, and the second condition while moving in the other direction (refer to Table 2.57).

The 2DFA starts from the left end-marker, and the initial state is $q_0$. From Table 2.57, we can see that upon reading the left end-marker in state $q_0$, the 2DFA moves one position to the right without changing the state. The machine changes its state to $q_1$ upon reading the first '$a$', then moves to state $q_2$ upon reading the second '$a$', and again moves to state $q_0$ from state $q_2$ upon reading the third '$a$'. Further, we notice that in states $q_0$, $q_1$, and $q_2$, the machine retains the state upon reading the symbol '$b$', indicating that the $b$'s are ignored while moving towards the right. States $q_0$, $q_1$, and $q_2$ form a loop, and are used to check whether the number of $a$'s is a multiple of 3. If the right end-marker is reached while reading the $a$'s, and if the current state is $q_0$, then the machine transits to state $q_3$, and moves one position to the left. If the right end-marker is reached while in state $q_1$ or $q_2$, the machine transits to the reject halt state $q_R$ because the number of $a$'s is not a multiple of 3.

**Table 2.57** State transition table for 2DFA

| $Q$ \ $\Sigma \cup \{\vdash \dashv\}$ | $\vdash$ | $a$ | $b$ | $\dashv$ |
|---|---|---|---|---|
| $q_0$ | $(q_0, R)$ | $(q_1, R)$ | $(q_0, R)$ | $(q_3, L)$ |
| $q_1$ | — | $(q_2, R)$ | $(q_1, R)$ | $(q_R, L)$ |
| $q_2$ | — | $(q_0, R)$ | $(q_2, R)$ | $(q_R, L)$ |
| $q_3$ | $(q_A, R)$ | $(q_3, L)$ | $(q_4, L)$ | — |
| $q_4$ | $(q_R, R)$ | $(q_4, L)$ | $(q_3, L)$ | — |
| $q_A$ | — | — | — | — |
| $q_R$ | — | — | — | — |

The 2DFA now starts reading in the reverse order, that is, from right to left. While moving towards the left, the 2DFA counts the number of *b*'s and ignores all *a*'s. State $q_3$ is reached if the right end-marker is read and the number of *a*'s are found to be a multiple of 3. In state $q_3$, if the machine reads '*b*', it transits to state $q_4$, and moves one position to the left; all the a's are ignored otherwise. While in state $q_4$, if the machine reads a second '*b*', it transits back to state $q_3$ and moves one position to the left. Thus, the loop formed by states $q_3$ and $q_4$ counts if the number of *b*'s is a multiple of 2—that is, if the number of *b*'s is an even number. In state $q_3$, if the machine reads the left end-marker, it moves to the accept halt state $q_A$, indicating that the string read contains an even number of *b*'s in addition to the number of *a*'s being a multiple of 3. Otherwise, it transits to the reject halt state, $q_R$.

Now, let us we consider:

$X$ = remainder of division of number of *a*'s in the input string by 3 (to check for multiples of 3)

$Y$ = remainder of division of number of '*b*'s in the input string by 2 (to check for even numbers)

Then, $X$ can take values: 0, 1, and 2; while $Y$ can take values: 0 and 1.

We see that states $q_0$, $q_1$, and $q_2$ in Table 2.57 represent the values 0, 1, and 2 respectively for $X$; and similarly, states $q_3$ and $q_4$ represent the values 0 and 1 respectively for $Y$.

Let us simulate the working of the 2DFA for an input string '*abaabbb*'. The string consists of 3 *a*'s and 4 *b*'s—we observe that the number of *a*'s are a multiple of 3, and the number of *b*'s is an even number. Hence, the string must be accepted by the 2DFA.

```
⊢ a b a a b b b ⊣          Initial configuration
↑
q0

⊢ a b a a b b b ⊣          δ (q0, ⊢) = (q0, R)
  ↑
  q0

⊢ a b a a b b b ⊣          δ (q0, a) = (q1, R)
    ↑
    q1

⊢ a b a a b b b ⊣          δ (q1, b) = (q1, R)
      ↑
      q1

⊢ a b a a b b b ⊣          δ (q1, a) = (q2, R)
        ↑
        q2

⊢ a b a a b b b ⊣          δ (q2, a) = (q0, R)
          ↑
          q0

⊢ a b a a b b b ⊣          δ (q0, b) = (q0, R)
            ↑
            q0
```

$\vdash$ a b a a b b b $\dashv$ (head at 6th symbol, state $q_0$) $\quad \delta(q_0, b) = (q_0, R)$

$\vdash$ a b a a b b b $\dashv$ (head at 7th symbol, state $q_0$) $\quad \delta(q_0, b) = (q_0, R)$

$\vdash$ a b a a b b b $\dashv$ (head at 6th symbol, state $q_3$) $\quad \delta(q_0, \dashv) = (q_3, L)$

$\vdash$ a b a a b b b $\dashv$ (head at 5th symbol, state $q_4$) $\quad \delta(q_3, b) = (q_4, L)$

$\vdash$ a b a a b b b $\dashv$ (head at 4th symbol, state $q_3$) $\quad \delta(q_4, b) = (q_3, L)$

$\vdash$ a b a a b b b $\dashv$ (head at 3rd symbol, state $q_4$) $\quad \delta(q_4, b) = (q_4, L)$

$\vdash$ a b a a b b b $\dashv$ (head at 2nd symbol, state $q_4$) $\quad \delta(q_4, a) = (q_4, L)$

$\vdash$ a b a a b b b $\dashv$ (head at 1st symbol, state $q_4$) $\quad \delta(q_4, a) = (q_4, L)$

$\vdash$ a b a a b b b $\dashv$ (head at 1st symbol, state $q_3$) $\quad \delta(q_4, b) = (q_3, L)$

$\vdash$ a b a a b b b $\dashv$ (head at $\vdash$, state $q_3$) $\quad \delta(q_3, a) = (q_3, L)$

$\vdash$ a b a a b b b $\dashv$ (head at 1st symbol, state $q_A$) $\quad \delta(q_3, \vdash) = (q_A, R)$

A 2FA is equivalent to a read-only turing machine (TM; refer to Chapter 4) that uses only a finite and constant amount of space on the input tape, which, of course, limits it ability. However, a 2FA cannot write anything onto the tape, while a TM can.

Though a 2FA seems to be more powerful than an FA, it is in fact equivalent to it. Hence, a 2FA can only accept regular languages. The only difference between the two is that an FA reads the input symbols only in one direction—left-to-right, and not in the reverse. This makes the FA a special case of the 2FA. Any FA which is equivalent of a 2FA generally has exponentially more number of states than its equivalent 2FA. For the above 2DFA, which has five states (excluding $q_A$ and $q_R$), the equivalent DFA can be constructed with six distinct states (refer to Fig. 2.50). The difference in the number of states is too small here, but this may not be the case every time.

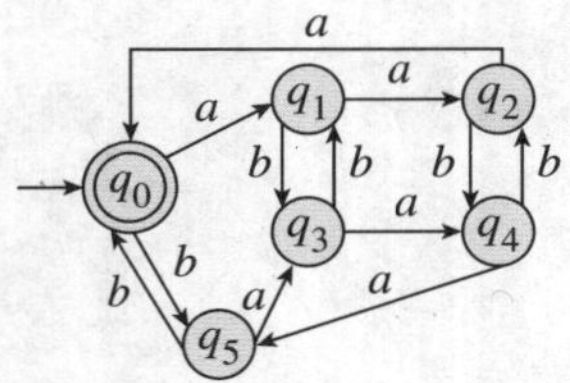


**Figure 2.50** DFA equivalent to the 2DFA in Table 2.56

Following is the explanation for the six states in the DFA in Fig. 2.50. Note that X and Y have the same meaning as stated earlier.

Let:

$q_0$: Represents $X = 0$ and $Y = 0$ (number of $a$'s is a multiple of 3 and number of $b$'s is even)
$q_1$: Represents $X = 1$ and $Y = 0$
$q_2$: Represents $X = 2$ and $Y = 0$
$q_3$: Represents $X = 1$ and $Y = 1$
$q_4$: Represents $X = 2$ and $Y = 1$
$q_5$: Represents $X = 0$ and $Y = 1$

State $q_0$ is an initial state as well as the final state. We observe that as the DFA makes a single read of the input string and only in one direction, each state needs to be associated with some value for $X$ as well as for $Y$. This means that each state needs to associate with the number of $a$'s and $b$'s read so far. This is unlike the 2DFA, which associates either the value of $X$ or $Y$ with the machine states. In case of 2DFA this is possible, as it makes the two passes of the input string—once while moving from left-to-right and the other in the reverse direction.

Thus, in case of 2DFA, we have three values for $X$ and two values for $Y$, making five states in total. For the equivalent DFA, the computation is equal to all combinations of values of $X$ and $Y$. Hence, in this example DFA, it is six ($3 \times 2 = 6$) states in total.

Let us consider an example, in which the machine accept strings whose number of $a$'s is a multiple of 6, and the number of $b$'s is a multiple of 4. In such a case, the 2DFA will have: $6 + 4 = 10$ states, while the equivalent DFA will have: $6 \times 4 = 24$ states. Thus, a DFA which is equivalent of a 2DFA generally has exponentially more number of states than the 2DFA.

## SUMMARY

The term 'machine' refers to a predictable program, whose behaviour can be understood without executing it. A 'state' is the term typically used for different functions that are constituents of a program. A 'program' is a collection of unique functions, each performing an atomic and unique task.

A basic machine is an abstract view of any program (or machine), where one is interested only in determining the output that is generated for a given input. A basic machine can be viewed as a function which maps the input set, $I$, to the output set, $O$. This function is called the machine function (MAF), and is defined as:

MAF: $I \to O$

A finite state machine (FSM) denotes all such programs that have a finite number of functions, but no memory (to store intermediate results). The power of this machine is limited due to lack of memory. An FSM is a simple and primitive computational model.

An FSM is represented by a pair of functions, namely:

Machine function:

MAF: $I \times S \to O$ and

State transition function:

STF: $I \times S \to S$

where, S: Finite set of internal states of the machine

*I*: Finite set of input symbols (or input alphabet)
*O*: Finite set of output symbols (or output alphabet)

Finite automata (FA) is the mathematical model (formalism) of an FSM. Mathematical models emphasize only the specific properties of these machines. An FA portrays an FSM as a language acceptor.

FA is formally denoted by the five-tuple:

$$M = (a, \Sigma, \delta, q_0, F)$$

where, $Q$: Finite set of states
$\Sigma$: Finite input alphabet
$q_0$: Initial state of FA; $q_0 \in Q$
$F$: Set of final states; it is a subset of $Q$, i.e., $F \subseteq Q$
$\delta$: State transition function (STF)

The '$\delta$' function for a deterministic FA or DFA is given by:

$$\delta : Q \times \Sigma \rightarrow Q$$

The '$\delta$' function for non-deterministic FA or NFA is given by:

$$\delta : Q \times \Sigma \rightarrow 2^Q$$

An FA is said to be deterministic if for every state there is a unique input symbol, which takes the state to the required next unique state. This is explained by an equation of the form, $\delta\ (q, a) = p$. This means that if the current state of the machine is $q$, and if the machine reads an input symbol '$a$', it makes transition to a unique next state, $p$.

An NFA may have more than one possible transition on the same input symbol from some state. Such a machine is not even probabilistic, as no weights are assigned to the different possible transitions from the state on the same symbol; hence, it can also be called a 'possibilistic' machine. This is explained by an example equation of the form: $\delta\ (q_0, 0) = \{q_0, q_1\}$. There could be multiple next states, and this is shown by the set entry. We note that $\{q_0, q_1\}$ is a member of $2^Q$ (the power set of $Q$, i.e., set of all subsets of $Q$).

NFA and DFA are equivalent to each other. In other words, for every NFA, there exists an equivalent DFA accepting the same set of words (or language). A DFA is, in a way, a specialization of an NFA. Hence, NFA and DFA have equal powers.

There is another formalism called 'NFA with $\epsilon$-transitions' (or $\epsilon$-moves). The $\delta$ function for an NFA with $\epsilon$-transitions is given by:

$$\delta : Q \times (\Sigma \cup \{\epsilon\}) \rightarrow 2^Q$$

An NFA with $\epsilon$-moves helps us divide a complex language acceptance problem into smaller problems; the solutions to these problems can then be integrated with the help of $\epsilon$-transitions. Further, an NFA with $\epsilon$-moves can be converted either to its equivalent NFA without $\epsilon$-moves, or directly to its equivalent DFA. These three machines are equivalent to one another and have equal powers.

FSMs can be classified as Moore and Mealy machines. 'Moore' and 'Mealy' machines are defined with the help of the six-tuple:

$$M = (Q, \Sigma, \Delta, \delta, \lambda, q_0)$$

where,

$Q$: Finite set of states
$\Sigma$: Finite input alphabet
$\Delta$: An output alphabet
$\delta$: State transition function (STF); $\delta : Q \times \Sigma \rightarrow Q$
$\lambda$: Machine function (MAF)
$q_0$: Initial state of the machine

The machine function for a Moore machine is given by:

$\lambda : Q \rightarrow \Delta$ (i.e., output depends only on the current state)

Whereas, the machine function for a Mealy machine is given by:

$\lambda : Q \times \Sigma \rightarrow \Delta$ (i.e., output depends on the current state as well as the input symbol read)

Moore and Mealy machines are equivalent to each other, which means that one can construct an equivalent Moore machine given a Mealy machine, and vice versa. Moore and Mealy machines can be implemented as finite state transducers (FST), which can write the output string onto the output tape.

Two or more states are said to be 'equivalent states' if they have the same transitions on the same input symbol, and this is true for all the transitions—but they should be of the same type, that is, either final or non-final. If there are multiple equivalent states in a given FSM, one can remove all but one and reduce (or minimize) the FSM.

FSMs lack the ability to store. We may say that an FSM is a program without variables and without assignment statement. Due to lack of memory, the FSM cannot solve problems such as checking whether a given input string is a palindrome or not; multiplication of numbers; and checking if parentheses are well-formed.

Two-way finite automata (2FA) are machines with a read head that can move in any direction from the current position—either towards the left or right. A 2FA is formally denoted by an eight-tuple (or octuple):

$M = (Q, \Sigma, \vdash, \dashv, \delta, q_0, q_A, q_R)$

where,

$Q$: Finite set of states

$\Sigma$: Finite input alphabet

$q_0$: Initial state of FA; $q_0 \in Q$

$q_A$: Accept halt (final) state of 2FA; $q_A \in Q$

$q_R$: Reject halt (final) state of 2FA; $q_R \in Q$

$\vdash$: Left end-marker symbol; $\notin \Sigma$

$\dashv$: Right end-marker symbol; $\notin \Sigma$

The '$\delta$' function for a 2DFA is given by:

$\delta : Q \times (\Sigma \cup \{\vdash, \dashv\}) \rightarrow (Q \times \{L, R\})$

The '$\delta$' function for a 2NFA is given by:

$\delta : Q \times (\Sigma \cup \{\vdash, \dashv\}) \rightarrow$ finite subsets of $(Q \times \{L, R\})$

Though the 2FA seems to be more powerful than an FA; it is in fact equivalent to the FA. Hence, a 2FA can only accept regular languages. The only difference between the two is that the FA reads the input symbols only in one direction—left-to-right—and not in the reverse. This makes the FA a special case of the 2FA. Any FA which is equivalent of a 2FA generally has exponentially more number of states than its equivalent 2FA.

## EXERCISES

This section lists a few unsolved problems for the readers to help understand the topic better and practice some FSM construction examples.

### Objective Questions

(E) 2.1 The smallest finite automata which accepts the language $\{x \mid \text{length of } x \text{ is divisible by } 3\}$ has

(a) 2 states
(b) 3 states
(c) 4 states
(d) 5 states

(U) 2.2 Which of the following is true?

(a) DFA and NFA have same power
(b) DFA is more powerful than NFA
(c) NFA is more powerful than DFA
(d) All of these

(U) 2.3 Which of the following is true about finite automata?

(a) It has no memory
(b) A finite automata can have more than one initial state
(c) Finite automaton uses stack as a memory
(d) All of these

(R) 2.4 The language accepted by DFA is called a __________ language.

(R) 2.5 NFA means __________.

(A) 2.6 Which of the following statements are true for the NFA: $(\{p, q, r, s\}, \{0, 1\}, \delta, p, \{q, s\})$, where '$\delta$' is given by:

**Table 2.58** State transition table

| $Q$ \ $\Sigma$ | 0 | 1 |
|---|---|---|
| $p$ | $q, r$ | $q$ |
| $q$ | $r$ | $q, r$ |
| $r$ | $s$ | $p$ |
| $s$ | — | $p$ |

(a) NFA accepts the string 00
(b) NFA does not accept the string 001
(c) NFA accepts the string 1111110
(d) All of these
(e) None of these

Ⓐ 2.7 If $M$ is a DFA accepting a language consisting of 0's and 1's that end in either '00' or '11'. What is the minimum number of states in $M$?
(a) 2
(b) 3
(c) 4
(d) 5
(e) 6

Ⓤ 2.8 Every DFA is also an NFA. Is this statement true or false?

## Review Questions

Ⓔ 2.1 Construct Mealy and Moore machines for the following:
For the input from $\Sigma^*$, where $\Sigma = \{0, 1, 2\}$ print the residue-modulo-5 of the input treated as a ternary (base 3 with digits 0, 1, and 2) number.

Ⓛ 2.2 Discuss the relative powers of NFA and DFA.

Ⓐ 2.3 Write the machine function and the state transition function for a binary adder. Support your answer with a transition diagram.

Ⓤ 2.4 Prove the following statement: 'Corresponding to every transition graph, there need not exist an FSM, but the converse is always true'.

Ⓡ 2.5 Define and give suitable examples for a transition graph.

Ⓔ 2.6 Construct a Mealy machine that accepts the strings from $(0 + 1)^*$ and produces the following output:

**Table 2.59** Output

| End of string | Output |
|---|---|
| 101 | $x$ |
| 110 | $y$ |
| Otherwise | $z$ |

Ⓛ 2.7 Explain whether a language of palindromes is accepted by an FSM. Justify.

Ⓤ 2.8 Describe the following:
(a) State equivalence
(b) FSM equivalence

Ⓤ 2.9 Write a short note on Mealy and Moore machines.

Ⓤ 2.10 Explain with an example, the process of converting a Mealy machine to its corresponding Moore machine.

Ⓛ 2.11 Write a short note on the properties and limitations of FSM.

Ⓛ 2.12 Compare Moore and Mealy machines.

Ⓔ 2.13 Design an FSM to check divisibility by three, where $\Sigma = \{0, 1, ..., 9\}$.

Ⓐ 2.14 What are finite automata? Construct the minimum state automata equivalent to the state transition diagram in Fig. 2.51.

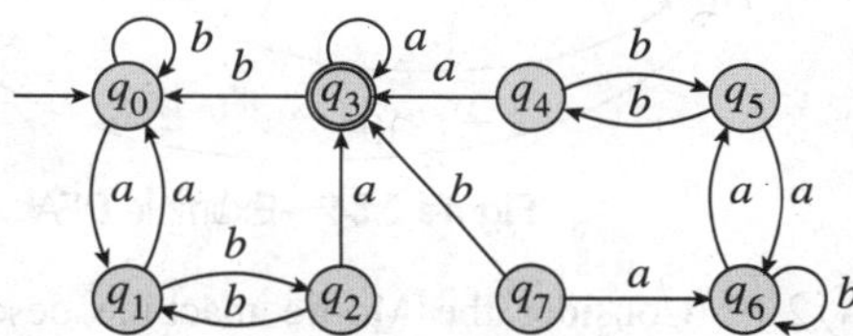


**Figure 2.51** Example automata

Ⓐ 2.15 Construct NFA without $\epsilon$-transitions for the NFA with $\epsilon$-transitions shown in Fig. 2.52.

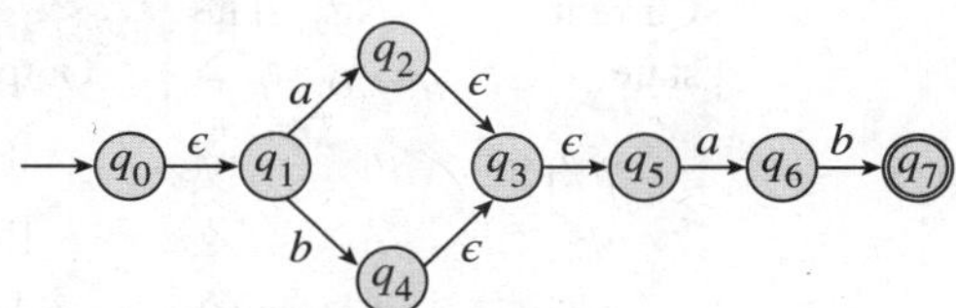


**Figure 2.52** Example NFA with $\epsilon$-transitions

Ⓔ 2.16 Design an FSM that reads strings made up of letters in the word 'CHARIOT' and recognizes those strings that contain the word 'CAT' as a substring.

Ⓐ 2.17 Construct a Moore machine equivalent to the Mealy machine represented by the TG in Fig. 2.53.

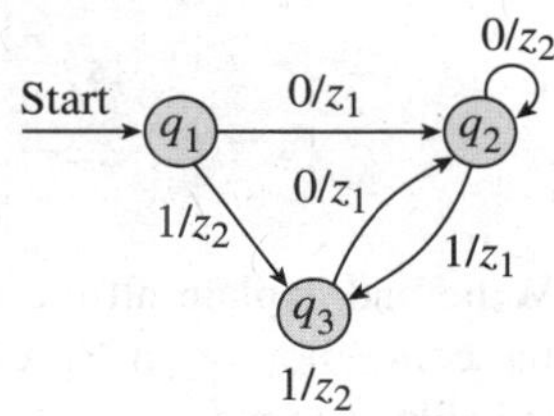


**Figure 2.53** Example Mealy machine

(A) 2.18 Consider the DFA as shown in Fig. 2.54. Obtain the minimum state DFA.

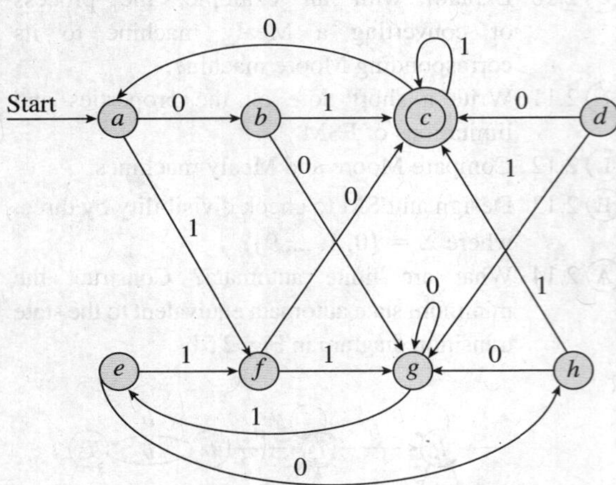


**Figure 2.54** Example DFA

(A) 2.19 Consider the Moore machine described by the transition table given here. Construct the corresponding Mealy machine.

**Table 2.60** Example Moore Machine

| Current state | Next state | | Output |
|---|---|---|---|
| | $a = 0$ | $a = 1$ | |
| $\rightarrow q_1$ | $q_1$ | $q_2$ | 0 |
| $q_2$ | $q_1$ | $q_3$ | 0 |
| $q_3$ | $q_1$ | $q_3$ | 1 |

(A) 2.20 Construct a DFA equivalent to the NFA: $(\{p, q, r, s\}, \{0, 1\}, \delta, p, \{q, s\})$, where '$\delta$' is given by:

**Table 2.61** Example NFA

| $Q$ \ $\Sigma$ | 0 | 1 |
|---|---|---|
| $p$ | $q, r$ | $q$ |
| $q$ | $r$ | $q, r$ |
| $r$ | $s$ | $p$ |
| $s$ | — | $p$ |

(U) 2.21 Write and explain all the steps required for the conversion of an NFA to a DFA using a suitable example.

(A) 2.22 Convert the Mealy machine in Fig. 2.55 to a Moore machine.

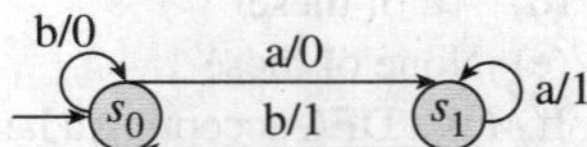


**Figure 2.55** Example Mealy machine

(A) 2.23 Consider the following NFA with $\epsilon$-transitions. Assume '$p$' to be the initial state and '$r$' as the final state.

**Table 2.62** Example NFA

| | $\epsilon$ | $a$ | $b$ | $c$ |
|---|---|---|---|---|
| $p$ | $\phi$ | $\{p\}$ | $\{q\}$ | $\{r\}$ |
| $q$ | $\{p\}$ | $\{q\}$ | $\{r\}$ | $\phi$ |
| $r$ | $\{q\}$ | $\{r\}$ | $\phi$ | $\{p\}$ |

(a) Compute the $\epsilon$-closure of each state
(b) List all the strings of length three or less accepted by the automata
(c) Convert the automaton to its equivalent DFA

(A) 2.24 Construct a DFA for the NFA, whose state transition function is given here. Assume '$p$' to be the initial state and $F = \{q, r\}$.

**Table 2.63** Example NFA

| | 0 | 1 |
|---|---|---|
| $p$ | $\{p, q\}$ | $\phi$ |
| $q$ | $r$ | $s$ |
| $f$ | $s$ | $\phi$ |
| $s$ | $s$ | $s$ |

(U) 2.25 Explain Moore and Mealy machines using suitable examples. How do we construct the equivalent Mealy machine for a given Moore machine? Give a suitable example.

(E) 2.26 Compare Mealy and Moore machines. Design a Mealy machine to replace each occurrence of sub-string '$abb$' by '$aba$', where $\Sigma = \{a, b\}$.

(E) 2.27 Design a Moore machine that changes all the vowels to '\$'.

Ⓐ 2.28 Construct a DFA equivalent to the NFA: $(\{p, q, r, s\}, \{0, 1\}, \delta_N, p, \{q, s\})$, where $\delta_N$ is as given in the following table:

**Table 2.64** Example NFA

| $Q$ \ $\Sigma$ | 0 | 1 |
|---|---|---|
| $\rightarrow p$ | $\{q, r\}$ | $\{q\}$ |
| $*q$ | $\{r\}$ | $\{q, r\}$ |
| $r$ | $\{s\}$ | $\{p\}$ |
| $*s$ | – | $\{p\}$ |

Ⓤ 2.29 Write short notes on:
(a) Deterministic finite automata
(b) Moore and Mealy machines
(c) Moore's algorithm for FSM equivalence
(d) Relative powers of NFA and DFA
(e) Limitations of FSM

Ⓡ 2.30 Give formal definitions for the following:
(a) Deterministic finite automata
(b) NFA with $\epsilon$-transitions
(c) Moore machine
(d) Acceptance of a string by FA

Ⓐ 2.31 Translate the Mealy machine in Fig. 2.56 into its equivalent Moore machine.

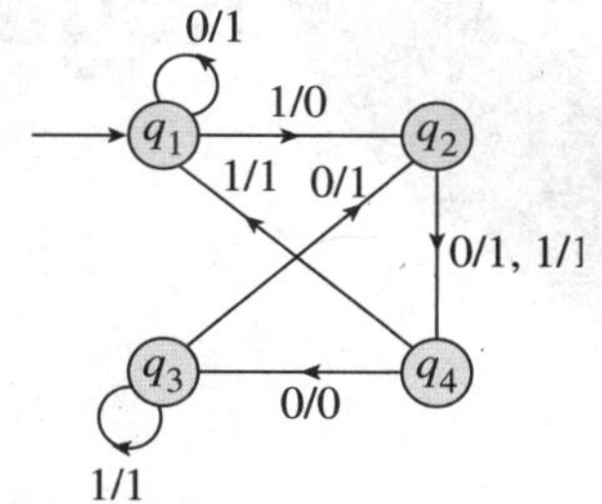


**Figure 2.56** Example Mealy machine

Ⓤ 2.32 Convert the following NFA into NFA without $\epsilon$-moves.

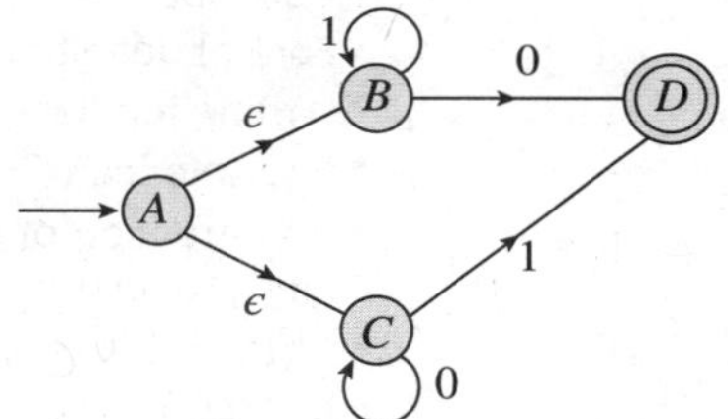


**Figure 2.57** Example NFA with $\epsilon$-moves

**Answers to Objective Questions**

2.1. (b) 2.2. (a) 2.3. (a) 2.4. regular 2.5. non-deterministic finite automata
2.6. (a) 2.7. (b) 2.8. True

# 3 Regular Expressions

**LEARNING OBJECTIVES**

After completing this chapter, the reader will be able to understand the following:

- Concept of regular expressions (REs)
- Formal definition of regular expressions
- Writing regular expressions from a given language description
- Equivalence of regular expressions and finite automata
- Construction of a deterministic finite automata (DFA) from the given regular expression
- Obtaining a regular expression for the language accepted by a DFA
- Arden's theorem
- Closure properties of regular languages (or sets)
- Pumping lemma for regular languages
- Applications of regular expressions/finite automata
- Myhill–Nerode theorem and Kleene's theorem

## 3.1 INTRODUCTION

The languages accepted by finite automata (FA) are described or represented by simple expressions called *regular expressions* (RE). Since FA accepts regular languages (RL), regular expressions are also used to denote regular languages.

Regular expressions are like the short-form notations that denote regular languages (or regular sets). This is analogous to the set labels such as $I$, which denotes the set of integers, and $\phi$, which denotes an empty set. The only difference in the case of regular expressions is that these are composed of few operators as well; hence, the term 'expressions'. As expressions are composed of some operands and some operators, it can be concluded that regular expressions are short notations that can even denote complex and infinite regular languages.

## 3.2 REGULAR EXPRESSION FORMALISM

The class of regular expressions over $\Sigma$ is defined recursively as follows:

1. Regular expressions over $\Sigma$, include letters, $\phi$ (empty set), and $\epsilon$ (empty string of length zero).
2. Every symbol $a \in \Sigma$ is a regular expression over $\Sigma$.
3. If $R_1$ and $R_2$ are regular expressions over $\Sigma$, then so are $(R_1 + R_2)$, $(R_1 \cdot R_2)$, and $(R_1)^*$, where '+' indicates *alternation* (parallel path), the operation '.' denotes *concatenation* (series connection), and '*' denotes *iteration* (*closure* or repetitive concatenation).
4. Regular expressions are only those that are obtained using rules 1–3.

As per the definition, $\phi$, $\epsilon$, and every input symbol from the input alphabet $\Sigma$, itself is a regular expression.

The expression, '$R_1 + R_2$' means *OR-ing* the two regular expressions, which is similar to the *exclusive OR* that we know. This operation is analogous to the 'if ... else ...' construct in programming languages. When the program is executed, only one of the two program paths is followed, based on whether the condition is true or false.

The expression '$R_1 \cdot R_2$' means $R_1$ followed by $R_2$. This is analogous to sequential execution in programmes—one step follows the other.

The expression '$R_1^*$' denotes zero or more occurrences of $R_1$, that is, repetitive (zero or more times) concatenation of $R_1$ to itself. Even an empty string $\epsilon$ is included herein, if $R_1$ is repeated zero times. This is analogous to the looping construct or recursion in programming languages.

The expression '$R_1^+$' is used to denote *positive closure* of $R_1$, and represents one or more occurrences of $R_1$. This means that at least one occurrence of $R_1$ is assured.

We can write this as: $R^+ = R \cdot R^*$.

Hence, we see that $R_1^+$ can be composed out of other primitive operations, and so it is not considered in the regular expression formalism.

Parallel paths, series connection, and repetitive concatenation can be explained with the help of transition graphs (TGs) as shown in Fig. 3.1. The TG in Fig. 3.1(a) represents the parallel paths operation, '$a + b$', which stands for either $a$ or $b$. Similarly, Fig. 3.1(b) represents the series operation, '$a \cdot b$', which stands for $a$ followed by $b$; and Fig. 3.1(c) represents repetitive concatenation, or the closure operation, '$a^*$', which stands for any number of occurrences of $a$, with the help of a self-loop.

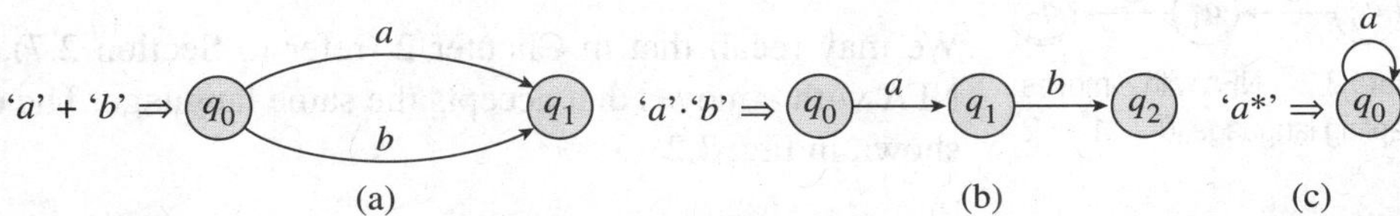


**Figure 3.1** Operators in regular expressions (a) Parallel paths (b) Series connection (c) Closure

If $r$ is a regular expression, then the language represented by $r$ is denoted by $L(r)$.

For example:

If $r = a + b$, then $L(r) = \{a, b\}$.
If $r = a \cdot b$, then $L(r) = \{ab\}$
If $r = a^*$, then $L(r) = \{\epsilon, a, aa, aaa, aaaa, \ldots\}$

Here $\epsilon$ stands for zero occurrences of $a$. Note that $a^*$ denotes an infinite set of strings, which includes all possible strings that can be composed out of $a$.

## 3.3 EXAMPLES OF REGULAR EXPRESSIONS

Let us look at some examples of regular expressions, and attempt to write regular expressions using a given regular language description.

---

**Example 3.1** Using a regular expression, describe the language consisting of all strings over $\Sigma = \{0, 1\}$ with at least two consecutive 0's.

***Solution*** The set of all strings over $\Sigma = \{0, 1\}$ is given as:

$$\Sigma^* = \{\epsilon, 0, 1, 00, 01, 10, 11, 000, 001, 010, \ldots\}$$

This set of all strings over $\Sigma = \{0, 1\}$ can be represented by the regular expression, $(0 + 1)^*$. This set includes all possible combinations of 0's and 1's.

However, we require at least one occurrence of '00', that is, two consecutive 0's. We might have any number of trailing 1's and 0's, and any number of leading 1's and 0's.

Therefore, the required regular expression for the language described is:

$$r = (0 + 1)^* \cdot 0 \cdot 0 \cdot (0 + 1)^*$$

---

**Example 3.2** Using a regular expression, represent the language defined over $\Sigma = \{0, 1, 2\}$, such that every string from the language contains 'any number of 0's followed by any number of 1's followed by any number of 2's'.

***Solution*** 'Any number of '0's' means zero or more occurrences of 0's. This can be denoted by '$0^*$'. Similarly, 'any number of 1's' can be denoted by '$1^*$', and 'any number of 2's' by '$2^*$'.

Therefore, the regular expression is given by:

$$r = 0^* \cdot 1^* \cdot 2^*$$

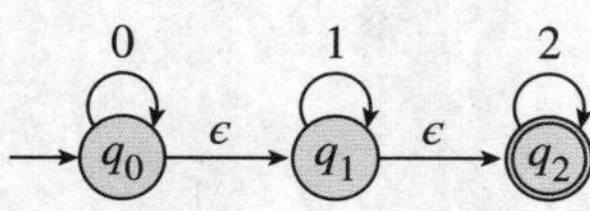


**Figure 3.2** NFA with $\epsilon$-moves accepting language, $0^* \cdot 1^* \cdot 2^*$

We may recall that in Chapter 2 (refer to Section 2.7), we have seen an NFA with $\epsilon$-moves that accepts the same language. The equivalent NFA is shown in Fig. 3.2.

---

**Example 3.3** If $L(r)$ = set of all strings over $\Sigma = \{0, 1, 2\}$, such that at least one 0 is followed by at least one 1, which is followed by at least one 2, find a regular expression $r$ representing this language.

***Solution*** This is very similar to the previous problem. The only difference here is that we require at least one occurrence of each symbol.

The phrase, 'at least one occurrence' means one or more occurrences of the symbol. Now, at least one occurrence of 0 can be represented by '$0 \cdot 0^*$', or $0^+$. We similarly represent at least one occurrence of 1's and 2's as well.

Therefore, we can write $r$ as:

$$r = 0 \cdot 0^* \cdot 1 \cdot 1^* \cdot 2 \cdot 2^*, \text{ or}$$
$$r = 0^+ \cdot 1^+ \cdot 2^+$$

---

**Example 3.4** Using a regular expression, represent the language over $\Sigma = \{a, b\}$ with all strings starting and ending with $a$'s and with any number of $b$'s in between.

***Solution*** In this language, each string must begin and end with an $a$, and in between there may be zero or more number of $b$'s.

Therefore, we may write $L(r)$ as:

$$L(r) = \{aa, aba, abba, abbba, \ldots\}$$

Hence, the regular expression for this language is:

$$r = a \cdot b^* \cdot a$$

---

**Example 3.5** If $L(r)$ = set of all strings over $\Sigma = \{0, 1\}$ ending with '011', then find $r$.

***Solution*** In this language, every string contains any combination of 0's and 1's, and always ends in '011'.

Therefore, we may write $L(r)$ as:

$$L(r) = \{011, 0011, 1011, \ldots\}$$

Hence, the regular expression $r$ is:

$$r = (0 + 1)^* \cdot 011$$

---

**Example 3.6** Describe in simple English the language represented by the regular expression

$$r = (1 + 10)^*$$

***Solution*** Let us try to list out all the strings in the language described by $r$:

$$L(r) = \{\epsilon, 1, 10, 11, 101, 110, 1010, \ldots\}$$

As per the regular expression, we have two parallel paths—'1' and '10', which are put into an iteration (or loop), that is, zero or more number of occurrences.

The empty string $\epsilon$ is obtained if we consider zero occurrences.

We get string '1' if we choose 1 from the two parallel paths, and consider only one occurrence. Similarly, we get string '10' if we choose the other path.

The string '11' is obtained if we choose path '1' for both the iterations.

The string '101' is obtained if we consider two occurrences (or iterations)—path '10' for the first iteration, and path '1' for the next.

Hence, we observe that this is an infinite language.

Now, let us attempt to describe the language looking at the string forms we have listed:

We see that the set $L(r)$ can be described as a language over $\Sigma = \{0, 1\}$ having strings beginning with '1', and not having two consecutive 0's.

---

**Example 3.7** Represent the language over $\Sigma = \{0, 1\}$ containing all possible combinations of 0's and 1's, but not having two consecutive 0's.

***Solution*** We have seen in the previous example that the language containing strings that start with '1' and do not have two consecutive 0's is represented by the regular expression:

$$r_1 = (1 + 10)^* \tag{3.1}$$

Similarly, the language containing strings that start with '0' and do not have two consecutive 0's can be represented as:

$$r_2 = 0 \cdot (1 + 10)^* \tag{3.2}$$

Combining Eqs (3.1) and (3.2), we write the required regular expression as:

$$r = (1 + 10)^* + 0 \cdot (1 + 10)^*$$

This can be simplified as:

$$r = (0 + \epsilon) \cdot (1 + 10)^*$$

---

**Example 3.8** If $r = ab^*a$, describe $L(r)$ in the form of a set.

***Solution*** $L(r)$ can be described in the form of a set of strings as shown here:

$$L(r) = \{aa, aba, abba, abbba, \ldots\}$$

The string $aa$ is obtained considering zero occurrences of the middle string $b$. The remaining strings, such as $aba$, $abba$, and so on, are obtained considering one, two, or more occurrences of $b$ respectively.

---

**Example 3.9** Show that $(a \cdot b)^* \neq a^* \cdot b^*$

***Solution*** Let $r_1 = (a \cdot b)^*$, and

$$r_2 = a^* \cdot b^*$$

Let us try listing the sets $L(r_1)$ and $L(r_2)$:

$$L(r_1) = \{\epsilon, ab, abab, ababab, \ldots\} \tag{3.3}$$

$L(r_2)$ is the concatenation of two sets $u$ and $v$; where,

$u = \{\epsilon, a, aa, aaa, \ldots\}$ that is represented by $a^*$; and

$v = \{\epsilon, b, bb, bbb, \ldots\}$, which is represented by $b^*$.

Therefore,

$$\begin{aligned} L(r_2) &= u \cdot v \\ &= \{\epsilon, a, aa, aaa, \ldots\} \cdot \{\epsilon, b, bb, bbb, \ldots\} \\ &= \{\epsilon, a, b, aa, bb, ab, \ldots\} \end{aligned} \tag{3.4}$$

Comparing Eqs (3.3) and (3.4), we can say that:

$$(a \cdot b)^* \neq a^* \cdot b^*$$

---

**Example 3.10** If $L(r) = \{a, c, ab, cb, abb, cbb, abbb, \ldots\}$, what is $r$ ?

***Solution*** We observe that the strings in $L(r)$ either begin with $a$ or $c$ and are followed by zero or more occurrences of $b$.

Hence, the regular expression $r$ that denotes this set is:

$$r = (a + c) \cdot b^*$$

---

**Example 3.11** If $L(r) = \{aaa, aab, aba, abb, baa, bab, bba, bbb\}$, find the regular expression $r$ which represents $L(r)$.

***Solution*** We observe that the length of each word in $L(r)$ is three, and $L(r)$ depicts all possible combinations of $a$'s and $b$'s.

We also observe that each letter in any word is either $a$ or $b$, that is, $(a + b)$.

Therefore, the regular expression $r$ can be written as:

$$\begin{aligned} r &= (a + b) \cdot (a + b) \cdot (a + b) \\ &= (a + b)^3 \end{aligned}$$

However, $(a + b)^3$ is not a formal notation. Hence, $(a + b) \cdot (a + b) \cdot (a + b)$ is the preferred answer.

---

**Example 3.12** Represent the set of all words over $\Sigma = \{a, b\}$ containing at least one $a$, using a regular expression.

***Solution*** According to the language description, every string must contain at least one $a$, with any number (zero or more) of $a$'s and $b$'s before and after it.

Thus, the regular expression may be written as:

$$r = (a + b)^* \cdot a \cdot (a + b)^*$$

---

**Example 3.13** Let $r = (a + b)^* \cdot a \cdot (a + b)^* \cdot a \cdot (a + b)^*$. Describe the language $L(r)$ represented by the given regular expression using simple English.

***Solution*** We can easily see that the regular expression $r$ denotes the languages $L(r)$ such that:

$$L(r) = \text{language over } \Sigma = \{a, b\} \text{ containing at least two } a\text{'s}$$

***Note***: Consider the regular expression:

$$r_1 = b^* \cdot a \cdot b^* \cdot a \cdot (a + b)^*$$

We see that $r_1$ also generates the same language as that of $r$. Therefore, regular expressions $r$ and $r_1$ are equivalent; so we can write:

$$(a + b)^* \cdot a \cdot (a + b)^* \cdot a \cdot (a + b)^* = b^* \cdot a \cdot b^* \cdot a \cdot (a + b)^*$$

Readers may verify this by generating both the languages as an exercise.

---

**Example 3.14** If $r = b^* \cdot a \cdot b^* \cdot a \cdot b^*$, describe $L(r)$ in simple English.

***Solution*** We see that the language description can be written as:

$L(r)$ = language over $\Sigma = \{a, b\}$ containing exactly two $a$'s

---

**Example 3.15** Represent the language over $\Sigma = \{a, b\}$ containing at least one $a$ and at least one $b$, using a regular expression.

***Solution*** Referring to Example 3.13, we may write the regular expression as:

$$r_1 = (a + b)^* \, a \, (a + b)^* \, b \, (a + b)^*$$

Please note that we have not shown the operator for concatenation '·' in the expression, as that is assumed if one symbol follows another.

The language may also be represented using the regular expression $r_2$, as the position of $a$ and $b$ can be interchanged:

$$r_2 = (a + b)^* \, b \, (a + b)^* \, a \, (a + b)^*$$

Thus, the end result is either of the aforementioned forms, and hence can be written as:

$$r = (a + b)^* \, a \, (a + b)^* \, b \, (a + b)^* + (a + b)^* \, b \, (a + b)^* \, a \, (a + b)^*$$

---

**Example 3.16** Show that $(a + b)^* = (a + b)^* + (a + b)^*$

***Solution***

Let $r_1 = (a + b)^*$ then, $L(r_1) = \{\epsilon, a, b, aa, ab, ba, bb, \ldots\}$ (3.5)

Let $r_2 = \underbrace{(a + b)^*}_{p} + \underbrace{(a + b)^*}_{q}$

Now, $L(p) = \{\epsilon, a, b, aa, ab, ba, bb, \ldots\}$,

and $L(q) = \{\epsilon, a, b, aa, ab, ba, bb, \ldots\}$

Therefore,

$$L(r_2) = L(p) \cup L(q) = \{\epsilon, a, b, aa, ab, ba, bb, \ldots\} \quad (3.6)$$

Comparing Eqs (3.5) and (3.6), we can say:

$$(a + b)^* = (a + b)^* + (a + b)^*$$

> ***Note***: Similarly, we can also show that:
> 1. $(a + b)^* = (a + b)^* \cdot (a + b)^*$
> 2. $(a + b)^* = a\,(a + b)^* + b\,(a + b)^* + \in$
> 3. $(a + b)^* = (a + b)^*\, ab\, (a + b)^* + b^*\, a^*$

---

**Example 3.17** Using a regular expression, represent the set of all strings of $a$'s and $b$'s containing at least one combination of double letters.

***Solution*** A double letter combination can either be $aa$ or $bb$.

Therefore, the regular expression can be written as:

$$r = (a + b)^* \cdot (aa + bb) \cdot (a + b)^*$$

---

**Example 3.18** If $L(r) = \{\epsilon, x, xx, xxx, xxxx, xxxxx\}$, what is $r$?

***Solution*** The regular expression can be written as:

$$\begin{aligned} r &= (\epsilon + x) \cdot (\epsilon + x) \cdot (\epsilon + x) \cdot (\epsilon + x) \cdot (\epsilon + x) \\ &= (\epsilon + x)^5 \end{aligned}$$

---

**Example 3.19** Let $L(r)$ = set of all strings over $\Sigma = \{a, b\}$ in which the strings either contain all $b$'s or else, there is an $a$ followed by some $b$'s; the set also contains $\in$. Find the regular expression that represents this language.

***Solution*** We may write the required $L(r)$ as:

$$L(r) = \{\in, a, b, ab, bb, abb, bbb, \ldots\}$$

Therefore,

$$\begin{aligned} r &= b^* + a \cdot b^* \\ &= (\epsilon + a) \cdot b^* \end{aligned}$$

---

**Example 3.20** Find the regular expression for the language consisting of all strings of $a$'s and $b$'s without any combination of double letters.

***Solution*** The required regular expression is given by:

$$r = (\epsilon + b) \cdot (ab)^* \cdot (\epsilon + a)$$

> ***Note***: We want all such strings that do not contain double letters. There are only two patterns that, if iterated, do not generate double letters; they are: $ab$ and $ba$. The aforementioned regular expression uses the pattern $ab$, which is iterated zero or more times. Any string that is the outcome of $(ab)^*$ never begins with $b$, and never ends with $a$. However, the strings can start with either $a$ or $b$ and end in either $a$ or $b$. Hence, '$(\epsilon + b)$' is concatenated in the beginning, and '$(\epsilon + a)$' at the end of the regular expression.

Using another pattern, that is, *ba*, we may write the regular expression as:

$$r = (\in + a) \cdot (ba)^* \cdot (\in + b)$$

Both are the equivalent regular expressions though they appear to be different.

---

**Example 3.21** Show that $(a^* b^*)^* = (a + b)^*$

***Solution***

Let $r_1 = (a^* b^*)^*$, and $r_2 = (a + b)^*$.

Then, $L(r_2) = \{\epsilon, a, b, aa, ab, ba, bb, \ldots\}$ (3.7)

$$\begin{aligned} L(r_1) &= \{(\epsilon, a, aa, \ldots) \cdot (\epsilon, b, bb, \ldots)\}^* \\ &= \{\epsilon, a, b, aa, bb, \ldots\}^* \\ &= \{\epsilon, a, b, aa, bb, ab, ba, \ldots\} \end{aligned} \quad (3.8)$$

From Eqs (3.7) and (3.8), it follows that:

$$(a^* b^*)^* = (a + b)^*$$

> ***Note***: Similarly, we can also show that:
> 1. $(a^* + b^*)^* = (a + b)^*$
> 2. $(ab)^* a = a (ba)^*$

---

**Example 3.22** Represent the language that contains strings over $\Sigma = \{0, 1\}$, and has even number of 0's.

***Solution*** An even number of 0's means either 0, 2, 4, 6, … number of 0's.

Hence, the required regular expression is:

$$r = (1^* \cdot 0 \cdot 1^* \cdot 0 \cdot 1^*)^* + 1^*$$

The path for $1^*$ ensures there are no 0's, while the path for $(1^* \cdot 0 \cdot 1^* \cdot 0 \cdot 1^*)^*$ ensures 2, 4, 6, … numbers of 0's.

We observe that for the path $(1^* \cdot 0 \cdot 1^* \cdot 0 \cdot 1^*)^*$, the two 0's are placed in such a way that they are preceded, followed, and separated by zero or more number of 1's. This generates all possible strings as required.

---

## 3.4 EQUIVALENCE OF REGULAR EXPRESSIONS AND FINITE AUTOMATA

Regular expressions denote a regular set, that is, the language accepted by some finite automata. Further, for every regular expression there exists an equivalent FA, which accepts the same language denoted by the regular expression. This is known as Kleene's theorem.

### 3.4.1 Kleene's Theorem

Kleene's theorem is stated in two parts:

1. Any regular language is accepted by a finite automaton.
2. Languages accepted by FA are regular.

*Proof*

1. Section 3.4.2 establishes the equivalence among regular expressions and FA. The way the regular languages are recursively defined is the reason why the regular expression is so constructed. One may refer to the definition of regular language in Section 3.5.1
2. Section 3.4.3 describes the method used to obtain the regular expression denoting the regular language accepted by any FA.

### 3.4.2 Regular Expression to FA Conversion

Our eventual goal is to construct a DFA that accepts the language denoted by the given regular expression. As per the mechanical process (algorithm), we first need to obtain the NFA with $\epsilon$-transitions, convert it to NFA, which in turn can be converted to its equivalent DFA. Alternately, we can directly construct the DFA from the constructed NFA with $\epsilon$-transitions as discussed in Chapter 2 (refer to sections 2.6 to 2.9).

#### *Regular Expression to NFA with $\epsilon$-moves Conversion*

If there is a simple regular expression, we can directly construct its equivalent DFA/NFA without much trouble. However, if the regular expression is complicated, then it is not possible to draw the FA by just looking at it.

There are certain rules to convert a given regular expression to its equivalent NFA with $\epsilon$-moves, which can then be transformed into its equivalent NFA or directly to its equivalent DFA, by the known methods. The rules for converting a given regular expression to its equivalent NFA with $\epsilon$-moves are depicted in Fig. 3.3.

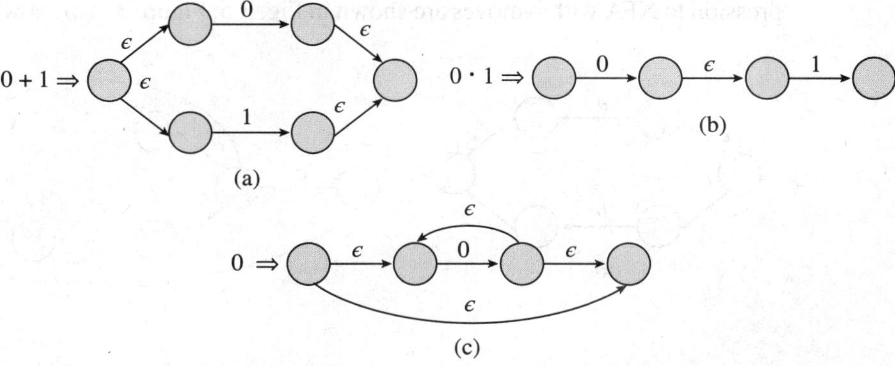


**Figure 3.3** Rules for constructing NFA with $\epsilon$-moves from given regular expression (a) Parallel paths (b) Series (c) Closure

Figure 3.3(a) shows how the '+' operator is converted to parallel paths.

One might question the use of $\epsilon$-moves in the figure: The figure illustrates a very simple example of '$r_1 + r_2$', where $r_1$ is 0 and $r_2$ is 1. In reality, these can be complex expressions themselves. In such a case, we introduce a new start state that connects with the initial states of the individual FA representing $r_1$ and $r_2$ using the $\epsilon$-moves. The individual final states of two FA are also similarly connected with a new final state.

Figure 3.3(b) shows how a final state of the FA for $r_1$ is connected to the start state for $r_2$; here $r_1$ is considered as 0 and $r_2$ as '1'. It is very important to note here that if these thumb rules are applied to obtain the NFA with $\epsilon$-moves, then each NFA with $\epsilon$-moves will always has a single final state.

Figure 3.3(c) shows a transition from the first state to the last state on $\epsilon$, which represents zero occurrences of $r$—taken here as 0. This is done to bypass $r$. The other path from the first state to the last state, which goes through some intermediate states, represents one or more occurrences of $r$. In all, the figure depicts 'zero or more' occurrences of $r$.

In order to represent $r^*$, we introduce a new start state and a new ending state: for this, we introduce a path from the start to the final state using $\epsilon$ to denote zero occurrences. We then connect the new start state to the start state of the FA for $r$ using $\epsilon$. Likewise, we connect the final state of the FA for $r$ to a new end state using $\epsilon$. Thus, the new FA denotes one occurrence of $r$. We then connect the original final state of FA for $r$ to its original initial state to achieve more than one occurrence. Overall, the new NFA with $\epsilon$-moves thus constructed represents zero or more occurrences of $r$, that is, $r^*$.

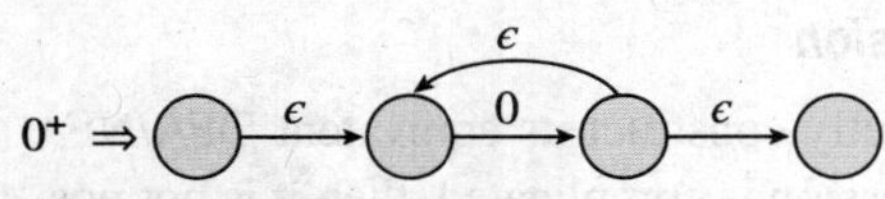


**Figure 3.4** NFA with $\epsilon$-moves representing positive closure of 0

Similarly, positive closure of 0, that is, $0^+$ is represented as an NFA with $\epsilon$-moves as shown in Fig. 3.4. This can be generalized to represent any complex $r$. Comparing Fig. 3.3(c) and Fig. 3.4, we note that the path from the new initial to new final state on symbol $\epsilon$, representing zero occurrences is removed now.

---

**Example 3.23** Draw an NFA with $\epsilon$-moves for the regular expression, $r = a \cdot (a + b)^*$, which represents the language consisting of strings of $a$'s and $b$'s, starting with $a$.

***Solution*** Using the rules given in Fig. 3.3, the steps for converting the given regular expression to NFA with $\epsilon$-moves are shown in Fig. 3.5. Figure 3.5(c) shows the required NFA.

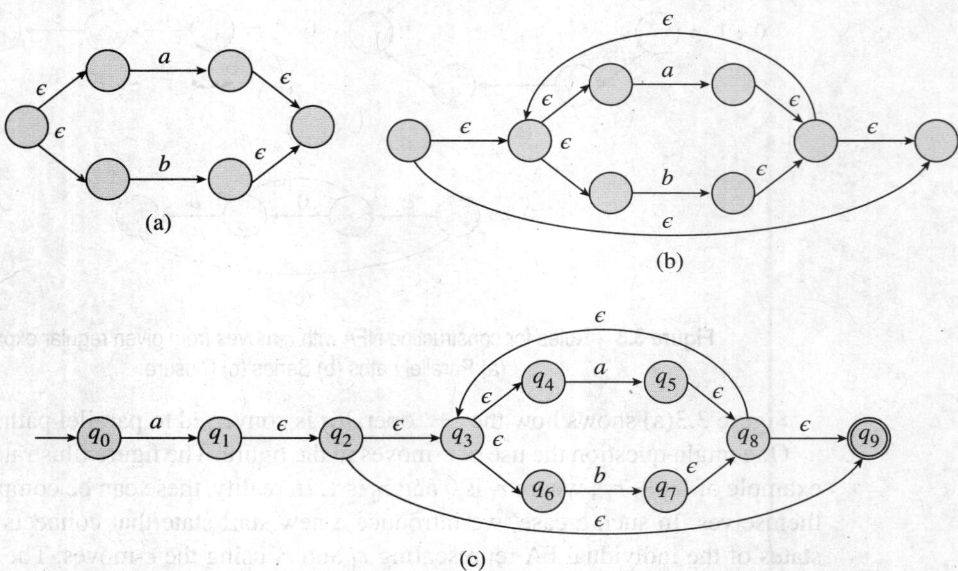


**Figure 3.5** Steps for constructing NFA with $\epsilon$-moves for $a \cdot (a + b)^*$ (a) Step 1: NFA with $\epsilon$-moves for $(a + b)$ (b) Step 2: NFA with $\epsilon$-moves for $(a + b)^*$ (c) Step 3: Final NFA with $\epsilon$-moves for $a \cdot (a + b)^*$

**Example 3.24** Draw the NFA with $\epsilon$-moves for the regular expression $r = (a^* + b^*)$.

***Solution*** Using the rules for converting the given regular expression to NFA with $\epsilon$-moves, we construct the NFA with $\epsilon$-moves for $(a^* + b^*)$ as shown in Fig. 3.6.

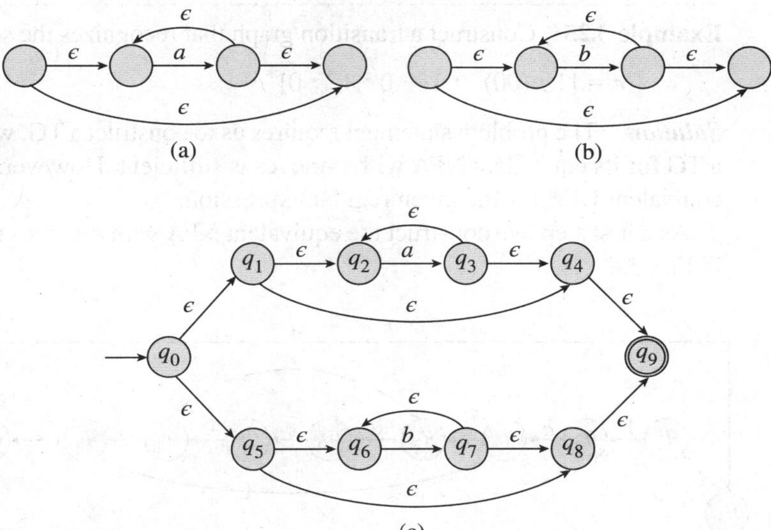


**Figure 3.6** NFA with $\epsilon$-moves for regular expression $(a^* + b^*)$ (a) Step 1: $a^*$ (b) Step 2: $b^*$ (c) Step 3: $(a^* + b^*)$

### *Regular Expression to NFA Conversion*

As discussed earlier, we can obtain the equivalent NFA with $\epsilon$-moves from a given regular expression; this can then be transformed into NFA without $\epsilon$-moves as discussed in Chapter 2 (refer to Section 2.8).

We may recall that the rule for obtaining the state function $\delta'$ for the equivalent NFA without $\epsilon$-moves from given NFA with $\epsilon$-moves is:

$$\delta'(q, a) = \epsilon\text{-closure } \{\delta\, [\hat{\delta}(q, \epsilon), a]\}$$

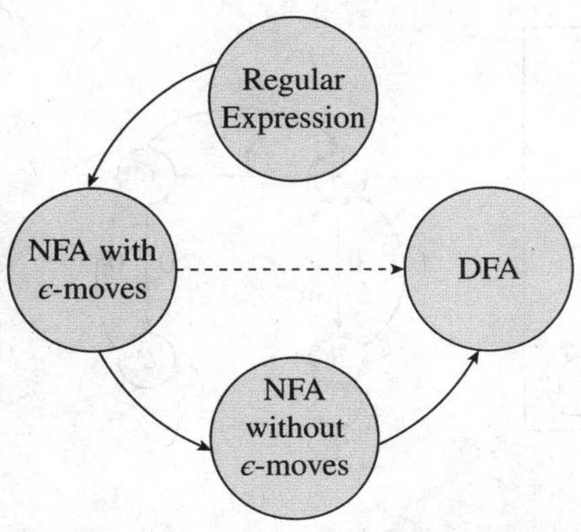


**Figure 3.7** Regular expression to DFA conversion

### *Regular Expression to DFA Conversion*

There are many ways to obtain the equivalent DFA from a given regular expression (refer to Fig. 3.7). The different methods are as follows:

1. Obtain from the given regular expression, the NFA with $\epsilon$-transitions, and by the direct method (refer to Chapter 2, Section 2.9.2), which uses the reachable states technique, convert it to its equivalent DFA.

2. Obtain the NFA with $\epsilon$-transitions from the given regular expression. Convert it to its equivalent NFA without $\epsilon$-moves. Convert this NFA to DFA (refer Chapter 2, Section 2.6). There are again two methods of conversion from NFA to DFA that we have discussed in Chapter 2. Use any one of these two methods.

---

**Example 3.25** Construct a transition graph that recognizes the set:

$$r = [1 \cdot (00)^* \cdot 1 + 0 \cdot 1^* \cdot 0]^*$$

***Solution*** The problem statement requires us to construct a TG, which means constructing a TG for its equivalent NFA with $\epsilon$-moves is sufficient. However, let us also construct the equivalent DFA for the given regular expression.

As a first step, we construct the equivalent NFA with $\epsilon$-moves using the rules, as shown in Fig. 3.8.

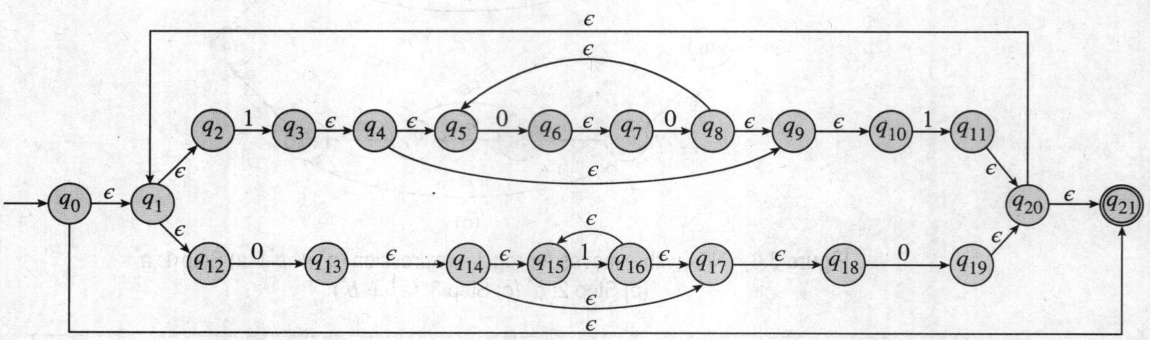


**Figure 3.8** NFA with $\epsilon$-moves for $[1 \cdot (00)^* \cdot 1 + 01^* \cdot 0]^*$

Using this NFA with $\epsilon$-transitions, we can obtain the equivalent DFA through the direct method, as shown in Fig. 3.9(a).

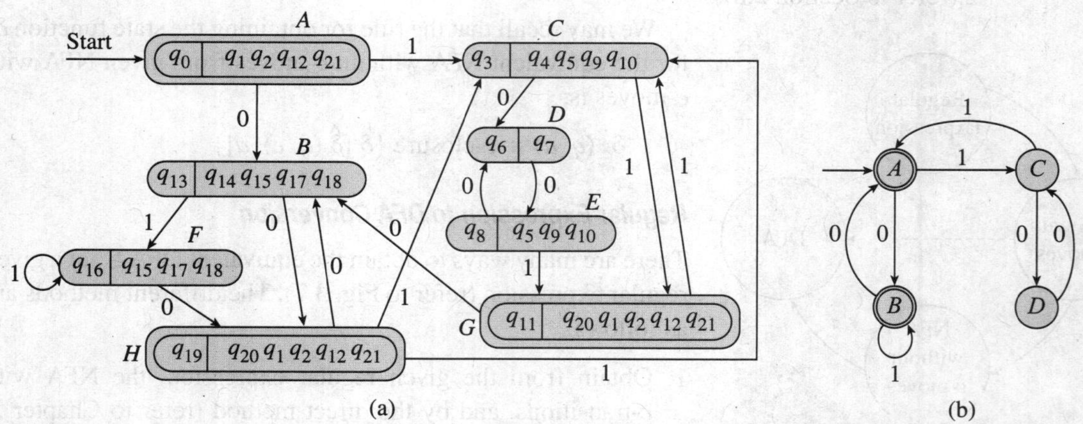


**Figure 3.9** DFA construction from NFA with $\epsilon$-moves (a) DFA directly obtained from NFA with $\epsilon$-moves in Fig. 3.8 (b) Final DFA for the regular expression $[1 \cdot (00)^* \cdot 1 + 01^* \cdot 0]^*$

We begin with the initial state $q_0$ of the given NFA with $\epsilon$-moves, and collect all reachable states (path labelled by $\epsilon$) from $q_0$. These are $q_1$, $q_2$, $q_{12}$, and $q_{21}$. As $q_{21}$ is the final state of the NFA and reachable from $q_0$, we mark this new state as final. Out of states $q_1$, $q_2$, $q_{12}$, and $q_{21}$, we see that there are no transitions on 0 or 1 from $q_1$. Similarly, there are no transitions from $q_{21}$ also, as it is the final state. However, $q_2$ goes to $q_3$ on reading 1, while $q_{12}$ goes to $q_{13}$ on reading 0.

**Table 3.1** State transition table for DFA in Fig. 3.9(a)

| Q \ Σ | 0 | 1 |
|---|---|---|
| *A | B | C |
| B | H | F |
| C | D | G |
| D | E | — |
| E | D | G |
| F | H | F |
| *G | B | C |
| *H | B | C |

'*': Final states

**Table 3.2** Reduced state transition table for DFA

| Q \ Σ | 0 | 1 |
|---|---|---|
| *A | B | C |
| B | A• | B• |
| C | D | A• |
| D | C• | — |

'*': Final states
'•': Modified entries

Therefore, we create two new state symbols: $q_3$, whose reachable states are $q_4$, $q_5$, $q_9$, and $q_{10}$; and $q_{13}$, whose reachable states are $q_{14}$, $q_{15}$, $q_{17}$, and $q_{18}$. We repeat the same process for the newly-created states $q_3$ and $q_{13}$, and continue till we reach to the stage where no more new states can be added.

Finally, we obtain eight states in the equivalent DFA, and relabel these states from *A* to *H*, as shown in Fig. 3.9 (a). Using these new labels, the state transition table for the equivalent DFA can be constructed as shown in Table 3.1.

We observe that *G* and *H* are equivalent to *A*; F is equivalent to *B*, and *E* is equivalent to *C*. The reduced state transition table after minimization based on the equivalent states is shown in Table 3.2.

Using Table 3.2, the transition graph for the final DFA equivalent to the given regular expression is drawn as shown in Fig. 3.9(b).

**Example 3.26** Construct the DFA that accepts the language represented by $0^* \cdot 1^* \cdot 2^*$.

***Solution*** First, let us convert $0^* \cdot 1^* \cdot 2^*$ to its equivalent NFA with $\epsilon$-moves, as shown in Fig. 3.10.

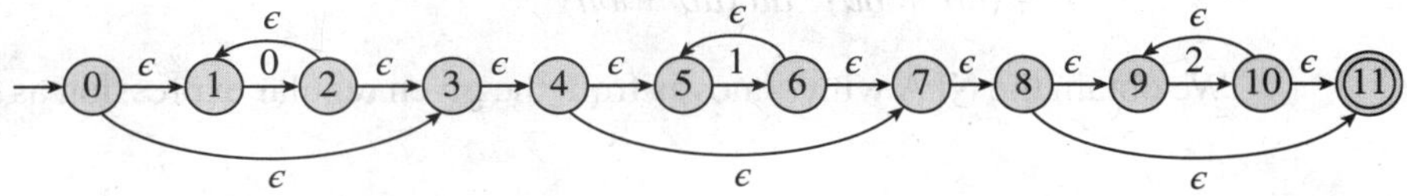


**Figure 3.10** NFA with $\epsilon$-moves for $0^* \cdot 1^* \cdot 2^*$

**Table 3.3** State transition table

| Q \ Σ | 0 | 1 | 2 |
|---|---|---|---|
| *A | B | C | D |
| *B | B | C | D |
| *C | — | C | D |
| *D | — | — | D |

'*': Final states

This can be converted to DFA using the direct method, as shown in Fig. 3.11(a).

Overall there are four states in the equivalent DFA that we have obtained. We relabel these states using letters from *A* to *D*, as shown in Fig. 3.11(a).

The state transition table for the DFA in Fig. 3.11(a) is as shown in Table 3.3.

We observe that state *B* is equivalent to state *A*; hence it can be replaced by state *A*. Thus, we get the reduced table as shown in Table 3.4.

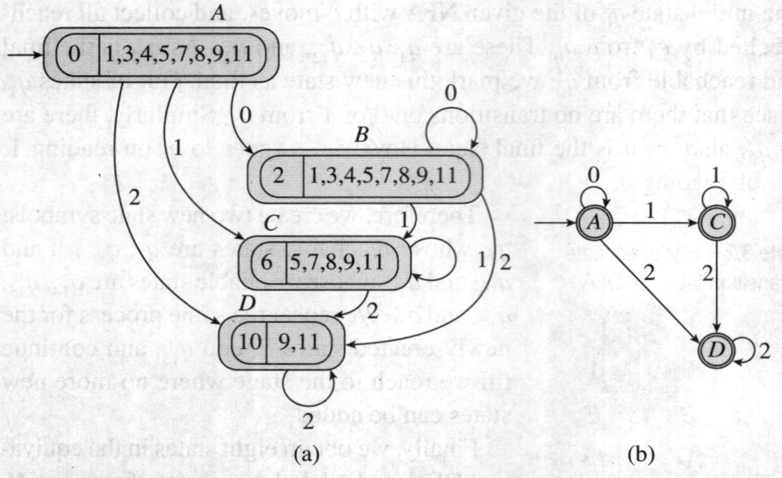


Figure 3.11 DFA construction from NFA with $\epsilon$-moves (a) DFA conversion using direct method (b) DFA for $0^* \cdot 1^* \cdot 2^*$

**Table 3.4** Reduced state transition table

| Q \ Σ | 0 | 1 | 2 |
|---|---|---|---|
| *A | A• | C | D |
| *C | — | C | D |
| *D | — | — | D |

'*': Final states
'•': Modified entry

Using the minimized state transition table for the final minimized DFA, as shown in Table 3.4, we can draw the final transition graph as shown in Fig. 3.11(b).

---

**Example 3.27** Construct a DFA that accepts the language represented by:

$$r = (ab \,/\, ba)^* \, aa \, (ab \,/\, ba)^*$$

***Solution*** Note that the operator '+' that is used to denote parallel paths can also be represented as '/'; though '+' is a more formal notation. Thus, the given regular expression is the same as:

$$r = (ab + ba)^* \, aa \, (ab + ba)^*$$

We obtain the NFA with $\epsilon$-moves from the given regular expression as shown in Fig. 3.12.

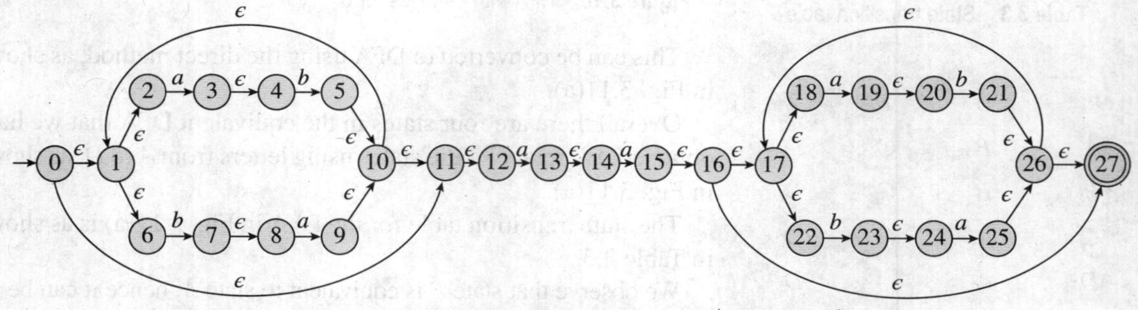

Figure 3.12 NFA with $\epsilon$-moves for $(ab \,/\, ba)^* \, aa \, (ab \,/\, ba)^*$

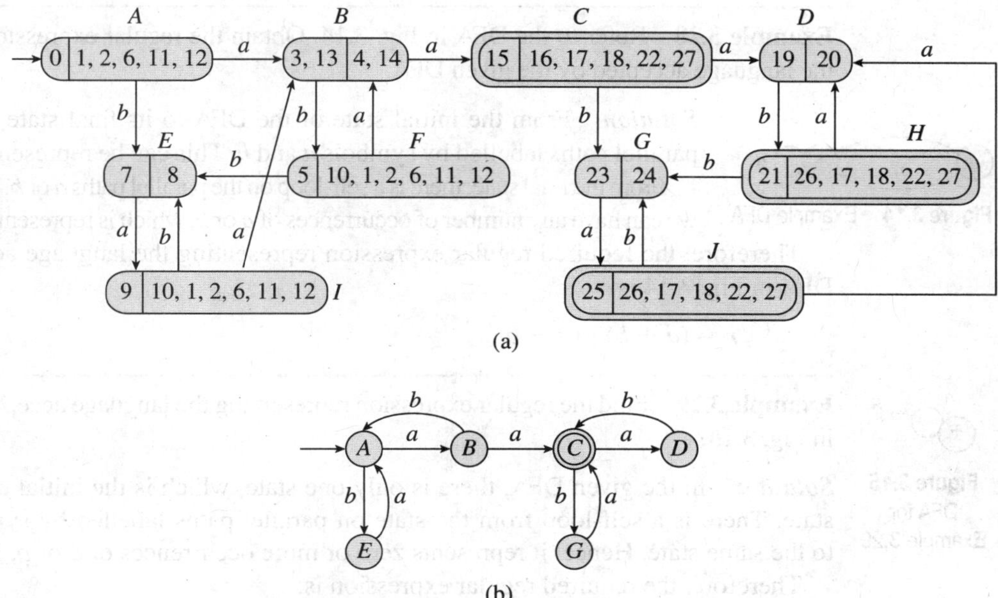


**Figure 3.13** Constructing DFA from NFA with $\epsilon$-moves (a) DFA obtained directly from Fig. 3.12 (b) Final DFA for $(ab / ba)^* aa (ab / ba)^*$

**Table 3.5** State transition table for the DFA in Fig. 3.13(a)

| Q \ Σ | a | b |
|---|---|---|
| A | B | E |
| B | C | F |
| *C | D | G |
| D | — | H |
| E | I | — |
| F | B | E |
| G | J | — |
| *H | D | G |
| I | B | E |
| *J | D | G |

'*': Final states

**Table 3.6** Reduced state transition table

| Q \ Σ | a | b |
|---|---|---|
| A | B | E |
| B | C | A• |
| *C | D | G |
| D | — | C• |
| E | A• | — |
| G | C• | — |

'*': Final states
'•': Modified entries

Using the direct method of conversion, the equivalent DFA is obtained as shown in Fig. 3.13(a). The state transition table for the DFA is shown in Table 3.5.

From the table, we identify the equivalent states. Hence, we can replace states *H* and *J* with state *C*, and states *I* and *F* with state *A*.

The reduced table is shown in Table 3.6.

Using Table 3.6, the final DFA that is equivalent to the given regular expression can be drawn as shown in Fig. 3.13(b).

### 3.4.3 DFA to Regular Expression Conversion

In the previous section, we have seen how to construct a DFA accepting the language denoted by a given regular expression. In this section, we shall prove the equivalence in the reverse direction. We start with a DFA and obtain the regular expression that denotes the language accepted by the DFA.

Let us first see some trivial examples, where we can write the regular expression by simply observing the DFA transitions. We shall discuss the conversion algorithms later in this section.

**Example 3.28** Refer to the DFA in Fig. 3.14. Obtain the regular expression that denotes the language accepted by the given DFA.

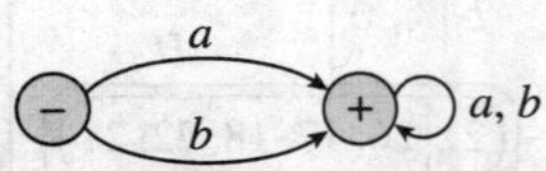

**Figure 3.14** Example DFA

***Solution*** From the initial state of the DFA to its final state, there are two parallel paths labelled by symbols $a$ and $b$. This can be represented as $(a + b)$.

From the final state, there is a self-loop on the parallel paths $a$ or $b$. This means that we can have any number of occurrences of $a$ or $b$, which is represented by $(a + b)^*$.

Therefore, the required regular expression representing the language accepted by the DFA in Fig. 3.14 is:

$$r = (a + b) \cdot (a + b)^*$$

**Example 3.29** Find the regular expression representing the language accepted by the DFA in Fig. 3.15.

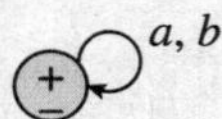

**Figure 3.15** DFA for Example 3.29

***Solution*** In the given DFA, there is only one state, which is the initial as well as final state. There is a self-loop from the state on parallel paths labelled by symbols $a$ and $b$ to the same state. Hence, it represents zero or more occurrences of $a$ or $b$, i.e., $(a + b)^*$.

Therefore, the required regular expression is:

$$r = (a + b)^*$$

**Example 3.30** Find the regular expression equivalent to the DFA in Fig. 3.16.

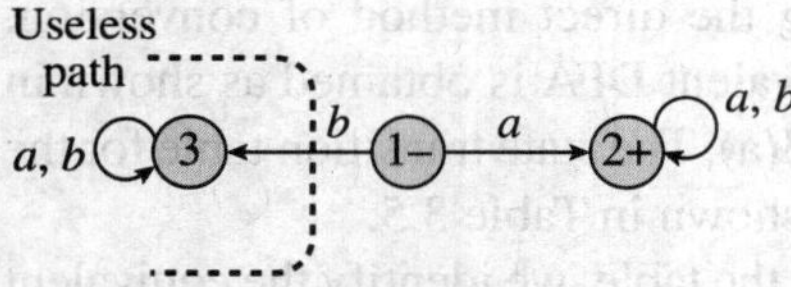

**Figure 3.16** DFA for Example 3.30

***Solution*** State 1 is the initial state from which, there is a transition on input $a$ to state 2, which is a final state. The other transition is on input $b$ to state 3, which is a non-final state. As we can see, state 3 is a dead (or trap) state. Therefore, that path is useless. We should remove the trap state and all the transitions that are incident on that trap state. Thus, the DFA without state 3 represents the regular expression:

$$r = a \cdot (a + b)^*$$

**Example 3.31** Find the regular expression equivalent to the DFA in Fig. 3.17.

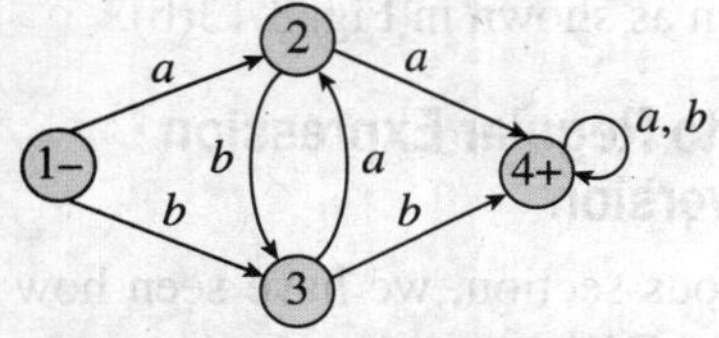

**Figure 3.17** DFA for Example 3.31

***Solution*** Let us consider the path for the input symbol $a$ from the initial state 1. We have two different regular expressions to reach the final state 4 from 1 via 2 (i.e., the path $1 \rightarrow 2 \rightarrow 3 \rightarrow 2 \rightarrow 4$), which are as follows:

$$r_1 = a\,(b\,a)^* \cdot a \cdot (a + b)^*$$

and

$$r_2 = a \cdot (b\,a)^* \cdot b\,b \cdot (a + b)^*$$

Similarly, let us consider the path for the input symbol $b$ from the initial state 1. We have the following two regular expressions to reach to final state via state 3 (i.e., path $1 \rightarrow 3 \rightarrow 2 \rightarrow 3 \rightarrow 4$):

$$r_3 = b \cdot (a\,b)^* \cdot b \cdot (a + b)^*$$

and

$$r_4 = b \cdot (a\,b)^* \cdot a\,a \cdot (a + b)^*$$

Therefore, the required regular expression is obtained by 'OR-ing' all the aforementioned regular expressions:

$$\begin{aligned} r &= r_1 + r_2 + r_3 + r_4 \\ &= [a \cdot (b\,a)^* \cdot a + a \cdot (b\,a)^* \cdot b\,b + b \cdot (a\,b)^* \cdot b + b \cdot (a\,b)^* \cdot a\,a] \cdot (a + b)^* \end{aligned}$$

We note that this example is slightly non-trivial for obtaining the required regular expression. Essentially, one needs to take into account all possible paths from the initial state to all final states (remember, there can be more than one final state).

---

**Example 3.32** Find the regular expression denoting the language accepted by the DFA in Fig. 3.18.

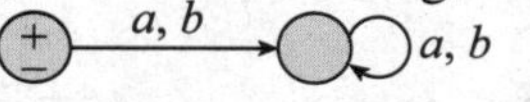


**Figure 3.18** DFA for Example 3.32

***Solution*** As the initial state is the only final state in Fig. 3.18, the other non-final state will never be reached in any string that is accepted by the machine. Hence, the non-final state here is a trap (or dead) state.

Thus, the only string accepted by this DFA is $\epsilon$. Therefore, the required regular expression is:

$$r = \epsilon$$

---

**Example 3.33** For the DFA in Fig. 3.19, find the equivalent regular expression.

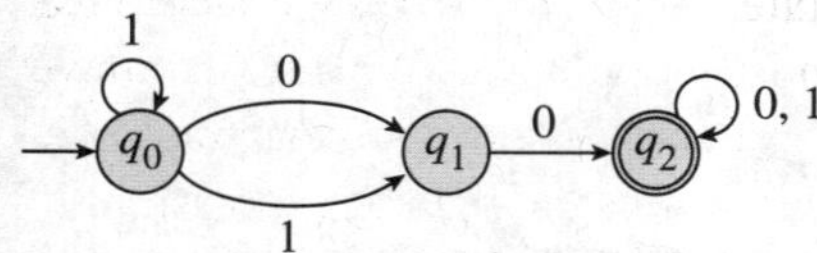


**Figure 3.19** DFA for Example 3.33

***Solution*** The first part of the regular expression is obtained by traversing the graph path, $q_0 \rightarrow q_1 \rightarrow q_2$:

$$r_1 = 1^*\,0\,0\,(0 + 1)^*$$

The second part is obtained from, $q_0 \rightarrow q_1 \rightarrow q_0 \rightarrow q_1 \rightarrow q_2$:

$$r_2 = (1^*\,01)^*\,00\,(0 + 1)^*$$

Hence, the required regular expression is:

$$\begin{aligned} r &= r_1 + r_2 \\ &= 1^*\,0\,0\,(0 + 1)^* + (1^*\,01)^*\,00\,(0 + 1)^* \end{aligned}$$

---

**Example 3.34** For the DFA in Fig. 3.20, find the equivalent regular expression.

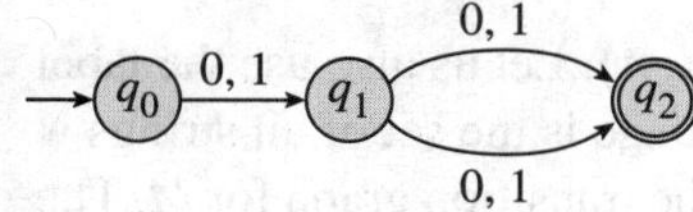


**Figure 3.20** DFA for Example 3.34

***Solution*** This DFA accepts all strings over $\Sigma = \{0, 1\}$, of even (but non-zero) length.

The regular expression is:

$$r = (0 + 1)\,(0 + 1)\,[(0 + 1)\,(0 + 1)]^*$$

**Example 3.35** For the DFA in Fig. 3.21, find equivalent regular expression.

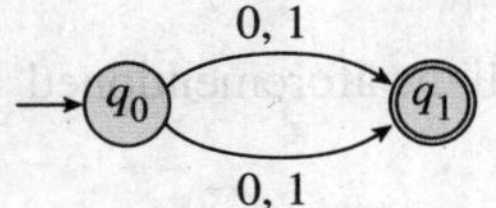


**Figure 3.21** DFA for Example 3.35

***Solution*** If we list all the strings for the DFA, we get:

$$L = \{0, 1, 000, 001, 010, 011, 100, 101, 110, 111, 00000, \ldots\}$$

We observe that the language consists of only odd length strings over $\Sigma = \{0, 1\}$. Hence, the required regular expression is:

$$r = (0 + 1) \cdot [(0 + 1) \cdot (0 + 1)]^*$$

**Example 3.36** For the DFA in Fig. 3.22, find the equivalent regular expression.

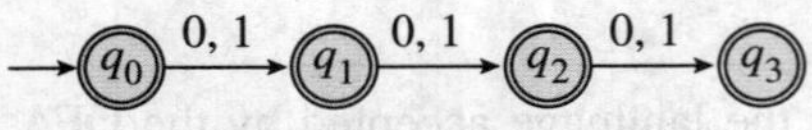


**Figure 3.22** DFA for Example 3.36

***Solution*** The language accepted by the DFA is:

$$L = \{0, 1, 00, 01, 10, 11, 000, 001, 010, 011, 100, 101, 110, 111\}$$

Hence, the regular expression is:

$$r = (0 + 1) + (0 + 1) \cdot (0 + 1) + (0 + 1) \cdot (0 + 1) \cdot (0 + 1)$$
$$= (0 + 1) + (0 + 1)^2 + (0 + 1)^3$$

**Example 3.37** Find the regular expression that represents the language that is accepted by the DFA in Fig. 3.23.

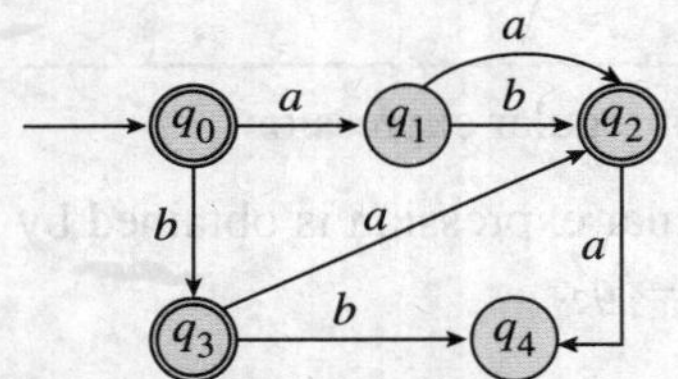


**Figure 3.23** DFA for Example 3.37

***Solution*** The language accepted by the DFA is:

$$L = \{\epsilon, ab, aa, ba\}$$

We observe that state $q_4$ is a dead state.

Therefore, the regular expression is:

$$r = \epsilon + aa + ab + ba$$

Here, $\epsilon$ is included as the initial state is also a final state.

### *Iterative Method for DFA to Regular Expression Conversion*

In the previous section, we have studied many examples, where we represented a language accepted by given DFAs using different regular expressions. Let us now discuss an algorithm, which obtains such regular expression for any given DFA as input.

**Theorem 3.1**

If $L = L(M)$ for some DFA $M$, then there is a regular expression $r$ such that $L(R) = L(M)$.

*Proof*

Let us consider any general DFA $M$, with $Q = \{1, 2, 3, 4, \ldots, n\}$. Let us also use the label $R_{ij}^{(k)}$, which represents a regular expression, and whose language is the set of all strings $w$ such that there is a path $w$ available from state $i$ to state $j$ in the transition graph for $M$. The only restriction here is that the path does not traverse through any state, whose number is greater than $k$. Note here that $i$ and $j$ may be greater than $k$, as they are not intermediate states, but the end points of the path.

Let us build the expression $R_{ij}^{(k)}$ through inductive definition, where we start with $k = 0$ and incrementally build the expression till $k = n$. In this way, we achieve all possible paths from $i$ to $j$ that traverse through all the possible states available in $M$.

As we have considered the state numbers to begin with 1, for $k = 0$ there will be no intermediate state. Hence, for $k = 0$, we rely only on the direct transitions that are available.

Now, there can only be two possibilities about $i$ and $j$ in such a case: Either $i = j$ or $i \neq j$, that is, there can be zero or more direct transitions available from $i$ to $j$ on some input symbol. Let us consider each case:

*Case 1*

If $i \neq j$, $k = 0$, and if:

1. There is no path from $i$ to $j$; then, $R_{ij}^0 = \phi$.
2. There is a single symbol $a$, which takes the DFA $M$ from $i$ to $j$ with single transition; then, $R_{ij}^0 = a$.
3. There are multiple symbols, say $l$ in number, on which $M$ makes transitions from $i$ to $j$ then, $R_{ij}^0 = a_1 + a_2 + \ldots + a_l$.

*Case 2*

If $i = j$, $k = 0$, and if:

1. There is no symbol which takes $M$ from $i$ to $j$ (i.e., from i to i); then, $R_{ij}^0 = \epsilon$. This is always true for any state $i$. Hence, there is always a path $\epsilon$ from $i$ to $i$.
2. There is a single symbol $a$ such that $\delta\ (i, a) = i$; then, $R_{ij}^0 = (\epsilon + a)$.
3. There are multiple symbols $a_1, a_2, \ldots, a_l$ such that, $\delta\ (i, a_1) = i$; $\delta\ (i, a_2) = i$; …, $\delta\ (i, a_l) = i$; then, $R_{ij}^0 = \epsilon + a_1 + a_2 + \ldots a_l$

Now, let us consider a path from state $i$ to $j$ that goes through intermediate states labelled either as $k$ or lower in number. When the path from $i$ to $j$ does not traverse through $k$ at all, then the regular expression can be represented as: $R_{ij}^{(k-1)}$. Alternatively, when the path traverses through $k$, it can be broken into three segments:

1. The first from $i$ to $k$, without passing through $k$, that is, $R_{ik}^{(k-1)}$.
2. There could be multiple sub-paths going from $k$ to $k$, without passing through $k$ as an intermediate state—this is equivalent to $R_{kk}^{(k-1)*}$.
3. The third segment is from $k$ to $j$, without passing through $k$—this is equivalent to $R_{kj}^{(k-1)}$.

Combining all the aforementioned expressions, that is, when there is a path from $i$ to $j$ that does not pass through $k$; and when it passes through $k$ at least once, we get the expression as:

$$R_{ij}^{k} = R_{ij}^{(k-1)} + R_{ik}^{(k-1)} (R_{kk}^{(k-1)})^{*} R_{kj}^{(k-1)}$$

The algorithm for obtaining the regular expression from the given DFA is thus based on the aforementioned rule, where we build the expressions in the order of increasing superscript. Observe that the regular expression $R_{ij}^{k}$ only depends upon the expression with smaller superscript, that is, '$k - 1$', which in turn depends on '$k - 2$', and so on, till $k = 0$, which is nothing but the direct transition.

We see that the algorithm does follow the inductive approach, where computation of the next step is in terms of the previous one. If we assume that state 1 is the initial state, and there are $n$ states in DFA $M$, then the sum of all expressions $R_{ij}^{n}$ gives the language accepted by $M$, provided all the $j$'s are final states, that is, $\sum_{j \in F} R_{ij}^{n}$, where $F$ is the set of all final states, as we know.

---

**Example 3.38** Obtain the regular expression for the DFA in Fig. 3.24.

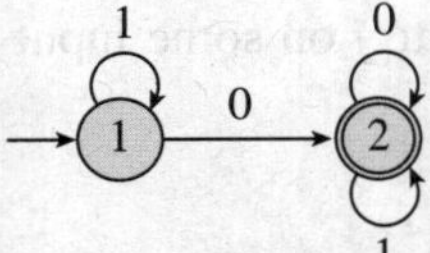


**Figure 3.24** DFA for Example 3.38

***Solution*** We see that the example DFA in Fig. 3.24 accepts language over {0, 1}, which contains strings having at least one 0. We can easily write the required regular expression as $r = 1^* 0 (0 + 1)^*$. However, let us apply the aforementioned algorithm and verify whether we get the same answer as expected.

For $k = 0$, the following table gives all the necessary regular expression components. Remember that for $k = 0$, we only consider direct transitions from $i$ to $j$, wherever available.

| | |
|---|---|
| $R_{11}^{(0)}$ | $(\epsilon + 1)$ |
| $R_{12}^{(0)}$ | $0$ |
| $R_{21}^{(0)}$ | $\phi$ |
| $R_{22}^{(0)}$ | $(\epsilon + 0 + 1)$ |

For $R_{11}^{(0)}$ we have $i = j = 1$, and there is exactly one symbol '1' on which there is a transition from state 1 to 1. For $R_{12}^{(0)}$, $i \neq j$, there is a single symbol '0' that takes the DFA from state 1 to 2. For $R_{21}^{(0)}$ $i \neq j$, there is no symbol that takes DFA from state 2 to 1; hence, it is considered as $\phi$. For $R_{22}^{(0)}$, $i = j = 2$ and there are two symbols '0' and '1', both making transition from $i$ to $j$.

Now, following the incremental step, we want to obtain the expressions labelled $R_{ij}^{(1)}$. We know from the algorithm that:

$$R_{ij}^{(1)} = R_{ij}^{(0)} + R_{i1}^{(0)} (R_{11}^{(0)})^* R_{1j}^{(0)}$$

Thus,

$$\begin{aligned} R_{11}^{(1)} &= R_{11}^{(0)} + R_{11}^{(0)} (R_{11}^{(0)})^* R_{11}^{(0)} \\ &= (\epsilon + 1) + (\epsilon + 1)(\epsilon + 1)^* (\epsilon + 1) \\ &= 1^* \end{aligned}$$

Similarly the rest of the expressions for $k = 1$, that is, $R_{12}^{(1)}$, $R_{21}^{(1)}$, and $R_{22}^{(1)}$ can be obtained. They are listed in the following table.

| | |
|---|---|
| $R_{11}^{(1)}$ | $1^*$ |
| $R_{12}^{(1)}$ | $1^* 0$ |
| $R_{21}^{(1)}$ | $\phi$ |
| $R_{22}^{(1)}$ | $(\epsilon + 0 + 1)$ |

Let us now obtain $R_{ij}^{(k)}$ for $k = 2$.

As we know,

$$R_{ij}^{(2)} = R_{ij}^{(1)} + R_{12}^{(1)} (R_{22}^{(2)})^* R_{2j}^{(1)}$$

Hence,

$$\begin{aligned} R_{11}^{(2)} &= R_{11}^{(1)} + R_{12}^{(1)} (R_{22}^{(1)})^* R_{21}^{(1)} \\ &= 1^* + 1^* 0 (\epsilon + 0 + 1)^* \phi \\ &= 1^* + \phi \\ &= 1^* \end{aligned}$$

This is obtained using the rule, $R \cdot \phi = \phi \cdot R = \phi$; since $\phi$ is an empty set, one cannot concatenate it with a string from $R$ to obtain $R \cdot \phi$ or $\phi \cdot R$. Hence, in Example 3.38:

$$1^* 0 (\epsilon + 0 + 1)^* \phi = \phi$$

Similarly,

$$\begin{aligned} R_{12}^{(2)} &= R_{12}^{(1)} + R_{12}^{(1)} (R_{22}^{(1)})^* R_{22}^{(1)} \\ &= 1^* 0 + 1^* 0 (\epsilon + 0 + 1)^* (\epsilon + 0 + 1) \\ &= 1^* 0 (0 + 1)^* \end{aligned}$$

The remaining two expressions, $R_{21}^{(1)}$ and $R_{22}^{(2)}$, can also be thus obtained.

| | |
|---|---|
| $R_{11}^{(2)}$ | $1^*$ |
| $R_{12}^{(2)}$ | $1^* 0 (0 + 1)^*$ |
| $R_{21}^{(2)}$ | $\phi$ |
| $R_{22}^{(2)}$ | $(0 + 1)^*$ |

Let us now attempt to represent the language accepted by the DFA in Fig. 3.24. Here, 1 is the start state and 2 is the final state; this means that the expression $R_{12}^{(2)}$ represents the language accepted by the DFA, as $R_{12}^{(2)}$ includes all the paths, starting from the initial state 1 to the final state 2, traversing through all the 2 states available in the DFA.

We see from the table:

$$R_{12}^{(2)} = 1^* 0 (0 + 1)^*$$

Hence, this is the regular expression denoting the language accepted by the DFA in Fig. 3.24.

---

**Example 3.39** Obtain the regular expression for the DFA described in Fig. 3.25.

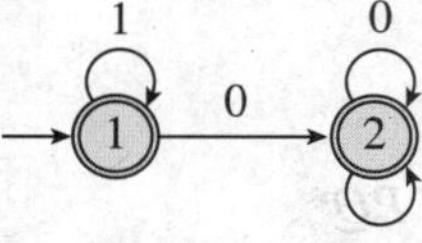


**Figure 3.25** DFA for Example 3.39

***Solution*** We see that the DFA in Fig. 3.25 is similar to the one in the previous example, except that here both state 1 and state 2 are final.

Since there are two final states now, the required regular expression is the summation of $R_{11}^{(2)}$ and $R_{12}^{(2)}$.

Therefore, the regular expression is given by:

$$R_{11}^{(2)} + R_{12}^{(2)} = 1^* + 1^* 0 (0 + 1)^*$$

---

***Note***: The algorithm we discussed for obtaining RE from the given DFA can be applied to NFA or NFA with $\epsilon$-moves as well. It actually does not depend on the type of FA being considered; rather, it only uses the state transition function for the computation.

### *DFA to Regular Expression Conversion using Arden's Theorem*

The method depicted in this section is much simpler as compared to the one in the previous section.

Let us assume that we have a DFA $M$ consisting of $n$ states $\{q_0, q_1, \ldots, q_n\}$. For each of these states, we identify the incoming transitions from all the states (including the state itself). In other words, in a transition graph for $M$, we identify all the directed edges incoming to each of the states.

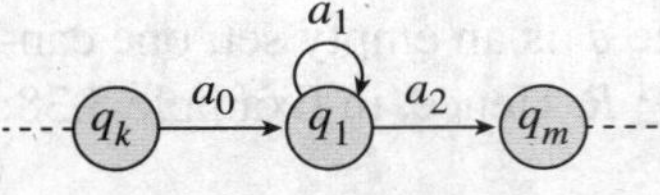


**Figure 3.26** Part of a DFA

For example, in the TG shown in Fig. 3.26, there are two incoming edges for the state $q_l$—one incoming from state $q_k$ labelled as $a_0$, and the other incoming from itself, labelled as $a_1$.

Once we identify all such incoming edges for every state, we can express each state as a state equation of the form:

$$q_n = q_0\, a_0 + q_1\, a_1 + \ldots + q_m\, a_m,$$

where, there are $m$ incoming edges from the states $q_0, q_1 \ldots q_m$ on input symbols labelled as $a_0, a_1, \ldots, a_m$ respectively.

Here, all the symbols from $q_0$ to $q_m$ may not necessarily represent different states; and similarly, all the symbols from $a_0$ to $a_m$ may not represent unique inputs.

The only restriction is that any such combination of a state symbol and input symbol should exist only once in the equation. For the example TG in Fig. 3.26, an equation for state $q_l$ can be written as:

$$q_l = q_k\, a_0 + q_l\, a_1 \tag{3.9}$$

We must also not forget to add $\epsilon$ if the state is initial as well as final.

This process needs to be repeated for all the $n$ states of the given FA. Once we have all the $n$ equations pertaining to the $n$ states, we substitute one into another to solve all the equations.

A solution here means that the right hand side of all such equations should contain only the input symbols and not the state labels (as in Eq. 3.9).

As we know for any DFA $M$, the set of final states, $F \subseteq Q$, hence, the language accepted by the DFA $M$ can be represented by the regular expression: $(S_1 + S_2 + \ldots + S_l)$, where $S_i$ are the solutions for the equations for state symbols $q_i \in F$.

We use Arden's theorem to solve the state equations.

**Theorem 3.2 (Arden's theorem)**

If $P$, $Q$, and $R$ are regular expressions, and:

1. If $R = P + RQ$, or $R = RQ + P$; then, $R$ can be simplified as, $R = PQ^*$.
2. If $R = P + QR$, or $R = QR + P$; then, $R$ can be simplified as, $R = Q^*\, P$.

*Proof*

1. Let us consider $R = P + RQ$.

Substituting the value of $R$ in the right hand side of the equation, we get:

$$R = P + (P + RQ)\, Q$$
$$\Rightarrow \quad R = P + PQ + RQ^2$$

Substituting again, we get:

$$R = P + PQ + (P + RQ)\, Q^2$$
$$\Rightarrow \quad R = P + PQ + PQ^2 + RQ^3$$

Thus, if we continue substituting for $R$ again and again, we get:

$$\Rightarrow \quad R = P + PQ + PQ^2 + PQ^3 + PQ^4 + PQ^5 + \ldots$$
$$\Rightarrow \quad R = P\,(\epsilon + Q + Q^2 + Q^3 + Q^4 + Q^5 + \ldots)$$
$$\Rightarrow \quad R = PQ^*$$

We can similarly prove this for $R = RQ + P$, as the '+' operation is commutative.

2. Let us consider $R = P + QR$.

Substituting the value of $R$ in the right hand side of the equation, we get:

$$R = P + Q\,(P + QR)$$
$$\Rightarrow \quad R = P + QP + Q^2R$$

Substituting again, we get:

$$R = P + QP + Q^2\,(P + QR)$$
$$\Rightarrow \quad R = P + QP + Q^2P + Q^3R$$

Thus, if we continue substituting for $R$ again and again, we get:

$$\Rightarrow \quad R = P + QP + Q^2P + Q^3P + Q^4P + Q^5P + \ldots$$
$$\Rightarrow \quad R = (\epsilon + Q + Q^2 + Q^3 + Q^4 + Q^5 + \ldots)\,P$$
$$\Rightarrow R = Q^*P$$

We can similarly prove this for $R = QR + P$, as the '+' operation is commutative.

Let us now look at some examples, which will help us understand the conversion method.

---

**Example 3.40** Construct a simplified regular expression corresponding to the transition diagram shown in Fig. 3.27, using Arden's theorem.

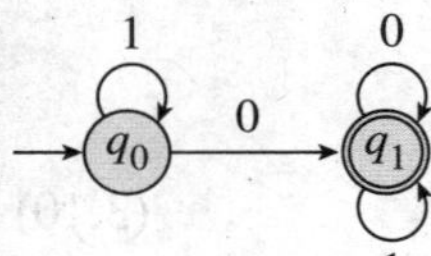


**Figure 3.27** DFA for Example 3.40

***Solution*** We observe from Fig. 3.27 that state $q_0$ has only one incoming edge; hence, the equation for $q_0$ can be written as:

$$q_0 = q_0\, 1$$

On the other hand, the equation for state $q_1$. which is the only final state, can be written as:

$$q_1 = q_0\, 0 + q_1\, 0 + q_1\, 1$$
$$= q_0\, 0 + q_1\, (0 + 1)$$

We can use Arden's theorem to simplify $q_0 = q_0\, 1$, by substituting the values: $R = q_0$, $Q = 1$ and $P = \epsilon$.

We get:

$$q_0 = q_0\, 1 + \epsilon$$

This is equivalent to:

$$q_0 = \epsilon\, 1^*$$
$$= 1^*$$

Here, we consider $P$ as $\epsilon$, as it is being used in the concatenation with $Q^*$, and $\epsilon$ has no effect when concatenated to any other string.

Now this simplified value of $q_0$ obtained by applying Arden's theorem, can be substituted into the equation for $q_1$.

We get:

$$q_1 = q_0\, 0 + q_1\,(0 + 1)$$
$$= 1^*\, 0 + q_1\,(0 + 1)$$

Let us now substitute the values: $R = q_1$, $P = 1^*0$, and $Q = (0 + 1)$ and apply Arden's theorem.

We get:

$$q_1 = 1^*\, 0\,(0 + 1)^*$$

As $q_1$ is the final state for the DFA in Fig. 3.27, the language accepted by the DFA can be represented by the regular expression:

$$R = q_1$$
$$= 1^*\, 0\,(0 + 1)^*$$

We observe that the DFAs in Fig. 3.24 (refer to Example 3.38) and Fig. 3.27 are equivalent, and so are the equivalent regular expressions that we have derived.

---

**Example 3.41** Consider the DFA $M$ shown in Fig. 3.28. Obtain a regular expression $R$ such that $L(R) = L(M)$. Apply Arden's theorem wherever appropriate.

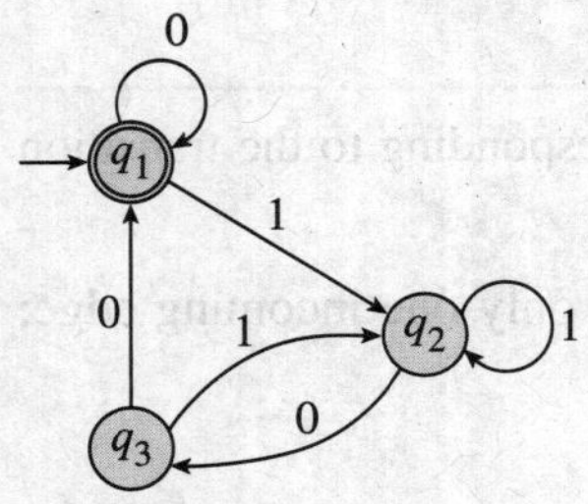


**Figure 3.28** DFA for Example 3.41

***Solution*** The state equations pertaining to the three states, $q_1$, $q_2$, and $q_3$, are:

$$q_1 = q_1\, 0 + q_3\, 0 + \epsilon \quad (q_1 \text{ is initial as well as final state; hence } \epsilon \text{ is added})$$
$$q_2 = q_1\, 1 + q_2\, 1 + q_3\, 1$$
$$q_3 = q_2\, 0$$

Substituting for $q_3$ in the equation for $q_1$, we get:

$$q_1 = q_1\, 0 + q_2\, 00 + \epsilon \tag{3.10}$$

Substituting for $q_3$ in the equation for $q_2$, we get:

$$q_2 = q_1 1 + q_2\, 1 + (q_2\, 0)\, 1$$
$$= q_1 1 + q_2\,(1 + 01)$$
$$= q_1 1\,(1 + 01)^* \quad (\text{using Arden's theorem, for } R = q_2,\ P = q_1 1,\ Q = 1 + 01)$$

Now, substituting for $q_2$ in the equation for $q_1$ i.e. in Eq. 3.10, we get:

$$q_1 = q_1\, 0 + [q_1\, 1\,(1 + 01)^*]\, 00 + \epsilon$$
$$= q_1\, 0 + q_1\, 1\,(1 + 01)^*\, 00 + \epsilon$$
$$= q_1\,(0 + 1\,(1 + 01)^*\, 00) + \epsilon$$

Using Arden's theorem for $R = q_1$, $P = \epsilon$, and $Q = (0 + 1\,(1 + 01)^*\,00)$, we get:

$$q_1 = \epsilon\,(0 + 1\,(1 + 01)^*\,00)^*$$
$$= (0 + 1\,(1 + 01)^*\,00)^*$$

As $q_1$ is the only final state of the DFA, the regular expression $R$ denoting the language accepted by the DFA can be written as:

$$R = (0 + 1\,(1 + 01)^*\,00)^*$$

> ***Note***: We need not solve the other two equations for $q_2$ and $q_3$, as these are non-final states. However, in case there is more than one final state, then we need to solve the equations pertaining to all the final states and add them up together. Refer to the next example, which is an illustration.

---

**Example 3.42** Consider the DFA $M$ in Fig. 3.29. Obtain a regular expression $R$ such that $L(R) = L(M)$. Apply Arden's theorem wherever appropriate.

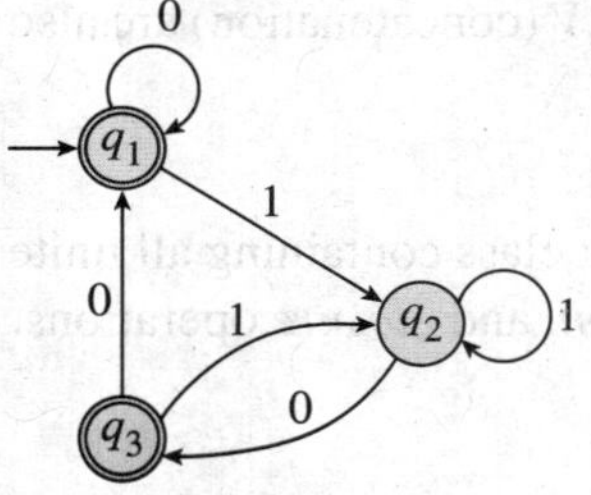


**Figure 3.29** DFA for Example 3.42

***Solution*** We observe that the DFA in Fig. 3.29 is similar to that in Fig. 3.28, except that state $q_3$ is also a final state. Since there are two final states, the regular expression $R$ is written as:

$$R = q_1 + q_3$$

We have already solved for $q_1$ in Example 4.41. Therefore, we shall solve the equation for $q_3$:

$$q_3 = q_2\,0$$

Since $q_3$ is dependent on $q_2$, we must solve the equation for $q_2$ as well:

$$q_2 = q_1\,1 + q_2\,1 + q_3\,1$$

Substituting t $q_3 = q_2\,0$ in $q_2$, we get:

$$q_2 = q_1\,1 + q_2\,1 + q_2\,0\,1$$
$$= q_1\,1 + q_2\,(1 + 0\,1)$$

Using Arden's theorem for $R = q_2$, $P = q_1\,1$, $Q = (1 + 0\,1)$, we get:

$$q_2 = q_1\,1\,(1 + 0\,1)^*$$

Substituting for $q_1 = (0 + 1\,(1 + 01)^*\,00)^*$, we get:

$$q_2 = (0 + 1\,(1 + 01)^*\,00)^*\,1\,(1 + 0\,1)^*$$

Now, substituting this value of $q_2$ in $q_3$, we get:

$$q_3 = q_2\,0$$
$$= (0 + 1\,(1 + 01)^*\,00)^*\,1\,(1 + 0\,1)^*\,0$$

Therefore, the regular expression $R$ denoting the language accepted by the DFA can be written as:

$$\begin{aligned} R &= q_1 + q_3 \\ &= (0 + 1\,(1 + 01)^*\,00)^* + (0 + 1\,(1 + 01)^*\,00)^*\,1\,(1 + 0\,1)^*\,0 \\ &= (0 + 1\,(1 + 01)^*\,00)^*\,(\epsilon + 1\,(1 + 0\,1)^*\,0) \end{aligned}$$

---

## 3.5 REGULAR SETS AND THEIR CLOSURE PROPERTIES

A regular set or a regular language is a language accepted by some FA that can be represented by a regular expression. Regular sets are thus closed under the same operations that are used to construct regular expressions such as '+' '·', and '*'.

### 3.5.1 Formal Definition for Regular Sets

The class of regular sets over $\Sigma$ is defined as:

1. Every finite set of words over $\Sigma$ (including $\phi$, the empty set or null set) is a regular set.
2. If $U$ and $V$ are regular sets over $\Sigma$, then $U \cup V$ (union) and $U.V$ (concatenation) are also regular sets.
3. If $S$ is a regular set over $\Sigma$, then so its closure, that is, $S^*$.

In other words, the class of regular sets over $\Sigma$ is the smallest class containing all finite sets of words over $\Sigma$, and is *closed under*: *Union*, *concatenation*, and *closure* operations.

### 3.5.2 Closure Properties of Regular Sets

Regular sets (or regular languages) are closed under the operations: Union, concatenation, and Kleene closure.

**Theorem 3.3**

If $L_1$ and $L_2$ are regular languages, then their union $L_1 \cup L_2$ is also a regular language. In other words, *regular languages are closed under union.*

*Proof*

Let us consider two regular languages, $L_1$ and $L_2$. This means that there exist regular expressions $R_1$ and $R_2$, such that $L_1 = L(R_1)$ and $L_2 = L(R_2)$.

From the definition of regular expressions (refer to Section 3.2), '$R_1 + R_2$' is also a regular expression. Therefore, $L(R_1 + R_2)$ is also a regular language.

Since the regular expression '$R_1 + R_2$' denotes all the strings that are either denoted by $R_1$ or $R_2$, we can say:

$$L(R_1 + R_2) = L(R_1) \cup L(R_2)$$

Hence, $L_1 \cup L_2$ is also a regular language.

**Theorem 3.4**

If $L_1$ and $L_2$ are regular languages, then their concatenation $L_1 \cdot L_2$ is also a regular language. In other words, *regular languages are closed under concatenation.*

*Proof*

Let us consider two regular languages, $L_1$ and $L_2$. This means that there exist regular expressions $R_1$ and $R_2$ such that:

$$L_1 = L(R_1), \text{ and } L_2 = L(R_2).$$

From the definition of regular expressions (refer to Section 3.2), '$R_1 \cdot R_2$' is also a regular expression. Therefore, $L(R_1 \cdot R_2)$ is also a regular language.

Since the regular expression '$R_1 \cdot R_2$' denotes all the strings that are denoted by $R_1$ concatenated with the strings denoted by $R_2$, we can say:

$$L(R_1 \cdot R_2) = L(R_1) \cdot L(R_2)$$

Hence, $L_1 \cdot L_2$ is also a regular language.

**Note**: Please refer to the section on set concatenation in Chapter 1 for the definition of two subsets *A* and *B*.

**Theorem 3.5**

If *L* is a regular language, then $L^*$ (Kleene closure of *L*) is also a regular language. In other words, *regular languages are closed under Kleene closure.*

*Proof*

Let *L* be a regular language. This means that there exists a regular expression *R* such that $L = L(R)$.

From the definition of regular expressions (refer to Section 3.2), $R^*$ is also a regular expression. Therefore, $L(R^*)$ is also a regular language.

Since the regular expression '$R_1{}^*$' denotes all the strings that are denoted by *R* concatenated to itself zero or more number of times, we can say:

$$L(R^*) = L(R) \cdot L(R) \cdot L(R) \cdot L(R) \cdot \ldots, \text{ zero or more number of times.}$$

We know that the concatenation of two or more regular languages yields a regular language. Therefore, we can say that Kleene closure is simply a repetitive concatenation. Hence, it follows that regular languages are closed under Kleene closure.

**Note**: Please refer to the section on set closure in Chapter 1 for more details.

## 3.6 PUMPING LEMMA FOR REGULAR LANGUAGES

Pumping lemma is an essential property of regular languages. This was first articulated by Y. Bar-Hillel, Micha A. Perles, and Eli Shamir in 1961. It is a useful tool for disproving the regularity of a given language in question. Pumping lemma for regular languages simply signifies the fact that if a regular language is infinite, then it must contain strings of a particular form.

**Lemma statement** It states that given any sufficiently long string accepted by an FSM, we can find a sub-string near the beginning of the string that may be repeated (or pumped) as many times as we like, and the resulting string will still be accepted by the same FSM.

*Proof*
Let $L(M)$ be a regular language accepted by a given DFA, $M = (Q, \Sigma, \delta, q_0, F)$, having $n$ number of states (nodes in the transition graph).

Let us consider an input string consisting of $n$ or more symbols, $a_1, a_2, a_3, \ldots, a_m, m \geq n$. Thus, the input string is of sufficiently long length.

If we consider $m = n$, then we require at least $(n + 1)$ state labels along the path. As per graph theory, in order to traverse the minimum linear path whose length is $x$, one needs to traverse through '$x + 1$' nodes.

Since there are only $n$ distinct states in the DFA $M$, it is not possible for each of the $(n + 1)$ state labels $q_0, q_1, q_2, \ldots, q_n$ to be distinct. Thus, to recognize the string of length $m = n$, we require at least $(n + 1)$ distinct states, which is not feasible.

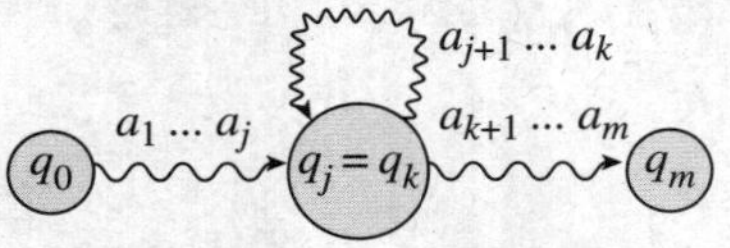

**Figure 3.30** Pumping lemma

Hence, there exist two integers $j$ and $k$ such that $0 \leq j < k \leq n$, for which, $q_j = q_k$. Let us consider the transition diagram for the DFA $M$, as given in Fig. 3.30.

Since, $j < k$, the length of string '$a_{j+1} \ldots a_k$' is *at least one*, and since $k \leq n$, its length is not more than $n$; that is, $1 \leq |a_{j+1} \ldots a_k| \leq n$.

Now, if $q_m \in F$, that is, if $q_m$ is a final state, it means that '$a_1, a_2 \ldots, a_m$' is in $L(M)$; hence, '$a_1, a_2 \ldots, a_j, a_{k+1}, a_{k+2}, \ldots, a_m$' is also in $L(M)$, since there is a path from $q_0$ to $q_m$ that goes through $q_j$ but not around the loop labelled '$a_{j+1} \ldots a_k$'. The maximum length of such a linear path without a loop is $(n - 1)$, as there are only $n$ possible distinct state (node) labels.

The loop '$a_{j+1} \ldots a_k$' is formed over the state $q_j = q_k$, because the sufficiently long string has length $m = n$. We can go over the loop as many times as we like, and the resultant string, of length $m \geq n$, will still be in $L(M)$.

Thus, we can conclude that:

$$a_1 \ldots a_j, (a_{j+1} \ldots a_k)^i, a_{k+1} \ldots a_m \in L(M), \text{ where } i \geq 0.$$

Here, $i = 0$ denotes the case when we do not go over the loop, that is, the string is not sufficiently long and its length is less than $n$; whereas $i > 0$ denotes one or more occurrences of the loop, that is, the string whose length is at least $n$ or more.

**Formal statement of pumping lemma** Let $L$ be a regular set. Then, there exists a constant $n$ such that, if $z$ is any word in $L$ such that the length of $z$ is at least $n$, that is, $|z| \geq n$; and we can write $z = uvw$ in such a way that:

1. $|uv| \leq n$, which means that the sub-string near the beginning of the string is not too long.
2. $|v| \geq 1$, which means that $v \neq \epsilon$; since $v$ is the sub-string that gets pumped.
3. For all $i \geq 0$, $u\,v^i\,w$ is in $L$. This means that the sub-string $v$ can be pumped as many times as we like and the resultant string will still be a member of $L$.

*Proof (of the formal statement)*
Let us consider:

$$z = a_1\, a_2 \ldots a_m$$
$$u = a_1\, a_2 \ldots a_j$$
$$v = a_j + {}_1 \ldots a_k$$
$$w = a_k + {}_1 \ldots a_m$$

Using this consideration, the previous proof can be a proof for the formal statement as well.

### 3.6.1 Applications of Pumping Lemma

Pumping lemma is used to check whether a given language is regular language or not. It is a powerful tool for disproving the regularity of certain languages.

The following procedure is used to show that a specific language is non-regular:

1. Assume that the given language $L$ is regular. Let $n$ be the constant of pumping lemma.
2. Choose a sufficiently long string $z$ from $L$ such that $|z| \geq n$; and write $z = uvw$ using pumping lemma.
3. Find a suitable $i$ such that '$uv^iw$' is not in $L$. This is a contradiction according to pumping lemma; and so, $L$ is not a regular language.

---

**Example 3.43** Prove that the set $L = \{0^{i^2} \mid i \text{ is an integer, } i \geq 1\}$, which consists of all strings of 0's whose length is a perfect square, is non-regular.

***Solution*** Given $i \geq 1$, we have:

For $i = 1$, $0^{i^2} = 0^{1^2} = 0$ (length $= 1^2$)
For $i = 2$, $0^{i^2} = 0^{2^2} = 0000$ (length $= 2^2$)
For $i = 3$, $0^{i^2} = 0^{3^2} = 000000000$ (length $= 3^2$)

As we can see, the length of each string is a perfect square.

1. Let us assume that the language $L$ is a regular language. Let $n$ be the constant of the pumping lemma.
2. Let us choose a sufficiently large string $z$ such that $z = 0^{l^2}$, for some large $l > 0$; the length of $z$ is given by: $|z| = l^2 \geq n$.
   Since we assumed that $L$ is a regular language and from the language definition, it is an infinite language, we can now apply pumping lemma. This means that we should be able to write $z$ as: $z = uvw$.
3. As per pumping lemma, every string '$uv^iw$', for all $i \geq 0$, is in $L$. Likewise, $|v| \geq 1$, which means that $v$ cannot be empty and must contain one or more symbols.

   Let us consider the case when $v$ contains a single symbol:
   In this case, $z = uvw = 0^{l^2}$, which means that the number of 0's in $z$ is a perfect square.
As per pumping lemma, we would expect '$uv^2w$' also to be a member of $L$; however, this cannot be possible, as $v$ contains only a single symbol, and adding one to the perfect square length would not always yield perfect square length. Thus, pumping $v$ would yield

strings with non-square lengths. Thus, '$uv^2w$' is not a member of $L$. This contradicts our assumption that $L$ is regular.

Let us now consider the case when $v$ contains perfect square number of 0's. A sample $v$ could be written as: '0000' (four 0's), or '000000000' (nine 0's), and so on. When we try to pump $v$ multiple times, such as, for example, $v^2$ = 00000000 (eight 0's), or $v^2$ = 000000000000000000 (18 0's), and so on, we find that the length does not remain a perfect square, and we get a string which is against the language definition, which is '$0^{i^2}$'. Thus, we can say that '$uv^2w$' is not a member of $L$. This contradicts our assumption that $L$ is regular.

Similarly, if we consider that $v$ contains any number of 0's, then on pumping it we will get into a situation where the string has non-square length, which is against the language definition. For example, if $v$ contains three zeros and if we pump it, say twice, we will get the string '000000', which does not have a perfect square length.

Hence, the language $L = \{0^{i^2} \mid i \geq 1\}$ is non-regular.

---

**Example 3.44** Prove that the following language is non-regular, using pumping lemma:

$$L = \{a^n\, b^n \mid n > 0\}$$

***Solution*** We must not confuse the $n$ in the language definition with the constant $n$ of pumping lemma. Hence, we rewrite the language definition as:

$$L = \{a^m b^m \mid m > 0\}.$$

1. Let us assume that the language $L$ is a regular language. Let $n$ be the constant of pumping lemma.
2. Let us choose a sufficiently large string $z$ such that $z = a^l b^l$, for some large $l > 0$; the length of $z$ is given by: $|z| = 2l \geq n$. Since we assumed that $L$ is a regular language and from the language definition, it is an infinite language, we can now apply pumping lemma. This means that we should be able to write $z$ as: $z = uvw$.
3. As per pumping lemma, every string '$uv^iw$', for all $i \geq 0$ is in $L$. Further, $|v| \geq 1$, which means that $v$ cannot be empty, and must contain one or more symbols.

Let us consider the case when $v$ contains a single symbol from $\{a, b\}$. Hence, $z = uvw = a^l b^l$, which means that the number of $a$'s and $b$'s in $z$ are the same. Therefore, as per pumping lemma, we would expect '$uv^2w$' also to be a member of $L$. However, this cannot be the case, as $v$ contains only a single symbol, and pumping $v$ would yield different number of $a$'s and $b$'s. Thus, '$uv^2w$' is not a member of $L$, contradicting our assumption that $L$ is regular.

Let us now consider the case when $v$ contains both the symbols, that is, $a$ as well as $b$. The sample $v$ could be written as '$ab$', or '$aabb$', and so on. When we try to pump $v$ multiple times, such as, for example, $v^2 = abab$, or $v^2 = aabbaabb$, and so on, we find that even $a$'s can follow $b$ in the string, which is against the language definition '$a^m b^m$', according to which, $a$'s are followed by $b$'s, and not vice versa. Thus, '$uv^2w$' is not a member of $L$, contradicting our assumption that $L$ is regular.

Hence, language $L = \{a^m b^m \mid m > 0\}$ is non-regular.

**Example 3.45** Show that the following language is non-regular, using pumping lemma:

$$L = \{ww \mid w \in (0, 1)^*\}$$

***Solution*** Each string in the language is represented as a concatenation of two equal sub-strings. Hence, language $L$ can be listed as:

$$L = \{\epsilon, 00, 11, 0101, 0000, 1010, 1111, \ldots\}$$

We observe that the length of every string is even.

1. Let us assume that the language $L$ is a regular language. Let $n$ be the constant of pumping lemma.
2. Let us choose a sufficiently large string $z$, such that $z = xx$, where $x = 0^p1^q$, for some large $p, q > 0$; the length of $z$ is given by: $|z| = 2\,(p + q) \geq n$.
   Since we assumed that $L$ is a regular language and from the language definition, it is an infinite language, we can now apply pumping lemma. Hence, we should be able to write $z$ as: $z = uvw$.
3. As per pumping lemma, every string '$uv^iw$', for all $i \geq 0$, is in $L$. Further, $|v| \geq 1$, which means that $v$ cannot be empty, and must contain one or more symbols.

Let us consider the case when $v$ contains a single symbol from $\{0, 1\}$. We assume $z = uvw = xx = 0^p1^q0^p1^q$. As per pumping lemma, we would expect '$uv^2w$' also to be a member of $L$. However, this cannot be the case as $v$ contains only a single symbol; hence, pumping $v$ would cause the first $x$ in string '$xx$' to end with $v$, and the second $x$ of string '$xx$' to begin with $v$. For example, for $z = 0^p1^q0^p1^q$, after pumping $v = 0$ once, we get, $z_1 = 0^p1^q000^p1^q$, which cannot be represented as a concatenation of two equal sub-strings. Thus, $uv^2w$ is not a member of $L$, as it modifies the string of the form $xx$ to $xvvx$ rather than $xvxv$. This contradicts our assumption that L is regular.

Let us now consider the case when $v$ contains both the symbols, that is, 0 as well as 1. The sample $v$ could be written as 01, or 100, and so on. When we try to pump $v$ multiple times, we obtain strings of the form, $xv^2v^2x$, $xv^3v^3x$, and so on, which is against the language definition $xx$—every string is represented as concatenation of two equal sub-strings. Thus, $uv^iw$, for all $i \geq 0$ is not a member of $L$. This contradicts our assumption that $L$ is regular.

Hence, language $L = \{ww \mid w \in (0, 1)^*\}$ is non-regular.

## 3.7 DECISION ALGORITHMS FOR REGULAR SETS

There are multiple decision algorithms that we can consider for verifying the properties of FSMs.

### *FSM Equivalence*

We have seen Moore's algorithm in Chapter 2 (refer to Section 2.12.1), which checks whether given two FSMs are equivalent or not.

### Emptiness, Finiteness, and Infiniteness

The set of sentences accepted by a finite automaton $M$ having $n$ states is:

1. Non-empty, if and only if the FA accepts a sentence whose length is less than $n$.
2. Infinite, if and only if the FA accepts some sentence whose length is $l$, where $n \le l < 2n$.

*Proof*

1. Let us consider the DFA in Fig. 3.30. The number of states in the given FA $M = n$.

In the figure, we observe that the shortest path accepted by the FA is '$a_1 \ldots a_j a_{k+1} \ldots a_m$' of length $= n - 1$, that is, less than $n$. The length is '$n - 1$' because the numbers of states (nodes) in the transition graph are $n$, and the maximum length of a linear (straight) path in such a case is '$n - 1$'.

Therefore, if we want the set to be non-empty, it should contain at least the minimum string length, that is, '$a_1 \ldots a_j a_{k+1} \ldots a_m$', whose length = '$n - 1$', which is less than $n$.

2. If $w$ is in $L(M)$ and $n \le |w| < 2n$, then using pumping lemma, we can write $w$ as:

$$w = w_1\, w_2\, w_3$$

Further, for all $i \ge 0$, '$w_1\, w_2^i\, w_3$' is in $L$.

Since $i = 0, 1, 2, \ldots, n$ (infinite), it follows that '$w_1\, w_2^i\, w_3$' represents an infinite set of strings. Therefore, $L(M)$ is infinite.

Now, we have to prove the converse, that is, if $L(M)$ is infinite, then there exists $w$ in $L(M)$, such that $|w| \ge n$, and $|w| < 2n$. Here, the first case, $|w| \ge n$ is obvious from pumping lemma; so the only part we have to prove is: $|w| < 2n$.

Let us assume that there is no word having length between $n$ and $2n - 1$, and let $2n$ be the minimum possible length of string $w$. Again, using pumping lemma, we can write:

$$w = w_1\, w_2\, w_3,$$

where $1 \le |w_2| \le n$ and '$w_1\, w_3$' is in $L(M)$—it is the linear path whose length is not more than '$n - 1$'.

However, as $|w| = 2n$, and $1 \le |w_2| \le n$, we have, $2n - 1 > |w_1\, w_3| > n$

This means that the length of '$w_1\, w_3$' is between $n$ and $2n - 1$, which is not possible. This is a contradiction of the lemma, according to which the length of '$w_1\, w_3$', the shortest word, should be less than $n$. Therefore, our assumption that $|w|$ should be at least $2n$ is wrong. Hence, $n \le |w| \le 2n$.

## 3.8 APPLICATIONS OF REGULAR EXPRESSIONS AND FINITE AUTOMATA

A variety of software applications from different areas can be simplified using the conversion of regular expression notation to efficient computer implementations of its corresponding finite automata. The applications of regular expressions and finite automata are spread from system software, such as language compilers, operating system utilities, and program development tools, to application programs such as text editors and syntactic pattern recognizers.

### 3.8.1 Lexical Analyser

As we know, the job of a compiler is to convert a source program written in a high-level language (HLL) such as 'C' to machine code, or low-level language (LLL).

Any compiler is sub-divided into five different phases/modules, namely:

1. Lexical analyser (also known as scanner or tokenizer)
2. Syntax analyser (also known as parser)
3. Intermediate code generator
4. Code optimizer
5. Code generator

The first phase of the compiler is the lexical analyser. Its job is to read the source file, character by character, and identify the valid words, called *tokens*. This is then passed to the second phase of the compiler—the parser—that tries to group these valid words as per the language grammar into meaningful programming statements, or constructs. The parser, thus, does the syntax checking, that is, checking if the tokens are in the right sequence as defined by the grammar for the language.

In order to recognize tokens from a text file (source program), the lexical analyser uses a set of regular expressions. It builds a general-purpose DFA from this set of regular expressions. Such a DFA is used to detect the valid words from a given source file. The validity of the words (or tokens) depends on whether they fit any one of the patterns defined by these regular expressions. Any programming language, for example 'C', contains mostly five different types of tokens, namely—identifiers, literals, punctuations, keywords, and operators.

For example, valid identifiers in 'C' are the sequences composed of a *letter*, followed by any number of *letters* and/or *digits*. The regular expression for identifiers can be written as: $(letter) \cdot (letter + digit)^*$, where:

$$letter = A, B, \ldots, Z, a, b, \ldots, z,$$

and

$$digit = 0, 1, \ldots, 9.$$

Similarly, integer literals such as '20' and '100' can be represented by, $(digit) \cdot (digit)^*$, that is, $(digit)^+$. Integer literals should consist of at least one digit.

One can write regular expressions for each class of tokens that are found in programming languages.

Normally, the regular expressions are converted to the DFA, and its state transition table is used to recognize the tokens. Each final state of the DFA indicates the particular token found. The DFAs for aforementioned two regular expressions are shown in Fig. 3.31.

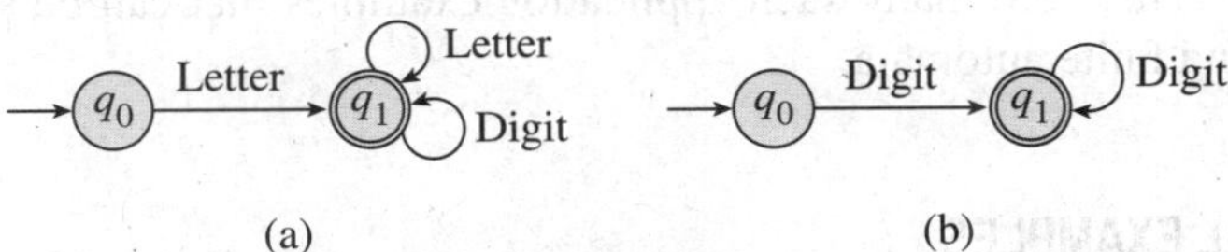


**Figure 3.31** Example DFAs (a) DFA for regular expression: $letter \cdot (letter + digit)^*$ (b) DFA for regular expression: $(digit)^+$

### 3.8.2 Text Editors

Certain modern text editors have some provisions to substitute other strings for any string matching a particular regular expression. 'Find and replace' is the common name used for such substitutions, which can replace every occurrence of a given string by the replacement string. This searching of every occurrence through a given text file is made simpler with the help of regular expressions. The UNIX/Linux text editor has been using this method since the very beginning. Nowadays, we find that most of the editors make searches based on the pattern specified by regular expressions.

### 3.8.3 'grep' Command

Originally written for the UNIX operating system, 'grep' is a command-line text-search utility. The name comes from the 'ed' command, 'g/re/p' (global / regular expression / print)—'ed' is a line editor for the UNIX operating system. The 'grep' command searches files or standard input globally for lines matching a given regular expression and prints the lines to the program's standard output. This command was created by Ken Thompson as a standalone application adapted from the regular expression interpreter, which he had written for 'ed'.

Syntax for the 'grep' command is:

```
grep [options] PATTERN [FILE...]
```

Here, 'pattern' is a regular expression that describes a set of strings that must be searched.

For example, the following 'grep' command prints all lines from the mentioned file containing the string 'vivek', regardless of capitalization. The string 'vivek' here is the simple pattern:

```
grep -i vivek peoplelist.txt
```

The following example is a grep command that searches for pairs of numeric digits in the file:

```
grep '[0-9][0-9]' file
```

Here, [0–9] means 'any digit between 0 to 9'. This is equivalent to writing the regular expression:

$$(0 + 1 + 2 + 3 + 4 + 5 + 6 + 7 + 8 + 9)$$

The pattern [0–9] is thus an extended version of the formal regular expression definition we have seen. The grep command thus makes use of the extended version of the regular expressions we have seen.

There are many such application examples that can be stated for regular expressions and finite automata.

## 3.9 ADDITIONAL EXAMPLES

Let us look at some more examples related to regular expressions.

**Example 3.46** Design a Mealy machine for the language represented as: $(0 + 1)^* (00 + 11)$

1. Construct a DFA for the same
2. Convert this Mealy machine to a Moore machine

***Solution***

1. Let us construct the equivalent NFA with $\epsilon$-moves to start with, as shown Fig. 3.32.

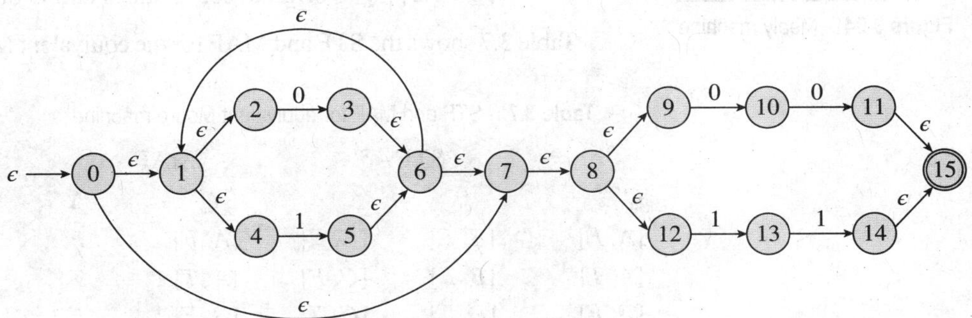


**Figure 3.32** NFA with $\epsilon$-moves for $(0 + 1)^* (00 + 11)$

We can now convert this NFA with $\epsilon$-moves to its equivalent DFA, as shown in Fig. 3.33.

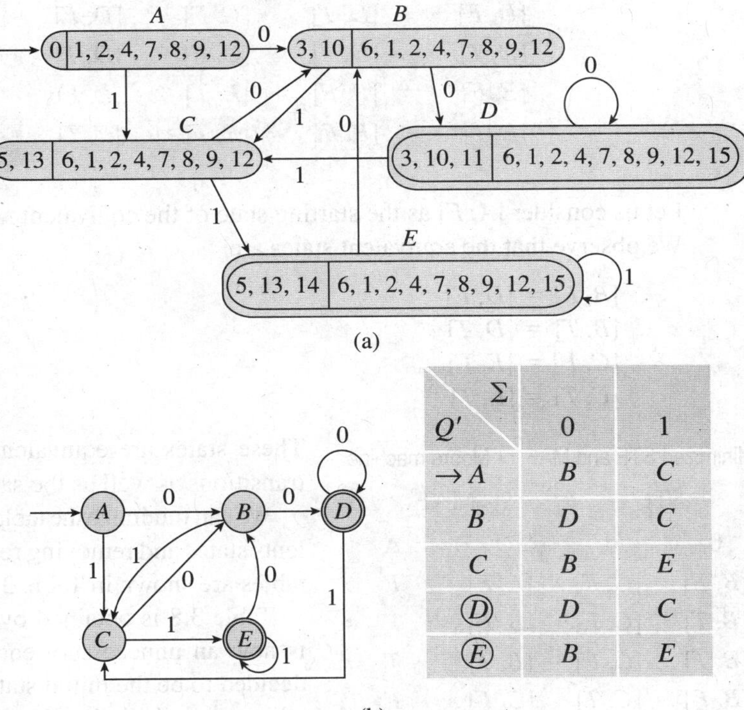


| $Q'$ \ $\Sigma$ | 0 | 1 |
|---|---|---|
| $\rightarrow A$ | $B$ | $C$ |
| $B$ | $D$ | $C$ |
| $C$ | $B$ | $E$ |
| (D) | $D$ | $C$ |
| (E) | $B$ | $E$ |

**Figure 3.33** NFA with $\epsilon$-moves to DFA conversion (a) Step 1 (b) Step 2

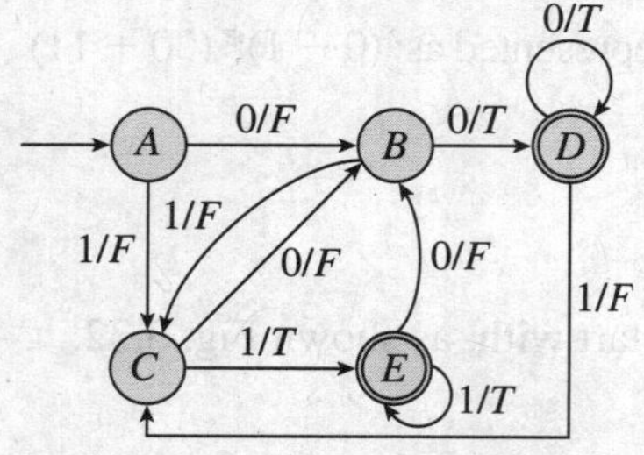


**Figure 3.34** Mealy machine

The DFA in Fig. 3.33(b) can be seen as a Mealy machine, where any edge approaching the final state will carry output $T$ (true); while the others will carry output $F$ (false). The Mealy machine thus can be drawn as shown in Fig. 3.34.

2. Let us now construct a Moore machine equivalent to the Mealy machine in Fig. 3.34. We need to consider a new set of states:

$$Q' = \{[Q \times \Delta] \mid Q \text{ is original set of states and is output alphabet}\}$$

Table 3.7 shows the STF and MAF for the equivalent Moore Machine.

**Table 3.7** STF and MAF for equivalent Moore machine

| $\Sigma$ / $Q'$ | STF - $\delta'$ | | MAF - $\lambda'$ | |
|---|---|---|---|---|
| | 0 | 1 | $Q'$ | $\Delta$ |
| $[A, F]$ | $[B, F]$ | $[C, F]$ | $[A, F]$ | $F$ |
| $[A, T]$ | $[B, F]$ | $[C, F]$ | $[A, T]$ | $T$ |
| $[B, F]$ | $[D, T]$ | $[C, F]$ | $[B, F]$ | $F$ |
| $[B, T]$ | $[D, T]$ | $[C, F]$ | $[B, T]$ | $T$ |
| $[C, F]$ | $[B, F]$ | $[E, T]$ | $[C, F]$ | $F$ |
| $[C, T]$ | $[B, F]$ | $[E, T]$ | $[C, T]$ | $T$ |
| $[D, F]$ | $[D, T]$ | $[C, F]$ | $[D, F]$ | $F$ |
| $[D, T]$ | $[D, T]$ | $[C, F]$ | $[D, T]$ | $T$ |
| $[E, F]$ | $[B, F]$ | $[E, T]$ | $[E, F]$ | $F$ |
| $[E, T]$ | $[B, F]$ | $[E, T]$ | $[E, T]$ | $T$ |

Let us consider $[A, F]$ as the starting state of the equivalent Moore machine. We observe that the equivalent states are:

$$[B, F] = [D, F]$$
$$[B, T] = [D, T]$$
$$[C, F] = [E, F]$$
$$[C, T] = [E, T]$$

These states are equivalent as they have the same transitions as well as the same output.

We can minimize the tables by replacing the equivalents states and removing repetitions. The minimized tables are shown in Table 3.8.

Table 3.8 is obtained by removing $[A, T]$, which is now an unnecessary entry point, since $[A, F]$ is decided to be the initial state. Further, all transitions which were depicting the removed states are altered by using their equivalent states.

**Table 3.8** Minimized STF and MAF for Moore machine

| $\Sigma$ / $Q'$ | STF | | MAF | |
|---|---|---|---|---|
| | 0 | 1 | $Q'$ | $\Delta$ |
| $[A, F]$ | $[B, F]$ | $[C, F]$ | $[A, F]$ | $F$ |
| $[B, F]$ | $[B, T]$ | $[C, F]$ | $[B, F]$ | $F$ |
| $[B, T]$ | $[B, T]$ | $[C, F]$ | $[B, T]$ | $T$ |
| $[C, F]$ | $[B, F]$ | $[C, T]$ | $[C, F]$ | $F$ |
| $[C, T]$ | $[B, F]$ | $[C, T]$ | $[C, T]$ | $T$ |

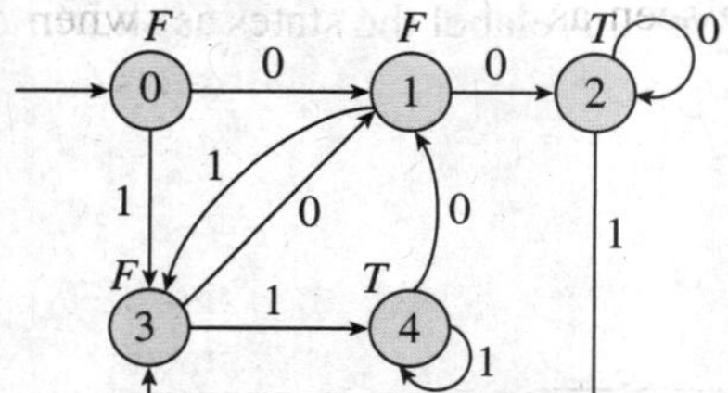

**Figure 3.35** Moore machine

Now, let us rename the state labels as follows:

$[A, F] = 0$
$[B, F] = 1$
$[B, T] = 2$
$[C, F] = 3$
$[C, T] = 4$

After renaming the state labels, the modified Moore machine can be drawn as shown in Fig. 3.35.

---

**Example 3.47** Construct the regular expressions for the following:

1. The set of all strings of 0's and 1's, such that the tenth symbol from the right is 1.
2. The set of strings in $(0 + 1)^*$, such that some two 0's are separated by a string, whose length is $4i$, for some $i \geq 0$.

***Solution***

1. It is required that the 10th symbol from the right should be 1. This means that the last nine symbols in the string, as well as those preceding the 10th symbol '1', are either 0 or 1.

   Therefore, the required regular expression is:

   $$r = (0 + 1)^* \cdot 1 \cdot (0 + 1)^9$$

2. It is required that some two 0's are separated by a string of length $4i$, $i \geq 0$. There can be any prefix or postfix string for these two 0's.

   Therefore, we may write the regular expression as:

   $$r = (0 + 1)^* \cdot 0 \cdot [(0 + 1)^{4*}] \cdot 0 \cdot (0 + 1)^*$$

---

**Example 3.48** Construct a DFA for the language over {0, 1} having all strings such that the third symbol from the right end is 0.

***Solution*** We require that the third symbol from the right end should be 0. The two symbols that follow it can be either 0 or 1. Similarly, all other symbols are also either 0 or 1.

Thus, the RE can be written as:

$$r = (0 + 1)^* \, 0 \, (0 + 1) \, (0 + 1)$$

The equivalent NFA with $\epsilon$-transitions can be drawn as shown in Fig. 3.36.

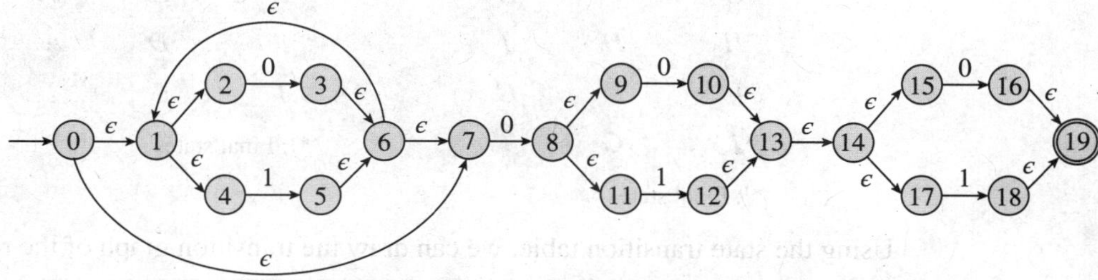

**Figure 3.36** NFA with $\epsilon$-transitions for $(0 + 1)^* \, 0 \, (0 + 1) \, (0 + 1)$

The equivalent DFA can be obtained as in Fig. 3.37. We can relabel the states as shown in the figure.

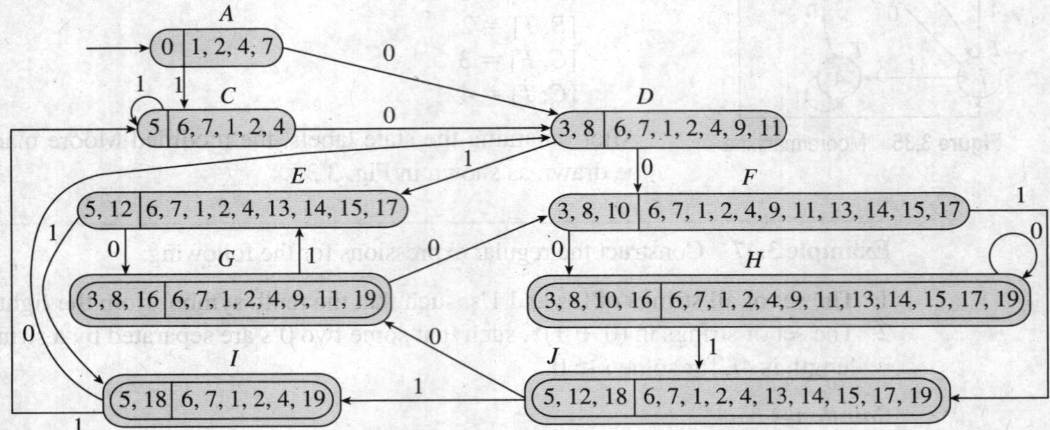


**Figure 3.37** DFA equivalent to NFA with $\epsilon$-transitions in Fig. 3.35

Let us draw the state transition table to see if we can reduce the diagram. Refer to Table 3.9.

We see that states $A$ and $C$ are equivalent, as both have the same transitions and both are non-final. Therefore, we can remove $C$ and replace it by $A$. Refer to the reduced Table 3.10.

**Table 3.9** State transition table for example DFA

| $Q'$ \ $\Sigma$ | 0 | 1 |
|---|---|---|
| $\rightarrow A$ | $D$ | $C$ |
| $C$ | $D$ | $C$ |
| $D$ | $F$ | $E$ |
| $E$ | $G$ | $I$ |
| $F$ | $H$ | $J$ |
| $*G$ | $F$ | $E$ |
| $*H$ | $H$ | $J$ |
| $*I$ | $D$ | $C$ |
| $*J$ | $G$ | $I$ |

'*': Final states

**Table 3.10** Reduced state transition table for example DFA

| $Q'$ \ $\Sigma$ | 0 | 1 |
|---|---|---|
| $\rightarrow A$ | $D$ | $A$ |
| $D$ | $F$ | $E$ |
| $E$ | $G$ | $I$ |
| $F$ | $H$ | $J$ |
| $*G$ | $F$ | $E$ |
| $*H$ | $H$ | $J$ |
| $*I$ | $D$ | $A$ |
| $*J$ | $G$ | $I$ |

'*': Final states

Using the state transition table, we can draw the transition graph of the required DFA.

## 3.10 MYHILL–NERODE THEOREM

In the theory of formal languages, Myhill–Nerode theorem provides a necessary and sufficient condition for a language to be regular. The theorem is named after John Myhill and Anil Nerode, who proved it at the University of Chicago in 1958.

**Theorem statement** A language $L$ is regular if and only if the equivalence set $R_L$ has a finite number of equivalence classes of strings, and the number of states in the smallest DFA recognizing $L$ is equal to the number of equivalence classes in $R_L$.

**Alternate statement** Given a regular language $L$ and a pair of strings $x$ and $y$, let the equivalence relation $R_L$ be defined as ${}_xR_{Ly}$ if and only if for all $z$ in $\Sigma^*$, '$xz$' is in $L$ exactly when '$yz$' is in $L$. Then, $R_L$ is of finite index.

*Proof*

If $L$ is a regular language, then by definition, there exists an FA $M$ that recognizes $L$, with only finite number of states. If there are $n$ states, then we partition the set of all strings into $n$ subsets, where subset $S_i$ is the set of strings that, when given as input to automaton $M$, causes it to end in state $i$.

For every two strings $x$ and $y$ that belong to the same state or same $S_i$, and for every choice of a third string $z$, the FA $M$ reaches the same state on input '$xz$' as it reaches on input '$yz$', and therefore, must either accept both the inputs '$xz$' and '$yz$', or reject both of them. Thus, $x$ and $y$ are indistinguishable with respect to language $L$.

Thus, we can say that strings $x$ and $y$ are related by an equivalence relation $R_L$, that is, ${}_xR_{Ly}$. Thus, every $S_i$ is a subset of an equivalence class of $R_L$, and every string member of one of these equivalence classes belongs to one of the sets $S_i$; this gives a many-to-one relation from the states of $M$ to the equivalence classes, implying that the number of equivalence classes is finite, and at most $n$.

In other words, if $R_L$ has finite equivalence classes, it is possible to design a DFA that has one state for each equivalence class. The start state of such a DFA corresponds to the equivalence class containing the empty string.

Thus, the existence of an FA recognizing $L$ implies that the Myhill–Nerode relation has a finite number of equivalence classes, which are, at most, equal to the number of states of the automaton. The existence of a finite number of equivalence classes implies the existence of an automaton with that many states. The Myhill–Nerode theorem may be used to show that a language $L$ is regular by showing that the number of equivalence classes of $R_L$ is finite.

For example, let us consider a language consisting of binary numbers that are divisible by 3. There can be three equivalence classes based on the remainder values, 0, 1, and 2. The minimal state DFA that can be obtained for such a language also has three states (refer to Chapter 2, Section 2.10.1, Example 2.14). Hence, the language is regular.

Another immediate corollary of the theorem is that if a language defines an infinite set of equivalence classes, it is not regular. It is this corollary that is frequently used to prove that a language is not regular.

## SUMMARY

The languages accepted by finite automata (FA) are described or represented by simple expressions called *regular expressions* (RE).

The class of regular expressions over $\Sigma$ is defined recursively as follows:

1. Regular expressions over $\Sigma$ include letters, $\phi$ (null set), and $\epsilon$ (empty string of length zero).
2. Every symbol $a \in \Sigma$ is a regular expression over $\Sigma$.
3. If $R_1$ and $R_2$ are regular expressions over $\Sigma$, then so are $(R_1 + R_2)$, $(R_1 \cdot R_2)$, and $(R_1)^*$, where '+' indicates *alternation* (parallel path), '.' denotes *concatenation* (series connection), and '*' denotes *iteration* (*closure* or repetitive concatenation).
4. Regular expressions are only those that are obtained using rules (1) to (3).

As per the definition, empty set $\phi$, empty string $\epsilon$, and every input symbol from the input alphabet $\Sigma$ itself is a regular expression.

The expression, '$R_1 + R_2$' is like considering $R_1$ and $R_2$ as two parallel paths in the equivalent DFA generated.

The expression '$R_1 \cdot R_2$' means $R_1$ followed by $R_2$.

The expression '$R_1^*$' denotes zero or more occurrences of $R_1$, that is, repetitive (zero or more times) concatenation of $R_1$ to itself. If $R_1$ is repeated zero times, the empty string $\epsilon$ gets generated as well.

The expression '$R_1^+$' is used to denote *positive closure* of $R_1$, and represents one or more occurrences of $R_1$. This means that at least one occurrence of $R_1$ is assured. That means, $R^+ = R \cdot R^*$. Hence, we see that $R_1^+$ can be composed out of other primitive operations, and so it is not considered in the formal definition of regular expressions.

For every regular expression, there exists an FA, which is equivalent to it and accepts the same language; the converse is also true. There are certain rules to convert a regular expression to NFA with $\epsilon$-moves, which can then be transformed into its equivalent NFA or directly to its equivalent DFA, using the known methods.

The operator '+' is converted to parallel paths. Consider a regular expression of the form '$r_1 + r_2$', where $r_1$ and $r_2$ are the complex expressions themselves. In such a case, we introduce a new start state that connects with the initial states of the individual FAs representing $r_1$ and $r_2$ using the $\epsilon$-moves. Similarly, we connect the individual final states of the two FAs into a new final state.

The operator '·' is converted to a series connection. In case of a regular expression of the form '$r_1 \cdot r_2$', the final state of the FA for $r_1$ is connected to the starting state of the FA for $r_2$ using an $\epsilon$-move.

In case of regular expression of the form '$r^*$', we introduce a new start state and a new ending state, apart from those of the FA equivalent to the regular expression $r$. We introduce a path from this new start to the new end state, using $\epsilon$-moves to denote zero occurrences of $r$. We then connect the new start state to the start state of the FA for $r$ using an $\epsilon$-move, and we connect the final state of the FA for $r$ to a new end state through $\epsilon$-moves. Thus, the new FA we constructed denotes one occurrence of $r$. We then connect the original final state of the FA for $r$ to its original initial state to achieve more than one occurrence.

We also have algorithmic solutions to obtain the regular expression from the given FA. The first algorithm is an iterative solution, while the other depends on Arden's theorem and is based on equation solving.

The iterative algorithm follows the formula:

$$R_{ij}^{(k)} = R_{ij}^{(k-1)} + R_{ik}^{(k-1)} (R_{kk}^{(k-1)})^* R_{kj}^{(k-1)}$$

In this equation, $R_{ij}^{(k)}$ denotes regular expression for all paths from state $i$ to state $j$, passing through all the states labelled $k$, or less than $k$. The state $k = 0$ is assumed as a direct transition from $i$ to $j$. The iterative method thus progresses from $k = 0$ (only direct transitions) to all $n$ states of the FA, $k = n$. At each stage, it applies the aforementioned formula to obtain the next level; thus, the method is inductive. If we have $i$ as the initial state, $j$ as the final state, and $k = n$ (all states), then $R_{ij}^{(k)}$ denotes the regular expression for the FA. If there is more than one final state, then the summation is considered as:

$\sum_{j \in F}, R_{ij}^{n}$ where $F$ is the set of all final states.

In the other method, we represent every state as an equation, and identify all incoming edges for every state. Each state can then be expressed as a state equation of the form:

$q_n = q_0\, a_0 + q_1\, a_1 + \ldots + q_m\, a_m$,

where, there are $m$ incoming edges from the states $q_0, q_1, \ldots, q_m$ on symbols labelled as $a_0, a_1, \ldots, a_m$, respectively.

These equations are solved by substitution using *Arden's theorem*, which states:

If $P$, $Q$, and $R$ are regular expressions, and:

(i) If $R = P + RQ$, or $R = RQ + P$; then, $R$ can be simplified as, $R = PQ*$.

(ii) If $R = P + QR$, or $R = QR + P$; then, $R$ can be simplified as, $R = Q*\, P$.

The class of regular sets over $\Sigma$ is defined as:

1. Every finite set of words over $\Sigma$ (including $\phi$, the empty set or null set) is a regular set.
2. If $U$ and $V$ are regular sets over $\Sigma$, then $U \cup V$ (union) and $U.V$ (concatenation) are also regular sets.
3. If $S$ is a regular set over $\Sigma$, then so its closure, that is, $S*$.

In other words, the class of regular sets over $\Sigma$ is the smallest class containing all finite sets of words over $\Sigma$, and is *closed under union*, *concatenation*, and *closure* operations.

Pumping lemma defines an important property of regular languages. It is used as a tool to disprove the regularity of certain specific languages.

*Pumping lemma*: Let $L$ be a regular set. Then, there exists a constant $n$ such that, if $z$ is any word in $L$ such that the length of $z$ is at least $n$, that is, $|z| \geq n$; and we can write $z = uvw$ in such a way that:

1. $|uv| \leq n$, which means that the sub-string near the beginning of the string is not too long.
2. $|v| \geq 1$, which means that $v \neq \epsilon$; since $v$ is the sub-string that gets pumped.
3. For all $i \geq 0$, $uv^iw$ is in $L$. This means that the sub-string $v$ can be pumped as many times as we like and the resultant string will still be a member of $L$.

The applications of regular expressions and finite automata range from system software such as language compilers, operating system utilities, and program development tools, to application programs such as text editors and syntactic pattern recognizers.

## EXERCISES

This section lists a few unsolved problems to help the readers understand the topic better and practise examples on regular expressions.

### Objective Questions

(E) 3.1 Let $P$ be the language represented by the regular expression $p^*q^*$, and $Q$ be $\{p^nq^n \mid n \geq 0\}$. Then which of the following is *always* regular?

(a) $P \cap Q$
(b) $P - Q$
(c) $\Sigma^* - P$
(d) $\Sigma^* - Q$

(U) 3.2 In a compiler, keywords of a language are recognized during

(a) parsing of the program
(b) code generation
(c) lexical analysis of the program
(d) dataflow analysis

(E) 3.3 Let $S$ and $T$ be languages over $\Sigma = \{a, b\}$ represented by the regular expressions $(a + b^*)^*$ and $(a + b)^*$, respectively. Which of the following is true?

(a) $S \neq T$
(b) $T \supseteq S$
(c) $S = T$
(d) $S \supseteq T$

(A) 3.4 Which of the following are regular languages?

$L1 = \{a^n \mid n \text{ is odd}\}$
$L2 = \{a^n \mid n \text{ is even}\}$
$L3 = \{a^n \mid n \text{ is prime}\}$
$L4 = \{a^n \mid n \text{ is a perfect square}\}$

(a) $L1$ and $L2$
(b) $L1$ only
(c) $L4$ only
(d) $L2$ and $L3$
(e) None of these
(f) All of these

(L) 3.5 Consider the regular expression (0 + 1) (0 + 1) … $n$ times. The minimum state finite automaton that recognizes the language represented by this regular expression contains:
(a) $n$ states
(b) $n + 1$ states
(c) $n + 2$ states
(d) None of these

(R) 3.6 A tokenizer is also called a ____________.

(U) 3.7 Regular languages are closed under:
(a) Union, intersection
(b) Union, Kleene closure
(c) Intersection, complement
(d) Complement, Kleene closure

(U) 3.8 Regular languages are:
(a) Closed under union
(b) Closed under complementation
(c) Closed under intersection
(d) All of these

(L) 3.9 Which of the following languages are regular?
(i) $L = \{a^n b^n \mid n = 0, 1, 2 \ldots\}$
(ii) The set of palindromes over alphabet $\{a, b\}$
(iii) $L = \{a^n, b^m c^{2m} \mid n, m \geq 0\}$
(a) Only (i)
(b) Only (ii)
(c) (i) and (iii)
(d) All of these
(e) None of these

(L) 3.10 Which of the following regular expressions over {0, 1} denotes the set of all strings not containing '100' as a substring?
(a) 0* (1 + 0)*
(b) 0* 1010*
(c) 0* 1 01
(d) 0* (10 + 1)*

(L) 3.11 Consider the following two statements:
$S1$: $\{0^{2n} \mid n \geq 1\}$ is a regular language
$S2$: $\{0^m 1^n 0^{m+n}) \mid m \geq 1$ and $n \geq 1\}$ is a regular language
Which of the following statements is true?
(a) Only $S1$
(b) Only $S2$
(c) Both $S1$ and $S2$
(d) Neither $S1$ nor $S2$

(U) 3.12 Given any regular expression, one can always construct a DFA that accepts the language denoted by it. Is this statement true or false?

(L) 3.13 Consider the following languages:
$L1 = \{ww \mid w$ belongs to $(a, b)^*\}$
$L2 = \{ww^R \mid w$ belongs to $(a, b)^*$; and $w^R$ is the reverse of $w\}$
$L3 = \{0^{2i} \mid i$ is an integer, $i \geq 0\}$
$L4 = \{0^{(i * i)} \mid i$ is an integer$\}$
Which of the languages are regular?
(a) $L1$ and $L2$
(b) $L2$, $L3$, and $L4$
(c) $L3$ and $L4$
(d) Only $L3$

(U) 3.14 Choose the false option:
Regular sets are closed under
(a) intersection
(b) union
(c) complement
(d) inverse substitution

(U) 3.15 Choose the false statement:
Let $L$ be any formal language, then:
(a) $L^*$ is regular
(b) $L^*$ is not necessarily regular
(c) $L^*$ is context-free and not regular
(d) $L^*$ is recursively enumerable and not recursive

## Review Questions

(R) 3.1 Define the following and give suitable examples:
(a) Regular set
(b) Regular expression

(A) 3.2 Prove that the language $L = \{a^n b^{n+1} \mid n > 0\}$ is non-regular, using pumping lemma.

(U) 3.3 Explain in brief the applications of finite automata.

(E) 3.4 Construct the NFA with $\epsilon$-transitions, which accepts the language defined by:

$(ab + ba)^* aa (ab + ba)^*$

Convert this NFA to a minimized DFA.

(C) 3.5 Construct regular expressions defined over the alphabet $\Sigma = \{a, b\}$, which denote the following languages:
(a) All strings without a double $a$.

(b) All strings in which any occurrence of the symbol $b$, is in groups of odd numbers.
(c) All strings in which the total number of $a$'s is divisible by 2.

(L) 3.6 Check the following regular expressions for equivalence and justify:
(a) $R_1 = (a + bb)^* (b + aa)^*$
$R_2 = (a + b)^*$
(b) $R_1 = (a + b)^* abab^*$
$R_2 = b^* a (a + b)^* ab^*$

(L) 3.7 Describe in English the sets denoted by the following regular expressions:
(a) $(a + \epsilon) (b + ba)^*$
(b) $(0^*1^*)^*$

(A) 3.8 Construct an NFA with $\epsilon$-moves, which accepts the language defined by:
$[(0 + 1)^* 10 + (00)^* (11)^*]^*$

(U) 3.9 Let $R_1$ and $R_2$ be two regular expressions. With the help of transition diagrams, illustrate the three operations (+, ·, $x$) on $R_1$ and $R_2$.

(A) 3.10 Show that the regular expressions, $(a^* bbb)^* a^*$ and $a^* (bbba^*)^*$, are equivalent.

(C) 3.11 Give a regular expression for representing all strings over $\{a, b\}$ that do not include the substrings '$bba$' and '$abb$'.

(L) 3.12 Consider the two regular expressions:
$R_1 = a^* + b^*$
$R_2 = ab^* + ba^* + b^* a + (a^* b)^*$
(a) Find a string corresponding to $R_1$ but not to $R_2$.
(b) Find a string corresponding to $R_2$ but not to $R_1$.
(c) Find a string corresponding to both $R_1$ and $R_2$.

(A) 3.13 Construct an NFA for the regular expression, $(a / b)^* ab$. Convert the NFA to its equivalent DFA and validate the answer with suitable examples.

(R) 3.14 Define the term regular language.

(U) 3.15 Write short note on: pumping lemma for regular sets.

(A) 3.16 Construct an NFA $(Q, \Sigma, \delta, q_0, F)$ for the following regular expression:
$01[((10)^+ + 111)^* + 0]^* 1$

(L) 3.17 Prove that the regular expressions given here are equivalent.
(a) $(a^* bbb)^* a^*$
(a) $a^* (bbb a^*)^*$

(L) 3.18 Describe the language accepted by the following finite automaton.

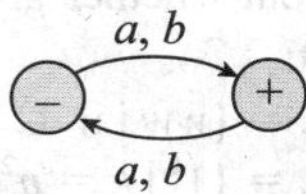


**Figure 3.38** Example DFA

(L) 3.19 Describe as simply as possible in English the language represented by: $(0/1)^* 0$.

(A) 3.20 Construct an NFA that recognizes the regular expression $(a / b)^* \cdot a \cdot b$. Convert it to a DFA, and draw the state transition table.

(A) 3.21 Construct a regular expression corresponding to the state diagram shown here, using Arden's theorem.

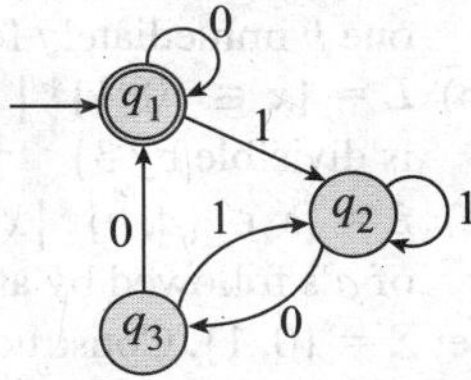


**Figure 3.39** Example FA

(U) 3.22 Is the following language regular? Justify.
$L = \{0^p 1^p p^{p+q} \mid p \geq 1, q \geq 1\}$

(C) 3.23 Construct the regular expression and finite automata for: $L = L_1 \cap L_2$ over alphabet $\{a, b\}$, where:
$L_1$ = all strings of even length
$L_2$ = all strings starting with $b$

(L) 3.24 Which of the following are true? Explain.
(a) $baa \in a^* b^* a^* b^*$
(b) $b^*a^* \cap a^* b^* = a^* \cup b^*$
(c) $a^* b^* \cap b^* c^* = \phi$
(d) $abcd \in [a (cd)^* b]^*$

(A) 3.25 Construct the regular expressions for the following DFAs:

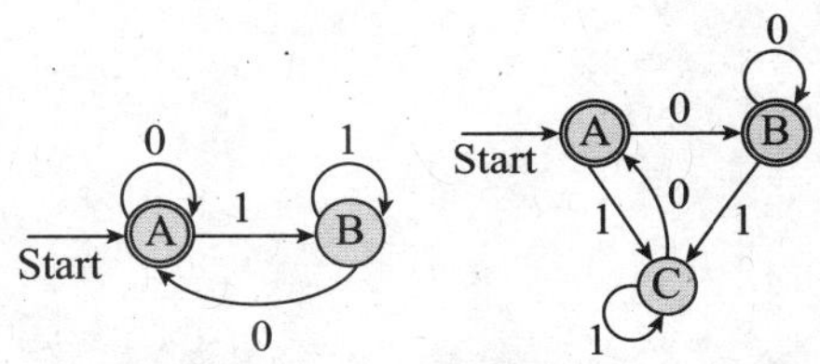


**Figure 3.40** Example DFAs

(U) 3.26 Which of the following languages are regular sets? Justify your answer.

(a) $\{0^{2n} \mid n \geq 1\}$
(b) $\{0^m 1^n 0^{m+n} \mid m \geq 1 \text{ and } n \geq 1\}$

(U) 3.27 Find out whether given languages are regular or not:
(a) $L = \{ww \mid w \in \{0, 1\}^*\}$
(b) $L = \{1^k \mid k = n^2, n >= 1\}$

(U) 3.28 With the help of a suitable example, prove that 'regular sets are closed under union, concatenation, and Kleene closure'.

(U) 3.29 Explain the following applications of regular expressions:
(a) grep utility in UNIX
(b) Finding pattern in text

(C) 3.30 Construct the NFA and DFA for the following languages:
(a) $L = \{x \in \{a, b, c\}^* \mid x$ contains exactly one $b$ immediately following $c\}$
(b) $L = \{x \in \{0, 1\}^* \mid x$ starts with 1 and $|x|$ is divisible by 3$\}$
(c) $L = \{x \in \{a, b\}^* \mid x$ contains any number of $a$'s followed by at least one $b\}$

(C) 3.31 Let $\Sigma = \{0, 1\}$. Construct regular expressions for each of the following:
(a) $L_1 = \{W = \Sigma^* \mid W$ has at least one pair of consecutive zeros$\}$
(b) $L_2 = \{W \in \Sigma^* \mid W$ has no pair of consecutive zeros$\}$
(c) $L_3 = \{W \in \Sigma^* \mid W$ starts with either '01' or '10'$\}$
(d) $L_4 = \{W \in \Sigma^* \mid W$ consists of even number of 0's followed by odd number of 1's$\}$

(A) 3.32 Construct a regular expression for the following DFA:

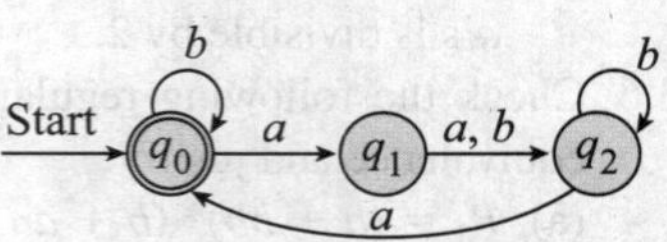


**Figure 3.41** Example DFA

(A) 3.33 Let $L = \{0^n \mid n$ is a prime number$\}$; show that $L$ is not regular.

(L) 3.34 Prove or disprove the following for regular expressions $r$, and $s$.
(a) $(rs + r)^* r = r (sr + r)^*$
(b) $s (rs + s)^* r = rr^* s (rr^* s)^*$
(c) $(r + s)^* = r^* + s^*$
(d) $(r^* s^*)^* = (r + s)^*$

(U) 3.35 State whether each of the following statements is true of false. Justify your answer. Assume that all languages are defined over the alphabet $\{0, 1\}$.
(a) If ($L1 \subseteq L2$) and ($L1$ is not regular), then $L2$ is not regular.
(b) If ($L1 \subseteq L2$) and ($L2$ is not regular), then $L1$ is not regular.
(c) If $L1$ and $L2$ are not regular, then ($L1 \cup L2$) is not regular.

(A) 3.36 Use pumping lemma to check whether the language, $L = \{ww \mid w \in (0, 1)^*\}$ is regular or not.

**Answers to Objective Questions**

3.1. (c) 3.2. (c) 3.3. (b) 3.4. (a) 3.5. (d) 3.6. lexical analyser 3.7. (b) 3.8. (a)
3.9. (e) 3.10. (c) 3.11. (a) 3.12. True 3.13. (d) 3.14. (a) 3.15. (a)

# Turing Machines

**LEARNING OBJECTIVES**

After completing this chapter, the reader will be able to understand the following:

- Computational problems that can be solved using a Turing machine (TM)
- Formal model of a TM
- Comparison of finite automata (FA) and TM on the basis of their relative computational powers
- Recursively enumerable languages and recursive languages
- Concept of composite TM and iterative TM
- Multi-tape TM, multi-stack TM, and multi-track TM
- Concept of universal Turing machine (UTM)
- Halting problem and limits of computability
- Church's Turing hypothesis
- Solvable, semi-solvable, and unsolvable problems
- Total and partial recursive functions
- Post's correspondence problem (PCP)

## 4.1 INTRODUCTION

The limitations of finite state machines (FSMs) necessitate the search for a more powerful machine. We have seen that an FSM cannot remember an arbitrarily long sequence of symbols. It has a read head that can move only in one direction—to the right always. It cannot move backwards to retrieve previous information stored onto the tape. Similarly, though the two-way finite automaton (2FA) has a read head that can move in any direction, it cannot store (write) anything onto the tape; hence, it cannot multiply two numbers, as the process requires intermediate results to be stored onto the tape. Furthermore, an FSM cannot check if a set of parentheses are well-formed, or for palindrome sequences. All these limitations arise because the FSMs do not have memory, and hence, they cannot solve problems that need to store data to be used for later computation.

We have already discussed the limitations of FSMs in detail in Chapter 2 (refer to Section 2.14). To overcome these limitations, we require a more powerful machine, which has the following properties:

1. Finite state control similar to that of the FSM—since any program needs a finite number of functions/states.
2. External memory capable of remembering arbitrarily long sequences of inputs—to achieve this, the machine should have unbounded one-dimensional memory from which, it can choose any required part, by moving to the left, right, or staying in one position (i.e., no movement)—the entire unbounded tape acts as an infinite memory.
3. Ability to store (write onto the tape)—the machine head should be a read/write head.
4. Ability to consume its own output as input during execution at a later time (like a complete feedback control system)—for this, all the intermediate information must be stored in the memory. For example, while multiplying numbers (multiplication is a process of repetitive addition), it is required to store the intermediate or partial sums, which are later added to get the final answer. Hence, the distinction between the input and output symbols needs to be dropped. This means that external communication as well as communication within the machine should rest on a common alphabet set.

All the aforementioned characteristics are satisfied by the *Turing machine* (TM), which was proposed by Alan Turing, a decade prior to the designing of the first shared-program computer. This concept of the Turing machine led to the concept of algorithms and finite procedures, since the basis of the TM is to first divide the process into primitive operations (functions/procedures/states) such that they cannot be further divisible, and then execute each operation in sequence.

## 4.2 ELEMENTS OF A TURING MACHINE

A TM consists of the following:

1. A head, which can read or write a symbol at a time, and move either to the left, right, or remain in the same position, depending on the symbol read from the tape cell.
2. An infinite tape, extending on either side of the head, marked-off into square cells, on which the symbols from an alphabet set can be written. The tape represents the unbounded one-dimensional memory (refer to Fig. 4.1), which is considered to be filled with blank characters, $\not{b}$'s, unless specified otherwise.
3. A finite set of symbols, called the external alphabet set $I$, which consists of lower-case English letters, digits, usual punctuation marks, and the blank character $\not{b}$.
4. A finite set of states denoted by $S$; the machine resides in one of these states.

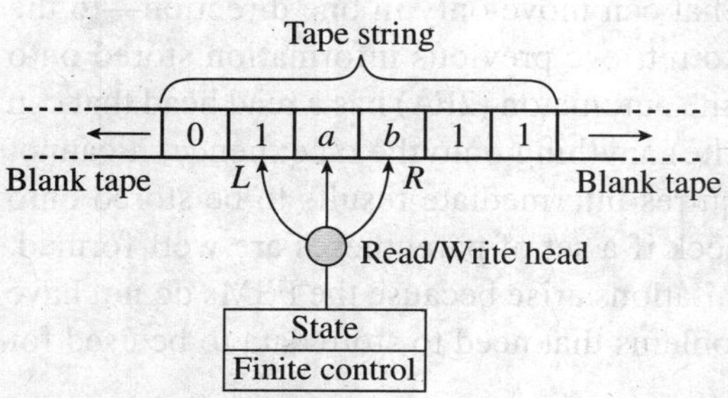


**Figure 4.1** Turing machine

The TM thus overcomes all the limitations of the FSM. It has infinite memory in the form of a tape that is unbounded at both the ends; a read/write head that can move in any direction, and helps the machine retrieve information from the tape that is stored earlier—in a way, this can be considered as converting the dumb storage into memory; it can consume its own output as input for use at a later stage in the algorithm execution. All these features make it a completely powerful machine. The TM and FSM are thus two extremes—an FSM is a minimal machine, whereas a TM is the most powerful machine.

## 4.3 TURING MACHINE FORMALISM

As we have already seen, a TM has a finite set of symbols $I$, and a finite set of states $S$ (one of which is the halt/final state).

A TM is denoted with the help of three functions, namely, the machine function (MAF), state transition function (STF), and the direction function (DIF), which are defined as:

MAF: $I \times S \rightarrow I$
STF: $I \times S \rightarrow S$
DIF: $I \times S \rightarrow D = \{L, R, N\}$

where, $L$ stands for 'move towards left by one tape cell position', $R$ stands for 'move towards right by one tape cell position', and $N$ stands for 'no movement, that is, stay in the same position or remain at the same tape cell, which has been read last'.

> ***Note***: Observe that the MAF for FSM is defined as: $I \times S \rightarrow O$, as there is a distinction between input and output; on the other hand, in case of a TM, it is defined as: $I \times S \rightarrow I$.

Based on the machine's state—which is an element of $S$—at any given time, and the input symbol read—which is an element of $I$—at any given time, the machine either takes no action (i.e., halt state) or performs the following three actions:

1. The input symbol read is erased and another symbol (possibly a blank character or the same symbol again) is printed on the tape cell.
2. The internal state of the machine is changed (possibly to the same state as it was initially in).
3. The head either moves one cell towards the right or left, or remains in the same position.

These actions can be described collectively by an ordered set of five elements, that is, a quintuple. For example, $(a, \alpha, b, \beta, L)$ represents such a quintuple, which exists if the head reads $a \in I$, while the machine is in state $\alpha \in S$, writes $b$ onto the tape cell after erasing $a$, changes the machine state to $\beta \in S$, and moves the head position to the left by one cell.

To represent these quintuples together, a table called a transition matrix or functional matrix (FM) is used. Such a matrix is a combination of the aforementioned three individual functions—the MAF, STF, and DIF. In this functional matrix, the rows and columns are labelled by symbols forms $S$ and $I$, respectively (as in FSMs), while the remaining triples, that is, $(b, \beta, L)$ are placed as the entries of the matrix.

**Table 4.1** Example functional matrix

| S \ I | 0 | 1 | ${b\!\!\!/}$ |
|---|---|---|---|
| $\alpha$ | $0\alpha R$ | $0\beta R$ | ${b\!\!\!/}\alpha R$ |
| $\beta$ | — | — | ${b\!\!\!/}\gamma N$ |
| $\gamma$ | — | — | — |

If the number of symbols in $S$, that is, the number of states = $|S| = m$, and the number of symbols in $I$, that is, number of tape symbols = $|I| = n$, then the size of the functional matrix is $(m \times n)$ number of output triples. For an example, refer to Table 4.1.

We see that in Table 4.1, $S$ has three states and $I$ has three tape symbols; hence, the functional matrix is of size $3 \times 3 = 9$.

If $\delta$ is a functional matrix, then an example transition can be expressed as:

$$\delta\ (a, \alpha) \rightarrow (a, \alpha, L)$$

This means, on reading symbol $a$ while in $\alpha$ state, the machine erases $a$, writes $a$ again, changes the state from $\alpha$ to itself, and moves the head position to the left by one tape cell.

In the aforementioned case, the significant change after transition is just the position of the head, because the symbol on the tape $a$ and the current state of the machine, that is, $\alpha$, remain the same even after the transition. Therefore, instead of writing the whole triple in the functional matrix, we can save space by writing only the significant changes. Hence, the aforementioned triple can be simplified as:

$$\delta\ (a, \alpha) \rightarrow (L)$$

The modified functional matrix, in which we only record the significant changes after deleting all other insignificant entries to save space, is called a *simplified functional matrix* (SFM). The SFM equivalent to the functional matrix in Table 4.1 is depicted in Table 4.2.

**Table 4.2** Simplified functional matrix

| S \ I | 0 | 1 | ${b\!\!\!/}$ |
|---|---|---|---|
| $\alpha$ | $R$ | $0\beta R$ | $R$ |
| $\beta$ | — | — | $\gamma N$ |
| $\gamma$ | — | — | — |

***Note***: It is also possible to convert a quintuple representation to a quadruple representation. For this, additional states may have to be introduced in $S$, so that the given TM is deterministic. For example, the quintuple $(a, \alpha, b, \beta, R)$ may be written as two quadruples: $(a, \alpha, b, \beta')$ and $(b, \beta', R, \beta)$, where, $\beta'$ is a new state. This quadruple notation essentially breaks two of the three operations into different transitions. The first transition $(a, \alpha, b, \beta')$ is about replacing the input symbol $a$ by $b$ and the second transition $(b, \beta', R, \beta)$ is about moving the head position one cell to the right. However, this quadruple notation is very rarely used; the quintuple notation discussed here is more popular.

### Formal Definition

A Turing machine (TM) is denoted here:

$$M = (Q, \Sigma, \Gamma, \delta, q_0, B, F),$$

where,

$Q$: Finite set of states

$\Gamma$: Finite set of allowable tape symbols, including blank character ${b\!\!\!/}$

$\Sigma$: The set of input symbols, which is a subset of $\Gamma$, excluding blank character ${b\!\!\!/}$

$B$: A symbol for blank character ${b\!\!\!/}$

$q_0$: Start (or initial) state $\in Q$
$F$: Set of final states (or halt states) $\subseteq Q$
$\delta$: Functional matrix, such that $\delta$: $(Q \times \Gamma) \rightarrow (Q \times \Gamma \times \{L, R, N\})$

In order to have a deterministic TM, there should be a unique triple $(b, \beta, d)$ for every state $\alpha$ on some symbol $a$, for $\delta(\alpha, a)$ in the functional matrix.

***Notes***:

1. $\delta$ may be undefined for some arguments, which are represented in the table as '—', (similar to the transition table of an FSM). Refer to Tables 4.1 and 4.2.
2. FSM is a special case of a TM. If we make the tape length finite and restrict the head movement only to one direction, then the functional matrix corresponding to this FSM will specify: $I \times S \rightarrow S$, which is, nothing but the state transition function (STF).

## 4.4 INSTANTANEOUS DESCRIPTION

Instantaneous description (ID) of a TM $M$ is denoted by '$\alpha_1\, q\, \alpha_2$', where $q$ is the current state of the TM, that is, $q \in Q$, and '$\alpha_1\, \alpha_2$' is the string in $\Gamma$*—that is, the contents of the tape bounded on both the ends by blank characters ($b\!\!\!/$'s). Note that $b\!\!\!/$ may occur within '$\alpha_1\, \alpha_2$' as well.

We define a move (or transition) of $M$ as follows:

Let '$a_0\, a_1 \ldots a_{i-1}\, q\, a_i \ldots a_n$' be an ID of $M$. This ID indicates that the current state of the machine is $q$ and the machine head is about to read symbol $a_i$ from the tape.

Suppose, $\delta(q, a_i) = (*, p, L)$ is a transition, where

If $i = n + 1$, then $a_i$ is taken to be $b\!\!\!/$, that is, blank character.

If $i = 0$, then the tape head moves one position to the left of the first symbol that is considered to be blank character $b\!\!\!/$, in the next ID.

If $i > 1$, then we can write the ID for the aforementioned transition as

$$a_0\, a_1 \ldots a_{i-1}\, q\, a_i \ldots a_n \underset{M}{\vdash} a_0\, a_1 \ldots a_{i-2}\, p\, a_{i-1} * a_{i+1} \ldots a_n$$

Similarly, for the move $\delta(q, a_i) = (*, p, R)$ we can write

$$a_0\, a_1 \ldots a_{i-1}\, q\, a_i \ldots a_n \underset{M}{\vdash} a_0\, a_1 \ldots a_{i-1} * p\, a_{i+1} \ldots a_n$$

If the two IDs are related by '$\underset{M}{\vdash}$', we say that the second results from the first by one move, as we have seen here. If one ID results from another by some finite number of moves (including zero number of moves), then they are related by the symbol, '$\underset{M}{\overset{*}{\vdash}}$'.

The language accepted by $M$ is denoted by $L(M)$ and is the set of those words in * that cause $M$ to enter a final state when $M$ is placed in state $q_0$ and the tape head of $M$ is at the leftmost cell.

Formally, we can define the language accepted by $M = (Q, \Sigma, \Gamma, \delta, q_0, B, F)$ as

$$L(M) = \{w \mid w \in \Sigma^*, \text{ and } q_0 W \underset{M}{\overset{*}{\vdash}} \alpha_1\, p\, \alpha_2 \text{ for some } p \text{ in } F \text{ and } \alpha_1 \text{ and } \alpha_2 \text{ in } \Gamma^*\}$$

Let us consider an example of a TM.

**Example 4.1** Consider an SFM for a TM with the following:

$$I = \{0, 1, ƀ\}$$
$$S = \{\alpha, \beta, \gamma = \text{halt}\}$$
$$D = \{L, R, N\}$$

The SFM is given in Table 4.3.

Find the purpose of the aforementioned TM, provided the initial configuration of the TM is as given in Fig. 4.2.

**Table 4.3** SFM for example TM

| S \ I | 0 | 1 | ƀ |
|---|---|---|---|
| $\alpha$ | $R$ | $0\beta R$ | $R$ |
| $\beta$ | — | — | $\gamma N$ |
| $\gamma$ | — | — | — |

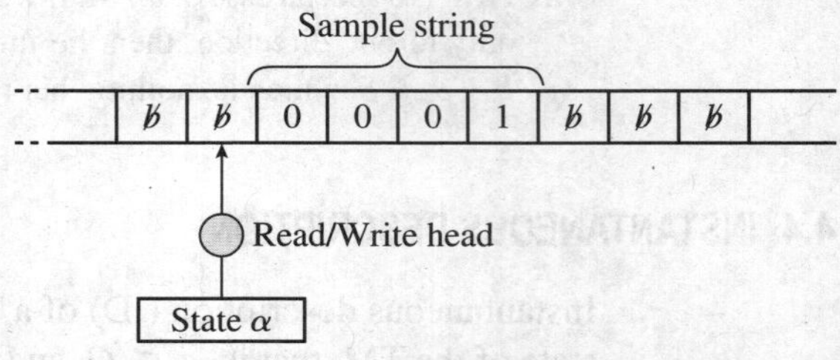


**Figure 4.2** Initial configuration of example TM

***Solution*** It is very important to note that the functional matrix gives us only half the information on what the TM does, and unless we know the initial configuration or initial ID of the TM, we cannot determine its purpose. Thus, the interpretation of the TM is highly dependent on its initial configuration, which includes the following: what the TM starts with, how the input string is assumed to be placed onto the tape, and the initial state of the machine. Note that the interpretation may differ for different initial configurations even for the same functional matrix.

Therefore, we can say that the initial configuration or the initial ID is like the assumption that forms the basis for the interpretation of the algorithm described by the functional matrix.

As we can see, initially the machine is the state $\alpha$, and the head points to the blank character ƀ just before the actual string begins; hence, $\alpha$ is the initial or start state of the TM.

We observe that the function of the aforementioned TM is to replace the last (or ending) 1 by 0, whenever a sequence of 0's followed by a 1 is encountered; it then moves to the next available blank, and halts.

Let us simulate the working of the TM using a sample string '0001':

| | |
|---|---|
| $\alpha$ ƀ 0 0 0 1 ƀ | initial configuration |
| $\vdash_M$ ƀ $\alpha$ 0 0 0 1 ƀ | $\delta(\alpha, ƀ) = (R)$ |
| $\vdash_M$ ƀ 0 $\alpha$ 0 0 1 ƀ | $\delta(\alpha, 0) = (R)$ |
| $\vdash_M$ ƀ 0 0 $\alpha$ 0 1 ƀ | $\delta(\alpha, 0) = (R)$ |

$\underset{M}{\vdash}$ $b\!\!\!/\,000\,\alpha\,1\,b\!\!\!/$ $\qquad \delta(\alpha, 0) = (R)$

$\underset{M}{\vdash}$ $b\!\!\!/\,0000\,\beta\,b\!\!\!/$ $\qquad \delta(\alpha, 1) = (0\,\beta\,R)$

$\underset{M}{\vdash}$ $b\!\!\!/\,0000\,\gamma\,b\!\!\!/$ $\qquad \delta(\beta, b\!\!\!/) = (\gamma\,N)$

The simulation of a TM for a particular input is a recording of the transition from one ID to another. The simulation given here is a formal notation. However, the IDs can also be represented using a slightly different notation as shown in the following simulation. We observe that in the changed notation, the head is clearly shown as a pointer pointing to the tape cell to be read. This change makes it visibly simple for the reader to understand. In this chapter, we are going to follow the same changed notation for representing the IDs for TM in preference to the formal one. Using the simpler ID notation, the aforementioned simulation can be shown as follows:

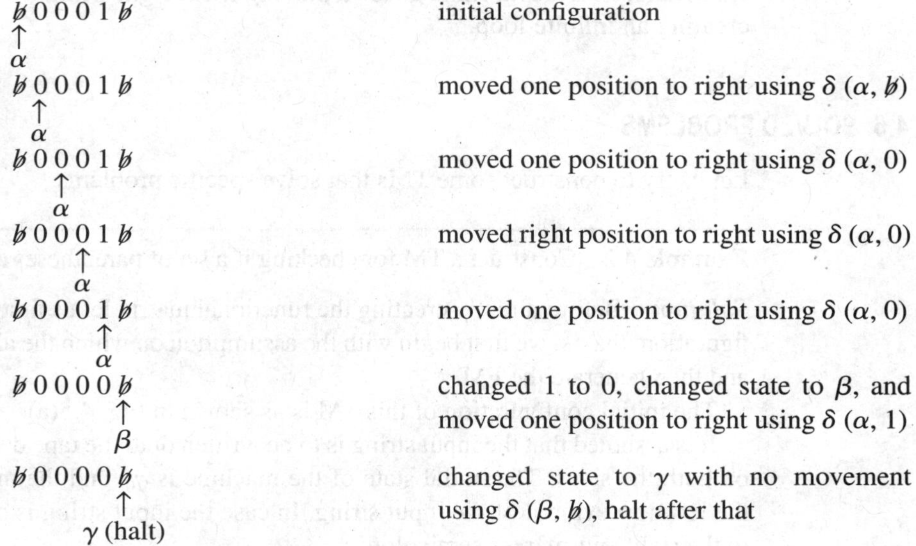

b̸ 0 0 0 1 b̸ ↑ α initial configuration
b̸ 0 0 0 1 b̸ ↑ α moved one position to right using δ (α, b̸)
b̸ 0 0 0 1 b̸ ↑ α moved one position to right using δ (α, 0)
b̸ 0 0 0 1 b̸ ↑ α moved right position to right using δ (α, 0)
b̸ 0 0 0 1 b̸ ↑ α moved one position to right using δ (α, 0)
b̸ 0 0 0 0 b̸ ↑ β changed 1 to 0, changed state to β, and moved one position to right using δ (α, 1)
b̸ 0 0 0 0 b̸ ↑ γ (halt) changed state to γ with no movement using δ (β, b̸), halt after that


## 4.5 TRANSITION GRAPH FOR TURING MACHINE

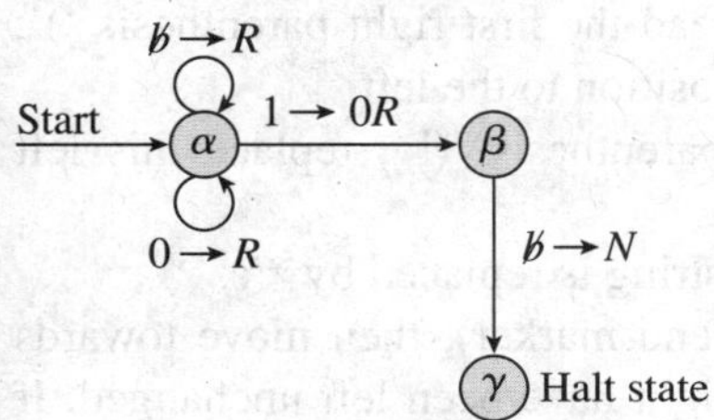


**Figure 4.3** TG for example TM

A TM can also be represented pictorially with the help of a transition graph (TG). In such a graph, the nodes denote the internal states from the set $S$. A pair of nodes is connected by a directed edge (or arc) labelled by the input symbol from the set $\Gamma$, followed by an arrow and the new output symbol again from the set $\Gamma$— this symbol is to be written after erasing the previous symbol; the direction of the move is selected from the set $D$. The transition graph for the TM in Example 4.1 is shown in Fig. 4.3.

> ***Note***: If a TM starts the run from an initial state and eventually reaches a halt state, the computation is stopped and we say that it has *accepted* the input word.

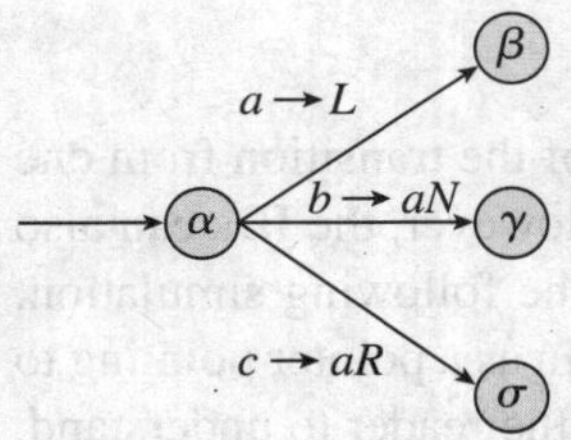


**Figure 4.4** Example transition graph

On the other hand, let us consider the transition graph in Fig. 4.4. If the machine is in state $\alpha$, and if the symbol read is different from $a$, $b$, and $c$, then we cannot proceed with the transition. This, in fact, corresponds to having unspecified entries in the functional matrix. Further, if the machine is in state $\beta$ and reads $a$ or $b$, then there is no way to proceed. In such situations, the computation is halted and we say that the machine has *rejected* the input word.

Sometimes, the machine may go into an infinite loop without ever halting. For example, if the triplet corresponding to ($\not{b}$, $\beta$) is ($\not{b}$, $\beta$, $R$), that is, $\delta(\beta, \not{b}) = (\not{b}, \beta, R)$, and the remainder of the tape consists of only blank characters, then the machine goes on moving to the right without ever changing the state, creating an infinite loop.

## 4.6 SOLVED PROBLEMS

Let us try to construct some TMs that solve specific problems.

---

**Example 4.2** Construct a TM for checking if a set of parentheses are well-formed.

***Solution*** Before directly creating the functional matrix let us first decide the initial configuration, that is, we first begin with the assumption on which the algorithm is to be fixed, and then generate the FM.

The initial configuration of this TM is as shown in Fig. 4.5(a).

It is assumed that the input string is to be written onto the tape delimited by semicolons on both the sides. The initial state of the machine is $q_0$, and the machine head points to the leftmost symbol of the input string. In case the input string is empty, the head points to the right end-marker semicolon.

**Algorithm**

1. From the initial state, move to the right until you read the first right parenthesis ')'; replace this right parenthesis by '*' and move one position to the left.
2. Continue moving left till you read the first left parenthesis '(' ; replace this left parenthesis by '*' and move to the right.
3. Repeat the aforementioned two steps till the whole string is replaced by *'s.
4. While moving right if you came across ';' (right end-marker), then move towards the left to search for any left parenthesis '(' that might have been left unchanged. If the parentheses are well-formed, there will be no more left parentheses '('; and the machine will only read the left end-marker ';'.

For this TM, we have:

$$I = \{(,*, ), ;, R_p, L_p, O\}$$
$$S = \{q_0, q_1, q_2, q_3 = \text{halt}\}$$
$$D = \{L, R, N\}$$

Here, $q_0$ is considered as the start state while $q_3$ is the halt state.

The SFM for the TM is as given in Table 4.4.

**Table 4.4** SFM of a TM that checks if parentheses are well-formed

| S \ I | ( | * | ) | ; | $R_p$ | $L_p$ | $O$ |
|---|---|---|---|---|---|---|---|
| $q_0$ | $R$ | $R$ | $*q_1L$ | $q_2L$ | — | — | — |
| $q_1$ | $*q_0R$ | $L$ | $L$ | $R_pq_3N$ | — | — | — |
| $q_2$ | $L_pq_3N$ | $L$ | $L$ | $Oq_3N$ | — | — | — |
| $q_3$ | — | — | — | — | — | — | — |

If the TM encounters an extra right parenthesis ')', it ends up in halt giving $R_p$ as output. If there is an extra left parenthesis '(', it moves to state $q_3$, that is, halt state, giving $L_p$ as output. If the entire sequence of parentheses is balanced, then the machine moves to the halt state $q_3$ giving the output $O$, indicating acceptable input.

We observe from Table 4.4 that state $q_0$ is responsible for searching for the first right parenthesis ')'. It moves towards the right, ignoring any left parenthesis '(' that is encountered. Once the right parenthesis is found, it is replaced with '*'; then the machine moves one position to the left and changes to state $q_1$. State $q_1$ is responsible for searching towards the left for the matching left parenthesis '('. Once the first left parenthesis '(' is found, it is replaced with '*', and the machine moves back to $q_0$. Thus, the states $q_0$ and $q_1$ represent the first two steps of the algorithm.

While moving towards the left and searching for the left parenthesis '(' while in state $q_1$, if the machine cannot find '(', that is, the machine reads ';' (left end-marker) instead, then it is an error condition. In such a case, the machine generates output symbol $R_p$, indicating an extra right parenthesis, and moves to the halt state $q_3$.

On the other hand, if while moving towards the right in $q_0$ and searching for the first right parenthesis, if the machine reads ';' (right end-marker), indicating there are no more right parentheses ')', to be changed to '*', the machine moves to state $q_2$. In state $q_2$, one needs to check for any unmatched left parentheses, '(', that are left. In state $q_2$, while moving to the left, if the machine comes across the symbol ';' (left end-marker), indicating that there are no more unmatched left parentheses '(', it is considered as the acceptance condition. Hence, the machine generates the output $O$, indicating that the input string is accepted, and moves to the halt state $q_3$.

However, in case while moving left it finds a left parenthesis '(', then it indicates the string is not well-formed and has at least one unmatched extra left parenthesis '('. This is an error condition and the machine generates output symbol $L_p$ and halts.

The transition graph for this TM is shown in Fig. 4.5(b).

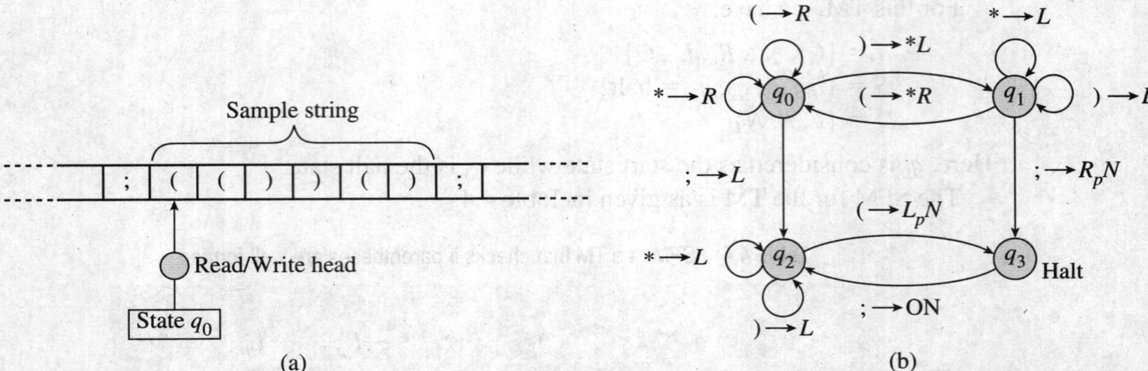


**Figure 4.5** TM for checking if a set of parentheses are well-formed (a) Initial configuration (b) TG for TM that checks if parentheses are well-formed

### *Simulation*

1. Let us simulate the working of the aforementioned TM on the sequence '( ( ) ( ) )'.

| | |
|---|---|
| ; ( ( ) ( ) ) ; ↑ $q_0$ | initial configuration |
| ; ( ( ) ( ) ) ; ↑ $q_0$ | $\delta(q_0, ( ) = (R)$ |
| ; ( ( ) ( ) ) ; ↑ $q_0$ | $\delta(q_0, ( ) = (R)$ |
| ; ( ( * ( ) ) ; ↑ $q_1$ | $\delta(q_0, ) ) = (* \; q_1, L)$ |
| ; ( * * ( ) ) ; ↑ $q_0$ | $\delta(q_1, ( ) = (* \; q_0 \; R)$ |
| ; ( * * ( ) ) ; ↑ $q_0$ | $\delta(q_0, *) = (R)$ |
| ; ( * * ( ) ) ; ↑ $q_0$ | $\delta(q_0, ( ) = (R)$ |
| ; ( * * ( * ) ; ↑ $q_1$ | $\delta(q_0, ) ) = (* \; q_1 \; L)$ |
| ; ( * * * * ) ; ↑ $q_0$ | $\delta(q_1, ( ) = (* \; q_0 \; R)$ |
| ; ( * * * * ) ; ↑ $q_0$ | $\delta(q_0 \; *) = (R)$ |
| ; ( * * * * * ; ↑ $q_1$ | $\delta(q_0, ) ) = (* \; q_1 \; L)$ |

; ( * * * * * ; $\delta(q_1, *) = (L)$
↑
$q_1$
; ( * * * * * ; $\delta(q_1, *) = (L)$
↑
$q_1$
; ( * * * * * ; $\delta(q_1, *) = (L)$
↑
$q_1$
; ( * * * * * ; $\delta(q_1, *) = (L)$
↑
$q_1$
; * * * * * * ; $\delta(q_1, () = (*\ q_0\ R)$
↑
$q_0$
; * * * * * * ; $\delta(q_0, *) = (R)$
↑
$q_0$
; * * * * * * ; $\delta(q_0, *) = (R)$
↑
$q_0$
; * * * * * * ; $\delta(q_0, *) = (R)$
↑
$q_0$
; * * * * * * ; $\delta(q_0, *) = (R)$
↑
$q_0$
; * * * * * * ; $\delta(q_0, *) = (R)$
↑
$q_0$
; * * * * * * ; $\delta(q_0, ;) = (q_2\ L)$
↑
$q_2$
; * * * * * * ; $\delta(q_2, *) = (L)$
↑
$q_2$
; * * * * * * ; $\delta(q_2, *) = (L)$
↑
$q_2$
; * * * * * * ; $\delta(q_2, *) = (L)$
↑
$q_2$
; * * * * * * ; $\delta(q_2, *) = (L)$
↑
$q_2$
; * * * * * * ; $\delta(q_2, *) = (L)$
↑
$q_2$
; * * * * * * ; $\delta(q_2, *) = (L)$
↑
$q_2$
*O* * * * * * * ; $\delta(q_2, ;) = (O\ q_3\ N)$
↑
$q_3$

The output symbol *O* indicates that the string '( ( ) ( ) )' is accepted by the TM as it is well-formed.

2. Let us now simulate the working of this TM for input sequence '('.

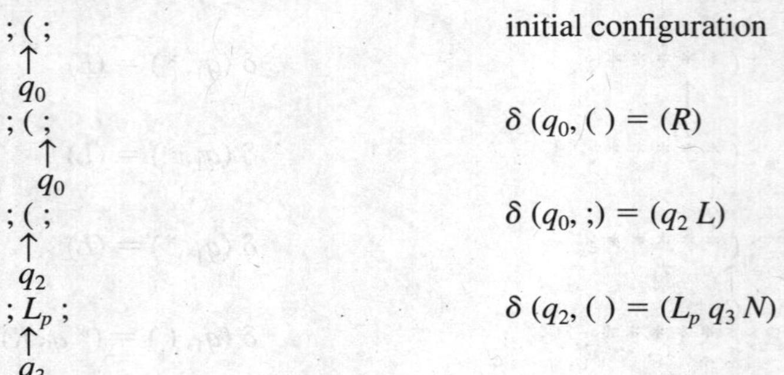

The output symbol $L_p$ indicates that there is at least one left parenthesis '(', which is unmatched, and the input string is not well-formed.

3. Finally, let us simulate the working of this TM for an empty sequence:

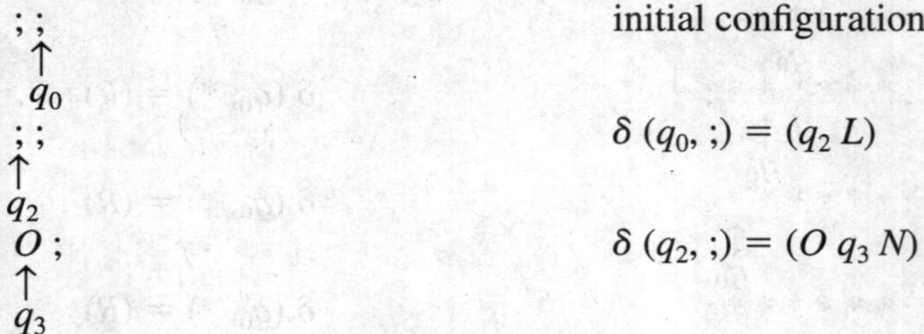

We observe that the empty string is accepted, as it is always well-formed.

---

**Example 4.3** Design a TM to find the 2's complement of a given binary number.

***Solution*** The initial configuration of the TM is considered as shown in Fig. 4.6(a). The initial state is $q_0$, and the head points to the first digit, that is, the most significant bit (MSB), of the binary number. The binary number is delimited by semicolons, which are used as the end-markers. The remaining tape is filled with blank characters, that is, $\not{b}$'s.

The algorithm we are going to use is the same as that used in Example 2.17 in Chapter 2.

**Algorithm**

1. Move towards the right till you reach ';', which is the right end-marker of the sequence.
2. Start moving towards the left till you reach the first 1; then move towards the left and replace each 0 by 1, and each 1 by 0, till you reach the left end-marker ';' of the sequence, then halt.

For this TM, we have

$$I = \{ 0, 1, ;\}$$
$$S = \{q_0, q_1, q_2, q_3 = \text{halt}\}$$
$$D = \{L, R, N\}$$

The SFM for the TM is given in Table 4.5.

**Table 4.5** SFM for a TM that finds 2's complement of a binary number

| S \ I | 0 | 1 | ; |
|---|---|---|---|
| $q_0$ | $R$ | $R$ | $q_1L$ |
| $q_1$ | $L$ | $q_2L$ | $q_3N$ |
| $q_2$ | $1L$ | $0L$ | $q_3N$ |
| $q_3$ | — | — | — |

The TG for the TM is as shown in Fig. 4.6(b).

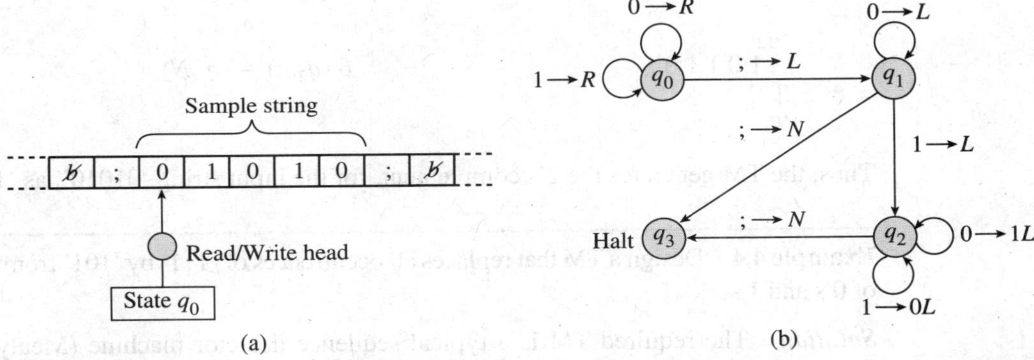


**Figure 4.6** TM to find the 2's complement of a given binary number (a) Initial configuration (b) TG for TM that finds 2's complement of a binary number

## *Simulation*

Let us simulate the working of this TM for the string '01010'.

$$\underset{\uparrow\, q_0}{;}\,0\,1\,0\,1\,0\,; \qquad \text{initial configuration}$$

$$;\,\underset{\uparrow\, q_0}{0}\,1\,0\,1\,0\,; \qquad \delta(q_0, 0) = (R)$$

$$;\,0\,\underset{\uparrow\, q_0}{1}\,0\,1\,0\,; \qquad \delta(q_0, 1) = (R)$$

$$;\,0\,1\,\underset{\uparrow\, q_0}{0}\,1\,0\,; \qquad \delta(q_0, 0) = (R)$$

$$;\,0\,1\,0\,\underset{\uparrow\, q_0}{1}\,0\,; \qquad \delta(q_0, 1) = (R)$$

$$;\,0\,1\,0\,1\,\underset{\uparrow\, q_0}{0}\,; \qquad \delta(q_0, 0) = (R)$$

$$
\begin{array}{ll}
; 0\,1\,0\,1\,0\,; & \delta(q_0, ;) = (q_1\,L) \\
\quad\quad\quad\quad\uparrow q_1 & \\
; 0\,1\,0\,1\,0\,; & \delta(q_1, 0) = (L) \\
\quad\quad\quad\uparrow q_1 & \\
; 0\,1\,0\,1\,0\,; & \delta(q_1, 1) = (q_2\,L) \\
\quad\quad\uparrow q_2 & \\
; 0\,1\,1\,1\,0\,; & \delta(q_2, 0) = (1\,L) \\
\quad\quad\uparrow q_2 & \\
; 0\,0\,1\,1\,0\,; & \delta(q_2, 1) = (0\,L) \\
\quad\uparrow q_2 & \\
; 1\,0\,1\,1\,0\,; & \delta(q_2, 0) = (1\,L) \\
\uparrow q_2 & \\
; 1\,0\,1\,1\,0\,; & \delta(q_2, ;) = (q_3\,N) \\
\uparrow q_3 &
\end{array}
$$

Thus, the TM generates the 2's complement, for the input string '01010', as '10110'.

---

**Example 4.4** Design a TM that replaces all occurrences of '111' by '101' from a sequence of 0's and 1's.

***Solution*** The required TM is a typical sequence detector machine (Mealy machine) that we have studied in Chapter 2. Let the initial configuration of the TM be as shown in Fig. 4.7(a).

The initial state is assumed to be $q_0$. The string is delimited at the rightmost end by a semicolon ';', which is used as the end-marker. The TM starts reading from the leftmost symbol in the input string.

**Table 4.6** SFM for a TM that replaces each occurrence of '111' by '101'

| S \ I | 0 | 1 | ; |
|---|---|---|---|
| $q_0$ | $R$ | $q_1R$ | $q_5N$ |
| $q_1$ | $q_0R$ | $q_2R$ | $q_5N$ |
| $q_2$ | $q_0R$ | $q_3L$ | $q_5N$ |
| $q_3$ | — | $0q_4R$ | — |
| $q_4$ | — | $q_0R$ | — |
| $q_5$ | — | — | — |

The SFM for the required TM, which converts each occurrence of '111' by '101' is as given in Table 4.6.

For this TM, we have

$$I = \{0, 1, ;\}$$
$$S = \{q_0, q_1, q_2, q_3, q_4, q_5 = \text{halt}\}$$
$$D = \{L, R, N\}$$

We see from Table 4.6 that states $q_0$, $q_1$, and $q_2$ collectively identify the sequence '111'. Once the sequence is identified, state $q_2$ makes a transition to state $q_3$ and points to the middle 1, which is replaced by 0 in state $q_3$; thus, the string is replaced by '101'. Once the replacement is done, the TM moves to state $q_4$, which resets to state $q_0$ for repeating the same process again to search for another sequence of '111' that may exist.

The TG for the TM is shown in Fig. 4.7(b).

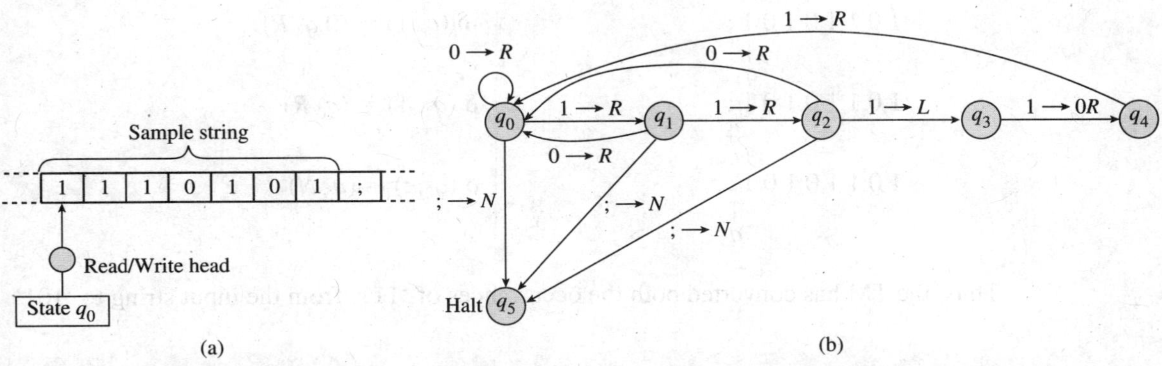


**Figure 4.7** TM that replaces all occurrences of '111' by '101' (a) Initial configuration (b) TG for TM that replaces each occurrence of '111' by '101'

### *Simulation*

Let us simulate the working of the TM that we have constructed for the input string '11110111'.

```
1 1 1 1 0 1 1 1 ;        initial configuration
↑
q0
1 1 1 1 0 1 1 1 ;        δ (q0, 1) = (q1 R)
  ↑
  q1
1 1 1 1 0 1 1 1 ;        δ (q1, 1) = (q2 R)
    ↑
    q2
1 1 1 1 0 1 1 1 ;        δ (q2, 1) = (q3 L)
  ↑
  q3
1 0 1 1 0 1 1 1 ;        δ (q3, 1) = (0 q4 R)
    ↑
    q4
1 0 1 1 0 1 1 1 ;        δ (q4, 1) = (q0 R)
      ↑
      q0
1 0 1 1 0 1 1 1 ;        δ (q0, 1) = (q1 R)
        ↑
        q1
1 0 1 1 0 1 1 1 ;        δ (q1, 0) = (q0 R)
          ↑
          q0
1 0 1 1 0 1 1 1 ;        δ (q0, 1) = (q1 R)
            ↑
            q1
1 0 1 1 0 1 1 1 ;        δ (q1, 1) = (q2 R)
              ↑
              q2
1 0 1 1 0 1 1 1 ;        δ (q2, 1) = (q3 L)
            ↑
            q3
```

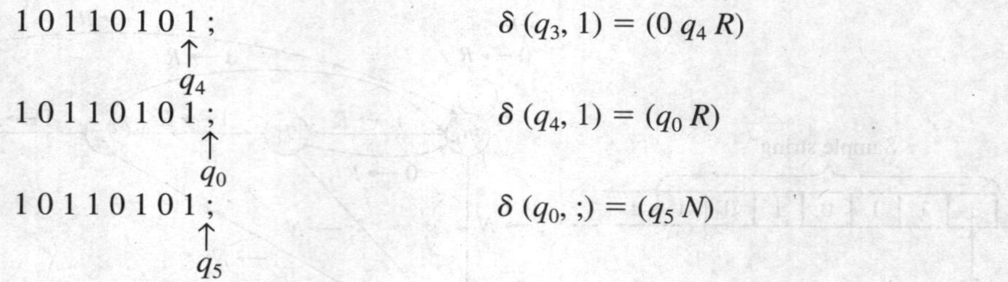


Thus, the TM has converted both the occurrences of '111' from the input string to '101'.

> ***Note***: As we know, the particular problem we have discussed can also be solved using Mealy machine. Since the TM is a more powerful machine, it can always solve problems that are solvable using an FSM.

**Example 4.5** Design a TM that recognizes words of the form $0^n\ 1^n$ for $n \geq 0$.

***Solution*** Let us assume the initial configuration as shown in Fig. 4.8(a). The transition graph for the TM is shown in Fig. 4.8(b).

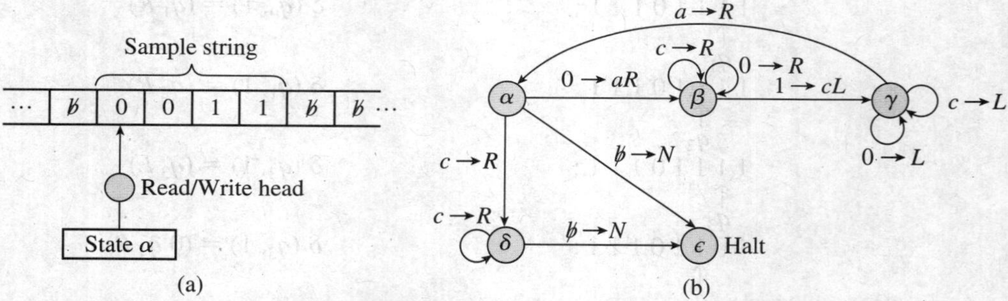


**Figure 4.8** TM that recognizes strings of the form $0^n\ 1^n$ for $n \geq 0$ (a) Initial configuration (b) Transition graph

**Algorithm**

1. Replace the first 0 by some other symbol, say $a$, and move towards the right till you reach the first 1.
2. Replace this first 1 by some other symbol, say $c$, and move towards the left till you reach the 0 immediately next to the one that was previously replaced by $a$.
3. Repeat the procedure till all 0's are replaced by $a$'s.

For this TM, we have

$$I = \{0, 1, a, c, ƀ\}$$
$$S = \{\alpha, \beta, \gamma, \delta, \epsilon = \text{halt}\}$$
$$D = \{L, R, N\}$$

The SFM for the TM is as shown in Table 4.7.

**Table 4.7** SFM for a TM that recognizes string $0^n 1^n$

| $S$ \ $I$ | 0 | 1 | $a$ | $c$ | $\not b$ |
|---|---|---|---|---|---|
| $\alpha$ | $a\beta R$ | — | — | $\delta R$ | $\epsilon N$ (accept) |
| $\beta$ | $R$ | $c\gamma L$ | — | $R$ | — |
| $\gamma$ | $L$ | — | $\alpha R$ | $L$ | — |
| $\delta$ | — | — | — | $R$ | $\epsilon N$ (accept) |
| $\epsilon$ | — | — | — | — | — |

Here, $\alpha$ is the initial state of the machine and $\epsilon$ is the halt state. The transition diagram is drawn as shown in Fig. 4.8(b).

***Simulation***

1. Let us simulate the working of the machine for the string '0011'.

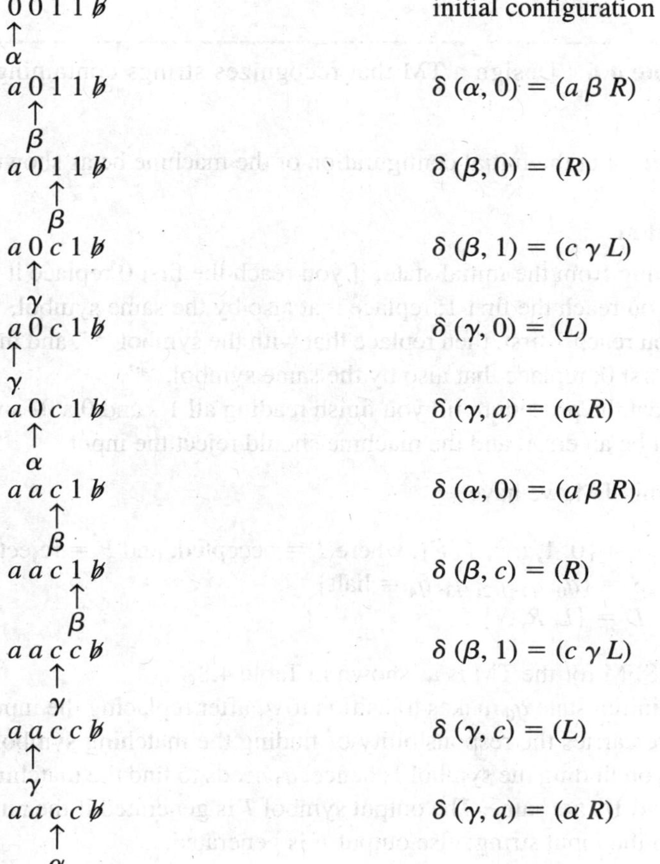

$0\ 0\ 1\ 1\ \not b$ (head on 1st symbol, state $\alpha$) — initial configuration

$a\ 0\ 1\ 1\ \not b$ (head on 2nd symbol, state $\beta$) — $\delta(\alpha, 0) = (a\ \beta\ R)$

$a\ 0\ 1\ 1\ \not b$ (head on 3rd symbol, state $\beta$) — $\delta(\beta, 0) = (R)$

$a\ 0\ c\ 1\ \not b$ (head on 2nd symbol, state $\gamma$) — $\delta(\beta, 1) = (c\ \gamma\ L)$

$a\ 0\ c\ 1\ \not b$ (head on 1st symbol, state $\gamma$) — $\delta(\gamma, 0) = (L)$

$a\ 0\ c\ 1\ \not b$ (head on 2nd symbol, state $\alpha$) — $\delta(\gamma, a) = (\alpha\ R)$

$a\ a\ c\ 1\ \not b$ (head on 3rd symbol, state $\beta$) — $\delta(\alpha, 0) = (a\ \beta\ R)$

$a\ a\ c\ 1\ \not b$ (head on 4th symbol, state $\beta$) — $\delta(\beta, c) = (R)$

$a\ a\ c\ c\ \not b$ (head on 3rd symbol, state $\gamma$) — $\delta(\beta, 1) = (c\ \gamma\ L)$

$a\ a\ c\ c\ \not b$ (head on 2nd symbol, state $\gamma$) — $\delta(\gamma, c) = (L)$

$a\ a\ c\ c\ \not b$ (head on 3rd symbol, state $\alpha$) — $\delta(\gamma, a) = (\alpha\ R)$

$$\begin{array}{ll} a\,a\,c\,c\,b\!\!\!/ & \delta\,(\alpha, c) = (\delta\, R) \\ \quad\;\; \uparrow & \\ \quad\;\; \delta & \\ a\,a\,c\,c\,b\!\!\!/ & \delta\,(\delta, c) = (R) \\ \quad\quad\;\; \uparrow & \\ \quad\quad\;\; \delta & \\ a\,a\,c\,c\,b\!\!\!/\,. & \delta\,(\delta, b\!\!\!/) = (\epsilon\, N) \\ \quad\quad\;\; \uparrow & \\ \quad\quad\;\; \epsilon & \end{array}$$

Thus, the string ‘0011’ is accepted by the TM.

2. Let us simulate the working of this TM for the empty string.

Empty string is accepted by the machine as it fits the pattern $0^n\ 1^n$ for $n = 0$. In case of empty string, the machine starts reading the trailing blank character, $b\!\!\!/$.

---

**Example 4.6** Design a TM that recognizes strings containing equal number of 0’s and 1’s.

***Solution*** Let the initial configuration of the machine be as shown in Fig. 4.9(a).

**Algorithm**

1. Starting from the initial state, if you reach the first 0 replace it by ‘*’, and move right till you reach the first 1; replace that also by the same symbol, ‘*’.
2. If you reach 1 first, then replace that with the symbol ‘*’, and move right till you reach the first 0; replace that also by the same symbol, ‘*’.
3. Repeat the procedure till you finish reading all 1’s and 0’s. If any 1 or 0 remains, there must be an error, and the machine should reject the input.

For this TM, we have

$I = \{0, 1, ;, *, T, F\}$, where $T$ = accepted; and $F$ = rejected
$S = \{q_0, q_1, q_2, q_3, q_4 = \text{halt}\}$
$D = \{L, R, N\}$

The SFM for the TM is as shown in Table 4.8.

The initial state $q_0$ makes transition to $q_1$ after replacing the input symbol 0 by *. State $q_1$ hence carries the responsibility of finding the matching symbol 1. State $q_3$ is reached from $q_0$ on finding the symbol 1; hence, $q_3$ needs to find the matching 0 so that the number of 0’s and 1’s are same. The output symbol $T$ is generated if the number of 0’s and 1’s are equal in the input string; else output $F$ is generated.

**Table 4.8** SFM for a TM that accepts strings containing equal number of 0's and 1's

| S \ I | 0 | 1 | ; | * | T | F |
|---|---|---|---|---|---|---|
| $q_0$ | $*q_1R$ | $*q_3R$ | $Tq_4N$ | $R$ | — | — |
| $q_1$ | $R$ | $*q_2L$ | $Fq_4N$ | $R$ | — | — |
| $q_2$ | $L$ | $L$ | $q_0R$ | $L$ | — | — |
| $q_3$ | $*q_2L$ | $R$ | $Fq_4N$ | $R$ | — | — |
| $q_4$ | — | — | — | — | — | — |

The transition diagram for the TM is as shown in Fig. 4.9(b).

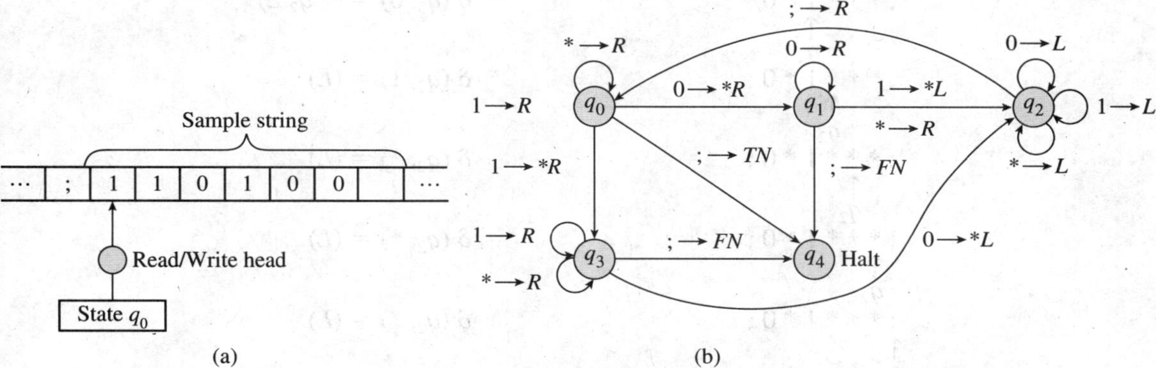


**Figure 4.9** TM that recognizes strings containing equal number of 0's and 1's (a) Initial configuration (b) TG for TM that accepts all strings containing equal number of 0's and 1's

### *Simulation*

1. Let us simulate the working of the TM for the string '110100'.

| | |
|---|---|
| ; 1 1 0 1 0 0 ; (head at first 1, state $q_0$) | initial configuration |
| ; * 1 0 1 0 0 ; (head at 1, state $q_3$) | $\delta(q_0, 1) = (*\ q_3\ R)$ |
| ; * 1 0 1 0 0 ; (head at 0, state $q_3$) | $\delta(q_3, 1) = (R)$ |
| ; * 1 * 1 0 0 ; (head at 1, state $q_2$) | $\delta(q_3, 0) = (*\ q_2\ L)$ |
| ; * 1 * 1 0 0 ; (head at *, state $q_2$) | $\delta(q_2, 1) = (L)$ |

| Configuration | Head | Transition |
|---|---|---|
| ; * 1 * 1 0 0 ; | ↑ $q_2$ | $\delta(q_2, *) = (L)$ |
| ; * 1 * 1 0 0 ; | ↑ $q_0$ | $\delta(q_2, ;) = (q_0\ R)$ |
| ; * 1 * 1 0 0 ; | ↑ $q_0$ | $\delta(q_0, *) = (R)$ |
| ; * * * 1 0 0 ; | ↑ $q_3$ | $\delta(q_0, 1) = (*\ q_3\ R)$ |
| ; * * * 1 0 0; | ↑ $q_3$ | $\delta(q_3, *) = (R)$ |
| ; * * * 1 0 0; | ↑ $q_3$ | $\delta(q_3, 1) = (R)$ |
| ; * * * 1 * 0 ; | ↑ $q_2$ | $\delta(q_3, 0) = (*\ q_2\ L)$ |
| ; * * * 1 * 0 ; | ↑ $q_2$ | $\delta(q_2, 1) = (L)$ |
| ; * * * 1 * 0 ; | ↑ $q_2$ | $\delta(q_2, *) = (L)$ |
| ; * * * 1 * 0 ; | ↑ $q_2$ | $\delta(q_2, *) = (L)$ |
| ; * * * 1 * 0 ; | ↑ $q_2$ | $\delta(q_2, *) = (L)$ |
| ; * * * 1 * 0 ; | ↑ $q_0$ | $\delta(q_2, ;) = (q_0\ R)$ |
| ; * * * 1 * 0 ; | ↑ $q_0$ | $\delta(q_0, *) = (R)$ |
| ; * * * 1 * 0 ; | ↑ $q_0$ | $\delta(q_0, *) = (R)$ |
| ; * * * 1 * 0 ; | ↑ $q_0$ | $\delta(q_0, *) = (R)$ |
| ; * * * * * 0 ; | ↑ $q_3$ | $\delta(q_0, 1) = (*\ q_3\ R)$ |
| ; * * * * * 0 ; | ↑ $q_3$ | $\delta(q_3, *) = (R)$ |
| ; * * * * * * ; | ↑ $q_2$ | $\delta(q_3, 0) = (*\ q_2\ L)$ |

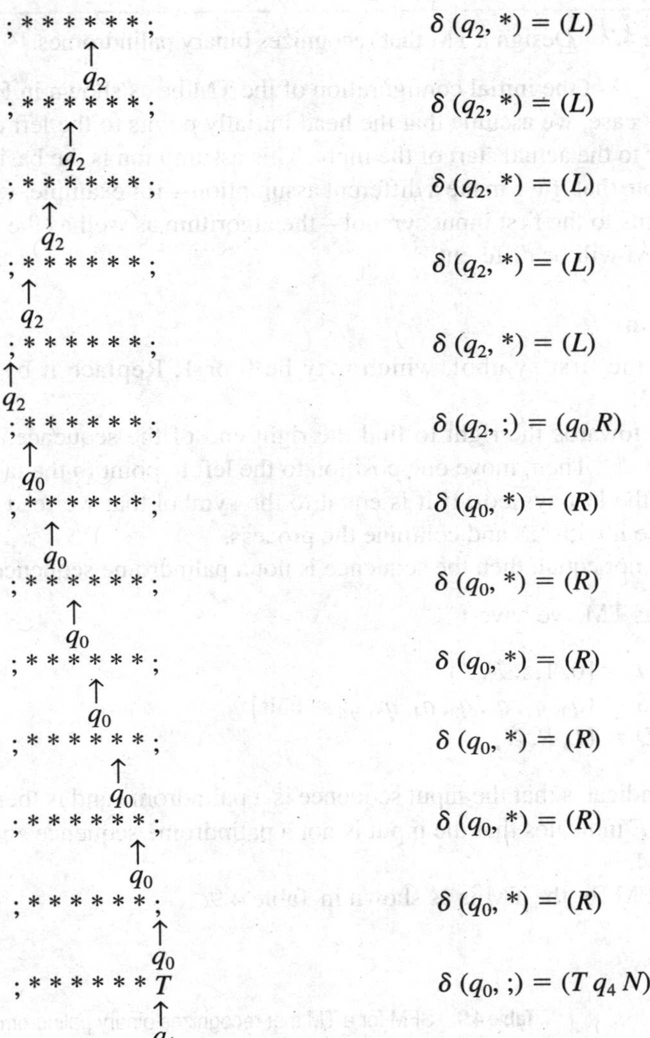


The output symbol $T$ indicates that the string is accepted by the TM.

2. Let us now simulate the working of the TM for the string '1'.

$$
\begin{array}{ll}
; 1 ; & \text{initial configuration} \\
\uparrow & \\
q_0 & \\
; * ; & \delta\,(q_0, 1) = (*\ q_3\ R) \\
\ \ \uparrow & \\
\ \ q_3 & \\
; * F & \delta\,(q_3, ;) = (F\ q_4\ N) \\
\ \ \uparrow & \\
\ \ q_4 &
\end{array}
$$

Thus, the string '1' is rejected by the machine as indicated by the output symbol $F$.

**Example 4.7** Design a TM that recognizes binary palindromes.

***Solution*** Let the initial configuration of the TM be as shown in Fig. 4.10(a).

In this case, we assume that the head initially points to the left end-marker ';', that is, just prior to the actual start of the input. This assumption is the basis for the algorithm we write. Note that if we make a different assumption—for example, we may assume that the head points to the first input symbol—the algorithm as well as the SFM that is generated for the TM will be different.

**Algorithm**

1. Read the first symbol, which may be 0 or 1. Replace it by some other symbol, say ';'.
2. Move towards the right to find the right end of the sequence, that is, the right end-marker ';'. Then, move one position to the left to point to the last symbol.
3. Read the last symbol. If it is equal to the symbol that we read at the other end, then replace it with ';', and continue the process.
4. If it is not equal, then the sequence is not a palindrome sequence.

For this TM, we have

$$I = \{0, 1, ;, F, T\}$$
$$S = \{q_0, q_1, q_2, q_3, q_4, q_5, q_6 = \text{halt}\}$$
$$D = \{L, R, N\}$$

Here, $T$ indicates that the input sequence is a palindrome and is therefore accepted by the TM; and $F$ indicates that the input is not a palindrome sequence and is therefore rejected by the TM.

The SFM for the TM is as shown in Table 4.9.

**Table 4.9** SFM for a TM that recognizes binary palindromes

| $S$ \ $I$ | 0 | 1 | ; | $F$ | $T$ |
|---|---|---|---|---|---|
| $q_0$ | $L$ | $L$ | $q_1R$ | — | — |
| $q_1$ | $;q_2R$ | $;q_4R$ | $Tq_6N$ | — | — |
| $q_2$ | $R$ | $R$ | $q_3L$ | — | — |
| $q_3$ | $;q_0L$ | $Fq_6N$ | $Tq_6N$ | — | — |
| $q_4$ | $R$ | $R$ | $q_5L$ | — | — |
| $q_5$ | $Fq_6N$ | $;q_0L$ | $Tq_6N$ | — | — |
| $q_6$ | — | — | — | — | — |

The transition graph is drawn as shown in Fig. 4.10(b).

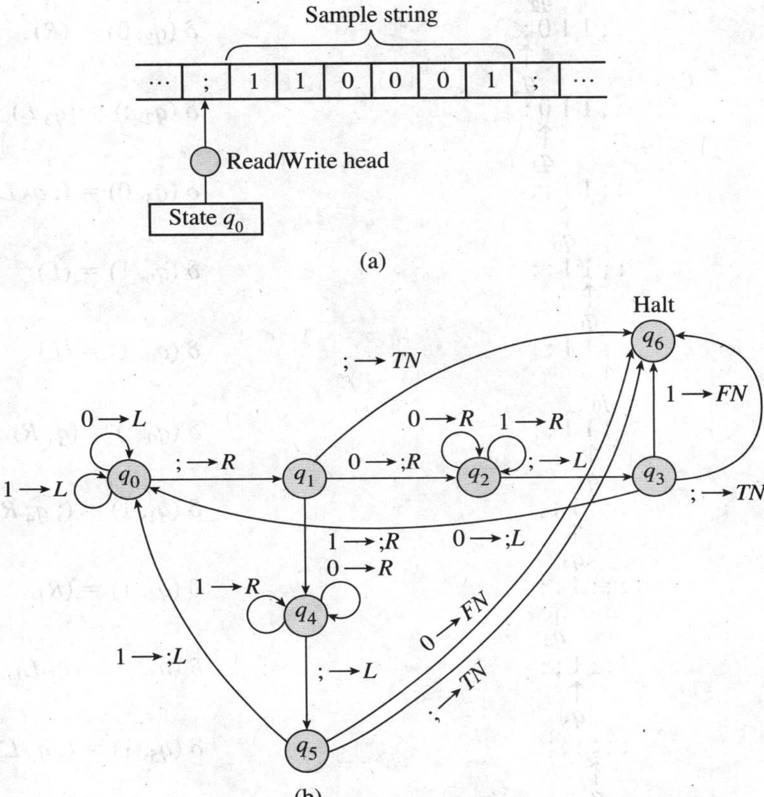


**Figure 4.10** TM that recognizes binary palindromes (a) Initial configuration (b) TG for TM that recognizes binary palindromes

### *Simulation*

1. Let us simulate the working of the TM that we have constructed for the string '0110', which is a binary palindrome sequence of even length.

| | |
|---|---|
| ; 0 1 1 0 ;<br>↑<br>$q_0$ | initial configuration |
| ; 0 1 1 0 ;<br>↑<br>$q_1$ | $\delta(q_0, ;) = (q_1\ R)$ |
| ; ; 1 1 0 ;<br>↑<br>$q_2$ | $\delta(q_1, 0) = (;\ q_2\ R)$ |
| ; ; 1 1 0 ;<br>↑<br>$q_2$ | $\delta(q_2, 1) = (R)$ |

| | |
|---|---|
| ; ; 1 1 0 ; ↑ $q_2$ | $\delta (q_2, 1) = (R)$ |
| ; ; 1 1 0 ; ↑ $q_2$ | $\delta (q_2, 0) = (R)$ |
| ; ; 1 1 0 ; ↑ $q_3$ | $\delta (q_2, ;) = (q_3\ L)$ |
| ; ; 1 1 ; ; ↑ $q_0$ | $\delta (q_3, 0) = (;\ q_0\ L)$ |
| ; ; 1 1 ; ; ↑ $q_0$ | $\delta (q_0, 1) = (L)$ |
| ; ; 1 1 ; ; ↑ $q_0$ | $\delta (q_0, 1) = (L)$ |
| ; ; 1 1 ; ; ↑ $q_1$ | $\delta (q_0, ;) = (q_1\ R)$ |
| ; ; ; 1 ; ; ↑ $q_4$ | $\delta (q_1, 1) = (;\ q_4\ R)$ |
| ; ; ; 1 ; ; ↑ $q_4$ | $\delta (q_4, 1) = (R)$ |
| ; ; ; 1 ; ; ↑ $q_5$ | $\delta (q_4, ;) = (q_5\ L)$ |
| ; ; ; ; ; ; ↑ $q_0$ | $\delta (q_5, 1) = (;\ q_0\ L)$ |
| ; ; ; ; ; ; ↑ $q_1$ | $\delta (q_0, ;) = (q_1\ R)$ |
| ; ; ; *T* ; ; ↑ $q_6$ | $\delta (q_1, ;) = (T\ q_6\ N)$ |

The output *T* indicates that the input string '0110' is a palindrome sequence.

2. Let us simulate the working of the TM for the input string '101', which is a palindrome sequence of odd length.

| | |
|---|---|
| ; 1 0 1 ; ↑ $q_0$ | initial configuration |
| ; 1 0 1 ; ↑ $q_1$ | $\delta (q_0, ;) = (q_1\ R)$ |
| ; ; 0 1 ; ↑ $q_4$ | $\delta (q_1, 1) = (;\ q_4\ R)$ |
| ; ; 0 1 ; ↑ $q_4$ | $\delta (q_4, 0) = (R)$ |

; ; 0 1 ; $\delta(q_4, 1) = (R)$
↑
$q_4$

; ; 0 1 ; $\delta(q_4, ;) = (q_5\ L)$
↑
$q_5$

; ; 0 ; ; $\delta(q_5, 1) = (;\ q_0\ L)$
↑
$q_0$

; ; 0 ; ; $\delta(q_0, 0) = (L)$
↑
$q_0$

; ; 0 ; ; $\delta(q_0, ;) = (q_1\ R)$
↑
$q_1$

; ; ; ; ; $\delta(q_1, 0) = (;\ q_2\ R)$
↑
$q_2$

; ; ; ; ; $\delta(q_2, ;) = (q_3\ L)$
↑
$q_3$

; ; $T$ ; ; $\delta(q_3, ;) = (T\ q_6\ N)$
↑
$q_6$

The output $T$ indicates that the input string '101' is recognized by the TM as a palindrome string.

3. Let us simulate the working of the TM for the string $\epsilon$, that is, the empty string, which is also a palindrome sequence with zero number of 0's and zero number of 1's.

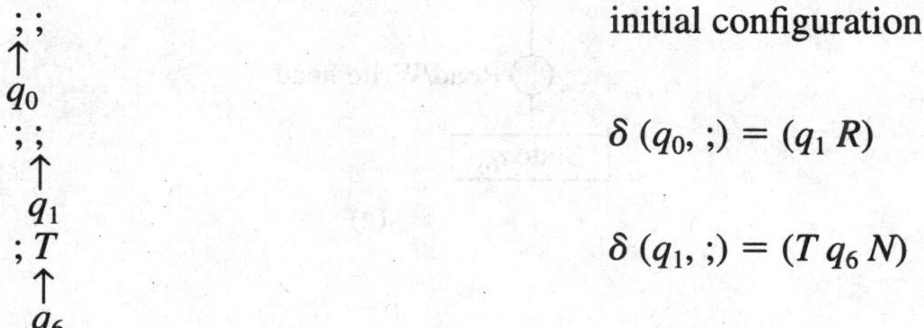


Thus, the empty palindrome string is also accepted by the TM.

4. Let us simulate the working of the TM for input string '01', which is not a palindrome string.

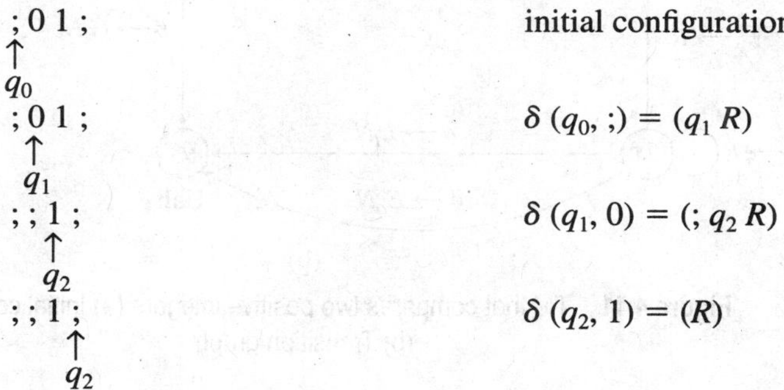

The output $F$ indicates that the string '01' is not a palindrome string, and hence, is rejected by the TM.

---

**Example 4.8** Design a TM, which compares two positive integers $m$ and $n$ and produces output $G_t$ if $m > n$; $L_t$ if $m < n$; and $E_q$ if $m = n$.

***Solution*** This TM is a symbol manipulation system. For this, we need to represent the numbers in the unary format. If we consider $\Sigma = \{a\}$, then the numbers can be represented using that many $a$'s. For example, '2' in unary format can be written as '*aa*' and '5' can be written as '*aaaaa*'.

The initial configuration of the TM is assumed as shown in Fig. 4.11(a). Notice that the two numbers, $m$ and $n$, are separated by a punctuation symbol ',' (comma).

The transition diagram for the required TM is shown in Fig. 4.11(b).

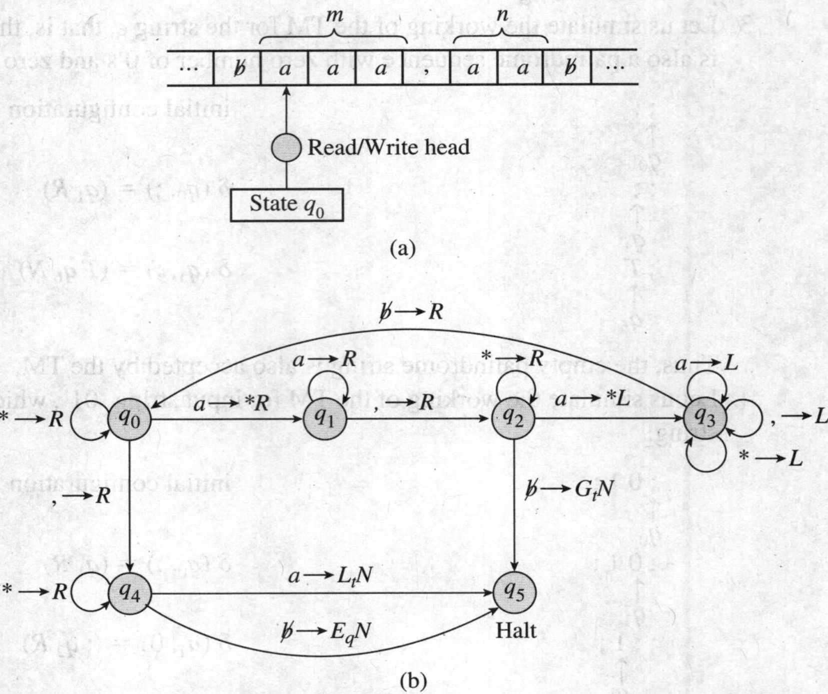


**Figure 4.11** TM that compares two positive integers (a) Initial configuration (b) Transition graph

**Algorithm**

1. Replace one $a$ from $m$ by '*'
2. Move right till you get the first $a$ of $n$, replace it with '*'
3. If no $a$ is remaining of $n$ that is to be replaced by '*' then $m > n$
4. Move left to find the next $a$ of $m$; if found repeat the aforementioned two steps
5. If no $a$ is remaining of $m$ then search if any $a$ is remaining that of $n$, if yes then, $m < n$; if no then, $m = n$

In short, keep replacing each $a$ of $m$ and $n$ by '*', until both or one of them gets fully replaced with *'s. If finally both are totally replaced by *'s, then they must be equal; otherwise, the one with some remaining $a$'s must be greater than the other.

For this TM, we have

$$I = \{a, , , *, \not{b}, G_t, L_t, E_q\}$$
$$S = \{q_0, q_1, q_2, q_3, q_4, q_5 = \text{halt}\}$$
$$D = \{L, R, N\}$$

The SFM for the TM is shown in Table 4.10.

**Table 4.10** SFM for a TM that compares two positive integers

| S \ I | $a$ | , | * | $\not{b}$ | $G$ | $L$ | $E$ |
|---|---|---|---|---|---|---|---|
| $q_0$ | $*q_1R$ | $q_4R$ | $R$ | — | — | — | — |
| $q_1$ | $R$ | $q_2R$ | — | — | — | — | — |
| $q_2$ | $*q_3L$ | — | $R$ | $G_tq_5N$ | — | — | — |
| $q_3$ | $L$ | $L$ | $L$ | $q_0R$ | — | — | — |
| $q_4$ | $L_tq_5N$ | — | $R$ | $E_qq_5N$ | — | — | — |
| $q_5$ | — | — | — | — | — | — | — |

Initially, the TM is in state $q_0$, which replaces one $a$ from $m$ by '*', and makes a transition to a new state $q_1$. State $q_1$ is responsible for finding the beginning of the next number $n$; on accomplishing this, $q_1$ makes transition to $q_2$. State $q_2$ replaces one $a$ from $n$ by '*' to match the one that we have replaced from $m$ earlier. Essentially, we subtract 1 from both the numbers.

Now, if the TM replaces one $a$ from $m$ by a '*', but there is no $a$ left to be replaced in $n$, then it means that in state $q_2$ the TM does not find any $a$; it instead reads a blank character $\not{b}$. In this case, the TM generates the output $G_t$ to indicate that the first number $m$ is greater than the second number $n$.

Let us consider another scenario. If there is no $a$ left in the number $m$, that is, the TM reads comma ',' while in state $q_0$; then, it changes to state $q_4$. State $q_4$ now needs to check whether there is any $a$ left in the second number $n$. If the TM finds an $a$ in $n$ while in state

$q_4$, then it means that the second number is greater, or that the first number $m$ is lesser than the second number $n$. Hence, the TM generates the output $L_t$.

On the other hand, if the TM reads a blank character $\not{b}$ in state $q_4$, then the TM generates output as $E_q$, indicating that both numbers are equal, and there are no more $a$'s left to be replaced in either of them.

The TM thus represents the numbers in unary format and performs the comparison by repetitive subtraction.

### *Simulation*

1. Let us simulate the working of the TM that we have constructed for $m = 3$, that is, $m =$ '$aaa$' and $n = 2$, that is, $n =$ '$aa$'.

| | |
|---|---|
| $\not{b}\ a\ a\ a\ ,\ a\ a\ \not{b}$ (head on 1st $a$, $q_0$) | initial configuration |
| $\not{b}\ *\ a\ a\ ,\ a\ a\ \not{b}$ (head on 2nd symbol $a$, $q_1$) | $\delta\ (q_0, a) = (*\ q_1\ R)$ |
| $\not{b}\ *\ a\ a\ ,\ a\ a\ \not{b}$ (head on 3rd symbol $a$, $q_1$) | $\delta\ (q_1, a) = (R)$ |
| $\not{b}\ *\ a\ a\ ,\ a\ a\ \not{b}$ (head on ',', $q_1$) | $\delta\ (q_1, a) = (R)$ |
| $\not{b}\ *\ a\ a\ ,\ a\ a\ \not{b}$ (head on $a$ after ',', $q_2$) | $\delta\ (q_1, ,) = (q_2\ R)$ |
| $\not{b}\ *\ a\ a\ ,\ *\ a\ \not{b}$ (head on ',', $q_3$) | $\delta\ (q_2, a) = (*\ q_3\ L)$ |
| $\not{b}\ *\ a\ a\ ,\ *\ a\ \not{b}$ (head on 3rd symbol $a$, $q_3$) | $\delta\ (q_3, ,) = (L)$ |
| $\not{b}\ *\ a\ a\ ,\ *\ a\ \not{b}$ (head on 2nd symbol $a$, $q_3$) | $\delta\ (q_3, a) = (L)$ |
| $\not{b}\ *\ a\ a\ ,\ *\ a\ \not{b}$ (head on $*$, $q_3$) | $\delta\ (q_3, a) = (L)$ |
| $\not{b}\ *\ a\ a\ ,\ *\ a\ \not{b}$ (head on $\not{b}$, $q_3$) | $\delta\ (q_3, *) = (L)$ |
| $\not{b}\ *\ a\ a\ ,\ *\ a\ \not{b}$ (head on $*$, $q_0$) | $\delta\ (q_3, \not{b}) = (q_0\ R)$ |
| $\not{b}\ *\ a\ a\ ,\ *\ a\ \not{b}$ (head on 2nd symbol $a$, $q_0$) | $\delta\ (q_0, *) = (R)$ |
| $\not{b}\ *\ *\ a\ ,\ *\ a\ \not{b}$ (head on $a$, $q_1$) | $\delta\ (q_0, a) = (*\ q_1\ R)$ |
| $\not{b}\ *\ *\ a\ ,\ *\ a\ \not{b}$ (head on ',', $q_1$) | $\delta\ (q_1, a) = (R)$ |

```
ƀ * * a , * a ƀ          δ (q1, ,) = (q2 R)
          ↑
          q2
ƀ * * a , * a ƀ          δ (q2, *) = (R)
            ↑
            q2
ƀ * * a , * * ƀ          δ (q2, a) = (* q3 L)
          ↑
          q3
ƀ * * a , * * ƀ          δ (q3, *) = (L)
        ↑
        q3
ƀ * * a , * * ƀ          δ (q3, ,) = (L)
      ↑
      q3
ƀ * * a , * * ƀ          δ (q3, a) = (L)
    ↑
    q3
ƀ * * a , * * ƀ          δ (q3, *) = (L)
  ↑
  q3
ƀ * * a , * * ƀ          δ (q3, *) = (L)
↑
q3
ƀ * * a , * * ƀ          δ (q3, ƀ) = (q0 R)
  ↑
  q0
ƀ * * a , * * ƀ          δ (q0, *) = (R)
    ↑
    q0
ƀ * * a , * * ƀ          δ (q0, *) = (R)
      ↑
      q0
ƀ * * * , * * ƀ          δ (q0, a) = (* q1 R)
        ↑
        q1
ƀ * * * , * * ƀ          δ (q1, ,) = (q2 R)
          ↑
          q2
ƀ * * * , * * ƀ          δ (q2, *) = (R)
            ↑
            q2
ƀ * * * , * * ƀ          δ (q2, *) = (R)
              ↑
              q2
ƀ * * * , * * Gt         δ (q2, ƀ) = (Gt q5 N)
              ↑
              q5
```

Thus, the output of the TM indicates that $m = 3$ is greater than $n = 2$.

2. Let us simulate the working of the TM for $m = 0$ (i.e., $\epsilon$), and $n = 1$ (i.e., '$a$'). As the first number is 0, the head points to the separator symbol ',', to begin with.

```
ƀ , a ƀ                  initial configuration
  ↑
  q0
```

ƀ , a ƀ   $\delta(q_0, ,) = (q_4\ R)$
↑
$q_4$

ƀ , $L_t$ ƀ   $\delta(q_4, a) = (L_t\ q_5\ N)$
↑
$q_5$

The output $L_t$ indicates that $m = 0$ is less than $n = 1$.

3. Let us consider the case when both numbers are equal: let $m = n = 1 =$ '$a$'.

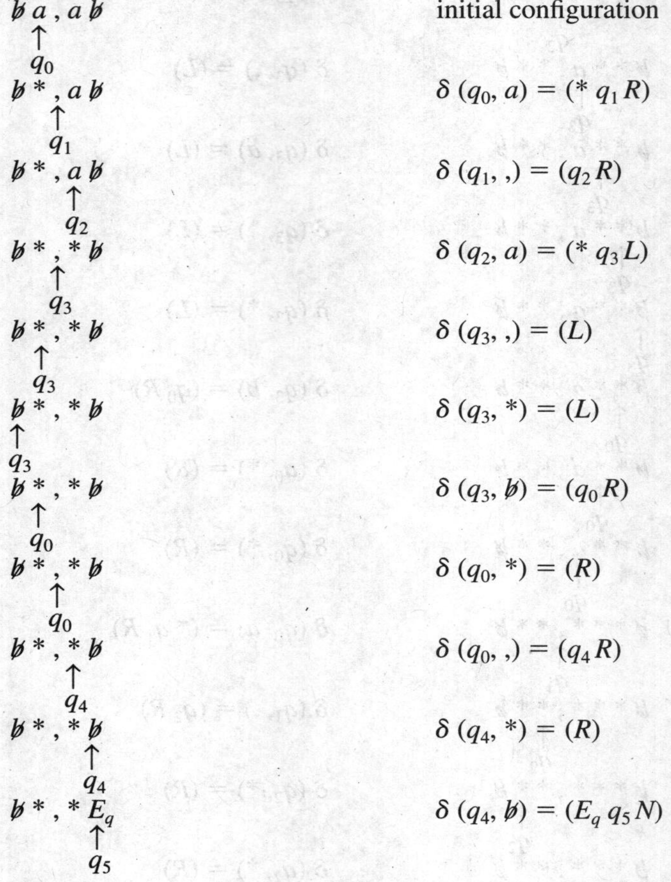


Thus, $m$ and $n$ are equal, which is indicated by the output $E_q$.

---

**Example 4.9** Design a TM that performs the addition of two unary numbers.

***Solution*** Let us consider the pair of numbers expressed in unary form using a symbol '$a$', that is, a number $x$ is represented by $x$ consecutive $a$'s. Let the initial configuration of the machine be as shown in Fig. 4.12(a). As both the unary numbers are represented using the letter '$a$', they are separated by the delimiter '$c$' on the tape. The initial state of the TM is $\alpha$, as specified in Fig. 4.12(a). The TG for this TM is shown in Fig. 4.12(b).

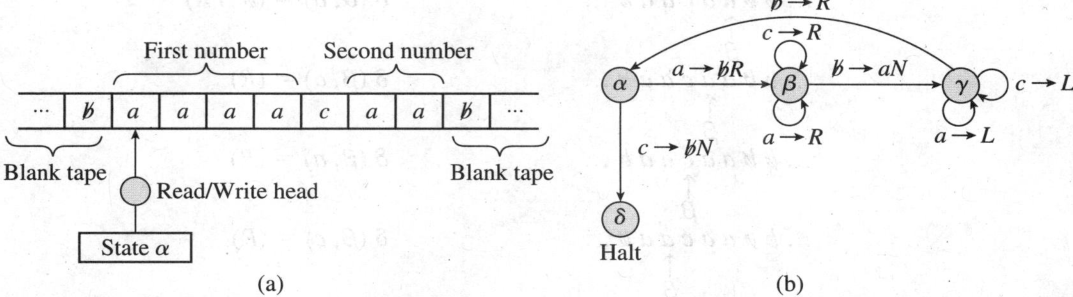


**Figure 4.12** TM that performs addition of two unary numbers (a) Initial configuration (b) TG for TM that adds two unary numbers

## Algorithm

Addition is nothing but concatenation. This is exactly similar to what is taught in pre-primary level mathematics. To achieve '$m + n$', let us represent $m$ and $n$ by some object such as blue balls and then perform aggregation. Put $m$ blue balls into a bucket and put $n$ blue balls into the same bucket; then count the total number of blue balls in the bucket. It gives the value after addition.

Replace each $a$ from the first number, that is, the string of $a$'s on the left side of $c$ by a blank character ƀ and add one $a$ after the string of $a$'s representing the second number. In this way, after completion of addition, the string of $a$'s equal to the result of addition resides on the right side of $c$. At the end, replace the $c$ with a blank character ƀ.

For this TM, we have

$$I = \{a, ƀ, c\}$$
$$S = \{\alpha, \beta, \gamma, \delta = \text{halt}\}$$
$$D = \{L, R, N\}$$

The simplified functional matrix for the TM is given in Table 4.11.

**Table 4.11** SFM for a TM that adds two unary numbers

| S \ I | a | ƀ | c |
|---|---|---|---|
| $\alpha$ | ƀ$\beta R$ | — | ƀ$\delta N$ |
| $\beta$ | $R$ | a$\gamma N$ | $R$ |
| $\gamma$ | $L$ | $\alpha R$ | $L$ |

***Note***: In this example, entries for $\delta$ state are not shown because they are null entries, as it is a halt state. In all previous examples, we have used '-' (hyphens) to indicate them as null/unspecified entries.

### *Simulation*

Let us simulate the working of the TM for the following example:

First number = 3 = '*aaa*'

Second number = 2 = '*aa*'

… ƀ *a a a c a a* ƀ … initial configuration
↑
$\alpha$

$\ldots \not b \not b\, a\, a\, c\, a\, a \not b \ldots$ $\qquad \delta(\alpha, a) = (\not b\, \beta\, R)$
$\uparrow$ $\beta$

$\ldots \not b \not b\, a\, a\, c\, a\, a \not b \ldots$ $\qquad \delta(\beta, a) = (R)$
$\uparrow$ $\beta$

$\ldots \not b \not b\, a\, a\, c\, a\, a \not b \ldots$ $\qquad \delta(\beta, a) = (R)$
$\uparrow$ $\beta$

$\ldots \not b \not b\, a\, a\, c\, a\, a \not b \ldots$ $\qquad \delta(\beta, c) = (R)$
$\uparrow$ $\beta$

$\ldots \not b \not b\, a\, a\, c\, a\, a \not b \ldots$ $\qquad \delta(\beta, a) = (R)$
$\uparrow$ $\beta$

$\ldots \not b \not b\, a\, a\, c\, a\, a \not b \ldots$ $\qquad \delta(\beta, a) = (R)$
$\uparrow$ $\beta$

$\ldots \not b \not b\, a\, a\, c\, a\, a\, a \not b \ldots$ $\qquad \delta(\beta, \not b) = (a\, \gamma\, N)$
$\uparrow$ $\gamma$

$\ldots \not b \not b\, a\, a\, c\, a\, a\, a \not b \ldots$ $\qquad \delta(\gamma, a) = (L)$
$\uparrow$ $\gamma$

$\ldots \not b \not b\, a\, a\, c\, a\, a\, a \not b \ldots$ $\qquad \delta(\gamma, a) = (L)$
$\uparrow$ $\gamma$

$\ldots \not b \not b\, a\, a\, c\, a\, a\, a \not b \ldots$ $\qquad \delta(\gamma, a) = (L)$
$\uparrow$ $\gamma$

$\ldots \not b \not b\, a\, a\, c\, a\, a\, a \not b \ldots$ $\qquad \delta(\gamma, c) = (L)$
$\uparrow$ $\gamma$

$\ldots \not b \not b\, a\, a\, c\, a\, a\, a \not b \ldots$ $\qquad \delta(\gamma, a) = (L)$
$\uparrow$ $\gamma$

$\ldots \not b \not b\, a\, a\, c\, a\, a\, a \not b \ldots$ $\qquad \delta(\gamma, a) = (L)$
$\uparrow$ $\gamma$

$\ldots \not b \not b\, a\, a\, c\, a\, a\, a \not b \ldots$ $\qquad \delta(\gamma, \not b) = (\alpha\, R)$
$\uparrow$ $\alpha$

$\ldots \not b \not b \not b\, a\, c\, a\, a\, a \not b \ldots$ $\qquad \delta(\alpha, a) = (\not b\, \beta\, R)$
$\uparrow$ $\beta$

$\ldots \not b \not b \not b\, a\, c\, a\, a\, a \not b \ldots$ $\qquad \delta(\beta, a) = (R)$
$\uparrow$ $\beta$

$\ldots \not b \not b \not b\, a\, c\, a\, a\, a \not b \ldots$ $\qquad \delta(\beta, c) = (R)$
$\uparrow$ $\beta$

$\ldots \not b \not b \not b\, a\, c\, a\, a\, a \not b \ldots$ $\qquad \delta(\beta, a) = (R)$
$\uparrow$ $\beta$

$\ldots \not b\, \not b\, \not b\, a\, c\, a\, a\, a\, \not b \ldots \qquad \delta(\beta, a) = (R)$

$\uparrow \beta$

$\ldots \not b\, \not b\, \not b\, a\, c\, a\, a\, a\, \not b \ldots \qquad \delta(\beta, a) = (R)$

$\uparrow \beta$

$\ldots \not b\, \not b\, \not b\, a\, c\, a\, a\, a\, a\, \not b \ldots \qquad \delta(\beta, \not b) = (a\, \gamma\, N)$

$\uparrow \gamma$

$\ldots \not b\, \not b\, \not b\, a\, c\, a\, a\, a\, a\, \not b \ldots \qquad \delta(\gamma, a) = (L)$

$\uparrow \gamma$

$\ldots \not b\, \not b\, \not b\, a\, c\, a\, a\, a\, a\, \not b \ldots \qquad \delta(\gamma, a) = (L)$

$\uparrow \gamma$

$\ldots \not b\, \not b\, \not b\, a\, c\, a\, a\, a\, a\, \not b \ldots \qquad \delta(\gamma, a) = (L)$

$\uparrow \gamma$

$\ldots \not b\, \not b\, \not b\, a\, c\, a\, a\, a\, a\, \not b \ldots \qquad \delta(\gamma, a) = (L)$

$\uparrow \gamma$

$\ldots \not b\, \not b\, \not b\, a\, c\, a\, a\, a\, a\, \not b \ldots \qquad \delta(\gamma, c) = (L)$

$\uparrow \gamma$

$\ldots \not b\, \not b\, \not b\, a\, c\, a\, a\, a\, a\, \not b \ldots \qquad \delta(\gamma, a) = (L)$

$\uparrow \gamma$

$\ldots \not b\, \not b\, \not b\, a\, c\, a\, a\, a\, a\, \not b \ldots \qquad \delta(\gamma, \not b) = (\alpha\, R)$

$\uparrow \alpha$

$\ldots \not b\, \not b\, \not b\, \not b\, c\, a\, a\, a\, a\, \not b \ldots \qquad \delta(\alpha, a) = (\not b\, \beta\, R)$

$\uparrow \beta$

$\ldots \not b\, \not b\, \not b\, \not b\, c\, a\, a\, a\, a\, \not b \ldots \qquad \delta(\beta, c) = (R)$

$\uparrow \beta$

$\ldots \not b\, \not b\, \not b\, \not b\, c\, a\, a\, a\, a\, \not b \ldots \qquad \delta(\beta, a) = (R)$

$\uparrow \beta$

$\ldots \not b\, \not b\, \not b\, \not b\, c\, a\, a\, a\, a\, \not b \ldots \qquad \delta(\beta, a) = (R)$

$\uparrow \beta$

$\ldots \not b\, \not b\, \not b\, \not b\, c\, a\, a\, a\, a\, \not b \ldots \qquad \delta(\beta, a) = (R)$

$\uparrow \beta$

$\ldots \not b\, \not b\, \not b\, \not b\, c\, a\, a\, a\, a\, \not b \ldots \qquad \delta(\beta, a) = (R)$

$\uparrow \beta$

$\ldots \not b\, \not b\, \not b\, \not b\, c\, a\, a\, a\, a\, a\, \not b \ldots \qquad \delta(\beta, \not b) = (a\, \gamma\, N)$

$\uparrow \gamma$

$\ldots \not b\, \not b\, \not b\, \not b\, c\, a\, a\, a\, a\, a\, \not b \ldots \qquad \delta(\gamma, a) = (L)$

$\uparrow \gamma$

$$\ldots \not{b}\,\not{b}\,\not{b}\,\not{b}\; c\; a\; a\; a\; a\; a\; \not{b} \ldots \qquad \delta(\gamma, a) = (L)$$
↑ $\gamma$

$$\ldots \not{b}\,\not{b}\,\not{b}\,\not{b}\; c\; a\; a\; a\; a\; a\; \not{b} \ldots \qquad \delta(\gamma, a) = (L)$$
↑ $\gamma$

$$\ldots \not{b}\,\not{b}\,\not{b}\,\not{b}\; c\; a\; a\; a\; a\; a\; \not{b} \ldots \qquad \delta(\gamma, a) = (L)$$
↑ $\gamma$

$$\ldots \not{b}\,\not{b}\,\not{b}\,\not{b}\; c\; a\; a\; a\; a\; a\; \not{b} \ldots \qquad \delta(\gamma, a) = (L)$$
↑ $\gamma$

$$\ldots \not{b}\,\not{b}\,\not{b}\,\not{b}\; c\; a\; a\; a\; a\; a\; \not{b} \ldots \qquad \delta(\gamma, c) = (L)$$
↑ $\gamma$

$$\ldots \not{b}\,\not{b}\,\not{b}\,\not{b}\; c\; a\; a\; a\; a\; a\; \not{b} \ldots \qquad \delta(\gamma, \not{b}) = (\alpha\ R)$$
↑ $\alpha$

$$\ldots \not{b}\,\not{b}\,\not{b}\,\not{b}\,\not{b}\; a\; a\; a\; a\; a\; \not{b} \ldots \qquad \delta(\alpha, c) = (\not{b}\ \delta\ N)$$
↑ $\delta$

Thus, the addition of the two numbers '3 + 2' is completed, and that is indicated by the five $a$'s that are left on the tape before the machine halts.

---

**Example 4.10** Design a TM that multiplies two unary numbers.

***Solution*** Multiplication, as we know, is repetitive addition of multiplicand to itself. We have already discussed unary addition using a TM in the previous example.

If $m$ is the multiplier and $n$ is the multiplicand, then $n \times m$ can be viewed as:

$$n \times m = n + n + \ldots\ m \text{ number of times}$$

Thus, we consider addition as the concatenation of $m$ number of $n$'s.

Let us consider the initial configuration of the TM as shown in Fig. 4.13(a). The multiplier and multiplicand are both unary representations of the decimal numbers. They are represented here using symbol 1; for example, the decimal number 2 in unary format is written as '11'. The rest of the tape is assumed to be filled with all 0's instead of $\not{b}$'s. The

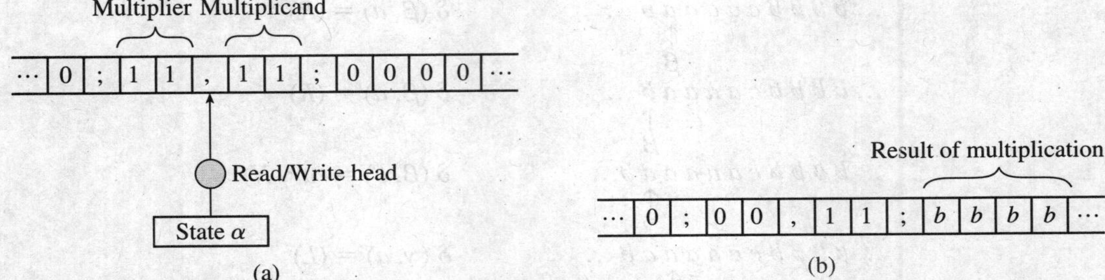


**Figure 4.13** TM that multiplies two unary numbers (a) Initial configuration (b) Final configuration of TM (for the operation $2 \times 2 = 4$).

multiplier and multiplicand are separated by a comma ',' and delimited at both the ends by semicolons ';'. The head points to the separator symbol ',' initially.

The result of the multiplication is written after the right end-marker semicolon (;). We have an example final configuration of the TM for a sample multiplication (2 × 2), as shown in Fig. 4.13(b). Observe how the result is written and where it is written onto the tape. The result is also represented in unary format but using the symbol *b*. The multiplier at the end gets replaced with 0's. The algorithm thus is a destructive one, as it modifies the parameters sent to it (in this case, the parameter modified is the multiplier).

**Algorithm**

1. Replace one '1' of the multiplier by '0', that is, subtract one from the multiplier.
2. To add the multiplicand to the result area, that is, beyond the right end-marker ';' replace one '1' of the multiplicand by some symbol, say '*a*'
3. Find the end of the result where '0' can be found, replace it with symbol '*b*' (result is represented by all '*b*'s)
4. Repeat the aforementioned steps 2 and 3 till all the '1's in the multiplicand are all replaced by '*a*'s
5. The multiplicand is added once to the result area; hence, reset the multiplicand to all '1's again and repeat the steps starting from 1.
6. Stop when all the '1's in the multiplier are replaced by all '0's

For this TM, we have:

$$I = \{0, 1, a, b, ;, ,\}$$
$$S = \{\alpha, \beta, \gamma, \delta, \epsilon, f = \text{halt}\}$$
$$D = \{L, R, N\}$$

The SFM for the TM is shown in Table 4.12.

**Table 4.12** SFM for a TM that multiplies two unary numbers

| S \ I | 0 | 1 | $a$ | $b$ | ; | , |
|---|---|---|---|---|---|---|
| $\alpha$ | $L$ | $0\beta R$ | — | — | $\phi N$ | $L$ |
| $\beta$ | $R$ | $aR$ | — | — | $\gamma L$ | $R$ |
| $\gamma$ | — | — | $1\,\delta\,R$ | — | $R$ | $L$ |
| $\delta$ | $b\epsilon L$ | $R$ | — | $R$ | $R$ | — |
| $\epsilon$ | $L$ | $L$ | $1\,\delta\,R$ | $L$ | $L$ | $\alpha N$ |
| $\phi$ | — | — | — | — | — | — |

In state $\alpha$, the TM starts by replacing one '1' from the multiplier by 0, that is, reducing the multiplier by 1. In state $\beta$, the TM moves right by replacing all 1's from the multiplicand by $a$'s, and changes the state to $\gamma$ once the right end-marker ';' is found. States $\gamma$,

$\delta$, and $\epsilon$ are responsible for concatenating the multiplicand to the right end once. In this process, all the 1's in the multiplicand that were replaced by all $a$'s are replaced again by 1's. The concatenated result is represented in unary form using the symbol $b$. The halt state $f$ is entered once all the multiplier 1's are replaced by 0's, which means that the TM halts when the multiplicand is added (concatenated) to itself multiplier number of times.

Let us see a simulation of this TM for a sample multiplication.

***Simulation***

Let us simulate the working of this TM for the following:

Multiplier = $m$ = 2 = '11'

Multiplicand = $n$ = 2 = '11'.

$\ldots 0 ; 1 1 , 1 1 ; 0 0 0 0 \ldots$ (head ↑ at ',', state $\alpha$) — initial configuration

$\ldots 0 ; 1 1 , 1 1 ; 0 0 0 0 \ldots$ (head ↑ at second 1 of multiplier, state $\alpha$) — $\delta(\alpha, ,) = (L)$

$\ldots 0 ; 1 0 , 1 1 ; 0 0 0 0 \ldots$ (head ↑ at ',', state $\beta$) — $\delta(\alpha, 1) = (0\, \beta\, R)$

(Decremented multiplier by 1)

$\ldots 0 ; 1 0 , 1 1 ; 0 0 0 0 \ldots$ (head ↑ at first 1 of multiplicand, state $\beta$) — $\delta(\beta, ,) = (R)$

(Concatenation of the multiplicand to the result area begins from here…)

$\ldots 0 ; 1 0 , a 1 ; 0 0 0 0 \ldots$ (head ↑ at second 1 of multiplicand, state $\beta$) — $\delta(\beta, 1) = (a\, R)$

(Replacing all '1's by '$a$'s from multiplicand is for performing concatenation of the multiplicand to the result)

$\ldots 0 ; 1 0 , a a ; 0 0 0 0 \ldots$ (head ↑ at ';', state $\beta$) — $\delta(\beta, 1) = (a\, R)$

$\ldots 0 ; 1 0 , a a ; 0 0 0 0 \ldots$ (head ↑ at second $a$, state $\gamma$) — $\delta(\beta, ;) = (\gamma\, L)$

$\ldots 0 ; 1 0 , a 1 ; 0 0 0 0 \ldots$ (head ↑ at ';', state $\delta$) — $\delta(\gamma, a) = (1\, \delta\, R)$

(This step again replaces the '$a$'s in the multiplicand with 1; therefore, after concatenation in the result area, the multiplicand will be restored as all '1's )

$\ldots 0 ; 1 0 , a 1 ; 0 0 0 0 \ldots$ (head ↑ at first 0 of result area, state $\delta$) — $\delta(\delta, ;) = (R)$

$\ldots 0 ; 1 0 , a 1 ; b 0 0 0 \ldots$ (head ↑ at ';', state $\epsilon$) — $\delta(\delta, 0) = (b\, \epsilon\, L)$

$\ldots 0 ; 1 0 , a 1 ; b 0 0 0 \ldots$ (head ↑ at 1, state $\epsilon$) — $\delta(\epsilon, ;) = (L)$

$\ldots 0 ; 1 0 , \underset{\substack{\uparrow \\ \epsilon}}{a} 1 ; b 0 0 0 \ldots$ $\qquad \delta(\epsilon, 1) = (L)$

$\ldots 0 ; 1 0 , \underset{\substack{\uparrow \\ \delta}}{1} 1 ; b 0 0 0 \ldots$ $\qquad \delta(\epsilon, a) = (1\ \delta\ R)$

(Multiplicand is completely replaced by 1's again)

$\ldots 0 ; 1 0 , 1 1 \underset{\substack{\uparrow \\ \delta}}{;} b 0 0 0 \ldots$ $\qquad \delta(\delta, 1) = (R)$

$\ldots 0 ; 1 0 , 1 1 ; \underset{\substack{\uparrow \\ \delta}}{b} 0 0 0 \ldots$ $\qquad \delta(\delta, ;) = (R)$

$\ldots 0 ; 1 0 , 1 1 ; b \underset{\substack{\uparrow \\ \delta}}{0} 0 0 \ldots$ $\qquad \delta(\delta, b) = (R)$

$\ldots 0 ; 1 0 , 1 1 ; \underset{\substack{\uparrow \\ \epsilon}}{b} b 0 0 \ldots$ $\qquad \delta(\delta, 0) = (b\ \epsilon\ L)$

(Concatenation of multiplicand to the result area is complete. Result is represented as a string of *b*'s)

$\ldots 0 ; 1 0 , 1 1 \underset{\substack{\uparrow \\ \epsilon}}{;} b b 0 0 \ldots$ $\qquad \delta(\epsilon, b) = (L)$

$\ldots 0 ; 1 0 , 1 \underset{\substack{\uparrow \\ \epsilon}}{1} ; b b 0 0 \ldots$ $\qquad \delta(\epsilon, ;) = (L)$

$\ldots 0 ; 1 0 , \underset{\substack{\uparrow \\ \epsilon}}{1} 1 ; b b 0 0 \ldots$ $\qquad \delta(\epsilon, 1) = (L)$

$\ldots 0 ; 1 0 \underset{\substack{\uparrow \\ \epsilon}}{,} 1 1 ; b b 0 0 \ldots$ $\qquad \delta(\epsilon, 1) = (L)$

$\ldots 0 ; 1 0 \underset{\substack{\uparrow \\ \alpha}}{,} 1 1 ; b b 0 0 \ldots$ $\qquad \delta(\epsilon, ,) = (\alpha\ N)$

$\ldots 0 ; 1 \underset{\substack{\uparrow \\ \alpha}}{0} , 1 1 ; b b 0 0 \ldots$ $\qquad \delta(\alpha, ,) = (L)$

$\ldots 0 ; \underset{\substack{\uparrow \\ \alpha}}{1} 0 , 1 1 ; b b 0 0 \ldots$ $\qquad \delta(\alpha, 0) = (L)$

$\ldots 0 ; 0 \underset{\substack{\uparrow \\ \beta}}{0} , 1 1 ; b b 0 0 \ldots$ $\qquad \delta(\alpha, 1) = (0\ \beta\ R)$

(Decremented the multiplier by 1 again; the second iteration begins)

$\ldots 0 ; 0 0 \underset{\substack{\uparrow \\ \beta}}{,} 1 1 ; b b 0 0 \ldots$ $\qquad \delta(\beta, 0) = (R)$

$\ldots 0 ; 0 0 , \underset{\substack{\uparrow \\ \beta}}{1} 1 ; b b 0 0 \ldots$ $\qquad \delta(\beta, ,) = (R)$

(Concatenation of the multiplicand, for the second time, to the result area begins here; since multiplication is repetitive addition, we use repetitive concatenation here)

$\ldots 0 ; 0 0 , a\, 1 ; b\, b\, 0\, 0 \ldots$ (head under 1, state $\beta$) $\quad \delta(\beta, 1) = (a\, R)$

(Replacing all '1's by '*a*'s from multiplicand is for performing concatenation of the multiplicand to the result)

$\ldots 0 ; 0 0 , a\, a ; b\, b\, 0\, 0 \ldots$ (head under ;, state $\beta$) $\quad \delta(\beta, 1) = (a\, R)$

$\ldots 0 ; 0 0 , a\, a ; b\, b\, 0\, 0 \ldots$ (head under second $a$, state $\gamma$) $\quad \delta(\beta, ;) = (\gamma\, L)$

$\ldots 0 ; 0 0 , a\, 1 ; b\, b\, 0\, 0 \ldots$ (head under ;, state $\delta$) $\quad \delta(\gamma, a) = (1\, \delta\, R)$

(Once it is concatenated to the result area, the *a* in the multiplicand is replaced again by 1)

$\ldots 0 ; 0 0 , a\, 1 ; b\, b\, 0\, 0 \ldots$ (head under first $b$, state $\delta$) $\quad \delta(\delta, ;) = (R)$

$\ldots 0 ; 0 0 , a\, 1 ; b\, b\, 0\, 0 \ldots$ (head under second $b$, state $\delta$) $\quad \delta(\delta, b) = (R)$

$\ldots 0 ; 0 0 , a\, 1 ; b\, b\, 0\, 0 \ldots$ (head under first 0, state $\delta$) $\quad \delta(\delta, b) = (R)$

$\ldots 0 ; 0 0 , a\, 1 ; b\, b\, b\, 0 \ldots$ (head under second $b$, state $\epsilon$) $\quad \delta(\delta, 0) = (b\, \epsilon\, L)$

$\ldots 0 ; 0 0 , a\, 1 ; b\, b\, b\, 0 \ldots$ (head under first $b$, state $\epsilon$) $\quad \delta(\epsilon, b) = (L)$

$\ldots 0 ; 0 0 , a\, 1 ; b\, b\, b\, 0 \ldots$ (head under ;, state $\epsilon$) $\quad \delta(\epsilon, b) = (L)$

$\ldots 0 ; 0 0 , a\, 1 ; b\, b\, b\, 0 \ldots$ (head under 1, state $\epsilon$) $\quad \delta(\epsilon, ;) = (L)$

$\ldots 0 ; 0 0 , a\, 1 ; b\, b\, b\, 0 \ldots$ (head under $a$, state $\epsilon$) $\quad \delta(\epsilon, 1) = (L)$

$\ldots 0 ; 0 0 , 1\, 1 ; b\, b\, b\, 0 \ldots$ (head under second 1, state $\delta$) $\quad \delta(\epsilon, a) = (1\, \delta\, R)$

(Multiplicand is completely replaced by 1's again)

$\ldots 0 ; 0 0 , 1\, 1 ; b\, b\, b\, 0 \ldots$ (head under ;, state $\delta$) $\quad \delta(\delta, 1) = (R)$

... 0 ; 0 0 , 1 1 ; *b b b* 0 ... $\delta\,(\delta, ;) = (R)$
↑ $\delta$

... 0 ; 0 0 , 1 1 ; *b b b* 0 ... $\delta\,(\delta, b) = (R)$
↑ $\delta$

... 0 ; 0 0 , 1 1 ; *b b b* 0 ... $\delta\,(\delta, b) = (R)$
↑ $\delta$

... 0 ; 0 0 , 1 1 ; *b b b* 0 ... $\delta\,(\delta, b) = (R)$
↑ $\delta$

... 0 ; 0 0 , 1 1 ; *b b b b* ... $\delta\,(\delta, 0) = (b\,\epsilon\,L)$
↑ $\epsilon$

(Concatenation of multiplicand to the result area is completed once again. The result is represented as a string of *b*'s)

... 0 ; 0 0 , 1 1 ; *b b b b* ... $\delta\,(\epsilon, b) = (L)$
↑ $\epsilon$

... 0 ; 0 0 , 1 1 ; *b b b b* ... $\delta\,(\epsilon, b) = (L)$
↑ $\epsilon$

... 0 ; 0 0 , 1 1 ; *b b b b* ... $\delta\,(\epsilon, b) = (L)$
↑ $\epsilon$

... 0 ; 0 0 , 1 1 ; *b b b b* ... $\delta\,(\epsilon, ;) = (L)$
↑ $\epsilon$

... 0 ; 0 0 , 1 1 ; *b b b b* ... $\delta\,(\epsilon, 1) = (L)$
↑ $\epsilon$

... 0 ; 0 0 , 1 1 ; *b b b b* ... $\delta\,(\epsilon, 1) = (L)$
↑ $\epsilon$

... 0 ; 0 0 , 1 1 ; *b b b b* ... $\delta\,(\epsilon, ,) = (\alpha\,N)$
↑ $\alpha$

... 0 ; 0 0 , 1 1 ; *b b b b* ... $\delta\,(\alpha, ,) = (L)$
↑ $\alpha$

... 0 ; 0 0 , 1 1 ; *b b b b* ... $\delta\,(\alpha, 0) = (L)$
↑ $\alpha$

... 0 ; 0 0 , 1 1 ; *b b b b* ... $\delta\,(\alpha, 0) = (L)$
↑ $\alpha$

... 0 ; 0 0 , 1 1 ; *b b b b* ... $\delta\,(\alpha, ;) = (\phi\,N)$
↑ $\phi$

(TM halts; multiplication is complete)

Thus, we see that the result of the multiplication: 2 × 2 is '*bbbb*', that is, 4.

> ***Note***: If we want to design a non-destructive TM, we must ensure that the original arguments (or parameters) are kept intact. Therefore, we must construct the TM such that before entering into the halt state, it replaces all '0's in the multiplier by all '1's again.

Thus, we see that multiplication, which is not possible for an FSM, is achieved using a TM.

---

**Example 4.11** Design a TM that finds the greatest common divisor (GCD) of two given numbers.

***Solution*** Let the initial configuration of the TM be as shown in Fig. 4.14(a). We observe that the two numbers—in this example, we consider the numbers, 4 and 2—are stored onto the tape without any separator in between; further, we observe that both the numbers are represented in unary format using the symbol 1.

The initial state of the TM is $\alpha$, and the head points to the last 1 of the unary representation of the first number among the given pair of numbers. As the sample pair is 4 and 2, we observe that the numbers in the tape are '1111' and '11'; and hence, the head points to the last 1 in '1111'.

**Algorithm**

Examine the numbers on the tape to find which of the two is larger. This is achieved by a repetitive subtraction process: First change one 1 in the first number to $a$; then change one 1 in the second number to $b$. Then return to the first number to change another 1 to $a$, and so on. This effectively subtracts the smaller number from the larger one.

If $x$ is the smaller number and $y$ is the larger number, then after the aforementioned processing, the pair $x$, $y$ is changed to $x$ and '$y$ - $x$'. This process is recursively carried out again on the newly-obtained pair. When the machine halts, it leaves one number in the pair as 0, and the other as the GCD.

The SFM for the TM is as shown in Table 4.13.

**Table 4.13** SFM for a TM that finds the GCD of two given numbers

| $S$ \ $I$ | 0 | 1 | $a$ | $b$ |
|---|---|---|---|---|
| $\alpha$ | $\delta R$ | $a\beta N$ | $L$ | $L$ |
| $\beta$ | $\gamma L$ | $b\alpha N$ | $R$ | $R$ |
| $\gamma$ | $\alpha R$ | $\alpha R$ | $1L$ | $0L$ |
| $\delta$ | *Halt* | $\alpha L$ | $0R$ | $1R$ |

For this TM, we have

$$I = \{0, 1, a, b\}$$
$$S = \{\alpha, \beta, \gamma, \delta\}$$

Halt state is not explicitly mentioned. One can introduce it if required, as we did for the examples so far. Wherever there is an entry 'Halt' in the transition Table 4.13, one can introduce a transition to such a halt state. The change is done to showcase a variation in the representation.

$$D = \{L, R, N\}$$

The transition diagram is as shown in Fig. 4.14(b).

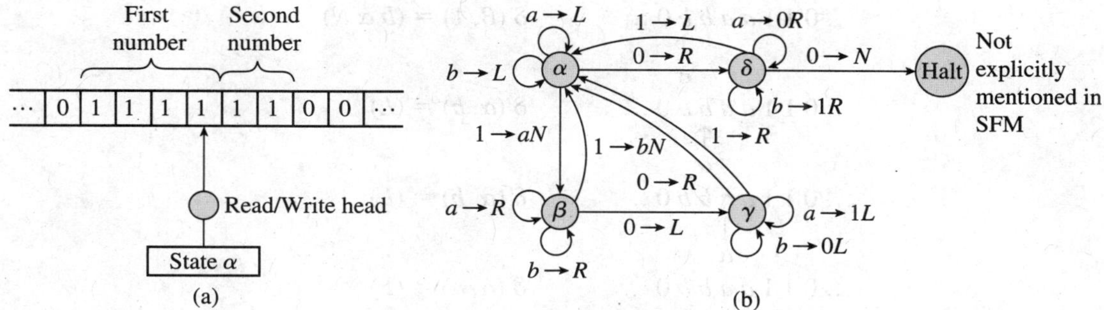


**Figure 4.14** TM that finds the GCD of two given numbers (a) Initial configuration (b) TG for TM that finds GCD of two given numbers

### *Simulation*

Let us simulate the working of the TM that we have constructed for the input numbers:

$x = 4 = $ '1111'

$y = 2 = $ '11'

```
... 0 1 1 1 1 1 1 0 ...        initial configuration
            ↑
            α
... 0 1 1 1 a 1 1 0 ...        δ (α, 1) = (a β N)
            ↑
            β
... 0 1 1 1 a 1 1 0 ...        δ (β, a) = (R)
              ↑
              β
... 0 1 1 1 a b 1 0 ...        δ (β, 1) = (b α N)
              ↑
              α
... 0 1 1 1 a b 1 0 ...        δ (α, b) = (L)
            ↑
            α
... 0 1 1 1 a b 1 0 ...        δ (α, a) = (L)
          ↑
          α
... 0 1 1 a a b 1 0 ...        δ (α, 1) = (a β N)
          ↑
          β
... 0 1 1 a a b 1 0 ...        δ (β, a) = (R)
            ↑
            β
... 0 1 1 a a b 1 0 ...        δ (β, a) = (R)
              ↑
              β
... 0 1 1 a a b 1 0 ...        δ (β, b) = (R)
                ↑
                β
```

```
... 0 1 1 a a b b 0 ...        δ (β, 1) = (b α N)
                ↑
                α
... 0 1 1 a a b b 0 ...        δ (α, b) = (L)
              ↑
              α
... 0 1 1 a a b b 0 ...        δ (α, b) = (L)
            ↑
            α
... 0 1 1 a a b b 0 ...        δ (α, a) = (L)
          ↑
          α
... 0 1 1 a a b b 0 ...        δ (α, a) = (L)
        ↑
        α
... 0 1 a a a b b 0 ...        δ (α, 1) = (a β N)
        ↑
        β
... 0 1 a a a b b 0 ...        δ (β, a) = (R)
          ↑
          β
... 0 1 a a a b b 0 ...        δ (β, a) = (R)
            ↑
            β
... 0 1 a a a b b 0 ...        δ (β, a) = (R)
              ↑
              β
... 0 1 a a a b b 0 ...        δ (β, b) = (R)
                ↑
                β
... 0 1 a a a b b 0 ...        δ (β, b) = (R)
                  ↑
                  β
... 0 1 a a a b b 0 ...        δ (β, 0) = (γ L)
                ↑
                γ
... 0 1 a a a b 0 0 ...        δ (γ, b) = (0 L)
              ↑
              γ
... 0 1 a a a 0 0 0 ...        δ (γ, b) = (0 L)
            ↑
            γ
... 0 1 a a 1 0 0 0 ...        δ (γ, a) = (1 L)
          ↑
          γ
... 0 1 a 1 1 0 0 0 ...        δ (γ, a) = (1 L)
        ↑
        γ
```

```
... 0 1 1 1 1 0 0 0 ...        δ (γ, a) = (1 L)
        ↑
        γ
... 0 1 1 1 1 0 0 0 ...        δ (γ, 1) = (α R)
        ↑
        α
```

The first iteration is complete. The pair obtained consists of (4 – 2) = 2 as the first number and 2 remains the second number, without any change.

```
... 0 1 a 1 1 0 0 0 ...        δ (α, 1) = (a, β N)
        ↑
        β
... 0 1 a 1 1 0 0 0 ...        δ (β, a) = (R)
          ↑
          β
... 0 1 a b 1 0 0 0 ...        δ (β, 1) = (b α N)
          ↑
          α
... 0 1 a b 1 0 0 0 ...        δ (α, b) = (L)
        ↑
        α
... 0 1 a b 1 0 0 0 ...        δ (α, a) = (L)
      ↑
      α
... 0 a a b 1 0 0 0 ...        δ (α, 1) = (a β N)
      ↑
      β
... 0 a a b 1 0 0 0 ...        δ (β, a) = (R)
      ↑
      β
... 0 a a b 1 0 0 0 ...        δ (β, a) = (R)
        ↑
        β
... 0 a a b 1 0 0 0 ...        δ (β, b) = (R)
          ↑
          β
... 0 a a b b 0 0 0 ...        δ (β, 1) = (b α N)
            ↑
            α
... 0 a a b b 0 0 0 ...        δ (α, b) = (L)
          ↑
          α
... 0 a a b b 0 0 0 ...        δ (α, b) = (L)
        ↑
        α
... 0 a a b b 0 0 0 ...        δ (α, a) = (L)
      ↑
      α
```

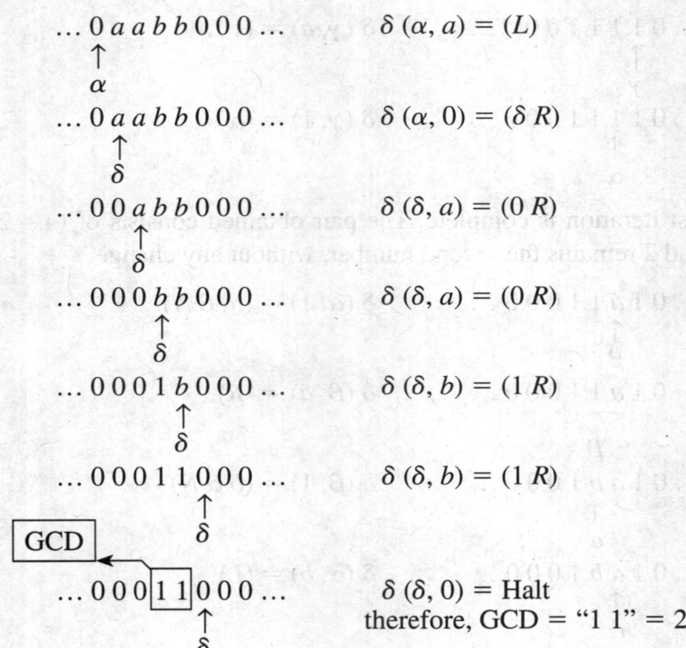


As the second number of the newly-obtained pair is 0, the GCD of 4 and 2 is represented by the number of 1's remaining on the tape. Hence, the answer is 2.

---

**Example 4.12** Design a TM that divides one number by the other, and finds the result of the division as well as the remainder if any.

***Solution*** Let us represent the numbers in the unary format using the symbol 1. For example, '3' can be represented as '111' in unary format. Let us assume the initial configuration of the TM as shown in the Fig. 4.15.

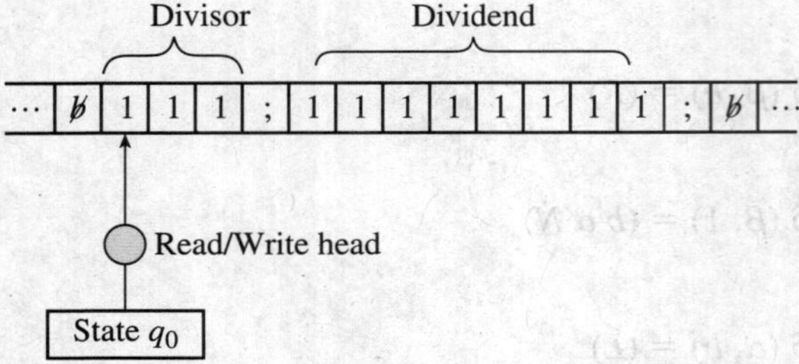


**Figure 4.15** Initial configuration of a TM that performs number division

We observe that the initial state of the TM is $q_0$; and that the divisor and dividend are separated by a comma ','. The machine head initially points to the start of the divisor.

After the division is performed, when the machine halts, the result of the division, which is also represented in unary format using the symbol 1, is written onto the tape immediately after the right end-marker ';'. The number of $a$'s in the divisor area represents the remainder of the division.

**Algorithm**

Division is repetitive subtraction of the divisor from the dividend. In the previous example, we have used repetitive subtraction to find the GCD of two numbers. Similarly, in Example 4.8, we designed a TM that compares two positive integers using subtraction. We now use a similar algorithm for division.

Replace one 1 of the divisor by *a*; and for each *a* in the divisor, replace one 1 of the dividend by *b*. Repeat the process until the whole divisor is subtracted from the dividend. Write 1 at the right end indicating that one cycle of subtraction is complete.

Iteratively, subtract the divisor again from the dividend till you have exhausted the dividend completely. At the end of every iteration, write 1 at the right end; after all the iterations are completed, the number of 1's at the right end represents the result of the division.

If the entire divisor cannot be subtracted from the dividend, then the number of *a*'s that replaces the 1's from the divisor represents the remainder of the division.

The SFM for the TM is as shown in Table 4.14.

**Table 4.14** SFM for a TM that performs number division

| S \ I | 1 | , | ; | $\not b$ | $a$ | $b$ |
|---|---|---|---|---|---|---|
| $q_0$ | $aq_1R$ | $q_4R$ | — | — | — | — |
| $q_1$ | $R$ | $q_2R$ | — | — | — | — |
| $q_2$ | $bq_3L$ | — | $q_7L$ | — | — | $R$ |
| $q_3$ | $L$ | $L$ | — | — | $q_0R$ | $L$ |
| $q_4$ | $R$ | — | $R$ | $1q_5R$ | — | $R$ |
| $q_5$ | $L$ | $q_6L$ | $L$ | — | — | $L$ |
| $q_6$ | — | — | — | $q_0R$ | $1L$ | — |
| $q_7$ | — | $q_8L$ | — | — | — | $L$ |
| $q_8$ | $L$ | — | — | — | $1q_9N$ | — |
| $q_9$ | — | — | — | — | — | — |

For this TM, we have:

$I = \{1, , , ; , \not b, a, b\}$
$S = \{q_0, q_1, q_2, q_3, q_4, q_5, q_6, q_7, q_8, q_9 = \text{halt}\}$
$D = \{L, R, N\}$

***Simulation***

Let us simulate the working of TM for

Divisor = 3 = '111'
Dividend = 8 = '11111111'

$\ldots \not b\, 1\, 1\, 1\, ,\, 1\, 1\, 1\, 1\, 1\, 1\, 1\, 1\, ;\, \not b \ldots$ initial configuration
$\uparrow$
$q_0$

$\ldots \not b\, a\, 1\, 1\, ,\, 1\, 1\, 1\, 1\, 1\, 1\, 1\, 1\, ;\, \not b \ldots$ $\delta(q_0, 1) = (a\, q_1\, R)$
$\uparrow$
$q_1$

(Subtraction of the divisor from dividend begins)

$\ldots \not{b}\, a\, 1\, 1\, ,\, 1\, 1\, 1\, 1\, 1\, 1\, 1\, 1\, ;\, \not{b} \ldots$ $\qquad \delta\,(q_1, 1) = (R)$
↑ $q_1$

$\ldots \not{b}\, a\, 1\, 1\, ,\, 1\, 1\, 1\, 1\, 1\, 1\, 1\, 1\, ;\, \not{b} \ldots$ $\qquad \delta\,(q_1, 1) = (R)$
↑ $q_1$

$\ldots \not{b}\, a\, 1\, 1\, ,\, 1\, 1\, 1\, 1\, 1\, 1\, 1\, 1\, ;\, \not{b} \ldots$ $\qquad \delta\,(q_1, ,) = (q_2\, R)$
↑ $q_2$

$\ldots \not{b}\, a\, 1\, 1\, ,\, b\, 1\, 1\, 1\, 1\, 1\, 1\, 1\, ;\, \not{b} \ldots$ $\qquad \delta\,(q_2, 1) = (b\, q_3\, L)$
↑ $q_3$

$\ldots \not{b}\, a\, 1\, 1\, ,\, b\, 1\, 1\, 1\, 1\, 1\, 1\, 1\, ;\, \not{b} \ldots$ $\qquad \delta\,(q_3, ,) = (L)$
↑ $q_3$

$\ldots \not{b}\, a\, 1\, 1\, ,\, b\, 1\, 1\, 1\, 1\, 1\, 1\, 1\, ;\, \not{b} \ldots$ $\qquad \delta\,(q_3, 1) = (L)$
↑ $q_3$

$\ldots \not{b}\, a\, 1\, 1\, ,\, b\, 1\, 1\, 1\, 1\, 1\, 1\, 1\, ;\, \not{b} \ldots$ $\qquad \delta\,(q_3, 1) = (L)$
↑ $q_3$

$\ldots \not{b}\, a\, 1\, 1\, ,\, b\, 1\, 1\, 1\, 1\, 1\, 1\, 1\, ;\, \not{b} \ldots$ $\qquad \delta\,(q_3, a) = (q_0\, R)$
↑ $q_0$

$\ldots \not{b}\, a\, a\, 1\, ,\, b\, 1\, 1\, 1\, 1\, 1\, 1\, 1\, ;\, \not{b} \ldots$ $\qquad \delta\,(q_0, 1) = (a\, q_1\, R)$
↑ $q_1$

$\ldots \not{b}\, a\, a\, 1\, ,\, b\, 1\, 1\, 1\, 1\, 1\, 1\, 1\, ;\, \not{b} \ldots$ $\qquad \delta\,(q_1, 1) = (R)$
↑ $q_1$

$\ldots \not{b}\, a\, a\, 1\, ,\, b\, 1\, 1\, 1\, 1\, 1\, 1\, 1\, ;\, \not{b} \ldots$ $\qquad \delta\,(q_1, ,) = (q_2\, R)$
↑ $q_2$

$\ldots \not{b}\, a\, a\, 1\, ,\, b\, 1\, 1\, 1\, 1\, 1\, 1\, 1\, ;\, \not{b} \ldots$ $\qquad \delta\,(q_2, b) = (R)$
↑ $q_2$

$\ldots \not{b}\, a\, a\, 1\, ,\, b\, b\, 1\, 1\, 1\, 1\, 1\, 1\, ;\, \not{b} \ldots$ $\qquad \delta\,(q_2, 1) = (b\, q_3\, L)$
↑ $q_3$

$\ldots \not{b}\, a\, a\, 1\, ,\, b\, b\, 1\, 1\, 1\, 1\, 1\, 1\, ;\, \not{b} \ldots$ $\qquad \delta\,(q_3, b) = (L)$
↑ $q_3$

$\ldots \not{b}\, a\, a\, 1\, ,\, b\, b\, 1\, 1\, 1\, 1\, 1\, 1\, ;\, \not{b} \ldots$ $\qquad \delta\,(q_3, ,) = (L)$
↑ $q_3$

$\ldots \not{b}\, a\, a\, 1\, ,\, b\, b\, 1\, 1\, 1\, 1\, 1\, 1\, ;\, \not{b} \ldots$ $\qquad \delta\,(q_3, 1) = (L)$
↑ $q_3$

$\ldots \not{b}\, a\, a\, 1\, ,\, b\, b\, 1\, 1\, 1\, 1\, 1\, 1\, ;\, \not{b} \ldots \qquad \delta\,(q_3, a) = (q_0\, R)$
$\uparrow$
$q_0$

$\ldots \not{b}\, a\, a\, a\, ,\, b\, b\, 1\, 1\, 1\, 1\, 1\, 1\, ;\, \not{b} \ldots \qquad \delta\,(q_0, 1) = (a\, q_1\, R)$
$\uparrow$
$q_1$

$\ldots \not{b}\, a\, a\, a\, ,\, b\, b\, 1\, 1\, 1\, 1\, 1\, 1\, ;\, \not{b} \ldots \qquad \delta\,(q_1, ,) = (q_2\, R)$
$\uparrow$
$q_2$

$\ldots \not{b}\, a\, a\, a\, ,\, b\, b\, 1\, 1\, 1\, 1\, 1\, 1\, ;\, \not{b} \ldots \qquad \delta\,(q_2, b) = (R)$
$\uparrow$
$q_2$

$\ldots \not{b}\, a\, a\, a\, ,\, b\, b\, 1\, 1\, 1\, 1\, 1\, 1\, ;\, \not{b} \ldots \qquad \delta\,(q_2, b) = (R)$
$\uparrow$
$q_2$

$\ldots \not{b}\, a\, a\, a\, ,\, b\, b\, b\, 1\, 1\, 1\, 1\, 1\, ;\, \not{b} \ldots \qquad \delta\,(q_2, 1) = (b\, q_3\, L)$
$\uparrow$
$q_3$

(One round of subtraction is complete)

$\ldots \not{b}\, a\, a\, a\, ,\, b\, b\, b\, 1\, 1\, 1\, 1\, 1\, ;\, \not{b} \ldots \qquad \delta\,(q_3, b) = (L)$
$\uparrow$
$q_3$

$\ldots \not{b}\, a\, a\, a\, ,\, b\, b\, b\, 1\, 1\, 1\, 1\, 1\, ;\, \not{b} \ldots \qquad \delta\,(q_3, b) = (L)$
$\uparrow$
$q_3$

$\ldots \not{b}\, a\, a\, a\, ,\, b\, b\, b\, 1\, 1\, 1\, 1\, 1\, ;\, \not{b} \ldots \qquad \delta\,(q_3, ,) = (L)$
$\uparrow$
$q_3$

$\ldots \not{b}\, a\, a\, a\, ,\, b\, b\, b\, 1\, 1\, 1\, 1\, 1\, ;\, \not{b} \ldots \qquad \delta\,(q_3, a) = (q_0\, R)$
$\uparrow$
$q_0$

$\ldots \not{b}\, a\, a\, a\, ,\, b\, b\, b\, 1\, 1\, 1\, 1\, 1\, ;\, \not{b} \ldots \qquad \delta\,(q_0, ,) = (q_4\, R)$
$\uparrow$
$q_4$

$\ldots \not{b}\, a\, a\, a\, ,\, b\, b\, b\, 1\, 1\, 1\, 1\, 1\, ;\, \not{b} \ldots \qquad \delta\,(q_4, b) = (R)$
$\uparrow$
$q_4$

$\ldots \not{b}\, a\, a\, a\, ,\, b\, b\, b\, 1\, 1\, 1\, 1\, 1\, ;\, \not{b} \ldots \qquad \delta\,(q_4, b) = (R)$
$\uparrow$
$q_4$

$\ldots \not{b}\, a\, a\, a\, ,\, b\, b\, b\, 1\, 1\, 1\, 1\, 1\, ;\, \not{b} \ldots \qquad \delta\,(q_4, b) = (R)$
$\uparrow$
$q_4$

$\ldots \not{b}\, a\, a\, a\, ,\, b\, b\, b\, 1\, 1\, 1\, 1\, 1\, ;\, \not{b} \ldots \qquad \delta\,(q_4, 1) = (R)$
$\uparrow$
$q_4$

```
... b̸ a a a , b b b 1 1 1 1 1 ; b̸ ...        δ (q4, 1) = (R)
                      ↑
                      q4
... b̸ a a a , b b b 1 1 1 1 1 ; b̸ ...        δ (q4, 1) = (R)
                        ↑
                        q4
... b̸ a a a , b b b 1 1 1 1 1 ; b̸ ...        δ (q4, 1) = (R)
                          ↑
                          q4
... b̸ a a a , b b b 1 1 1 1 1 ; b̸ ...        δ (q4, 1) = (R)
                            ↑
                            q4
... b̸ a a a , b b b 1 1 1 1 1 ; b̸ ...        δ (q4, ;) = (R)
                              ↑
                              q4
... b̸ a a a , b b b 1 1 1 1 1 ; 1 b̸ ...      δ (q4, b̸) = (1 q5 L)
                              ↑
                              q5
```

(1 is written to the result area as one round of subtraction is complete)

```
... b̸ a a a , b b b 1 1 1 1 1 ; 1 b̸ ...      δ (q5, ;) = (L)
                            ↑
                            q5
... b̸ a a a , b b b 1 1 1 1 1 ; 1 b̸ ...      δ (q5, 1) = (L)
                          ↑
                          q5
... b̸ a a a , b b b 1 1 1 1 1 ; 1 b̸ ...      δ (q5, 1) = (L)
                        ↑
                        q5
... b̸ a a a , b b b 1 1 1 1 1 ; 1 b̸ ...      δ (q5, 1) = (L)
                      ↑
                      q5
... b̸ a a a , b b b 1 1 1 1 1 ; 1 b̸ ...      δ (q5, 1) = (L)
                    ↑
                    q5
... b̸ a a a , b b b 1 1 1 1 1 ; 1 b̸ ...      δ (q5, 1) = (L)
                  ↑
                  q5
... b̸ a a a , b b b 1 1 1 1 1 ; 1 b̸ ...      δ (q5, b) = (L)
                ↑
                q5
... b̸ a a a , b b b 1 1 1 1 1 ; 1 b̸ ...      δ (q5, b) = (L)
              ↑
              q5
... b̸ a a a , b b b 1 1 1 1 1 ; 1 b̸ ...      δ (q5, b) = (L)
            ↑
            q5
... b̸ a a a , b b b 1 1 1 1 1 ; 1 b̸ ...      δ (q5, ,) = (q6 L)
          ↑
          q6
```

$\dots \not b\ a\ a\ 1\ ,\ b\ b\ b\ 1\ 1\ 1\ 1\ 1\ ;\ 1\ \not b \dots \qquad \delta(q_6, a) = (1\ L)$

$\uparrow q_6$

$\dots \not b\ a\ 1\ 1\ ,\ b\ b\ b\ 1\ 1\ 1\ 1\ 1\ ;\ 1\ \not b \dots \qquad \delta(q_6, a) = (1\ L)$

$\uparrow q_6$

$\dots \not b\ 1\ 1\ 1\ ,\ b\ b\ b\ 1\ 1\ 1\ 1\ 1\ ;\ 1\ \not b \dots \qquad \delta(q_6, a) = (1\ L)$

$\uparrow q_6$

(Divisor is retrieved by replacing all *a*'s by 1's; it is now ready for the next iteration)

$\dots \not b\ 1\ 1\ 1\ ,\ b\ b\ b\ 1\ 1\ 1\ 1\ 1\ ;\ 1\ \not b \dots \qquad \delta(q_6, \not b) = (q_0\ R)$

$\uparrow q_0$

$\dots \not b\ a\ 1\ 1\ ,\ b\ b\ b\ 1\ 1\ 1\ 1\ 1\ ;\ 1\ \not b \dots \qquad \delta(q_0, 1) = (a\ q_1\ R)$

$\uparrow q_1$

(Subtraction of the divisor from the dividend begins for the second time)

$\dots \not b\ a\ 1\ 1\ ,\ b\ b\ b\ 1\ 1\ 1\ 1\ 1\ ;\ 1\ \not b \dots \qquad \delta(q_1, 1) = (R)$

$\uparrow q_1$

$\dots \not b\ a\ 1\ 1\ ,\ b\ b\ b\ 1\ 1\ 1\ 1\ 1\ ;\ 1\ \not b \dots \qquad \delta(q_1, 1) = (R)$

$\uparrow q_1$

$\dots \not b\ a\ 1\ 1\ ,\ b\ b\ b\ 1\ 1\ 1\ 1\ 1\ ;\ 1\ \not b \dots \qquad \delta(q_1, ,) = (q_2\ R)$

$\uparrow q_2$

$\dots \not b\ a\ 1\ 1\ ,\ b\ b\ b\ 1\ 1\ 1\ 1\ 1\ ;\ 1\ \not b \dots \qquad \delta(q_2, b) = (R)$

$\uparrow q_2$

$\dots \not b\ a\ 1\ 1\ ,\ b\ b\ b\ 1\ 1\ 1\ 1\ 1\ ;\ 1\ \not b \dots \qquad \delta(q_2, b) = (R)$

$\uparrow q_2$

$\dots \not b\ a\ 1\ 1\ ,\ b\ b\ b\ 1\ 1\ 1\ 1\ 1\ ;\ 1\ \not b \dots \qquad \delta(q_2, b) = (R)$

$\uparrow q_2$

$\dots \not b\ a\ 1\ 1\ ,\ b\ b\ b\ b\ 1\ 1\ 1\ 1\ ;\ 1\ \not b \dots \qquad \delta(q_2, 1) = (b\ q_3\ L)$

$\uparrow q_3$

$\dots \not b\ a\ 1\ 1\ ,\ b\ b\ b\ b\ 1\ 1\ 1\ 1\ ;\ 1\ \not b \dots \qquad \delta(q_3, b) = (L)$

$\uparrow q_3$

$\dots \not b\ a\ 1\ 1\ ,\ b\ b\ b\ b\ 1\ 1\ 1\ 1\ ;\ 1\ \not b \dots \qquad \delta(q_3, b) = (L)$

$\uparrow q_3$

$\dots \not b\ a\ 1\ 1\ ,\ b\ b\ b\ b\ 1\ 1\ 1\ 1\ ;\ 1\ \not b \dots \qquad \delta(q_3, b) = (L)$

$\uparrow q_3$

$$\ldots \not{b}\; a\; 1\; \underset{\underset{q_3}{\uparrow}}{1}\; ,\; b\; b\; b\; b\; 1\; 1\; 1\; 1\; ;\; 1\; \not{b} \ldots \qquad \delta(q_3, ,) = (L)$$

$$\ldots \not{b}\; a\; \underset{\underset{q_3}{\uparrow}}{1}\; 1\; ,\; b\; b\; b\; b\; 1\; 1\; 1\; 1\; ;\; 1\; \not{b} \ldots \qquad \delta(q_3, 1) = (L)$$

$$\ldots \not{b}\; \underset{\underset{q_3}{\uparrow}}{a}\; 1\; 1\; ,\; b\; b\; b\; b\; 1\; 1\; 1\; 1\; ;\; 1\; \not{b} \ldots \qquad \delta(q_3, 1) = (L)$$

$$\ldots \not{b}\; a\; \underset{\underset{q_0}{\uparrow}}{1}\; 1\; ,\; b\; b\; b\; b\; 1\; 1\; 1\; 1\; ;\; 1\; \not{b} \ldots \qquad \delta(q_3, a) = (q_0\, R)$$

$$\ldots \not{b}\; a\; a\; \underset{\underset{q_1}{\uparrow}}{1}\; ,\; b\; b\; b\; b\; 1\; 1\; 1\; 1\; ;\; 1\; \not{b} \ldots \qquad \delta(q_0, 1) = (a\, q_1\, R)$$

$$\ldots \not{b}\; a\; a\; 1\; \underset{\underset{q_1}{\uparrow}}{,}\; b\; b\; b\; b\; 1\; 1\; 1\; 1\; ;\; 1\; \not{b} \ldots \qquad \delta(q_1, 1) = (R)$$

$$\ldots \not{b}\; a\; a\; 1\; ,\; \underset{\underset{q_2}{\uparrow}}{b}\; b\; b\; b\; 1\; 1\; 1\; 1\; ;\; 1\; \not{b} \ldots \qquad \delta(q_1, ,) = (q_2\, R)$$

$$\ldots \not{b}\; a\; a\; 1\; ,\; b\; \underset{\underset{q_2}{\uparrow}}{b}\; b\; b\; 1\; 1\; 1\; 1\; ;\; 1\; \not{b} \ldots \qquad \delta(q_2, b) = (R)$$

$$\ldots \not{b}\; a\; a\; 1\; ,\; b\; b\; \underset{\underset{q_2}{\uparrow}}{b}\; b\; 1\; 1\; 1\; 1\; ;\; 1\; \not{b} \ldots \qquad \delta(q_2, b) = (R)$$

$$\ldots \not{b}\; a\; a\; 1\; ,\; b\; b\; b\; \underset{\underset{q_2}{\uparrow}}{b}\; 1\; 1\; 1\; 1\; ;\; 1\; \not{b} \ldots \qquad \delta(q_2, b) = (R)$$

$$\ldots \not{b}\; a\; a\; 1\; ,\; b\; b\; b\; b\; \underset{\underset{q_2}{\uparrow}}{1}\; 1\; 1\; 1\; ;\; 1\; \not{b} \ldots \qquad \delta(q_2, b) = (R)$$

$$\ldots \not{b}\; a\; a\; 1\; ,\; b\; b\; b\; \underset{\underset{q_3}{\uparrow}}{b}\; b\; 1\; 1\; 1\; ;\; 1\; \not{b} \ldots \qquad \delta(q_2, 1) = (b\, q_3\, L)$$

$$\ldots \not{b}\; a\; a\; 1\; ,\; b\; b\; \underset{\underset{q_3}{\uparrow}}{b}\; b\; b\; 1\; 1\; 1\; ;\; 1\; \not{b} \ldots \qquad \delta(q_3, b) = (L)$$

$$\ldots \not{b}\; a\; a\; 1\; ,\; b\; \underset{\underset{q_3}{\uparrow}}{b}\; b\; b\; b\; 1\; 1\; 1\; ;\; 1\; \not{b} \ldots \qquad \delta(q_3, b) = (L)$$

$$\ldots \not{b}\; a\; a\; 1\; ,\; \underset{\underset{q_3}{\uparrow}}{b}\; b\; b\; b\; b\; 1\; 1\; 1\; ;\; 1\; \not{b} \ldots \qquad \delta(q_3, b) = (L)$$

$$\ldots \not{b}\; a\; a\; 1\; \underset{\underset{q_3}{\uparrow}}{,}\; b\; b\; b\; b\; b\; 1\; 1\; 1\; ;\; 1\; \not{b} \ldots \qquad \delta(q_3, b) = (L)$$

$$\ldots\ \not{b}\ a\ a\ \underset{\substack{\uparrow\\ q_3}}{1}\ ,\ b\ b\ b\ b\ b\ 1\ 1\ 1\ ;\ 1\ \not{b}\ \ldots \qquad \delta\,(q_3, ,) = (L)$$

$$\ldots\ \not{b}\ a\ \underset{\substack{\uparrow\\ q_3}}{a}\ 1\ ,\ b\ b\ b\ b\ b\ 1\ 1\ 1\ ;\ 1\ \not{b}\ \ldots \qquad \delta\,(q_3, 1) = (L)$$

$$\ldots\ \not{b}\ a\ a\ \underset{\substack{\uparrow\\ q_0}}{1}\ ,\ b\ b\ b\ b\ b\ 1\ 1\ 1\ ;\ 1\ \not{b}\ \ldots \qquad \delta\,(q_3, a) = (q_0\, R)$$

$$\ldots\ \not{b}\ a\ a\ a\ \underset{\substack{\uparrow\\ q_1}}{,}\ b\ b\ b\ b\ b\ 1\ 1\ 1\ ;\ 1\ \not{b}\ \ldots \qquad \delta\,(q_0, 1) = (a\, q_1\, R)$$

$$\ldots\ \not{b}\ a\ a\ a\ ,\ \underset{\substack{\uparrow\\ q_2}}{b}\ b\ b\ b\ b\ 1\ 1\ 1\ ;\ 1\ \not{b}\ \ldots \qquad \delta\,(q_1, ,) = (q_2\, R)$$

$$\ldots\ \not{b}\ a\ a\ a\ ,\ b\ \underset{\substack{\uparrow\\ q_2}}{b}\ b\ b\ b\ 1\ 1\ 1\ ;\ 1\ \not{b}\ \ldots \qquad \delta\,(q_2, b) = (R)$$

$$\ldots\ \not{b}\ a\ a\ a\ ,\ b\ b\ \underset{\substack{\uparrow\\ q_2}}{b}\ b\ b\ 1\ 1\ 1\ ;\ 1\ \not{b}\ \ldots \qquad \delta\,(q_2, b) = (R)$$

$$\ldots\ \not{b}\ a\ a\ a\ ,\ b\ b\ b\ \underset{\substack{\uparrow\\ q_2}}{b}\ b\ 1\ 1\ 1\ ;\ 1\ \not{b}\ \ldots \qquad \delta\,(q_2, b) = (R)$$

$$\ldots\ \not{b}\ a\ a\ a\ ,\ b\ b\ b\ b\ \underset{\substack{\uparrow\\ q_2}}{b}\ 1\ 1\ 1\ ;\ 1\ \not{b}\ \ldots \qquad \delta\,(q_2, b) = (R)$$

$$\ldots\ \not{b}\ a\ a\ a\ ,\ b\ b\ b\ b\ b\ \underset{\substack{\uparrow\\ q_2}}{1}\ 1\ 1\ ;\ 1\ \not{b}\ \ldots \qquad \delta\,(q_2, b) = (R)$$

$$\ldots\ \not{b}\ a\ a\ a\ ,\ b\ b\ b\ b\ \underset{\substack{\uparrow\\ q_3}}{b}\ b\ 1\ 1\ ;\ 1\ \not{b}\ \ldots \qquad \delta\,(q_2, 1) = (b\, q_3\, L)$$

$$\ldots\ \not{b}\ a\ a\ a\ ,\ b\ b\ b\ \underset{\substack{\uparrow\\ q_3}}{b}\ b\ b\ 1\ 1\ ;\ 1\ \not{b}\ \ldots \qquad \delta\,(q_3, b) = (L)$$

$$\ldots\ \not{b}\ a\ a\ a\ ,\ b\ b\ \underset{\substack{\uparrow\\ q_3}}{b}\ b\ b\ b\ 1\ 1\ ;\ 1\ \not{b}\ \ldots \qquad \delta\,(q_3, b) = (L)$$

$$\ldots\ \not{b}\ a\ a\ a\ ,\ b\ \underset{\substack{\uparrow\\ q_3}}{b}\ b\ b\ b\ b\ 1\ 1\ ;\ 1\ \not{b}\ \ldots \qquad \delta\,(q_3, b) = (L)$$

$$\ldots\ \not{b}\ a\ a\ a\ ,\ \underset{\substack{\uparrow\\ q_3}}{b}\ b\ b\ b\ b\ b\ 1\ 1\ ;\ 1\ \not{b}\ \ldots \qquad \delta\,(q_3, b) = (L)$$

$$\ldots\ \not{b}\ a\ a\ a\ \underset{\substack{\uparrow\\ q_3}}{,}\ b\ b\ b\ b\ b\ b\ 1\ 1\ ;\ 1\ \not{b}\ \ldots \qquad \delta\,(q_3, b) = (L)$$

$\ldots \not{b}\; a\, a\, a\, ,\, b\, b\, b\, b\, b\, b\, 1\, 1\, ;\, 1\, \not{b} \ldots$ $\qquad \delta\,(q_3, ,) = (L)$

$\uparrow$
$q_3$

$\ldots \not{b}\; a\, a\, a\, ,\, b\, b\, b\, b\, b\, b\, 1\, 1\, ;\, 1\, \not{b} \ldots$ $\qquad \delta\,(q_3, a) = (q_0\, R)$

$\uparrow$
$q_0$

(Second round of subtraction is complete)

$\ldots \not{b}\; a\, a\, a\, ,\, b\, b\, b\, b\, b\, b\, 1\, 1\, ;\, 1\, \not{b} \ldots$ $\qquad \delta\,(q_0, ,) = (q_4\, R)$

$\uparrow$
$q_4$

$\ldots \not{b}\; a\, a\, a\, ,\, b\, b\, b\, b\, b\, b\, 1\, 1\, ;\, 1\, \not{b} \ldots$ $\qquad \delta\,(q_4, b) = (R)$

$\uparrow$
$q_4$

$\ldots \not{b}\; a\, a\, a\, ,\, b\, b\, b\, b\, b\, b\, 1\, 1\, ;\, 1\, \not{b} \ldots$ $\qquad \delta\,(q_4, b) = (R)$

$\uparrow$
$q_4$

$\ldots \not{b}\; a\, a\, a\, ,\, b\, b\, b\, b\, b\, b\, 1\, 1\, ;\, 1\, \not{b} \ldots$ $\qquad \delta\,(q_4, b) = (R)$

$\uparrow$
$q_4$

$\ldots \not{b}\; a\, a\, a\, ,\, b\, b\, b\, b\, b\, b\, 1\, 1\, ;\, 1\, \not{b} \ldots$ $\qquad \delta\,(q_4, b) = (R)$

$\uparrow$
$q_4$

$\ldots \not{b}\; a\, a\, a\, ,\, b\, b\, b\, b\, b\, b\, 1\, 1\, ;\, 1\, \not{b} \ldots$ $\qquad \delta\,(q_4, b) = (R)$

$\uparrow$
$q_4$

$\ldots \not{b}\; a\, a\, a\, ,\, b\, b\, b\, b\, b\, b\, 1\, 1\, ;\, 1\, \not{b} \ldots$ $\qquad \delta\,(q_4, b) = (R)$

$\uparrow$
$q_4$

$\ldots \not{b}\; a\, a\, a\, ,\, b\, b\, b\, b\, b\, b\, 1\, 1\, ;\, 1\, \not{b} \ldots$ $\qquad \delta\,(q_4, 1) = (R)$

$\uparrow$
$q_4$

$\ldots \not{b}\; a\, a\, a\, ,\, b\, b\, b\, b\, b\, b\, 1\, 1\, ;\, 1\, \not{b} \ldots$ $\qquad \delta\,(q_4, 1) = (R)$

$\uparrow$
$q_4$

$\ldots \not{b}\; a\, a\, a\, ,\, b\, b\, b\, b\, b\, b\, 1\, 1\, ;\, 1\, \not{b} \ldots$ $\qquad \delta\,(q_4, ;) = (R)$

$\uparrow$
$q_4$

$\ldots \not{b}\; a\, a\, a\, ,\, b\, b\, b\, b\, b\, b\, 1\, 1\, ;\, 1\, \not{b} \ldots$ $\qquad \delta\,(q_4, 1) = (R)$

$\uparrow$
$q_4$

$\ldots \not{b}\; a\, a\, a\, ,\, b\, b\, b\, b\, b\, b\, 1\, 1\, ;\, 1\, 1\, \not{b} \ldots$ $\qquad \delta\,(q_4, \not{b}) = (1\, q_5\, L)$

$\uparrow$
$q_5$

(One more 1 is written to the result area as second subtraction round is complete)

$\ldots \not{b}\; a\, a\, a\, ,\, b\, b\, b\, b\, b\, b\, 1\, 1\, ;\, 1\, 1\, \not{b} \ldots$ $\qquad \delta\,(q_5, 1) = (L)$

$\uparrow$
$q_5$

… ƀ a a a , b b b b b b 1 1 ; 1 1 ƀ … $\delta(q_5, ;) = (L)$
↑
$q_5$

… ƀ a a a , b b b b b b 1 1 ; 1 1 ƀ … $\delta(q_5, 1) = (L)$
↑
$q_5$

… ƀ a a a , b b b b b b 1 1 ; 1 1 ƀ … $\delta(q_5, 1) = (L)$
↑
$q_5$

… ƀ a a a , b b b b b b 1 1 ; 1 1 ƀ … $\delta(q_5, b) = (L)$
↑
$q_5$

… ƀ a a a , b b b b b b 1 1 ; 1 1 ƀ … $\delta(q_5, b) = (L)$
↑
$q_5$

… ƀ a a a , b b b b b b 1 1 ; 1 1 ƀ … $\delta(q_5, b) = (L)$
↑
$q_5$

… ƀ a a a , b b b b b b 1 1 ; 1 1 ƀ … $\delta(q_5, b) = (L)$
↑
$q_5$

… ƀ a a a , b b b b b b 1 1 ; 1 1 ƀ … $\delta(q_5, b) = (L)$
↑
$q_5$

… ƀ a a a , b b b b b b 1 1 ; 1 1 ƀ … $\delta(q_5, b) = (L)$
↑
$q_5$

… ƀ a a a , b b b b b b 1 1 ; 1 1 ƀ … $\delta(q_5, ,) = (q_6 L)$
↑
$q_6$

… ƀ a a 1 , b b b b b b 1 1 ; 1 1 ƀ … $\delta(q_6, a) = (1\,L)$
↑
$q_6$

… ƀ a 1 1 , b b b b b b 1 1 ; 1 1 ƀ … $\delta(q_6, a) = (1\,L)$
↑
$q_6$

… ƀ 1 1 1 , b b b b b b 1 1 ; 1 1 ƀ … $\delta(q_6, a) = (1\,L)$
↑
$q_6$

(Divisor is retrieved by replacing all *a*'s with 1's; it is now ready for the next iteration)

… ƀ 1 1 1 , b b b b b b 1 1 ; 1 1 ƀ ƀ … $\delta(q_6, ƀ) = (q_0 R)$
↑
$q_0$

… ƀ a 1 1 , b b b b b b 1 1 ; 1 1 ƀ … $\delta(q_0, 1) = (a\, q_1 R)$
↑
$q_1$

(Subtraction of the divisor from dividend begins for the third time)

$$\ldots \not{b}\; a\; 1\; \underset{\substack{\uparrow\\ q_1}}{1}\; ,\; b\; b\; b\; b\; b\; b\; 1\; 1\; ;\; 1\; 1\; \not{b} \ldots \qquad \delta\,(q_1, 1) = (R)$$

$$\ldots \not{b}\; a\; 1\; 1\; \underset{\substack{\uparrow\\ q_1}}{,}\; b\; b\; b\; b\; b\; b\; 1\; 1\; ;\; 1\; 1\; \not{b} \ldots \qquad \delta\,(q_1, 1) = (R)$$

$$\ldots \not{b}\; a\; 1\; 1\; ,\; \underset{\substack{\uparrow\\ q_2}}{b}\; b\; b\; b\; b\; b\; 1\; 1\; ;\; 1\; 1\; \not{b} \ldots \qquad \delta\,(q_1, ,) = (q_2\, R)$$

$$\ldots \not{b}\; a\; 1\; 1\; ,\; b\; \underset{\substack{\uparrow\\ q_2}}{b}\; b\; b\; b\; b\; 1\; 1\; ;\; 1\; 1\; \not{b} \ldots \qquad \delta\,(q_2, b) = (R)$$

$$\ldots \not{b}\; a\; 1\; 1\; ,\; b\; b\; \underset{\substack{\uparrow\\ q_2}}{b}\; b\; b\; b\; 1\; 1\; ;\; 1\; 1\; \not{b} \ldots \qquad \delta\,(q_2, b) = (R)$$

$$\ldots \not{b}\; a\; 1\; 1\; ,\; b\; b\; b\; \underset{\substack{\uparrow\\ q_2}}{b}\; b\; b\; 1\; 1\; ;\; 1\; 1\; \not{b} \ldots \qquad \delta\,(q_2, b) = (R)$$

$$\ldots \not{b}\; a\; 1\; 1\; ,\; b\; b\; b\; b\; \underset{\substack{\uparrow\\ q_2}}{b}\; b\; 1\; 1\; ;\; 1\; 1\; \not{b} \ldots \qquad \delta\,(q_2, b) = (R)$$

$$\ldots \not{b}\; a\; 1\; 1\; ,\; b\; b\; b\; b\; b\; \underset{\substack{\uparrow\\ q_2}}{b}\; 1\; 1\; ;\; 1\; 1\; \not{b} \ldots \qquad \delta\,(q_2, b) = (R)$$

$$\ldots \not{b}\; a\; 1\; 1\; ,\; b\; b\; b\; b\; b\; b\; \underset{\substack{\uparrow\\ q_2}}{1}\; 1\; ;\; 1\; 1\; \not{b} \ldots \qquad \delta\,(q_2, b) = (R)$$

$$\ldots \not{b}\; a\; 1\; 1\; ,\; b\; b\; b\; b\; b\; \underset{\substack{\uparrow\\ q_3}}{b}\; b\; 1\; ;\; 1\; 1\; \not{b} \ldots \qquad \delta\,(q_2, 1) = (b\; q_3\; L)$$

$$\ldots \not{b}\; a\; 1\; 1\; ,\; b\; b\; b\; b\; \underset{\substack{\uparrow\\ q_3}}{b}\; b\; b\; 1\; ;\; 1\; 1\; \not{b} \ldots \qquad \delta\,(q_3, b) = (L)$$

$$\ldots \not{b}\; a\; 1\; 1\; ,\; b\; b\; b\; \underset{\substack{\uparrow\\ q_3}}{b}\; b\; b\; b\; 1\; ;\; 1\; 1\; \not{b} \ldots \qquad \delta\,(q_3, b) = (L)$$

$$\ldots \not{b}\; a\; 1\; 1\; ,\; b\; b\; \underset{\substack{\uparrow\\ q_3}}{b}\; b\; b\; b\; b\; 1\; ;\; 1\; 1\; \not{b} \ldots \qquad \delta\,(q_3, b) = (L)$$

$$\ldots \not{b}\; a\; 1\; 1\; ,\; b\; \underset{\substack{\uparrow\\ q_3}}{b}\; b\; b\; b\; b\; b\; 1\; ;\; 1\; 1\; \not{b} \ldots \qquad \delta\,(q_3, b) = (L)$$

$$\ldots \not{b}\; a\; 1\; 1\; ,\; \underset{\substack{\uparrow\\ q_3}}{b}\; b\; b\; b\; b\; b\; b\; 1\; ;\; 1\; 1\; \not{b} \ldots \qquad \delta\,(q_3, b) = (L)$$

$$\ldots \not{b}\; a\; 1\; 1\; \underset{\substack{\uparrow\\ q_3}}{,}\; b\; b\; b\; b\; b\; b\; b\; 1\; ;\; 1\; 1\; \not{b} \ldots \qquad \delta\,(q_3, b) = (L)$$

$$\ldots\ \not b\ a\ 1\ \underset{\substack{\uparrow\\ q_3}}{1}\ ,\ b\ b\ b\ b\ b\ b\ b\ 1\ ;\ 1\ 1\ \not b\ \ldots \qquad \delta\,(q_3, ,) = (L)$$

$$\ldots\ \not b\ a\ \underset{\substack{\uparrow\\ q_3}}{1}\ 1\ ,\ b\ b\ b\ b\ b\ b\ b\ 1\ ;\ 1\ 1\ \not b\ \ldots \qquad \delta\,(q_3, 1) = (L)$$

$$\ldots\ \not b\ \underset{\substack{\uparrow\\ q_3}}{a}\ 1\ 1\ ,\ b\ b\ b\ b\ b\ b\ b\ 1\ ;\ 1\ 1\ \not b\ \ldots \qquad \delta\,(q_3, 1) = (L)$$

$$\ldots\ \not b\ a\ \underset{\substack{\uparrow\\ q_0}}{1}\ 1\ ,\ b\ b\ b\ b\ b\ b\ b\ 1\ ;\ 1\ 1\ \not b\ \ldots \qquad \delta\,(q_3, a) = (q_0\, R)$$

$$\ldots\ \not b\ a\ a\ \underset{\substack{\uparrow\\ q_1}}{1}\ ,\ b\ b\ b\ b\ b\ b\ b\ 1\ ;\ 1\ 1\ \not b\ \ldots \qquad \delta\,(q_0, 1) = (a\, q_1\, R)$$

$$\ldots\ \not b\ a\ a\ 1\ \underset{\substack{\uparrow\\ q_1}}{,}\ b\ b\ b\ b\ b\ b\ b\ 1\ ;\ 1\ 1\ \not b\ \ldots \qquad \delta\,(q_1, 1) = (R)$$

$$\ldots\ \not b\ a\ a\ 1\ ,\ \underset{\substack{\uparrow\\ q_2}}{b}\ b\ b\ b\ b\ b\ b\ 1\ ;\ 1\ 1\ \not b\ \ldots \qquad \delta\,(q_1, ,) = (q_2\, R)$$

$$\ldots\ \not b\ a\ a\ 1\ ,\ b\ \underset{\substack{\uparrow\\ q_2}}{b}\ b\ b\ b\ b\ b\ 1\ ;\ 1\ 1\ \not b\ \ldots \qquad \delta\,(q_2, b) = (R)$$

$$\ldots\ \not b\ a\ a\ 1\ ,\ b\ b\ \underset{\substack{\uparrow\\ q_2}}{b}\ b\ b\ b\ b\ 1\ ;\ 1\ 1\ \not b\ \ldots \qquad \delta\,(q_2, b) = (R)$$

$$\ldots\ \not b\ a\ a\ 1\ ,\ b\ b\ b\ \underset{\substack{\uparrow\\ q_2}}{b}\ b\ b\ b\ 1\ ;\ 1\ 1\ \not b\ \ldots \qquad \delta\,(q_2, b) = (R)$$

$$\ldots\ \not b\ a\ a\ 1\ ,\ b\ b\ b\ b\ \underset{\substack{\uparrow\\ q_2}}{b}\ b\ b\ 1\ ;\ 1\ 1\ \not b\ \ldots \qquad \delta\,(q_2, b) = (R)$$

$$\ldots\ \not b\ a\ a\ 1\ ,\ b\ b\ b\ b\ b\ \underset{\substack{\uparrow\\ q_2}}{b}\ b\ 1\ ;\ 1\ 1\ \not b\ \ldots \qquad \delta\,(q_2, b) = (R)$$

$$\ldots\ \not b\ a\ a\ 1\ ,\ b\ b\ b\ b\ b\ b\ \underset{\substack{\uparrow\\ q_2}}{b}\ 1\ ;\ 1\ 1\ \not b\ \ldots \qquad \delta\,(q_2, b) = (R)$$

$$\ldots\ \not b\ a\ a\ 1\ ,\ b\ b\ b\ b\ b\ b\ b\ \underset{\substack{\uparrow\\ q_2}}{1}\ ;\ 1\ 1\ \not b\ \ldots \qquad \delta\,(q_2, b) = (R)$$

$$\ldots\ \not b\ a\ a\ 1\ ,\ b\ b\ b\ b\ b\ b\ \underset{\substack{\uparrow\\ q_3}}{b}\ b\ ;\ 1\ 1\ \not b\ \ldots \qquad \delta\,(q_2, 1) = (b\, q_3\, L)$$

$$\ldots\ \not b\ a\ a\ 1\ ,\ b\ b\ b\ b\ b\ \underset{\substack{\uparrow\\ q_3}}{b}\ b\ b\ ;\ 1\ 1\ \not b\ \ldots \qquad \delta\,(q_3, b) = (L)$$

$$\ldots \not b\, a\, a\, 1\, ,\, b\, b\, b\, b\, \underset{\substack{\uparrow\\ q_3}}{b}\, b\, b\, b\, ;\, 1\, 1\, \not b \ldots \qquad \delta\,(q_3, b) = (L)$$

$$\ldots \not b\, a\, a\, 1\, ,\, b\, b\, b\, \underset{\substack{\uparrow\\ q_3}}{b}\, b\, b\, b\, b\, ;\, 1\, 1\, \not b \ldots \qquad \delta\,(q_3, b) = (L)$$

$$\ldots \not b\, a\, a\, 1\, ,\, b\, b\, \underset{\substack{\uparrow\\ q_3}}{b}\, b\, b\, b\, b\, b\, ;\, 1\, 1\, \not b \ldots \qquad \delta\,(q_3, b) = (L)$$

$$\ldots \not b\, a\, a\, 1\, ,\, b\, \underset{\substack{\uparrow\\ q_3}}{b}\, b\, b\, b\, b\, b\, b\, ;\, 1\, 1\, \not b \ldots \qquad \delta\,(q_3, b) = (L)$$

$$\ldots \not b\, a\, a\, 1\, ,\, \underset{\substack{\uparrow\\ q_3}}{b}\, b\, b\, b\, b\, b\, b\, b\, ;\, 1\, 1\, \not b \ldots \qquad \delta\,(q_3, b) = (L)$$

$$\ldots \not b\, a\, a\, 1\, \underset{\substack{\uparrow\\ q_3}}{,}\, b\, b\, b\, b\, b\, b\, b\, b\, ;\, 1\, 1\, \not b \ldots \qquad \delta\,(q_3, b) = (L)$$

$$\ldots \not b\, a\, a\, \underset{\substack{\uparrow\\ q_3}}{1}\, ,\, b\, b\, b\, b\, b\, b\, b\, b\, ;\, 1\, 1\, \not b \ldots \qquad \delta\,(q_3, ,) = (L)$$

$$\ldots \not b\, a\, \underset{\substack{\uparrow\\ q_3}}{a}\, 1\, ,\, b\, b\, b\, b\, b\, b\, b\, b\, ;\, 1\, 1\, \not b \ldots \qquad \delta\,(q_3, 1) = (L)$$

$$\ldots \not b\, a\, a\, \underset{\substack{\uparrow\\ q_0}}{1}\, ,\, b\, b\, b\, b\, b\, b\, b\, b\, ;\, 1\, 1\, \not b \ldots \qquad \delta\,(q_3, a) = (q_0\, R)$$

$$\ldots \not b\, a\, a\, a\, \underset{\substack{\uparrow\\ q_1}}{,}\, b\, b\, b\, b\, b\, b\, b\, b\, ;\, 1\, 1\, \not b \ldots \qquad \delta\,(q_0, 1) = (a\, q_1\, R)$$

$$\ldots \not b\, a\, a\, a\, ,\, \underset{\substack{\uparrow\\ q_2}}{b}\, b\, b\, b\, b\, b\, b\, b\, ;\, 1\, 1\, \not b \ldots \qquad \delta\,(q_1, ,) = (q_2\, R)$$

$$\ldots \not b\, a\, a\, a\, ,\, b\, \underset{\substack{\uparrow\\ q_2}}{b}\, b\, b\, b\, b\, b\, b\, ;\, 1\, 1\, \not b \ldots \qquad \delta\,(q_2, b) = (R)$$

$$\ldots \not b\, a\, a\, a\, ,\, b\, b\, \underset{\substack{\uparrow\\ q_2}}{b}\, b\, b\, b\, b\, b\, ;\, 1\, 1\, \not b \ldots \qquad \delta\,(q_2, b) = (R)$$

$$\ldots \not b\, a\, a\, a\, ,\, b\, b\, b\, \underset{\substack{\uparrow\\ q_2}}{b}\, b\, b\, b\, b\, ;\, 1\, 1\, \not b \ldots \qquad \delta\,(q_2, b) = (R)$$

$$\ldots \not b\, a\, a\, a\, ,\, b\, b\, b\, b\, \underset{\substack{\uparrow\\ q_2}}{b}\, b\, b\, b\, ;\, 1\, 1\, \not b \ldots \qquad \delta\,(q_2, b) = (R)$$

$$\ldots \not b\, a\, a\, a\, ,\, b\, b\, b\, b\, b\, \underset{\substack{\uparrow\\ q_2}}{b}\, b\, b\, ;\, 1\, 1\, \not b \ldots \qquad \delta\,(q_2, b) = (R)$$

$$\ldots \not b\, a\, a\, a\, ,\, b\, b\, b\, b\, b\, b\, \underset{\substack{\uparrow\\ q_2}}{b}\, b\, ;\, 1\, 1\, \not b \ldots \qquad \delta\,(q_2, b) = (R)$$

$\ldots \not{b}\, a\, a\, a\, ,\, b\, b\, b\, b\, b\, b\, b\, b\, ;\, 1\, 1\, \not{b} \ldots \quad \delta(q_2, b) = (R)$ (head at the 8th $b$, state $q_2$)

$\ldots \not{b}\, a\, a\, a\, ,\, b\, b\, b\, b\, b\, b\, b\, b\, ;\, 1\, 1\, \not{b} \ldots \quad \delta(q_2, b) = (R)$ (head at ;, state $q_2$)

(Subtraction cannot be completed in the third round)

$\ldots \not{b}\, a\, a\, a\, ,\, b\, b\, b\, b\, b\, b\, b\, b\, ;\, 1\, 1\, \not{b} \ldots \quad \delta(q_2, ;) = (q_7\, L)$ (head at the 8th $b$, state $q_7$)

$\ldots \not{b}\, a\, a\, a\, ,\, b\, b\, b\, b\, b\, b\, b\, b\, ;\, 1\, 1\, \not{b} \ldots \quad \delta(q_7, b) = (L)$ (head at the 7th $b$, state $q_7$)

$\ldots \not{b}\, a\, a\, a\, ,\, b\, b\, b\, b\, b\, b\, b\, b\, ;\, 1\, 1\, \not{b} \ldots \quad \delta(q_7, b) = (L)$ (head at the 6th $b$, state $q_7$)

$\ldots \not{b}\, a\, a\, a\, ,\, b\, b\, b\, b\, b\, b\, b\, b\, ;\, 1\, 1\, \not{b} \ldots \quad \delta(q_7, b) = (L)$ (head at the 5th $b$, state $q_7$)

$\ldots \not{b}\, a\, a\, a\, ,\, b\, b\, b\, b\, b\, b\, b\, b\, ;\, 1\, 1\, \not{b} \ldots \quad \delta(q_7, b) = (L)$ (head at the 4th $b$, state $q_7$)

$\ldots \not{b}\, a\, a\, a\, ,\, b\, b\, b\, b\, b\, b\, b\, b\, ;\, 1\, 1\, \not{b} \ldots \quad \delta(q_7, b) = (L)$ (head at the 3rd $b$, state $q_7$)

$\ldots \not{b}\, a\, a\, a\, ,\, b\, b\, b\, b\, b\, b\, b\, b\, ;\, 1\, 1\, \not{b} \ldots \quad \delta(q_7, b) = (L)$ (head at the 2nd $b$, state $q_7$)

$\ldots \not{b}\, a\, a\, a\, ,\, b\, b\, b\, b\, b\, b\, b\, b\, ;\, 1\, 1\, \not{b} \ldots \quad \delta(q_7, b) = (L)$ (head at the 1st $b$, state $q_7$)

$\ldots \not{b}\, a\, a\, a\, ,\, b\, b\, b\, b\, b\, b\, b\, b\, ;\, 1\, 1\, \not{b} \ldots \quad \delta(q_7, b) = (L)$ (head at ",", state $q_7$)

$\ldots \not{b}\, a\, a\, a\, ,\, b\, b\, b\, b\, b\, b\, b\, b\, ;\, 1\, 1\, \not{b} \ldots \quad \delta(q_7, ,) = (q_8\, L)$ (head at the 3rd $a$, state $q_8$)

$\ldots \not{b}\, a\, a\, 1\, ,\, b\, b\, b\, b\, b\, b\, b\, b\, ;\, 1\, 1\, \not{b} \ldots \quad \delta(q_8, a) = (1\, q_9\, N)$ (head at 1, state $q_9$)

(The additional *a*, for which no matching 1 can be replaced by *b* in the dividend is changed back to 1)

$\ldots \not{b}\, \boxed{a\, a}\, 1\, ,\, b\, b\, b\, b\, b\, b\, b\, b\, ;\, \boxed{1\, 1}\, \not{b} \ldots \quad \delta(q_8, a) = (1\, q_9\, N)$ (head at 1, state $q_9$)

Remainder = '*aa*' = 2 Result of division = '11' = 2

The number of $a$'s in the divisor area represents the remainder, and the number of 1's after the right end-marker ';' represents the result of the division. Hence, the result obtained when 8 is divided by 3 is 2, and the remainder is 2.

---

**Example 4.13** Design a TM to find the value of $\log_2(n)$, where $n$ is any binary number and a perfect power of 2.

***Solution*** It is given that $n$ is a binary number and a perfect power of 2.

We know:

$2^0 = 1 = 1$ (binary)
$2^1 = 2 = 10$ (binary)
$2^2 = 4 = 100$ (binary)
$2^3 = 8 = 1000$ (binary)

From the aforementioned listing, we have

$\log_2(2^0) = \log_2(1) = 0$ (zero number of 0's after first 1 in the binary format)
$\log_2(2^1) = \log_2(2) = 1$ (one 0 after first 1 in the binary format, which is 10)
$\log_2(2^2) = 2\log_2(2) = 2 \times 1 = 2$ (two 0's after first 1 in binary format, which is 100)

The conclusion is that, the value of $\log_2(n)$, where $n$ is a binary number and a perfect power of 2, is equal to the number of 0's after the first 1 in the given number $n$.

**Algorithm**

Count of the number of zeros after the beginning '1' of the binary number '$n$'; it gives us the required answer.

1. Read the first digit, that is, 1, and ignore it.
2. Read the following 0 from the string that follows the 1, replace it by a symbol, $a$, and write a symbol, $c$, after the right end-marker.
3. Repeat the procedure till all the 0's that follow 1 get replaced by $a$'s.
4. The number of $c$'s written after the right end-marker gives the required value of $\log_2(n)$.

Thus, the input string is in binary format and the resultant value is in unary format using symbol $c$.

> ***Note***: We could use a simpler algorithm as well, which simply replaces the first digit 1 with a blank character $\not{b}$; the remaining number of 0's gives the required answer. However, this would destroy the input parameter, and hence we do not use this algorithm.

The initial configuration of the required TM is shown in Fig. 4.16(a), and its transition graph is shown in Fig. 4.16(b).

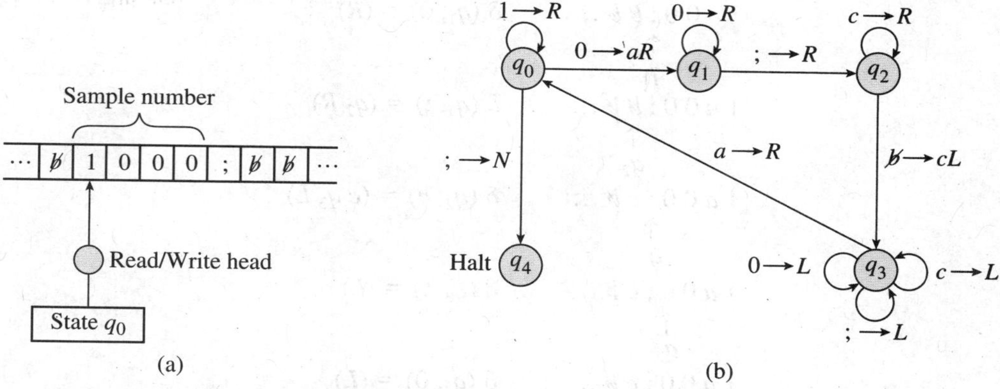


**Figure 4.16** Finding the value of $\log_2(n)$ (a) Initial configuration (b) TG for TM that finds $\log_2(n)$

The SFM is created as shown in Table 4.15.

**Table 4.15** SFM for a TM that finds $\log_2$ (n)

| S \ I | 1 | 0 | ; | a | c | $\not{b}$ |
|---|---|---|---|---|---|---|
| $q_0$ | $R$ | $aq_1R$ | $q_4N$ | — | — | — |
| $q_1$ | — | $R$ | $q_2R$ | — | — | — |
| $q_2$ | — | — | — | — | $R$ | $cq_3L$ |
| $q_3$ | — | $L$ | $L$ | $q_0R$ | $L$ | — |
| $q_4$ | — | — | — | — | — | — |

### Simulation

Let us simulate the working of the TM that we have constructed for $n = 1000$ $(= 8 = 2^3)$. We know that for this number $n$, $\log_2(n) = 3$, which can be represented as $ccc$ in unary form.

1 0 0 0 ; $\not{b}$ $\not{b}$ ... initial configuration
↑
$q_0$

1 0 0 0 ; $\not{b}$ $\not{b}$ ... $\delta(q_0, 1) = (R)$
  ↑
  $q_0$

1 $a$ 0 0 ; $\not{b}$ $\not{b}$ ... $\delta(q_0, 0) = (a\, q_1\, R)$
    ↑
    $q_1$

1 $a$ 0 0 ; $\not{b}$ $\not{b}$ ... $\delta(q_1, 0) = (R)$
      ↑
      $q_1$

$1\,a\,0\,0\,;\,\not b\,\not b \ldots \qquad \delta\,(q_1, 0) = (R)$
↑ $q_1$

$1\,a\,0\,0\,;\,\not b\,\not b \ldots \qquad \delta\,(q_1, ;) = (q_2\,R)$
↑ $q_2$

$1\,a\,0\,0\,;\,c\,\not b \ldots \qquad \delta\,(q_2, \not b) = (c\,q_3\,L)$
↑ $q_3$

$1\,a\,0\,0\,;\,c\,\not b \ldots \qquad \delta\,(q_3, ;) = (L)$
↑ $q_3$

$1\,a\,0\,0\,;\,c\,\not b \ldots \qquad \delta\,(q_3, 0) = (L)$
↑ $q_3$

$1\,a\,0\,0\,;\,c\,\not b \ldots \qquad \delta\,(q_3, 0) = (L)$
↑ $q_3$

$1\,a\,0\,0\,;\,c\,\not b \ldots \qquad \delta\,(q_3, a) = (q_0\,R)$
↑ $q_0$

$1\,a\,a\,0\,;\,c\,\not b \ldots \qquad \delta\,(q_0, 0) = (a\,q_1\,R)$
↑ $q_1$

$1\,a\,a\,0\,;\,c\,\not b\,\not b \ldots \qquad \delta\,(q_1, 0) = (R)$
↑ $q_1$

$1\,a\,a\,0\,;\,c\,\not b\,\not b \ldots \qquad \delta\,(q_1, ;) = (q_2\,R)$
↑ $q_2$

$1\,a\,a\,0\,;\,c\,\not b\,\not b \ldots \qquad \delta\,(q_2, c) = (R)$
↑ $q_2$

$1\,a\,a\,0\,;\,c\,c\,\not b \ldots \qquad \delta\,(q_2, \not b) = (c\,q_3\,L)$
↑ $q_3$

$1\,a\,a\,0\,;\,c\,c\,\not b \ldots \qquad \delta\,(q_3, c) = (L)$
↑ $q_3$

$1\,a\,a\,0\,;\,c\,c\,\not b \ldots \qquad \delta\,(q_3, ;) = (L)$
↑ $q_3$

$1\,a\,a\,0\,;\,c\,c\,\not b \ldots \qquad \delta\,(q_3, 0) = (L)$
↑ $q_3$

$1\,a\,a\,0\,;\,c\,c\,\not b \ldots \qquad \delta\,(q_3, a) = (q_0\,R)$
↑ $q_0$

$1\,a\,a\,a\,;c\,c\,\not{b}\,\not{b}\ldots$ $\quad\uparrow q_1\quad$ $\delta(q_0, 0) = (a\,q_1\,R)$

$1\,a\,a\,a\,;c\,c\,\not{b}\,\not{b}\ldots$ $\quad\uparrow q_2\quad$ $\delta(q_1, ;) = (q_2\,R)$

$1\,a\,a\,a\,;c\,c\,\not{b}\,\not{b}\ldots$ $\quad\uparrow q_2\quad$ $\delta(q_2, c) = (R)$

$1\,a\,a\,a\,;c\,c\,\not{b}\,\not{b}\ldots$ $\quad\uparrow q_2\quad$ $\delta(q_2, c) = (R)$

$1\,a\,a\,a\,;c\,c\,c\,\not{b}\ldots$ $\quad\uparrow q_3\quad$ $\delta(q_2, \not{b}) = (c\,q_3\,L)$

$1\,a\,a\,a\,;c\,c\,c\,\not{b}\ldots$ $\quad\uparrow q_3\quad$ $\delta(q_3, c) = (L)$

$1\,a\,a\,a\,;c\,c\,c\,\not{b}\ldots$ $\quad\uparrow q_3\quad$ $\delta(q_3, c) = (L)$

$1\,a\,a\,a\,;c\,c\,c\,\not{b}\ldots$ $\quad\uparrow q_3\quad$ $\delta(q_3, ;) = (L)$

$1\,a\,a\,a\,;c\,c\,c\,\not{b}\ldots$ $\quad\uparrow q_0\quad$ $\delta(q_3, a) = (q_0\,R)$

$1\,a\,a\,a\,;c\,c\,c\,\not{b}\ldots$ $\quad\uparrow q_4\quad$ $\delta(q_0, ;) = (q_4\,N)$

The TM halts with the result *ccc*, which is the expected value, that is, 3.

We could also replace all the *a*'s by 0's again, in order to retain the input parameter, so as to have a non-destructing algorithm.

---

## 4.7 COMPLEXITY OF A TURING MACHINE

The complexity of a TM is directly proportional to the size of the functional matrix. In other words, we can say that the complexity of a TM depends on the number of symbols that are being used and the number of states of the TM. Hence

$$\text{Complexity of a TM} = |\Gamma| \times |Q| \qquad (\text{or } |I| \times |S|),$$

where, $|\Gamma|$ = Cardinality of tape alphabet (i.e., number of tape symbols),
and $|Q|$ = Number of states of the TM.

Let us consider Example 4.13 in which we designed a TM that finds $\log_2(n)$, where $n$ is a perfect power of 2, and is represented in binary format. For this example, we have

$$\Gamma = \{1, 0, a, c, ;, \not{b}\}$$
$$Q = \{q_0, q_1, q_2, q_3, q_4 = \text{halt}\}$$

Therefore, the complexity of the TM $= |\Gamma| \times |Q| = 6 \times 5 = 30$

Thus, while designing a TM, we must ensure that it has minimum complexity, that is, we should design a TM such that it has lesser number of input symbols and states.

## 4.8 COMPOSITE AND ITERATIVE TURING MACHINES

Two or more Turing machines can be combined to solve a complex problem, such that the output of one TM forms the input to the next TM, and so on. This is called *composition*.

For realizing a composite TM (or a CTM), the functional matrices of the component TMs are combined by re-labeling the symbols, as required, and suitably branching to an appropriate state rather than the halt state at the completion of the performance of each component TM. Figure 4.17(a) depicts a composition of $n$ TMs.

Another way of having a combination TM is by applying its own output as input repetitively. This is called *iteration* or *recursion*, and the TM is said to be an iterative TM (or ITM). For an example, refer to Fig. 4.17(b).

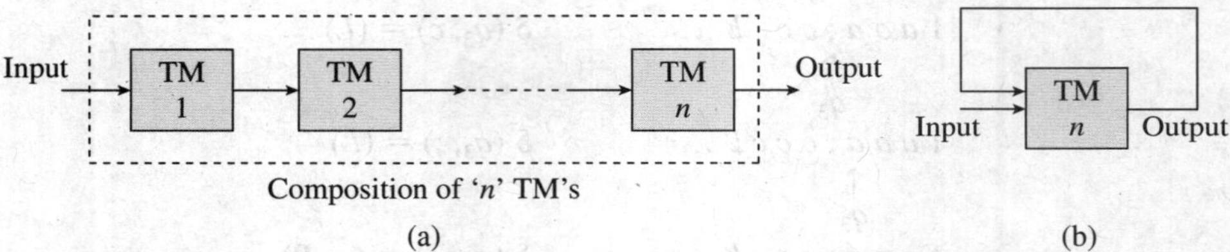


**Figure 4.17** Composite and iterative TMs (a) Composite TM (CTM) (b) Iterative TM (ITM)

The idea of a composite TM gives rise to the concept of breaking a complicated job into a number of smaller jobs, implementing each separately, and then combining them together to get the answer for the job required to be done. Therefore, we can divide a problem into simple jobs and design different TMs for each job. This is a typical *separation of concerns* achieved in software development; it is analogous to the function composition that we know from discrete mathematics: $f \circ g\ (x) = f\,(g\ (x))$. The output of $g\ (x)$ is given as input to function $f$. In a way, modular programming can be considered to be influenced by CTM.

Functionally, most of the TMs that we have implemented earlier in the chapter, for example, multiplication as repetitive addition, division as repetitive subtraction, and so on, are examples of iterative TMs.

---

**Example 4.14** Design a TM to find the value of $n^2$, where $n$ is any integer $\geq 0$.

***Solution*** Let us consider the initial configuration to be as shown in Fig. 4.18 (a).

The number $n$ is represented in unary form using 0's, as shown in Fig. 4.18(a). We find $n^2$ is in terms of the multiplication '$n \times n$'. This involves copying $n$ after the comma ',', onto the tape, and using that as the multiplicand—represented in unary form using symbol 1—as shown in Fig. 4.18(b). We can then perform the multiplication '$n \times n$', as we have done in Example 4.10. Figure 4.18(b) is the initial configuration for the TM that performs multiplication as we have seen earlier.

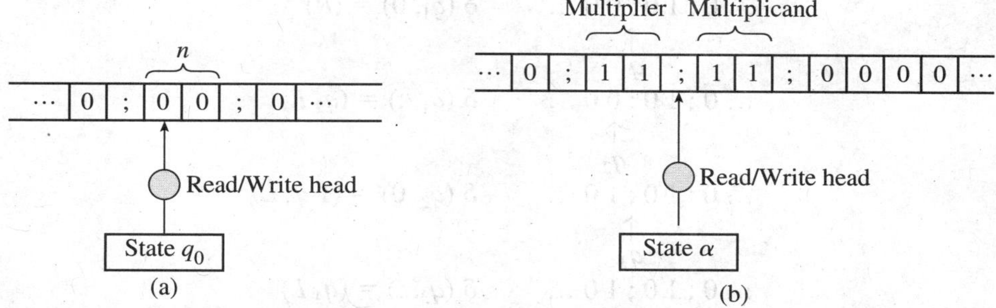


**Figure 4.18** TM that computes $n^2$ ($n \geq 0$) (a) Initial configuration (b) Configuration after copying $n$ onto tape

Observe that the TM that computes $n^2$ can be considered as a composition of two TMs. The first TM prepares the output in the form suggested in Figure 4.18(b), which can be used as input for the second TM that performs multiplication. The second TM is similar to the one that we have already designed in Example 4.10; the SFM for this TM is described in Table 4.12 with $\alpha$ as the initial state. Hence, we need to design the first TM, which converts the initial configuration shown in Fig. 4.18(a) into the form that can be used as input by the second TM, whose initial configuration is shown in Fig. 4.18(b).

**Algorithm**

1. Replace one 0 at a time by symbol 1 and copy it after the right end-marker, ';'.
2. Repeat this process till all the 0's from $n$ are replaced by 1's.
3. Thus, another copy of $n$ gets prepared after the right end-marker, ';'. This is done to store $n$ as the multiplier as well as multiplicand onto the tape.
4. Now, replace the end-marker, ';', by a comma, ',', and add another end-marker, ';', at the end of the copy of $n$ created at the right end.

The SFM for the required TM is shown in Table 4.16.

**Table 4.16** SFM for the TM that prepares input for multiplication

| S \ I | 0 | ; | 1 | , |
|---|---|---|---|---|
| $q_0$ | $1q_1R$ | $,q_5R$ | — | — |
| $q_1$ | $R$ | $q_2R$ | — | — |
| $q_2$ | $1q_3L$ | — | $R$ | — |
| $q_3$ | — | $q_4L$ | $L$ | — |
| $q_4$ | $L$ | — | $q_0R$ | — |
| $q_5$ | $;q_6L$ | — | $R$ | — |
| $q_6$ | — | — | $L$ | $\alpha N$ |

***Simulation***

Let us simulate the working of the TM for $n = 2$.

$$\begin{array}{ll} \ldots 0\,;\,0\,0\,;\,0\,0 \ldots & \text{initial configuration} \\ \quad\quad\uparrow & \\ \quad\quad q_0 & \\ \ldots 0\,;\,1\,0\,;\,0\,0 \ldots & \delta(q_0, 0) = (1\, q_1\, R) \\ \quad\quad\quad\uparrow & \\ \quad\quad\quad q_1 & \end{array}$$

$$\ldots 0\,;1\,0\,;0\,0\ldots \quad \delta(q_1, 0) = (R)$$
$$\uparrow q_1$$

$$\ldots 0\,;1\,0\,;0\,0\ldots \quad \delta(q_1, ;) = (q_2\, R)$$
$$\uparrow q_2$$

$$\ldots 0\,;1\,0\,;1\,0\ldots \quad \delta(q_2, 0) = (1\, q_3\, L)$$
$$\uparrow q_3$$

$$\ldots 0\,;1\,0\,;1\,0\ldots \quad \delta(q_3, ;) = (q_4\, L)$$
$$\uparrow q_4$$

$$\ldots 0\,;1\,0\,;1\,0\ldots \quad \delta(q_4, 0) = (L)$$
$$\uparrow q_4$$

$$\ldots 0\,;1\,0\,;1\,0\ldots \quad \delta(q_4, 1) = (q_0\, R)$$
$$\uparrow q_0$$

$$\ldots 0\,;1\,1\,;1\,0\ldots \quad \delta(q_0, 0) = (1\, q_1\, R)$$
$$\uparrow q_1$$

$$\ldots 0\,;1\,1\,;1\,0\ldots \quad \delta(q_1, ;) = (q_2\, R)$$
$$\uparrow q_2$$

$$\ldots 0\,;1\,1\,;1\,0\ldots \quad \delta(q_2, 1) = (R)$$
$$\uparrow q_2$$

$$\ldots 0\,;1\,1\,;1\,1\,0\ldots \quad \delta(q_2, 0) = (1\, q_3\, L)$$
$$\uparrow q_3$$

$$\ldots 0\,;1\,1\,;1\,1\,0\ldots \quad \delta(q_3, 1) = (L)$$
$$\uparrow q_3$$

$$\ldots 0\,;1\,1\,;1\,1\,0\ldots \quad \delta(q_3, ;) = (q_4\, L)$$
$$\uparrow q_4$$

$$\ldots 0\,;1\,1\,;1\,1\,0\ldots \quad \delta(q_4, 1) = (q_0\, R)$$
$$\uparrow q_0$$

**(*n* is completely copied to the right end)**

$$\ldots 0\,;1\,1\,,1\,1\,0\ldots \quad \delta(q_0, ;) = (,\, q_5\, R)$$
$$\uparrow q_5$$

$$\ldots 0\,;1\,1\,,1\,1\,0\ldots \quad \delta(q_5, 1) = (R)$$
$$\uparrow q_5$$

$$\ldots 0\,;1\,1\,,1\,1\,0\ldots \quad \delta(q_5, 1) = (R)$$
$$\uparrow q_5$$

$$\ldots 0 ; 1\,1 , 1\,1 ; 0 \ldots \quad \delta\,(q_5, 0) = (; q_6\, L)$$
$$\uparrow$$
$$q_6$$

$$\ldots 0 ; 1\,1 , 1\,1 ; 0 \ldots \quad \delta\,(q_6, 1) = (L)$$
$$\uparrow$$
$$q_6$$

$$\ldots 0 ; 1\,1 , 1\,1 ; 0 \ldots \quad \delta\,(q_6, 1) = (L)$$
$$\uparrow$$
$$q_6$$

$$\ldots 0 ; 1\,1 , 1\,1 ; 0 \ldots \quad \delta\,(q_6, ,) = (\alpha\, N)$$
$$\uparrow$$
$$\alpha$$

Thus, we see that the original sequence, '…0 ; 0 0 ; 0 …' got replaced by '… 0 ; 1 1 , 1 1 ; 0 …'. The number $n$, which was originally represented as '00' is now represented as '11', and is also duplicated in order to act as a multiplicand/multiplier pair for computing $n^2 = n \times n$. The new sequence now matches the initial configuration of the TM that performs multiplication. Hence, $\delta\,(q_6, ,) = (\alpha\, N)$ thus moves the TM to the initial state of the second (multiplication) TM.

Thus, the SFM in Table 4.16 is followed by the SFM for the TM that performs multiplication (refer to Table 4.12). This makes a composite TM, as required. The square of a given number is thus represented as a function composition (refer to Fig. 4.19).

In Fig. 4.19, $TM_n$ is the TM whose SFM is shown in Table 4.16, and $TM_{n \times n}$ is the TM which performs the multiplication. $TM_{n^2}$ is thus implemented as a composition of two TMs.

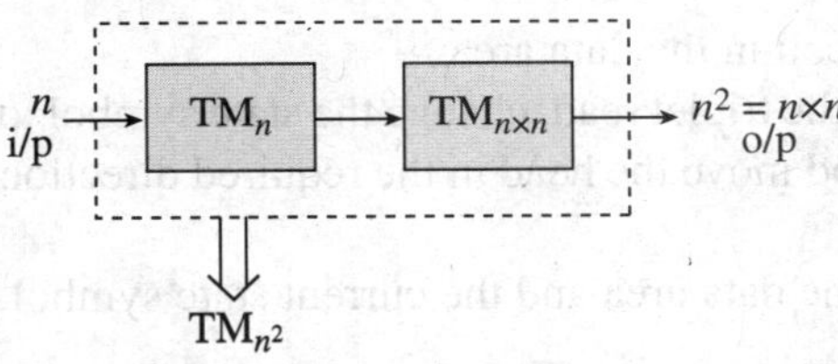


**Figure 4.19** Computing $n^2$ using composite TM

## 4.9 UNIVERSAL TURING MACHINE

Visualize a TM that simulates a given TM for a given input. So far, we have been simulating the working of a TM using a series of IDs. However, it is feasible to build a simulating TM if the input tape and the SFM of the TM to be simulated are available on the simulating TM's tape, along with the simulating algorithm to be implemented in the form of an SFM. Here, we are essentially building a program, which simulates another program for a given input.

Let us call the simulating program (or TM) as a meta-program (or meta-TM). The meta-TM takes the SFM for the TM to be simulated as one of the inputs (*program area* on the meta-TM's tape). We will also need the initial ID or initial configuration, along with the input string for the simulation (*data area* on the meta-TM tape).

We now implement the SFM for the meta-TM that represents the simulating algorithm (*system area*). The simulating algorithm is responsible for checking the current state and the current input symbol of the TM to be simulated by visiting the data area; it then, accordingly, picks the quintuple from the program area, and visits the data area again to simulate the action specified by the quintuple—it changes the state, if any, the symbol read, if any, and the direction as required. After one such simulation step, the data area of the meta-TM starts depicting the next ID of the TM being simulated.

A universal Turing machine (UTM) is capable of simulating any TM $T$, if the following information is available on its tape:

1. The description of $T$ in terms of its SFM (*program area* of the tape)
2. The initial configuration of $T$ with the processing data (input string) to be fed to $T$ (*data area* of the tape)

This means that the UTM should have an *imitation algorithm* (simulating logic in the form of its SFM) in order to correctly interpret the rules of the operation given in the SFM of the TM being simulated, that is, $T$.

The UTM should also have a table look-up facility and should perform the following steps:

**Imitation algorithm**

1. Scan the tape cell on the data area of the tape and read the symbol from the same area that $T$ reads from to start with; next, read the initial state of $T$.
2. Move the tape to the program area containing the SFM of $T$, and find the row in the SFM for the state symbol read in Step 1.
3. Find the column for the input symbol read in Step 1 and read the triplet (new symbol, new state, direction to move) stored as the entry, which is the entry at the intersection of the required row and column.
4. Move the tape to reach the appropriate tape cell in the data area.
5. Replace the symbol by the new symbol from the triplet read, change the state symbol to the next state symbol from the triplet read, and move the head in the required direction as specified in the triplet.
6. Read the next symbol to be read by $T$ from the data area and the current state symbol. Then, go to Step 2.

Since the UTM is a TM, the aforementioned imitation algorithm is implemented as an SFM.

We know that every TM, including the UTM, has a linear tape. Hence, we cannot arrange the SFM (which is a matrix or a table) for the TM to be simulated as it is, onto the UTM's tape. Hence, we must store it linearly either in row-major order or column-major order. For example, let us consider the SFM for $T$ (sample TM) as shown in Table 4.17.

**Table 4.17** Example SFM

| $S$ \ $I$ | 0 | 1 | $\not b$ |
|---|---|---|---|
| $\alpha$ | $1\beta R$ | $1\alpha R$ | $\not b\alpha R$ |
| $\beta$ | *** | *** | $\not b\gamma N$ |

This SFM can be represented as a linear sequence (column-major ordering) as follows:

$$0\ \alpha\ 1\ \beta\ R\ 0\ \beta * * *\ 1\ \alpha\ 1\ \alpha\ R\ 1\ \beta * * *\ \not b\ \alpha\ \not b\ \alpha\ R\ \not b\ \beta\ \not b\ \gamma\ N$$

The unspecified entry ('-') here is translated to '***', in order to keep the size of the quintuple intact, that is, to ensure that there are five symbols to represent each cell. This helps identifying the end of one quintuple and start of the next, in the linear storage.

The UTM tape consists of the program area, which is the SFM for the other TM stored either in row-major or column-major order, as we have just seen in the case of the example SFM in Table 4.17. Thus, we see that the UTM needs to consume not only the input symbols but also the state symbols, as well as the direction symbols as inputs on its tape. As a result, the new tape alphabet for UTM will have an additional ten symbols, namely: $\Gamma = \{0, 1, b\!\!\!/, \alpha, \beta, \gamma, L, R, N, *\}$. As we know, the symbols are user-defined, and different users assume different symbols while designing TMs. Now, if we expect the UTM to simulate all these TMs, it becomes practically impossible to impose finiteness onto the tape alphabet, $\Gamma$. Hence, there is a need to encode the symbols in some unique way.

For this, let us assume that there are altogether $m$ distinct symbols. Hence, we can assign a unique and easy-to-decode binary code to each of these symbols with $n$ or more bits, where $2^n \geq m$.

Let us consider the aforementioned example, in which we have ten different symbols, namely, $\{0, 1, b\!\!\!/, \alpha, \beta, \gamma, L, R, N, *\}$, that is, $m = 10$.

We can represent or encode these symbols using a 4-bit binary code ($2^4 > 10 > 2^3$) as follows:

$0 = 0\,0\,0\,0$; $1 = 0\,0\,0\,1$; $b = 0\,0\,1\,0$;
$\alpha = 0\,0\,1\,1$; $\beta = 0\,1\,0\,0$; $\gamma = 0\,1\,0\,1$;
$L = 0\,1\,1\,0$; $R = 0\,1\,1\,1$; $N = 1\,0\,0\,0$;
$* = 1\,0\,0\,1$

There are more encoding techniques as well. We shall discuss one such technique later in Chapter 9. Essentially, the binary encoding restricts the size of the tape alphabet for UTM to two letters—0 and 1.

***Note***: The concept of UTM laid the foundation for *stored-program computers* and interpretive implementation of *programming languages*. The SFM for UTM can be visualized as part of the *operating system*, which is the program (or finite set of programs) capable of loading and simulating the other programs.

Hence, we see that the UTM is a meta-program that takes other programs as input and simulates them. This is based the concept of *program as data*, which was later adopted in Lambda-calculus as well.

## 4.10 MULTI-TAPE TURING MACHINE

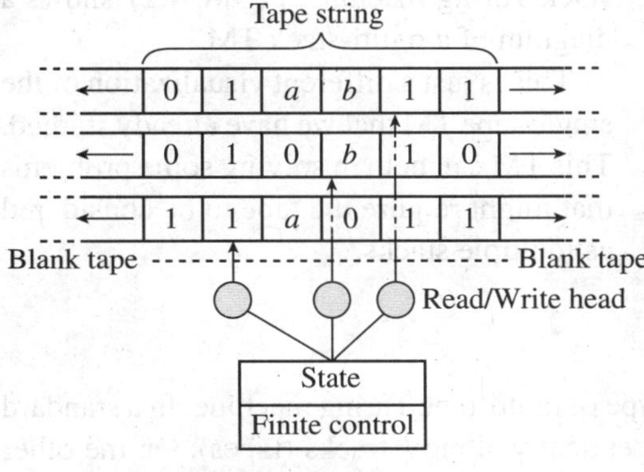


**Figure 4.20** Multi-tape TM

Multi-tape Turing machines are similar to the single-tape Turing machines that we have discussed so far, but with some constant $k$ number of independent tapes, having their own read/write heads. These machines have independent control over all the heads—any of these can move and read/write their own tapes. All these tapes are unbounded at both the ends just as in the single-tape TM. Figure 4.20 shows a multi-tape TM.

The multi-tape TM model intuitively seems to be much more powerful than the single-tape model. However, any multi-tape machine, no matter how large the $k$ may be, can be simulated only by a single-tape machine using quadratically more computation time. Thus, multi-tape machines cannot calculate any more functions than the single-tape machines do, and the computational complexity (the time taken to perform the computation) is also not affected dramatically by a change between single-tape and multi-tape machines. In short, the multi-tape TM and single-tape TM are equivalent in power (except for some difference in execution time). In turn, the multi-tape TM just adds to the convenience and not to the power of computation.

***Formal Definition***

A $k$-tape Turing machine is denoted by:

$$M = \{Q, \Sigma, \Gamma, \delta, q_0, B, F\}$$

where,

$Q$: Finite set of states
$\Gamma$: Finite set of allowable tape symbols including blank character $\not{b}$
$\Sigma$: Subset of $\Gamma$, excluding blank character $\not{b}$; it is the set of input symbols
$B$: A symbol in $\Gamma$; it is the blank character $\not{b}$.
$q_0$: Start (or initial) state $\in Q$
$F$: Set of final states (or halt states) $\subseteq Q$
$\delta$: Functional matrix, such that, $\delta$: $(Q \times \Gamma^k) \rightarrow (Q \times (\Gamma \times \{L, R, N\})^k)$

A $k$-tape TM can read up to $k$ symbols at every instance, while in a current state. It then can change the state, erase the current symbol and write a new symbol for each of the $k$ symbols, and can also decide the direction for each of the $k$ heads, independent of each other.

## 4.11 MULTI-STACK TURING MACHINE

The symbols to the left of the head of the TM can be stored onto one stack, while the symbols on the right of the head can be placed on the other stack.

On each stack, symbols closer to the Turing machine's head are placed closer to the top of the stack. This type of organization is called multi-stack Turing machine or two-stack Turing machine. Figure 4.21 shows a diagram of a multi-stack TM.

This is just a different visualization of the single-tape TM that we have already studied. This TM can help in solving some problems that might require the tape to be considered as multiple stacks.

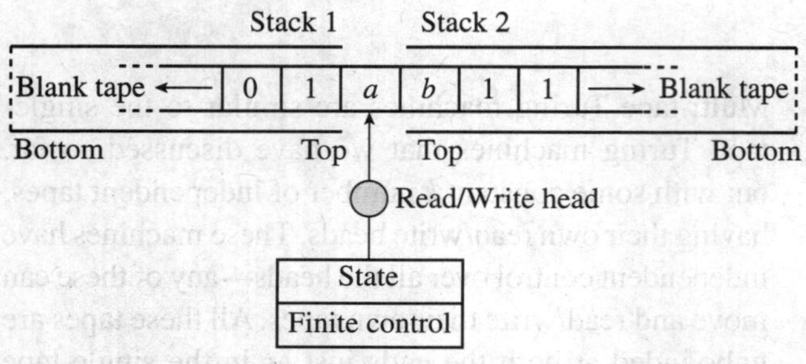


**Figure 4.21** Multi-stack TM

## 4.12 MULTI-TRACK TURING MACHINE

A multi-track Turing machine is a specific type of multi-tape Turing machine. In a standard $k$-tape Turing machine, $k$ heads move independently along $k$ tracks (tapes). On the other hand, in a $k$-track Turing machine, one head reads and writes on all tracks simultaneously.

A tape position in a $k$-track Turing machine denotes $k$ symbols from the tape alphabet. This is equivalent to the standard single-tape Turing machine except that it reads/writes $k$ symbols at one go, and therefore, accepts recursively enumerable languages.

### Formal Definition

A $k$-track Turing machine is denoted by

$$M = (Q, \Sigma, \Gamma, \delta, q_0, B, F),$$

where,

Q: Finite set of states

$\Gamma$: Finite set of allowable tape symbols including blank $\not b$

$\Sigma$: Subset of '$\Gamma$' excluding the blank $\not b$; it is the set of input symbols

$B$: A symbol for blank character $\not b$

$q_0$: Start (or initial) state $\in Q$

$F$: Set of final states (or halt states) $\subseteq Q$

$\delta$: Functional matrix, such that $\delta: (Q \times \Gamma^k) \rightarrow (Q \times \Gamma^k \times \{L, R, N\})$

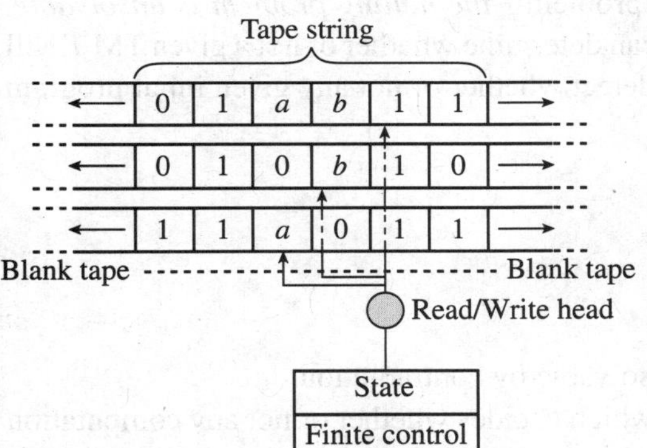

**Figure 4.22** Multi-track TM

Note the difference in the definition of the functional matrix for multi-tape and multi-track TMs. Multi-track TMs can only read $k$ symbols and print $k$ new symbols after erasing the old symbols, but the direction change can only be done once. This is because they do not have $k$ independent heads as the multi-tape TMs do; they only have $k$ tracks and one head. Figure 4.22 helps us visualise a multi-track TM.

## 4.13 SOLVABLE, SEMI-SOLVABLE, AND UNSOLVABLE PROBLEMS

If there is a TM, which when applied to any problem, always eventually terminates with the correct 'yes' or 'no' answer, we call the problem *solvable*. For example, consider the problem of determining whether or not a given binary number is a palindrome (refer to Example 4.7). For any input binary number, the TM halts with the answer $T$ (i.e., 'yes') or $F$ (i.e., 'no'), based on whether it is a palindrome sequence or not, respectively. Most of the problems we have solved so far are solvable problems.

Now, if there is a TM, which when applied to any problem, always eventually terminates when the answer is 'yes', and may or may not terminate when the answer is 'no', we call the problem *semi-solvable* or *partially solvable*. For instance, let us consider Example 4.12. Any division problem is undefined if the divisor is zero. In such a case the TM we have designed might loop forever. This problem is thus partially solvable.

However, if there is no TM, which when applied to a problem, eventually terminates with the answer 'yes', we call the problem *unsolvable*. We are yet to see any such problem that is unsolvable, though there are many such problems existing in the world. One such problem is the *halting problem* that we are going to discuss in this chapter.

## 4.14 HALTING PROBLEM

For a given initial configuration of a TM, two cases arise:

1. The machine starting at this configuration will halt after a finite number of steps.
2. The machine starting at this configuration never halts no matter how long it runs.

Given any TM, the problem of determining whether or not it ever halts is called the *halting problem*.

To solve the halting problem, we need some mechanism that consumes any functional matrix, input data tape, and the initial configuration of a TM, and determines whether or not the TM will ever halt. Any such mechanism essentially should be an algorithm (or TM) that needs to simulate any given TM for checking whether or not it halts.

In reality, one cannot solve the halting problem—*the halting problem is unsolvable.* This means that there exists no TM, which can determine whether or not a given TM $T$ will ever halt. In other words, no program can detect whether or not any given input program (including itself), will ever halt.

**Theorem 4.1**

The halting problem is unsolvable.

*Proof*

Let us prove that the halting problem is unsolvable by contradiction.

Let us assume that there exists a TM $A$, which decides whether or not any computation by any TM $T$ will ever halt, given the description $d_T$ (SFM) of $T$, and the input tape $t$ of $T$. Then, for every input ($t$, $d_T$) to $A$, if $T$ halts, then $A$ reaches an 'accept halt' state; else, $A$ reaches a 'reject halt' state. Figure 4.23(a) shows a diagrammatic representation of the working of TM $A$.

We now attempt to construct another TM $B$, which takes ($t$, $d_T$) as the input; it functions as follows:

First it copies the input and duplicates the same onto its tape. Then it takes this duplicated information tape as the input to $A$. Whenever $A$ reaches the 'accept halt' state, $B$ loops forever, and whenever $A$ reaches the 'reject halt' state, $B$ halts. Figure 4.23(b) shows a diagrammatic representation of the working of TM $B$.

Considering the original behaviour of $A$, we find that $B$ acts as follows:

It loops if $T$ halts for input $t$, and halts if $T$ does not halt for the input $t$. Thus, the working of TM $B$ is exactly opposite to that of TM $T$.

Now, since $B$ itself is a TM, let us set $T = B$. In this case, $B$ halts for the input if and only if $B$ does not halt for the same input, and loops forever if and only if $B$ halts for the input. Figure 4.23(c) shows the working of the TM $B$, which takes itself as input.

This is a contradiction.

Hence, we conclude that the machine $A$, which can decide whether or not any other TM will ever halt cannot exist. Therefore, we conclude that the halting problem is unsolvable.

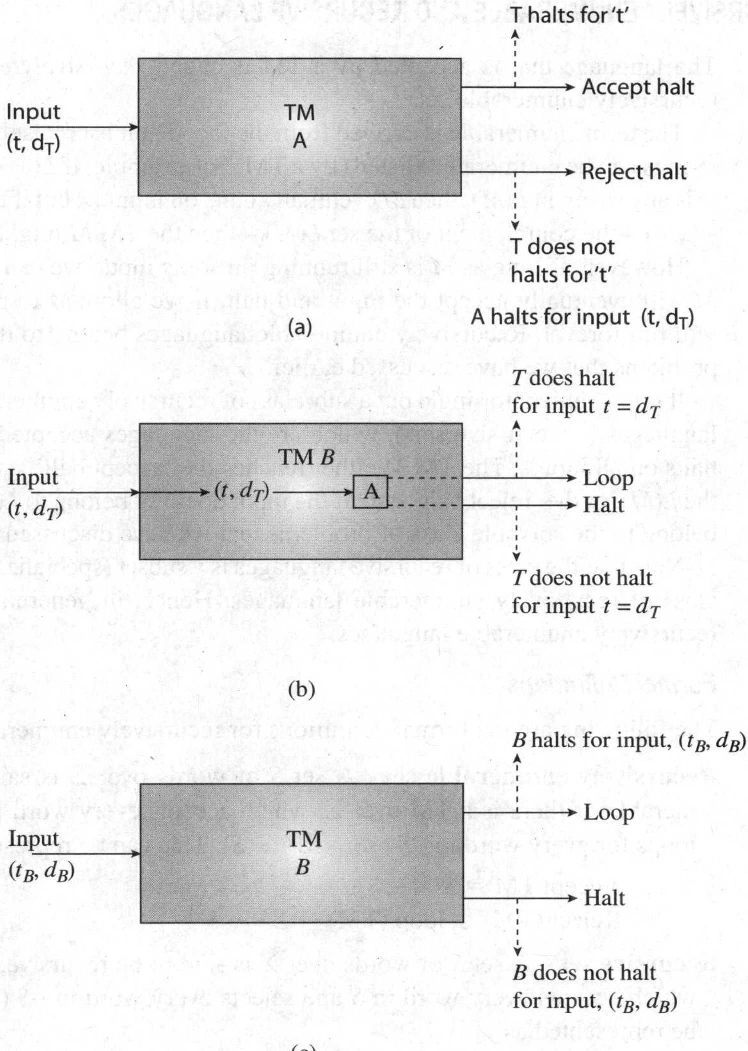


**Figure 4.23** Working of a TM (a) Working of TM *A* (b) Working of TM *B* (c) Working of TM *B*, which takes itself as input

### *Consequences of the Halting Problem*

1. We cannot decide whether or not a TM will ever print a given symbol $a$ of its alphabet. This is also unsolvable.
2. Two TMs with the same alphabet cannot be checked for equivalence or non-equivalence by an algorithm. This means that there is no effective general way to decide whether or not a given computational process will ever terminate, or whether or not two given processes are equivalent. This is also another unsolvable problem.

There are many other unsolvable problems that we will discuss in the subsequent chapters.

## 4.15 RECURSIVELY ENUMERABLE AND RECURSIVE LANGUAGES

The language that is accepted by a TM is called *recursively enumerable language* (or recursively enumerable set).

The term enumerable is derived from the fact that it is precisely these languages, whose strings can be enumerated (listed) by a TM. For example, if $L(M)$ is such a language and if $w$ is any string in $L(M)$, then $M$ eventually halts on input $w$; but if the input string belongs to $\sim L(M)$—the complement of the set $L(M)$—then the TM $M$ might fail to halt on this input.

However, as long as $M$ is still running on some input, we can never tell whether or not $M$ will eventually accept the input and halt, if we allow $M$ to run long enough; or if $M$ will run forever. Recursively enumerable languages belong to the semi-solvable class of problems that we have discussed earlier.

It is convenient to single out a sub-class of recursively enumerable sets, called recursive languages (or recursive sets), which are the languages accepted by at least one TM that halts on all inputs. The TM $M$ either reaches the 'accept halt' state if the input belongs to the $L(M)$, or the 'reject halt' state if the input does not belong to $L(M)$. Recursive languages belong to the solvable class of problems that we have discussed earlier.

Note that the class of recursive languages is a subset (specialization) of the more generic class of recursively enumerable languages. Hence, in general, TMs are said to accept recursively enumerable languages.

### *Formal Definitions*

The following are the formal definitions for recursively enumerable and recursive sets.

**Recursively enumerable set** A set $S$ of words over $\Sigma$ is said to be recursively enumerable, if there is a TM over $\Sigma$, which accepts every word in $S$ and either rejects or loops for every word in $\sim S$ ($\sim S = \Sigma^* - S$). This can be represented as

$$\text{Accept TM} = S$$
$$\text{Reject (TM)} \cup \text{loop (TM)} = \Sigma^* - S$$

**Recursive set** A set $S$ of words over $\Sigma$ is said to be recursive, if there is a TM over $\Sigma$, which accepts every word in $S$ and rejects every word in $\sim S$ ($\sim S = \Sigma^* - S$). This can be represented as

$$\text{Accept (TM)} = S$$
$$\text{Reject (TM)} = \Sigma^* - S$$
$$\text{Loop (TM)} = \phi$$

## 4.16 FUNCTIONS

A TM may be viewed as a computer of functions that accept arguments (input parameters) in unary form and produce results (outputs) in unary form.

For example, let us assume that an integer $i \geq 0$ is represented by the string $a^i$. If a function has $k$ integer arguments, that is, $i_1, i_2, \ldots, i_k$, then these integers are initially placed on the tape separated by some delimiter, such as ','. For example, $a^{i1}, a^{i2}, \ldots, a^{ik}$. If the TM halts (i.e., accepts or rejects) with a tape consisting of $a^m$ for some $m$, then we say that

$$f(i_1, i_2, \ldots, i_k) = m,$$

where, $f$ is the function of $k$ arguments computed by this TM.

Note that the TMs can be designed to compute a function of one argument, a different function of two arguments, and so on. Furthermore, if the TM $M$ computes a function $f$ of $k$ arguments, then $f$ need not have a value for all different $k$-tuples of integers, $i_1, i_2, \ldots, i_k$. In other words, the function $f$ may not be defined for all combinations of values for all the arguments. For example, division is not defined for all values of divisors—it is undefined for divisor = 0.

### 4.16.1 Total Recursive Functions

If $f(i_1, i_2, \ldots i_k)$ is defined for all values of arguments, $i_1, \ldots, i_k$, then $f$ is said to be a total recursive function. These total recursive functions correspond to the recursive languages, since they are computed by a TM that always halts.

All common arithmetic functions on integers, such as multiplication, $[\log_2 n]$, and $2^{2n}$, are total recursive functions. Most of the examples that we have solved so far are total recursive functions.

### 4.16.2 Partial Recursive Functions

If $f(i_1, i_2, \ldots, i_k)$ is not defined for all values of arguments $i_1, \ldots, i_k$, then $f$ is said to be a partial recursive function. In other words, a function $f(i_1, \ldots, i_k)$ computed by a TM, which may or may not halt on a given input, is said to be a partial recursive function.

Partial recursive functions are analogous to recursively enumerable languages, since they are computed by a TM that halts on acceptance, while for any other input it may or may not halt. For example, factorial ($n!$) is only defined for integers, $n \geq 0$; it is undefined for negative integers. Another example that we have seen is that of division, which is undefined if divisor = 0.

Most of the real world problems are partial functions (or recursively enumerable). For example, while using an ATM, we cannot withdraw amount zero, or an amount that is more than the balance in the account (except in case of overdraft facility). Similarly, one cannot have negative weight; hence, the weighing machine must show positive values only.

## 4.17 CHURCH–TURING HYPOTHESIS

This hypothesis is also known as *Church–Turing conjecture*, *Church's Thesis*, or *Church's conjecture*. It essentially states that everything that is algorithmically computable is computable by a Turing machine. If some method (algorithm) exists to carry out a calculation, then the same calculation can also be carried out by a Turing machine.

American mathematician, Alonzo Church, created a method called $\lambda$-calculus (Lambda-calculus) for defining functions. It is an equivalent computational model of the UTM.

**Statement of the hypothesis** The intuitive notion of a computable function can be identified with the class of partial recursive functions. In other words, every problem having an algorithmic solution can be solved using a machine having the foregoing set of instructions.

## 4.18 POST'S CORRESPONDENCE PROBLEM

Let $A = w_1, w_2, \ldots, w_k$, and $B = x_1, x_2, \ldots, x_k$ be strings over some alphabet $\Sigma$.

Post's correspondence problem (PCP) is to find the correspondence sequence of integers, $i_1, i_2, \ldots, i_m$, for $m \geq 1$ such that

$$w_{i1}, w_{i2}, \ldots, w_{im} = x_{i1}, x_{i2}, \ldots, x_{im}$$

The sequence, '$i_1, i_2, \ldots, i_m$' is considered to be the solution for the PCP instance. Each PCP instance is constituted by some set of values for $A$ and $B$.

Note that the entire class of PCP instances is unsolvable. If we consider the PCP as a generic class of all such instances, then it is *unsolvable*. Furthermore, there exists no generic algorithm that can find a solution for any such PCP instance; hence, it is also an *undecidable* problem. However, for a few values of $A$ and $B$, it might have a solution.

Let us now look at a few examples to understand this better.

---

**Example 4.15** Let $\Sigma = \{1, 0\}$ and let $A$ and $B$ be defined as shown in Table 4.18. Find the correspondence sequence of integers, $i_1, i_2, \ldots, i_m$, for $m \geq 1$, such that

$$w_{i1}, w_{i2}, \ldots, w_{im} = x_{i1}, x_{i2}, \ldots, x_{im}$$

**Table 4.18** Post's correspondence problem with a solution

| | A | B |
|---|---|---|
| i | $w_i$ | $x_i$ |
| 1 | 0 | 000 |
| 2 | 01000 | 01 |
| 3 | 01 | 1 |

***Solution*** The given PCP instance has a solution for $m = 4$:

$i_1 = 2$
$i_2 = 1$
$i_3 = 1$
$i_4 = 3$

Observe that

$$w_2\, w_1\, w_1\, w_3 = (0\,1\,0\,0\,0)\,(0)\,(0)\,(0\,1) = 0\,1\,0\,0\,0\,0\,0\,0\,1$$
$$x_2\, x_1\, x_1\, x_3 = (0\,1)\,(0\,0\,0)\,(0\,0\,0)\,(1) = 0\,1\,0\,0\,0\,0\,0\,0\,1$$

Hence, $w_2\, w_1\, w_1\, w_3 = x_2\, x_1\, x_1\, x_3$

---

**Example 4.16** Let $\Sigma = \{1, 0\}$ and let $A$ and $B$ be defined as shown in Table 4.19. Find the correspondence sequence of integers, $i_1, i_2, \ldots i_m$, for $m \geq 1$, such that

$$w_{i1}, w_{i2}, \ldots w_{im} = x_{i1}, x_{i2}, \ldots, x_{im}$$

**Table 4.19** Post's Correspondence problem without a solution

| | A | B |
|---|---|---|
| i | $w_i$ | $x_i$ |
| 1 | *ba* | *bab* |
| 2 | *abb* | *bb* |
| 3 | *bab* | *Abb* |

***Solution*** We see that this PCP instance is unsolvable, since we cannot find any correspondence sequence of integers as required.

Thus, every instance of the given PCP might not have a solution. In other words, the given PCP is undecidable; it means that the given PCP does not have any algorithmic solution.

There are a wide variety of other problems, which are undecidable.

As there is no algorithm that can handle an entire class of PCP instances, PCP is considered an unsolvable problem. There is no TM (no algorithmic solution) that can be built to solve a class of PCP instances. This also indicates that mathematics cannot always be reduced to the construction of algorithms, as even in narrow areas of mathematics, such as group theory, there are many algorithmically unsolvable problems.

## 4.19 ADDITIONAL TURING MACHINE EXAMPLES

Let us now look at some more examples of TMs.

**Example 4.17** Design a TM that increments the value of any binary number by one. The output should also be a binary number, whose value is one more than the given number.

***Solution*** Recall that we have designed a Mealy machine for solving the same problem in Chapter 2 (refer to Section 2.10.2, Example 2.16).

The following was the algorithm for the machine:

1. Read bit by bit from least significant bit (LSB) to most significant bit (MSB), that is, from right to left.
2. Keep on replacing the 1's by 0's till you reach the first 0.
3. Replace this first 0 by 1.
4. Keep the remaining bits as they are.

For example, let us consider the binary number '1001'. According to the aforementioned method, the following changes are made stepwise:

1 0 0 1 → replace by 0

1 0 0 0 → first 0, replace by 1

1 0 1 0 → remaining bits as they are without any change

Thus, '1010' is the output obtained after incrementing value of '1001' by one. We shall apply the same algorithm to build the SFM for the TM we want to design.

The initial configuration of the TM is considered as shown in Fig. 4.24(a). Using the aforementioned algorithm, we form the SFM as shown in Table 4.20. The transition graph for the same can be drawn as shown in Fig. 4.24(b).

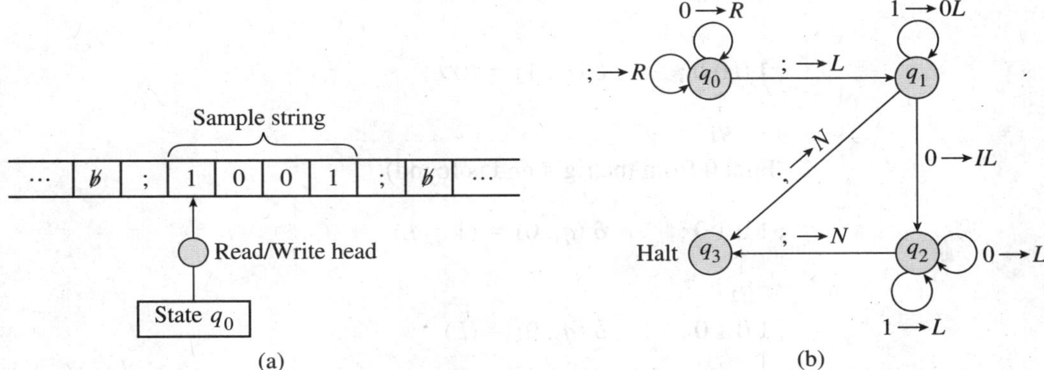


**Figure 4.24** TM that adds one to any binary number (a) Initial configuration (b) Transition graph

**Table 4.20** SFM for TM that adds one to any binary number

| S \ I | 0 | 1 | ; |
|---|---|---|---|
| $q_0$ | $R$ | $R$ | $q_1L$ |
| $q_1$ | $1q_2L$ | $0L$ | $q_3N$ |
| $q_2$ | $L$ | $L$ | $q_3N$ |
| $q_3$ | — | — | — |

For this TM, we have

$$I = \{0, 1, ;\}$$
$$S = \{q_0, q_1, q_2, q_3 = \text{halt}\}$$
$$D = \{L, R, N\}$$

State $q_0$ is responsible for finding the right end of the string so that the TM can start reading from the LSB. State $q_1$, while searching for the first 0 from the right end, replaces all the 1's by 0's. It then replaces the first 0 also by 1 and transits to state $q_2$. State $q_2$ ignores the remaining 0's and 1's—that is, it keeps all remaining bits as they are.

Now, let us simulate the working of the TM on some input binary strings.

***Simulation***

1. Let us simulate the working of the aforementioned TM for binary number '1001'.

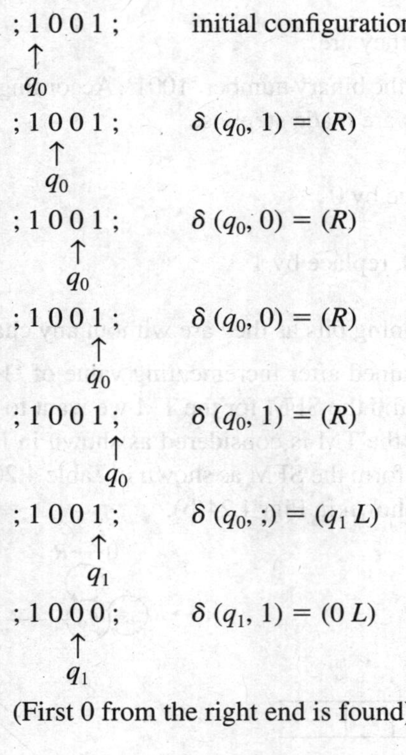

; 1 0 0 1 ; initial configuration
↑ $q_0$ (on the first ;)

; 1 0 0 1 ; $\delta(q_0, 1) = (R)$
↑ $q_0$ (on the first 1)

; 1 0 0 1 ; $\delta(q_0, 0) = (R)$
↑ $q_0$ (on the second symbol)

; 1 0 0 1 ; $\delta(q_0, 0) = (R)$
↑ $q_0$ (on the third symbol)

; 1 0 0 1 ; $\delta(q_0, 1) = (R)$
↑ $q_0$ (on the last 1)

; 1 0 0 1 ; $\delta(q_0, ;) = (q_1\, L)$
↑ $q_1$ (on the last 1)

; 1 0 0 0 ; $\delta(q_1, 1) = (0\, L)$
↑ $q_1$ (on the third symbol)

(First 0 from the right end is found)

; 1 0 1 0 ; $\delta(q_1, 0) = (1\, q_2\, L)$
↑ $q_2$ (on the second symbol)

; 1 0 1 0 ; $\delta(q_2, 0) = (L)$
↑ $q_2$ (on the first 1)

$$;1010; \quad \delta(q_2, 1) = (L)$$
$$\uparrow$$
$$q_2$$

$$;1010; \quad \delta(q_2, ;) = (q_3\ N)$$
$$\uparrow$$
$$q_3$$

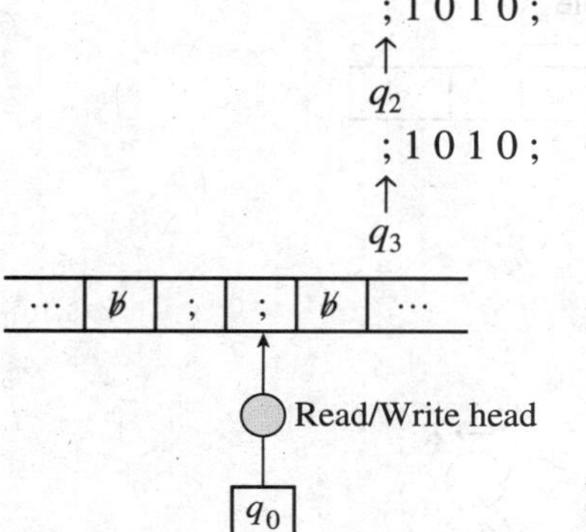

**Figure 4.25** Initial configuration when input is $\epsilon$

2. Let us check the working of the aforementioned TM for a boundary condition, that is, when an empty string is fed as the input.

When the input is an empty string, then the initial configuration will be as shown in Fig. 4.25. Initially, the head points to the right end-marker, ';', to indicate that the input string is empty.

The simulation will be as follows:

$$;; \quad \text{Initial configuration}$$
$$\uparrow$$
$$q_0$$

$$;; \quad \delta(q_0, ;) = (q_1\ L)$$
$$\uparrow$$
$$q_0$$

$$;; \quad \delta(q_1, ;) = (q_3\ N)$$
$$\uparrow$$
$$q_0$$

---

**Example 4.18** Design a TM that computes the function $f(x, y)$, which is defined as follows:

$$f(x, y) = x - y, \text{ if } x > y$$
$$= 0, \text{ if } x \leq y$$

***Solution*** Let us consider $x$ and $y$ as integers represented in unary format using symbol $a$. For computing the aforementioned function, we must compare $x$ and $y$, and then subtract $y$ from $x$, if $x > y$.

We have already designed a TM that compares two numbers in Example 4.8 in Section 4.6.

We are now going to use the same technique, but with a little modification to sets $I$ and $S$, because here, we do not have to produce the result of the comparison; we need to show the result of the subtraction only if $x > y$.

The initial configuration of the TM will be as shown in Fig. 4.26(a) and the TG for the same is shown in Fig. 4.26(b).

If $x > y$, then the TM will write the result of the subtraction, '$x - y$', after the semicolon (;). Else the machine will not write anything onto the tape.

For this TM, we have

$$I = \{a, *, ', ;, \not{b}\}$$
$$S = \{q_0, q_1, q_2, q_3, q_4, q_5, q_6, q_7 = \text{halt}\}$$
$$D = \{L, R, N\}$$

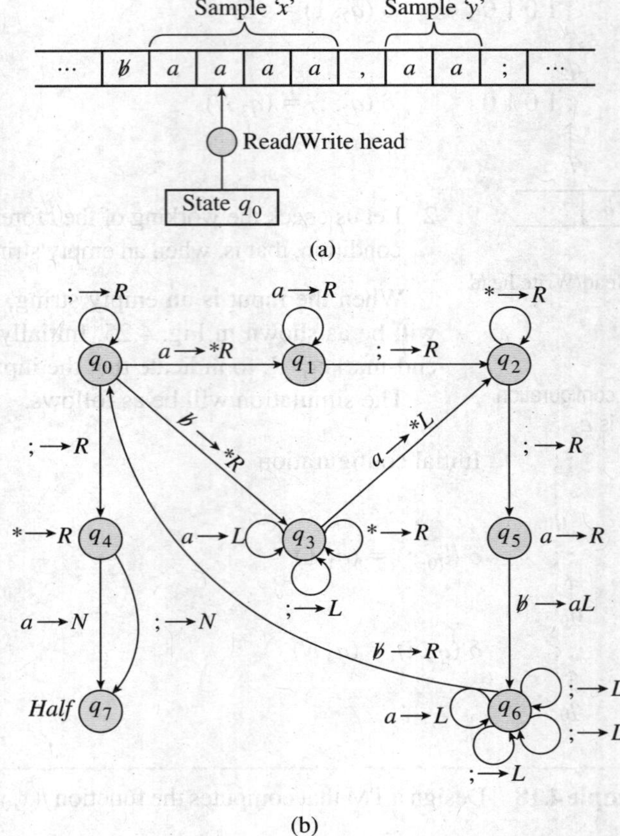


**Figure 4.26** TM that computes *f*(*x*, *y*) (a) Initial configuration (b) Transition graph

The SFM for the TM that computes *f*(*x*, *y*) is given in Table 4.21.

**Table 4.21** SFM for a TM that computes *f*(*x*, *y*)

| | *a* | , | * | ; | ƀ |
|---|---|---|---|---|---|
| $q_0$ | $*q_1R$ | $q_4R$ | $R$ | — | — |
| $q_1$ | $R$ | $q_2R$ | — | — | — |
| $q_2$ | $*q_3L$ | — | $R$ | $q_5R$ | — |
| $q_3$ | $L$ | $L$ | $L$ | — | $q_0R$ |
| $q_4$ | $q_7N$ | — | $R$ | $q_7N$ | — |
| $q_5$ | $R$ | — | — | — | $a\ q_6L$ |
| $q_6$ | $L$ | $L$ | $L$ | $L$ | $q_0R$ |

### *Simulation*

1. Let us simulate the working of the TM that we have constructed for $x = 4$ and $y = 2$, that is, for the case $x > y$. In unary from, $x$ will be represented as '*aaaa*' and $y$ is represented as '*aa*'.

```
... ƀ a a a a , a a ; ƀ ...      initial configuration
      ↑
      q0
... ƀ * a a a , a a ; ƀ ...      δ (q0, a) = (* q1 R)
        ↑
        q1
... ƀ * a a a , a a ; ƀ ...      δ (q1, a) = (R)
          ↑
          q1
... ƀ * a a a , a a ; ƀ ...      δ (q1, a) = (R)
            ↑
            q1
... ƀ * a a a , a a ; ƀ ...      δ (q1, a) = (R)
              ↑
              q1
... ƀ * a a a , a a ; ƀ ...      δ (q1, ,) = (q2 R)
                ↑
                q2
... ƀ * a a a , * a ; ƀ ...      δ (q2, a) = (* q3 L)
              ↑
              q3
... ƀ * a a a , * a ; ƀ ...      δ (q3, ,) = (L)
            ↑
            q3
... ƀ * a a a , * a ; ƀ ...      δ (q3, a) = (L)
          ↑
          q3
... ƀ * a a a , * a ; ƀ ...      δ (q3, a) = (L)
        ↑
        q3
... ƀ * a a a , * a ; ƀ ...      δ (q3, a) = (L)
      ↑
      q3
... ƀ * a a a , * a ; ƀ ...      δ (q3, *) = (L)
    ↑
    q3
... ƀ * a a a , * a ; ƀ ...      δ (q3, ƀ) = (q0 R)
      ↑
      q0
... ƀ * a a a , * a ; ƀ ...      δ (q0, *) = (R)
        ↑
        q0
... ƀ * * a a , * a ; ƀ ...      δ (q0, a) = (* q1 R)
          ↑
          q1
```

$\ldots \not{b} * * a\, a , * a ; \not{b} \ldots \qquad \delta(q_1, a) = (R)$
$\uparrow q_1$

$\ldots \not{b} * * a\, a , * a ; \not{b} \ldots \qquad \delta(q_1, a) = (R)$
$\uparrow q_1$

$\ldots \not{b} * * a\, a , * a ; \not{b} \ldots \qquad \delta(q_1, ,) = (q_2\, R)$
$\uparrow q_2$

$\ldots \not{b} * * a\, a , * a ; \not{b} \ldots \qquad \delta(q_2, *) = (R)$
$\uparrow q_2$

$\ldots \not{b} * * a\, a , * * ; \not{b} \ldots \qquad \delta(q_2, a) = (*\, q_3\, L)$
$\uparrow q_3$

$\ldots \not{b} * * a\, a , * * ; \not{b} \ldots \qquad \delta(q_3, *) = (L)$
$\uparrow q_3$

$\ldots \not{b} * * a\, a , * * ; \not{b} \ldots \qquad \delta(q_3, ,) = (L)$
$\uparrow q_3$

$\ldots \not{b} * * a\, a , * * ; \not{b} \ldots \qquad \delta(q_3, a) = (L)$
$\uparrow q_3$

$\ldots \not{b} * * a\, a , * * ; \not{b} \ldots \qquad \delta(q_3, a) = (L)$
$\uparrow q_3$

$\ldots \not{b} * * a\, a , * * ; \not{b} \ldots \qquad \delta(q_3, *) = (L)$
$\uparrow q_3$

$\ldots \not{b} * * a\, a , * * ; \not{b} \ldots \qquad \delta(q_3, *) = (L)$
$\uparrow q_3$

$\ldots \not{b} * * a\, a , * * ; \not{b} \ldots \qquad \delta(q_3, \not{b}) = (q_0\, R)$
$\uparrow q_0$

$\ldots \not{b} * * a\, a , * * ; \not{b} \ldots \qquad \delta(q_0, *) = (R)$
$\uparrow q_0$

$\ldots \not{b} * * a\, a , * * ; \not{b} \ldots \qquad \delta(q_0, *) = (R)$
$\uparrow q_0$

$\ldots \not{b} * * * a , * * ; \not{b} \ldots \qquad \delta(q_0, a) = (*\, q_1\, R)$
$\uparrow q_1$

$\ldots \not{b} * * * a , * * ; \not{b} \ldots \qquad \delta(q_1, a) = (R)$
$\uparrow q_1$

$$\ldots \not{b} * * * a , \underset{\substack{\uparrow \\ q_2}}{*} * ; \not{b} \ldots \qquad \delta\,(q_1, ,) = (q_2\, R)$$

$$\ldots \not{b} * * * a , * \underset{\substack{\uparrow \\ q_2}}{*} ; \not{b} \ldots \qquad \delta\,(q_2, *) = (R)$$

$$\ldots \not{b} * * * a , * * \underset{\substack{\uparrow \\ q_2}}{;} \not{b} \ldots \qquad \delta\,(q_2, *) = (R)$$

$$\ldots \not{b} * * * a , * * ; \underset{\substack{\uparrow \\ q_5}}{\not{b}} \ldots \qquad \delta\,(q_2, ;) = (q_5\, R)$$

($x$ is found to be greater than $y$)

$$\ldots \not{b} * * * a , * * \underset{\substack{\uparrow \\ q_6}}{;} a \not{b} \ldots \qquad \delta\,(q_5, \not{b}) = (a\, q_6\, L)$$

$$\ldots \not{b} * * * a , * \underset{\substack{\uparrow \\ q_6}}{*} ; a \not{b} \ldots \qquad \delta\,(q_6, ;) = (L)$$

$$\ldots \not{b} * * * a , \underset{\substack{\uparrow \\ q_6}}{*} * ; a \not{b} \ldots \qquad \delta\,(q_6, *) = (L)$$

$$\ldots \not{b} * * * a \underset{\substack{\uparrow \\ q_6}}{,} * * ; a \not{b} \ldots \qquad \delta\,(q_6, *) = (L)$$

$$\ldots \not{b} * * * \underset{\substack{\uparrow \\ q_6}}{a} , * * ; a \not{b} \ldots \qquad \delta\,(q_6, ,) = (L)$$

$$\ldots \not{b} * * \underset{\substack{\uparrow \\ q_6}}{*} a , * * ; a \not{b} \ldots \qquad \delta\,(q_6, a) = (L)$$

$$\ldots \not{b} * \underset{\substack{\uparrow \\ q_6}}{*} * a , * * ; a \not{b} \ldots \qquad \delta\,(q_6, *) = (L)$$

$$\ldots \not{b} \underset{\substack{\uparrow \\ q_6}}{*} * * a , * * ; a \not{b} \ldots \qquad \delta\,(q_6, *) = (L)$$

$$\ldots \underset{\substack{\uparrow \\ q_6}}{\not{b}} * * * a , * * ; a \not{b} \ldots \qquad \delta\,(q_6, *) = (L)$$

$$\ldots \not{b} \underset{\substack{\uparrow \\ q_0}}{*} * * a , * * ; a \not{b} \ldots \qquad \delta\,(q_6, \not{b}) = (q_0\, R)$$

$$\ldots \not{b} * \underset{\substack{\uparrow \\ q_0}}{*} * a , * * ; a \not{b} \ldots \qquad \delta\,(q_0, *) = (R)$$

$$\ldots \not{b} * * \underset{\substack{\uparrow \\ q_0}}{*} a , * * ; a \not{b} \ldots \qquad \delta\,(q_0, *) = (R)$$

… ƀ * * * a , * * ; a ƀ … $\qquad \delta (q_0, *) = (R)$
↑
$q_0$

… ƀ * * * * , * * ; a ƀ … $\qquad \delta (q_0, a) = (* \; q_1 \; R)$
↑
$q_1$

… ƀ * * * * , * * ; a ƀ … $\qquad \delta (q_1, ,) = (q_2 \; R)$
↑
$q_2$

… ƀ * * * * , * * ; a ƀ … $\qquad \delta (q_2, *) = (R)$
↑
$q_2$

… ƀ * * * * , * * ; a ƀ … $\qquad \delta (q_2, *) = (R)$
↑
$q_2$

… ƀ * * * * , * * ; a ƀ … $\qquad \delta (q_2, ;) = (q_5 \; R)$
↑
$q_5$

… ƀ * * * * , * * ; a ƀ … $\qquad \delta (q_5, a) = (R)$
↑
$q_5$

… ƀ * * * * , * * ; a a ƀ … $\qquad \delta (q_5, ƀ) = (a \; q_6 \; L)$
↑
$q_6$

… ƀ * * * * , * * ; a a ƀ … $\qquad \delta (q_6, a) = (L)$
↑
$q_6$

… ƀ * * * * , * * ; a a ƀ … $\qquad \delta (q_6, ;) = (L)$
↑
$q_6$

… ƀ * * * * , * * ; a a ƀ … $\qquad \delta (q_6, *) = (L)$
↑
$q_6$

… ƀ * * * * , * * ; a a ƀ … $\qquad \delta (q_6, *) = (L)$
↑
$q_6$

… ƀ * * * * , * * ; a a ƀ … $\qquad \delta (q_6, ,) = (L)$
↑
$q_6$

… ƀ * * * * , * * ; a a ƀ … $\qquad \delta (q_6, *) = (L)$
↑
$q_6$

… ƀ * * * * , * * ; a a ƀ … $\qquad \delta (q_6, *) = (L)$
↑
$q_6$

… ƀ * * * * , * * ; a a ƀ … $\qquad \delta (q_6, *) = (L)$
↑
$q_6$

$$\ldots \not{b} * * * * , * * ; a\, a\, \not{b} \ldots \qquad \delta(q_6, *) = (L)$$
$\uparrow q_6$

$$\ldots \not{b} * * * * , * * ; a\, a\, \not{b} \ldots \qquad \delta(q_6, \not{b}) = (q_0\, R)$$
$\uparrow q_0$

$$\ldots \not{b} * * * * , * * ; a\, a\, \not{b} \ldots \qquad \delta(q_0, *) = (R)$$
$\uparrow q_0$

$$\ldots \not{b} * * * * , * * ; a\, a\, \not{b} \ldots \qquad \delta(q_0, *) = (R)$$
$\uparrow q_0$

$$\ldots \not{b} * * * * , * * ; a\, a\, \not{b} \ldots \qquad \delta(q_0, *) = (R)$$
$\uparrow q_0$

$$\ldots \not{b} * * * * , * * ; a\, a\, \not{b} \ldots \qquad \delta(q_0, *) = (R)$$
$\uparrow q_0$

$$\ldots \not{b} * * * * , * * ; a\, a\, \not{b} \ldots \qquad \delta(q_0, ,) = (q_4\, R)$$
$\uparrow q_4$

$$\ldots \not{b} * * * * , * * ; a\, a\, \not{b} \ldots \qquad \delta(q_4, *) = (R)$$
$\uparrow q_4$

$$\ldots \not{b} * * * * , * * ; a\, a\, \not{b} \ldots \qquad \delta(q_4, *) = (R)$$
$\uparrow q_4$

$$\ldots \not{b} * * * * , * * ; a\, a\, \not{b} \ldots \qquad \delta(q_4, ;) = (q_7, N)$$
$\uparrow q_7$ — $a\,a$ → result of $(x - y)$ Halt

2. Let us simulate the working of this TM for $x = 1$ and $y = 2$, that is, for the condition $x < y$.

$$\ldots \not{b}\, a , a\, a ; \not{b} \ldots \qquad \text{initial configuration}$$
$\uparrow q_0$

$$\ldots \not{b} * , a\, a ; \not{b} \ldots \qquad \delta(q_0, a) = (*\, q_1\, R)$$
$\uparrow q_1$

$$\ldots \not{b} * , a\, a ; \not{b} \ldots \qquad \delta(q_1, ,) = (q_2\, R)$$
$\uparrow q_2$

$$\ldots \not{b} * , * a ; \not{b} \ldots \qquad \delta(q_2, a) = (*\, q_3\, L)$$
$\uparrow q_3$

$$\ldots \not{b} * , * a ; \not{b} \ldots \qquad \delta(q_3, ,) = (L)$$
$\uparrow q_3$

$\ldots \not b * , * a ; \not b \ldots$ $\delta (q_3, *) = (L)$
↑ $q_3$

$\ldots \not b * , * a ; \not b \ldots$ $\delta (q_3, \not b) = (q_0\ R)$
↑ $q_0$

$\ldots \not b * , * a ; \not b \ldots$ $\delta (q_0, *) = (R)$
↑ $q_0$

$\ldots \not b * , * a ; \not b \ldots$ $\delta (q_0, ,) = (q_4\ R)$
↑ $q_4$

$\ldots \not b * , * a ; \not b \ldots$ $\delta (q_4, *) = (R)$
↑ $q_4$

$\ldots \not b * , * a ; \not b \ldots$ $\delta (q_4, a) = (q_7, N)$
↑ $q_7$
Halt
'$x$' found less than '$y$'
→ blank after ';' indicates result zero as $x < y$

3. Let us simulate the working of the TM for $x = y = 1$.

$\ldots \not b\ a , a ; \not b \ldots$ initial configuration
↑ $q_0$

$\ldots \not b * , a ; \not b \ldots$ $\delta (q_0, a) = (*\ q_1\ R)$
↑ $q_1$

$\ldots \not b * , a ; \not b \ldots$ $\delta (q_1, ,) = (q_2\ R)$
↑ $q_2$

$\ldots \not b * , * ; \not b \ldots$ $\delta (q_2, a) = (*\ q_3\ L)$
↑ $q_3$

$\ldots \not b * , * ; \not b \ldots$ $\delta (q_3, ,) = (L)$
↑ $q_3$

$\ldots \not b * , * ; \not b \ldots$ $\delta (q_3, *) = (L)$
↑ $q_3$

$\ldots \not b * , * ; \not b \ldots$ $\delta (q_3, \not b) = (q_0\ R)$
↑ $q_0$

$\ldots \not b * , * ; \not b \ldots$ $\delta (q_0, *) = (R)$
↑ $q_0$

$\ldots \not b * , * ; \not b \ldots$ $\delta (q_0, ,) = (q_4\ R)$
↑ $q_4$

... ƀ * , * ; ƀ ... $\delta(q_4, *) = (R)$
↑
$q_4$
... ƀ * , * ; ƀ ... $\delta(q_4, ;) = (q_7, N)$
↑ Halt
$q_7$ 'x' found less than 'y'
→ blank after ';' indicates result zero as $x = y$

---

**Example 4.19** Design a TM to obtain the reversed string from the given input string over $\Sigma = \{a, b\}$.

***Solution*** Let us consider the initial configuration of the TM as shown in Fig. 4.27(a). The TG for this TM is shown in Fig. 4.27(b).

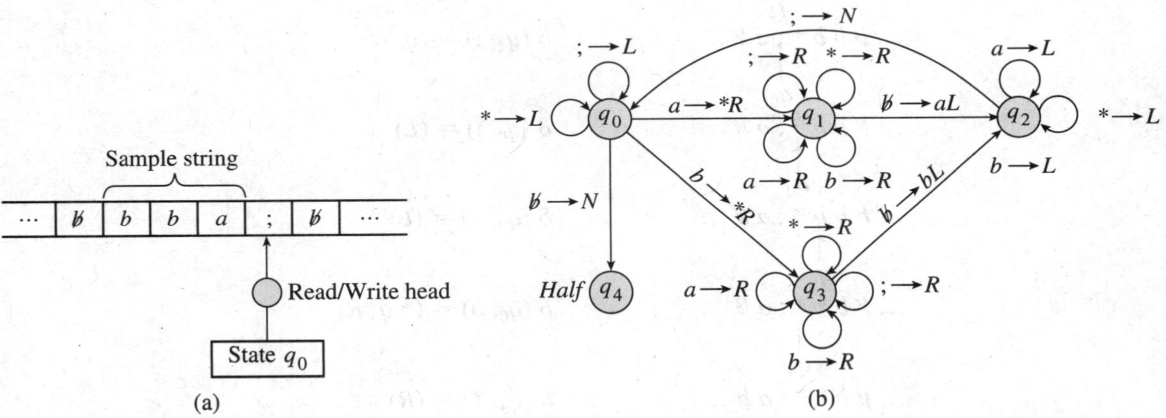


**Figure 4.27** TM that reverses input string (a) Initial configuration (b) Transition graph

For this TM, we have

$$I = \{a, b, *, ;, ƀ\}$$
$$S = \{q_0, q_1, q_2, q_3, q_4 = \text{halt}\}$$
$$D = \{L, R, N\}$$

Initially, the head points to the right end of the input string. The TM reads one character at a time from the end of the string and copies it after the end-marker, ';'. Thus, the TM reads the string characters in the reverse order and copies them to the result area to achieve the required reversed string.

The SFM for the TM is given in Table 4.22.

**Table 4.22** SFM for TM that reverses the given string

| S \ I | a | b | ; | ƀ | * |
|---|---|---|---|---|---|
| $q_0$ | $*q_1R$ | $q_3R$ | $L$ | $q_4N$ | $L$ |
| $q_1$ | $R$ | $R$ | $R$ | $a\,q_2L$ | $R$ |
| $q_2$ | $L$ | $L$ | $q_0N$ | — | $L$ |
| $q_3$ | $R$ | $R$ | $R$ | $b\,q_2L$ | $R$ |
| $q_4$ | — | — | — | — | — |

***Simulation***

1. Let us simulate the working of TM for the input string '*bba*'.

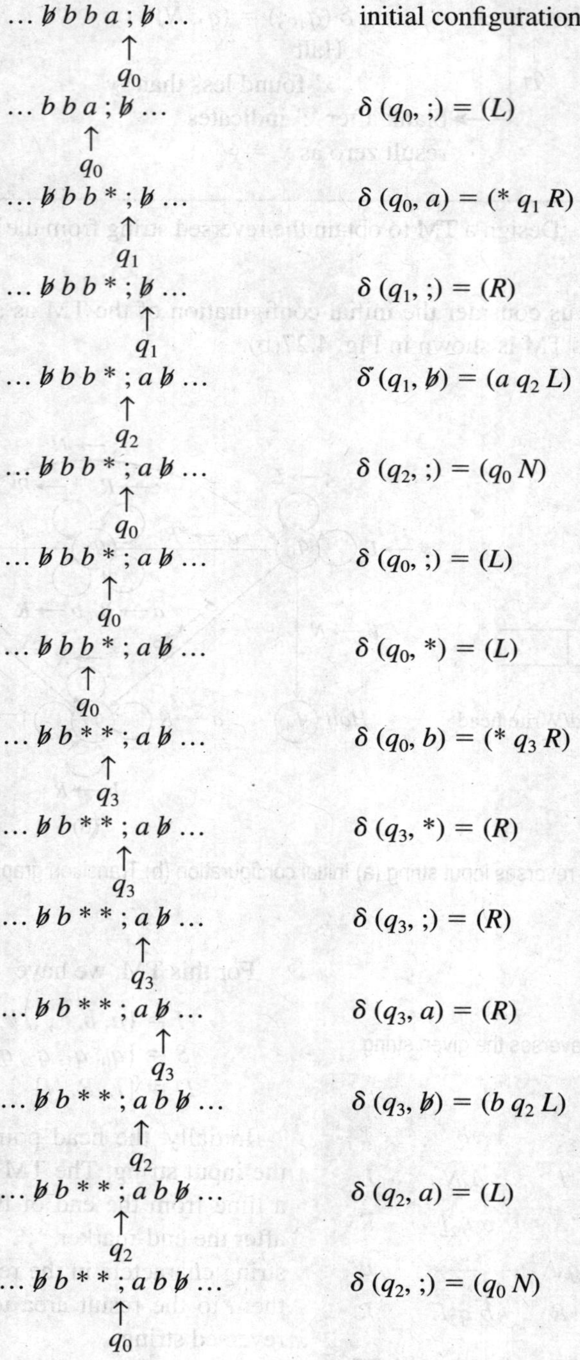

| | | |
|---|---|---|
| … $\not b$ *b b a* ; $\not b$ … | $q_0$ | initial configuration |
| … *b b a* ; $\not b$ … | $q_0$ | $\delta\ (q_0, ;) = (L)$ |
| … $\not b$ *b b* * ; $\not b$ … | $q_1$ | $\delta\ (q_0, a) = (*\ q_1\ R)$ |
| … $\not b$ *b b* * ; $\not b$ … | $q_1$ | $\delta\ (q_1, ;) = (R)$ |
| … $\not b$ *b b* * ; *a* $\not b$ … | $q_2$ | $\delta\ (q_1, \not b) = (a\ q_2\ L)$ |
| … $\not b$ *b b* * ; *a* $\not b$ … | $q_0$ | $\delta\ (q_2, ;) = (q_0\ N)$ |
| … $\not b$ *b b* * ; *a* $\not b$ … | $q_0$ | $\delta\ (q_0, ;) = (L)$ |
| … $\not b$ *b b* * ; *a* $\not b$ … | $q_0$ | $\delta\ (q_0, *) = (L)$ |
| … $\not b$ *b* * * ; *a* $\not b$ … | $q_3$ | $\delta\ (q_0, b) = (*\ q_3\ R)$ |
| … $\not b$ *b* * * ; *a* $\not b$ … | $q_3$ | $\delta\ (q_3, *) = (R)$ |
| … $\not b$ *b* * * ; *a* $\not b$ … | $q_3$ | $\delta\ (q_3, ;) = (R)$ |
| … $\not b$ *b* * * ; *a* $\not b$ … | $q_3$ | $\delta\ (q_3, a) = (R)$ |
| … $\not b$ *b* * * ; *a b* $\not b$ … | $q_2$ | $\delta\ (q_3, \not b) = (b\ q_2\ L)$ |
| … $\not b$ *b* * * ; *a b* $\not b$ … | $q_2$ | $\delta\ (q_2, a) = (L)$ |
| … $\not b$ *b* * * ; *a b* $\not b$ … | $q_0$ | $\delta\ (q_2, ;) = (q_0\ N)$ |

$\ldots \not{b}\; b * * \;;\; a\; b\; \not{b} \ldots \qquad \delta(q_0, ;) = (L)$

$\uparrow q_0$

$\ldots \not{b}\; b * * \;;\; a\; b\; \not{b} \ldots \qquad \delta(q_0, *) = (L)$

$\uparrow q_0$

$\ldots \not{b}\; b * * \;;\; a\; b\; \not{b} \ldots \qquad \delta(q_0, *) = (L)$

$\uparrow q_0$

$\ldots \not{b} * * * \;;\; a\; b\; \not{b} \ldots \qquad \delta(q_0, b) = (*\; q_3\; R)$

$\uparrow q_3$

$\ldots \not{b} * * * \;;\; a\; b\; \not{b} \ldots \qquad \delta(q_3, *) = (R)$

$\uparrow q_3$

$\ldots \not{b} * * * \;;\; a\; b\; \not{b} \ldots \qquad \delta(q_3, *) = (R)$

$\uparrow q_3$

$\ldots \not{b} * * * \;;\; a\; b\; \not{b} \ldots \qquad \delta(q_3, ;) = (R)$

$\uparrow q_3$

$\ldots \not{b} * * * \;;\; a\; b\; \not{b} \ldots \qquad \delta(q_3, a) = (R)$

$\uparrow q_3$

$\ldots \not{b} * * * \;;\; a\; b\; \not{b} \ldots \qquad \delta(q_3, b) = (R)$

$\uparrow q_3$

$\ldots \not{b} * * * \;;\; a\; b\; b\; \not{b} \ldots \qquad \delta(q_3, \not{b}) = (b\; q_2\; L)$

$\uparrow q_2$

$\ldots \not{b} * * * \;;\; a\; b\; b\; \not{b} \ldots \qquad \delta(q_2, b) = (L)$

$\uparrow q_2$

$\ldots \not{b} * * * \;;\; a\; b\; b\; \not{b} \ldots \qquad \delta(q_2, a) = (L)$

$\uparrow q_2$

$\ldots \not{b} * * * \;;\; a\; b\; b\; \not{b} \ldots \qquad \delta(q_2, ;) = (q_0\; N)$

$\uparrow q_0$

$\ldots \not{b} * * * \;;\; a\; b\; b\; \not{b} \ldots \qquad \delta(q_0, ;) = (L)$

$\uparrow q_0$

$\ldots \not{b} * * * \;;\; a\; b\; b\; \not{b} \ldots \qquad \delta(q_0, *) = (L)$

$\uparrow q_0$

$\ldots \not{b} * * * \;;\; a\; b\; b\; \not{b} \ldots \qquad \delta(q_0, *) = (L)$

$\uparrow q_0$

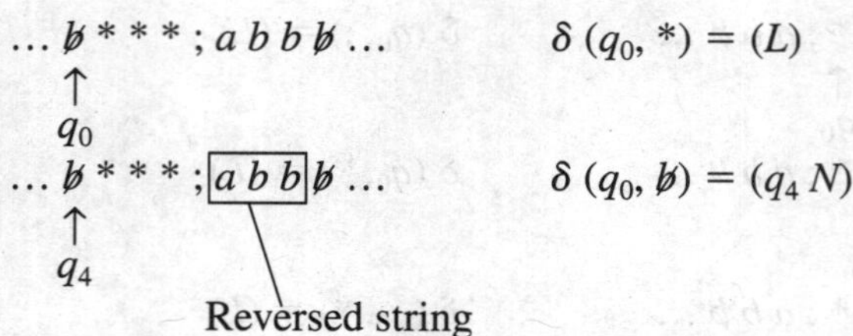


2. Let us check the working of this TM for a boundary condition, that is, for empty input.

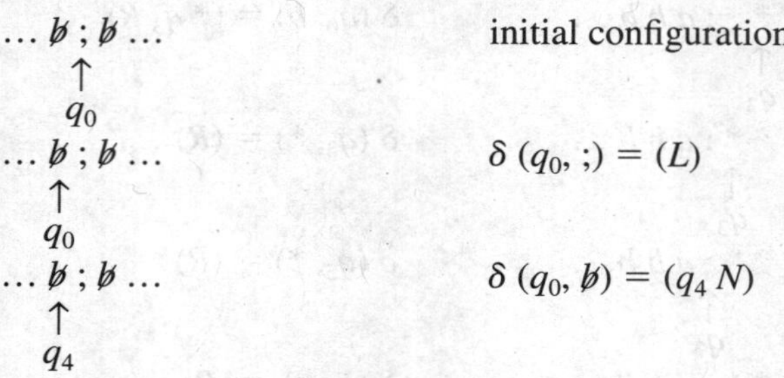


---

**Example 4.20** Draw a transition table for a TM that accepts the language of all non-palindromes over $\{a, b\}$.

***Solution*** In Section 4.6 (refer to Example 4.7), we designed a TM that accepts all palindrome sequences over {0, 1}. This problem is exactly the reverse.

Let us assume the initial configuration to be as shown in Fig. 4.28.

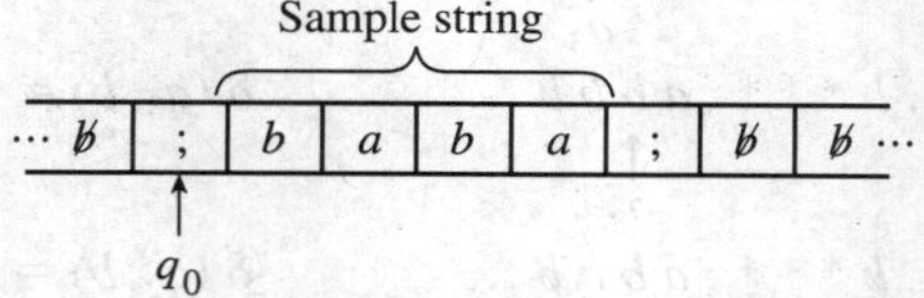


**Figure 4.28** Initial configuration

Let us assume that the TM will output $T$ if the string is non-palindrome; else, it outputs $F$. The SFM for the TM is as shown in Table 4.23.

**Table 4.23** SFM for a TM that accepts non-palindromes

| $\delta$ Q \ Σ | $a$ | $b$ | ; |
|---|---|---|---|
| $q_0$ | $L$ | $L$ | $q_1R$ |
| $q_1$ | $;q_2R$ | $;q_4R$ | $Fq_6N$ |
| $q_2$ | $R$ | $R$ | $q_3L$ |
| $q_3$ | $;q_0L$ | $Tq_6N$ | $Fq_6N$ |
| $q_4$ | $R$ | $R$ | $q_5L$ |
| $q_5$ | $Tq_6N$ | $;q_0L$ | $Fq_6N$ |
| Halt $q_6$ | — | — | — |

Observe that this transition table generates $T$ wherever the SFM in Table 4.9 (refer to Example 4.7) generates $F$, and vice versa. These two TMs are complements of each other, except that they work on different input symbols.

---

## 4.20 LINEAR BOUNDED AUTOMATA

A linear bounded automaton (LBA) is a restricted form of Turing machine, which follows three main restrictions:

1. The tape alphabet includes two special symbols, serving as left and right end-markers (just as in the case of two-way finite automata; refer to Chapter 2).

2. The end-markers cannot be erased. Hence, one cannot write anything at the end-marker positions.
3. Transitions do not make the head move to the left of the left end-marker or to the right of the right end-marker.

Just as in a Turing machine, the LBA consists of a tape made up of cells that can contain symbols from a finite tape alphabet—a head that can read from or write to one cell on the tape at a time, and can either be moved one position to the left or right, or remain in the same position (within the boundaries of the end-markers) and a finite number of states.

The difference between the two is that while a Turing machine has a tape, which is considered unbounded at both the ends, the LBA has only a finite contiguous portion of the tape, whose length is a linear function of the length of the initial input. Hence, the name linear bounded automata. It is computationally equivalent to a Turing machine, though restricted. Instead of having an infinite tape to compute, the computation in the LBA is restricted to the portion of the tape containing the input, plus the two tape cells holding the end-markers. This limitation makes the LBA a somewhat more *realistic* model of computers than a Turing machine.

## SUMMARY

A *Turing machine* (TM) is a computational model that we can use to solve any problem that has an algorithmic solution. A problem for which we cannot build a TM is said to be unsolvable.

A TM accepts or recognizes *recursively enumerable languages* (REL), as well as *regular languages*—the set of all regular languages is a proper subset of the class of RELs. Therefore, for every finite state machine (FSM) there exists an equivalent TM, but the converse is not true. The TM is the most powerful machine among other computation models, including the FSM.

A TM consists of the following:

1. A head that can read or write a symbol and move either to the left or right, or stay in its position, depending on the symbol read from the tape cell.
2. An infinite tape, extending on either side of the head, marked off into square cells, on which the symbols from an alphabet set can be written. The tape represents the unbounded one-dimensional memory of the TM (refer to Fig. 4.1).
3. A finite set of symbols, known as an external alphabet set $I$, which consists of lower-case English letters, digits, usual punctuation marks, and the blank character '$\not{b}$'.
4. A finite set of states denoted by $S$, in one of which the machine can reside.

A TM has an infinite memory in the form of a tape that is unbounded at both ends—a read/write head that can move in any direction and helps the machine retrieve information that has been stored earlier. In a way, it converts the dumb storage into memory. A TM can consume its own output as input at a later stage while executing the algorithm, which makes it a very powerful machine. There is no distinction between the input and output alphabet sets.

A TM is denoted with the help of three functions, namely, the *machine function* (MAF), the *state transition function* (STF), and the *direction function* (DIF), which are defined as follows:

MAF: $I \times S \rightarrow I$
STF: $I \times S \rightarrow S$
DIF: $I \times S \rightarrow D = \{L, R, N\}$,

where,
$L$ stands for 'move towards left by one tape cell position';
$R$ stands for 'move towards right by one tape cell position';

and $N$ stands for 'no movement, that is, stay in the same position, or remain at the same tape cell position'.

Note that the MAF for an FSM is defined as $I \times S \rightarrow O$, as there is a distinction between the input and the output, while in case of a TM it is defined as $I \times S \rightarrow I$, as there is no distinction between the input and output.

A Turing machine (TM) is denoted by

$M = (Q, \Sigma, \Gamma, \delta, q_0, B, F)$,

where,

$Q$: Finite set of states

$\Gamma$: Finite set of allowable tape symbols including blank character ƀ

$\Sigma$: Subset of '$\Gamma$', excluding blank character ƀ; it is the set of input symbols

$B$: A symbol for blank character ƀ

$q_0$: Start (or initial) state $\in Q$

$F$: Set of final states (or halt states) $\subseteq Q$

$\delta$: Functional matrix, such that $\delta$: $(Q \times \Gamma) \rightarrow (Q \times \Gamma \times \{L, R, N\})$

In order to have a deterministic TM, for every state $\alpha$ on some symbol $a$, there should be a unique triple $(b, \beta, D)$ for the entry $\delta(\alpha, a)$ in the functional matrix. For some arguments, $\delta$ might be undefined. For such arguments, we write '-' in the SFM (just as we do in a state transition table of a finite state machine).

The FSM can be considered as a special case of the TM, whose tape length is finite and the head movement is restricted only to one direction.

An *instantaneous description* (ID) of a TM $M$ is denoted by '$\alpha_1\ q\ \alpha_2$', where $q$ is the current state of the TM, $q \in Q$, and '$\alpha_1\ \alpha_2$' is the string in $\Gamma^*$ that is contained in the tape bounded on both ends by the blank character ƀ. Note that the blank character may occur within '$\alpha_1\ \alpha_2$' as well.

We can define a move (or transition) of $M$ as follows:

Let '$a_0\ a_1 \ldots a_{i-1}\ q\ a_i \ldots a_n$' be an ID of $M$. This ID indicates that the current machine state is $q$ and the machine head is about to read symbol $a_i$ from the tape.

Suppose, $\delta(q, a_i) = (*, p, L)$ is a transition, where if $i = n + 1$, then $a_i$ is taken to be ƀ;

if $i = 0$, then in the next ID, the tape head goes one position to the left of the first symbol that is considered to be blank character ƀ; and

If $i > 1$, we can write the ID for the aforementioned transition as

$$a_0\ a_1 \ldots a_{i-1}\ q\ a_i \ldots a_n \underset{M}{\vdash} a_0\ a_1 \ldots a_{i-2}\ p\ a_{i-1} * a_{i+1} \ldots a_n$$

Similarly, for the move $\delta(q, a_i) = (*, p, R)$ we can write

$$a_0\ a_1 \ldots a_{i-1}\ q\ a_i \ldots a_n \underset{M}{\vdash} a_0\ a_1 \ldots a_{i-1} * p\ a_{i+1} \ldots a_n$$

The language accepted by a TM, $M = (Q, \Sigma, \Gamma, \delta, q_0, B, F)$ is described as

$L(M) = \{w \mid w \in \Sigma^*$, and $q_0 W \overset{*}{\underset{M}{\vdash}} \alpha_1\ p\ \alpha_2$ for some $p$ in $F$, and $\alpha_1$ and $\alpha_2$ in $\Gamma^*\}$

The *complexity of a TM* is directly proportional to the size of its functional matrix. In turn, we can say that the complexity of a TM depends on the number of symbols and the number of states of the TM.

Complexity of a TM $= |\Gamma| \times |Q|$,

where,

$|\Gamma|$ = Cardinality of tape alphabet (i.e., number of tape symbols)

$|Q|$ = Number of states of the TM

Two or more TMs can be combined to solve a complex problem, such that the output of one TM forms the input to the next TM, and so on. This is called a *composition*. Another way of having a combination TM is by applying its own output as input repetitively. This is called *iteration* or *recursion*.

A *universal Turing machine* (UTM) is capable of simulating any TM $T$, if the following information is available onto its tape:

- The description of $T$ in terms of its SFM (*program area* of the tape)
- The initial configuration of $T$ along with the processing data (input string) to be fed to $T$ (*data area* of the tape).

A UTM requires an *imitation algorithm* (simulating logic in the form of its SFM) to correctly interpret the rules of the operation given in the SFM for $T$.

The concept of UTM laid the foundation for *stored-program computers*. The SFM for UTM can be visualized as part of the operating system, that is, the program (or finite set of programs) capable of loading and executing other programs. Hence, the

UTM is a meta-program that takes other programs as input and simulates them. *Program as data* is the concept used here, which was later adopted in Lambda-calculus as well.

*Multi-tape Turing machines* are similar to single-tape machines, but have a constant $k$ number of independent tapes with their own read/write heads. This TM has independent control over all the heads, and any of these can move and read/write their own tapes. All these tapes are unbounded at both the ends just as in a single-tape TM. Though the multi-tape TM model intuitively seems to be much more powerful than the single-tape model, any multi-tape machine, no matter how large $k$ may be, can be simulated by a single-tape machine using quadratically more computation time.

The organization of a TM, in which the symbols to the left of the head of the TM are stored onto one stack, while the symbols on the right of the head are placed onto the other stack, is known as a *multi-stack Turing machine* or a two-stack Turing machine. In this system, the symbols closer to the Turing machine's head are placed closer to the top of each stack.

A *multi-track Turing machine* is a specific type of multi-tape Turing machine. In a standard $k$-tape Turing machine, there are $k$ heads that move independently along $k$ tracks (tapes). On the other hand, in a $k$-track Turing machine, one head reads and writes on all tracks simultaneously. This is equivalent to a standard single-tape Turing machine, except that it reads/writes $k$ symbols at one go, and therefore, accepts the recursively enumerable languages.

If there is a TM, which when applied to any problem, always terminates with the correct 'yes' or 'no' answer, then we call the problem *solvable*. For example, consider the problem of determining whether or not a given binary number is a palindrome (refer to Example 4.7). For any input binary number, the TM halts with the answer $T$ (i.e., 'yes') or $F$ (i.e., 'no'), respectively, based on whether or not the given binary number is a palindrome sequence.

If there is a TM, which when applied to any problem, always terminates when the answer is 'yes' but may or may not terminate when the answer is 'no', we call the problem *semi-solvable* or *partially solvable*. For example, division is undefined if the divisor is zero; hence, the TM may not terminate if the divisor is zero. This is a semi-solvable problem.

If there is no TM, which when applied to a problem eventually terminates with the answer 'yes', we call the problem *unsolvable*. *Post's correspondence problem* (PCP) is one such unsolvable problem.

Let $A = w_1, w_2, \ldots, w_k$, and $B = x_1, x_2, \ldots, x_k$ be strings over some alphabet $\Sigma$. Post's correspondence problem (PCP) is to find the correspondence sequence of integers, $i_1, i_2, \ldots, i_m$, for $m \geq 1$ such that

$$w_{i1}, w_{i2}, \ldots, w_{im} = x_{i1}, x_{i2}, \ldots, x_{im}$$

The sequence, '$i_1, i_2, \ldots, i_m$' is considered as the solution for the PCP instance. Each PCP instance is constituted by some set of values for $A$ and $B$.

Given any TM, the problem of determining whether or not it ever halts, is called the *halting problem*. The halting problem is unsolvable, meaning that there exists no TM, which can determine whether or not a given TM $T$ will ever halt. In other words, no program can detect whether or not any given input program (including itself), will ever halt. This limits what can be computed using a computer.

The language that is accepted by a TM is called a *recursively enumerable language*. The term enumerable is derived from the fact that it is precisely these languages, whose strings can be enumerated (listed) by a TM. For example, if $L(M)$ is such a language, and if $w$ is any string in $L(M)$, then $M$ eventually halts on input $w$; however, if the input string belongs to $\sim L(M)$—the complement of the set $L(M)$—then the TM $M$ might fail to halt on this input. Recursively enumerable languages belong to the semi-solvable class of problems.

It is convenient to single out a sub-class of recursively enumerable sets called *recursive languages* (or recursive sets), which are the languages that are accepted by at least one TM that halts on all inputs. The TM $M$ either reaches the 'accept halt' state if the input belongs to the $L(M)$ or reaches the 'reject halt' state if the input does not belong to $L(M)$. Recursive languages belong to the solvable class of problems discussed earlier.

If $f(i_1, i_2, \ldots, i_k)$ is defined for all values of arguments $i_1, \ldots, i_k$, then $f$ is said to be a *total recursive function*. These total recursive functions correspond to the recursive languages, since they are computed by a TM that always halts.

If $f(i_1, i_2, \ldots, i_k)$ is not defined for all values of arguments $i_1, \ldots, i_k$, then $f$ is said to be a *partial recursive function*. In other words, a function $f(i_1, \ldots, i_k)$ computed by a TM, which may or may not halt on a given input, is said to be a partial recursive function. Partial recursive functions are analogous to the recursively enumerable languages, since they are computed by a TM that halts on acceptance and may or may not halt for any other input.

A *linear bounded automaton* (LBA) is a restricted form of a TM. While a TM has a tape, which is considered unbounded at both the ends, the LBA only has a finite contiguous portion of tape, whose length is a linear function of the length of the initial input. However, it is computationally equivalent to a Turing machine. The LBA is a somewhat more *realistic* model of computers than a Turing machine.

## EXERCISES

This section lists a few unsolved problems to help the readers understand the topic better and practice a few examples related to TMs.

### Objective Questions

Ⓛ 4.1 An arbitrary TM $M$ is given, and a language $L$ is defined as follows

$L = (0 + 00)^*$ if $M$ accepts at least one string.

$L = (0 + 00 + 000)^*$ if $M$ accepts at least two strings.

$L = (0 + 00 + 000 + 0000)^*$ if $M$ accepts at least three strings

Similarly,

$L = (0 + 00 + 000 + \ldots +0\text{^}n)^*$ if $M$ accepts at least $n - 1$ strings.

Choose the correct statement.

(a) We cannot say anything about $L$, as the question of whether or not a TM accepts a string is undecidable.

(b) $L$ is context-sensitive but not regular.

(c) $L$ is context-free but not regular.

(d) $L$ is not a finite set.

Ⓛ 4.2 If the strings of a language $L$ that is accepted by a TM can be effectively enumerated in lexicographic (i.e., alphabetic) order, which of the following statements is true?

(a) $L$ is necessarily finite.

(b) $L$ is regular but not necessarily finite.

(c) $L$ is context-free but not necessarily regular.

(d) $L$ is recursive but not necessarily context-free.

Ⓛ 4.3 If the strings of a language $L$ that are accepted by a multi-track TM $M$ can be effectively enumerated in lexicographic (i.e., alphabetic) order, which of the following statements is true?

(a) $L$ is necessarily finite.

(b) $L$ is regular but not necessarily finite.

(c) $L$ is context-free but not necessarily regular.

(d) $L$ is recursive but not necessarily context-free.

Ⓡ 4.4 The language accepted by a TM is called __________ language.

Ⓤ 4.5 State whether the following statements are true or false.

(a) FSM and TM are equivalent machines.

(b) For every FSM there exists an equivalent TM.

(c) For every TM there exists an equivalent FSM.

(d) FSM is more powerful than TM.

Ⓡ 4.6 SFM means __________.

Ⓛ 4.7 A single-tape TM $M$ has two states, $q_0$ and $q_1$, of which $q_0$ is the starting state. The tape alphabet of $M$ is $\{0, 1, \not{b}\}$ and its input alphabet is $\{0, 1\}$. The symbol $\not{b}$ is used to indicate the end of the input string. The transition function of $M$ is described in Table 4.24.

**Table 4.24** Transition function of *M*

| | 0 | 1 | $b\!\!/$ |
|---|---|---|---|
| $q_0$ | $q_1\ 1\ R$ | $q_1\ 1\ R$ | Halt |
| $q_1$ | $q_1\ 1\ R$ | $q_0\ 1\ L$ | $q_0\ b\!\!/\ L$ |

Which of the following statements is false about *M*?

(a) *M* halts on any string in $(0 + 1)^+$
(b) *M* halts on any string in $(00 + 1)^*$
(c) *M* does not halt on all strings ending in 0
(d) *M* does not halt on all strings ending in 1

(L) 4.8 Consider a TM *M* whose SFM is as shown in Table 4.25, where $Q_0$ is the initial state and $Q_f$ is a final (halt) state.

**Table 4.25** Simplified functional matrix

| | 0 | 1 | B |
|---|---|---|---|
| $Q_0$ | $Q_0\ 0\ R$ | $Q_2\ 1\ L$ | $Q_f\ N$ |
| $Q_1$ | $Q_2\ 1\ L$ | $Q_1\ 1\ R$ | $Q_f\ N$ |
| $Q_2$ | $Q_2\ 1\ L$ | $Q_2\ 0\ L$ | $Q_f\ N$ |
| $Q_f$ | — | — | — |

Choose the correct statement:

(a) The machine accepts all strings over {0, 1} ending with 1.
(b) The machine accepts $0^*$.
(c) The machine accepts 01.
(d) The machine accepts 001.

(U) 4.9 Which of the following languages are accepted by a TM?

(i) $L = \{a^n b^n \mid n = 0, 1, 2, \ldots\}$
(ii) The set of palindromes over alphabet $\{a, b\}$
(iii) $L = \{a^n, b^m c^{2m} \mid n, m \geq 0\}$

(a) Only (i)
(b) Only (ii)
(c) (i) and (iii)
(d) All of these
(e) None of these

(U) 4.10 With respect to the power of recognition of languages, which of the following statements is false?

(a) Linear bound automata are equivalent to Turing machines.
(b) Linear bound automata are equivalent to multi-track TMs.
(c) Linear bound automata are equivalent to deterministic finite automata.
(d) Linear bound automata are equivalent to multi-tape TMs.

(U) 4.11 The C language is

(a) a context-free language
(b) a context-sensitive language
(c) a regular language.
(d) completely parsable only by TMs.

(U) 4.12 Choose the correct statement:

(a) There exists a universal TM, which can simulate any TM *M* on its input *w*.
(b) There does not exist a universal Turing machine, which can simulate any TM *M* on its input *w*.
(c) The universal language is recursive.

(U) 4.13 State whether the following statement is true of false:
Total recursive function is a special case of partial recursive function.

## Review Questions

(L) 4.1 Compare FSM and TM.

(U) 4.2 Explain the halting problem.

(C) 4.3 Design a TM for multiplying two unary numbers. Show the stepwise functioning of the TM for the input sequences:
(a) 111 × 1111 (b) 111 × 11

(C) 4.4 Design a TM to recognize an arbitrary string divisible by 4 from $\Sigma = \{0, 1, 2\}$.

(C) 4.5 Design a TM to compute *n*! (factorial *n*). Show the stepwise functioning of the TM for the input $n = 3$.

(C) 4.6 Design a TM to convert a binary-coded decimal number into a unary number. Validate the design for:
(a) 1001 (b) 0000

(U) 4.7 What is a universal Turing machine?

(C) 4.8 Design a TM to find the GCD of two given numbers.

(U) 4.9 Write a short note on the halting problem.

(C) 4.10 Design a TM to compare two numbers, which will produce the output *L* if the first number is lesser than the second number, output *G* if the first number is greater than the second number, and output *E* otherwise.

Ⓒ 4.11 Design a TM, which computes the 2's complement of a given binary number.

Ⓒ 4.12 Construct a TM for the language, $L = \{a^m b^n \mid m \geq n, n \geq 1\}$.

Ⓒ 4.13 Construct a TM for checking if a given set of parentheses are well-formed.

Ⓤ 4.14 Write a short note on solvability and semi-solvability.

Ⓤ 4.15 Write a short note on recursive TM.

Ⓛ 4.16 Consider the TM $M = \{(q_0, q_1, q_2, q_f), (0, 1), (0, 1, B), \delta, q_0, B, (q_f)\}$.
Describe the language $L(M)$, if $\delta$ consists of the following sets of rules:
$\delta(q_0, 0) = (q_1\ 1\ R)$;
$\delta(q_1, 1) = (q_0\ 0\ R)$;
$\delta(q_1, B) = (q_f\ B\ R)$.

Ⓒ 4.17 Design a TM that accepts the language $\{0^n 1^n 0^n \mid n \geq 1\}$. In addition, give the transition function and the transition diagram.

Ⓔ 4.18 Construct a TM that accepts the language $(a^* b a^* b)$.

Ⓒ 4.19 Design TMs that recognize the following languages:
(a) $\{0^n 1^n 0^n \mid n \geq 1\}$
(b) $\{WW^R \mid W \text{ is in } (0 + 1)^*\}$
(c) The set of strings with equal number of 0's and 1's

Ⓤ 4.20 Define the TM, explain its working, and give the applications of the same.

Ⓒ 4.21 Construct TMs that recognize the following languages:
(a) $L = \{0^n 1^m \mid n, m >= 0\}$
(b) $L = \{x \in \{0, 1\}^* \mid x \text{ ends in } 00\}$

Ⓤ 4.22 Define and explain a multi-tape TM.

Ⓤ 4.23 Define recursive and recursively enumerable languages.

Ⓤ 4.24 Explain the following for a TM:
(a) Power of TM over finite state machine
(b) Universal TM

Ⓔ 4.25 Design a TM to replace '110' by '101' in a binary input string.

Ⓤ 4.26 Write a short note on Post's correspondence problem (PCP).

Ⓒ 4.27 Draw transitions tables for TMs that accept the following languages:
(a) $\{a^i b^j \mid i < j\}$
(b) The language of balanced string of parentheses

Ⓒ 4.28 Draw a transition table for a TM that accepts the language of all non-palindromes over $\{a, b\}$.

Ⓡ 4.29 Define the following:
(a) Multi-track TM
(b) Multi-tape TM
(c) Recursively enumerable language
(d) Recursive language

Ⓒ 4.30 Design a TM to compute the function $n^2$.

Ⓒ 4.31 Design a TM to accept the language, $L = \{x \in \{0, 1\}^* \mid x$ contains equal number of 0's and 1's$\}$. Simulate the operation for the string '110100'.

Ⓒ 4.32 Design a TM to find the value of $\log_2 n$, where $n$ is any binary number and a perfect power of 2.

Ⓔ 4.33 Determine the solution for the following instance of Post's correspondence problem in Table 4.26.

**Table 4.26** Post's correspondence problem

| | A | B |
|---|---|---|
| $i$ | $w_i$ | $x_i$ |
| 1 | 01 | 0 |
| 2 | 110010 | 0 |
| 3 | 1 | 1111 |
| 4 | 11 | 01 |

**Answers to Objective Questions**

4.1. (a) 4.2. (d) 4.3. (d) 4.4. recursively enumerable 4.5. (a) False (b) True (c) False (d) True 4.6. simplified functional matrix 4.7. (a) 4.8. (b) 4.9. (d) 4.10. (c) 4.11. (a) 4.12. (a) 4.13. True

# Grammars

**LEARNING OBJECTIVES**

After completing this chapter, the reader will be able to understand the following:

- Concept of context-free grammars (CFGs)
- Formalism of CFGs and context-free languages (CFLs)
- Leftmost/Rightmost derivations and derivation tree
- Concept of ambiguous grammar and removal of ambiguity
- Simplification of CFG
- Chomsky normal form (CNF) and Greibach normal form (GNF)
- Chomsky hierarchy
- Equivalence of regular grammars and finite automata
- Concept of derivation graph
- Applications of CFG
- Backus–Naur form (BNF)
- Kuroda normal form
- Dyck language
- Pumping lemma and Ogden's lemma

## 5.1 INTRODUCTION

Grammar, for a particular language, is defined as a finite set of formal rules for generating syntactically correct sentences. The language may be a formal programming language, such as C, C++, and Java, or natural language such as English and French. Any type of language requires a grammar, which defines syntactically correct statement formats or constructs allowed for that particular language. Hence, we can also call a grammar for a language as the *syntactic definition* of the language; and we can, therefore, say that *grammar defines syntax of a language.*

For example, if we want to generate the English statement 'dog runs', we may use the following rules:

| | | |
|---|---|---|
| < Sentence > | → | < noun > < verb > |
| < Noun > | → | dog |
| < Verb > | → | runs |

These rules describe how the sentence of the form 'noun' followed by 'verb' can be generated. As we know, there are many such rules in the English language; and these are collectively called the grammar for the language.

In this chapter, we are going to discuss the grammar for formal languages, particularly context-free grammar (CFG).

## 5.2 CONSTITUENTS OF GRAMMAR

Grammar consists of two types of symbols—terminals and non-terminals (also called variables or auxiliary symbols).

Terminal symbols are those symbols that are part of a generated sentence. For example, in the aforementioned example, 'dog' and 'runs' are the terminal symbols as they collectively formulate the statement and are part of the generated statement.

Non-terminal symbols are those symbols that take part in the formation (or generation) of the statement, but are not part of the generated statement. No statement that is generated using grammar rules will ever contain non-terminals. For example, in the aforementioned example, 'sentence', 'noun', and 'verb' are non-terminals, which are not present in the generated statement; but they took part in the formation of the statement.

We see that:

$$\langle\text{sentence}\rangle \xrightarrow{\text{gives}} \langle\text{noun}\rangle\ \langle\text{verb}\rangle$$
$$\xrightarrow{\text{gives}} \text{dog runs}$$

Therefore, non-terminals are essential while declaring the rules; without these, the grammar cannot be defined. These rules for grammar are also called *productions*, *production rules*, or *syntactical rules.* The word 'production' is used in relation with the statement-generation process (or derivation process).

## 5.3 FORMAL DEFINITION OF GRAMMAR

For building a formal model, we must consider two aspects of the given grammar:

1. The generative capacity of the grammar, that is, the grammar used should generate all and only those sentences of the language for which it is written.
2. Constituents of the grammar—terminals and non-terminals.

A grammar that is based on the constituent structure described here is called *constituent structure grammar* or *phase structure grammar.*

A phrase structure grammar is denoted by a quadruple of the form:

$$G = \{V, T, P, S\},$$

where,

$V$: Finite set of non-terminals (or variables); sometimes this is also denoted by $N$ instead of $V$
$T$: Finite set of terminals

$S$: $S$ is a non-terminal, which is a member of $N$; it usually denotes the starting symbol
$P$: Finite set of productions (or syntactical rules)

Productions have the generic form '$\alpha \rightarrow \beta$', where $\alpha, \beta \subset (V \cup T)^*$, and $\alpha \neq \epsilon$. As we know, $V \cap T = \phi$. Note that $\alpha$ and $\beta$ may consist of any number of terminals as well as non-terminals and they are usually termed as *sentential forms.*

If the production rules have the form: '$A \rightarrow \alpha$', where $A$ is any non-terminal and $\alpha$ is any sentential form, then such grammar is called *context-free grammar (CFG).*

Observe that in this type of grammar has a restriction that on the left-hand side of each production there is only one non-terminal. For example, the grammar that we have considered for generating the statement 'dog runs' is context-free grammar (with some notational differences; these will be discussed in sections 5.4 and 5.16).

## 5.4 GRAMMAR NOTATIONS

There are some typical notations used for grammars. The following are some simple CFG notations:

1. Non-terminals are usually denoted by capital letters: $A, B, C, D$, etc.
2. Terminals are denoted by small case letters: $a$, $b$, $c$, etc.
3. Strings of terminals (that is, valid words in the language for which the grammar is written) are usually denoted by $u$, $v$, $w$, $x$, $y$, $z$, etc.
4. Sentential forms, that is, strings of the form $(V \cup T)^*$ that are formed using any combination of terminals and non-terminals are denoted by $\alpha$, $\beta$, $\gamma$, etc.
5. The arrow symbol, '$\rightarrow$', stands for production. For example, a production denoted by '$A \rightarrow b$' indicates, '*A produces b*'.
6. If the same non-terminal has multiple productions, that is, there is more than one rule for the same non-terminal, we use '|' (which means 'or') to represent the grammar in a simplified form.

   For example, let us consider the following grammar $G$:

   $$G = \{(E), (+, *, a), P, E\},$$

   where, $P$ consists of the following productions:

   $$P = \{E \rightarrow E + E,\; E \rightarrow E * E,\; E \rightarrow a\;\}$$

   We see that all the three productions mentioned are for the non-terminal $E$, that is, all the three productions have the same left-hand side. In such a case, we can combine these with the help of the '|' operator as shown here:

   $$P = \{E \rightarrow E + E \mid E * E \mid a\}$$

7. The '$\Rightarrow$' symbol stands for the process of derivation (or generation) of any string belonging to some language.

For example, let us consider the production set $P$ that consists of the productions: $\{S \rightarrow AB; A \rightarrow a; B \rightarrow b\}$. Let us try to derive or generate the string '*ab*' using this set of productions. Every grammar has a start symbol and that is the starting point for any derivation process. Hence, we begin with the start symbol $S$.

As $S$ produces $AB$, we can derive or generate $AB$ from $S$.

$$S \overset{\text{derives}}{\Rightarrow} AB$$

Since $A$ produces $a$, we have:

$$S \overset{\text{derives '}a\text{'}}{\Rightarrow} a\,B$$

Since $B$ produces $b$, we have:

$$S \overset{\text{derives '}b\text{'}}{\Rightarrow} ab$$

Here, the symbol '$\Rightarrow$' stands for 'derived in a single step'. Similarly, the symbol '$\overset{*}{\Rightarrow}$' stands for 'derived in any number of steps'. For example, we can write, $S \overset{*}{\Rightarrow} ab$, for the aforementioned generation process. We shall discuss more about the derivation process in the next section.

8. It is possible to have a production of the form '$A \rightarrow \epsilon$', which is termed as an '*ϵ-production*'.

## 5.5 DERIVATION PROCESS

Any string that can be derived using the grammar rules is said to be part of the language represented by the grammar. If $G$ is the grammar, then the language generated by the grammar is represented as:

$$L(G) = \{x \mid x \text{ can be derived using productions in } G\}$$

Derivation of a string begins with the start symbol of the grammar, and we may apply multiple grammar rules to get the string of all terminals.

There are two different types of derivations—leftmost derivation and rightmost derivation.

### 5.5.1 Leftmost Derivation

If at each step in a derivation, a production is applied to the leftmost variable (or non-terminal), then the derivation is called leftmost derivation.

For example, if the grammar $G$ consists of:

$$\{(E), (+, *, \text{a}), P, E\},$$

where $P$ consists of the following productions:

1. $E \rightarrow E + E$
2. $E \rightarrow E * E$
3. $E \rightarrow a$

Using this grammar, let us generate the string '$a + a$'.

We begin the derivation with the start symbol, that is, $E$.

At every stage, the symbol to be replaced by the right-hand side of the applicable production is <u>underlined</u>.

The string is generated as follows:

$E \Rightarrow \underline{E} + E,$ using production 1
$\Rightarrow a + \underline{E},$ using production 3 applied to the leftmost non-terminal $E$
$\Rightarrow a + a,$ using production 3 applied to $E$, which is the only non-terminal

Observe that in each step of the derivation, the leftmost non-terminal symbol is replaced by the right-hand side of the production applicable.

We also observe that at each step in the derivation, we get some string containing both terminals and non-terminals, that is, sentential form. In the leftmost derivation, these are termed as *left sentential forms*.

In this example, '$E + E$', '$a + E$', and '$a + a$' are left sentential forms. As we know, the final left sentential form, '$a + a$', is the generated string, and does not contain any non-terminal.

***Note***: Leftmost derivation generates any string from left to right. Hence, it is mainly applicable for top-down parsing. A top-down parser is a program that uses context-free grammar to generate the input string using leftmost derivation. If the input string can be generated, it is considered as a valid input string. As the input string is read from left to right, it is expected to be generated in the same order while checking the validity, terminal by terminal (refer to Chapter 6, Section 6.7 on equivalence of CFG and PDA).

### 5.5.2 Rightmost Derivation

If at each step in the derivation of a string, a production is always applied to the rightmost non-terminal, then the derivation is called rightmost derivation. It is also termed as *canonical derivation*.

For example, let us consider the same grammar $G$, where $P$ consists of:

1. $E \rightarrow E + E$
2. $E \rightarrow E * E$
3. $E \rightarrow a$

Let us derive the string '$a + a * a$' using the aforementioned grammar, applying rightmost derivation.

We begin with the start symbol $E$.

At every stage, the symbol to be replaced by the right-hand side of the applicable production is underlined.

$E \Rightarrow E + \underline{E},$ using production 1
$\Rightarrow E + E * \underline{E},$ using production 2, applied to the rightmost $E$
$\Rightarrow E + \underline{E} * a,$ using production 3, applied to the rightmost $E$
$\Rightarrow \underline{E} + a * a,$ using production 3, applied to the rightmost $E$
$\Rightarrow a + a * a,$ using production 3, applied to the only $E$ left

The aforementioned derivation is a rightmost derivation, as we are replacing the rightmost variable by the right-hand side of the production at every step in the derivation. The sentential forms at every step in the rightmost derivation are termed as *right sentential forms*.

For example, in the aforementioned derivation, '$E + E$', '$E + E * E$', '$E + E * a$', '$E + a * a$', and '$a + a * a$' are all right sentential forms. The last right sentential form, that is, '$a + a * a$' is the string that we have derived.

### 5.5.3 Derivation Examples

Let us now solve some problems illustrating leftmost and rightmost derivations.

---

**Example 5.1** Consider the following CFG:

$$G = \{(S, A), (a, b), P, S\},$$

where $P$ consists of:

$$S \to a\,A\,S \mid a$$
$$A \to S\,b\,A \mid S\,S \mid b\,a$$

Derive string '*aabbaa*' using leftmost derivation and rightmost derivation.

***Solution*** From the given information, $S$ is the start symbol. Let us number the productions as:

1. $S \to aAS$
2. $S \to a$
3. $A \to SbA$
4. $A \to SS$
5. $A \to ba$

The leftmost derivation for the string '*aabbaa*' can be shown as given here:

*Leftmost derivation:*

$S \Rightarrow a\,\underline{A}\,S,$ using rule 1
$\Rightarrow a\,\underline{S}\,b\,A\,S,$ using rule 3
$\Rightarrow a\,a\,b\,\underline{A}\,S,$ using rule 2
$\Rightarrow a\,a\,b\,b\,a\,\underline{S},$ using rule 5
$\Rightarrow a\,a\,b\,b\,a\,a,$ using rule 2

The rightmost derivation for the same string is as shown here:

*Rightmost derivation:*

$S \Rightarrow a\,A\,\underline{S},$ using rule 1
$\Rightarrow a\,\underline{A}\,a,$ using rule 2
$\Rightarrow a\,S\,b\,\underline{A}\,a,$ using rule 3
$\Rightarrow a\,\underline{S}\,b\,b\,a\,a,$ using rule 5
$\Rightarrow a\,a\,b\,b\,a\,a,$ using rule 2

---

**Example 5.2** For the grammar $G$, which is defined as:

$$S \to a\,B \mid b\,A,$$
$$A \to a \mid a\,S \mid b\,A\,A, \text{ and}$$
$$B \to b \mid b\,S \mid a\,B\,B,$$

where $S$ is the starting symbol, write the leftmost and rightmost derivations for the string '*bbaaba*'.

***Solution*** Let us number the rules as follows

1. $S \to a\,B$
2. $S \to b\,A$
3. $A \to a$
4. $A \to a\,S$
5. $A \to b\,A\,A$
6. $B \to b$
7. $B \to b\,S$
8. $B \to a\,B\,B$

*Leftmost derivation:*

| | |
|---|---|
| $S \Rightarrow b\,\underline{A},$ | using rule 2 |
| $\Rightarrow b\,b\,\underline{A}\,A,$ | using rule 5 |
| $\Rightarrow b\,b\,a\,\underline{S}\,A,$ | using rule 4 |
| $\Rightarrow b\,b\,a\,a\,\underline{B}\,A,$ | using rule 1 |
| $\Rightarrow b\,b\,a\,a\,b\,\underline{A},$ | using rule 6 |
| $\Rightarrow b\,b\,a\,a\,b\,a,$ | using rule 3 |

*Rightmost derivation:*

| | |
|---|---|
| $S \Rightarrow b\,\underline{A},$ | using rule 2 |
| $\Rightarrow b\,b\,A\,\underline{A},$ | using rule 5 |
| $\Rightarrow b\,b\,\underline{A}\,a,$ | using rule 3 |
| $\Rightarrow b\,b\,a\,\underline{S}\,a,$ | using rule 4 |
| $\Rightarrow b\,b\,a\,a\,\underline{B}\,a,$ | using rule 1 |
| $\Rightarrow b\,b\,a\,a\,b\,a,$ | using rule 6 |

---

**Example 5.3** For the following grammar, give the leftmost and rightmost derivations for the string '*aaabbb*'.

$$S \to a\,S\,b \mid a\,b$$

***Solution*** Let us number the productions as follows:

1. $S \to a\,S\,b$
2. $S \to a\,b$

*Leftmost derivation:*

| | |
|---|---|
| $S \Rightarrow a\,\underline{S}\,b,$ | using rule 1 |
| $\Rightarrow a\,a\,\underline{S}\,b\,b,$ | using rule 1 |
| $\Rightarrow a\,a\,a\,b\,b\,b,$ | using rule 2 |

*Rightmost derivation:*

Rightmost derivation is exactly same as leftmost derivation, as in each step there is only one non-terminal to be replaced by its right-hand side.

## 5.6 DERIVATION TREE

Derivation tree is a graphical representation, or description, of how the sentence (or string) has been derived, or generated, using a grammar. For every string derivable from the start symbol, there is an associated derivation tree. Derivation tree is also known as *rule tree*, *parse tree*, or *syntax tree.*

Thus, the generation of any string or statement can be represented with the help of a leftmost derivation, rightmost derivation, or derivation tree. All these three representations are equivalent, which means that given any one of them, the other two can be constructed.

### *Formal Definition*

Let $G = \{V, T, P, S\}$ be a CFG. A tree is a derivation tree for $G$ if:

1. Every vertex (or node) has a label, which is a symbol from the set $\{V \cup T \cup (\epsilon)\}$.
2. The label of the root vertex is $S$, the start symbol of $G$.
3. If a vertex is interior (or an intermediate node) in the tree and has label $A$, then $A$ must be in $V$, that is, $A$ is a non-terminal.
4. If vertex $n$ has label $A$ and vertices $n_1, n_2, \ldots, n_k$ are the children nodes of vertex $n$, in order from the left, with labels $X_1, X_2, \ldots, X_k$ respectively, then '$A \rightarrow X_1 X_2 \ldots X_k$' must be a production in $P$.
5. If vertex $n$ has label $\epsilon$, then $n$ is a leaf and is the only son of its father, (i.e., $\epsilon$-production).

---

**Example 5.4** Consider the grammar, $G = \{(S, A), (a, b), P, S\}$,

where $P$ consists of:

$$S \rightarrow a\,A\,S \mid a$$
$$A \rightarrow S\,b\,A \mid S\,S \mid b\,a$$

Draw derivation tree for the string '*aabbaa*'.

***Solution*** In Section 5.5.3, we have seen both leftmost as well the rightmost derivations for the aforementioned string. The third way to represent the derivation of the string is with the help of a derivation tree, as shown in Fig. 5.1.

If we read the leaf nodes from left to right in sequence, it gives us the string '*aabbaa*'. The tree gives us a pictorial representation of the derivation steps for generating the string '*aabbaa*'.

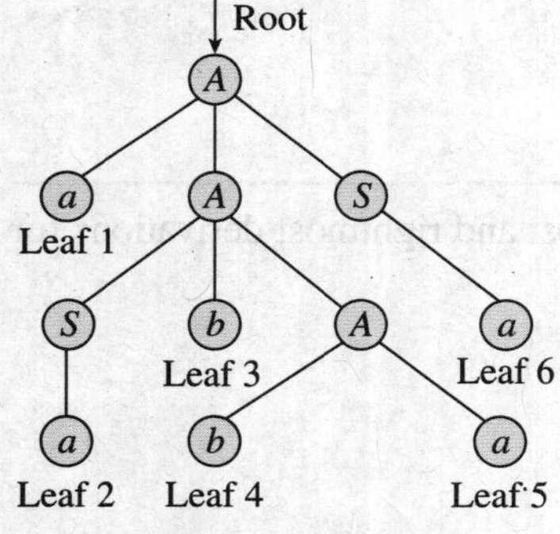


**Figure 5.1** Derivation tree for string '*aabbaa*'

---

## 5.7 CONTEXT-FREE LANGUAGES

A context-free language (CFL) is the language generated by a context-free grammar $G$. This can be described as:

$$L(G) = \{w \mid w \subset T^*, \text{ and is derivable from the start symbol } S\}$$

All the CFGs that we have seen so far represent CFLs.

### 5.7.1 Examples

Let us discuss some examples of CFLs, and attempt to write their CFGs.

**Example 5.5** Let $G$ be a context-free grammar, which is defined as:

$$S \rightarrow a\,S\,b \mid a\,b$$

Find the CFL generated by $G$.

***Solution*** Let us begin by listing the strings that we can generate using the given CFG, $G$. We start with minimal length string. Let us number the productions as:

1. $S \rightarrow a\,S\,b$
2. $S \rightarrow a\,b$

Let us now derive different strings using $G$.

Using production 2, we can derive string '*ab*' in one step as:

$$S \Rightarrow a\,b$$

Let us derive another string as follows:

$S \Rightarrow a\,\underline{S}\,b,$ using rule 1
$\Rightarrow a\,a\,b\,b,$ using rule 2

Similarly, we have:

$S \Rightarrow a\,\underline{S}\,b,$ using rule 1
$\Rightarrow a\,a\,\underline{S}\,b\,b,$ using rule 1
$\Rightarrow a\,a\,a\,b\,b\,b,$ using rule 2
$S \Rightarrow a\,\underline{S}\,b,$ using rule 1
$\Rightarrow a\,a\,\underline{S}\,b\,b,$ using rule 1
$\Rightarrow a\,a\,a\,\underline{S}\,b\,b\,b,$ using rule 1
$\Rightarrow a\,a\,a\,a\,b\,b\,b\,b,$ using rule 2

Thus, the language can be listed in the form of a set, as:

$$L(G) = \{ab, aabb, aaabbb, aaaabbbb, \ldots\},$$

or

$$L(G) = \{a^n b^n \mid n \geq 1\}$$

Thus, the CFG $G$ defines the language containing strings of the form $a^n b^n$ for $n \geq 1$; which can be expressed as, '$n$ number of $a$'s followed by the same number of $b$'s'.

**Example 5.6** Find the CFL associated with the CFG, $G$, which is defined as follows:

$$S \rightarrow a\,B \mid b\,A$$
$$A \rightarrow a \mid a\,S \mid b\,A\,A$$
$$B \rightarrow b \mid b\,S \mid a\,B\,B$$

***Solution*** Let us number the productions (or rules) as follows:

1. $S \rightarrow a\,B$
2. $S \rightarrow b\,A$
3. $A \rightarrow a$
4. $A \rightarrow a\,S$

5. $A \to b\,A\,A$
6. $B \to b$
7. $B \to b\,S$
8. $B \to a\,B\,B$

Let us derive different strings using the given CFG, $G$:

$S \Rightarrow a\,\underline{B}$, using rule 1
$\Rightarrow a\,b$, using rule 6
$S \Rightarrow b\,\underline{A}$, using rule 2
$\Rightarrow b\,a$, using rule 3
$S \Rightarrow a\,\underline{B}$ using rule 1
$\Rightarrow a\,b\,\underline{S}$, using rule 7
$\Rightarrow a\,b\,a\,\underline{B}$, using rule 1
$\Rightarrow a\,b\,a\,b$, using rule 6
$S \Rightarrow a\,\underline{B}$, using rule 1
$\Rightarrow a\,b\,\underline{S}$, using rule 7
$\Rightarrow a\,b\,b\,\underline{A}$, using rule 2
$\Rightarrow a\,b\,b\,a$, using rule 3
$S \Rightarrow a\,\underline{B}$, using rule 1
$\Rightarrow a\,a\,\underline{B}\,B$, using rule 8
$\Rightarrow a\,a\,b\,\underline{B}$, using rule 6
$\Rightarrow a\,a\,b\,b$, using rule 6
$S \Rightarrow b\,\underline{A}$, using rule 2
$\Rightarrow b\,a\,\underline{S}$, using rule 4
$\Rightarrow b\,a\,a\,\underline{B}$, using rule 1
$\Rightarrow b\,a\,a\,b$, using rule 6
$S \Rightarrow b\,\underline{A}$, using rule 2
$\Rightarrow b\,b\,\underline{A}\,A$, using rule 5
$\Rightarrow b\,b\,a\,\underline{A}$, using rule 3
$\Rightarrow b\,b\,a\,a$, using rule 3
$S \Rightarrow b\,\underline{A}$, using rule 2
$\Rightarrow b\,b\,\underline{A}\,A$, using rule 5
$\Rightarrow b\,b\,a\,\underline{S}\,A$, using rule 4
$\Rightarrow b\,b\,a\,a\,\underline{B}\,A$, using rule 1
$\Rightarrow b\,b\,a\,a\,b\,\underline{A}$, using rule 6
$\Rightarrow b\,b\,a\,a\,b\,a$, using rule 3
$S \Rightarrow b\,\underline{A}$, using rule 2
$\Rightarrow b\,a\,\underline{S}$, using rule 4
$\Rightarrow b\,a\,b\,\underline{A}$, using rule 2
$\Rightarrow b\,a\,b\,b\,\underline{A}\,A$, using rule 5
$\Rightarrow b\,a\,b\,b\,a\,\underline{S}\,A$, using rule 4
$\Rightarrow b\,a\,b\,b\,a\,a\,\underline{B}\,A$, using rule 1
$\Rightarrow b\,a\,b\,b\,a\,a\,b\,\underline{A}$, using rule 6
$\Rightarrow b\,a\,b\,b\,a\,a\,b\,a$, using rule 3

Thus, we see that all the strings that we have derived have equal number of $a$'s and $b$'s. Thus, the CFL generated by the given CFG, $G$ is:

$$L(G) = \{x \mid x \text{ containing equal number of } a\text{'s and } b\text{'s}\}.$$

---

**Example 5.7** Write the grammar for generating strings over $\Sigma = \{a\}$, containing any (zero or more) number of $a$'s, and comment upon the language generated by this grammar.

***Solution*** Zero number of $a$'s can be generated using the production:

$S \rightarrow \epsilon$ (i.e., $\epsilon$-production)

If we want one or more $a$'s, we can generate them using the productions:

$$S \rightarrow a \mid a\,S$$

Combining the two, the grammar that we get is:

$$S \rightarrow a\,S \mid a \mid \epsilon$$

We see that the production '$S \rightarrow a$' is unnecessary, as that can be generated by applying the rule '$S \rightarrow aS$', followed by substituting for $S$ using '$S \rightarrow \epsilon$'.

Thus, we can represent the grammar formally as:

$$G = \{(S), (a, \epsilon), (S \rightarrow aS, S \rightarrow \epsilon), S\}$$

Let us try deriving the string '$aaa$'. For this grammar, using leftmost derivation:

$S \Rightarrow a\,\underline{S}$, using rule 1
$\Rightarrow a\,a\,\underline{S}$, using rule 1
$\Rightarrow a\,a\,a\,\underline{S}$, using rule 1
$\Rightarrow a\,a\,a$, using rule 2, this substitutes $\epsilon$ for $S$

> ***Note***: The language described in this example is a regular language, and we can denote it using the regular expression, $a^*$. Hence, the grammar, $G$, and the regular expression, $a^*$, are equivalent as they both represent the same language $L$, containing any number (zero or more) of $a$'s.

---

**Example 5.8** Write a grammar for the language represented by the regular expression, $(a + b)^*$.

***Solution*** The regular expression $(a + b)^*$ represents a regular language containing any number of $a$'s or $b$'s.

The grammar is given by:

$$S \rightarrow \underset{1}{a\,S} \mid \underset{2}{b\,S} \mid \underset{3}{\epsilon}$$

Let us try deriving the string '$aaba$' for this grammar:

$S \Rightarrow a\,\underline{S}$, using rule 1
$\Rightarrow a\,a\,\underline{S}$, using rule 1
$\Rightarrow a\,a\,b\,\underline{S}$, using rule 2

$\Rightarrow a\,a\,b\,a\,\underline{S},$ using rule 1
$\Rightarrow a\,a\,b\,a,$ using rule 3

***Note***: If we want to write the CFG for the language $(a + b)^+$, that is, strings containing at least one occurrence of $a$ or $b$, it can be written as:

$$S \rightarrow a\,S \mid b\,S \mid a \mid b$$

This grammar now cannot generate an empty string, that is, the string containing zero number of $a$'s and zero number of $b$'s, because $P$ does not contain a production of the form, $S \rightarrow \epsilon$.

---

**Example 5.9** Write the grammar generating all strings consisting of $a$'s and $b$'s with at least two $a$'s.

***Solution*** The given language can be represented using the following regular expression:

$$(a + b)^*\, a\, (a + b)^*\, a\, (a + b)^*$$

The grammar generating this language can be written as:

$$G = \{(S, A), (a, b, \epsilon), P, S\},$$

where, $P$ consists of:

$$S \rightarrow A\,a\,A\,a\,A \qquad (5.1)$$
$$A \rightarrow a\,A \mid b\,A \mid \epsilon$$
$$\quad 2 \quad 3 \quad 4$$

We observe that $A$ generates the language represented by $(a + b)^*$.

Let us generate string '$aa$' for grammar $G$, using rightmost derivation:

$S \Rightarrow A\,a\,A\,a\,\underline{A},$ using rule 1
$\Rightarrow A\,a\,\underline{A}\,a,$ using rule 4
$\Rightarrow \underline{A}\,a\,a,$ using rule 4
$\Rightarrow a\,a,$ using rule 4

Thus, '$aa$' is the minimal length string from the given language.

---

**Example 5.10** Write the grammar for generating the variable names, which can be given by the regular expression: (*letter*) (*letter / digit*)*, which means, a letter followed by any number of letters or digits.

***Solution*** Let non-terminal $L$ denote and produce letters, and let non-terminal $D$ produce digits.

The grammar $G$ can be written as:

$$S \rightarrow LS'$$
$$S' \rightarrow LS' \mid DS' \mid \epsilon$$
$$L \rightarrow a \mid b \mid \ldots \mid z \mid A \mid B \mid C \mid \ldots \mid Z$$
$$D \rightarrow 0 \mid 1 \mid 2 \mid 3 \ldots \mid 9$$

Here, $S$ is the start symbol.

Let us derive the variable name '*flag12*', using the aforementioned grammar. The steps in the (leftmost) derivation are:

$$\begin{aligned} S &\Rightarrow \underline{L}S' \\ &\Rightarrow f\,\underline{S'} \\ &\Rightarrow f\,\underline{L}\,S' \\ &\Rightarrow f\,l\,\underline{S'} \\ &\Rightarrow f\,l\,\underline{L}\,S' \\ &\Rightarrow f\,l\,a\,\underline{S'} \\ &\Rightarrow f\,l\,a\,\underline{L}\,S' \\ &\Rightarrow f\,l\,a\,g\,\underline{S'} \\ &\Rightarrow f\,l\,a\,g\,\underline{D}\,S' \\ &\Rightarrow f\,l\,a\,g\,1\,S' \\ &\Rightarrow f\,l\,a\,g\,1\,\underline{D}\,S' \\ &\Rightarrow f\,l\,a\,g\,1\,2\,\underline{S'} \\ &\Rightarrow f\,l\,a\,g\,1\,2 \qquad \text{(using } S' \rightarrow \epsilon\text{)} \end{aligned}$$

---

**Example 5.11** Describe the CFL generated by the following grammar $G$:

$$G = \{(S), (a, b, \epsilon), P, S\},$$

where, $P$ consists of:

$$\begin{array}{l} S \rightarrow a\,S\,a \mid b\,S\,b \mid a \mid b \mid \epsilon \\ \qquad\ \ 1 \qquad\ \ 2 \quad\ 3\ \ 4\ \ 5 \end{array}$$

***Solution*** Let us try to derive different strings from the CFL, so that we can list them in the form of a set:

$$\begin{aligned} S &\Rightarrow a\,\underline{S}\,a, && \text{using rule 1} \\ &\Rightarrow a\,a, && \text{using rule 5} \\ S &\Rightarrow b\,\underline{S}\,b, && \text{using rule 2} \\ &\Rightarrow b\,b, && \text{using rule 5} \\ S &\Rightarrow a\,\underline{S}\,a, && \text{using rule 1} \\ &\Rightarrow a\,a\,a, && \text{using rule 3} \\ S &\Rightarrow a\,\underline{S}\,a, && \text{using rule 1} \\ &\Rightarrow a\,b\,a, && \text{using rule 4} \\ S &\Rightarrow b\,\underline{S}\,b, && \text{using rule 2} \\ &\Rightarrow b\,a\,b, && \text{using rule 3} \\ S &\Rightarrow b\,\underline{S}\,b, && \text{using rule 2} \\ &\Rightarrow b\,b\,b, && \text{using rule 4} \end{aligned}$$

The set of all strings will thus be:

$$L = \{\epsilon, a, b, aa, bb, aaa, aba, bbb, bab, \ldots\}$$

Thus, the CFL is a language consisting of all palindrome strings over $\Sigma = \{a, b\}$.

---

---

**Example 5.12** Write a grammar for the language over $\Sigma = \{a, b\}$ containing at least one occurrence of '*aa*'.

***Solution*** We are given a regular language, which can be represented using $(a + b)^*\ a\ a\ (a + b)^*$. The grammar can be written as follows:

$$S \to X\ a\ a\ X$$
$$X \to a\ X \mid b\ X \mid \epsilon$$

Here, $S$ is the start symbol.

Let us derive the string, '*bbaaab*' using leftmost derivation, as follows:

$$\begin{aligned} S &\Rightarrow \underline{X}\ a\ a\ X, && \text{using } (S \to X\ a\ a\ X) \\ &\Rightarrow b\ \underline{X}\ a\ a\ X, && \text{using } (X \to b\ X) \\ &\Rightarrow b\ b\ \underline{X}\ a\ a\ X, && \text{using } (X \to b\ X) \\ &\Rightarrow b\ b\ a\ a\ \underline{X}, && \text{using } (X \to \epsilon) \\ &\Rightarrow b\ b\ a\ a\ a\ \underline{X}, && \text{using } (X \to a\ X) \\ &\Rightarrow b\ b\ a\ a\ a\ b\ X, && \text{using } (X \to b\ X) \\ &\Rightarrow b\ b\ a\ a\ a\ b, && \text{using } (X \to \epsilon) \end{aligned}$$

---

**Example 5.13** Find the CFL generated by following grammar:

$$S \to X\,Y$$
$$X \to a\ X \mid b\ X \mid a$$
$$Y \to Y\,a \mid Y\,b \mid a$$

***Solution*** If we consider only the productions associated with $X$, which are:

$$X \to a\ X \mid b\ X \mid a$$

we see that $X$ produces strings containing any number of $a$'s or $b$'s, ending with $a$.

If we consider the productions associated with $Y$, which are:

$$Y \to Y\,a \mid Y\,b \mid a$$

we see that $Y$ produces strings starting with $a$ followed by any number of $a$'s or $b$'s.

Now considering the production '$S \to X\,Y$', we can conclude that $S$ produces strings with at least one occurrence of '*aa*'. The first $a$ comes from strings ending with $a$ that are derivable from $X$, and the second $a$ comes from the strings beginning with $a$ that are derivable from $Y$.

Therefore, this grammar is equivalent to the CFG that we have seen in previous problem—both the CFGs produce the same language consisting of strings over $\Sigma = \{a, b\}$ with at least two consecutive $a$'s.

---

**Example 5.14** Write the grammar to generate the strings containing consecutive $a$'s but not consecutive $b$'s.

***Solution*** The required grammar will contain the following productions:

$$S \to a\,S \mid b\,X \mid a \mid b \mid \epsilon$$
$$X \to a\,S \mid a \mid \epsilon$$

with, $V = \{S, X\}$, $T = \{a, b\}$, and $S$ as the start symbol.

We observe from the aforementioned productions that as soon as $b$ is generated, the rammar tries to generate $a$ as the next symbol. This is done using the production '$S \to b\,X$'.

---

**Example 5.15** Consider the CFG:

$$S \to X\,Y\,X$$
$$X \to a\,X \mid b\,X \mid \epsilon$$
$$Y \to b\,b\,b$$

Show that this generates the language defined by $(a + b)^*\ bbb\ (a + b)^*$.

***Solution*** Let us derive a few strings so that we can list them in the form of a set:

| | |
|---|---|
| $S \Rightarrow \underline{X}\,Y\,X,$ | using $(S \to X\,Y\,X)$ |
| $\Rightarrow \underline{Y}\,X,$ | using $(X \to \epsilon)$ |
| $\Rightarrow b\,b\,b\,\underline{X},$ | using $(Y \to b\,b\,b)$ |
| $\Rightarrow b\,b\,b,$ | using $(X \to \epsilon)$ |
| $S \Rightarrow \underline{X}\,Y\,X,$ | using $(S \to X\,Y\,X)$ |
| $\Rightarrow a\,\underline{X}\,Y\,X,$ | using $(X \to a\,X)$ |
| $\Rightarrow a\,\underline{Y}\,X,$ | using $(X \to \epsilon)$ |
| $\Rightarrow a\,b\,b\,b\,\underline{X},$ | using $(Y \to b\,b\,b)$ |
| $\Rightarrow a\,b\,b\,b,$ | using $(X \to \epsilon)$ |

$$L = \{bbb, abbb, bbbb, bbba, \ldots\}$$

We also see that since $X \to a\,X \mid b\,X \mid \epsilon$, the non-terminal $X$ produces all strings containing any number of $a$'s and $b$'s, that is, the language can be represented as $(a + b)^*$.

Hence, the given CFG generates the language defined by $(a + b)^*\ bbb\ (a + b)^*$.

---

**Example 5.16** Write a CFG to generate the language of all strings that have more number of $a$'s than $b$'s.

***Solution*** The expected language set can be written as:

$$L = \{a, aa, aab, aba, baa, aaaa, aaaab, \ldots\}$$

Earlier, in Example 5.6, we have discussed the grammar for a language containing equal number of $a$'s and $b$'s.

The grammar was defined as:

$$S \to aB \mid bA$$
$$A \to a \mid aS \mid bAA$$
$$B \to b \mid bS \mid aBB$$

Using the aforementioned grammar, the grammar for the required language $L$ can be written as:

$$X \rightarrow YS \mid SY \mid YSY \mid Y$$
$$S \rightarrow aB \mid bA$$
$$A \rightarrow a \mid aS \mid bAA$$
$$B \rightarrow b \mid bS \mid aBB$$
$$Y \rightarrow aY \mid a$$

Here, $X$ is the start symbol.

---

**Example 5.17** Find a CFG for each of the languages defined by the following regular expressions:

(a) $ab^*$
(b) $a^*b^*$
(c) $(baa + abb)^*$

***Solution***

(a) The required CFG for $ab^*$ is given by:

$$S \rightarrow a\,B$$
$$B \rightarrow b\,B \mid \epsilon$$

Here, $S$ is the start symbol.

(b) The required CFG for $a^*b^*$ is:

$$S \rightarrow A\,B$$
$$A \rightarrow a\,A \mid \epsilon$$
$$B \rightarrow b\,B \mid \epsilon$$

Here, $S$ is the start symbol.

(c) The required CFG for $(baa + abb)^*$ is:

$$S \rightarrow A\,S \mid B\,S \mid \epsilon$$
$$\text{A} \rightarrow b\,a\,a$$
$$\text{B} \rightarrow a\,b\,b$$

Here, $S$ is the start symbol.

---

**Example 5.18** Find a CFG for the language over $\Sigma = \{a, b\}$ containing words that have different first and last letters.

***Solution*** It is required that the words should have different first and last letters. This means that if the first letter is $a$, then the last letter in the word should be $b$. Similarly, if the first letter is $b$, then the last letter in the word should be $a$. In between, we can have any combination of $a$'s and $b$'s.

The regular language can be represented using the regular expression:

$$a\,(a + b)^*\,b + b\,(a + b)^*\,a$$

The required CFG, therefore, can be written as:

$$S \to a\,A\,b \mid b\,A\,a$$
$$A \to a\,A \mid b\,A \mid \epsilon$$

Here, $S$ is the starting symbol.

---

**Example 5.19** Find the context-free grammar that generates the language:

$$L = \{a^i\, b^j\, c^k \mid i = j + k\}$$

***Solution*** The grammar that generates the given language $L$ can be written as follows:

$$S \to a\,S\,c \mid A \mid \epsilon$$
$$A \to a\,A\,b \mid \epsilon$$

Here, $S$ is the starting symbol; and the production '$S \to \epsilon$' is added to include the case when the values of $i$, $j$, and $k$ are all zero.

The non-terminal $S$, with the help of the production '$S \to aSc$', generates as many $c$'s as the number of $a$'s. The middle $A$ in the production '$A \to aAb$' generates equal number of $a$'s and $b$'s; and '$S \to A$' is added to include the case when the value of $k$ is zero.

---

**Example 5.20** Write a CFG for the following language:

$$L = \{a^{m+n}\, b^m\, c^n \mid n, m \geq 0\}$$

***Solution*** We observe that this language is exactly the same as the language in the previous example, that is, Example 5.19. Hence, the CFG is defined as:

$$S \to a\,S\,c \mid A \mid \epsilon$$
$$A \to a\,A\,b \mid \epsilon$$

---

**Example 5.21** Write the CFG for the language:

$$L = \{0^m\, 1^n\, 0^{m+n} \mid m, n \geq 0\}$$

***Solution*** The grammar for the language is defined as:

$$S \to 0\,S\,0 \mid A \mid \epsilon$$
$$A \to 1\,S\,0 \mid \epsilon$$

Here, $S$ is the starting symbol. The rule '$S \to 0S0$' adds equal (i.e., $m$) number of 0's at the beginning and towards the end. The rule '$A \to 1S0$' adds equal number (i.e., $n$) of 0's and 1's, in order to fulfil the requirement for '$m + n$' number of 0's towards the end.

---

**Example 5.22** Find the CFG that generates each of the following languages:

(a) Set of odd length strings in $\{a, b\}^*$ having $a$ as the middle symbol
(b) Set of even length strings in $\{a, b\}^*$ having the same symbols in the middle

***Solution***

(a) The required grammar can be written as follows:

$$S \to a\,S\,a \mid a\,S\,b \mid b\,S\,a \mid b\,S\,b \mid a$$

(b) The required grammar can be written as follows:

$$S \to a\,S\,a \mid a\,S\,b \mid b\,S\,a \mid b\,S\,b \mid a\,a \mid b\,b$$

---

**Example 5.23** Give the CFG for the following language:

$$L = \{a^n\, b^m\, a^n \mid n \geq 0, m \geq 1\}$$

***Solution*** The grammar generating the required language $L$ can be written as follows:

$$S \to a\,S\,a \mid B$$
$$B \to b\,B \mid b$$

Here, $S$ is the starting symbol. After generating the starting and ending $a$'s, the $S$ in the middle can be replaced by $B$ using the rule '$S \to B$'. The non-terminal $B$ generates one or more $b$'s in the middle as required.

---

**Example 5.24** Construct the CFG for the language:

$$L = \{a^n b^n c^m d^m \mid n, m \geq 1\} \cup \{a^m b^n c^n d^m \mid n, m \geq 1\}$$

***Solution*** The first part $\{a^n b^n c^m d^m \mid n, m \geq 1\}$ can be expressed with the help of the following grammar, $G_1$:

$$S_1 \to A\,C$$
$$A \to a\,A\,b \mid a\,b$$
$$C \to c\,C\,d \mid c\,d$$

The second part $\{a^m b^n c^n d^m \mid n, m \geq 1\}$ can be expressed with the help of the following grammar, $G_2$:

$$S_2 \to a\,S_2\,d \mid a\,B\,d$$
$$B \to b\,B\,c \mid b\,c$$

As we want to obtain the union of these two languages, the equivalent grammar, $G$ can be obtained as follows:

$$G = G_1 \cup G_2$$

Thus, the final grammar, $G$, can be written as follows:

$$S \to S_1 \mid S_2$$
$$S_1 \to A\,C$$
$$A \to a\,A\,b \mid a\,b$$
$$C \to c\,C\,d \mid c\,d$$
$$S_2 \to a\,S_2\,d \mid a\,B\,d$$
$$B \to b\,B\,c \mid b\,c$$

**Example 5.25** Construct the CFG for the language containing the set of strings over $\{a, b\}$ with exactly twice as many $a$'s as $b$'s.

***Solution*** Let us consider the case when the string has one $b$; then, there there will be two $a$'s in the string. The following are the string combinations with one $b$ and two $a$'s:

$$\{aab, aba, baa\}$$

These combinations can be pumped (or repeated) to achieve all possible combinations of such strings. Hence, we can use the following regular expression to represent the set of strings:

$$(aab + aba + baa)^*$$

This is a regular language, and we can write a CFG for this language as follows:

$$S \rightarrow A\,S \mid \epsilon$$
$$A \rightarrow a\,a\,b \mid a\,b\,a \mid b\,a\,a$$

**Example 5.26** Construct a CFG for the following language set:

$$L = \{a^{2n}b^n \mid n \geq 1\}$$

***Solution*** The grammar for the required language can be written as follows:

$$S \rightarrow a\,a\,S\,b \mid a\,a\,b$$

For every two $a$'s in the beginning, one $b$ is generated at the end.

**Example 5.27** Find the context-free grammar for the following language:

$$L = \{a^n\,b^m\,c^k \mid n = m \text{ or } m \leq k; n \geq 0, m \geq 0, k \geq 0\}$$

***Solution*** There are two alternatives discussed here:

(a) $n = m$; therefore, $k$ can be any number, and is not related to either $n$ or $m$.
(b) $m \leq k$; therefore, $n$ can be any number, and is not related to $m$ or $k$.

For alternative (a), the grammar can be written as:

$S_1 \rightarrow A\,C$
$A \rightarrow a\,A\,b \mid \epsilon$; $\quad n = m$
$C \rightarrow c\,C \mid \epsilon$; generates any number of $c$'s

For alternative (b), the grammar can be written as:

$S_2 \rightarrow B\,D\,E$
$B \rightarrow a\,B \mid \epsilon$; generates any number of $a$'s
$D \rightarrow b\,D\,c \mid \epsilon$; for $m = k$
$E \rightarrow c\,E \mid \epsilon$; for $m < k$

We now combine these two grammars by taking their union as follows:

$$S \rightarrow S_1 \mid S_2$$

The rest of the productions remain as they are.

**Example 5.28** Construct a CFG for the following set:

$$\{a^{2n}\, b\, c \mid n \geq 1\}$$

***Solution*** The grammar $G$ for the given set can be written as follows:

$S \rightarrow A\, b\, c$
$A \rightarrow a\, a\, A \mid a\, a$; for $n \geq 1$

We see that the number of $a$'s generated is always even.

## 5.8 AMBIGUOUS CONTEXT-FREE GRAMMAR

A CFG for a language is said to be *ambiguous*, if there exists at least one string, which can be generated (or derived) in more than one way. This means that there exists more than one leftmost derivation, more than one rightmost derivation, and more than one derivation tree associated with such a string.

For an *unambiguous* CFG, there exists exactly one way of deriving any string of the language. This means that there is exactly one way to depict the leftmost derivation, one way to describe the rightmost derivation, and exactly one derivation tree that can be associated with such a string. The examples we have seen in Section 5.7.1 are all unambiguous grammars.

Let us now look at an example of ambiguous grammar. Consider the following grammar:

$$E \rightarrow \underset{1}{E + E} \mid \underset{2}{E * E} \mid \underset{3}{id}$$

Let us try deriving the string '$\underline{id} + id \times id$':

Using leftmost derivation, there are two different ways of deriving the given string:

(a) $E \Rightarrow \underline{E} + E$, using rule 1
$\Rightarrow id + \underline{E}$, using rule 3
$\Rightarrow id + \underline{E} * E$, using rule 2
$\Rightarrow id + id * \underline{E}$, using rule 3
$\Rightarrow id + id * id$, using rule 3

(b) $E \Rightarrow \underline{E} \times E$, using rule 2
$\Rightarrow \underline{E} + E * E$, using rule 1
$\Rightarrow id + \underline{E} * E$, using rule 3
$\Rightarrow id + id * \underline{E}$, using rule 3
$\Rightarrow id + id * id$, using rule 3

Similarly, there are two ways of deriving the same string using rightmost derivation:

(a) $E \Rightarrow E + \underline{E}$, using rule 1
$\Rightarrow E + E * \underline{E}$, using rule 2
$\Rightarrow E + \underline{E} * id$, using rule 3
$\Rightarrow \underline{E} + id * id$, using rule 3
$\Rightarrow id + id * id$, using rule 3

(b) $E \Rightarrow E * \underline{E}$, using rule 2
$\Rightarrow \underline{E} * id$, using rule 3
$\Rightarrow E + \underline{E} * id$, using rule 1
$\Rightarrow \underline{E} + id * id$, using rule 3
$\Rightarrow id + id * id$, using rule 3

Likewise, we can draw two different derivation trees to depict the derivation for the same string, as shown in Fig. 5.2.

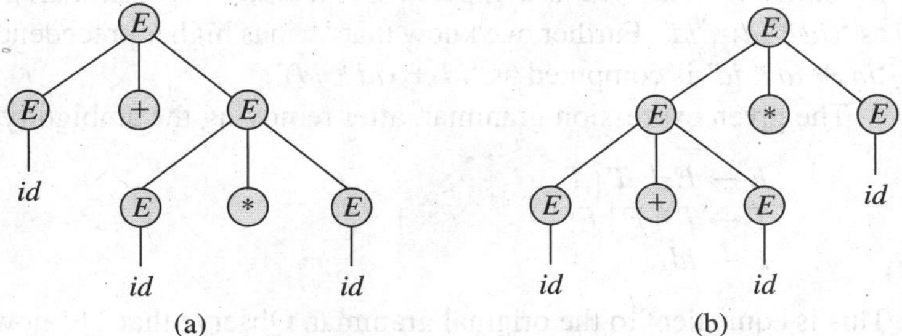


**Figure 5.2** Derivation trees for the string '*id* + *id* * *id*' (a) First derivation tree for '*id* + *id* * *id*' (b) Second derivation tree for '*id* + *id* * *id*'

Thus, there are two different ways of deriving the string '*id* + *id* * *id*', based on the production that is used first. Hence, the grammar given is ambiguous.

As there are more than one ways of deriving a string, one might wonder which one is the right derivation, or if both are correct. The first derivation, that is, to start with the production '$E \rightarrow E + E$', is considered to be correct as '*id* + *id* * *id* = *id* + (*id* * *id*)' because '*' has higher priority than '+'. Therefore, the basic operation is '+', that is, addition of '*id*' and '*id* * *id*'. Hence, the derivation tree in Fig. 5.2(a) is correct. The grammar described here is ambiguous as the information of the operators' precedence is missing.

The reader can try deriving the string '*id* + *id* + *id*', which also has more than one ways of deriving, using the aforementioned grammar. Though the same operator '+' is used twice in the string, the information that '+' is left associative is missing from the grammar. Though '(*id* + *id*) + *id*' is the right way to group the operands, the grammar also allows '*id* + (*id* + *id*)'; that introduces an ambiguity.

### 5.8.1 Removal of Ambiguity

There is no algorithm for removing ambiguity in any given CFG. Every ambiguous grammar has a different cause for the ambiguity, and hence, the remedy for each would be different. Removing the ambiguity for a specific grammar is feasible; but creating a generic solution to remove the ambiguity of any ambiguous grammar is an *unsolvable problem*.

While we remove the ambiguity of any grammar, we must ensure that the resultant grammar is equivalent to the original one; in other words, it should generate the same CFL as the original grammar generates.

For example, let us consider the grammar we have seen earlier:

$$E \rightarrow E + E \mid E * E \mid id$$

Here, the cause of ambiguity is that the grammar does not use the precedence information and associative properties of the operators '+' (addition) and '*' (multiplication). Since both '+' and '*' are left associative, the order of the operations is from left to right. For example, '*id* + *id* + *id*' is computed as '(*id* + *id*) + *id*'; similarly, '*id* * *id* * *id*' is computed as '(*id* * *id*) * *id*'. Further, we know that '*' has higher precedence over '+'; for example, '*id* + *id* * *id*' is computed as '*id* + (*id* * *id*)'.

The given expression grammar, after removing the ambiguity, can be written as:

$$\begin{aligned} &E \rightarrow E + T \mid T \\ &T \rightarrow T * F \mid F \\ &F \rightarrow id \end{aligned}$$

This is equivalent to the original grammar. Observe that '+' now can be derived only using non-terminal *E*; thus the left operands are automatically grouped now. We further see that only non-terminal *T* can derive a string containing '×'; hence, when '+' and '×' are used together, '*' is given higher priority.

Let us derive the same string '*id* + *id* * *id*', using the new unambiguous grammar. Leftmost derivation of '*id* + *id* * *id*' can be depicted as:

$$\begin{aligned} E &\Rightarrow \underline{E} + T \\ &\Rightarrow \underline{T} + T \\ &\Rightarrow \underline{F} + T \\ &\Rightarrow id + T \\ &\Rightarrow id + \underline{T} * F \\ &\Rightarrow id + \underline{F} * F \\ &\Rightarrow id + id * \underline{F} \\ &\Rightarrow id + id * id \end{aligned}$$

Rightmost derivation can be written as:

$$\begin{aligned} E &\Rightarrow E + \underline{T} \\ &\Rightarrow E + T * \underline{F} \\ &\Rightarrow E + \underline{T} * id \\ &\Rightarrow E + \underline{F} * id \\ &\Rightarrow \underline{E} + id * id \\ &\Rightarrow \underline{T} + id * id \\ &\Rightarrow \underline{F} + id * id \\ &\Rightarrow id + id * id \end{aligned}$$

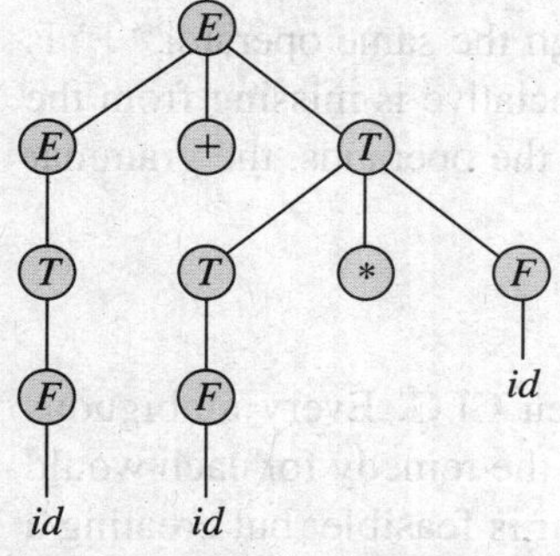

**Figure 5.3** Derivation tree for '*id* + *id* * *id*' using unambiguous grammar

The derivation tree for the string is shown in Fig. 5.3. Observe that there is only one way of deriving the required string.

**Example 5.29** Check whether or not the following grammar is ambiguous; if it is ambiguous, remove the ambiguity and write an equivalent unambiguous grammar.

$$\begin{array}{l} S \to i\,C\,t\,S \mid i\,C\,t\,S\,e\,S \mid a \\ C \to b \end{array}$$

***Solution*** Let us number the productions as follows:

$$\begin{array}{l} S \to \underset{1}{i\,C\,t\,S} \mid \underset{2}{i\,C\,t\,S\,e\,S} \mid \underset{3}{a} \\ \underset{4}{C \to b} \end{array}$$

Let us derive the string '*ibtibtaea*'.

The leftmost derivation for the string yields the following two different derivations:

$$\begin{array}{lll} S & \Rightarrow i\,\underline{C}\,t\,S, & \text{using rule 1} \\ & \Rightarrow i\,b\,t\,\underline{S}, & \text{using rule 4} \\ & \Rightarrow i\,b\,t\,i\,\underline{C}\,t\,S\,e\,S, & \text{using rule 2} \\ & \Rightarrow i\,b\,t\,i\,b\,t\,\underline{S}\,e\,S, & \text{using rule 4} \\ & \Rightarrow i\,b\,t\,i\,b\,t\,a\,e\,\underline{S}, & \text{using rule 3} \\ & \Rightarrow i\,b\,t\,i\,b\,t\,a\,e\,a, & \text{using rule 3} \\ S & \Rightarrow i\,\underline{C}\,t\,S\,e\,S, & \text{using rule 2} \\ & \Rightarrow i\,b\,t\,\underline{S}\,e\,S, & \text{using rule 4} \\ & \Rightarrow i\,b\,t\,i\,\underline{C}\,t\,S\,e\,S, & \text{using rule 1} \\ & \Rightarrow i\,b\,t\,i\,b\,t\,\underline{S}\,e\,S, & \text{using rule 4} \\ & \Rightarrow i\,b\,t\,i\,b\,t\,a\,e\,\underline{S}, & \text{using rule 3} \\ & \Rightarrow i\,b\,t\,i\,b\,t\,a\,e\,a, & \text{using rule 3} \end{array}$$

There are also two different rightmost derivations as depicted here:

$$\begin{array}{lll} S & \Rightarrow i\,C\,t\,\underline{S}, & \text{using rule 1} \\ & \Rightarrow i\,C\,t\,i\,C\,t\,S\,e\,\underline{S}, & \text{using rule 2} \\ & \Rightarrow i\,C\,t\,i\,C\,t\,\underline{S}\,e\,a, & \text{using rule 3} \\ & \Rightarrow i\,C\,t\,i\,\underline{C}\,t\,a\,e\,a, & \text{using rule 3} \\ & \Rightarrow i\,\underline{C}\,t\,i\,b\,t\,a\,e\,a, & \text{using rule 4} \\ & \Rightarrow i\,b\,t\,i\,b\,t\,a\,e\,a, & \text{using rule 4} \\ S & \Rightarrow i\,C\,t\,S\,e\,\underline{S}, & \text{using rule 2} \\ & \Rightarrow i\,C\,t\,\underline{S}\,e\,a, & \text{using rule 3} \\ & \Rightarrow i\,C\,t\,i\,C\,t\,\underline{S}\,e\,a, & \text{using rule 1} \\ & \Rightarrow i\,C\,t\,i\,\underline{C}\,t\,a\,e\,a, & \text{using rule 3} \\ & \Rightarrow i\,\underline{C}\,t\,i\,b\,t\,a\,e\,a, & \text{using rule 4} \\ & \Rightarrow i\,b\,t\,i\,b\,t\,a\,e\,a, & \text{using rule 4} \end{array}$$

We have seen that there can be two leftmost derivations instead of one. Similarly, there are two rightmost derivations instead of one. This means that there are two different ways of deriving the same string: one that starts with '$i\,C\,t\,s$' and the other starts with '$i\,C\,t\,S\,e\,S$'.

These two ways can be reflected in the two derivation trees shown in Fig. 5.4.

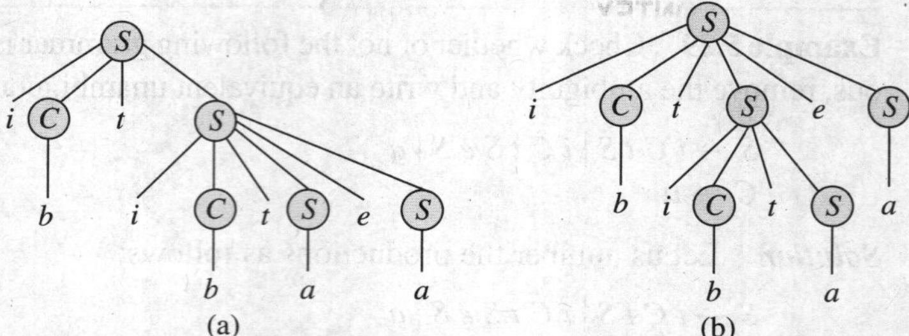

**Figure 5.4** Derivation trees for '*ibtibtaea*' using ambiguous grammar (a) First derivation tree (b) Second derivation tree

Hence, we conclude that the given grammar is ambiguous.

The given grammar is the grammar for the 'if-statement'. Here, the 'else' part is considered associated with the later 'if' part. This information is not used by the grammar writer. Hence, there is ambiguity.

The equivalent unambiguous grammar is:

$$S \to A \mid B$$
$$A \to i\,C\,t\,A\,e\,A \mid a$$
$$B \to i\,C\,t\,S \mid i\,C\,t\,A\,e\,B$$
$$C \to b$$

Using this unambiguous grammar, we now attempt to derive the string '*ibtibtaea*'. We observe that in this case, there is only one way of deriving the string. Therefore, the grammar is now unambiguous.

Leftmost derivation:

$$S \Rightarrow \underline{B}$$
$$\Rightarrow i\,\underline{C}\,t\,S$$
$$\Rightarrow i\,b\,t\,\underline{S}$$
$$\Rightarrow i\,b\,t\,\underline{A}$$
$$\Rightarrow i\,b\,t\,i\,\underline{C}\,t\,A\,e\,A$$
$$\Rightarrow i\,b\,t\,i\,b\,t\,\underline{A}\,e\,A$$
$$\Rightarrow i\,b\,t\,i\,b\,t\,a\,e\,\underline{A}$$
$$\Rightarrow i\,b\,t\,i\,b\,t\,a\,e\,a$$

Rightmost derivation:

$$S \Rightarrow \underline{B}$$
$$\Rightarrow i\,C\,t\,\underline{S}$$
$$\Rightarrow i\,C\,t\,\underline{A}$$
$$\Rightarrow i\,C\,t\,i\,C\,t\,A\,e\,\underline{A}$$
$$\Rightarrow i\,C\,t\,i\,C\,t\,\underline{A}\,e\,a$$
$$\Rightarrow i\,C\,t\,i\,\underline{C}\,t\,a\,e\,a$$
$$\Rightarrow i\,\underline{C}\,t\,i\,b\,t\,a\,e\,a$$
$$\Rightarrow i\,b\,t\,i\,b\,t\,a\,e\,a$$

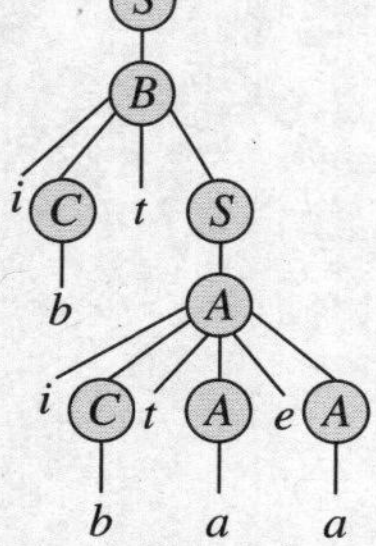

**Figure 5.5** Derivation tree for '*ibtibtaea*' using unambiguous grammar

Similarly, the derivation tree for the string is shown in Fig. 5.5.

## 5.9 SIMPLIFICATION OF CONTEXT-FREE GRAMMAR

A context-free grammar $G$ can be simplified, and written in a *reduced form*, using the following rules:

1. Each variable and terminal of the CFG should appear in the derivation of at least one word in the $L(G)$.
2. There should not be any production of the form '$A \to B$', where $A$ and $B$ are both non-terminals.

We shall discuss some simplification techniques in the following subsections.

### 5.9.1 Removal of Useless Symbols

A symbol $X$ is considered useful if there is a derivation of the form, $S \overset{*}{\Rightarrow} \alpha X \beta \overset{*}{\Rightarrow} w$, where $\alpha$, $\beta$ are sentential forms and $w$ is any string of terminals, that is, ($w \subset T^*$).

If no such derivation exists, then the symbol $X$ will not appear in any of the derivations; in this case, $X$ is a *useless symbol*.

Three aspects of usefulness of a non-terminal $X$ are as follows:

1. There must be some string that can be derived from $X$
2. The symbol $X$ must appear in the derivation of at least one string derivable from $S$ (start symbol).
3. The symbol $X$ should not occur in any sentential form that contains a variable from which no terminal string can be derived.

In order to remove the useless symbols, we must either delete the production rules that contain these symbols or rewrite the grammar. Let us now discuss a few example grammars.

---

**Example 5.30** Consider the following grammar:

$$G = \{(S, A), (1, 0), P, S\},$$

where, $P$ consists of the following productions:

$$S \to 10 \mid 0\,S\,1 \mid 1\,S\,0 \mid A \mid S\,S$$

Simplify the grammar by removing the useless symbols, if any.

***Solution*** We observe that there is a non-terminal $A$, which cannot derive any string of terminals, in the given grammar $G$. This is represented as follows:

$$S \Rightarrow A \Rightarrow ?$$

Hence, $A$ is a useless symbol and we should remove it.

To remove the useless symbol $A$, we should delete the production '$S \to A$'.

Therefore, the simplified or reduced form grammar is:

$$S \to 1\,0 \mid 0\,S\,1 \mid 1\,S\,0 \mid S\,S$$

---

*Note*: The grammar, after removing the productions containing useless symbols, should be checked for the purpose it was written for. One should rewrite the grammar if the resultant language is changed in the process.

**Example 5.31** Consider the grammar $G$ defined as:

$$G = \{(S, A, B), (a), P, S\},$$

where, $P$ consists of:

$$S \rightarrow A\,B \mid a$$
$$A \rightarrow a$$

Simplify the grammar by removing useless symbols, if any.

***Solution*** We observe that in the given grammar, there is a variable $B$, which does not derive any string of terminals. Thus, it is a useless symbol.

In order to simplify the grammar, we should delete all the productions that contain $B$. There is one such production '$S \rightarrow AB$'; hence, we drop this production and write the simplified grammar without useless symbols as:

$$S \rightarrow a$$
$$A \rightarrow a$$

Here, though $A$ produces a string of terminals, it cannot occur in any derivation of any string derivable from $S$. Therefore, $A$ is also a useless symbol now and hence, we should drop the production '$A \rightarrow a$'.

Hence, the simplified grammar can be written with only one production rule:

$$G = \{(S), (a), (S \rightarrow a), S\}$$

This grammar is obviously equivalent to the given grammar, but is in a simplified form.

### 5.9.2 Removal of Unit Productions

A production rule of the form '$A \rightarrow B$', where, $A$ and $B$ are both non-terminals, is called a *unit production*. All other productions (including $\epsilon$-productions) are non-unit productions.

#### *Elimination Rule*

For every pair of non-terminals $A$ and $B$,

1. If the CFG has a unit production of the form '$A \rightarrow B$', or
2. If there is a chain of unit productions leading from $A$ to $B$, such as:

$$A \Rightarrow X_1 \Rightarrow X_2 \Rightarrow \ldots \Rightarrow B,$$

where, all $X_i$ $(i > 0)$ are non-terminals, then introduce new production(s) according to the following rule:

'If the non-unit productions for $B$ are:

$$B \rightarrow \alpha_1 \mid \alpha_2 \mid \ldots,$$

where, $\alpha_1$, $\alpha_2$, …, are sentential forms (not containing only one non-terminal); then create the productions for $A$ as:

$$A \rightarrow \alpha_1 \mid \alpha_2 \mid \ldots\text{'}$$

---

**Example 5.32** Consider the grammar $G$ defined as:

$$G = \{(A, B), (a, b), P, A\},$$

where, $P$ consists of:

$$A \rightarrow B$$
$$B \rightarrow a \mid b$$

Simplify the grammar by eliminating the unit productions, if any.

***Solution*** We see that '$A \rightarrow B$' is the unit production that we need to eliminate. Applying the elimination rule, we have:

$$B \rightarrow \alpha_1 \mid \alpha_2,$$

where $\alpha_1 = a$,
and $\alpha_2 = b$.

Therefore, we can write the reduced form grammar without the unit production as:

$$A \rightarrow a \mid b$$

Thus, the simplified $G$ can be written as:

$$G = \{(A), (a, b), (A \rightarrow a, A \rightarrow b), A\}$$

---

**Example 5.33** Consider the grammar $G$, which consists of the following productions with $S$ as the start symbol:

$$S \rightarrow A \mid b\,b$$
$$A \rightarrow B \mid b$$
$$B \rightarrow S \mid a$$

Simplify the grammar by eliminating the unit productions, if any.

***Solution*** We see that there is a chain of unit productions: $S \rightarrow A \rightarrow B \rightarrow S$. Using the productions, '$A \rightarrow B$' and '$B \rightarrow S \mid a$', we add a new production to $A$, as follows:

$$A \rightarrow S \mid a$$

Therefore, the grammar becomes:

$$S \rightarrow A \mid b\,b$$
$$A \rightarrow S \mid a \mid b$$

We have another unit production, '$S \to A$'; after removing this, the grammar is reduced to:

$$S \to S \mid a \mid b \mid b\,b$$

However, there is still one more unit production, namely, '$S \to S$', which we can directly remove as the symbol on the left and right are the same. Therefore, the equivalent grammar without unit productions can be written as:

$$S \to a \mid b \mid b\,b$$

---

**Example 5.34** Eliminate unit productions from the following grammar:

$$S \to a \mid X\,b \mid a\,Y\,a \mid b \mid a\,a$$
$$X \to Y$$
$$Y \to b \mid X$$

***Solution*** In the aforementioned grammar, we see that there are two unit productions: '$X \to Y$' and '$Y \to X$'.

From the productions, '$X \to Y$' and '$Y \to b \mid X$', we can derive:

$$Y \to b \mid Y$$

Hence, we can now delete '$X \to Y$'.

Further, we observe that the new rule '$Y \to Y$' does not make any sense, and hence, can be deleted.

After these additions and deletions, we rewrite the given grammar as follows:

$$S \to a \mid Y\,b \mid a\,Y\,a \mid b \mid a\,a, \qquad \text{(replacing } X \text{ by } Y)$$
$$Y \to b$$

---

### 5.9.3 Elimination of $\epsilon$-Productions

A production of the form '$A \to \epsilon$', where $A$ is a non-terminal, is known as an *$\epsilon$-production*. If $\epsilon$ is a member of $L(G)$ for a given grammar $G$, then we cannot eliminate all $\epsilon$-productions from $G$; whereas, if $\epsilon$ is not in $L(G)$, then we can remove all the $\epsilon$-productions.

**Theorem 5.1**

If $L$ is a CFL generated by a CFG that includes $\epsilon$-productions, then there exists another CFG without $\epsilon$-productions, which generates either the whole language $L$ (if $L$ does not contain $\epsilon$), or a language containing all the words in $L$, except $\epsilon$; that is, $L - \{\epsilon\}$.

*Proof*

The elimination method is based on the concept of nullable non-terminals:

In a given CFG, if there is a non-terminal $N$ and a production '$N \to \epsilon$', or if $N$ produces $\epsilon$ in one or more steps, that is, '$N \overset{*}{\Rightarrow} \epsilon$', then $N$ is called a *nullable non-terminal*.

For example, consider the grammar:

$$A \to B \mid \epsilon$$
$$B \to a$$

In this grammar, $A$ is a nullable non-terminal, but $B$ is not.

On the other hand, consider the grammar:

$A \to B \mid a$
$B \to a \mid \epsilon$

In this grammar, since '$B \to \epsilon$' is one of the productions, $B$ is a nullable non-terminal. Likewise, since $A \Rightarrow B \Rightarrow \epsilon$, that is, $A \stackrel{*}{\Rightarrow} \epsilon$, $A$ is also a nullable non-terminal.

The steps in the process of eliminating $\epsilon$-productions are as follows:

1. Delete all $\epsilon$-productions from the grammar.
2. Identify nullable non-terminals.
3. If there is a production of the form '$A \to \alpha$', where $\alpha$ is any sentential form containing at least one nullable non-terminal, then add new productions, whose right-hand side is formed by deleting all possible subsets of nullable non-terminals from $\alpha$.
4. If using step 3, we get a production of the form '$A \to \epsilon$', then do not add that to the final grammar.

Let us now work on some examples to illustrate this method.

---

**Example 5.35** Eliminate $\epsilon$-productions from $G$, where $G$ consists of the following productions:

$$S \to a\,S\,a \mid b\,S\,b \mid \epsilon$$

***Solution***

After deleting the $\epsilon$-productions we have:

$$S \to a\,S\,a \mid b\,S\,b$$

Since '$S \to \epsilon$' is a production in the given grammar, $S$ is a nullable non-terminal.

The following two productions contain nullable non-terminals on the right-hand side:

$$S \to a\,S\,a$$
$$S \to b\,S\,b$$

In the production '$S \to a\,S\,a$', if we delete $S$ from the right-hand side we can add a new production as:

$$S \to a\,a$$

Similarly, from '$S \to b\,S\,b$', deleting $S$ from the right-hand side, we have a new production as follows:

$$S \to b\,b,$$

which we can add to the final grammar.

Thus, the final grammar, $G'$, without $\epsilon$-productions is as follows:

$$S \to a\,S\,a \mid b\,S\,b \mid a\,a \mid b\,b$$

Comparing $G$ and $G'$, we see that:

$$L(G') = L(G) - \{\epsilon\}$$

**Example 5.36** Eliminate $\epsilon$-productions from the grammar $G$, which is defined as:

$$S \rightarrow a \mid X b \mid a Y a$$
$$X \rightarrow Y \mid \epsilon$$
$$Y \rightarrow b \mid X$$

Compare the language generated by the new grammar with the language generated by $G$.

***Solution***

Delete '$X \rightarrow \epsilon$' from the final set of productions.

Since there is a production, $X \rightarrow \epsilon$, therefore $X$ is a nullable non-terminal. We also have:

$$Y \Rightarrow X \Rightarrow \epsilon$$
$$\text{Or, } Y \overset{*}{\Rightarrow} \epsilon$$

Since $Y$ produces $\epsilon$ in two steps, therefore, $Y$ is also a nullable non-terminal.

Consider the following productions having nullable non-terminals existing on their right-hand side:

$$S \rightarrow X b$$
$$S \rightarrow a Y a$$
$$X \rightarrow Y$$
$$Y \rightarrow X$$

From '$S \rightarrow X b$', if we delete $X$, we can add the production:

$$S \rightarrow b$$

to the final set.

Similarly, from '$S \rightarrow a Y a$', if we delete $Y$ we can add:

$$S \rightarrow a a$$

to the final set of productions.

From the production '$X \rightarrow Y$' and '$Y \rightarrow X$' if we delete the nullable non-terminals on the right-hand side, we get productions, '$X \rightarrow \epsilon$' and '$Y \rightarrow \epsilon$', which we cannot add to the final set.

Thus, the final grammar $G'$ is written as:

$$S \rightarrow a \mid X b \mid a Y a \mid b \mid a a$$
$$X \rightarrow Y$$
$$Y \rightarrow b \mid X$$

We observe that, both the languages $L(G)$ and $L(G')$ do not contain $\epsilon$. Therefore, by Theorem 5.1, we can say:

$$L(G) = L(G')$$

Recall that in Example 5.34, we have further reduced this grammar by eliminating the unit productions.

**Example 5.37** Eliminate the $\epsilon$-productions from grammar $G$ defined as:

$$S \rightarrow X\,a$$
$$X \rightarrow a\,X \mid b\,X \mid \epsilon$$

***Solution*** We can delete production '$X \rightarrow \epsilon$' from final set of productions. Since '$X \rightarrow \epsilon$' is a production in the given set, $X$ is a nullable non-terminal.

Let us consider all productions with at least one nullable non-terminal on the right-hand side:

$$S \rightarrow X\,a$$
$$X \rightarrow a\,X$$
$$X \rightarrow b\,X$$

Deleting $X$ from the right-hand side from these, we obtain three new productions to be added to the final set of productions:

$$S \rightarrow a$$
$$X \rightarrow a$$
$$X \rightarrow b$$

Therefore, the final grammar $G'$ is defined as:

$$S \rightarrow X\,a \mid a$$
$$X \rightarrow a\,X \mid b\,X \mid a \mid b$$

We observe that $\epsilon$ is not a member of $L(G)$

Therefore,

$$L(G) = L(G')$$

**Example 5.38** Eliminate $\epsilon$-productions from the grammar $G$, which is defined as:

$$A \rightarrow a\,B\,b \mid b\,B\,a$$
$$B \rightarrow a\,B \mid b\,B \mid \epsilon$$

***Solution*** We delete '$B \rightarrow \epsilon$' from the final set. Since there is a production '$B \rightarrow \epsilon$' in the given set, $B$ is a nullable non-terminal.

Let us consider all productions having $B$ on the right-hand side:

$$A \rightarrow a\,B\,b \mid b\,B\,a$$
$$B \rightarrow a\,B \mid b\,B$$

Deleting $B$ from these productions, we get four more new productions to add to the final set:

$$A \rightarrow a\,b$$
$$A \rightarrow b\,a$$
$$B \rightarrow a$$
$$B \rightarrow b$$

Thus, the final grammar $G'$ can be written as:

$$A \to a\,B\,b \mid b\,B\,a \mid a\,b \mid b\,a$$
$$B \to a\,B \mid b\,B \mid a \mid b$$

We further observe that:

$$L(G) = L(G')$$

---

**Example 5.39** Eliminate the $\epsilon$-productions from the grammar $G$, which is defined as:

$$S \to A\,B\,A$$
$$A \to a\,A \mid \epsilon$$
$$B \to b\,B \mid \epsilon$$

***Solution***

We delete the productions '$A \to \epsilon$' and '$B \to \epsilon$' from the final set of productions.

Since '$A \to \epsilon$' and '$B \to \epsilon$' are productions in the given set, both $A$ and $B$ are nullable non-terminals.

Further, we have:

$$S \Rightarrow ABA \Rightarrow BA \Rightarrow A \Rightarrow \epsilon, \text{ using rules '}A \to \epsilon\text{' and '}B \to \epsilon\text{', i.e., } S \overset{*}{\Rightarrow} \epsilon$$

Since, $S$ produces $\epsilon$, $S$ is also a nullable non-terminal.

Let us consider the following productions having nullable non-terminals on the right-hand side:

$$S \to A\,B\,A$$
$$A \to a\,A$$
$$B \to b\,B$$

From the production '$S \to A\ B\ A$', after deleting all possible subsets of nullable non-terminals, we get following new productions:

$$S \to A\,B$$
$$S \to B\,A$$
$$S \to A\,A$$
$$S \to A$$
$$S \to B$$
$$S \to \epsilon$$

Among these, we can add all productions to the final set, except '$S \to \epsilon$'.

Similarly, from '$A \to a\ A$', we get '$A \to a$', and from '$B \to b\ B$', we get '$B \to b$' to add to the final set.

Therefore, the final grammar $G'$ is defined as follows:

$$S \to A\,B\,A \mid A\,B \mid B\,A \mid A\,A \mid A \mid B$$
$$A \to a\,A \mid a$$
$$B \to b\,B \mid b$$

Further, we observe that:

$$L(G') = L(G) - \{\epsilon\}$$

## 5.10 NORMAL FORMS

Context-free grammars can be written in certain standard forms, known as *normal forms*. These normal forms impose certain restrictions on the productions in the CFG. Complex CFGs can thus be reduced to simple forms after modifying them or rewriting them using these normal forms. In this section, we shall discuss two normal forms: Chomsky normal form (CNF) and Greibach normal form (GNF).

Every CFG without $\epsilon$-productions has an equivalent grammar in Chomsky normal form or Greibach normal form. Equivalent here means that the two grammars generate the same language. Let us discuss these two normal forms in detail.

### 5.10.1 Chomsky Normal Form

Any CFL without $\epsilon$, which is generated by a grammar in which all productions are of the form:

'$A \to B\ C$', or '$A \to a$',

where, $A$, $B$, and $C$ are non-terminals and $a$ is a terminal symbol, is said to be in Chomsky normal form (CNF).

We see that there are restrictions on the form of productions in CNF, as they can be expressed in only two ways: '$A \to BC$' and '$A \to a$'. In other words, we can only have either two non-terminals or a single terminal on the right-hand side of every production.

If the language has an empty string, that is, $\epsilon$, then only the following $\epsilon$-production is allowed in CNF:

$$S \to \epsilon,$$

where, $S$ is the start symbol.

**Example 5.40** Convert the following CFG to CNF.

$$S \to a\,S\,a \mid b\,S\,b \mid a \mid b \mid a\,a \mid b\,b$$

***Solution*** In CNF, we can have only two types of productions: either '$A \to B\ C$' or '$A \to a$'.

If we add two productions for the aforementioned grammar, namely:

$$A \to a$$
$$B \to b$$

We can rewrite the aforementioned grammar as:

$$S \to A\,S\,A \mid B\,S\,B \mid a \mid b \mid A\,A \mid B\,B \qquad \text{(using '}A \to a\text{' and '}B \to b\text{')}$$
$$A \to a$$
$$B \to b$$

We need not change the productions '$S \to a$' and '$S \to b$', because they are already in CNF.

Now, there are only two productions which are not in CNF and hence need to be changed:

$$S \to A\,S\,A$$
$$S \to B\,S\,B$$

To bring them to CNF we introduce two new variables, $R_1$ and $R_2$, such that:

$$S \to A\,R_1$$
$$S \to B\,R_2$$
$$R_1 \to S\,A$$
$$R_2 \to S\,B$$

Thus, an equivalent grammar expressed in CNF can be written as:

$$S \to A\,R_1 \mid B\,R_2 \mid a \mid b \mid A\,A \mid B\,B$$
$$A \to a$$
$$B \to b$$
$$R_1 \to S\,A$$
$$R_2 \to S\,B$$

---

**Example 5.41** Convert the following grammar to Chomsky normal form.

$$S \to b\,A \mid a\,B$$
$$A \to b\,A\,A \mid a\,S \mid a$$
$$B \to a\,B\,B \mid b\,S \mid b$$

***Solution*** We see that productions '$A \to a$' and '$B \to b$' are already in CNF.

Now, if we introduce two more productions, $R_1$ and $R_2$, such that:

$$R_1 \to a$$
$$R_2 \to b$$

then, the given grammar can be written as:

$$S \to R_2 A \mid R_1 B$$
$$A \to R_2\,A\,A \mid R_1\,S \mid a$$
$$B \to R_1\,B\,B \mid R_2\,S \mid b$$
$$R_1 \to a$$
$$R_2 \to b$$

We see that there are still two more productions which are not in CNF; namely, '$A \to R_2 A\,A$' and '$B \to R_1 B\,B$'.

After introducing two more new symbols—$R_3$ and $R_4$—and further break-up, we write the given grammar in CNF as:

$$S \to R_2 A \mid R_1 B$$
$$A \to R_2\,R_3 \mid R_1\,S \mid a$$
$$B \to R_1\,R_4 \mid R_2\,S \mid b$$
$$R_1 \to a$$

$R_2 \rightarrow b$
$R_3 \rightarrow A\,A$
$R_4 \rightarrow B\,B$

---

**Example 5.42** Express the following grammar using CNF.

$S \rightarrow ABA$
$A \rightarrow a\,A \mid \epsilon$
$B \rightarrow b\,B \mid \epsilon$

***Solution*** As we know, before we express a grammar in CNF, we should first remove the $\epsilon$-productions. Hence, we get a new grammar $G'$ such that:

$$L(G') = L(G) - \{\epsilon\}$$

Refer to Example 5.39 in which we have already dealt with this grammar.

The new grammar $G'$ without the $\epsilon$-productions is:

$S \rightarrow A\,B\,A \mid A\,B \mid B\,A \mid A\,A \mid A \mid B$
$A \rightarrow a\,A \mid a$
$B \rightarrow b\,B \mid b$

Let us first eliminate the unit productions; namely, '$S \rightarrow A$' and '$S \rightarrow B$'.

This is achieved by substituting '$A \rightarrow a\,A \mid a$' in '$S \rightarrow A$', and '$B \rightarrow b\,B \mid b$' in '$S \rightarrow B$'. After removing the unit productions the grammar can be written as follows:

$S \rightarrow A\,B\,A \mid A\,B \mid B\,A \mid A\,A \mid a\,A \mid a \mid b\,B \mid b$
$A \rightarrow a\,A \mid a$
$B \rightarrow b\,B \mid b$

Now, let us introduce three new variables, $R_1$, $R_2$, and $R_3$, as shown in the final grammar. Observe that we have also added the $\epsilon$-productions for $S$ because the language generates the empty string $\epsilon$.

The final grammar is written as follows:

$S \rightarrow A\,R_1 \mid A\,B \mid B\,A \mid A\,A \mid R_2A \mid a \mid R_3B \mid b \mid \epsilon$
$A \rightarrow R_2A \mid a$
$B \rightarrow R_3B \mid b$
$R_1 \rightarrow B\,A$
$R_2 \rightarrow a$
$R_3 \rightarrow b$

---

### 5.10.2 Greibach Normal Form

Every CFL without $\epsilon$ can be generated by a grammar, whose every production is of the form, $A \rightarrow a\alpha$, where $A$ is a non-terminal, $a$ is a terminal, and $\alpha$ is a (possibly empty) string containing only non-terminals. This type of grammar is said to be in *Greibach normal form* (GNF).

Thus, in GNF, the right-hand side of each production should contain only one terminal symbol—and that should be the first symbol on the right-hand side—followed by zero or more non-terminals.

If the language has an empty string, that is, $\epsilon$, then only the following $\epsilon$-production is allowed:

$$S \to \epsilon,$$

where, $S$ is the start symbol.

---

**Example 5.43** Convert the following grammar to GNF.

$$S \to A\,B\,A \mid A\,B \mid B\,A \mid A\,A \mid A \mid B$$
$$A \to a\,A \mid a$$
$$B \to b\,B \mid b$$

***Solution*** We see that the productions from $S$ are not in GNF. To bring them to the proper form, we replace the leading $A$'s and $B$'s by their right-hand sides in the productions, '$A \to a\,A$', '$A \to a$', '$B \to b\,B$', and '$B \to b$'.

Therefore, the final grammar in GNF is:

$$S \to a\,A\,B\,A \mid a\,B\,A \mid a\,A\,B \mid a\,B \mid b\,B\,A \mid b\,A \mid a\,A\,A \mid a\,A \mid a\,A \mid a \mid b\,B \mid b$$
$$A \to a\,A \mid a$$
$$B \to b\,B \mid b$$

---

**Example 5.44** Convert the following grammar $G$ to GNF:

$$G = \{(A_1, A_2, A_3), (a, b), P, A_1\},$$

where, $P$ consists of the following productions:

$$A_1 \to A_2\,A_3$$
$$A_2 \to A_3\,A_1 \mid b$$
$$A_3 \to A_1\,A_2 \mid a$$

***Solution*** We observe that '$A_1 \to A_2\,A_3$' is the only production with $A_1$ on the left-hand side. Let us substitute $A_2\,A_3$ for $A_1$ in the production '$A_3 \to A_1\,A_2$'.

The resulting set of productions is:

$$A_1 \to A_2\,A_3$$
$$A_2 \to A_3\,A_1 \mid b$$
$$A_3 \to A_2\,A_3\,A_2 \mid a$$

Similarly, let us substitute for the first occurrence of $A_2$ in the production rule for $A_3$ with $A_3\,A_1$ and $b$.

The new set will be:

$$A_1 \to A_2\,A_3$$
$$A_2 \to A_3\,A_1 \mid b$$
$$A_3 \to A_3\,A_1\,A_3\,A_2 \mid b\,A_3\,A_2 \mid a$$

The production '$A_3 \rightarrow A_3\, A_1\, A_3\, A_2$' is recursive (the first symbol on the right-hand side of the production is the same as the non-terminal on the the left-hand side). Hence, we introduce a new symbol $B_3$, and write the following productions:

$$A_3 \rightarrow b\, A_3\, A_2\, B_3$$
$$A_3 \rightarrow a\, B_3$$
$$B_3 \rightarrow A_1\, A_3\, A_2 \mid A_1\, A_3\, A_2\, B_3$$

The resulting set is:

$$A_1 \rightarrow A_2\, A_3$$
$$A_2 \rightarrow A_3\, A_1 \mid b$$
$$A_3 \rightarrow b\, A_3\, A_2\, B_3 \mid a\, B_3 \mid b\, A_3\, A_2 \mid a$$
$$B_3 \rightarrow A_1\, A_3\, A_2 \mid A_1\, A_3\, A_2\, B_3$$

Now, the productions for $A_3$ are all in GNF. Therefore, we can substitute for $A_3$ in the production '$A_2 \rightarrow A_3\, A_1$'. The resulting set of productions is:

$$A_1 \rightarrow A_2\, A_3$$
$$A_2 \rightarrow b\, A_3\, A_2\, B_3\, A_1 \mid a\, B_3 A_1 \mid b\, A_3\, A_2\, A_1 \mid a\, A_1 \mid b$$
$$A_3 \rightarrow b\, A_3 A_2\, B_3 \mid a\, B_3 \mid b\, A_3\, A_2 \mid a$$
$$B_3 \rightarrow A_1\, A_3\, A_2 \mid A_1\, A_3\, A_2\, B_3$$

Now, the productions for $A_2$ are also in GNF.

Hence, we substitute for $A_2$ in '$A_1 \rightarrow A_2\, A_3$'. We now have:

$$A_1 \rightarrow b\, A_3\, A_2\, B_3\, A_1\, A_3 \mid a\, B_3\, A_1\, A_3 \mid b\, A_3\, A_2\, A_1\, A_3 \mid a\, A_1\, A_3 \mid b\, A_3$$
$$A_2 \rightarrow b\, A_3\, A_2\, B_3\, A_1 \mid a\, B_3\, A_1 \mid b\, A_3\, A_2\, A_1 \mid a\, A_1 \mid b$$
$$A_3 \rightarrow b\, A_3\, A_2\, B_3 \mid a\, B_3 \mid b\, A_3\, A_2 \mid a$$
$$B_3 \rightarrow A_1\, A_3\, A_2 \mid A_1\, A_3\, A_2\, B_3$$

Now, we see that the productions for $A_1$ are also in GNF. Hence, we substitute these in the production for $B_3$ to get the final grammar in GNF.

An equivalent grammar in GNF, thus, can be written as:

$$A_1 \rightarrow b\, A_3\, A_2\, B_3\, A_1\, A_3 \mid a\, B_3\, A_1\, A_3 \mid b\, A_3\, A_2\, A_1\, A_3 \mid a\, A_1\, A_3 \mid b\, A_3$$
$$A_2 \rightarrow b\, A_3\, A_2\, B_3\, A_1 \mid a\, B_3\, A_1 \mid b\, A_3\, A_2\, A_1 \mid a\, A_1 \mid b$$
$$A_3 \rightarrow b\, A_3\, A_2\, B_3 \mid a\, B_3 \mid b\, A_3\, A_2 \mid a$$
$$\begin{aligned} B_1 \rightarrow\ & b\, A_3\, A_2\, B_3\, A_1\, A_3\, A_3\, A_2 \mid b\, A_3\, A_2\, B_3\, A_1\, A_3\, A_3\, A_2\, B_3 \\ & \mid a\, B_3\, A_1\, A_3\, A_3\, A_2 \mid a\, B_3\, A_1\, A_3\, A_3\, A_2\, B_3 \\ & \mid bA_3\, A_2\, A_1\, A_3\, A_3\, A_2 \mid b\, A_3\, A_2\, A_1\, A_3\, A_3\, A_2\, B_3 \\ & \mid a\, A_1 A_3\, A_3\, A_2 \mid a\, A_1\, A_3\, A_3\, A_2\, B_3 \\ & \mid b\, A_3\, A_3\, A_2 \mid bA_3\, A_3\, A_2\, B_3 \end{aligned}$$

## 5.11 CHOMSKY HIERARCHY

The class of phrase structure grammars is very large. However, imposing certain constraints on the production rules, different classes of phrase structure grammar can be obtained. It is more of a containment hierarchy, as one class of grammars is more powerful than the other, and so on. The hierarchy thus obtained is called *Chomsky hierarchy*. This hierarchy of grammars was described by Noam Chomsky in 1956. It is occasionally referred to as *Chomsky–Schützenberger hierarchy*, after Marcel-Paul Schützenberger, who played a crucial role in the development of the theory of formal languages.

Chomsky suggested four different classes of phrase structure grammars, as follows:

1. Type-0 (unrestricted grammar)
2. Type-1 (context-sensitive grammar)
3. Type-2 (context-free grammar)
4. Type-3 (regular grammar)

### 5.11.1 Unrestricted Grammar (Type-0 Grammar)

There are no restrictions on the productions of a grammar of this type. This type of grammar permits productions of the form '$\alpha \to \beta$'; $\alpha \neq \epsilon$, where, $\alpha$ and $\beta$ are sentential forms; that is, any combination of any number of terminals and non-terminals, $\alpha, \beta \subset (V \cup T)^*$; and $\alpha \neq \epsilon$, because there must be something to be replaced by the right-hand side of the production. Such a grammar is called *semi-Thue grammar* or *unrestricted grammar*.

Type-0 grammars (unrestricted grammars) include all formal grammars; they generate exactly all languages that can be recognized by a Turing machine. These languages are also known as *recursively enumerable languages*. This means that we need to construct Turing machines (TMs) to recognize the languages generated by this class of grammars.

For example, let us consider the following grammar:

$$V = \{A, B, C\}$$
$$T = \{a, b, c\}$$
$$G = \{V, T, P, A\},$$

where, $P$ consists of:

$$A \to A\ B$$
$$A\ B \to B\ C$$
$$B \to A\ c\ D$$
$$A\ c \to a\ b\ c$$
$$D \to \epsilon$$

As we can see, there are no restrictions on the production forms, except that $\alpha \neq \epsilon$. Therefore, it is a type-0 grammar.

### 5.11.2 Context-sensitive Grammar (Type-1 Grammar)

The restrictions on this type of grammar are as follows:

1. For each production of the form '$\alpha \to \beta$', the length of $\beta$ is at least as much as the length of $\alpha$, except for '$S \to \epsilon$'.
2. The rule '$S \to \epsilon$' is allowed only if the start symbol $S$ does not appear on the right-hand side of any production.

3. The term 'context sensitive' is used because the grammar has productions of the form:

$$\alpha_1 A \alpha_2 \rightarrow \alpha_1 \beta \alpha_2; (\beta \neq \epsilon),$$

where, the replacement of a non-terminal $A$ by $\beta$ is allowed only if $\alpha_1$ precedes $A$ and $\alpha_2$ succeeds $A$; $\alpha_1$ and $\alpha_2$ may or may not be empty.

Context-sensitive grammar (CSG) or type-1 grammar generates *context-sensitive language* (CSL). Turing machines can be constructed to recognize such context-sensitive languages.

For example, consider the grammar $G$, which is defined as:

$$G = \{(A, B, C), (a, b), P, A\},$$

where, $P$ consists of the productions:

$$A \rightarrow A\,B$$
$$A\,B \rightarrow A\,C$$
$$A\,C \rightarrow a\,b$$

We observe that this grammar is in accordance with the restrictions placed in type-1 or context-sensitive grammar.

### 5.11.3 Context-free Grammar (Type-2 Grammar)

In this class of grammar:

The only allowed type of production is '$A \rightarrow \alpha$', where, $A$ is a non-terminal, and $\alpha$ is in sentential form, that is, $\alpha \subset (V \cup T)^*$; and $\alpha$ may also be equal to $\epsilon$. The left-hand side of the production, thus, contains only one non-terminal.

The start symbol of the grammar can also appear on right-hand side.

*Non-deterministic pushdown automata* (NPDA) can accept the whole class of context-free languages (CFL), generated by CFG.

For example, let us consider the following grammar $G$, which is a CFG:

$$G = \{(S), (a, b), P, S\},$$

where, $P$ consists of the following productions:

$$S \rightarrow a\,S\,a \mid b\,S\,b \mid a \mid b$$

We have already seen many examples and discussed many concepts regarding CFGs in the previous sections.

### 5.11.4 Regular Grammar (Type-3 Grammar)

This type of grammar has the following restrictions on its productions:

1. The left-hand side of each product should contain only one non-terminal.
2. The right-hand side can contain at most one non-terminal symbol, which is allowed to appear as the rightmost symbol or the leftmost symbol.

The language generated using this grammar is called a *regular language* (RL). Regular languages are too primitive and can be generated and recognized by *finite state machines* (FSMs). These languages are denoted by simpler expressions called regular expressions.

Depending on whether the position of a non-terminal on the right-hand side of the production (if it exists) is leftmost or rightmost, the regular grammar is further classified as follows: Left-linear grammar ($G_L$) and Right-linear grammar ($G_R$)

#### *Left-linear Grammar*

As we know, regular grammar can contain at the most one non-terminal on the right-hand side of every production. If this non-terminal appears as the leftmost symbol on the right-hand side, then it is said to be left-linear grammar.

The allowed types of productions in left-linear grammar are:

$$A \to B\,w$$
$$A \to w,$$

where, $A$ and $B$ are non-terminals, and $w$ is a string of terminals.

The rule '$S \to \epsilon$' is allowed only if the start symbol $S$ does not appear on the right-hand side of any production.

Consider the following grammar $G$:

$$G = \{(S, B, C), (a, b), P, S\}$$

where, $P$ consists of:

$$S \to C\,a \mid B\,b$$
$$C \to B\,b$$
$$B \to B\,a \mid b$$

The aforementioned grammar is left-linear, as each production has at the most one non-terminal at the leftmost position on the right-hand side.

#### *Right-linear Grammar*

A regular grammar consisting of productions with at most one non-terminal as the rightmost symbol on the right-hand side of every production (if it exists), is said to be right-linear grammar.

The allowed forms of the productions are:

$$A \to w\,B$$
$$A \to w,$$

where, $A$ and $B$ are non-terminals and $w$ is the string of terminals.

The rule '$S \to \epsilon$' is allowed only if the start symbol $S$ does not appear on the right-hand side of any production.

For example, the following grammar $G$ is right-linear:

$$G = \{(S, A), (0, 1), P, S\},$$

where, $P$ consists of:

$$S \to 0A$$
$$A \to 0A \mid 1$$

## 5.12 EQUIVALENCE OF RIGHT-LINEAR AND LEFT-LINEAR GRAMMARS

The left and the right-linear grammars are said to be equivalent if the sets generated (languages) by them are equal. For every right-linear grammar $G_R$ there exists an equivalent left-linear grammar $G_L$. Further, we can say that a language is said to be regular if it is either generated by a right-linear grammar or a left-linear grammar.

### 5.12.1 Conversion of Right-linear Grammar to Equivalent Left-linear Grammar

The following are the steps to convert right-linear grammar to its equivalent left linear grammar:

1. Represent the given right-linear grammar by a transition diagram with vertices labelled by the symbols from $\{V \cup (\epsilon)\}$ and transitions labelled by the symbols from $\{T \cup (\epsilon)\}$.
2. Interchange the positions of the initial and final states.
3. Reverse the directions of all the transitions, keeping the positions of all intermediate states unchanged.
4. Rewrite the grammar from this new transition graph in the left-linear fashion.

The reversal proposed here is due to the fact that right-linear grammar derives the string from left to right, while left-linear grammar derives it in the reverse way, that is, from right to left. This means that the terminal symbol first generated in the case of right-linear grammar will be generated last in case of its equivalent left-linear grammar.

---

**Example 5.45** Convert the following right-linear grammar $G_R$ to its equivalent left-linear grammar:

$$S \to b\,B$$
$$B \to b\,C$$
$$B \to a\,B$$
$$B \to b$$
$$C \to a$$

***Solution*** Let us construct a transition graph (TG) using the given right-linear grammar. The initial state will be labelled by start symbol $S$, and the final state will be labelled by $\epsilon$. The TG is shown in Fig. 5.6(a).

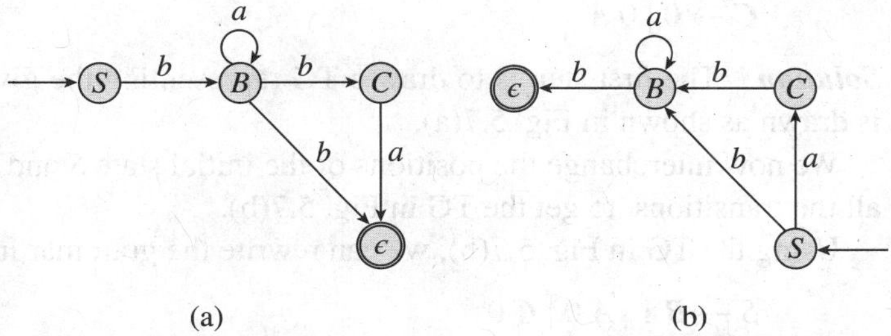


**Figure 5.6** Conversion of right-linear grammar to equivalent left-linear grammar (a) TG constructed from right-linear grammar (b) Resultant TG after interchanging initial and final states and reversing all the transitions

After interchanging the positions of the initial and the final states and reversing the directions of all the transitions of the TG, we get the TG for the equivalent left-linear grammar as shown in Fig. 5.6(b).

From the TG in Fig. 5.6(b), we can rewrite the left-linear grammar $G_L$ as follows:

$$S \to C\,a$$
$$S \to B\,b$$
$$C \to B\,b$$
$$B \to B\,a$$
$$B \to b$$

This left-linear grammar is equivalent to the given right-linear grammar. Let us check this for a string '*baab*'.

Using $G_R$, we can derive the given string as:

$$S \Rightarrow b\,B \Rightarrow b\,a\,B \Rightarrow b\,a\,a\,B \Rightarrow b\,a\,a\,b$$

Now, using the equivalent left-linear grammar $G_L$, we derive the same string as:

$$S \Rightarrow B\,b \Rightarrow B\,a\,b \Rightarrow B\,a\,a\,b \Rightarrow b\,a\,a\,b$$

Thus, we see that the left-linear grammar that we have obtained generates the same language as that of the given right-linear grammar. The only change we observe is that the right-linear grammar begins to derive the given string from the leftmost symbol, while the left-linear grammar derives it in the reverse direction, that is, from the rightmost symbol. In this example, we see that the first symbol of the string '*baab*', that is, '*b*', is generated first using right-linear grammar, and last using left-linear grammar.

We also see that the intermediate sentential forms in both the derivations are mirror images of each other. For example, '*B b* and '*b B*'; '*b a B*' and '*B a b*'; and '*b a a B*' and '*B a a b*'.

---

**Example 5.46** Write an equivalent left-linear grammar for the right-linear grammar, which is defined as:

$$S \to 0\,A \mid 1\,B$$
$$A \to 0\,C \mid 1\,A \mid 0$$
$$B \to 1\,B \mid 1\,A \mid 1$$
$$C \to 0 \mid 0\,A$$

***Solution*** The first step is to draw a TG representing the given right-linear grammar. It is drawn as shown in Fig. 5.7(a).

We now interchange the positions of the initial state *S* and the final state $\epsilon$ and reverse all the transitions, to get the TG in Fig. 5.7(b).

Using the TG in Fig. 5.7(b), we can rewrite the grammar in left-linear fashion as:

$$S \to B\,1 \mid A\,0 \mid C\,0$$
$$B \to B\,1 \mid 1$$
$$A \to A\,1 \mid B\,1 \mid C\,0 \mid 0$$
$$C \to A\,0$$

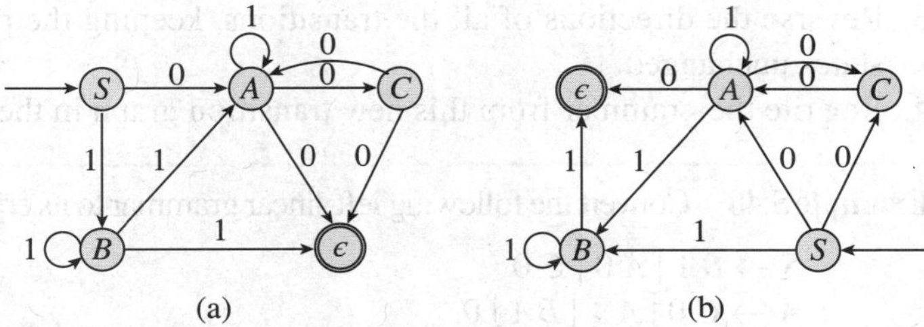


**Figure 5.7** $G_R$ to $G_L$ conversion (a) TG representing $G_R$ (right-linear grammar) (b) TG after interchanging initial and final states and reversing the transitions

---

**Example 5.47** Write an equivalent left-linear grammar for the following right-linear grammar:

$S \rightarrow 0\,A$
$A \rightarrow 1\,0\,A \mid \epsilon$

***Solution*** To start with, we draw the TG representing the aforementioned right-linear grammar, as shown in Fig. 5.8(a).

After interchanging the positions of the initial state $S$ and final state $\epsilon$, and reversing all the transitions of the TG in Fig. 5.8(a), we get the TG as shown in Fig. 5.8(b).

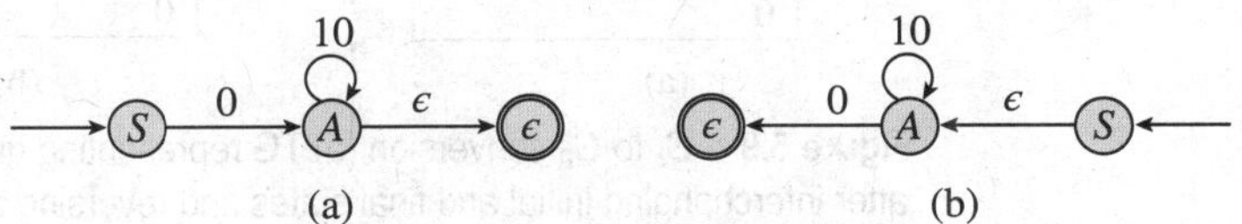


**Figure 5.8** $G_R$ to $G_L$ conversion (a) TG representing $G_R$ (b) TG after interchanging initial and final vertices and reversing the transitions

From the TG in Fig. 5.8(b), we can write the left-linear grammar as follows:

$S \rightarrow A\,\epsilon$
$A \rightarrow A\,1\,0 \mid 0$

The grammar can be further simplified as follows:

$S \rightarrow A$
$A \rightarrow A\,1\,0 \mid 0$

---

## 5.12.2 Conversion of Left-linear Grammar to Equivalent Right-linear Grammar

A method similar to that we have seen while converting $G_R$ to $G_L$ can be applied to convert a given $G_L$ to its equivalent $G_R$.

1. Represent the given left-linear grammar by a transition diagram (or transition graph) with vertices labelled by the symbols from $\{V \cup (\epsilon)\}$, and transitions labelled by the symbols from $\{T \cup (\epsilon)\}$.
2. Interchange the positions of the initial and final states.

3. Reverse the directions of all the transitions, keeping the positions of all intermediate states unchanged.
4. Rewrite the grammar from this new transition graph in the right-linear fashion.

---

**Example 5.48** Convert the following left-linear grammar to its equivalent right-linear grammar.

$S \to B1 \mid A0 \mid C0$
$A \to C0 \mid A1 \mid B1 \mid 0$
$B \to B1 \mid 1$
$C \to A0$

***Solution*** The transition graph (TG) representing the given $G_L$ is drawn as shown in Fig. 5.9(a).

The TG can be modified by interchanging the positions of the initial and final states and reversing all the transitions as shown in Fig. 5.9(b).

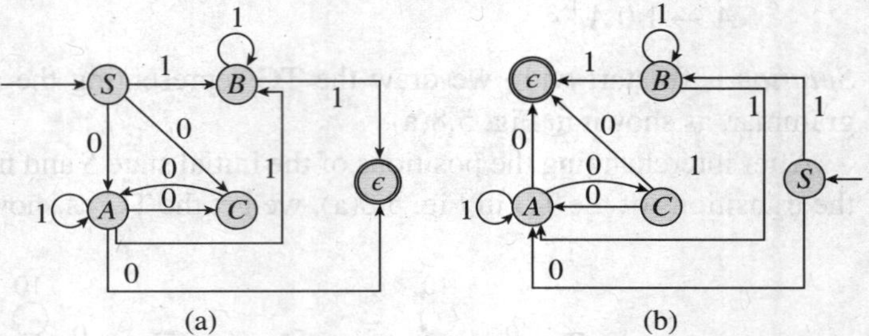


**Figure 5.9** $G_L$ to $G_R$ conversion (a) TG representing given $G_L$ (b) TG after interchanging initial and final states and reversing the transitions

Using the TG in Fig. 5.9(b), we can write the equivalent $G_R$ as:

$S \to 0A \mid 1B$
$A \to 1A \mid 0C \mid 0$
$B \to 1B \mid 1A \mid 1$
$C \to 0A \mid 0$

---

**Example 5.49** Write an equivalent $G_R$ for the following $G_L$:

$S \to S10 \mid 0$

***Solution*** The TG for the given $G_L$ can be drawn as shown in Fig. 5.10(a).

After interchanging the positions of the initial and final states, and reversing all the transitions, we can get the TG as shown in Fig. 5.10(b).

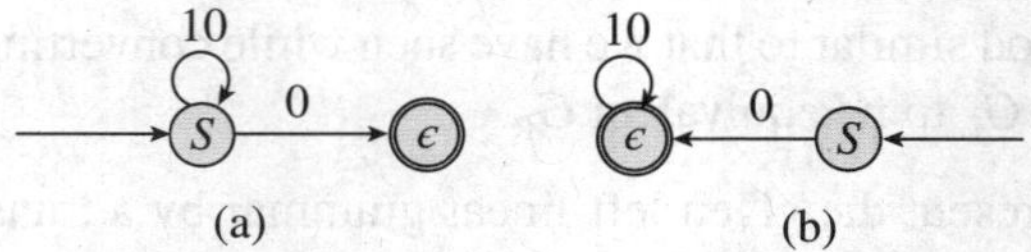


**Figure 5.10** $G_L$ to $G_R$ conversion (a) TG representing $G_L$ (b) TG after interchanging initial and final states and reversing the transitions

Using the TG in Fig. 5.10(b), we write the required $G_R$ as follows:

$$S \rightarrow 0\,\epsilon$$
$$\epsilon \rightarrow 1\,0\,\epsilon$$

In this case, there is a problem, because $\epsilon$ seems to be part of a production, which is not really allowed in any grammar. An alternative approach is to change the label of the $\epsilon$ state. However, this does not solve the problem, as the grammar we obtained is not equivalent.

This problem occurs because $S$ has a self-loop in the TG in Fig. 5.10(a), because of the production '$S \rightarrow S\,1\,0$'. As a result, in Fig. 5.10(b), the loop is on the state labelled $\epsilon$; obviously the language generated has changed.

---

In order to solve this problem, we first modify the given $G_L$ by introducing a new variable $A$, and rewriting the productions as follows:,

$$S \rightarrow A$$
$$A \rightarrow A\,1\,0 \mid 0$$

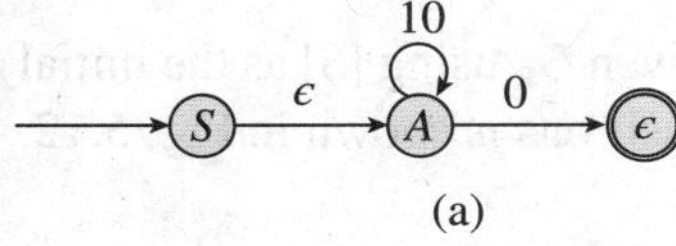

(a)

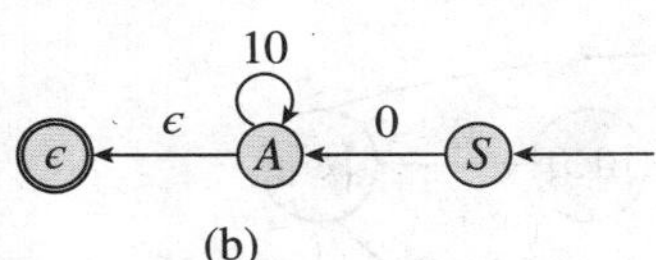

(b)

**Figure 5.11** $G_L$ to $G_R$ conversion (a) TG representing $G_L$ (b) TG after modification

We see that now there is no loop on the start symbol $S$. Hence, we can solve the problem using the usual method:

The modified $G_L$ is represented as a TG shown in Fig. 5.11(a). After reversing the transitions and interchanging the initial and final vertices, we get the TG shown in Fig. 5.11(b).Using the TG in Fig. 5.11(b), we write the required $G_R$ as follows:

$$S \rightarrow 0\,A$$
$$A \rightarrow 1\,0\,A \mid \epsilon$$

We see that the right-linear grammar obtained is now equivalent to the original left-linear grammar.

## 5.13 EQUIVALENCE OF REGULAR GRAMMARS AND FINITE AUTOMATA

As we know, regular grammars can generate regular languages (or regular sets) and the same can be accepted by an FA. In Section 5.12, we have represented right-linear as well the left-linear grammar using TGs, which are nothing but finite automata. This means that while inter-converting $G_R$ and $G_L$, we have assumed the fact that FA and regular grammars are equivalent. Observe that he transition graphs that we have obtained are NFA.

Hence, let us discuss the conversion algorithm for obtaining FA equivalent to a given regular grammar in more detail.

### 5.13.1 Right-linear Grammar and FA

Let us suppose that $G = \{V, T, P, S\}$ is some right-linear grammar. We can construct an NFA with $\epsilon$-moves ($\epsilon$-transitions), $M = \{Q, T, \delta, (S), (\epsilon)\}$, that simulates derivations in $G$, where:

1. $Q$ consists of a symbol $[\alpha]$ such that $\alpha$ is either $S$ or a (not necessarily proper) suffix of some right-hand side of a production in $P$;

2. $\delta$ is defined as:
   (a) If $A$ is a variable, then $\delta$ ([$A$], $\epsilon$) = {[$\alpha$] | $A \to \alpha$ is a production)
   (b) If $a$ is in $T$, and $\alpha$ is in ($T^* \cup T^* \cdot V$), then $\delta$ ([$a\alpha$], $a$) = {[$\alpha$]}

This NFA with $\epsilon$-moves can then be converted to DFA (refer to Chapter 2 for the detailed conversion algorithm).

Let us discuss some examples to illustrate the construction of FA from a given right-linear grammar.

---

**Example 5.50** Find the equivalent DFA accepting the regular language defined by the following right-linear grammar:

$$S \to 0\,A \mid 1\,B$$
$$A \to 0\,C \mid 1\,A \mid 0$$
$$B \to 1\,B \mid 1\,A \mid 1$$
$$C \to 0 \mid 0\,A$$

***Solution*** We can construct an NFA with $\epsilon$-moves for the given $G_R$ using [$S$] as the initial state and [$\epsilon$] as the final state. The resultant NFA with $\epsilon$-transitions is shown in Fig. 5.12.

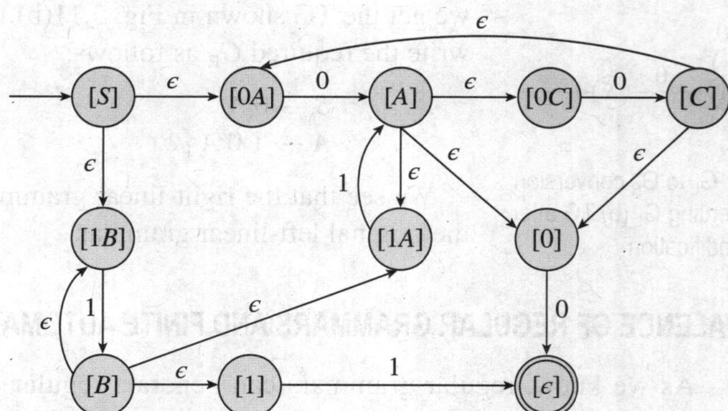


**Figure 5.12** NFA with $\epsilon$-moves drawn from given $G_R$

**Table 5.1** Transition table for DFA in Fig. 5.13(a)

| Q \ Σ | 0 | 1 |
|---|---|---|
| A | B | D |
| B | C | B |
| *C | E | — |
| D | — | F |
| *E | C | B |
| *F | C | F |

'*': Final states

As $S$ produces '$S \to 0\ A$' and '$S \to 1\ B$', we have introduced two $\epsilon$-transitions from [$S$]. Since [$0A$] is in the form [$a\alpha$], the transition from [$0A$] to [$A$] is shown on symbol 0.

Similarly, for state [$1B$] it is shown on 1 to state [$B$]. Repeating the same procedure for [$A$] and [$B$], we get the NFA with $\epsilon$-moves as shown in Fig. 5.12. In the process, we must *take care that no state is repeated.*

The equivalent DFA can then be obtained as shown in Fig. 5.13(a).

We can change the labels of the states as shown in Fig. 5.13(a). The new labels are the symbols from $A$ to $F$.

The state transition table for the same is shown in Table 5.1.

We see that it is not possible to reduce this table further—though states $B$ and $E$ have the same transitions, they are not equivalent because $B$ is a non-final state and $E$ is a final state. Hence, the final DFA remains with the six states as shown in Fig. 5.13(b).

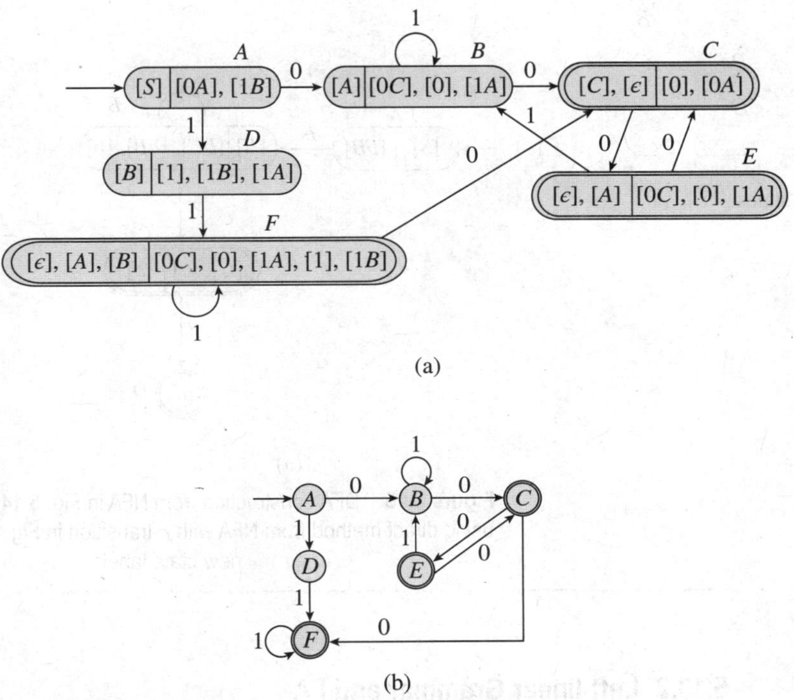


**Figure 5.13** Equivalent DFA (a) DFA obtained from NFA with $\epsilon$-moves in Fig. 5.12 (b) DFA for the right-linear grammar

---

**Example 5.51** Construct a DFA that accepts the same regular language defined by the following right-linear grammar:

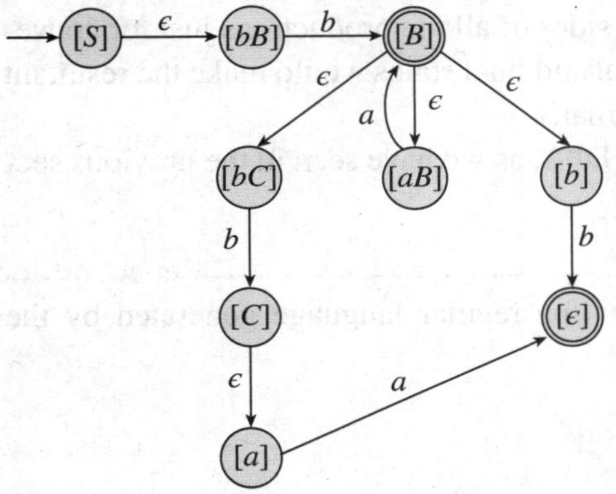


**Figure 5.14** NFA with $\epsilon$-moves for given $G_R$

$S \rightarrow b\,B$
$B \rightarrow b\,C \mid a\,B \mid b$
$C \rightarrow a$

***Solution*** Using the given $G_R$, we construct an NFA with $\epsilon$-transitions as shown in Fig. 5.14.

The NFA with $\epsilon$-moves thus obtained contains $[S]$ as the initial state and $[\epsilon]$ as the final state. Starting with the production '$S \rightarrow bB$', and thereafter repeatedly applying the rules given, we obtain this diagram.

This NFA with $\epsilon$-moves can be directly converted to its equivalent DFA as shown in Fig. 5.15(a).

**Table 5.2** State transition table for DFA in Fig. 5.15(a)

| | $a$ | $b$ |
|---|---|---|
| $A$ | — | $B$ |
| $B$ | $B$ | $C$ |
| $*C$ | $D$ | — |
| $*D$ | — | — |

'*': Final states

We can change the labels of the states as shown in Fig. 5.15(a). The state transition table for the resultant DFA is as shown in Table 5.2.

The table cannot be reduced further and therefore, we proceed to draw the required DFA with new labels as shown in Fig. 5.15(b).

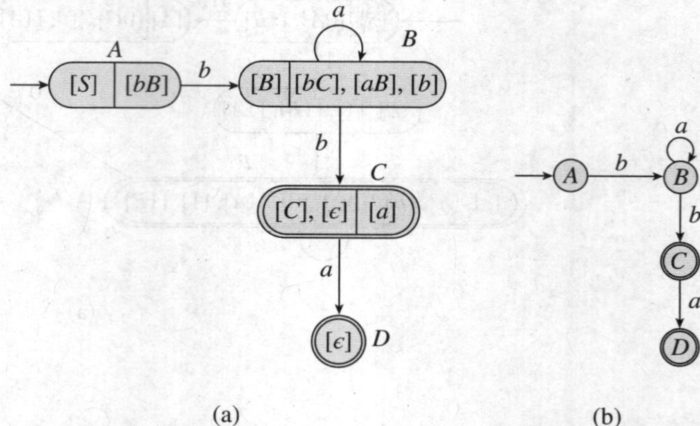


**Figure 5.15** DFA construction from NFA in Fig. 5.14 (a) DFA obtained using direct method from NFA with $\epsilon$-transition in Fig. 5.14 (b) DFA with new state labels

### 5.13.2 Left-linear Grammar and FA

Let $G = \{V, T, P, S\}$ be a left-linear grammar. The first step is to obtain $G' = \{V, T, P', S\}$, the right-linear grammar with P′ consisting of the productions in $G$ with right sides reversed, which are not equivalent to the original $G_L$.

From this right-linear grammar, an NFA with $\epsilon$-moves is constructed as discussed in Section 5.13.1. We now reverse all the transitions and interchange the positions of the initial and final states to obtain the NFA with $\epsilon$-moves equivalent to the original left-linear grammar. Note that we reversed the right-hand sides of all the productions just for convenience—the reversal of transitions and the initial and final states would make the resultant NFA equivalent to the original left-linear grammar.

This NFA is now converted to its equivalent DFA, as we have seen in the previous section (and in Chapter 2).

**Example 5.52** Construct a DFA that accepts the regular language generated by the following left-linear grammar:

$$S \to C\,a \mid B\,b$$
$$C \to B\,b$$
$$B \to B\,a \mid b$$

***Solution*** As the first step, we reverse the right-hand sides of the productions in the given $G_L$, to obtain a right-linear grammar (not equivalent to the given $G_L$). After reversing we get the productions:

$$S \to a\,C \mid b\,B$$
$$C \to b\,B$$
$$B \to a\,B \mid b$$

Using this $G_R$, we draw the NFA with $\epsilon$-moves as shown in Fig. 5.16(a), which is obtained with the help of the rules discussed in Section 5.13.1.

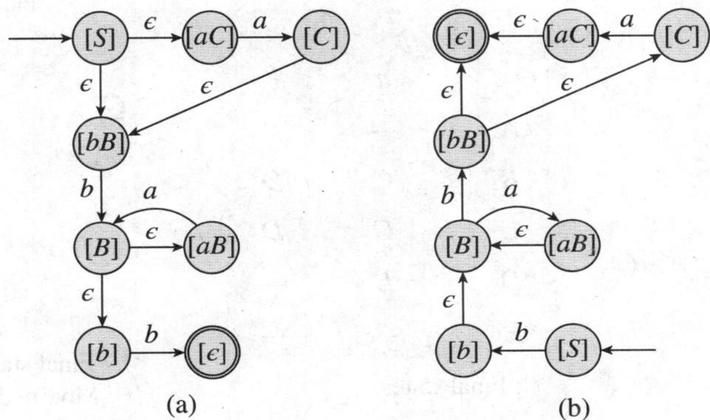


**Figure 5.16** Construction of NFA with $\epsilon$-moves for given $G_L$ (a) Construction of NFA with $\epsilon$-moves from $G_R$ (b) NFA with $\epsilon$-moves equivalent to given $G_L$

Figure 5.16(a) can be modified by interchanging the positions of the initial and final states, and by reversing the transitions to get the modified NFA with $\epsilon$-moves equivalent to the given $G_L$. This is shown in Fig. 5.16(b).

This NFA with $\epsilon$-moves can then be converted to its equivalent DFA as shown in Fig. 5.17(a).

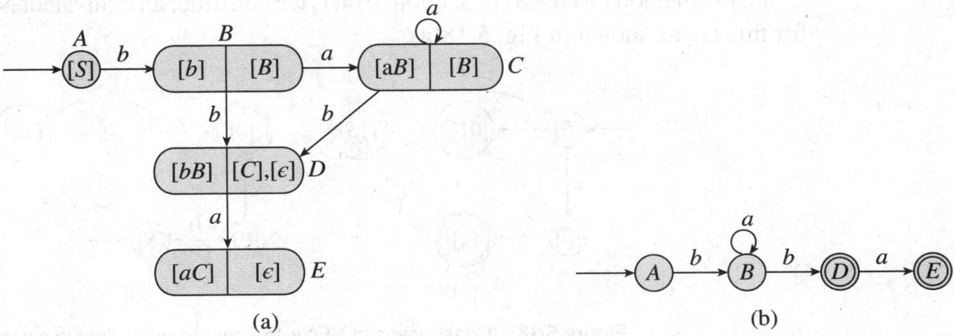


**Figure 5.17** DFA construction from the NFA in Fig. 5.16 (a) DFA obtained from NFA with $\epsilon$-moves in Fig. 5.16(b) (b) Final minimized DFA after relabelling the states

The DFA states are relabelled using letters from $A$ to $E$, as shown in Fig. 5.17(a), Now, let us check if we can reduce this diagram further. For this, we draw the state transition table for the DFA as shown in Table 5.3.

We observe that states $B$ and $C$ are equivalent, as both are non-final states and have the same transitions on $a$ and $b$.

Thus, we replace $C$ by $B$ and accordingly modify the state transition table as shown in Table 5.4.

**Table 5.3** State transition table for the DFA in Fig. 5.17(a)

| $Q$ \ $\Sigma$ | $a$ | $b$ |
|---|---|---|
| $A$ | — | $B$ |
| $B$ | $C$ | $D$ |
| $C$ | $C$ | $D$ |
| $*D$ | $E$ | — |
| $*E$ | — | — |

'*': Final states

**Table 5.4** Reduced state transition table for the DFA in Fig. 5.17(b)

| $Q$ \ $\Sigma$ | $a$ | $b$ |
|---|---|---|
| $A$ | — | $B$ |
| $B$ | $B$• | $D$ |
| $*D$ | $E$ | — |
| $*E$ | — | — |

'*': Final states
'•': Modified entry

The final minimized DFA is shown in Fig. 5.17(b).

**Example 5.53** Construct a DFA equivalent to the following left-linear grammar:

$$S \rightarrow S\,1\,0 \mid 0$$

***Solution*** We first reverse the right-hand sides of all the productions of the given $G_L$ to obtain a right-linear grammar (not equivalent to the given $G_L$).

Thus, we have:

$$S \rightarrow 0\,1\,S \mid 0$$

Using the method discussed in Section 5.14.1, we construct an equivalent NFA with $\epsilon$-moves for this $G_R$ as shown in Fig. 5.18(a).

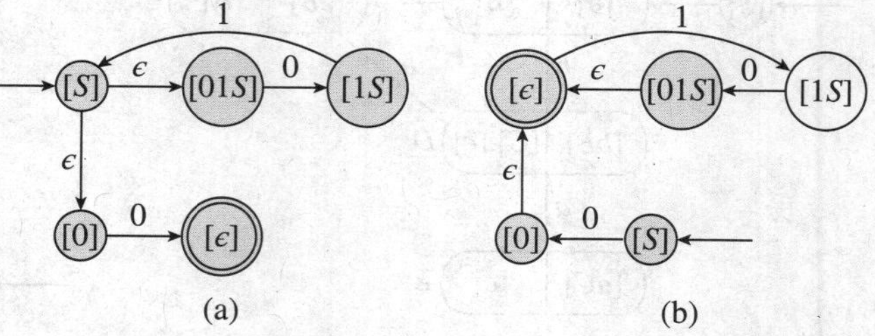


**Figure 5.18** Construction of NFA with $\epsilon$-moves equivalent to given $G_L$ (a) NFA with $\epsilon$-moves for $G_R$ obtained by reversing productions of given $G_L$ (b) NFA with $\epsilon$-moves equivalent to given $G_L$

We then interchange the positions of the initial and final states and reverse the transitions to get the NFA with $\epsilon$-moves that is equivalent to the given left-linear grammar. This is shown in Fig. 5.18(b).

This NFA with $\epsilon$-moves is converted into its equivalent DFA as shown in Fig. 5.19(a).

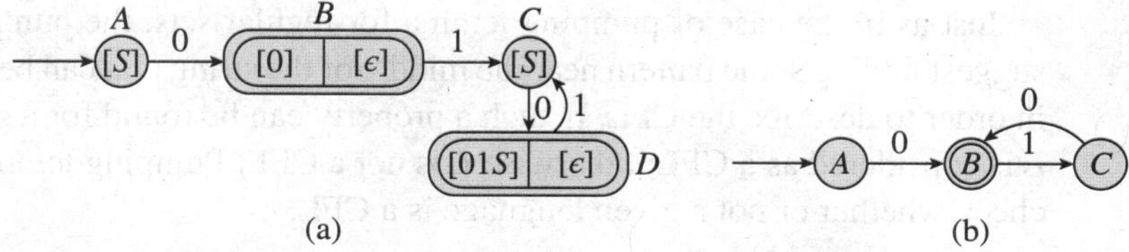


**Figure 5.19** Construction of DFA equivalent to NFA in Fig. 5.18 (a) DFA equivalent to NFA with $\epsilon$-moves in Fig. 5.18(b) (b) Final DFA

Next, the state transition table for the DFA in Fig. 5.19(a) is constructed as shown in Table 5.5.

We observe that states $B$ and $D$ are equivalent as both are final states and both have the same transitions. Therefore, we replace $D$ by $B$ to get the reduced state transition table as shown in Table 5.6.

**Table 5.5** State transition table for DFA in Fig. 5.19(a)

| $Q$ \ $\Sigma$ | 0 | 1 |
|---|---|---|
| $A$ | $B$ | — |
| $*B$ | — | $C$ |
| $C$ | $D$ | — |
| $*D$ | — | $C$ |

'*': Final states

**Table 5.6** Modified state transition table for the DFA in Fig. 5.19(b)

| $Q$ \ $\Sigma$ | 0 | 1 |
|---|---|---|
| $A$ | $B$ | — |
| $*B$ | — | $C$ |
| $C$ | $B$• | — |

'*': Final states
'•': Modified entry

Using this reduced transition table, we draw the TG for the final DFA as shown in Fig. 5.19(b).

## 5.14 PUMPING LEMMA FOR CONTEXT-FREE LANGUAGES

Pumping lemma for regular languages signify the fact that if the regular language is infinite, then it must contain strings of a particular form (refer to Chapter 3). The pumping lemma for CFLs is similar, and is an important property.

**Lemma statement** Let $L$ be a CFL. Then, there exists a constant $n$ such that if $z$ is any string in $L$ such that its length is at least $n$, that is, $|z| \geq n$, then we can write $z = uvwxy$, where:

1. $|vwx| \leq n$; that is, the middle portion of the string is not too long.

2. $|vx| \geq 1$; that is, $vx \neq \epsilon$. Since, $v$ and $x$ are the substrings that get pumped, it is required that at least one of them should be non-empty.
3. For all values of $i$; $i \geq 0$, $uv^iwx^iy$ is in $L$; that is, the two substrings $v$ and $x$ can be pumped as many times as required and the resultant string obtained will be a member of $L$.

Just as in the case of pumping lemma for regular sets, the pumping lemma for CFLs suggest finding some pattern near the middle of the string that can be pumped (or repeated) in order to describe the CFL. If such a property can be found for a given language $L$, then $L$ is considered as a CFL; otherwise $L$ is not a CFL. Pumping lemma can thus be used to check whether or not a given language is a CFL.

**Alternate statement** Let $G = \{V, T, P, S\}$ be a context-free grammar represented in Chomsky normal form with $m$ number of non-terminals, that is, $|V| = m$. Then if $z$ is any string in $L(G)$, and $|z| \geq 2^{m-1} + 1$, then $z$ can be written as, $z = uvwxy$ such that, $|vx| \geq 1$ and $|vwx| \leq 2^m$; and for all $i \geq 0$, $uv^iwx^iy$ is in $L(G)$.

*Proof*

Since $G$ is in CNF, each production is of the form '$A \to BC$' or '$A \to a$'. Thus, any sub-tree of a parse tree of height $h$ will have a yield at most $2^{h-1}$ number of leaves. This is the property of any binary tree, and is true even in case of CNF grammar—as any parse (or derivation) tree for a CNF grammar is a binary tree.

For example, consider grammar $G$ expressed in CNF with the following productions:

$$S \to AB \mid a$$
$$A \to AA \mid a$$
$$B \to b$$

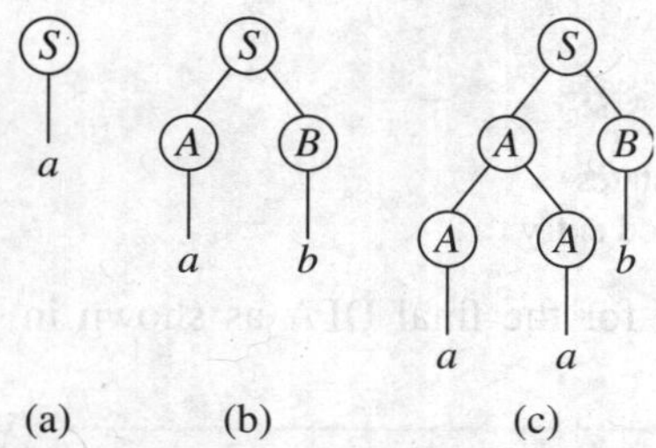


**Figure 5.20** Parse trees with different heights for CNF grammar (a) Height = 1 (b) Height = 2 (c) Height = 3

Parse trees of heights 1, 2, and 3 for these productions are depicted as shown in Fig. 5.20.

We observe that in Fig. 5.20(a), the parse tree with height 1 has $2^{1-1} = 2^0 = 1$ leaf. Similarly, in Fig. 5.20(b), the parse tree with height 2 has $2^{2-1} = 2^1 = 2$ leaves; that is, its yield length is 2.

However, Fig. 5.20(c) is not a complete binary tree and has yield 3. Still, even if we consider a balanced binary tree with height 3, it can have a maximum of 4 leaves: $2^{3-1} = 2^2 = 4$. Hence, the maximum possible yield for a parse tree of height $h$ is $2^{h-1}$.

We also observe that the longest path for a binary parse tree of height $h$ is $h$; and it contains at least $h$ non-terminals.

For example, in Fig. 5.20(b) with parse tree of height 2, the length of the longest path is 2—there are 2 paths actually, both of length 2; one leads to $a$ and the other leads to $b$—and each path has 2 non-terminals in it—the path that leads to $a$ has $S$ followed by $A$, and the path that leads to $b$ has $S$ followed by $B$ in it. Similarly, we see that for the binary parse tree in Fig. 5.20(c) with height 3, the length of the longest path is 3, and has 3 non-terminals in it.

Now, if there is a string $z$ in $L(G)$ such that $|z| \geq 2^{m-1} + 1$ then, from the aforementioned properties of the binary trees, we can say that the height of the parse tree for $z$ is

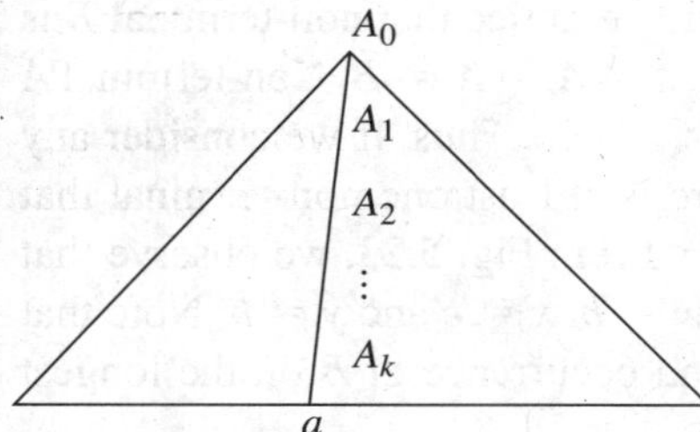

**Figure 5.21** Longest path *LP* in a parse tree for a sufficiently long string *z*

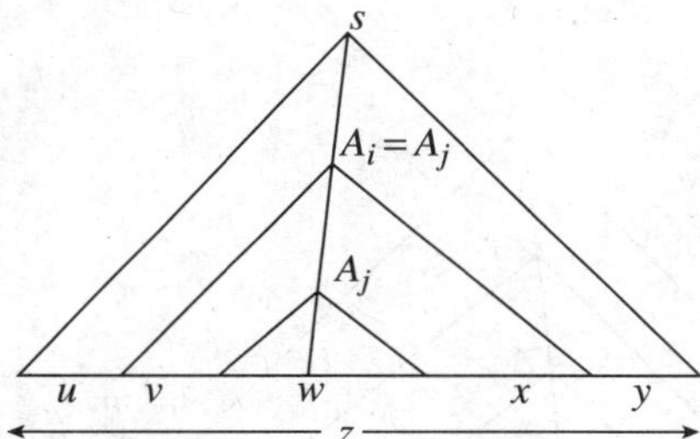

**Figure 5.22** Dividing the string so that it can be pumped

greater than $m$. The minimum height of such a parse tree is '$m$ + 1', which means that the length of any longest path, *LP*, on this parse tree is more than $m$; that is, $|LP| \geq m + 1$. Thus, the longest path *LP* contains more than $m$ non-terminals in it.

Since grammar $G$ has only $m$ non-terminals and any longest path *LP* in the parse tree for $z$ has more than $m$ non-terminals, we conclude that there are a few non-terminals that are repeated on the *LP*.

Let us consider one such longest path *LP* as shown in Fig. 5.21 with more than $m$ non-terminals in it, labelled as, $A_0, A_1, \ldots, A_k$.

Since there are only $m$ distinct non-terminals in set $V$, at least two of the *last '$m$ + 1' non-terminals* on the longest path *LP* must be the same non-terminals.

Let us suppose $A_i = A_j$, where $k - m \leq i < j \leq k$. Hence, it is possible to divide the parse tree for string $z$ as shown in Fig. 5.22.

Substring $w$ is the yield of the sub-tree, whose root node is $A_j$; and substrings $v$ and $x$ that are to the left and right of $w$ respectively, are part of the yield of the larger sub-tree, whose root is $A_i$. Similarly, $u$ and $y$ are the portions of $z$ that are to the left and right respectively of the sub-tree rooted at $A_i$.

Remember that we picked up $A_i$ to be close to the bottom of the parse tree, that is, $k - i \leq m$. We have seen earlier that at least two of the *last m* + 1 *non-terminals* on the longest path *LP* must be the same non-terminals. Hence, we conclude that the longest path for the sub-tree rooted at $A_i$ is no longer than $m$ + 1; this means that the length of the yield of the sub-tree rooted at $A_i$, which is $vwx$, is given by: $|vwx| \leq 2^m$. This proves condition one of the pumping lemma.

Next, we note that both $v$ and $x$ cannot be $\epsilon$ at the same time; but, one of them could be. This is because, in CNF we do not have any unit productions. Hence, if a non-terminal is repeated on the longest path to the second occurrence of the same non-terminal, there would be some non-empty substring already derived to the left of the second occurrence of the same non-terminal. This means that $|vx| \geq 1$. This proves condition two of the pumping lemma.

In order to prove condition three of the pumping lemma, let us consider the grammar $G$ expressed in CNF having productions:

$$\{S \rightarrow AB \mid a; A \rightarrow AB \mid a; B \rightarrow BA \mid b\}$$

The parse tree for the string '*ababb*' using these productions is shown in Fig. 5.23.

*x* is empty here, $x = \epsilon$

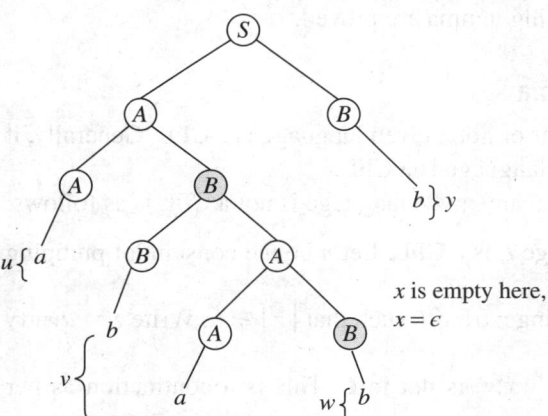

**Figure 5.23** Parse tree illustrating the string division

We see that there are only 3 non-terminals in $G$: $A$, $B$, and $S$, that is, $m = 3$. Refer to the longest path, $S \rightarrow A \rightarrow B \rightarrow A \rightarrow B \rightarrow b$. We see that the length of the path is 6, which is more than the number of non-terminals. We also see that the string $z$ is '*ababb*', which satisfies the condition $|z| \geq 2^{m-1} + 1$. However, we notice that non-terminal $B$ is marked grey in Fig. 5.23, showing that it is repeated, that is, $A_i = A_j = B$. Non-terminal $A$ is also repeated, but we are considering the example of $B$ here. Thus, if we consider any sufficiently long string $z$ from the language, then, there is at least one non-terminal that is repeated in the longest path from the parse tree for $z$. From Fig. 5.23, we observe that $z$ can be written as $z = uvwxy$, where $u = a$, $v = ba$, $w = b$, $x = \epsilon$ and $y = b$. Note that $v = ba$, is the string generated to the left of the second occurrence of $B$ on the longest path considered here.

Since $A_i$ and $A_j$ are the same non-terminals in the parse tree in Fig. 5.22, we replace $A_i$ by $A_j$ and draw a new parse tree as shown in Fig. 5.24(a). Similarly, if we replace, $A_j$ by $A_i$, we get a parse tree as shown in Fig. 5.24(b).

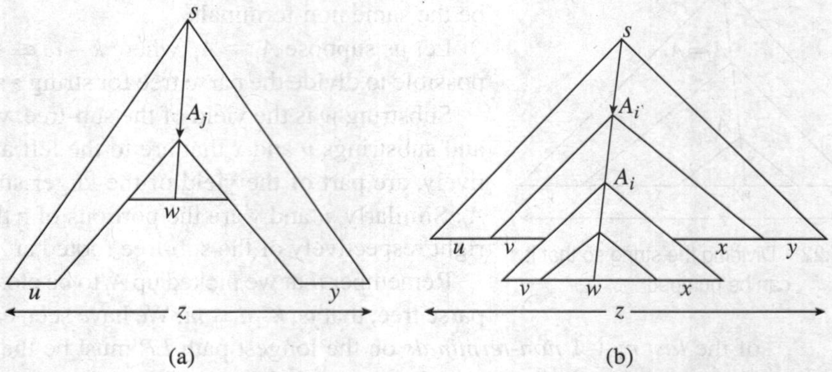


**Figure 5.24** Pumping the substrings $v$ and $x$ (a) Parse tree after replacing $A_i$ with $A_j$ (b)Parse tree after replacing $A_j$ with $A_i$

In the parse tree shown in Fig. 5.24(a), the yield is '$uwy$', as we have replaced $A_i$ by $A_j$; on the other hand, in parse tree shown in Fig. 5.24(b), the yield is '$uv^2wx^2y$' as we have replaced $A_j$ by $A_i$. Thus, both represent the yield of the form '$uv^iwx^iy$', for $i = 0$ and $i = 2$ respectively. This proves condition 3. of the pumping lemma.

Hence, all the conditions of the pumping lemma are proved.

### 5.14.1 Application of Pumping Lemma

Pumping lemma is used to check whether or not a given language is a CFL. Generally, it is used as a tool to disprove that a given language is a CFL.

The procedure that is used to show that any given language is not a CFL is as follows:

*Step 1*: Assume that the given language $L$ is a CFL. Let $n$ be the constant of pumping lemma.

*Step 2*: Choose a sufficiently long string $z$ from $L$ such that $|z| \geq n$. Write $z = uvwxy$ using pumping lemma.

*Step 3*: Find a suitable $k$ so that '$uv^kwx^ky$' is not in $L$. This is a contraction as per pumping lemma; hence, $L$ is not a CFL.

**Example 5.54** Show that $L = \{a^n b^n c^n \mid n \geq 1\}$ is not a context-free language.

***Solution*** Let us not confuse with the $n$ used in the language definition as the constant $n$ of pumping lemma. Hence, we rewrite the language definition as:

$$L = \{a^m b^m c^m \mid m \geq 1\}.$$

*Step 1*: Let us assume that the language $L$ is a CFL.

*Step 2*: Let us choose a sufficiently large string $z$, such that $z = a^l b^l c^l$, for some large $l > 0$. Since we have assumed that $L$ is a CFL and is an infinite language, pumping lemma can be applied. This means that we should be able to write $z$ as: $z = uvwxy$.

*Step 3*: As per pumping lemma, every string '$uv^i wx^i y$', for all $i \geq 0$ is in $L$. Since $|vx| \geq 1$, only one among $v$ and $x$ can be empty. Without loss of generality, let us assume that $v$ is non-empty. As $v$ is a substring, it can contain any of the three symbols from the alphabet $\{a, b, c\}$ for the language $L$.

Let us consider the case in which $v$ contains a single symbol from $\{a, b, c\}$. Therefore, $z = uvwxy = a^l b^l c^l$; this means that the number of $a$'s, $b$'s, and $c$'s in $z$ are same. As per pumping lemma, we would expect '$uv^2wx^2y$' to be a member of $L$, which does not seem to be the case as $v$ contains only a single symbol and pumping $v$ would yield different number of $a$'s, $b$'s, and $c$'s. Thus, '$uv^2wx^2y$' is not a member of $L$. This contradicts our assumption that $L$ is a CFL.

Now, let us consider the case in which $v$ contains two of the three symbols, say, $a$ and $b$. The sample $v$ could be written as $ab$, $aabb$, and so on. When we try to pump $v$ multiple times; for example, $v^2 = abab$, or $v^2 = aabbaabb$, and so on, we find that even number of $b$'s follow $a$ in the string, which is against the language definition: '$a^m b^m c^m$' where the $a$'s are followed by $b$'s, which are followed by $c$'s. Thus, $uv^2wx^2y$ is not a member of $L$. This again contradicts our assumption that $L$ is a CFL.

Similarly, let us consider the case in which $v$ contains all the three symbols; pumping it will result in a situation, where we will have $b$'s or $c$'s followed by $a$'s, which is not allowed as per language definition.

Finally, let us consider the case when $v$ contains one symbol; $x$ is also non-empty and contains one symbol; for example, $v = a^i$, and $x = c^j$, for some $i, j \leq m$. Even if we pump $v$ and $x$, the resultant string might not contain the same number of $a$'s, $b$'s, and $c$'s. Thus, '$uv^i wx^i y$' for all $i \geq 0$ might not be a member of $L$. This contradicts our assumption that $L$ is a CFL.

Hence, $L = \{a^m b^m c^m \mid m \geq 1\}$ is not a CFL.

**Example 5.55** Show that $L = \{a^p \mid p \text{ is prime}\}$ is not a context-free language.

***Solution***

*Step 1*: Let us assume that the language $L$ is a CFL.

*Step 2*: Let us choose a sufficiently large string $z$ such that $z = a^l$ for some large $l$, which is prime. Since we assumed that $L$ is a CFL and an infinite language; pumping lemma can be applied now. This means that we should be able to write a string: $z = uvwxy$.

*Step 3*: As per pumping lemma, every string '$uv^i wx^i y$', for all $i \geq 0$ is in $L$.

That is, if we consider $i = 0$, then $uv^0wx^0y = uwy$ is in $L$. Let us assume $|uwy|$ is a prime number, say $k$.

As per pumping lemma, let us have $|vx| = r \geq 1$; and let $i = k$. Then, as per pumping lemma, '$uv^kwx^ky$' should be in $L$. However, $|uv^kwx^ky| = |uwy| + k * |vx| = k + k * r = k(1 + r)$, which is not a prime number as it is divisible by $k$. Thus, '$uv^kwx^ky$' is not in $L$. This contradicts our assumption that $L$ is a CFL. Hence, $L$ is not a CFL.

---

### 5.14.2 Ogden's Lemma

There is a stronger version of pumping lemma for CFLs, known as Ogden's lemma, named after William F. Ogden. It differs from the pumping lemma by allowing us to focus on any $n$ distinguished (or marked) positions of a string $z$, and guaranteeing that the strings to be pumped have distinguished (or marked) positions between 1 and $n$.

**Lemma statement** If $L$ is a CFL, then there exists a constant $n$, such that:

If $z$ is any string in language $L$ having length at least $n$, and in which we select at least $n$ positions to be distinguished (or marked), then we can write $z = uvwxy$ such that:

1. $vwx$ has at most $n$ distinguished (or marked) positions.
2. $vx$ has at least one distinguished (or marked) position.
3. For all $i$, $uv^iwx^iy$ is in $L$.

*Proof*

Let $b$ be the maximum number of symbols in the right-hand side of any grammar rule. A sufficiently long string $z$ in $L$ has at least $n$ marked positions. Let us assume that a leaf in the parse tree for $z$ is marked if its position in $z$ is marked; and let an internal node of the parse tree be marked if the sub-trees rooted at two or more of its children each contain a marked leaf.

If any path from root to leaves in the parse tree contains $k$ marked internal nodes, then the parse tree has at the most $b^k$ marked leaves. If we consider $n = b^{|V|+1}$, where $|V|$ is the total number of non-terminals in the grammar, then the minimum number of marked internal nodes in any path is '$|V| + 1$'. Thus, there exists at least one such marked internal node, that is, non-terminal, that appears twice on the path.

Then, using a similar method as that in the pumping lemma, we can proceed to prove the Ogden's lemma.

## 5.15 KURODA NORMAL FORM

Just like the normal forms that we have discussed for context-free grammars, the Kuroda normal form is for context-sensitive languages. It is named after a linguist Sige-Yuki Kuroda.

A context-sensitive grammar is said to be in Kuroda normal form, if all the production rules are of the form:

$$AB \to CD, \text{ or } A \to BC, \text{ or } A \to B, \text{ or } A \to a,$$

where $A$, $B$, $C$, and $D$ are all non-terminal symbols and $a$ is a terminal symbol.

Every grammar in Kuroda normal form is monotonic or non-contracting. That is, none of the rules decreases the size of the string that is being generated. Thus, every context-sensitive language, which does not generate the empty string, can be generated by a grammar expressed in Kuroda normal form.

Note that the production $AB \rightarrow CD$ can be replaced by any of the following productions:

1. $AB \rightarrow AX$
2. $AX \rightarrow YX$
3. $YX \rightarrow YD$
4. $YD \rightarrow CD$

The productions numbered 1 and 2 are called *right context-sensitive*, while the rules numbered 3 and 4 are called *left context-sensitive*.

## 5.16 DYCK LANGUAGE

Dyck language is the language consisting of well-formed parentheses. For such a language, the alphabet set can be written as $\Sigma = \{ (, ) \}$; and the grammar for such a language can be written as:

$$S \rightarrow S ( S ) \mid \epsilon$$

Given any word $x$ over $\Sigma$, if:

$$D(x) = (\text{number of left parentheses in } x) - (\text{number of right parentheses in } x),$$

then $x$ is a member of Dyck language if and only if:

1. $D(x) = 0$; and
2. $D(y) \geq 0$,

for any prefix $y$ of $x$.

Dyck language is also called *parenthesis language* and is a CFL, as we can see. It is named after the mathematician Walther von Dyck.

## 5.17 DERIVATION GRAPH

We have already discussed derivation trees or rule trees in Section 5.6. Derivation trees are used to describe the derivation process of any string from the language generated by any context-free (type-2) grammar. Since type-3 grammar, that is, regular grammar, is a subset of context-free grammars, derivation of any string from regular languages can also be expressed with the help of derivation trees.

However, the use of derivation trees is neither efficient nor appealing when the recursive definition is found in the grammars, since the same node, denoting a non-terminal, repeatedly occurs in the tree.

For example, consider the following CFG:

$$S \rightarrow a\, S\, a \mid b\, S\, b \mid b$$

Let us derive the string '*abbba*':

$S \Rightarrow a\, \underline{S}\, a,$ using rule 1

$\Rightarrow a\, b\, \underline{S}\, b\, a,$ using rule 2

$\Rightarrow a\, b\, b\, b\, a,$ using rule 3

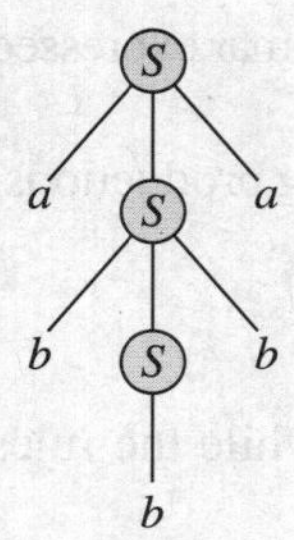


Figure 5.25 Derivation tree for '*abbba*'

The derivation tree for the same can be drawn as shown in Fig. 5.25. We see that the node $S$ occurs three times in the tree.

Moreover, the derivation tree does not give any information about the production rule that has been applied at each particular stage in the derivation.

On the other hand, in the derivation graph, the nodes are labelled by the production rule numbers that are applied at each stage in the derivation process; and there is no repetition of any node unless the same rule is applied again.

Usually, derivations of any string from the languages generated using type-0 and type-1 grammars are represented by a more general directed planar graph, known as a *derivation graph.*

> ***Note***: A planar graph is one that can be drawn on a two-dimensional plane without intersecting any two edges, except at the nodes.

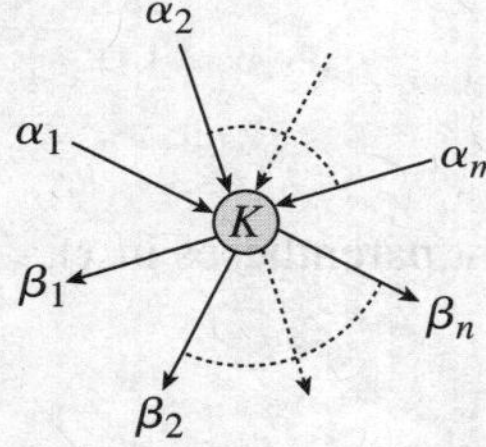


Figure 5.26 Node $K$ in a derivation graph representing the production, $K: \alpha \to \beta$

Let a set $P$ of productions be ordered and labelled as $\{1, 2, 3, \ldots, K\}$, and let '$\alpha \to \beta$' be the $K$th production rule in $P$. Further, let $\alpha_1, \alpha_2, \ldots, \alpha_m$, and $\beta_1, \beta_2, \ldots, \beta_n$, be the left to right ordering of the symbols in the sentential forms, $\alpha$ and $\beta$ respectively. Then, the node representing the production $K$, whose incoming directed edges (or arcs) from left to right are labelled as $\alpha_1, \alpha_2, \ldots, \alpha_m$ and outgoing arcs from left to right are labelled as $\beta_1, \beta_2, \ldots, \beta_n$ in the derivation graph for any string, as shown in Fig. 5.26.

Further, when $\beta_i$ for $i = 1, 2, \ldots, n$ is a terminal, it ends in a node labelled $\epsilon$. The set of edges ending in the $\epsilon$-nodes is called the *frontier* and the sequence of edge labels from left to right is called the *yield*, and gives a sentential form in the derivation.

The sequence of labels of edges ending in the $\epsilon$-nodes from left to right gives us the string for which the derivation graph is prepared.

---

**Example 5.56** Consider a type-0 grammar $G$ defined as:

$$G = \{(S, A, B, C, D), (a, b, +), P, S\},$$

where $P$ consists of the following productions:

1: $S \to ACS$
2: $S \to BDS$
3: $S \to +$
4: $CA \to AC$
5: $CB \to BC$
6: $DA \to AD$
7: $DB \to BD$
8: $D+ \to +b$
9: $C+ \to +a$
10: $A \to a$
11: $B \to b$

Prepare the derivation graph for the string '$ab+ab$'.

***Solution*** Let us first derive the string '*ab*+*ab*' using the given set of productions:

$$
\begin{aligned}
S &\Rightarrow AC\underline{S}, && \text{(rule 1)}\\
&\Rightarrow ACBD\underline{S}, && \text{(rule 2)}\\
&\Rightarrow ACB\underline{D+}, && \text{(rule 3)}\\
&\Rightarrow AC\underline{B}+b, && \text{(rule 8)}\\
&\Rightarrow AB\underline{C}+b, && \text{(rule 5)}\\
&\Rightarrow \underline{A}B+ab, && \text{(rule 9)}\\
&\Rightarrow a\underline{B}+ab, && \text{(rule 10)}\\
&\Rightarrow ab+ab, && \text{(rule 11)}
\end{aligned}
$$

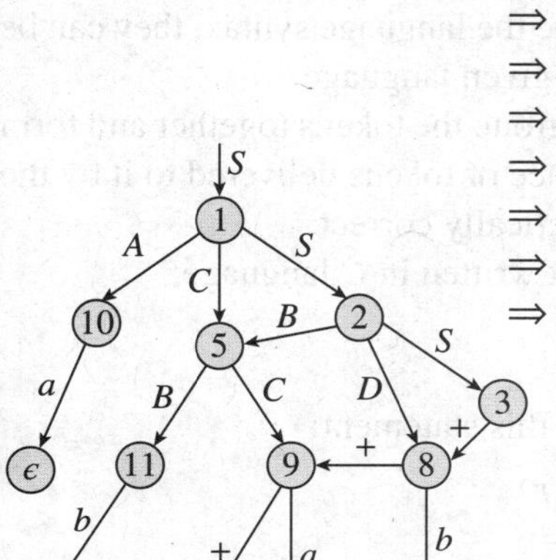


**Figure 5.27** Derivation graph for '*ab* +*ab*'

This derivation process can now be represented with the help of a derivation graph, as shown in Fig. 5.27.

Observing the figure, we can easily conclude that derivation graphs are more helpful than derivation trees, as we get exact information about how the string is derived and which productions are applied at every stage in the derivation. Moreover, the derivation graph is suitable for all types of grammars unlike derivation trees, which only can support type-2 and type-3 grammars.

## 5.18 APPLICATIONS OF CONTEXT-FREE GRAMMAR

Context-free grammars have applications in many areas, from compiler construction to syntactic pattern recognition. Some subsets of deterministic CFLs (DCFLs) are being used to represent the programming languages. Hence, CFGs are used to denote the syntax of these programming languages.

### 5.18.1 Parser (or Syntax Analyser)

In Chapter 3, we have discussed in detail, the applications of regular expressions and FA, and how these can be used in the construction of lexical analysers, which is the first phase of a compiler. Any compiler can be subdivided into five different phases/modules; namely:

1. Lexical analyser (or scanner)
2. Syntax analyser (or parser)
3. Intermediate code generator
4. Code optimizer
5. Code generator

Lexical analyser uses a set of regular expressions and builds a general-purpose DFA. Such DFA are used to detect the valid words—called tokens—from a given source file, considering it as a text file. The validity of the words depends on whether or not they fit any one of the patterns defined by the set of regular expressions. Any programming language, for example C, contains only five types of valid words, namely, identifiers, literals, punctuations, keywords, and operators.

After identifying the tokens, the lexical analyser passes these tokens to the second phase of the compiler, that is, the parser or syntax analyser, which checks the syntax. Syntax checking here means checking whether the tokens are in the right sequence as defined by the context-free grammar. Since CFGs are used to define the language syntax, they can be used to check the syntax of any program written in the given language.

A parser basically uses the context-free grammar to group the tokens together and form sentences. If it is able to form a sentence from a sequence of tokens delivered to it by the lexical analyser, the sentence is considered to be syntactically correct.

For example, let us consider the following statement written in *C* language:

$$\underline{a} = b;$$

The lexical analyser identifies the following tokens for this statement:

| | | |
|---|---|---|
| $a$ | identifier | token: '*id*' |
| $=$ | operator | token: '=' |
| $b$ | identifier | token: '*id*' |
| ; | punctuation | token: ';' |

These four tokens are then passed on to the parser.

The CFG for an assignment statement (in the limited form, as required here) is written as follows:

$$S \rightarrow id \cdot O \cdot id \cdot P$$
$$O \rightarrow =$$
$$P \rightarrow ;$$

The parser can derive the string '*id O id* ;' using the aforementioned CFG, as follows:

$$\begin{aligned} S &\Rightarrow id \cdot \underline{O} \cdot id \cdot P \\ &\Rightarrow id \cdot = \cdot id \cdot \underline{P} \\ &\Rightarrow id \cdot = \cdot id \cdot ; \end{aligned}$$

This matches with the sequence of tokens received. Hence, the parser declares the input to be syntactically correct. Thus, syntax checking is done with the help of CFGs for formal (or programming) languages such as *C*.

## 5.19 BACKUS–NAUR FORM

Backus–Naur form (or Backus-normal Form; abbreviated as BNF) is a notational technique used for context-free grammars. It is mainly used to denote the syntax for the programming languages; it used by most of the tools that consume context-free grammars.

The simple context-free grammar notation that has been used in this chapter so far, and is described in Section 5.4, has limited capabilities. For example, in simple notation, non-terminal symbols are denoted by capital letters. As there are only 26 capital letters, we cannot use this notation for any complex CFG that may require more than 26 non-terminals. In most programming languages, the syntax needs to be defined with much complex CFGs that require more than 1000 grammar rules, and more than 100 non-terminals; and simple

CFG notation cannot really suffice this need. Hence, BNF notation is introduced. It is important to remember that by introducing BNF, we are not increasing the power of the CFGs; we are only suggesting a better notation for the CFLs. However, we can safely say that BNF is a more powerful notation for type-2 (and hence, type-3) languages.

In BNF notation, non-terminals can be represented by any word—similar to JAVA identifiers delimited by angular brackets on both the ends, whereas, terminals are represented by words consisting of capital letters. For example, '<ifStatement>', '<program>', and '<postalAddress>' are valid non-terminals in BNF, while 'NEWLINE', 'ID', and 'NUMBER' are valid terminals.

The production rules have a slightly different format compared to simple CFG notation. The productions in BNF are represented as:

<symbol> ::= *expression*

Here, '<symbol>' is any non-terminal, and '*expression*' is any sentential form, that is, any combination of terminals and non-terminals.

For example, consider the following CFG written in BNF format:

| | | |
|---|---|---|
| <assignmentStatement> | ::= | ID <operator> ID <punctuation> |
| <operator> | ::= | '=' |
| <punctuation> | ::= | ';' |

We observe that this CFG is the same as the one discussed in Section 5.15, except for notational changes; and also that any CFG that is expressed in BNF is more readable as well.

## SUMMARY

Grammar can be defined as a finite set of formal rules for generating syntactically correct sentences for a particular language for which it is written.

Grammar consists of two types of symbols, namely: Terminals and Non-terminals (also called variables, or auxiliary symbols)

Terminal symbols are those symbols, which are part of the generated sentence. Non-terminal symbols are those symbols, which take part in the formation or generation of the statement, but are not part of the generated statement.

A phrase structure *grammar* is formally denoted by a quadruple of the form:

$G = \{V, T, P, S\}$,

where,

$V$: Finite set of non-terminals (or variables)

$T$: Finite set of terminals

$S$: $S$ is a non-terminal, which is a member of $N$; it is the starting symbol

$P$: Finite set of productions (or syntactical rules)

Productions have the generic form as, '$\alpha \to \beta$', where $\alpha, \beta \subset (V \cup T)^*$, and $\alpha \neq \epsilon$. As we know, $V \cap T = \phi$. Note that $\alpha$ and $\beta$ consist of any number of terminals as well as non-terminals and they are usually termed as *sentential forms*.

If the production rules have the form: '$A \to \alpha$', where $A$ is any non-terminal and $\alpha$ is any sentential form, then such grammar is called *context-free grammar* (CFG).

*Context-free language* (CFL) is the language generated by a context-free grammar G. This can be described as:

$L(G) = \{w \mid w \subset T^*$, and is derivable from the start symbol $S\}$

In simple CFG notation, non-terminals are usually denoted by capital letters $A$, $B$, $C$, $D$, etc., while terminals are denoted by small case letters $a$, $b$, $c$, etc. A string of terminals (i.e., valid words in the language for which the grammar is written) are usually denoted by $u, v, w, x, y, z$, etc. Sentential forms, that is, strings formed using any combination of terminals and non-terminals—that is, strings of the form $(V \cup T)^*$—are denoted by $\alpha, \beta, \gamma$, etc.

Simple context-free grammar notation has limited capabilities. For example, in simple notation, non-terminal symbols are denoted by capital letters. As there are only 26 capital letters, we cannot use this notation for any complex CFG that may require more than 26 non-terminals. In most programming languages, the syntax needs to be defined using complex CFGs that require more than 1000 grammar rules and more than 100 non-terminals; and simple CFG notation cannot really suffice this need. Hence, *Backus-Naur form* (BNF) notation is introduced. In BNF notation, non-terminals can be represented by any word—similar to JAVA identifiers delimited by angular brackets on both the ends, whereas, terminals are represented by words consisting of all capitals.

Derivation of a string begins with the start symbol of the grammar. One can apply multiple grammar rules to derive strings of all terminals. There are two different derivations possible; namely:

*Leftmost derivation*: At each step in a derivation, a production is applied to the leftmost variable.
*Rightmost derivation*: At each step in a derivation, a production is applied to the rightmost variable.

A *derivation tree* is a graphical representation or description of how the sentence (or string) has been derived or generated using the grammar $G$. The root node of the derivation tree is the start symbol of the grammar; intermediate nodes are the non-terminal symbols, and the leaves are the terminal symbols. A depth-first search of a derivation tree denotes the string for which it is drawn. The derivation tree, though simple, cannot support more generic forms of the grammars, namely, type-0 and type-1.

A *derivation graph* is a more generic graphical representation of the derivation of any string that supports all type of grammars. Apart from this, the derivation graph also records the information of the rules that are applied at every stage in the derivation, which is otherwise not recorded in any derivation tree.

The CFG for a given language is said to be *ambiguous* if there exists at least one string, which can be generated (or derived) in more than one way. In other words, there exists more than one leftmost derivation, more than one rightmost derivation, and also more than one derivation tree, associated with a string in such grammar. For an *unambiguous* CFG, there exists exactly one way of deriving any string in the language. In other words, there is exactly one way to depict the leftmost derivation, one way to describe the rightmost derivation, and exactly one derivation tree that can be drawn for any given string.

Following are the rules for writing a given context-free grammar $G$ in the *reduced form*:

1. Each variable and each terminal of the given CFG should appear in the derivation of at least one word in $L(G)$.
2. There should not be unit productions of the form '$A \to B$', where $A$ and $B$ are both non-terminals.
3. There should not be $\epsilon$-productions of the form, '$A \to \epsilon$', unless the language contains the empty string, $\epsilon$.

There are certain standard ways of writing context-free grammars, which impose certain restrictions on the productions in the CFG. These are called normal forms. We have mainly discussed two normal forms in this chapter:

*Chomsky normal form* (CNF): Production forms allowed in CNF are: '$A \to BC$', or '$A \to a$', where $A$, $B$, and $C$ are non-terminals and $a$ is a terminal symbol.
*Greibach normal form* (GNF): The only allowed form of the production in GNF is: '$A \to a\alpha$', where $A$ is a non-terminal, $a$ is a terminal, and $\alpha$ is a (possibly empty) string of only non-terminals.

The class of phrase structure grammars is very large. By imposing certain constraints on the production rules, different classes of phrase structure grammar, depending on the different restrictions that are imposed, can be obtained. This is more of a containment hierarchy of grammars.

Chomsky has suggested four different classes of phrase structure grammars, called *Chomsky hierarchy*, which is described as follows—Type-0 (unrestricted grammar), Type-1 (context-sensitive grammar), Type-2 (context-free grammar), Type-3 (regular grammar)

Regular grammars are further classified as left-linear or right-linear, depending on whether the only non-terminal (if it exists) on the right-hand side of the production is a leftmost symbol or a rightmost symbol, respectively. Regular grammar is equivalent to finite automata as well as regular expressions.

Pumping lemma for context-free languages is used to check whether or not a given language $L$ is a CFL. It is an important property of the CFLs; and is stated as follows:

Let $L$ be a CFL. Then there exists a constant $n$ such that:

If $z$ is any string in $L$ such that the length of $z$ is at least $n$, that is, $|z| \geq n$, then we can write $z = uvwxy$, where:

1. $|vwx| \leq n$; this means that the middle portion of the string is not too long
2. $|vx| \geq 1$; this means that $vx \neq \epsilon$. Since, $v$ and $x$ are the substrings that get pumped, it is required that at least one of them should be non-empty.
3. For all values of $i$ such that $i \geq 0$, $uv^iwx^iy$ is in $L$; this means that the two substrings $v$ and $x$ can be pumped as many times as required, and the resultant string obtained will still be a member of $L$.

Context-free grammars have applications mainly in the area of compiler construction. CFGs are used to describe the syntax of most programming languages. Syntax analysers or parsers are built to check the syntax of any input based on the CFG rules. Parsers are generally implemented as deterministic pushdown automata (DPDA).

Kuroda normal form is a normalization suggested for context-sensitive languages. It is named after a linguist Sige-Yuki Kuroda. A context-sensitive grammar is said to be in Kuroda normal form, if all the production rules are of the form:

$AB \to CD$, or $A \to BC$, or $A \to B$, or $A \to a$,

where $A$, $B$, $C$, and $D$ are all non-terminal symbols and $a$ is a terminal symbol.

Dyck language is the language consisting of well-formed parentheses. For such a language, the alphabet set can be written as $\Sigma = \{ (, ) \}$; and the grammar for such a language can be written as:

$S \to S ( S ) \mid \epsilon.$

Given any word $x$ over $\Sigma$, if:

$D(x) =$ (number of left parentheses in $x$) – (number of right parentheses in $x$),

then $x$ is a member of Dyck language if and only if:

1. $D(x) = 0$; and
2. $D(y) \geq 0$,

for any prefix $y$ of $x$.

Dyck language is also called *parenthesis language* and is a CFL, as we can see. It is named after the mathematician Walther von Dyck.

There is a stronger version of pumping lemma for CFLs, known as Ogden's lemma, named after William F. Ogden. It differs from the pumping lemma by allowing us to focus on any $n$ distinguished (or marked) positions of a string $z$, and guaranteeing that the strings to be pumped have distinguished (or marked) positions between 1 and $n$. It states:

If $L$ is a CFL, then there exists a constant $n$, such that:

If $z$ is any string in language $L$ having length at least $n$, and in which we select at least $n$ positions to be distinguished (or marked), then we can write $z = uvwxy$ such that:

1. $vwx$ has at most $n$ distinguished (or marked) positions.
2. $vx$ has at least one distinguished (or marked) position.

For all $i$, $uv^iwx^iy$ is in $L$.

## EXERCISES

This section lists a few unsolved problems to help the readers understand the topic better and practise examples on context-free grammars.

## Objective Questions

(L) 5.1 The language generated by the grammar $G = \{(S), (0, 1), P, S\}$, where $P = \{S \rightarrow 0S1 \mid 0S \mid S1 \mid 0\}$ is:
(a) a regular language
(b) a context-free language
(c) a context-sensitive language
(d) a recursively enumerable language

(U) 5.2 Which of the following statements is true about the language $L = \{0^{2n} \mid n > 0\}$?
(a) $L$ is a recursively enumerable language.
(b) $L$ is not a regular language.
(c) $L$ is not a context-free language.
(d) $L$ is an ambiguous language.

(L) 5.3 Which sentence can be generated by the following CFG?
$S \rightarrow a\,B \mid b\,A$
$A \rightarrow a \mid a\,S \mid b\,A\,A$
$B \rightarrow b \mid b\,S \mid a\,B\,B$
(a) *ababbbaaa*
(b) *babababbaa*
(c) *bbbaa*
(d) *bbbbbb*

(U) 5.4 Which of the following statements is true?
S1: Every context-free grammar can be transformed into CNF
S2: It is possible to obtain an equivalent unambiguous grammar for every ambiguous CFG
S3: CNF is more powerful than GNF
S4: A CFG is normalized in order to remove ambiguity
(a) S1 and S2
(b) S1 only
(c) S4 only
(d) S2 and S3
(e) None of these
(f) All of these

(L) 5.5 Let $L$ denote the language generated by the grammar:
$S \rightarrow 0\,S\,0 \mid 0\,0$
Which of the following statements is true?
(a) $L$ generates the language $0^+$
(b) $L$ is a regular language but not $0^+$
(c) $L$ is context-free but not regular
(d) $L$ is not context-free

(R) 5.6 GNF means ________.

(U) 5.7 Which of the following languages are CFLs?
(i) $L = \{a^n\,b^n \mid n = 0, 1, 2, \ldots\}$
(ii) The set of palindromes over alphabet $\{a, b\}$
(iii) $L = \{a^n\,b^m\,c^{2m} \mid n, m \geq 0\}$
(a) Only (i)
(b) Only (ii)
(c) (i) and (iii)
(d) All of these
(e) None of these

(U) 5.8 Consider the following statements:
$S1$: $\{0^{2n} \mid n \geq 1\}$ is a regular language
$S2$: $\{0^m\,1^n\,0^{m+n}) \mid m \geq 1 \text{ and } n \geq 1\}$ is a regular language
Which of the following statements is true?
(a) Only S1
(b) Only S2
(c) Both S1 and S2
(d) None of these

(U) 5.9 State whether the following statement is true or false:
Every regular language is also context-free.

(U) 5.10 Consider the following languages:
$L1 = \{ww \mid w \text{ belongs to } (a, b)^*\}$
$L2 = \{ww^R \mid w \text{ belongs to } (a, b)^*;\ w^R \text{ is the reverse of } w\}$
$L3 = \{0^{2i} \mid i \text{ is an integer, } i \geq 0\}$
$L4 = \{0^{(i * i)} \mid i \text{ is an integer}\}$
Which of the languages is regular?
(a) Only $L1$ and $L2$
(b) Only $L2$, $L3$, and $L4$
(c) Only $L3$ and $L4$
(d) Only $L3$

(U) 5.11 The language $L = \{a^k b^k \mid k \geq 1\}$ is:
(a) Type-3 language
(b) Type-2 language
(c) Type-1 language
(d) Type-0 language

(U) 5.12 The set of productions for the grammar $G$ is $P = \{A \rightarrow a\,b \mid a\,A;\ a\,A\,b \rightarrow a\,B\,C\,b\}$. Hence, $G$ is:
(a) Type-3 grammar
(b) Type-2 grammar
(c) Type-1 grammar
(d) Type-0 grammar

## Review Questions

(A) 5.1 Write a context-free grammar (CFG) which generates the language $L$ denoted by:
$(a + b)^* \, bbb \, (a + b)^*$

(L) 5.2 Distinguish between the type-0 and type-1 grammars.

(U) 5.3 Explain Greibach normal form (GNF) with the help of an example.

(A) 5.4 Consider the grammar $G = \{(S, A), (0, 1), P, S\}$, where $P$ consists of:
$S \to 0 \, A \, S \mid 0$
$A \to S \, 1 \, A \mid S \, S \mid 1 \, 0$
Show the leftmost derivation and rightmost derivation for the input string '001100'.

(U) 5.5 What is a derivation tree? Give suitable examples.

(A) 5.6 Convert the following grammar to Chomsky normal form (CNF):
$S \to A \, B \, A$
$A \to a \, A \mid \epsilon$
$B \to b \, B \mid \epsilon$

(L) 5.7 Find the context-free language associated with the following CFG:
$S \to a \, B \mid b \, A$
$A \to a \mid a \, S \mid b \, A \, A$
$B \to b \mid b \, S \mid a \, B \, B$

(L) 5.8 Is the following grammar ambiguous?
$S \to 0 \, A \, 1 \mid 0 \, B \, A$
$A \to S \, 0 \, 1 \mid 0$
$B \to 1 \, B \mid 1$

(A) 5.9 Show that the following CFG is ambiguous. Remove the ambiguity and write an equivalent unambiguous CFG.
$S \to S + S \mid S * S \mid 4$

(R) 5.10 Define the following and give appropriate examples:
(a) Derivation graph
(b) Unrestricted grammar
(c) CFG

(U) 5.11 What is regular grammar? State its category in Chomsky hierarchy.

(A) 5.12 Write a CFG, which accepts the language $L$, where:
$L = \{0^i \, 1^j \, 0^k \mid j > i + k\}$.
Using this grammar, show the derivation of the string '0111100'.

(A) 5.13 Convert the following right-linear grammar to its equivalent left-linear grammar:
$S \to a \, A \mid b \, B \mid a \, S \mid a$
$A \to b \, A \mid \epsilon$
$B \to a \, B \mid \epsilon$

(C) 5.14 Write the CFG for each of the following languages:
(a) The set of palindromes over alphabet $\{a, b\}$
(b) The set of all strings over alphabet $\{a, b\}$ with exactly twice many $a$'s as $b$'s
(c) $L = \{a^i \, b^j \, c^k \mid i \neq j \text{ or } j \neq k\}$

(A) 5.15 Consider the following languages:
$L_1 = \{a^n \, b^{2n} \, c^m \mid n, m \geq 0\}$
$L_2 = \{a^n \, b^m \, c^{2m} \mid n, m \geq 0\}$
Write the CFG for each of them.

(U) 5.16 Write a short note on the applications of CFG.

(C) 5.17 Write a CFG, which defines a language $L$ over $\Sigma = \{a, b\}$ such that $L$ contains the words in which, the letter $b$ does not appear consecutively three times.

(A) 5.18 Remove the unit productions from the following CFG.
$S \to a \, X \mid Y \, b$
$X \to S$
$Y \to b \, Y \mid b$

(L) 5.19 Consider grammar $G$ defined using the productions:
$E \to E + E \mid E * E \mid (E) \mid id$
Is the grammar $G$ ambiguous? Justify your answer.

(A) 5.20 Write a CFG that will generate the language:
$L = \{WCW^R \mid W \in (a, b)^*$, and $W^R$ is the reverse of $W\}$
Using this grammar, show the leftmost derivation, rightmost derivation, and derivation tree for the input string '*ababCbaba*'.

(A) 5.21 Write the CFGs generating the following languages, for $n > 0$:
(a) $(bdb)^n C^n$
(b) $(ab)^n \, (cd)^n$

(A) 5.22 Find the CFG without $\epsilon$-productions equivalent to the following grammar. Assume $S$ is the start symbol.
$S \to A \, B \, a \, C$
$A \to B \, C$

$B \rightarrow b \mid \epsilon$
$C \rightarrow D \mid \epsilon$
$D \rightarrow C$

(L) 5.23 Is the language $L = \{a^n b^m \mid n \neq m\}$ context-free? If yes, write the CFG defining this language.

(A) 5.24 Convert the following grammar into CNF:
$S \rightarrow a\,B \mid b\,A$
$A \rightarrow a \mid a\,S \mid b\,A\,A$
$B \rightarrow b \mid b\,S \mid a\,B\,B$

(A) 5.25 Write the CFG for the language:
$L = \{a^{2n} b^n \mid n \geq 1\}$

(U) 5.26 What is an ambiguous grammar? Explain with the help of an example, the removal of ambiguity in CFGs.

(A) 5.27 Convert the following CFG into CNF:
$S \rightarrow a\,S\,a \mid b\,S\,b \mid a \mid b \mid a\,a \mid b\,b$

(U) 5.28 Write a short note on Chomsky hierarchy.

(A) 5.29 Find the context-free grammar with no useless symbols equivalent to:
$S \rightarrow A\,B \mid C\,a$
$B \rightarrow B\,C \mid A\,B$
$A \rightarrow a$
$C \rightarrow a\,B \mid b$

(L) 5.30 If the grammar $G$ is given by the productions:
$S \rightarrow a\,S\,a \mid b\,S\,b \mid a\,a \mid b\,b \mid \epsilon,$
show that $L(G)$ has no strings of odd length.

(A) 5.31 Construct a DFA equivalent to the following grammar:
$S \rightarrow a\,S \mid b\,S \mid a\,A$
$A \rightarrow b\,B$
$B \rightarrow a\,C$
$C \rightarrow b\,A$

(A) 5.32 Construct a regular grammar for the DFA shown in Fig. 5.28.

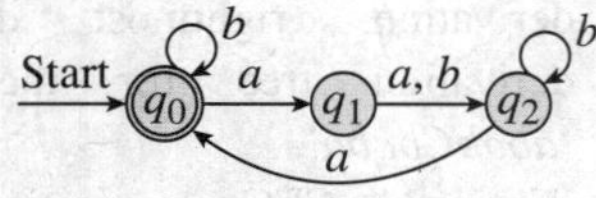


**Figure 5.28**

(A) 5.33 Convert the following grammar into its equivalent GNF:
$S \rightarrow A\,B;\ A \rightarrow B\,S \mid b;\ B \rightarrow S\,A \mid a$

(A) 5.34 Show that the following grammar is ambiguous:
$S \rightarrow a \mid a\,b\,S\,b \mid a\,A\,b$
$A \rightarrow b\,S \mid a\,A\,A\,b$

(A) 5.35 Describe the terms 'left-linear' and 'right-linear' grammars; and convert the following left-linear grammar to its equivalent right-linear grammar.
$S \rightarrow B1 \mid A0 \mid C0$
$A \rightarrow C0 \mid A1 \mid B1 \mid 0$
$B \rightarrow B1 \mid 1$
$C \rightarrow A0$

(A) 5.36 For the following grammar, find an equivalent grammar, which is in reduced form and has no unit productions.
$S \rightarrow AB$
$A \rightarrow a$
$B \rightarrow C \mid b$
$C \rightarrow D$
$D \rightarrow E$
$E \rightarrow a$

(L) 5.37 Give the regular expression for the language generated by the following grammar:
$S \rightarrow A \mid B;\ A \rightarrow 0A \mid \epsilon;\ B \rightarrow 0B \mid B \mid \epsilon$

(A) 5.38 For the following grammar $G$, construct an NFA $M$ such that $L(M) = L(G)$:
$S \rightarrow a\,b\,A \mid b\,a\,B$
$A \rightarrow b\,S \mid b$
$B \rightarrow a\,S \mid a$

(A) 5.39 Show that the following language $L$ is a CFL.
$L = \{0^n 1^n \mid n \leq 1\} \cup \{0^n 1^{2n} \mid n \geq 1\}$

(A) 5.40 Construct the right-linear grammar corresponding to the regular expression:
$R = (0 + 1)^* (1 + (01)^*)$

(A) 5.41 Convert the following grammar to GNF:
$S \rightarrow B\,S;\ S \rightarrow A\,a;\ A \rightarrow b\,c;\ B \rightarrow A\,c$

(A) 5.42 Show that the following languages are context-free languages.
(a) $L_1 = \{a^i b^i c^j \mid i, j >= 1\}$
(b) $L_2 = \{a^i b^j c^j \mid i, j >= 1\}$

(L) 5.43 Find whether the string '*aabbb*' is a member of $L(G)$, where $G$ is defined as:
$S \rightarrow XY$
$X \rightarrow YY \mid a$
$Y \rightarrow XY \mid b$

(L) 5.44 Is the following CFG is ambiguous?
$G = \{(S, A), (a, b), P, S\}$, where $P$ consists of:
$S \rightarrow a\,A\,S \mid a$
$A \rightarrow S\,b\,A \mid S\,S \mid b\,a$

(A) 5.45 Convert the following grammar to GNF, assuming $A_1$ as the start symbol.
$A_1 \rightarrow A_2\,A_3$

$A_2 \rightarrow A_3 A_1 \mid b$
$A_3 \rightarrow A_1 A_2 \mid a$

Ⓒ 5.46 Find context-free grammars generating each of the following languages:
(a) $L_1 = \{a^i b^j c^k \mid i = j + k\}$
(b) $L_2 = \{a^i b^j c^k \mid j = i + k\}$
(c) $L_3 = \{a^i b^j c^k \mid i = j \text{ or } j = k\}$

Ⓐ 5.47 Draw an NFA that accepts the language generated by the following grammar, and explain the language it generates.
$S \rightarrow a A \mid b C \mid b$
$A \rightarrow a S \mid b B$
$B \rightarrow a C \mid b A \mid a$
$C \rightarrow a B \mid b S$

Ⓤ 5.48 What is a normal form? Explain CNF and GNF with the help of suitable examples.

Ⓒ 5.49 Find the CFG generating the following languages:
(a) The set of odd length strings in $\{a, b\}^*$ having $a$ as the middle symbol
(b) The set of even length strings over $\{a, b\}^*$ whose middle symbols are same

Ⓐ 5.50 Convert the following CFG into GNF:
$S \rightarrow A B \mid 0$
$A \rightarrow B X \mid 1$
$B \rightarrow C D \mid 2$
$C \rightarrow A D \mid 0$
$D \rightarrow 1$

Ⓒ 5.51 Construct a CFG for the following sets:
(a) $\{a^{2n} bc \mid n \geq 1\}$
(b) $\{a^n b^m c^m d^n \mid m, n \geq 1\}$

Ⓐ 5.52 Convert the following CFG to CNF:
$S \rightarrow A A C D$
$A \rightarrow a A b \mid \epsilon$
$C \rightarrow a C \mid a$
$D \rightarrow a D a \mid b D b \mid \epsilon$

Ⓛ 5.53 Show that the language $L = \{0^{2^i} \mid i \geq 1\}$ is not a CFL.

Ⓐ 5.54 Using pumping lemma, show that the language $L = \{0^{i^2} \mid i \geq 1\}$ is not a CFL.

**Answers to Objective Questions**

5.1 (a) 5.2. (a) 5.3. (b) 5.4. (b) 5.5. (b) 5.6. Greibach normal form 5.7. (d)
5.8. (a) 5.9. True 5.10. (d) 5.11. (b) 5.12. (d)

# 6 Pushdown Stack-memory Machine

**LEARNING OBJECTIVES**

After completing this chapter, the reader will be able to understand the following:

- Computational problems that can be solved using a single stack
- Formal model of pushdown stack-memory machine, called pushdown automaton (PDA)
- Comparison of finite automata (FA) and PDA on the basis of their relative computational powers
- Difference between deterministic PDA (DPDA) and non-deterministic PDA (NPDA), and their relative computational powers
- Equivalence between PDA and context-free grammars (CFGs)
- Acceptance of a CFL by an empty stack against acceptance by a final state
- Application of Chomsky normal form (CNF) for controlling stack growth
- Closure properties of context-free languages (CFLs)

## 6.1 INTRODUCTION

A pushdown stack-memory machine (PDM) is a computational model that is used to solve any problem that has an algorithmic solution and requires a single stack memory (infinite memory, ideally) as storage. Thus, a PDM can remember arbitrarily long input strings, which is not feasible for a finite state machine (FSM) as it does not have any memory at all.

The PDMs can accept or recognize context-free languages (CFLs). A set of all regular languages is a proper subset of CFLs; hence, PDMs can also accept regular languages. Therefore, one can say that a PDM is an FSM having an external stack memory, which makes it a more powerful tool comparatively. A PDM however, is less powerful when compared to a Turing machine (TM). Stacks have limited ability. They can only be used to implement LIFO, whereas a tape is more powerful when compared to a stack in usage. A TM can consume its own output as input using the tape, which is impossible in case of a PDM as the stack is external to the tape.

## 6.2 ELEMENTS OF A PDM

A PDM is collectively described with the help of the following elements:

1. An input alphabet, (Σ), that is, a finite set of input symbols.
2. An unbounded input tape, bounded only by the input length. The input string is written onto the tape, which is initially assumed to contain blank characters (ƀ). The left end of the input tape is fixed and the tape is unbounded towards the right end.
3. An alphabet of stack symbols (Γ).
4. A pushdown stack. Initially the stack is empty and is assumed to contain a blank character ƀ at the bottom to represent the stack empty position.
5. Start, accept, and reject indicators.
6. Branching state—read.
7. Stack operations, namely push and pop.

The input tape of a PDM is visualized to be divided into cells having one input symbol from Σ written into each—a finite control (head assembly that moves one cell at a time towards the right upon reading a symbol from the tape) and an external stack, which is an external memory. Figure 6.1 shows a pictorial representation of the memory of a PDM.

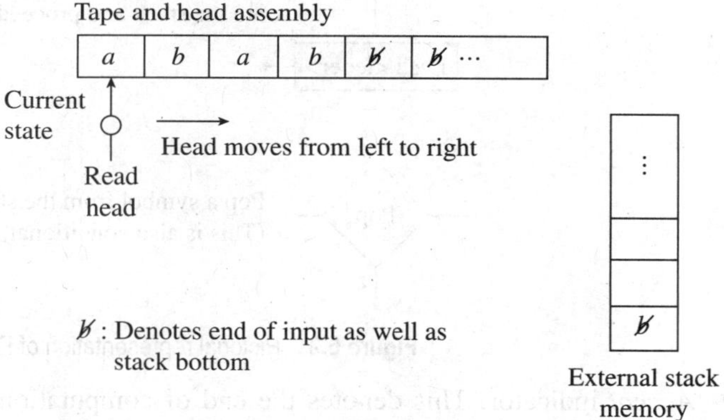


**Figure 6.1** Memory of PDM

A PDM can only read from the tape and cannot write onto it; the read head always moves in one direction, that is, from left to right. The stack is external to the reading assembly and acts as an auxiliary memory. Thus, a PDM can be considered as an FSM having an external stack memory.

### 6.2.1 Pictorial Representation of PDM Elements

Instead of using a state transition diagram that is the usual notation for describing machines, a PDM is represented using flowcharts.

Figure 6.2 depicts the different elements that are used in the flowchart representation of a PDM. The typical elements are as follows:

- *Start* indicator: This is a very common element found in flowcharts. It denotes the beginning of the computation.

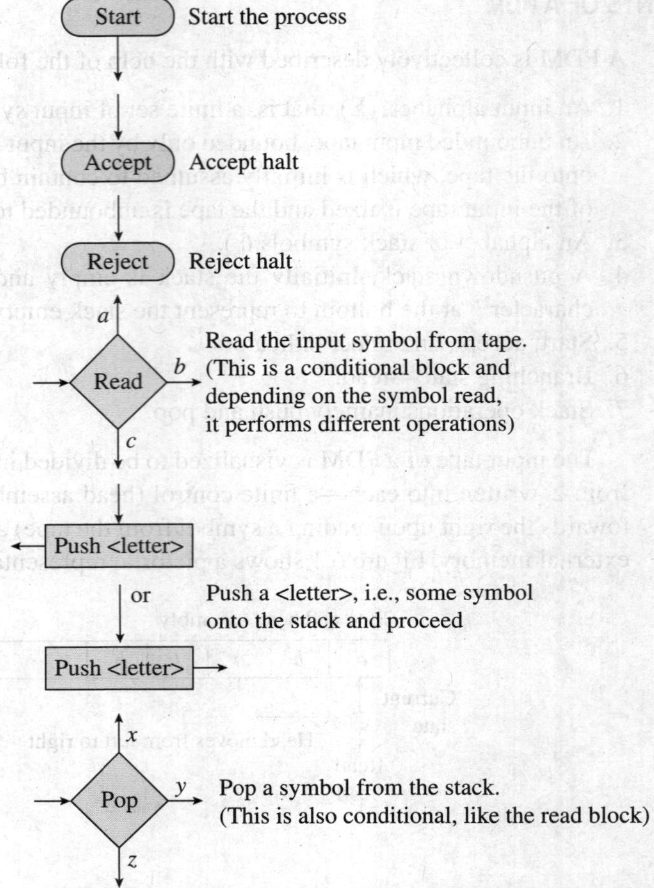


**Figure 6.2** Pictorial representation of PDA elements

- *Accept* indicator: This denotes the end of computation that results in accepting the input string. It means that the input string has a valid pattern as defined by the context-free grammar (CFG). We know that a PDM accepts or recognizes CFLs.
- *Reject* indicator: This denotes the end of computation that results in the rejection of the input string. This means that the input is invalid with respect to the CFG rules.
- *Push* action: Push is an operation that is carried over the external stack and is denoted by a rectangular block. One symbol can be pushed at a time.
- *Pop* action: Pop is an operation that results in a decision block. The program flow is specified based on the symbol that is retrieved from the stack.
- *Read* state: Read state is represented as a decision block. The program flow is specified, based on the input symbol that is read.

## 6.3 PUSHDOWN AUTOMATA

Pushdown automaton (plural—automata; abbreviated as PDA) is the mathematical model (formalism) of the PDM.

### *Formal Definition*

A pushdown automaton $M$ is denoted as

$$M = \{Q, \Sigma, \Gamma, \delta, q_0, Z_0, F)$$

where,

$Q$: Finite set of states
$\Sigma$: Input alphabet (input strings are composed of symbols from $\Sigma$)
$\Gamma$: Stack alphabet
$q_0$: Initial state $q_0$, which is a member of $Q$
$Z_0$: $Z_0$, which is a member of $\Gamma$, is a particular stack symbol called the start symbol. It indicates the bottom of the stack, and is considered as $\not{b}$ (blank character) in many designs
$F$: Set of final states, $F \subseteq Q$
$\delta$: $Q \times \Sigma \times \Gamma \rightarrow Q \times \Gamma^*$ (This defines the transition function $\delta$ for a *deterministic PDA* or *DPDA*. The transition function for a non-deterministic PDA or NPDA is different, and is stated later)

The stack is an external storage system. Hence, one can store any symbol onto the stack, though it may not really be the symbol that has been read from the input tape. Moreover, one can push multiple symbols onto the stack, upon reading a single symbol from the input tape. Hence, there is a distinction between input alphabet ($\Sigma$) and stack alphabet ($\Gamma$). These two sets may overlap or may be completely distinct sets, depending on the problem that we are solving.

Any subset of $Q$ can be marked as the set of final states $F$, depending on the solution. Upon reading the entire input string, if the machine resides in any of the final states, then the input string is considered as 'accepted' by the machine. Otherwise, the machine resides in any of the non-final states, and the input is considered as 'rejected' by the machine. Usually, in the pictorial representation of the problem solution, rejection is not explicitly shown. The paths that are unspecified in the flowchart are considered rejection paths. We shall discuss more about this in the examples.

A stack is initially assumed to contain the symbol $Z_0$, that is, the blank character $\not{b}$. Any PDM solution is based on this assumption.

In case of a DPDA, $\delta$ $(q, a, Z)$ does not contain more than one element for any state $q$ in $Q$, any symbol $Z$ in $\Gamma$ on top of the stack, and input symbol $a$ in $\Sigma$. Thus, the transition would be of the form

$$\delta\ (q, a, Z) = (p, \gamma)$$

where, $p$ is the unique next state in $Q$ to which the machine makes the transition ($p$ may or may not be equal to $q$), and $\gamma$ is a member of $\Gamma^*$(zero or more occurrences of symbols from $\Gamma$). The symbol $\gamma$ can be one of the following:

- Empty, that is, $\epsilon$, if the stack operation performed is pop. This means that $Z$ is popped out of the stack.
- $Z$, if the stack is not updated—only a state transition is performed.
- $xx\ldots xxZ$, if multiple symbols $xx\ldots xx$ are pushed onto the stack.
- $xx\ldots xx$, if $Z$ is popped out of the stack and multiple symbols $xx\ldots xx$ are pushed onto the stack.

Therefore, if the DPDA is in state $q$, it reads symbol $a$ from the tape cell, and if $Z$ is on top of the stack, it changes the state to $p$, replaces $Z$ on the stack top by $\gamma$ (considering the aforementioned four scenarios), and moves the head one cell position to the right on the tape.

For an NPDA, the transition function $\delta$ is defined as follows:

$$\delta: Q \times \{\Sigma \cup (\epsilon)\} \times \Gamma \rightarrow \text{finite subsets of } Q \times \Gamma^*$$

For example, consider the following transition:

$$\delta\ (q, a, Z) = \{(p_1, \gamma_1), (p_2, \gamma_2), \ldots, (p_m, \gamma_m)\},$$

where, $q, p_1, p_2, \ldots, p_m$ are states from $Q$, $a$ is any input symbol in $\Sigma$, $Z$ is any stack symbol in $\Gamma$, and all $\gamma_i$ for $1 \leq i \leq m$ are members of $\Gamma^*$.

The interpretation of this definition is that the NPDA in state $q$ reads input symbol $a$ while $Z$ is the topmost symbol on the stack, possibly makes transition to any state $p_i$, replaces symbol $Z$ on the stack by any string $\gamma_i$ (as per the aforementioned four scenarios), and advances the read head one cell position to the right on the input tape. The NPDA, hence, is considered as an unpredictable (non-deterministic or possibilistic) machine as it can perform any of the possible transitions during its execution, though the current machine state, current input symbol being read, and the stack state are the same.

## 6.4 FINITE AUTOMATA VS PDA

As we have discussed, a PDA can be visualized as an FA having an external stack. Thus, a PDA has infinite storage in the form of a stack, which is missing in the FA. Hence, the FA has lesser computational power compared to the PDA. Furthermore, an FA cannot solve any problem that requires to store intermediate results in the memory for further computation.

As we know, FA are capable of accepting (or recognizing) regular languages (RLs), while PDA can accept CFLs. Since the set of all RLs is a subset of the class of CFLs, we can say that every RL is also a CFL; however, the vice versa may not be true. Hence, PDAs can accept all RLs. This is demonstrated through the following examples.

### 6.4.1 Examples of PDA Accepting Regular Languages

**Example 6.1** Construct a PDA that recognizes the language accepted by the DFA shown in Fig. 6.3.

***Solution*** The DFA given in Fig. 6.3 accepts the regular language represented by the following regular expression:

$$b^*\ a\ a^*\ (b\ b^*\ a\ a^*)^*$$

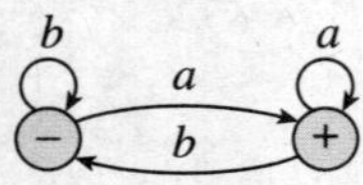

**Figure 6.3** Example DFA

We can construct a DPDA equivalent to the given DFA, as shown in Fig. 6.4.

In Fig. 6.4, we see that $Read_1$ state of the DPDA is analogous to the initial state of the DFA and $Read_2$ state is analogous to the final state of the given DFA. Since $Read_2$ state is analogous to the final state, if the input ends in $Read_1$, that is, if we get a blank

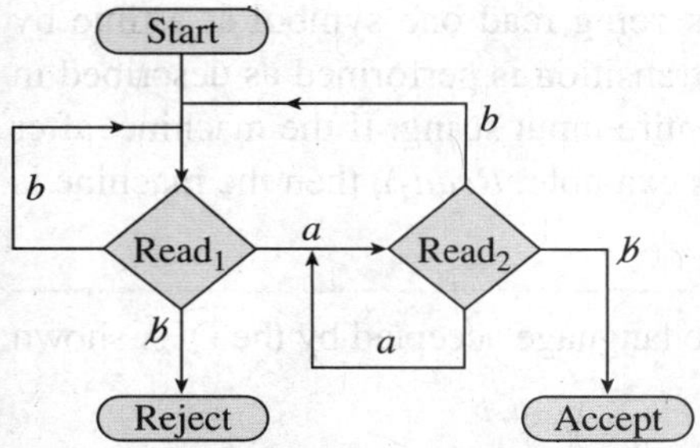


**Figure 6.4** DPDA equivalent to DFA in Fig. 6.3

character b̸ on the tape in *Read*$_1$, the machine rejects the input string; else it transits to 'accept' state as shown in the figure.

Please note that the external stack is not required for this example as the language being accepted is a regular language. Hence, the DFA and the DPDA are equivalent machines and the changes are only notational.

In this example, we have demonstrated the PDA as a regular language acceptor.

Let us simulate the working of the PDA for the strings '*bbaaba*' and '*baaabab*'.

1. Simulation for string '*bbaaba*':

| Current state | Input symbol | Next state | Head point position |
|---|---|---|---|
| Start | — | Read$_1$ | b b a b a b̸ ... |
| Read$_1$ | *b* | Read$_1$ | b b a a b a b̸ ... |
| Read$_1$ | *b* | Read$_1$ | b b a a b a b̸ ... |
| Read$_1$ | *a* | Read$_2$ | b b a a b a b̸ ... |
| Read$_2$ | *a* | Read$_2$ | b b a a b a b̸ ... |
| Read$_2$ | *b* | Read$_1$ | b b a a b a b̸ ... |
| Read$_1$ | *a* | Read$_2$ | b b a a b a b̸ ... |
| Read$_2$ | *b* | Accept | b b a a b a b b̸ ... |

Thus, the string '*bbaaba*' is accepted by the PDA.

2. Simulation for string '*baaabab*':

| Current state | Input symbol | Next state | Head point position |
|---|---|---|---|
| Start | — | Read$_1$ | b a a a b a b b̸ ... |
| Read$_1$ | *b* | Read$_1$ | b a a a b a b b̸ ... |
| Read$_1$ | *a* | Read$_2$ | b a a a b a b b̸ ... |
| Read$_2$ | *a* | Read$_2$ | b a a a b a b b̸ ... |
| Read$_2$ | *a* | Read$_2$ | b a a a b a b b̸ ... |
| Read$_2$ | *b* | Read$_1$ | b a a a b a b b̸ ... |
| Read$_1$ | *a* | Read$_2$ | b a a a b a b b̸ ... |
| Read$_2$ | *b* | Read$_1$ | b a a a b a b b̸ ... |
| Read$_1$ | b̸ | Reject | b a a a b a b b̸ b̸ ... |

Thus, the string '*baaabab*' is rejected by the PDA

This simulation depicts how the input string is being read one symbol at a time by the machine. Upon reading every symbol, a state transition is performed as described in Fig. 6.4. The machine stops after consuming the entire input string. If the machine, after reading the entire input, is in the final state (in this example, *Read*$_2$), then the machine is said to accept the string; else it rejects the string.

---

**Example 6.2** Construct a PDA that recognizes the language accepted by the DFA shown in Fig. 6.5.

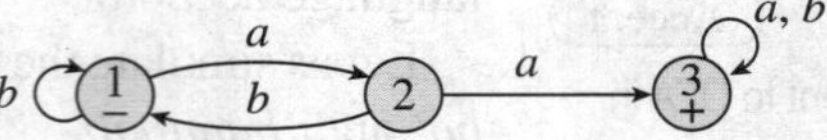


**Figure 6.5** Example DFA

***Solution*** The equivalent DPDA can be constructed as shown in Fig. 6.6.

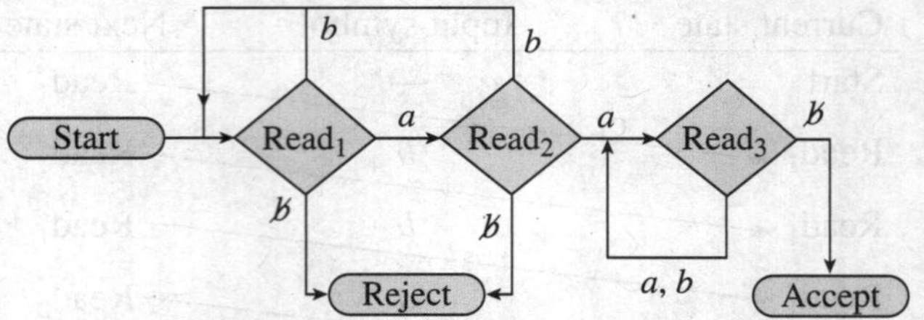


**Figure 6.6** DPDA equivalent to DFA in Fig. 6.5

We see that the *Read*$_1$ state in the PDA is analogous to state 1 in the given DFA. Similarly, *Read*$_2$ is analogous to state 2, and *Read*$_3$ is analogous to state 3 in the given DFA. Hence, *Read*$_1$ and *Read*$_2$ are non-final states. If the PDA reads a blank character ƀ indicating the end of the input string while in these states, the machine rejects the input string. Upon reading the entire input string, if the PDA reaches the final state, that is, *Read*$_3$, then the input string is accepted by the PDA.

Let us simulate the working of the PDA for the input given as '*abaab*'. The acceptance of the input can be shown as follows:

| Current state | Input symbol | Next state | Head point position |
|---|---|---|---|
| Start | — | Read$_1$ | *a b a a b ƀ* ... |
| Read$_1$ | *a* | Read$_2$ | *a b a a b ƀ* ... |
| Read$_2$ | *b* | Read$_1$ | *a b a a b ƀ* ... |
| Read$_1$ | *a* | Read$_2$ | *a b a a b ƀ* ... |
| Read$_2$ | *a* | Read$_3$ | *a b a a b ƀ* ... |
| Read$_3$ | *b* | Read$_3$ | *a b a a b ƀ ƀ* ... |
| Read$_3$ | ƀ | Accept | *a b a a b b ƀ* ... |

---

### 6.4.2 Relative Computational Powers of PDA and FA

We have seen in the previous subsection that PDA can accept regular languages just as FA. However, a PDA is much more powerful when compared to the FA, as it has infinite memory in the form of an external stack that is absent in the case of FA. In other words, we can say that FA is a special case of PDA—it is a PDA without an external stack.

For every FA, we can construct an equivalent PDA that accepts the same regular language. Such a PDA does not require a stack and its operations such as push and pop.

We have already discussed earlier that PDA can accept CFLs that are the superset of the class of RLs. In the following section, we shall look at some examples of PDA that accept CFLs.

## 6.5 PDA ACCEPTING CFLs

We have seen that a PDA accepts not only RLs, but also CFLs. Further, we also know that building a DPDA or an NPDA that accepts RLs does require an external stack. However, this is not possible while designing a PDA solution for the CFLs.

The following examples will illustrate this further.

---

**Example 6.3** Construct a PDA that accepts the following language:

$$L = \{a^n\, b^n \mid n \geq 0\}$$

***Solution*** As per the definition, every string in the language contains $n$ number of $a$'s followed by the same number of $b$'s; also, it contains an empty string $\epsilon$, whenever $n = 0$.

**Algorithm**

1. Keep on pushing all $a$'s onto the stack till the machine reads the first $b$.
2. Each time it reads $b$, it pops one $a$ from the stack.
3. If the number of $a$'s are equal to the number of $b$'s, then at the end of the input string, that is, when blank character $\not{b}$ is read from the tape, the top of the stack should also contain the blank character $\not{b}$, indicating that the stack is empty. The string is accepted only in this case; else it is rejected.

The required DPDA is constructed as shown in Fig. 6.7.

We see from Fig. 6.7 that $Read_1$ state pushes all $a$'s onto the stack. On reading the first $b$, it performs the pop operation; $Read_2$ state checks whether or not the same number of $b$'s are following the $a$'s, by repeatedly popping the $a$'s from the stack for every matching $b$ that is read.

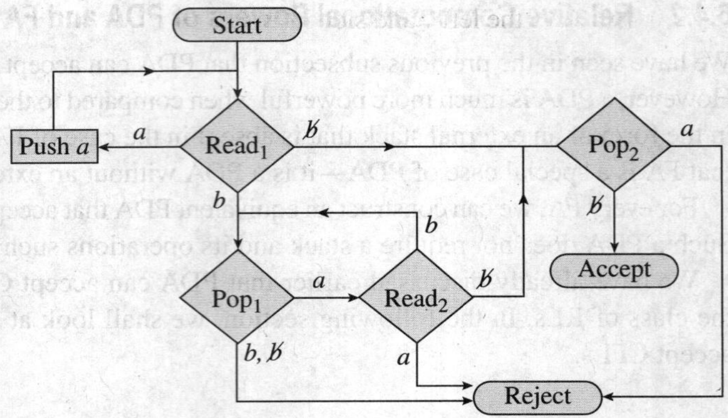


*Read*$_1$: Keep on pushing $a$'s till you get the first $b$
*Pop*$_1$: Pop an $a$ when you read one $b$
*Read*$_2$: When you get $b$ while reading $b$'s go to 'Pop$_2$'
*Pop*$_1$: Input is finished, so check whether the stack is empty or not. If empty go to 'Accept'

**Figure 6.7** PDA that accepts $\{a^n b^n \mid n \geq 0\}$

***Simulation***

1. Let us simulate the acceptance of the string '*aabb*':

| Current state | Stack contents | Tape and head |
|---|---|---|
| Start | $\not{b}$ | $\underset{\uparrow}{a}\ a\ b\ b\ \not{b}\ \not{b}\ \ldots$ |
| ↓ | | |
| *Read*$_1$ | $\not{b}$ | $a\ \underset{\uparrow}{a}\ b\ b\ \not{b}\ \not{b}\ \ldots$ |
| $a$ ↓ | | |
| Push $a$ | $\not{b}\ a$ | $a\ \underset{\uparrow}{a}\ b\ b\ \not{b}\ \not{b}\ \ldots$ |
| ↓ | | |
| *Read*$_1$ | $\not{b}\ a$ | $a\ a\ \underset{\uparrow}{b}\ b\ \not{b}\ \not{b}\ \ldots$ |
| $a$ ↓ | | |
| Push $a$ | $\not{b}aa$ | $a\ a\ \underset{\uparrow}{b}\ b\ \not{b}\ \not{b}\ \ldots$ |
| ↓ | | |
| *Read*$_1$ | $\not{b}aa$ | $a\ a\ b\ \underset{\uparrow}{b}\ \not{b}\ \not{b}\ \ldots$ |
| $b$ ↓ | | |
| *Pop*$_1$ | $\not{b}a$ | $a\ a\ b\ \underset{\uparrow}{b}\ \not{b}\ \not{b}\ \ldots$ |
| $a$ ↓ | | |
| *Read*$_2$ | $\not{b}a$ | $a\ a\ b\ b\ \underset{\uparrow}{\not{b}}\ \not{b}\ \ldots$ |
| $b$ ↓ | | |
| *Pop*$_1$ | $\not{b}$ | $a\ a\ b\ b\ \underset{\uparrow}{\not{b}}\ \not{b}\ \ldots$ |
| $a$ ↓ | | |
| *Read*$_2$ | $\not{b}$ | $a\ a\ b\ b\ \not{b}\ \underset{\uparrow}{\not{b}}\ \ldots$ |
| $\not{b}$ ↓ | | |
| *Pop*$_2$ | — | $a\ a\ b\ b\ \not{b}\ \underset{\uparrow}{\not{b}}\ \ldots$ |
| $\not{b}$ ↓ | | |
| Accept | | |

The arrows on the left-hand side indicate transitions from one state to another on reading the same symbol. The operations 'push' and 'pop' are performed while processing the input.

In the beginning, the stack is assumed to contain the blank character b̸ to indicate the bottom of the stack. In the aforementioned simulation, the first two characters in the input string are pushed onto the stack as both are *a*'s. Then, for every *b* read, an *a* is popped out of the stack. Once the blank character b̸ is read, indicating the end of the input, 'pop' operation is performed to check whether the stack is empty as well. If the stack is empty, that is, if pop operation returns the bottommost element as b̸, then the input string is accepted by the PDA. Thus, the input string '*aabb*' is found to match the expected pattern, $a^n b^n$. This is also referred to as *acceptance by empty stack* (refer to Section 6.5.2).

2. Let us now simulate the rejection of '*abbba*':

| Current state | Stack contents | Tape and head |
|---|---|---|
| Start | b̸ | *a b b b a* b̸ b̸ ... |
| ↓ | | ↑ |
| *Read*$_1$ | b̸ | *a b b b a* b̸ b̸ ... |
| *a* ↓ | | ↑ |
| Push *a* | b̸*a* | *a b b b a* b̸ b̸ ... |
| ↓ | | ↑ |
| *Read*$_1$ | b̸*a* | *a b b b a* b̸ b̸ ... |
| *b* ↓ | | ↑ |
| *Pop*$_1$ | b̸ | *a b b b a* b̸ b̸ ... |
| *a* ↓ | | ↑ |
| *Read*$_2$ | b̸ | *a b b b a* b̸ b̸ ... |
| *b* ↓ | | ↑ |
| *Pop*$_1$ | — | *a b b b a* b̸ b̸ ... |
| b̸ ↓ | | ↑ |
| Reject | | |

In this simulation, the first *a* gets pushed onto the stack. When the second input symbol *b* is read, the topmost stack symbol *a* is popped to match the read symbol *b*. The stack becomes empty after the first pop. The third symbol *b* is read but the stack is found to be empty—it does not contain any more *a*'s to match with the *b* that is read. Hence, the input string is rejected.

***Notes***:

1. The given language $L = \{a^n b^n \mid n \geq 0\}$, is not a regular language; therefore, it cannot be recognized by an FA. It is actually a CFL and the CFG for the same can be written as follows:

$$S \rightarrow a\,S\,b \mid \epsilon$$

2. We observe that the PDA in Fig. 6.7 is a DPDA because from every state there is a unique transition for a symbol that is read.
3. We need not restrict ourselves to using the same alphabet for the input strings as well as the stack. Since the stack is an external memory component, the stack alphabet ($\Gamma$) is considered to be distinct from the input alphabet ($\Sigma$). In this example, it is possible to read an $a$ from the tape and push $x$ onto the stack. In this case, the number of $x$'s represents the count of the number of $a$'s present, as shown in Fig. 6.8.

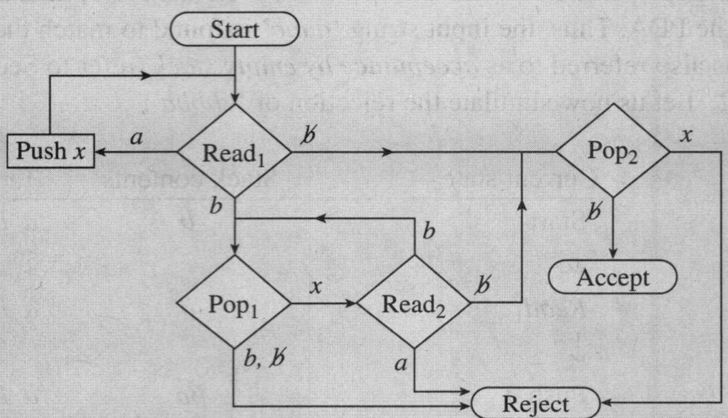


**Figure 6.8** DPDA using distinct sets of input and stack alphabets

The DPDA in Fig. 6.7 can also be specified using the following set of equations, which are based on the formal notations discussed in Section 6.3.

The following two equations denote the pushing of symbol $a$ onto the stack if the symbol read is $a$; the stack is either empty or contains $a$ as its topmost symbol. These two equations collectively signify the process of pushing all the $a$'s onto the stack (till the first $b$ is read). Refer to program block 1 in Fig. 6.9.

$$\delta\ (Read_1, a, \not{b}) = (Read_1, a\not{b})$$
$$\delta\ (Read_1, a, a) = (Read_1, aa)$$

The following two equations denote the pop operation of $a$ out of the stack for every $b$ that is read. This is indicated by the stack state, which changes from $a$ to $\epsilon$ (refer to program block 2 in Fig. 6.9). The two transitions indicate moving from $Read_1$ to $Read_2$ for the first $b$ that is read and $Read_2$ to itself for the subsequent $b$'s that are read.

$$\delta\ (Read_1, b, a) = (Read_2, \epsilon)$$
$$\delta\ (Read_2, b, a) = (Read_2, \epsilon)$$

The following two equations denote the two program paths that lead to the acceptance of the input string, if it matches the required pattern, $a^n b^n$. The first equation represents the case $n = 0$, that is, when the input string is empty ($\epsilon$). The second equation represents the case $n > 0$.

$$\delta\ (Read_1, \not{b}, \not{b}) = \text{Accept}$$
$$\delta\ (Read_2, \not{b}, \not{b}) = \text{Accept}$$

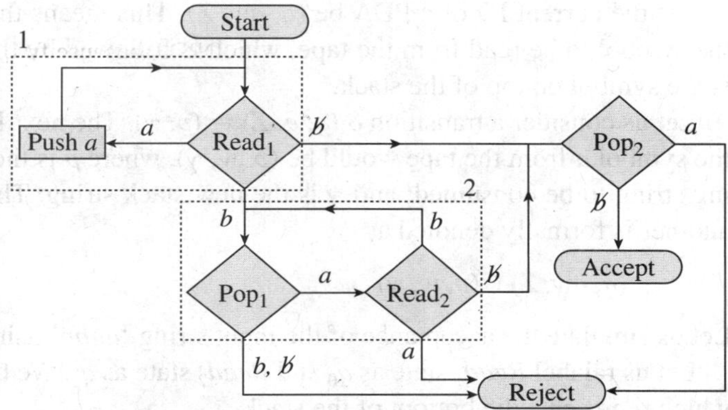


**Figure 6.9** PDA that accepts $\{a^n b^n \mid n \geq 0\}$

In principle, the aforementioned six equations are sufficient to denote the DPDA that accepts the given CFL. The following six are additional equations that denote rejections and may not be specified—since anyway, what is not specified is always rejected.

The following two rejection equations represent the presence of additional number of $a$'s.

$$\delta\,(Read_1, \not b, a) = \text{Reject}$$
$$\delta\,(Read_2, \not b, a) = \text{Reject}$$

The following two rejections represent that the number of $b$'s is more than the number of $a$'s.

$$\delta\,(Read_1, b, \not b) = \text{Reject}$$
$$\delta\,(Read_2, b, \not b) = \text{Reject}$$

These two equations are reached when the DPDA reads $a$ while in $Read_2$ state, no matter what is on the top of the stack. This is something that is against the expected pattern. These equations represent the case where there are some $a$'s even after all the $b$'s have been read. Hence, they are considered as rejection equations.

$$\delta\,(Read_2, a, \not b) = \text{Reject}$$
$$\delta\,(Read_2, a, a) = \text{Reject}$$

---

### 6.5.1 Instantaneous Description of PDA

Instantaneous description (ID) of a PDA, as the name suggests, is its description at a given instance, while computing a given input string. It is described with the help of a triple $(q, w, z)$, where $q$ denotes the current state of the machine; $w$ denotes the input string remaining to be read from the tape; and $z$ denotes the topmost stack symbol.

While consuming any given input string (symbol by symbol), the PDA moves from one ID to another. This process continues as long as the input lasts. This means that the simulations we have seen in the examples can also be described more formally with the help of a series of IDs.

Let the current ID of a PDA be $(q, aw, Z)$. This means that $q$ is the current state; $a$ is the symbol to be read from the tape, which is followed by the remaining string $w$; and $Z$ is the symbol on top of the stack.

Let us consider a transition $\delta(q, a, Z) = (p, \gamma)$. The next ID for the PDA after reading the symbol $a$ from the tape would be $(p, w, \gamma)$, where $p$ is the next state; $w$ is the remaining string to be consumed; and $\gamma$ is the new stack string. This transition from one ID to another is formally denoted as

$$(q, aw, Z) \vdash (p, w, \gamma)$$

Let us simulate the acceptance of the input string '*aabb*' using the series of IDs.

Let us relabel $Read_1$ state as $q_0$ and $Read_2$ state as $q_1$. We have already labelled $Z_0$ as $\not{b}$, which represents the bottom of the stack.

$$\begin{aligned}(q_0, aabb\not{b}, \not{b}) &\vdash (q_0, abb\not{b}, a\not{b})\\ &\vdash (q_0, bb\not{b}, aa\not{b})\\ &\vdash (q_1, b\not{b}, a\not{b})\\ &\vdash (q_1, \not{b}, \not{b})\\ &\vdash (\text{Accept}, \epsilon, \epsilon)\end{aligned}$$

### 6.5.2 Acceptance of CFL by Empty Stack

The acceptance of an input string '*aabb*' as depicted in the previous section is an example of acceptance by an empty stack. Observe that neither $Read_1$ nor $Read_2$ is designated as a final state in the DPDA shown in Fig. 6.7. In this chapter, we have implemented acceptance by empty stack for all the solved examples, as it is the most common way of implementation. Readers may attempt to build the acceptance by final state for these examples, if interested.

A string $w$ is said to be accepted by a PDA, if

$$(q_0, w, Z_0) \vdash^* (p, \epsilon, \epsilon)$$

where, $p$ is any state in $Q$, and '$\vdash^*$' denotes an ID after reading the entire input string. '$\vdash^*$' denotes multiple steps in reading the string, while '$\vdash$' denotes one step at a time (refer to Fig. 6.10).

### 6.5.3 Acceptance of CFL by Final State

Acceptance by final state is not very commonly implemented for PDA and is not very different from acceptance by empty stack.

A string $w$ is said to be accepted by a PDA if:

$$(q_0, w, Z_0) \vdash^* (p, \epsilon, \gamma)$$

where, $p$ is a member of $F$, which is a designated set of final states (refer to Section 6.3), and $\gamma$ is any stack string. This means that upon reading the entire string $w$, if the PDA transits to a final state, then the string $w$ is said to be accepted by the PDA (refer to Fig. 6.11).

### 6.5.4 State Transition Diagram for PDA

We can also represent PDAs using the state transition diagram, just as we did in the case of FA and Turing machines. However, there is a slight change in the notation, based on whether a given PDA accepts a CFL with an empty stack or a final state.

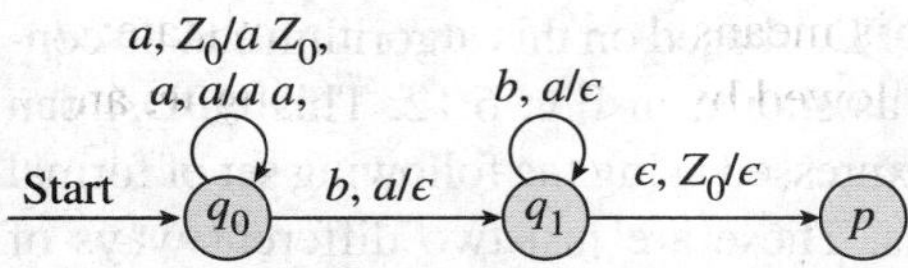


**Figure 6.10** State transition diagram for PDA that accepts $\{a^n b^n \mid n \geq 0\}$ by empty stack

As per the usual notations, the state transition diagram is a directed graph, where each node represents a state and an edge represents a transition. The state transition diagram for the DPDA in Fig. 6.7 is drawn as shown in Fig. 6.10.

The edges are labelled in the form '$a$, $Z/\gamma$' where, $a$ is the input symbol read; $Z$ denotes the topmost stack symbol; and $\gamma$ denotes the stack string after transition is complete.

In Fig. 6.10, which is a state transition diagram for the DPDA in Fig. 6.7, we have relabelled $Read_1$ as $q_0$; $Read_2$ as $q_1$; and accept indicator as $p$. Note that though $p$ is not a final state, it is reached when the input ends and the stack becomes empty.

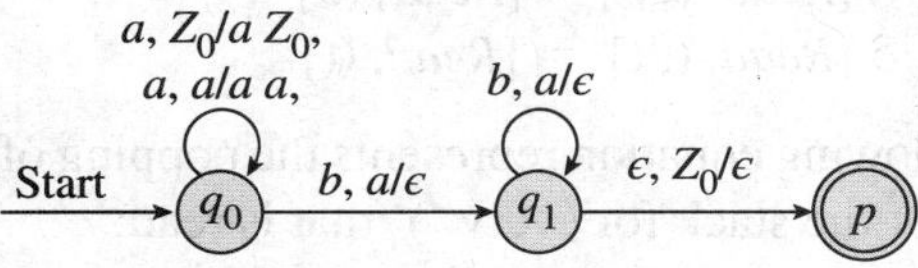


**Figure 6.11** State transition diagram for PDA that accepts $\{a^n b^n \mid n \geq 0\}$ by final state

The state transition diagram in Fig. 6.10 can be modified to depict the DPDA accepting the same CFL by the final state, as shown in Fig. 6.11.

We observe that the only change in Fig. 6.11 is that $p$ is now marked with double circles to indicate that it is a final state; and the stack string $Z_0$ remains unchanged while approaching the state $p$.

---

**Example 6.4** Design a PDA that checks for well-formed parentheses.

***Solution*** As we know, a string of parentheses that is well-formed should start with the opening bracket '(' and must end with the closing bracket ')'. This is a CFL and can be described with the help of the following grammar:

$$S \rightarrow (\,S\,)\,S \mid \epsilon$$

The language can be expressed as

$$L = \{\epsilon, (\,), (\,(\,)\,), (\,)\,(\,), (\,)\,(\,(\,)\,), (\,(\,)\,)\,(\,), \ldots\}$$

**Algorithm**

The problem is similar to that in the previous example, in which we have seen that the string should begin with $a$, and is matched with the subsequent $b$'s; in this example, all '('s are pushed onto the stack to be matched later with the subsequent ')'s. The only difference is that the machine can read opening parenthesis '('even after reading the closing parenthesis ')', rather than all '('s being read first followed by all ')'s. In other words, the language is not of the form $(^n\,)^n$; for example, there may be strings of the form '( ) ( )' or '( ) ( ( ) )' as well. Due to this, the algorithm and the PDA will be a little different, as follows:

1. If you read symbol '(', push '(' onto the stack.
2. On reading every ')' pop one '(' from the stack.
3. Repeat the aforementioned two steps till you finish with all the parentheses in the string.
4. When the input ends, that is, on reading $\not{b}$, the top of the stack should also contain $\not{b}$; this indicates that the string consists of well-formed parentheses.

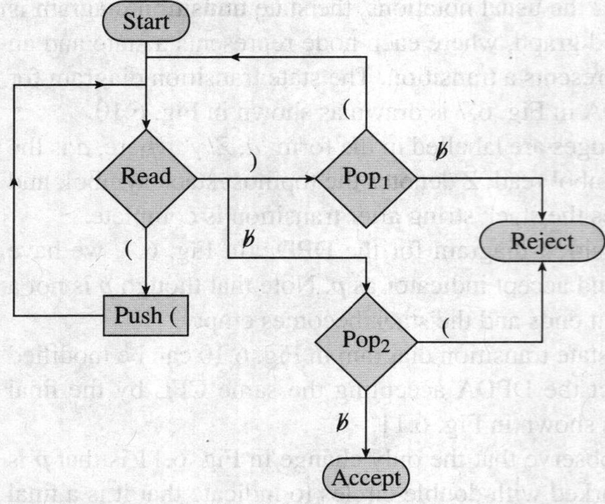


**Figure 6.12** DPDA that checks for well-formed parentheses

The DPDA based on this algorithm can be constructed as shown in Fig. 6.12. This DPDA can also be expressed using the following set of formal equations. These are just two different ways of representing the given solution and are equivalent to each other.

When the symbol '(' is read, push it onto the stack. This is expressed using the following two equations:

$$\delta\ [Read, (, \not{b}] = [Read, (\not{b}]$$
$$\delta\ [Read, (, (] = [Read, ((]$$

The following equation represents the popping of '(' out of the stack for every ')' that is read:

$$\delta\ [Read, ), (] = [Read, \epsilon]$$

The following equation is the only path to acceptance. When the input ends, the stack must be empty as well.

$$\delta\ (Read, \not{b}, \not{b}) = \text{Accept}$$

Rejection paths are expressed with the help of the following two equations:

$\delta\ [Read, ), \not{b}] = \text{Reject}$ … number of ')'s is more
$\delta\ [Read, \not{b}, (] = \text{Reject}$ … number of '('s is more

### *Simulation*

Let us simulate the acceptance of the string '(( ) ( ))' by an empty stack.

| Current state | Stack contents | Tape and head |
|---|---|---|
| Start | $\not{b}$ | ( ( ) ( ) ) $\not{b}\,\not{b}$ … |
| ↓ | | ↑ |
| *Read* | $\not{b}$ | ( ( ) ( ) ) $\not{b}\,\not{b}$ … |
| ( ↓ | | ↑ |
| Push ( | $\not{b}$ ( | ( ( ) ( ) ) $\not{b}\,\not{b}$ … |
| ↓ | | ↑ |
| *Read* | $\not{b}$ ( | ( ( ) ( ) ) $\not{b}\,\not{b}$ … |
| ( ↓ | | ↑ |
| Push ( | $\not{b}$ ( ( | ( ( ) ( ) ) $\not{b}\,\not{b}$ … |
| ↓ | | ↑ |
| *Read* | $\not{b}$ ( ( | ( ( ) ( ) ) $\not{b}\,\not{b}$ … |
| ) ↓ | | ↑ |
| *Pop$_1$* | $\not{b}$ ( | ( ( ) ( ) ) $\not{b}\,\not{b}$ … |
| ( ↓ | | ↑ |

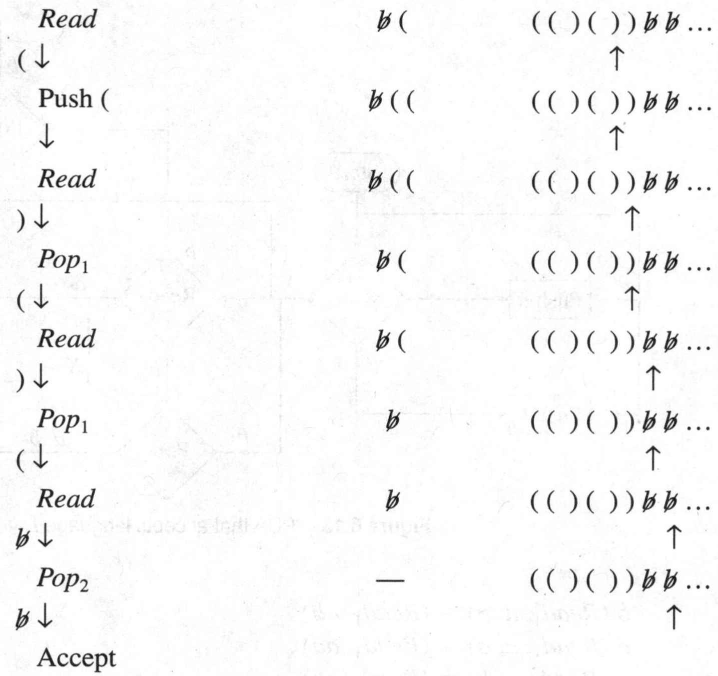

| | | |
|---|---|---|
| *Read* | ƀ ( | ( ( ) ( ) ) ƀ ƀ ... |
| ( ↓ | | ↑ |
| Push ( | ƀ ( ( | ( ( ) ( ) ) ƀ ƀ ... |
| ↓ | | ↑ |
| *Read* | ƀ ( ( | ( ( ) ( ) ) ƀ ƀ ... |
| ) ↓ | | ↑ |
| *Pop*$_1$ | ƀ ( | ( ( ) ( ) ) ƀ ƀ ... |
| ( ↓ | | ↑ |
| *Read* | ƀ ( | ( ( ) ( ) ) ƀ ƀ ... |
| ) ↓ | | ↑ |
| *Pop*$_1$ | ƀ | ( ( ) ( ) ) ƀ ƀ ... |
| ( ↓ | | ↑ |
| *Read* | ƀ | ( ( ) ( ) ) ƀ ƀ ... |
| ƀ ↓ | | ↑ |
| *Pop*$_2$ | — | ( ( ) ( ) ) ƀ ƀ ... |
| ƀ ↓ | | ↑ |
| Accept | | |

**Example 6.5** Construct a PDA that accepts the following language:

$$L = \{X, aXa, bXb, aaXaa, abXba, baXab, bbXbb, aaaXaaa, \ldots\}$$

***Solution*** We see that the language consists of all odd length palindrome strings over $\Sigma = \{a, b\}$ having $X$ as their middle symbol. This is a CFL with the grammar expressed as

$$S \to a\,S\,a \mid b\,S\,b \mid X$$

**Algorithm**

1. Push all symbols onto the stack till $X$ is read by the machine.
2. Beyond $X$, for every input symbol that is read, pop a symbol from the stack and check for the equality with the recently-read symbol.
3. If the symbol on the stack matches with the symbol read, then continue step 2; else, reject the string.
4. If the end of the input is reached, that is, the symbol read is ƀ, pop the symbol onto the top of the stack. If the symbol popped is also ƀ (indicates stack empty), then accept the input string; else, reject the string.

The DPDA based on this algorithm is constructed as shown in Fig. 6.13. The set of equations equivalent to the DPDA are given here:

The following six equations are responsible for pushing all $a$'s and $b$'s till the symbol $X$ has been read.

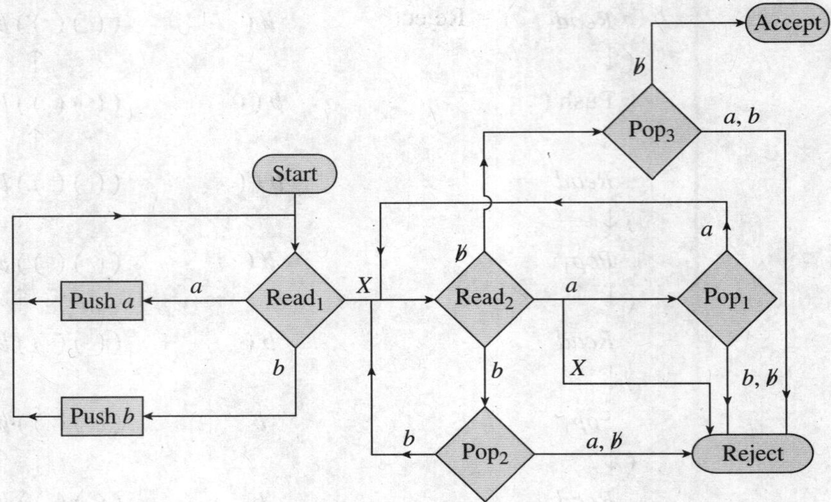


**Figure 6.13** PDA that accepts language $L$

$$\delta\,(Read_1, a, \not b) = (Read_1, a\not b)$$
$$\delta\,(Read_1, a, a) = (Read_1, aa)$$
$$\delta\,(Read_1, a, b) = (Read_1, ab)$$

$$\delta\,(Read_1, b, \not b) = (Read_1, b\not b)$$
$$\delta\,(Read_1, b, b) = (Read_1, bb)$$
$$\delta\,(Read_1, b, a) = (Read_1, ba)$$

The following three equations represent the case when the middle symbol $X$ is read. A transition is made from $Read_1$ state to the next state, $Read_2$, and the stack remains unchanged.

$$\delta\,(Read_1, X, a) = (Read_2, a)$$
$$\delta\,(Read_1, X, b) = (Read_2, b)$$
$$\delta\,(Read_1, X, \not b) = (Read_2, \not b)$$

Once the symbol $X$ is read, the steps are followed to match the remaining half of the input string to the first half, which is already present on the stack. This is expressed with the help of the following three equations:

If the symbol read is the same as the symbol on top of the stack, then it gets popped off.

$$\delta\,(Read_2, b, b) = (Read_2, \epsilon)$$
$$\delta\,(Read_2, a, a) = (Read_2, \epsilon)$$
$$\delta\,(Read_2, \not b, \not b) = \text{Accept}$$

The invalid input strings are rejected by the DPDA. This is expressed through the following equations:

$$\delta\,(Read_2, a, \not b) = \text{Reject}$$
$$\delta\,(Read_2, a, b) = \text{Reject}$$

$\delta\ (Read_2, b, \not b) = \text{Reject}$
$\delta\ (Read_2, b, a) = \text{Reject}$

$\delta\ (Read_2, \not b, b) = \text{Reject}$
$\delta\ (Read_2, \not b, a) = \text{Reject}$
$\delta\ (Read_2, X, b) = \text{Reject}$
$\delta\ (Read_2, X, a) = \text{Reject}$
$\delta\ (Read_2, X, \not b) = \text{Reject}$

### *Simulation*

Let us simulate the acceptance of the string '*abXba*'.

| Current state | Stack contents | Tape and head |
|---|---|---|
| Start | $\not b$ | $a\ b\ X\ b\ a\ \not b\ \not b\ \ldots$ |
| $\downarrow$ | | $\uparrow$ |
| $Read_1$ | $\not b$ | $a\ b\ X\ b\ a\ \not b\ \not b\ \ldots$ |
| $a \downarrow$ | | $\phantom{a\ }\uparrow$ |
| Push $a$ | $\not b\ a$ | $a\ b\ X\ b\ a\ \not b\ \not b\ \ldots$ |
| $\downarrow$ | | $\phantom{a\ }\uparrow$ |
| $Read_1$ | $\not b\ a$ | $a\ b\ X\ b\ a\ \not b\ \not b\ \ldots$ |
| $b \downarrow$ | | $\phantom{a\ b\ }\uparrow$ |
| Push $b$ | $\not b\ a\ b$ | $a\ b\ X\ b\ a\ \not b\ \not b\ \ldots$ |
| $\downarrow$ | | $\phantom{a\ b\ }\uparrow$ |
| $Read_1$ | $\not b\ a\ b$ | $a\ b\ X\ b\ a\ \not b\ \not b\ \ldots$ |
| $X \downarrow$ | | $\phantom{a\ b\ X\ }\uparrow$ |
| $Read_2$ | $\not b\ a\ b$ | $a\ b\ X\ b\ a\ \not b\ \not b\ \ldots$ |
| $b \downarrow$ | | $\phantom{a\ b\ X\ b\ }\uparrow$ |
| $Pop_2$ | $\not b\ a$ | $a\ b\ X\ b\ a\ \not b\ \not b\ \ldots$ |
| $b \downarrow$ | | $\phantom{a\ b\ X\ b\ }\uparrow$ |
| $Read_2$ | $\not b\ a$ | $a\ b\ X\ b\ a\ \not b\ \not b\ \ldots$ |
| $a \downarrow$ | | $\phantom{a\ b\ X\ b\ a\ }\uparrow$ |
| $Pop_1$ | $\not b$ | $a\ b\ X\ b\ a\ \not b\ \not b\ \ldots$ |
| $a \downarrow$ | | $\phantom{a\ b\ X\ b\ a\ }\uparrow$ |
| $Read_2$ | $\not b$ | $a\ b\ X\ b\ a\ \not b\ \not b\ \ldots$ |
| $\not b \downarrow$ | | $\phantom{a\ b\ X\ b\ a\ \not b\ }\uparrow$ |
| $Pop_3$ | — | $a\ b\ X\ b\ a\ \not b\ \not b\ \ldots$ |
| $\not b \downarrow$ | | $\phantom{a\ b\ X\ b\ a\ \not b\ }\uparrow$ |
| Accept | | |

## 6.6 DPDA VS NPDA

Consider a CFL that consists of all possible palindrome strings over $\Sigma = \{a, b\}$. Such a CFL can be expressed with the help of the following CFG:

$$S \rightarrow a\,S\,a \mid b\,S\,b \mid a \mid b \mid \epsilon \qquad (G)$$

Odd length palindrome strings over $\Sigma = \{a, b\}$ can be generated using the following grammar rules:

$$S \rightarrow a\,S\,a \mid b\,S\,b \mid a \mid b \qquad (G1)$$

This is obtained by replacing the middle symbol $X$ in the CFG we have seen in Example 6.5 by $a$ or $b$.

Similarly, all even length palindrome strings over $\Sigma = \{a, b\}$ can be generated using the following grammar rules:

$$S \rightarrow a\,S\,a \mid b\,S\,b \mid \epsilon \qquad (G2)$$

Here, the middle symbol $X$ in Example 6.5 is replaced by $\epsilon$.

We see that the grammar $G$ is a combination of the rules for odd as well as even length palindrome strings over $\Sigma = \{a, b\}$.

Using this grammar, and with the help of the following example, let us attempt to compare DPDA and NPDA.

---

**Example 6.6** Construct a PDA, which accepts the language denoted by the following grammar:

$$S \rightarrow a\,S\,a \mid b\,S\,b \mid a \mid b \mid \epsilon \qquad (G)$$

***Solution*** The given language consists of all possible palindrome strings over $\Sigma = \{a, b\}$.

The required PDA can be obtained by making the following changes in the DPDA shown in Fig. 6.13.

In Fig. 6.13, the middle symbol $X$ separates the first half of the string that is pushed onto the stack, from the second half that is used for comparison. If we wish to accept all odd length palindrome strings over $\Sigma = \{a, b\}$, this middle symbol $X$ must be replaced by either $a$ or $b$, as shown in grammar $G1$. Hence, the transition from $Read_1$ state to $Read_2$ state is changed either to symbol $a$ or $b$ (refer to Fig. 6.14).

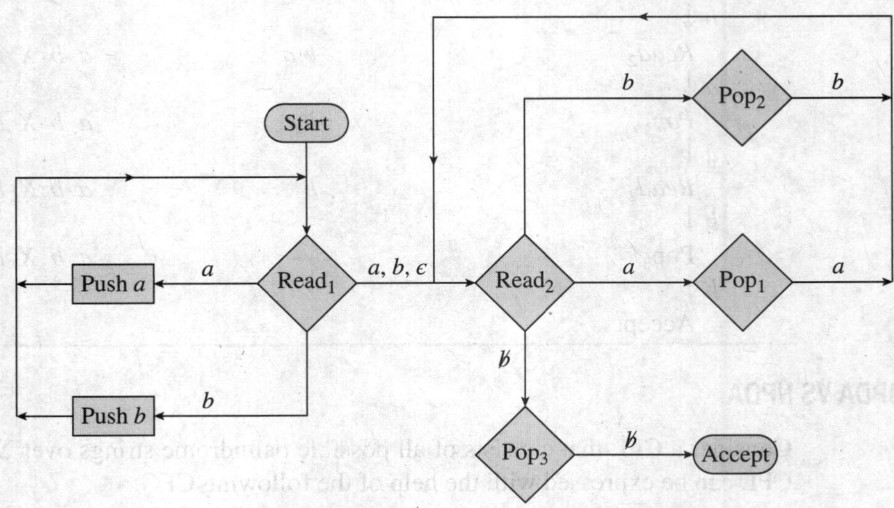


**Figure 6.14** NPDA that accepts all palindrome strings over $\Sigma = \{a, b\}$

Similarly, as per grammar $G2$, the middle symbol $X$ becomes $\epsilon$ for even length palindrome strings; hence, the transition from $Read_1$ state to $Read_2$ state. Therefore, in the required PDA (refer to Fig. 6.14), we change the symbol $X$ to $\epsilon$.

Thus, there are now three possible transitions from $Read_1$ to $Read_2$ depending on the input symbol read—$a$, $b$, or $\epsilon$.

Please note that the PDA that we have obtained in Fig. 6.14 is non-deterministic. Further, the rejection paths are not shown in the figure for further simplification. The NPDA in Fig. 6.14 can also be expressed using the equations mentioned here.

The following set of equations denotes the operation of pushing $a$'s or $b$'s onto the stack, till the mid-point is reached:

$$\left.\begin{aligned}
\delta\,(Read_1, a, \not{b}) &= (Read_1, a\not{b})\\
\delta\,(Read_1, a, a) &= (Read_1, aa)\\
\delta\,(Read_1, a, b) &= (Read_1, ab)\\
\delta\,(Read_1, b, \not{b}) &= (Read_1, b\not{b})\\
\delta\,(Read_1, b, b) &= (Read_1, bb)\\
\delta\,(Read_1, b, a) &= (Read_1, ba)
\end{aligned}\right\} \tag{6.1}$$

The following set of six equations ignores the middle symbol. The transition from $Read_1$ state to $Read_2$ state is made without changing the stack string.

$$\left.\begin{aligned}
\delta\,(Read_1, a, a) &= (Read_2, a)\\
\delta\,(Read_1, a, b) &= (Read_2, b)\\
\delta\,(Read_1, b, a) &= (Read_2, a)\\
\delta\,(Read_1, b, b) &= (Read_2, b)\\
\delta\,(Read_1, \epsilon, a) &= (Read_2, a)\\
\delta\,(Read_1, \epsilon, b) &= (Read_2, b)
\end{aligned}\right\} \tag{6.2}$$

The following three equations denote the process of matching the second half of the input string with the stacked symbols in order to check whether or not the string is a palindrome, and accept the string in case it is a palindrome.

$$\begin{aligned}
\delta\,(Read_2, b, b) &= (Read_2, \epsilon)\\
\delta\,(Read_2, a, a) &= (Read_2, \epsilon)\\
\delta\,(Read_2, \not{b}, \not{b}) &= \text{Accept}
\end{aligned}$$

We notice that Eq. sets (6.1) and (6.2) have some conflicting entries, which are mentioned here:

$$\delta\,(Read_1, a, a) = (Read_1, aa) \text{ from Eqs (6.1)}$$
$$\delta\,(Read_1, a, a) = (Read_2, a) \text{ from Eqs (6.2)}$$

This is because the PDA is non-deterministic.

We have already discussed in Section 6.3, the differences between the transition function $\delta$ in a DPDA and an NPDA.

The conflicting entries can be explained using the transition function $\delta$ of the NPDA, which is defined as

$$\delta: Q \times \{\Sigma \cup (\epsilon)\} \times \Gamma \rightarrow \text{finite subsets of } Q \times \Gamma^*$$

The aforementioned example of conflicting entries can formally be written as

$$\delta\,(Read_1, a, a) = \{(Read_1, aa), (Read_2, a)\}$$

Thus, the NPDA in Fig. 6.14 is capable of accepting the language of all palindrome strings over $= \{a, b\}$. We see that it is however not possible to build a DPDA for the same CFL, as we cannot really decide when the mid-point is reached, in order to match the two halves of the input string using a single stack.

***Simulation***

Let us see a possible simulation for the acceptance of the string '*aba*'.

| Current state | Stack contents | Tape and head |
|---|---|---|
| Start | $\not{b}$ | $a\ b\ a\ \not{b}\ \not{b}\ \ldots$ <br> ↑ |
| ↓ | | |
| $Read_1$ | $\not{b}$ | $a\ b\ a\ \not{b}\ \not{b}\ \ldots$ <br> ↑ |
| $a$ ↓ | | |
| Push $a$ | $\not{b}\ a$ | $a\ b\ a\ \not{b}\ \not{b}\ \ldots$ <br>   ↑ |
| ↓ | | |
| $Read_1$ | $\not{b}\ a$ | $a\ b\ a\ \not{b}\ \not{b}\ \ldots$ <br>   ↑ |
| $b$ ↓ | | |
| $Read_2$ | $\not{b}\ a$ | $a\ b\ a\ \not{b}\ \not{b}\ \ldots$ <br>     ↑ |
| $a$ ↓ | | |
| $Pop_1$ | $\not{b}$ | $a\ b\ a\ \not{b}\ \not{b}\ \ldots$ <br>     ↑ |
| $a$ ↓ | | |
| $Read_2$ | $\not{b}$ | $a\ b\ a\ \not{b}\ \not{b}\ \ldots$ <br>       ↑ |
| $\not{b}$ ↓ | | |
| $Pop_3$ | — | $a\ b\ a\ \not{b}\ \not{b}\ \ldots$ <br>       ↑ |
| $\not{b}$ ↓ | | |
| Accept | | |

Since NPDA is a possibilistic machine, the aforementioned simulation is one possible machine transition that leads to acceptance. This is interpreted considering the fact that $b$ is a mid-point of '*aba*'.

---

***Note***: No DPDA exists, which can accept the CFL expressed by the given grammar $G$. Thus, we can say that NPDA is more powerful than DPDA; NPDA accepts many more CFLs for which no DPDA can be built. In other words, the class of CFLs accepted by DPDA is a proper subset of the CFLs accepted by NPDA.

### 6.6.1 Relative Powers of DPDA/NPDA and NFA/DFA

From the aforementioned discussion, we can conclude that a language accepted by an NPDA may not be accepted by a DPDA. As a result, for every NPDA, there may not exist an equivalent DPDA. This is comparatively different from the NFA/DFA scenario.

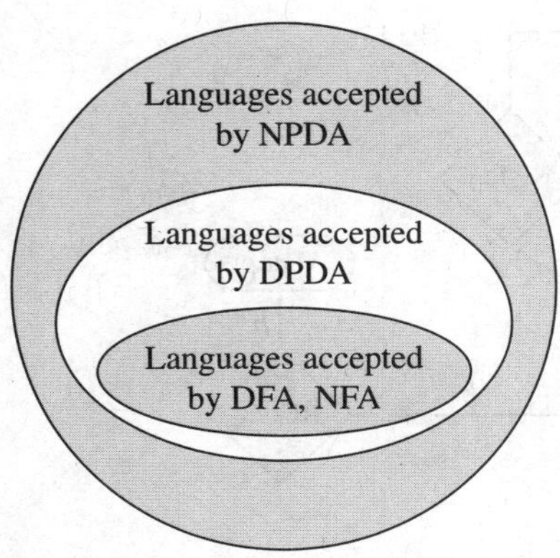


**Figure 6.15** Venn diagram explaining relative powers of DPDA/NPDA and DFA/NFA

Refer to the Venn diagram shown in Fig. 6.15 that depicts the relative powers of DFA, NFA, DPDA, and NPDA. Since, for every NFA there exists an equivalent DFA accepting the same regular language, we can say that DFA and NFA have equal powers. However, this does not hold true for PDAs—NPDA and DPDA have different capabilities. The NPDA can accept any CFL, while DPDA is a special case of NPDA that accepts only a subset of the CFLs accepted by the NPDA. Thus, DPDA is less powerful than NPDA.

## 6.7 EQUIVALENCE OF CFG AND PDA

So far in the examples, we have not directly used the CFG for building the PDA. Instead, we have used the language properties and a simple algorithm that uses a single stack to achieve the acceptance.

In this section, we shall discuss the algorithm to build an NPDA directly, based on the given CFG. This algorithm treats the NPDA mainly as a syntax analyser (or parser) that validates the input string based on the given grammar or CFG. Precisely, the NPDA is considered as a top-down parser, which uses leftmost derivation to generate the input string to be validated. The NPDA thus constructed uses the CFG to apply one grammar rule at a time and generates the input string, symbol by symbol. Each generated symbol is then matched with the input symbol read. If all the input symbols are matched, then the NPDA considers the input string as valid.

---

**Example 6.7** Construct a PDA that accepts the language generated by the following CFG:

$$S \rightarrow SS \mid (S) \mid (\,)$$

***Solution*** The required NPDA is constructed as shown in Fig. 6.16.

The algorithm is based on the leftmost derivation process as mentioned earlier. As we are aware, the leftmost derivation process involves replacing the leftmost non-terminal at every step by the right-hand side of the grammar rule. For example, if the provided grammar rule is of the form '$A \rightarrow \alpha$', then $A$ is replaced by $\alpha$. Further, whenever a terminal symbol is generated on the stack, an input symbol is read to match it.

**Algorithm**

1. Start with pushing the start symbol onto the stack.
2. After popping the start symbol, push the right-hand side of the production rule that is applicable in the leftmost derivation of the string onto the stack, but in the reverse way. Please note that the right-hand side of the production rule is pushed in the reverse order so as to receive the leftmost non-terminal symbol onto the top of the stack. In this way, the leftmost non-terminal symbol can be popped out of the stack and expanded further to achieve the leftmost derivation.
3. Whenever a terminal symbol is generated after popping from the stack, read an input symbol from the tape and check whether it matches the currently popped symbol.

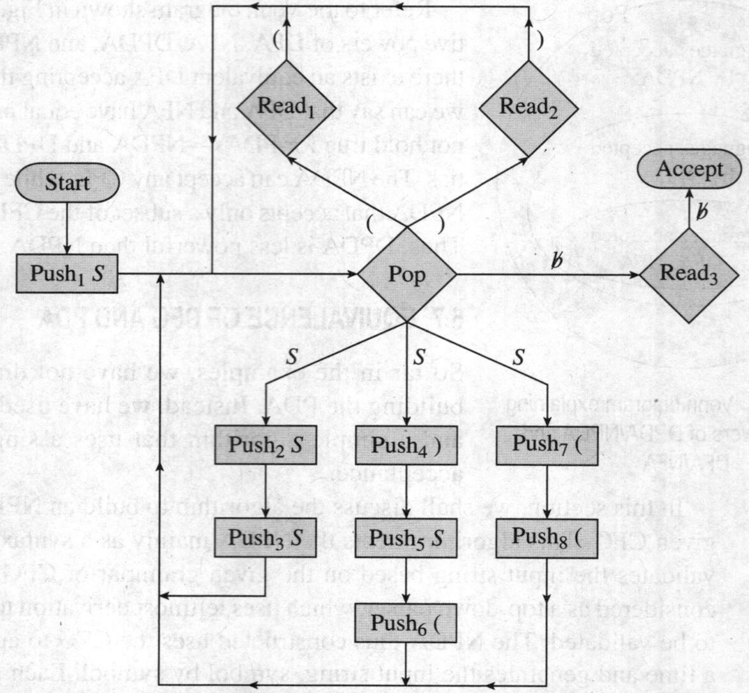


**Figure 6.16** NPDA that accepts the language generated by $S \rightarrow SS \mid (S) \mid (\ )$

4. Continue the process till the entire input string is consumed.
5. When the stack is empty, that is, the popped symbol is $\not b$, read the input. If the symbol read from the input stream is $\not b$ (indicates end of input), then declare acceptance. This also denotes that the input string is entirely derived using the NPDA and that the input string is syntactically valid.

***Simulation***

Let us simulate the working of the NPDA in Fig. 6.16 for the string '( ( ) ( ) )'.

Leftmost derivation for the string '( ( ) ( ) )' is:

$$
\begin{aligned}
S &\Rightarrow (\,S\,) \\
&\Rightarrow (\,S\,S\,) \\
&\Rightarrow (\,(\,)\,S\,) \\
&\Rightarrow (\,(\,)\,(\,)\,)
\end{aligned}
$$

We shall use this derivation for the simulation, as follows:

| Current state | Stack contents | Tape and head |
|---|---|---|
| Start | $\not b$ | ( ( ) ( ) ) $\not b$ $\not b$ … |
| ↓ | | ↑ |
| $\text{Push}_1\ S$ | $\not b\ S$ | ( ( ) ( ) ) $\not b$ $\not b$ … |
| ↓ | | ↑ |

| | | |
|---|---|---|
| Pop | b̸ | (( )( )) b̸ b̸ … |
| S ↓ | | ↑ |
| Push$_4$ ) | b̸ ) | (( )( )) b̸ b̸ … |
| ↓ | | ↑ |
| Push$_5$ *S* | b̸ ) *S* | (( )( )) b̸ b̸ … |
| ↓ | | ↑ |
| Push$_6$ ( | b̸ ) *S* ( | (( )( )) b̸ b̸ … |
| ↓ | | ↑ |
| *Pop* | b̸ ) *S* | (( )( )) b̸ b̸ … |
| ( ↓ | | ↑ |
| *Read*$_1$ | b̸ ) *S* | (( )( )) b̸ b̸ … |
| ( ↓ | | ↑ |
| *Pop* | b̸ ) | (( )( )) b̸ b̸ … |
| S ↓ | | ↑ |
| Push$_2$ *S* | b̸ ) *S* | (( )( )) b̸ b̸ … |
| S ↓ | | ↑ |
| Push$_3$ *S* | b̸ ) *SS* | (( )( )) b̸ b̸ … |
| ↓ | | ↑ |
| *Pop* | b̸ ) *S* | (( )( )) b̸ b̸ … |
| S ↓ | | ↑ |
| Push$_7$ ) | b̸ ) *S* ) | (( )( )) b̸ b̸ … |
| ↓ | | ↑ |
| Push$_8$ ( | b̸ ) *S* ) ( | (( )( )) b̸ b̸ … |
| ↓ | | ↑ |
| *Pop* | b̸ ) *S* ) | (( )( )) b̸ b̸ … |
| ( ↓ | | ↑ |
| *Read*$_1$ | b̸ ) *S* ) | (( )( )) b̸ b̸ … |
| ( ↓ | | ↑ |
| *Pop* | b̸ ) *S* | (( )( )) b̸ b̸ … |
| ) ↓ | | ↑ |
| *Read*$_2$ | b̸ ) *S* | (( )( )) b̸ b̸ … |
| ) ↓ | | ↑ |
| *Pop* | b̸ ) | (( )( )) b̸ b̸ … |
| S ↓ | | ↑ |
| Push$_7$ ) | b̸ )) | (( )( )) b̸ b̸ … |
| ↓ | | ↑ |
| Push$_8$ ( | b̸ )) ( | (( )( )) b̸ b̸ … |
| ↓ | | ↑ |
| *Pop* | b̸ )) | (( )( )) b̸ b̸ … |
| ( ↓ | | ↑ |
| *Read*$_1$ | b̸ )) | (( )( )) b̸ b̸ … |
| ( ↓ | | ↑ |
| *Pop* | b̸ ) | (( )( )) b̸ b̸ … |
| ) ↓ | | ↑ |

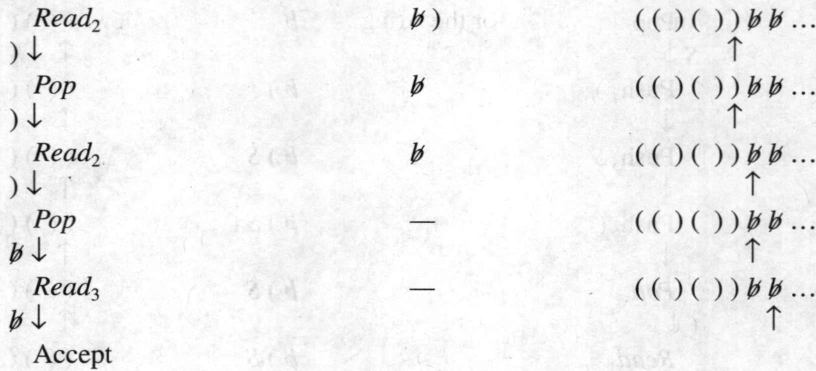

| | | |
|---|---|---|
| *Read*$_2$ | $\not b$ ) | ( ( ) ( ) ) $\not b$ $\not b$ ... ↑ |
| ) ↓ | | |
| *Pop* | $\not b$ | ( ( ) ( ) ) $\not b$ $\not b$ ... ↑ |
| ) ↓ | | |
| *Read*$_2$ | $\not b$ | ( ( ) ( ) ) $\not b$ $\not b$ ... ↑ |
| ) ↓ | | |
| *Pop* | — | ( ( ) ( ) ) $\not b$ $\not b$ ... ↑ |
| $\not b$ ↓ | | |
| *Read*$_3$ | — | ( ( ) ( ) ) $\not b$ $\not b$ ... ↑ |
| $\not b$ ↓ | | |
| Accept | | |

**Example 6.8** Construct a PDA that accepts the language generated by the grammar

$$S \to S + S \mid S * S \mid 4$$

***Solution*** The required NPDA is constructed as shown in Fig. 6.17.

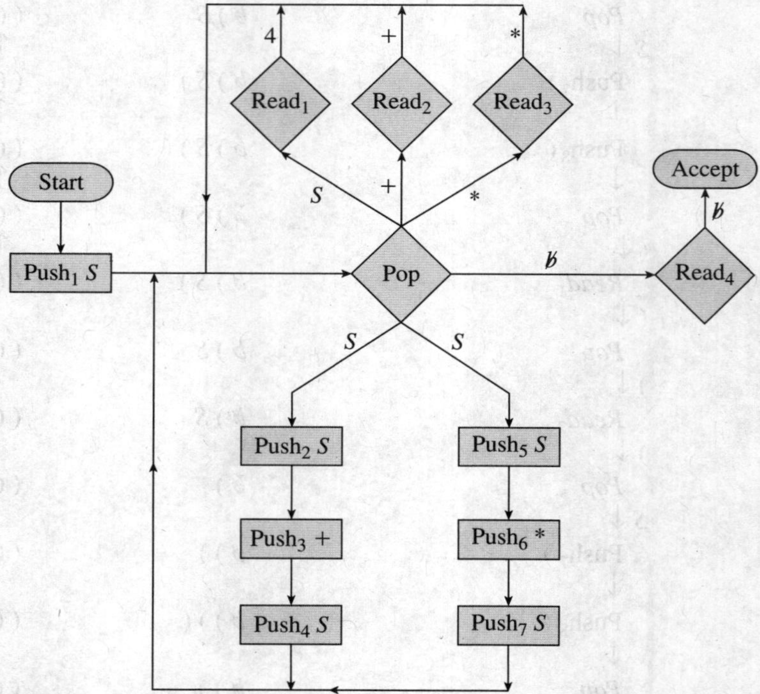


**Figure 6.17** NPDA that accepts the language generated by $S \to S + S \mid S * S \mid 4$

### *Simulation*

Let us simulate the working of the NPDA that we have constructed for the string '4 + 4 * 4'

Leftmost derivation for the string '4 + 4 * 4' is as follows:

$$\begin{aligned} S &\Rightarrow S + S \\ &\Rightarrow 4 + S \\ &\Rightarrow 4 + S * S \\ &\Rightarrow 4 + 4 * S \\ &\Rightarrow 4 + 4 * 4 \end{aligned}$$

Based on the leftmost derivation, the simulation for the acceptance of the string '4 + 4 * 4' is as follows:

| Current state | Stack contents | Tape and head | | | | | | | | |
|---|---|---|---|---|---|---|---|---|---|---|
| Start | ƀ | 4 | + | 4 | * | 4 | ƀ | ƀ | ... |
| ↓ | | ↑ | | | | | | | |
| Push$_1$ $S$ | ƀ $S$ | 4 | + | 4 | * | 4 | ƀ | ƀ | ... |
| ↓ | | ↑ | | | | | | | |
| *Pop* | ƀ | 4 | + | 4 | * | 4 | ƀ | ƀ | ... |
| $S$ ↓ | | ↑ | | | | | | | |
| Push$_2$ $S$ | ƀ $S$ | 4 | + | 4 | * | 4 | ƀ | ƀ | ... |
| $S$ ↓ | | ↑ | | | | | | | |
| Push$_3$ + | ƀ $S$ + | 4 | + | 4 | * | 4 | ƀ | ƀ | ... |
| ↓ | | ↑ | | | | | | | |
| Push$_4$ $S$ | ƀ $S$ + $S$ | 4 | + | 4 | * | 4 | ƀ | ƀ | ... |
| ↓ | | ↑ | | | | | | | |
| *Pop* | ƀ $S$ + | 4 | + | 4 | * | 4 | ƀ | ƀ | ... |
| $S$ ↓ | | ↑ | | | | | | | |
| *Read*$_1$ | ƀ $S$ + | 4 | + | 4 | * | 4 | ƀ | ƀ | ... |
| 4 ↓ | | | ↑ | | | | | | |
| *Pop* | ƀ $S$ | 4 | + | 4 | * | 4 | ƀ | ƀ | ... |
| + ↓ | | | ↑ | | | | | | |
| *Read*$_2$ | ƀ $S$ | 4 | + | 4 | * | 4 | ƀ | ƀ | ... |
| + ↓ | | | | ↑ | | | | | |
| *Pop* | ƀ | 4 | + | 4 | * | 4 | ƀ | ƀ | ... |
| $S$ ↓ | | | | ↑ | | | | | |
| Push$_5$ $S$ | ƀ $S$ | 4 | + | 4 | * | 4 | ƀ | ƀ | ... |
| ↓ | | | | ↑ | | | | | |
| Push$_6$ * | ƀ $S$* | 4 | + | 4 | * | 4 | ƀ | ƀ | ... |
| ↓ | | | | ↑ | | | | | |
| Push$_7$ $S$ | ƀ $S$ * $S$ | 4 | + | 4 | * | 4 | ƀ | ƀ | ... |
| ↓ | | | | ↑ | | | | | |
| *Pop* | ƀ $S$ * | 4 | + | 4 | * | 4 | ƀ | ƀ | ... |
| $S$ ↓ | | | | ↑ | | | | | |
| *Read*$_1$ | ƀ $S$ * | 4 | + | 4 | * | 4 | ƀ | ƀ | ... |
| 4 ↓ | | | | | ↑ | | | | |

| | | |
|---|---|---|
| *Pop* | $\not{b}\, S$ | $4 + 4 * 4 \not{b}\ \not{b} \ldots$ |
| $* \downarrow$ | | ↑ |
| *Read*$_3$ | $\not{b}\, S$ | $4 + 4 * 4 \not{b}\ \not{b} \ldots$ |
| $* \downarrow$ | | ↑ |
| *Pop* | $\not{b}$ | $4 + 4 * 4 \not{b}\ \not{b} \ldots$ |
| $S \downarrow$ | | ↑ |
| *Read*$_1$ | $\not{b}$ | $4 + 4 * 4 \not{b}\ \not{b} \ldots$ |
| $4 \downarrow$ | | ↑ |
| *Pop* | — | $4 + 4 * 4 \not{b}\ \not{b} \ldots$ |
| $\not{b} \downarrow$ | | ↑ |
| *Read*$_4$ | — | $4 + 4 * 4 \not{b}\ \not{b} \ldots$ |
| $\not{b} \downarrow$ | | ↑ |
| Accept | | |

### 6.7.1 NPDA Construction using Chomsky Normal Form

As we know, Chomsky normal form (CNF) mandates only two forms of production rules:

1. $S \to AB$
2. $S \to a$

Production rule of type 1 has exactly two non-terminals on the right-hand side, while the production rule of type 2 contains a single terminal symbol at the right-hand side.

In the previous two examples, we observe that even the terminal symbols are pushed onto the stack and again popped to match the input symbols. The complexity of this algorithm can be reduced using CNF. If we express the grammar in CNF, then the production rule of type 1 is used to push the right-hand side onto the stack, while the rule of type 2 is directly used to match the input symbols from the tap. This has two benefits:

1. Terminals are not pushed onto the stack.
2. At most, two non-terminal symbols are pushed onto the stack at every step in the derivation process.

This in turn helps control the stack growth, which as we have seen, is much more without CNF. On the other hand, grammar without CNF may have multiple symbols on the right-hand side of production rules.

**Example 6.9** Construct a PDA that accepts the following language:

$$L = \{a^{2n} \mid n > 0\}$$

***Solution*** The CFG for the given language can be written as

$$S \to SS \mid aa$$

Let us express the grammar in CNF:

$$S \to SS \mid AA$$
$$A \to a$$

The NPDA is constructed using the CFG expressed in CNF as shown in Fig. 6.18.

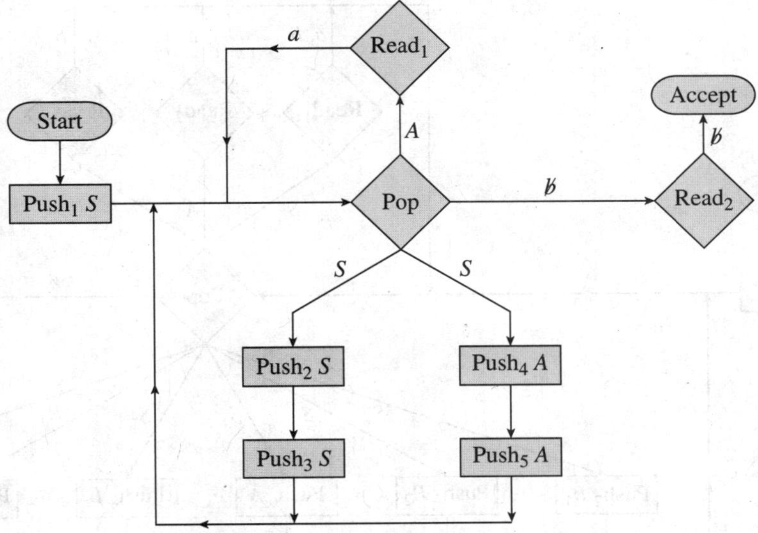


**Figure 6.18** NPDA that accepts $\{a^{2n} \mid n > 0\}$

We see from Fig. 6.18 that in the grammar expressed in CNF, no terminal gets pushed onto the stack.

---

**Example 6.10** Construct a PDA that accepts all palindrome strings over $\Sigma = \{a, b\}$.

***Solution*** This is the same as Example 6.6 that we solved earlier. Let us apply the CNF and then compare the efficiency of the resultant PDA.

The CFG for the language is defined as

$$S \rightarrow a\,S\,a \mid b\,S\,b \mid a \mid b \mid \epsilon$$

Removing the $\epsilon$-production, the grammar can be written as

$$S \rightarrow a\,S\,a \mid b\,S\,b \mid a \mid b \mid a\,a \mid b\,b$$

Now, let us convert this grammar to CNF:

$$S \rightarrow A\,S\,A \mid B\,S\,B \mid A\,A \mid B\,B \mid a \mid b$$
$$A \rightarrow a$$
$$B \rightarrow b$$

Therefore, the final CFG expressed in the CNF, which can be considered for constructing the required PDA is as follows:

$$S \rightarrow A\,R_1 \mid B\,R_2 \mid A\,A \mid B\,B \mid a \mid b$$
$$R_1 \rightarrow SA$$
$$R_2 \rightarrow SB$$
$$A \rightarrow a$$
$$B \rightarrow b$$

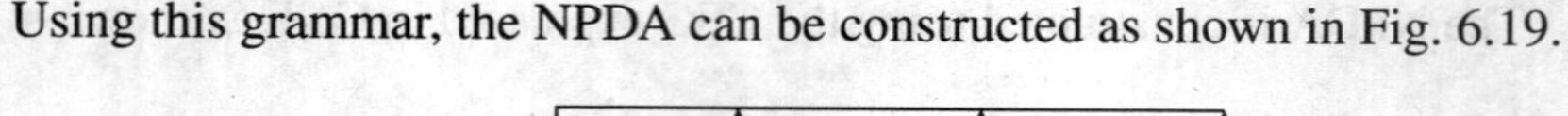
Using this grammar, the NPDA can be constructed as shown in Fig. 6.19.

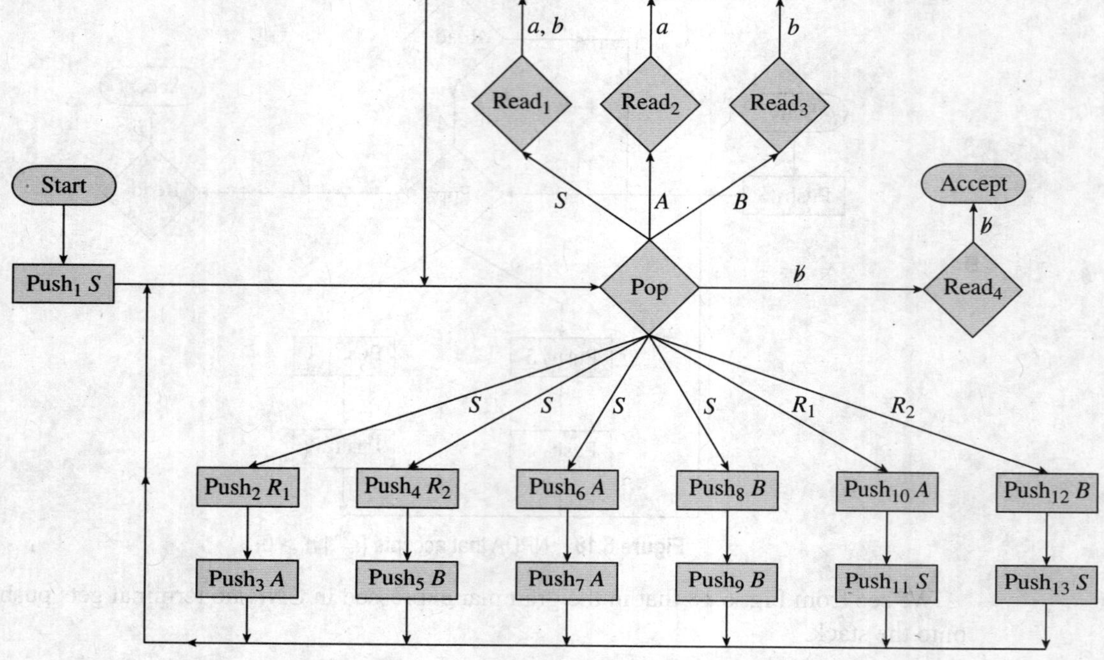


**Figure 6.19** NPDA that accepts all palindrome strings

### *Simulation*

Let us simulate the working of the NPDA in Fig. 6.19 for the string '*aba*'.

| Current state | Stack contents | Tape and head |
|---|---|---|
| Start | $\not b$ | $a\ b\ a\ \not b\ \not b \ldots$ |
| ↓ | | ↑ |
| Push$_1$ $S$ | $\not b\, S$ | $a\ b\ a\ \not b\ \not b \ldots$ |
| ↓ | | ↑ |
| *Pop* | $\not b$ | $a\ b\ a\ \not b\ \not b \ldots$ |
| $S$ ↓ | | ↑ |
| Push$_2$ $R_1$ | $\not b\, R_1$ | $a\ b\ a\ \not b\ \not b \ldots$ |
| ↓ | | ↑ |
| Push$_3$ $A$ | $\not b\, R_1 A$ | $a\ b\ a\ \not b\ \not b \ldots$ |
| ↓ | | ↑ |
| *Pop* | $\not b\, R_1$ | $a\ b\ a\ \not b\ \not b \ldots$ |
| $A$ ↓ | | ↑ |
| *Read$_2$* | $\not b\, R_1$ | $a\ b\ a\ \not b\ \not b \ldots$ |
| $a$ ↓ | | ↑ |
| *Pop* | $\not b$ | $a\ b\ a\ \not b\ \not b \ldots$ |
| $R_1$ ↓ | | ↑ |

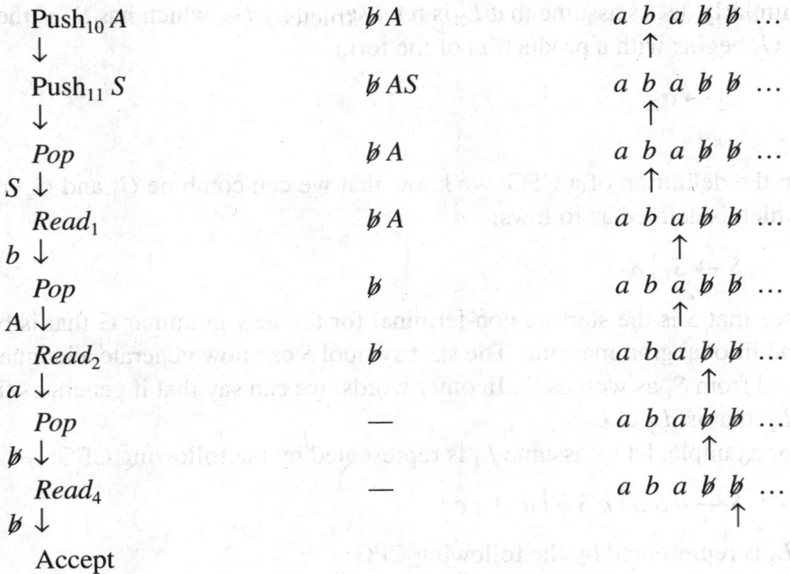


This simulation is based on the following leftmost derivation:

$$
\begin{aligned}
S &\Rightarrow \underline{A}\, R_1 \\
&\Rightarrow a\, \underline{R_1} \\
&\Rightarrow a\, \underline{S}\, A \\
&\Rightarrow a\, b\, \underline{A} \\
&\Rightarrow a\, b\, a
\end{aligned}
$$

## 6.8 CLOSURE PROPERTIES OF CFLs

Context-free languages (CFLs), like RLs, are also closed under union, concatenation, and Kleene closure. Let us attempt to prove these facts using CFG and PDA concepts.

**Theorem 6.1**

If $L_1$ and $L_2$ are CFLs, then their union '$L_1 \cup L_2$' is also a CFL. In other words, *CFLs are closed under union.*

*Proof*

Let us consider two context-free languages, $L_1$ and $L_2$. This means that these languages can be represented using context-free grammars (CFGs).

Let us assume that $L_1$ is represented by the CFG $G_1$, which has $S_1$ as its starting non-terminal (or start symbol). Hence, $G_1$ begins with a production of the form

$$S_1 \rightarrow \alpha_1$$

…

Similarly, let us assume that $L_2$ is represented by $G_2$, which has $S_2$ as the start symbol; then $G_2$ begins with a production of the form

$$S_2 \rightarrow \alpha_2$$
$$\ldots$$

From the definition of a CFG, we know that we can combine $G_1$ and $G_2$ into a grammar $G$, which is defined as follows:

$$S \rightarrow S_1 \mid S_2$$

We see that $S$ is the starting non-terminal for the new grammar $G$ that is built with only one additional grammar rule. The start symbol $S$ can now generate a language that can be derived from $S_1$ as well as $S_2$. In other words, we can say that it generates the union of $L_1$ and $L_2$, that is, $L_1 \cup L_2$.

For example, let us assume $L_1$ is represented by the following CFG:

$$S \rightarrow a\,S\,a \mid b\,S\,b \mid a \mid b \mid \epsilon$$

and $L_2$ is represented by the following CFG:

$$S \rightarrow a\,S\,b \mid \epsilon$$

Then, the CFG for '$L_1 \cup L_2$' is defined as

$$S \rightarrow S_1 \mid S_2$$
$$S_1 \rightarrow a\,S_1\,a \mid b\,S_1\,b \mid a \mid b \mid \epsilon$$
$$S_2 \rightarrow a\,S_2\,b \mid \epsilon$$

We can also prove this closure property by constructing individual PDAs for $L_1$ and $L_2$ and combining the two to form an NPDA with a new 'start' state having two outgoing edges, each incident onto the start states of these PDAs. Thus, the resulting NPDA accepts a language, which is also a CFL, and equal to '$L_1 \cup L_2$'.

**Theorem 6.2**

If $L_1$ and $L_2$ are CFLs, then their concatenation '$L_1 \cdot L_2$' is also a CFL. In other words, *CFLs are closed under concatenation.*

*Proof*

Let us consider two context-free languages, $L_1$ and $L_2$ that can be represented using CFGs.

Let us assume that $L_1$ is represented by the CFG $G_1$, which has $S_1$ as its starting non-terminal (or start symbol). Hence, $G_1$ begins with a production of the form

$$S_1 \rightarrow \alpha_1$$
$$\ldots$$

Similarly, if we assume that $L_2$ is represented by the CFG $G_2$, which has $S_2$ as the start symbol, then $G_2$ begins with a production of the form

$$S_2 \rightarrow \alpha_2$$
$$\ldots$$

From the definition of a CFG, we know that we can combine $G_1$ and $G_2$ into $G$, which is described as follows:

$$S \rightarrow S_1\, S_2$$

We see that $S$ is the starting non-terminal for the new grammar $G$ that is built with only one additional grammar rule. Now, $S$ can generate a language that is the concatenation of $L_1$ and $L_2$, that is, '$L_1 \cdot L_2$'.

Let us assume that $L_1$ is represented by the CFG

$$S \rightarrow a\,S\,a \mid b\,S\,b \mid a \mid b \mid \epsilon$$

and $L_2$ is represented by the CFG

$$S \rightarrow a\,S\,b \mid \epsilon$$

The CFG for '$L_1 \cdot L_2$' is defined as

$$S \rightarrow S_1\, S_2$$
$$S_1 \rightarrow a\,S_1\,a \mid b\,S_1\,b \mid a \mid b \mid \epsilon$$
$$S_2 \rightarrow a\,S_2\,b \mid \epsilon$$

This can be represented using two individual PDA for $L_1$ and $L_2$ respectively such that the final state of the PDA for $L_1$ is merged with the start state of the PDA for $L_2$.

**Theorem 6.3**

If $L$ is a CFL, then $L^*$ (Kleene closure of $L$) is also a CFL. In other words, *CFLs are closed under Kleene closure.*

*Proof*

Let us assume that $L$ is represented by a CFG $G$ that has a starting non-terminal $S$ and is defined as follows:

$$S \rightarrow \alpha$$
$$\ldots$$

Let us construct a grammar $G_1$ having starting symbol $S_1$ with the following production rules:

$$S_1 \rightarrow S\,S_1 \mid \epsilon$$

Thus, $G_1$ can generate a language obtained from repetitive concatenation of $L$. The resultant language is thus obtained by concatenating $L$ to itself zero or more times; this is the same as $L^*$.

For example, let the CFG for language $L$ be defined as

$$S \rightarrow a\,S\,a \mid b\,S\,b \mid a \mid b \mid \epsilon$$

then, the CFG for $L^*$ is

$$S_1 \rightarrow S\,S_1 \mid \epsilon$$
$$S \rightarrow a\,S\,a \mid b\,S\,b \mid a \mid b \mid \epsilon$$

We can represent $L$ by a PDA. If we combine the start state and the final state of this PDA, it will represent the PDA for $L^*$.

## 6.9 ADDITIONAL PDA EXAMPLES

In this section, let us discuss some more examples on the construction of PDA.

---

**Example 6.11** Construct a PDA that recognizes the following language:

$$\{a^n x \mid n \geq 0, x \in \{a, b\}^* \text{ and } |x| \leq n\}$$

***Solution*** We see that for the given language, it is not possible to determine where the string of $a$'s—that is, $a^n$—ends, and the string $x$ starts. This is because $x$ also consists of $a$'s. Hence, we design an NPDA as shown in Fig. 6.20.

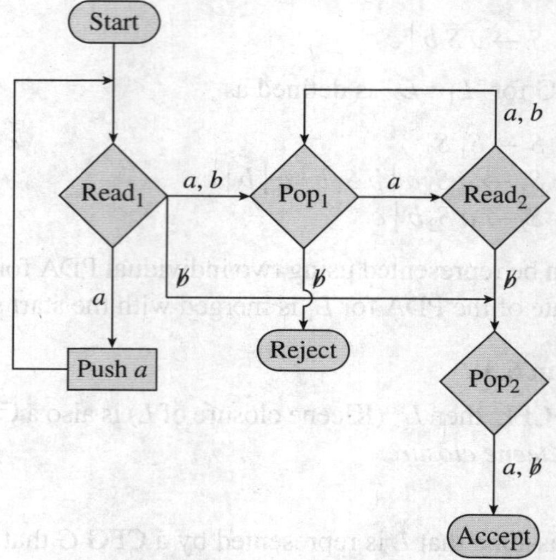


**Figure 6.20** NPDA that accepts $\{a^n x \mid n \geq 0, x \in \{a, b\}^* \text{ and } |x| \leq n\}$

**Algorithm**

1. Push all $a$'s onto the stack till we reach the beginning of $x$. (Remember that $x$ may start with either $a$ or $b$. Determinism is impossible to achieve if $x$ starts with $a$).
2. Read one symbol from $x$—either $a$ or $b$—and pop one $a$ from the stack.
3. Continue the process till you reach the end of the input.
4. When the input ends, that is, when you read b̸ on the tape, the stack may either be empty (if $|x| = n$) or may have a few $a$'s left (if $|x| < n$).
5. In either case, the stack cannot be empty before the input ends, as $|x| > n$ is not allowed. Hence, in such a case, the input string should be rejected.

---

**Example 6.12** Construct a PDA for the language described as follows:
The set of all strings over alphabet $\{a, b\}$ with exactly equal number of $a$'s and $b$'s.

***Solution*** We need to consider the fact that the string might begin with either $a$ or $b$. Therefore, pushing only $a$'s or only $b$'s will not work. We need to push whenever the stack is empty or the top of the stack carries the same symbol as the one just read. Refer to the algorithm that follows. The required DPDA is depicted in Fig. 6.21.

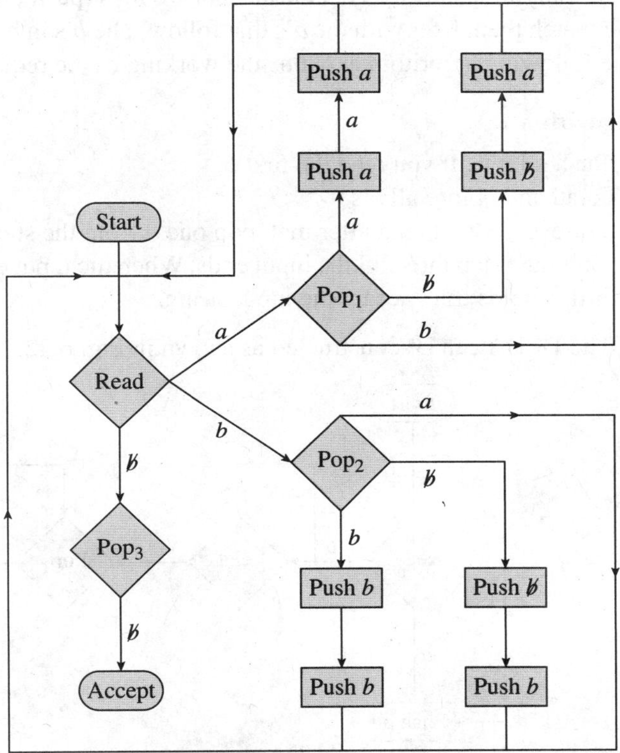


**Figure 6.21** DPDA that accepts equal number of *a*'s and *b*'s

**Algorithm**

1. Read a symbol, either *a* or *b*.
2. If the stack is empty, that is, the top of the stack top contains ƀ, push the symbol that has been read.
3. If the top of the stack contains the same symbol as the symbol that has been read, then also push this symbol.
4. If the top of the stack carries a symbol that is different from what has been read—for example, if the symbol read is *a* and the top of the stack contains *b*, or vice versa—pop the symbol onto the top of the stack. This contributes to matching *a*'s with *b*'s, or vice versa.
5. Continue with the aforementioned four steps until the input string ends, that is, until you read ƀ on the tape.
6. When the input string ends, then the top of this stack should be ƀ. If this holds true, then accept the input string.

**Example 6.13** Construct a PDA that accepts the language $L = \{a^n\, b^m\, a^n \mid m, n \geq 1\}$.

***Solution*** For this language, we need to match the number of $a$'s at the beginning and the end of any input string. This means that we must push all the $a$'s before the string of $b$'s and match them later with the $a$'s that follow. The $b$'s in between can be read and ignored. The following algorithm explains the working of the required PDA.

**Algorithm**

1. Push all $a$'s till you read the first $b$.
2. Read and ignore all $b$'s.
3. For every $a$ you read after that, pop one $a$ from the stack.
4. Continue step three till the input ends. When the input ends, the stack should be empty; if this holds true, accept the input string.

The DPDA can be constructed as shown in Fig. 6.22.

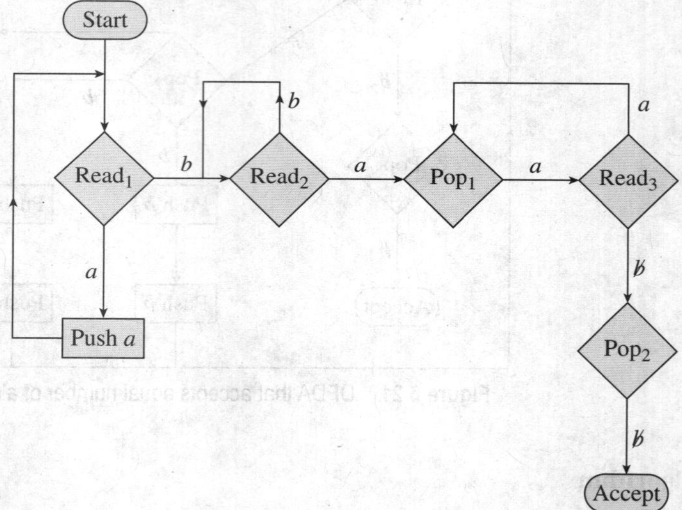


**Figure 6.22** PDA that accepts $a^n b^m a^n$

## SUMMARY

A pushdown stack-memory machine (PDM) is a computational model that we can use to solve any problem that has an algorithmic solution and requires a single stack memory.

A PDM accepts or recognizes regular languages (RLs) as well as context-free languages (CFLs).

Since the set of RLs is a proper subset of the class of CFLs, for every finite state machine (FSM), there exists an equivalent PDM, but not vice versa. Hence, a PDM is more powerful than the FSM due to its infinite memory in the form of an external stack.

Most commonly, a PDM is represented with the help of a flowchart-like diagram. Its formalism is obtained using a pushdown automaton (PDA), which is the mathematical model of a PDM.

A pushdown automaton $M$ is denoted as

$$M = (Q, \Sigma, \Gamma, \delta, q_0, Z_0, F)$$

where,

$Q$: Finite set of states
$\Sigma$: Input alphabet (input strings are composed of the symbols from $\Sigma$)
$\Gamma$: Stack alphabet
$q_0$: Initial state; $q_0 \in Q$
$Z_0$: $Z_0 \in \Gamma$ is a particular stack symbol called the start symbol, usually considered as a blank character $\not{b}$ in many designs.
$F$: Set of final states; $F \subseteq Q$

The $\delta$ function for deterministic PDA or DPDA is defined as

$$\delta: Q \times \Sigma \times \Gamma \rightarrow Q \times \Gamma^*$$

The $\delta$ function for non-deterministic PDA or NPDA is defined as

$$\delta: Q \times \{\Sigma \cup (\epsilon)\} \times \Gamma \rightarrow \text{finite subsets of } Q \times \Gamma^*$$

In the case of a DPDA, the transition function $\delta$ ($q$, $a$, $Z$) does not contain more than one element for any state $q$ in $Q$, any symbol $Z$ in $\Gamma$ on top of the stack, and any input symbol $a$ in $\Sigma$. Thus, the transition would be of the form

$$\delta\,(q, a, Z) = (p, \gamma)$$

where, $p$ is the unique next state in $Q$ to which the machine makes the transition, and $\gamma$ is a member of $\Gamma^*$(zero or more occurrences of symbols from $\Gamma$), and can be one of the following:

1. Empty, that is, $\epsilon$, if the stack operation performed is 'pop'. This means that $Z$ is popped out of the stack.
2. $Z$, if the stack is not updated; only a state transition is performed.
3. '$xx...xxZ$', if multiple symbols '$xx...xx$' are pushed onto the stack.
4. '$xx...xx$', if $Z$ is popped out of the stack and multiple symbols '$xx...xx$' are pushed onto the stack.

An NPDA performs any one of the multiple actions available for an input symbol read and the same stack symbol that is on top of the stack. Hence, NPDA is a possibilistic machine.

For example, let us consider the following transition:

$$\delta\,(q, a, Z) = \{(p_1, \gamma_1), (p_2, \gamma_2), \ldots, (p_m, \gamma_m)\},$$

where, $q, p_1, p_2, \ldots, p_m$ are states in $Q$, $a$ is any input symbol in $\Sigma$, $Z$ is any stack symbol in $\Gamma$, and all $\gamma_i$, for $1 \leq i \leq m$, are members of $\Gamma^*$.

The NPDA accepts the entire class of CFLs, while DPDA cannot be constructed to accept a few CFLs. Hence, DPDA is less powerful than NPDA. In other words, DPDA can only accept a subset of the class of CFLs. We see that this is slightly different from the finite automata (FA) scenario, where non-deterministic FA (NFA) is equivalent in power to the deterministic FA (DFA). Thus, for every NFA we can construct an equivalent DFA; however, every NPDA cannot be transformed into an equivalent DPDA.

There exists an algorithm to automatically build an NPDA from the given context-free grammar (CFG). The NPDA thus built is more like a simple top-down parser, which uses the leftmost derivation to regenerate the input string and check its validity. If it can generate all the input symbols in the same order as in the input string using the given CFG, it is considered to be a valid input string for the parser.

If a parser is generated using a CFG, which is expressed in Chomsky normal form (CNF), it has the advantage of controlled stack growth. It is also more efficient since no terminal symbol gets unnecessarily pushed onto the stack.

Context-free languages (CFLs) are closed under these operations—union, concatenation, and Kleene closure.

## EXERCISES

This section lists a few unsolved problems to help the readers understand the topic better and practise a few examples on PDA construction.

### Objective Questions

(L) 6.1 If $L$ is a language generated by the grammar $S \to 0\,S\,0 \mid 00$, which of the following statements is true?
(a) It is possible to construct a DPDA that accepts the language $L$.
(b) It is not possible to construct a DPDA that accepts the language $L$.
(c) It is not possible to construct an NPDA that accepts the language $L$.
(d) It is not possible to construct a PDA that accepts the language $L$.

(L) 6.2 We are given a language $L = \{0^{2n} \mid n > 0\}$. Consider the following statements:
$S1$: One can construct a DFA that accepts the language $L$
$S2$: One can construct a DPDA that accepts the language $L$
$S3$: One can construct a PDA that accepts the language $L$
Which of the following statements is correct?
(a) Only $S1$ is correct
(b) Only $S2$ is correct
(c) Only $S3$ is correct
(d) $S1$ and $S2$ are correct
(e) $S1$ and $S3$ are correct
(f) $S2$ and $S3$ are correct
(g) All three are correct
(h) None are correct

(U) 6.3 Which of the following statements is true?
(a) If a language is context-free, it can always be accepted by a deterministic pushdown automaton.
(b) The union of two context-free languages is also a context-free language.
(c) The intersection of two context-free languages is also a context-free language.
(d) The complement of a context-free language is also a context-free language.

(R) 6.4 The language accepted by a PDA is called a __________ language.

(U) 6.5 State whether the following statements are true or false.
(a) DPDA and NPDA are equivalent machines.
(b) For every NFA there exists an equivalent DFA.
(c) A PDA cannot accept regular languages.
(d) Only an NPDA accepts all CFLs.

(R) 6.6 CNF means __________.

(U) 6.7 Context-free languages are closed under which of the following?
(a) Union, intersection
(b) Union, Kleene closure
(c) Intersection, complement
(d) Complement, Kleene closure

(U) 6.8 Context-free languages are
(a) closed under union
(b) closed under complementation
(c) closed under intersection
(d) All of these

(L) 6.9 Which of the following languages are accepted by a DPDA?
(i) $L = \{a^n\, b^n \mid n = 0, 1, 2, \ldots\}$
(ii) The set of palindromes over alphabet $\{a, b\}$
(iii) $L = \{a^n\, b^m\, c^{2m} \mid n, m \geq 0\}$
(a) Only (i)
(b) Only (ii)
(c) (i) and (iii)
(d) All of these
(e) None of these

(U) 6.10 With respect to the power of recognition of languages, which of the following statements is false?
(a) Non-deterministic finite-state automata are equivalent to deterministic finite state automata.
(b) Non-deterministic pushdown automata are equivalent to deterministic pushdown automata.

(c) Non-deterministic Turing machines are equivalent to deterministic pushdown automata.
(d) Non-deterministic Turing machines are equivalent to deterministic Turing machines.

(U) 6.11 If $L1$ is a CFL and $L2$ is an RL, which of the following is false?
(a) $(L1 = L2)$ is not a CFL.
(b) $L1 \cap L2$ is a CFL.
(c) $\sim L2$ (complement of $L2$) is a CFL.
(d) $\sim L1$ (complement of $L1$) is an RL.

(U) 6.12 Every regular language is also context-free. Is this statement true or false?

## Review Questions

(A) 6.1 Convert the given FA, $M = \{(q_0, q_1, q_2), (0, 1), \delta, (q_0), (q_2)\}$ into its equivalent PDA; the transition function $\delta$ for $M$ is defined as

| | 0 | 1 |
|---|---|---|
| $q_0$ | $q_0$ | $q_1$ |
| $q_1$ | $q_1$ | $q_2$ |
| $q_2$ | $q_2$ | $q_2$ |

(L) 6.2 Discuss the relative powers of DPDA and NPDA.

(A) 6.3 Construct a PDA that accepts the language defined by the following regular grammar:
$S \to 0\,A \mid 1\,B \mid 0$
$A \to A\,0 \mid B$
$B \to c \mid d$
Here, $N = \{S, A, B\}$, $T = \{0, 1, c, d\}$, and $S$ is the start symbol.

(U) 6.4 With the help of PDAs, show that context-free languages are closed under union, concatenation, and Kleene closure.

(R) 6.5 Give the formal definition of PDA.

(E) 6.6 Construct a PDA (or NPDA) that accepts the language over $\Sigma = \{a, b\}$ and is defined as $L = \{a^n b^n \mid n = 0, 1, 2 \ldots\}$.
Simulate the working of this PDA (or NPDA) for the inputs:
(a) *aaabbb* (b) *aab* (c) *aaa*

(L) 6.7 Which machine accepts the language of palindromes, FSM or PDM? Justify your answer.

(A) 6.8 Construct a PDA equivalent to the following CFG:
$S \to 0\,A\,1 \mid 0\,B\,A$
$A \to S\,0\,1 \mid 0$
$B \to 1\,B \mid 1$

(A) 6.9 Give the graphical representation of the language generated by the following CFG:
$S \to S + S \mid S * S \mid 4$
Show the stack and tape contents for the expression: '4 + 4 * 4'.

(A) 6.10 Construct a PDA that accepts the following language by an empty stack:
$S \to 0\,S\,1 \mid A$
$A \to 1\,A\,0 \mid S \mid \epsilon$

(A) 6.11 Construct a PDA equivalent to the following grammar:
$S \to a\,A\,A$
$A \to a\,S \mid b\,S \mid a$

(U) 6.12 Define pushdown automata. What are the different types of PDA? What are the applications of PDA?

(A) 6.13 Let the grammar $G$ be defined as
$S \to a\,A\,B\,B \mid a\,A\,A$
$A \to a\,B\,B \mid a$
$B \to b\,B\,B \mid A$
Construct an NPDA that accepts the language generated by this grammar.

(C) 6.14 Construct pushdown automata for each of the following languages:
(a) The set of palindromes over alphabet $\{a, b\}$
(b) The set of all strings over alphabet $\{a, b\}$ with exactly twice as many $a$'s as $b$'s
(c) $L = \{a^i b^j c^k \mid i + j \text{ or } j + k\}$

(L) 6.15 Consider the following two languages:
$L_1 = \{a^n b^{2n} c^m \mid n, m \geq 0\}$
$L_2 = \{a^n b^m c^{2m} \mid n, m \geq 0\}$
Is $L_1 \cap L_2$ a context-free language? Justify your answer.

Ⓒ 6.16 Construct a pushdown automaton to accept the language:

$L = \{WW^R \mid W \in \{a, b\}^*$, and $W^R$ is the reverse of $W\}$

Show all possible states, transition inputs, and the contents of the stack.

Ⓛ 6.17 $WW^R$ is accepted by an NPDA but not by any DPDA. Justify.

Ⓛ 6.18 Discuss the relative powers of FSM, PDM, and Turing machine (TM).

Ⓐ 6.19 What is PDA? Construct a PDA for the grammar $E \to E + E \mid E * E \mid (E) \mid id$

Ⓒ 6.20 Construct a DPDA that will recognize the following language:

$L = \{WCW^R \mid W \in (a, b)^*$ and $W^R$ is the reverse of $W\}$.

Simulate the working of this PDA for input string '*ababCbaba*'.

Ⓐ 6.21 Design a PDA to accept the following languages for $n > 0$:

(a) $(bdb)^n C^n$

(b) $(ab)^n (cd)^n$

Ⓒ 6.22 Design a pushdown automaton to accept the language containing all odd length palindromes over $\Sigma = \{0, 1\}$.

Ⓛ 6.23 Construct a context-free grammar equivalent to the following PDA (described with the help of the given set of equations):

$\delta(q_0, b, Z_0) = \{(q_0, ZZ_0)\}$
$\delta(q_0, \epsilon, Z_0) = \{(q_0, \epsilon)\}$
$\delta(q_0, b, Z) = \{(q_0, ZZ)\}$
$\delta(q_0, a, Z) = \{(q_1, Z)\}$
$\delta(q_1, b, Z) = \{(q_0, \epsilon)\}$
$\delta(q_1, a, Z_0) = \{(q_0, Z_0)\}$

Ⓛ 6.24 Give a grammar for the language $L(M)$, where $M = (\{q_0, q_1\}, \{0, 1\}, \{z_0, x\}, \delta, q_0, z_0, \phi)$, and $\delta$ is given by:

$\delta(q_0, 1, z_0) = (q_0, xz_0)$ $\quad \delta(q_0, \epsilon, z_0) = (q_0, \epsilon)$
$\delta(q_0, 1, x) = (q_0, xx)$ $\quad \delta(q_1, 1, x) = (q_1, \epsilon)$
$\delta(q_0, 0, x) = (q_1, x)$ $\quad \delta(q_0, 0, z_0) = (q_0, z_0)$

Ⓒ 6.25 Construct a PDA for the following language set:

$L = \{a^{2n} b^n \mid n \geq 1\}$

Ⓐ 6.26 Convert the following CFG into PDA:

$S \to a\,B \mid b\,A$
$A \to a \mid a\,S \mid b\,A\,A$
$B \to b \mid b\,S \mid a\,B\,B$

Ⓤ 6.27 Prove the following:

(a) CFLs are not closed under intersection.

(b) CFLs are closed under Kleene closure.

Ⓒ 6.28 Construct an NPDA defined over $\Sigma = \{a, b, c\}$ that accepts the language

$L = \{\omega_1 c \omega_2 \mid \omega_1, \omega_2 \in \{a, b\}^*, \omega_1 \neq \omega_2\}$

Ⓤ 6.29 Write short notes on the following:

(a) Deterministic pushdown automata

(b) Equivalence of PDA and CFG

(c) Relative powers of NFA/DFA and NPDA/DPDA

(d) Use of CNF in PDA construction

(e) Closure properties of CFLs

Ⓒ 6.30 Construct a deterministic PDA recognizing the following language:

$L = \{x \in (ab)^* \mid$ number of $a$'s is more than number of $b$'s$\}$

**Answers to Objective Questions**

6.1. (a) 6.2. (g) 6.3. (b) 6.4. context-free 6.5. (a) False; (b) True; (c) False; (d) True
6.6. Chomsky normal form 6.7. (b) 6.8. (a) 6.9. (c) 6.10. (b) 6.11. (c) 6.12. True

# Parsing Techniques

**LEARNING OBJECTIVES**

After completing this chapter, the reader will be able to understand the following:

- Basics of parsing techniques
- Concepts of top-down and bottom-up parsing
- Recursive descent parsing (RDP)
- Application of leftmost and rightmost derivations during parsing
- Operator precedence parsing
- Automatic construction of SLR, canonical-LR, and LALR parsers

## 7.1 INTRODUCTION

In Chapter 5, we have seen how formal languages are classified into different types. We also discussed the Chomsky hierarchy of grammars associated with each class of languages, the applications of context-free grammars (CFGs), as well as ambiguity of grammars, and the construction of derivation or parse tree.

CFGs are mainly applied in areas related to compiler construction, syntactic pattern recognition, and the like. The present chapter discusses in more detail, various parsing techniques and the commonly-used approaches of syntactic analysis. It also discusses automatic construction of parsers from context-free grammars. However, the approach here is not as detailed as required from the perspective of compiler design, as the primary intent is only to introduce the reader to various applications of CFGs.

## 7.2 PARSING

A compiler is a meta-program that converts a source language program to machine code. Its construction involves different phases. The first phase, which is called lexical analysis, processes the source input program and identifies the valid words (or tokens) from it. We have discussed lexical analysis in Chapter 3 (refer to Section 3.8.1) as one of the applications of regular languages and automata. Parsing is the second phase of the compiler-construction process. The parser (or syntax analyser) receives the token stream identified by the lexical analyser (refer to Chapter 5, Section 5.18.1). In this section, we shall discuss parsing in greater detail.

A parser is a program that groups the tokens (that are received from the lexical analyser) together to formulate statements, using some context-free grammar (CFG) as reference. If a statement can be formulated (or constructed) from the given stream of tokens as per the reference CFG, then the stream of tokens and hence, the source input program is considered to be syntactically correct. If no statement can be formulated as per the reference CFG, then the source input program is considered syntactically incorrect, and errors are generated.

For example, if the reference grammar is

$$S \rightarrow D + D$$
$$D \rightarrow 0 \mid 1 \mid 2 \mid 3 \mid 4 \mid 5 \mid 6 \mid 7 \mid 8 \mid 9,$$

then the statement '1 + 7' is syntactically correct; whereas the statement '+ 2' is syntactically incorrect.

A parser analyses the syntax of the input program code as per the definition of the CFG, and tells us whether or not it is syntactically correct.

For example, if the input is '1 + 7', the lexical analyser generates three tokens: '1', '+', and '7'. Using the grammar rule, '1' and '7' can be derived from the non-terminal *D*. Thus, the statement '1 + 7' has the form '*D* + *D*', as suggested by the CFG, and is hence syntactically correct.

The parser is a program that is deterministic in nature. Since ambiguity of grammar introduces non-determinism, ambiguous grammars are not suitable for parsing. Therefore, the ambiguity must be removed, and this modified unambiguous grammar is used for parsing. We shall discuss more about this later in the chapter.

Parsers are classified as top-down parsers and bottom-up (or shift-reduce) parsers; both these techniques are fundamentally different from each other. We shall discuss these techniques in the following sections.

## 7.3 TOP-DOWN PARSING

As the name suggests, a top-down parser begins with the start symbol of the grammar and attempts to re-construct the statement for which the syntax needs to be analysed for correctness; it uses the grammar to derive the statement. If it can derive the statement, the statement is considered to be syntactically correct; else it is considered to be incorrect.

As we know, the derivation involves construction of a derivation tree (or parse tree). The reader may refer to Chapter 5, Section 5.6 to revise the concept if required. The top-down parser begins from the start symbol, which is the root node (*top*) of the parse tree, and moves towards the terminals, which are the leaves of the derivation tree and represent the bottom (*down*) of the tree.

For example, for the grammar discussed in Section 7.2, the parse (or derivation) tree for the statement '1 + 7' can be constructed stepwise as shown in Fig. 7.1.

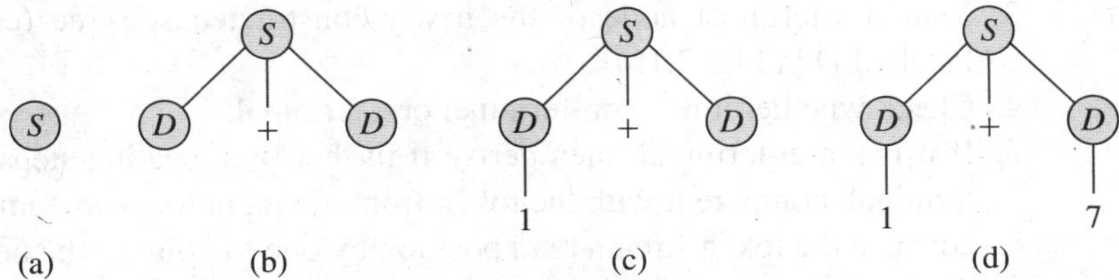


**Figure 7.1** Construction of top-down parse tree (a) Root node as start symbol (b) Intermediate form of the parse tree (c) Intermediate form of the parse tree (d) Complete parse tree for '1 + 7'

Figure 7.1 shows the reconstruction of the statement '1 + 7' in the form of a parse tree. Since the reconstruction is possible, the statement is considered to be syntactically correct. We observe that the tree is constructed from top to bottom; hence the name, top-down parser.

We observe that in Fig. 7.1(c), the leftmost non-terminal $D$ is first derived to '1'. This means that leftmost derivation has been applied in this technique. One might wonder if we can use rightmost derivation in top-down parsing. The answer is, no. We shall discuss this in detail in the next section.

### 7.3.1 Use of Leftmost Derivation

The input to any parser is received from the lexical analyser as a stream of tokens. A stream is a finite sequence, which needs to be read from left to right for the correct sequence. Thus, for the example that we have considered, token '1' is to be read first, followed by '+', and then '7'.

The top-down parser, which constructs the parse tree, needs to consume the generated tokens, one at a time from the token stream received from the lexical analyser. In Fig. 7.1(c), the top-down parser generates '1' using leftmost derivation, checks it with the first token in the token stream, which is also '1'. If they are matched, as they are in this case, it continues with the process of derivation; else, it abruptly stops and declares the input as incorrect.

The leftmost derivation for the statement '1 + 7' can be written as

$$\begin{aligned} S &\Rightarrow \underline{D} + D \\ &\Rightarrow 1 + \underline{D} \\ &\Rightarrow 1 + 7 \end{aligned}$$

We see that the string '1 + 7' is generated from left to right, that is, in the same order of the token stream that is received from the lexical analyser. Thus, we conclude that only leftmost derivation is suitable for a top-down parser, as it helps regenerate the string in the same order to check correctness.

### 7.3.2 Working of a Top-down Parser

In Chapter 6 (refer to Section 6.7), we saw how a pushdown automaton (PDA) can act as a top-down parser, and discussed the parsing process. Let us now discuss the working of a top-down parser, step by step.

1. Begin with the start symbol in the grammar (refer to Fig. 7.1a).
2. Apply the first grammar rule for the start symbol and construct the second level of the parse tree (refer to Fig. 7.1b).

3. Visit the leftmost node of the newly-constructed sub-tree (e.g., the leftmost node labelled $D$ in Fig. 7.1b).
4. Check whether it is a non-terminal or a terminal.
5. If it is a non-terminal, then derive it further by repeating steps 3 to 5. Else, if it is a terminal, compare it with the token from the input token stream. If they are matching, advance the token stream read position by one to point to the next token; else, declare the input as incorrect. In our example, the leftmost node in Fig. 7.1(b) happens to be a non-terminal. Therefore, it has been derived as shown in Fig. 7.1(c).
6. Visit the next node in the sub-tree from the aforementioned step 3 and repeat steps 4 to 6.

There are some potential problems in this algorithm. For example, refer to step 5. If we get a non-terminal, it is expected to derive it further. However, if there are multiple derivation rules available for the non-terminal, step 5 does not mention which of the available rules to apply. For example, in the given grammar, the first rule for $D$ is '$D \rightarrow 0$' and not '$D \rightarrow 1$'. Therefore, if we apply the first rule first, we may have to construct the tree with '$D \rightarrow 0$', and then backtrack and apply the second rule '$D \rightarrow 1$' to get the desired symbol '1' to match with the token stream. This problem arises because the sequence of rules is followed in the order they are given. Similarly, in order to generate symbol '7', the first six rules need to be applied and rejected. A lot of rework is required, which may delay the parsing. In the next section, we shall discuss some potential problems and how they can be overcome.

### 7.3.3 Some Potential Problems and their Solutions

There are a few problems related to top-down parsing, which are mostly related to the grammar and the order of production rules applied. Let us discuss a few important problem situations, and how they can be overcome while constructing the top-down parser.

#### Backtracking

Consider the following grammar:

$$S \rightarrow c\,A\,d$$
$$A \rightarrow a\,b \mid a$$

Let us consider the input string '*cad*', which needs to be checked using the algorithm discussed in the previous section. We begin with the start symbol $S$ and apply the only production rule for $S$, which is '$S \rightarrow c\,A\,d$'. The intermediate parse tree is as shown in Fig. 7.2(a).

The leftmost symbol of the newly-constructed sub-tree is $c$. It is a terminal symbol and matches with the first token $c$ from the input stream '*cad*'.

The next symbol of the newly-constructed sub-tree is $A$. It is a non-terminal and needs to be derived further. The first production rule for $A$ is '$A \rightarrow a\,b$'. Applying this rule, we construct the next level of the tree as shown in Fig. 7.2(b).

The leftmost symbol of the newly constructed sub-tree, as shown in Fig. 7.2(b), is $a$, which is a terminal symbol. This matches with the second token $a$ from the stream '*cad*'.

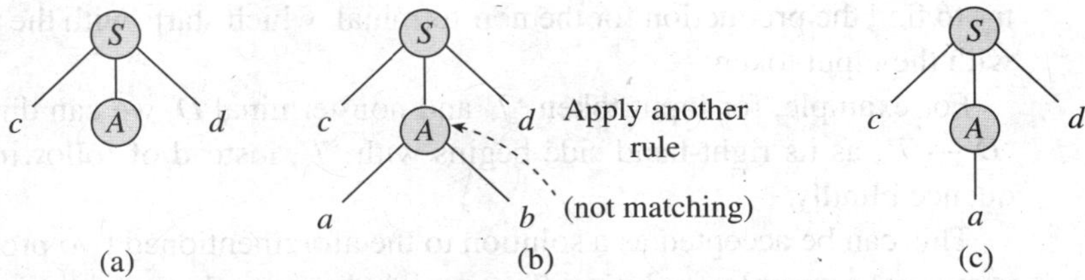


**Figure 7.2** Top-down parsing with backtracking (a) Intermediate parse tree (b) Leftmost symbol of the newly constructed sub-tree (c) Application of the second production rule to get the tree

The next symbol of the newly-constructed sub-tree is *b*. It is also a terminal symbol. We try to match it with the third token, which is *d*. This does not match. This means that we have applied the wrong rule and need to backtrack.

Thus, we delete the sub-tree for *A* and apply the second production rule to get the tree shown in Fig. 7.2(c). This leads to the correct derivation.

This problem is called *backtracking*, and causes a delay in parsing. The problem arises because the sequence of productions is followed blindly in the same order as they are given in the grammar.

### *Incorrect Parsing Decisions*

This is a comparatively more serious problem. In this problem, the order in which the productions are applied may sometimes affect the language accepted. For example, if we apply the production '$A \rightarrow a$' before '$A \rightarrow a\,b$', and the input string to be parsed is '*cabd*', the top-down parser designed to analyse this syntax may not accept this input (refer to Fig. 7.3).

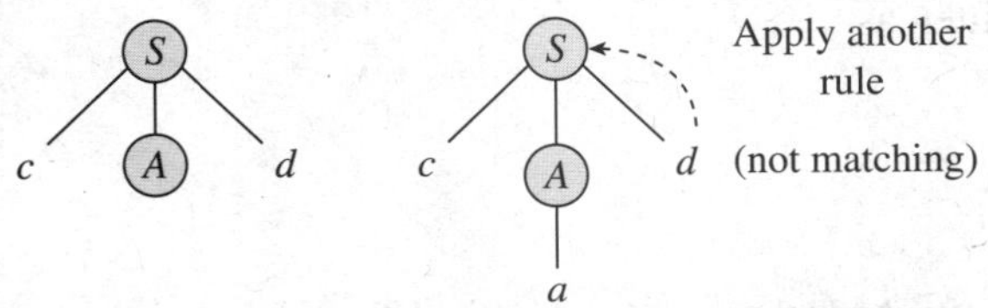


**Figure 7.3** Incorrect parsing decisions

We see from Fig. 7.3 that if we apply the rule '$A \rightarrow a$' first, and the input to be checked for correctness is '*cabd*', then the tokens '*c*' and '*a*' are matched but '*d*' cannot be matched with '*b*'. The parser thus deletes the sub-tree associated with the parent node of '*d*', which is '*S*', and tries to apply the second rule for '*S*' as per the backtracking process. As there is no second rule for '*S*' in the given grammar, the parser declares the string '*cabd*' to be syntactically incorrect, though it is actually a correct string as per the grammar. Hence, this is a much more serious problem compared to backtracking and questions the usability of such a top-down parser.

### *Read Input First*

The solution to these two problems is to apply the productions with some more intelligence. We now understand that we cannot apply productions as per their default ordering. Let us discuss this in more detail with the help of an example.

Consider the following grammar:

$$S \rightarrow D + D$$
$$D \rightarrow 0 \mid 1 \mid 2 \mid 3 \mid 4 \mid 5 \mid 6 \mid 7 \mid 8 \mid 9$$

When we need to match '7', there is no need to apply the first six productions for *D* and reject them. In order to avoid this, the strategy is to read the input token beforehand and try to find the production for the non-terminal, which starts with the terminal and matches with the input token.

For example, for input token '7' and non-terminal $D$, we can directly choose the rule '$D \rightarrow 7$', as its right-hand side begins with '7', instead of following the production sequence blindly.

This can be accepted as a solution to the aforementioned two problems. However, this is still not a complete solution. There might be more than one production rule that begins with the same symbol.

For example, in the following example grammar, we have

$$S \rightarrow c\,A\,d$$
$$A \rightarrow a\,b \mid a$$

Here, both the productions for $A$ start with $a$. In such a case, we perform *left-factoring* for these production rules. This is explained in the following section.

### Left-factoring

Left-factoring introduces a new non-terminal to the common symbol in the multiple productions; this takes care of the rest of the productions.

For example, the left-factoring of the two productions of $A$, as seen in the previous section, is as follows:

$$A \rightarrow a\,B$$
$$B \rightarrow b \mid \epsilon$$

The modified grammar can thus be written as

$$S \rightarrow c\,A\,d$$
$$A \rightarrow a\,B$$
$$B \rightarrow b \mid \epsilon$$

We see that the common part $a$ has been attached to a new non-terminal $B$, which derives the rest of the portions, which are $b$ and $\epsilon$. The modified grammar has thus retained the same language. With this new left-factored grammar, both the example strings, '*cad*' and '*cabd*', can be parsed without any problem as there is always a unique rule that starts with a single terminal.

> ***Note***: We observe that to make every production rule begin with a terminal symbol, the grammar should be expressed in Greibach normal form (GNF), as discussed in Chapter 5 (refer to Section 5.10.2).

### Left Recursion

There is another major difficulty while constructing top-down parsers, which is called *left recursion*.

A grammar is said to be left-recursive if there exists a non-terminal, $A$, such that some derivation from $A$ yields a sentential form '$A\,\alpha$' for some $\alpha$.

$$A \overset{+}{\Rightarrow} A\,\alpha$$

This means that $A$, in one or more steps of derivation, gives a string that again starts with $A$. This may cause a top-down parser to go into an infinite loop. Whenever a parser tries to expand $A$, it will reach $A$ again, and the process will continue forever. However, this problem also has a solution.

If there is a left-recursive pair of productions of the form

$$A \rightarrow A\,\alpha \mid \beta,$$

where, $\beta$ does not begin with $A$, we can get rid of these productions by introducing the following new set of productions:

$$A \rightarrow \beta\, A'$$
$$A' \rightarrow \alpha\, A' \mid \epsilon$$

We see that both these sets of productions are equivalent and represent the same language.

Consider the left-recursive grammar given here:

$$S \rightarrow S\,a \mid e$$

The left recursion can be removed, as shown here:

$$S \rightarrow e\,S'$$
$$S' \rightarrow a\,S' \mid \epsilon$$

We see that these two grammars are equivalent. This can be seen from the two equivalent parse trees constructed using these two grammars for the string '*eaa*' (refer to Fig. 7.4).

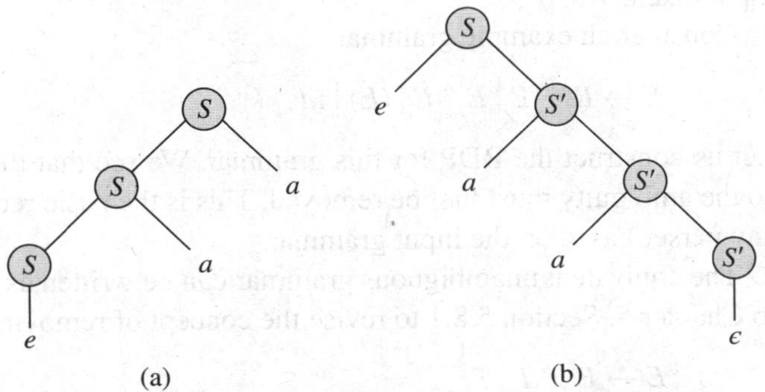


**Figure 7.4** Removal of left recursion (a) Parse tree using left-recursive grammar (b) Parse tree after removing left recursion

The elimination rule for left recursion can be generalized as follows:

Left-recursive productions of the form

$$A \rightarrow A\,\alpha_1 \mid A\,\alpha_2 \mid \ldots \mid A\,\alpha_m \mid \beta_1 \mid \beta_2 \mid \ldots \mid \beta_n,$$

can be replaced by the following set of productions:

$$A \rightarrow \beta_1\, A' \mid \beta_2\, A' \mid \ldots \mid \beta_n\, A'$$
$$A' \rightarrow \alpha_1\, A' \mid \alpha_2\, A' \mid \ldots \mid \alpha_m\, A' \mid \epsilon$$

Let us consider another example of left-recursive grammar:

$$S \rightarrow S\,a \mid S\,b\,c \mid b\,d \mid e$$

An equivalent grammar can be obtained after removing left recursion using the generalized elimination rule as follows:

$$S \rightarrow b\,d\,S' \mid e\,S'$$
$$S' \rightarrow a\,S' \mid b\,c\,S' \mid \epsilon$$

### 7.3.4 Recursive Descent Parsing

A recursive descent parser (RDP) is a type of top-down parser that needs no backtracking. This parser makes use of recursive procedures to validate the input for correctness. It does not require backtracking as every procedure checks the input token before taking any action. This minimizes the delay caused due to backtracking. Thus, the solution to the backtracking problem is inbuilt in this type of top-down parser.

Though this parser is free from backtracking, left factoring and removal of left recursion are still required. Moreover, a common rule applicable to any type of parsing is that the context-free grammar at hand must be unambiguous.

However, construction of this type of parser is fairly simple. For every non-terminal, one needs to write an equivalent procedure. If there are $n$ productions for a non-terminal, then there must be as many mutually exclusive code segments in the procedure representing the non-terminal.

If a non-terminal appears on the right-hand side of a production, it is treated as a procedure call. If a terminal appears on the right-hand side of a production, it is matched with the input token.

Consider an example grammar:

$$E \rightarrow E + E \mid E * E \mid (E) \mid id$$

Let us construct the RDP for this grammar. We see that the grammar is ambiguous and so the ambiguity must first be removed. This is the basic requirement before constructing any parser based on the input grammar.

The equivalent unambiguous grammar can be written as follows (the reader may refer to Chapter 5, Section 5.8.1 to revise the concept of removing ambiguity).

$$E \rightarrow E + T \mid T$$
$$T \rightarrow T * F \mid F$$
$$F \rightarrow (E) \mid id$$

Note that this grammar is left-recursive. After eliminating the left recursion, the equivalent grammar can be written as

$$E \rightarrow T\,E' \qquad \text{(here, } \beta = T, \alpha = +\,T\text{)}$$
$$E' \rightarrow +\,T\,E' \mid \epsilon$$
$$T \rightarrow F\,T' \qquad \text{(here, } \beta = F, \alpha = *\,F\text{)}$$
$$T' \rightarrow *\,F\,T' \mid \epsilon$$
$$F \rightarrow (E) \mid id$$

The grammar is now ready for constructing an RDP as it has no ambiguity, no left-recursion problem, and does not require left factoring.

The RDP consisting of the mutually recursive procedures can be written as shown in Program 7.1. We see that every non-terminal is represented as a recursive procedure in the program. In Program 7.1, the procedure 'ADVANCE ( )' increments a token stream pointer to the next token and the procedure 'ERROR ( )' declares the input to be erroneous.

```
Procedure E ( )
{
        T ( );
        E_dash ( );
}
Procedure E_dash ( )
{
        if (input_token == '+')
        {
                ADVANCE ( );
                T ( );
                E_dash ( );
        }
}
Procedure T ( )
{
        F ( );
        T_dash ( );
}
Procedure T_dash ( )
{
        if (input_token == '*')
        {
                ADVANCE ( );
                F ( );
                T_dash ( );
        }
}
Procedure F ( )
{
        if (input_token = = 'id')
                ADVANCE ( );
        else if (input_token = = '(')
        {
                ADVANCE ( );
                E ( );
                if (input_token = = ')')
                    ADVANCE ( );
                else
                    ERROR ( );
        }
        else
                ERROR ( );
}
```

**Program 7.1** Example recursive descent parser

Once a procedure calls another (or even itself recursively), an entry into the call-stack is created to recognize the call. The stack is a last-in-first-out (LIFO) type, as seen in Chapter 6, while discussing PDA.

Let us try to simulate the working of Program 7.1 for the input '*id* + *id*'. Since the RDP is a top-down parser, it uses leftmost derivation internally. This is evident from the call-stack we are going to prepare. Refer to Fig. 7.5 for the simulation.

We begin with the start symbol *E* of the grammar—as indicated in Fig. 7.5(a)—by pushing *E* onto the stack first. Procedure *E* calls *T*, which in turn calls *F* (refer to Program 7.1). The call-stack shown in Fig. 7.5(a) indicates the same.

Procedure *F* matches the token *id* and advances the token stream pointer by one position. Procedure *F* returns after matching the token, as seen in Fig. 7.5(b).

Once procedure *F* returns as per Program 7.1, procedure *T* calls procedure *T_dash*. This can be seen from the call-stack in Fig. 7.5(c).

Procedure *T_dash* does not match the next token '+' and hence returns. Since procedure *T* is complete, it returns. Procedure *E*, which initially called *T*, now executes the next statement as per Program 7.1. It calls procedure *E_dash*. This can be seen from the call-stack in Fig. 7.5(d).

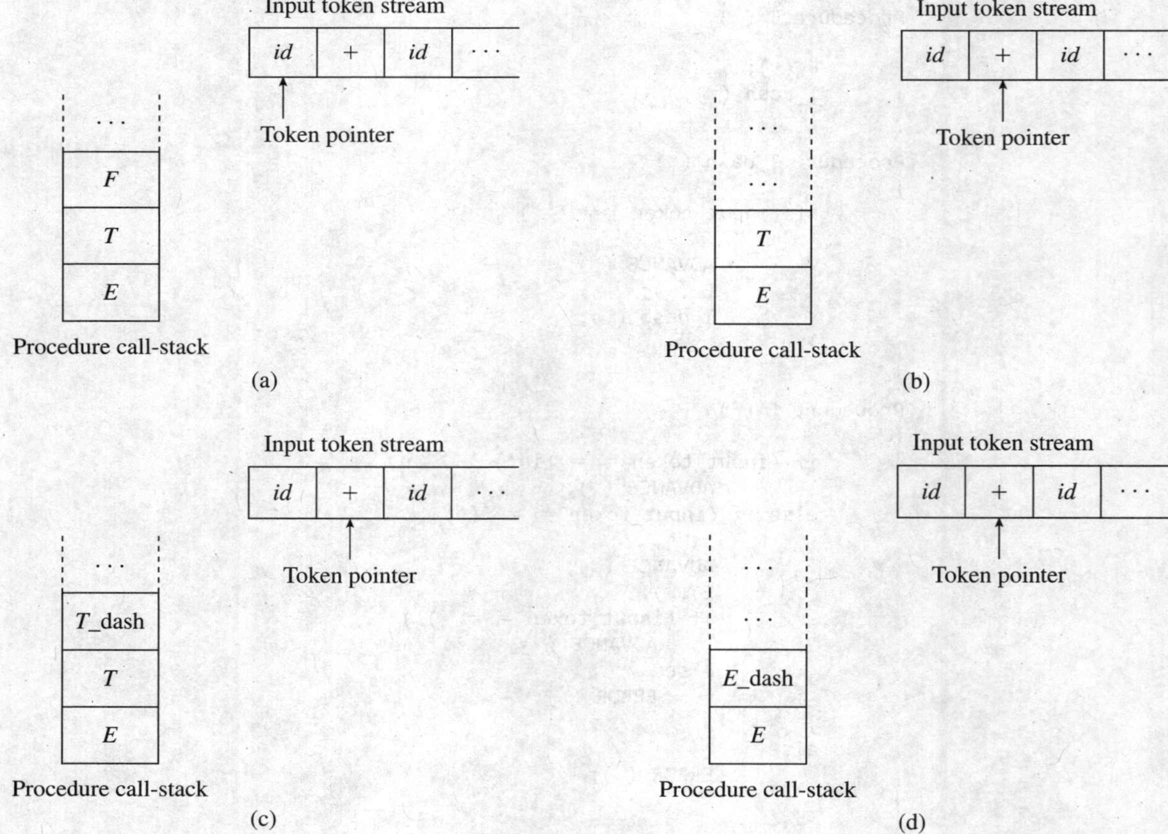


**Figure 7.5** Simulation of the working of Program 7.1 (a) No token matched yet (b) First token 'id' matched (c) *T* or *T_dash* does not generate '+' (d) Yet to match token '+'

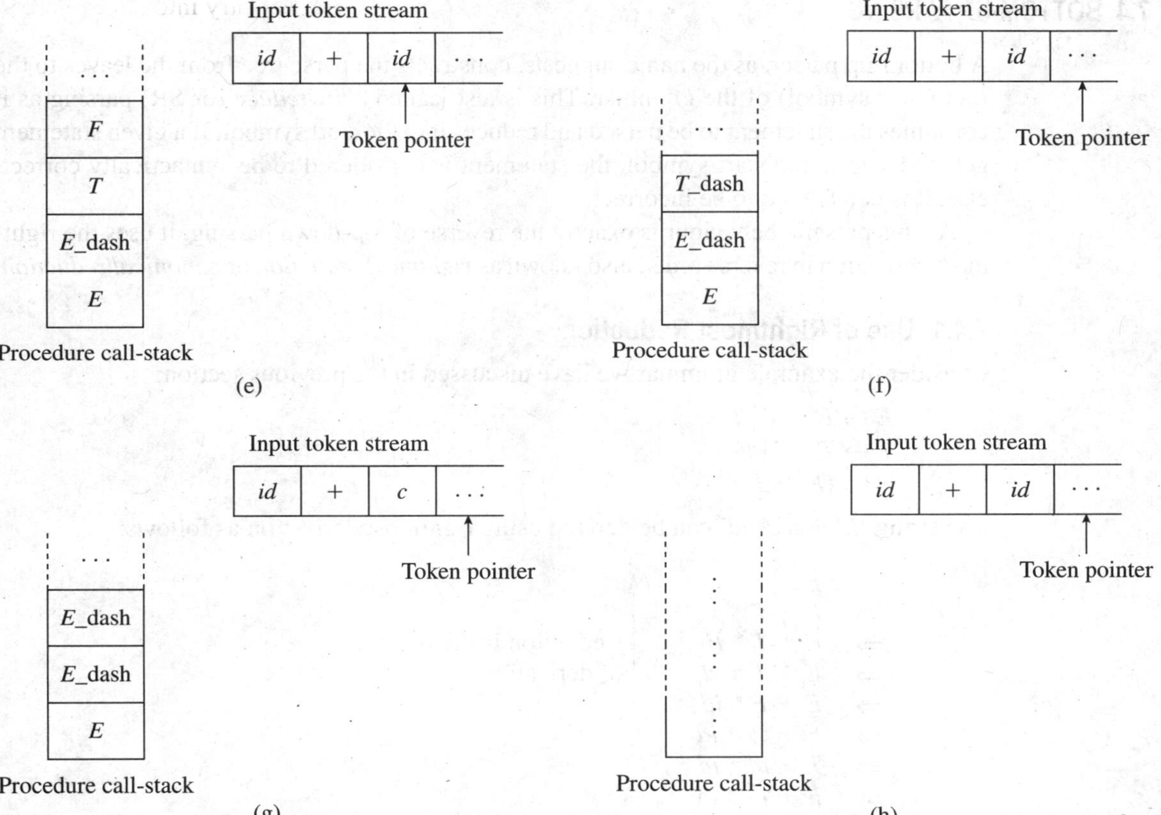


**Figure 7.5** *(Continued)* (e) Token '+' matched (f) Token '*id*' matched (g) *E_dash* calls itself recursively (h) *E* returns successfully without error

Procedure *E_dash* matches the token '+', advances the token stream pointer to point to the next token, and calls *T*, which in turn calls procedure *F* as shown in Fig. 7.5(e).

Procedure *F* matches the token *id*, advances the input token stream pointer, and returns. Hence, procedure *T* executes the next statement by calling *T_dash* as per Program 7.1. This can be seen in Fig. 7.5(f).

Once procedures *T_dash* and *T* return, procedure *E_dash* calls itself, as it executes the next statement. Refer to Fig. 7.5(g) to see the call-stack at this stage.

However, both the calls to *E_dash* return, as no other token is found. Finally, procedure *E*, which initially called *E_dash*, returns, leaving the stack empty. The whole of the input stream is already matched and no error is generated. Hence, the input '*id* + *id*' is considered to be syntactically correct. Acceptance is done by empty stack, as shown in Fig. 7.5(h).

> ***Note***: We have already discussed acceptance by empty stack by a PDA in Chapter 6 (refer to Section 6.5.2). Further, it is important to remember that every parser is nothing but a DPDA. Therefore, every parser is bound to use a stack, either directly or indirectly. This is also evident from the example RDP that we have just discussed.

## 7.4 BOTTOM-UP PARSING

A bottom-up parser, as the name suggests, constructs the parse tree from the leaves to the root (start symbol) of the grammar. This is also called *shift-reduce* (or SR) parsing as it consumes the statement to be parsed and reduces it to the start symbol. If a given statement gets reduced to the start symbol, the statement is considered to be syntactically correct; else, it is considered to be incorrect.

As this parser's behaviour is exactly the reverse of top-down parsing, it uses the rightmost derivation in reverse order, also known as *rightmost reduction* or *canonical reduction*.

### 7.4.1 Use of Rightmost Reduction

Consider the example grammar we have discussed in the previous section:

$$E \to E + T \mid T$$
$$T \to T * F \mid F$$
$$F \to (E) \mid id$$

The string '*id* + *id* * *id*' can be derived using rightmost derivation as follows:

$$\begin{aligned} & E \\ \Rightarrow\ & E + T \\ \Rightarrow\ & E + T * F \\ \Rightarrow\ & E + T * id \\ \Rightarrow\ & E + F * id \\ \Rightarrow\ & E + id * id \\ \Rightarrow\ & T + id * id \\ \Rightarrow\ & F + id * id \\ \Rightarrow\ & id + id * id \end{aligned}$$

↑ Reduction is the reverse of derivation

The shift-reduce parser, like all other parsers, receives the input stream of tokens, to be read from left-to-right. The shift-reduce parser reduces the input string to the start symbol, and it is evident from the aforementioned reduction that rightmost reduction is the only suitable process of reduction. The leftmost symbol is consumed first, followed by the next, and so on.

Let us read in the reverse direction of the aforementioned rightmost derivation, that is, from the last sentential form towards the start symbol. In the given canonical reduction, *id* is the first token, which gets reduced to *F*. The symbol *F* then gets reduced to *T*, which in turn gets reduced to *E*. Then the next token *id* from the input token stream gets consumed, and the process continues till we reach the start symbol of the grammar.

### 7.4.2 Working of a Bottom-up Parser

Reaching from one sentential form to the previous in the reduction process requires a production of the form '$A \to \alpha$', whose right-hand side is $\alpha$ and can be reduced to the left-hand side symbol *A* (the symbol identified to be reduced is called a *handle*). At every step, a handle is identified to perform the reduction. A handle is always the right-hand side of some production. For example, in the canonical reduction we discussed in the previous section, the token *id* gets reduced to *F* using the production '$F \to id$', in the first step; in this step, *id* is the handle. Towards the end of the reduction, we see the reduction of the handle '$T * F$' to $T$, and at the end, '$E + T$' gets reduced to the start symbol '$E$'. This process of identifying a handle at every step and reducing it appropriately to reach a start symbol eventually is known as *handle pruning*.

The bottom-up (or shift-reduce) parser also makes use of a stack for handle pruning. Thus, the 'shift' operation shifts a symbol onto the stack from the token stream while reduction using the production rule '$A \rightarrow \alpha$' means popping out the handle '$\alpha$' from the stack and pushing '$A$' instead.

Table 7.1 illustrates the working of a shift-reduce parser for the example string '$id + id * id$'. Here, \$ identifies the bottom of the stack as well as the end of the input.

**Table 7.1** Working of a shift-reduce parser

| Input | Stack | Action |
|---|---|---|
| $id + id * id$ \$ | \$ | Shift '$id$' |
| $+ id * id$ \$ | $id$ \$ | Reduce using $F \rightarrow id$ |
| $+ id * id$ \$ | $F$ \$ | Reduce using $T \rightarrow F$ |
| $+ id * id$ \$ | $T$ \$ | Reduce using $E \rightarrow T$ |
| $+ id * id$ \$ | $E$ \$ | Shift '+' |
| $id * id$ \$ | $+ E$ \$ | Shift '$id$' |
| $* id$ \$ | $id + E$ \$ | Reduce using $F \rightarrow id$ |
| $* id$ \$ | $F + E$ \$ | Reduce using $T \rightarrow F$ |
| $* id$ \$ | $T + E$ \$ | Shift '*' |
| $id$ \$ | $* T + E$ \$ | Shift '$id$' |
| \$ | $id * T + E$ \$ | Reduce using $F \rightarrow id$ |
| \$ | $F * T + E$ \$ | Reduce using $T \rightarrow T * F$ |
| \$ | $T + E$ \$ | Reduce using $E \rightarrow E + T$ |
| \$ | $E$ \$ | Accept |

### 7.4.3 Operator Precedence Parsing

This is a type of shift-reduce parsing, which handles a small class of parsers that use the precedence and associative relations among operators to make decisions for actions.

Let us consider a simple operator grammar.

$$E \rightarrow E + E \mid E * E \mid id$$

In this grammar, we have three terminals—*id*, '+', and '*'. Further, \$ is assumed to be a special symbol used to denote the end of input token stream as well as the bottom of the parser stack. Since '*' has higher precedence over '+', an expression like '$a + b * c$' is treated as '$a + (b * c)$'.

Let us refer to the highlighted entry from Table 7.1. We have '$E + T$' on top of the stack, and '*' is the next input token. We could have reduced '$E + T$' to $E$ using the rule, '$E \to E + T$'. However, '*' is shifted onto the stack instead, because '*' has higher precedence over '+'. Thus, the operator precedence parser builds this type of information into a table that helps making shift or reduce decisions.

**Table 7.2** Operator precedence relations

| | *id* | + | * | $ |
|---|---|---|---|---|
| *id* | | > | > | > |
| + | < | > | < | > |
| * | < | > | > | > |
| $ | < | < | < | |

Further, both these operators '+ and '*' are left associative, which means that if an expression contains the same operator more than once, the first (leftmost) operator gets the first priority, and so on. For example, an expression such as '1 + 2 + 3' is treated as '(1 + 2) + 3'.

Using these known relations among operators, we can formulate the relations among these symbols, as shown in Table 7.2.

If the input string to be parsed is '$id + id * id$', then after inserting the aforementioned precedence relations, the modified string will look like:

$$\$ < id > + < id > * < id > \$$$

Now, this string can be used for parsing. Whatever is included in a pair of angular brackets '< >' is considered as a handle and needs to be reduced.

Processing the handles from left to right, we get the following string:

$$\$ E + E * E \$$$

Since the non-terminals cannot be compared for the precedence relations, we assume them to be non-existing and re-insert the relations. Hence we get

$$\$ < + < * > \$$$

This means '$E * E$' needs to be reduced first to $E$ to get

$$\$ E + E \$$$

This can further be reduced with the inserted relations to $E$, as follows:

$$\$ < + > \$$$

## 7.5 AUTOMATIC CONSTRUCTION OF BOTTOM-UP PARSERS

Before introducing other types of shift-reduce table-driven parsers such as the SLR parsers and canonical LR parsers, some background about some special class of CFGs is required. These special types of grammars are called LR-grammars, and are used in the construction of LR-parsers, which are efficient bottom-up or shift-reduce parsers. In this section, we shall discuss LR(0) and LR(1) grammars, and different algorithms for constructing the LR-parsers.

### 7.5.1 LR(0) Grammar

Many systems for writing a compiler require syntactic specification in restricted form of CFGs, which allow only the representation of deterministic CFLs (DCFL). The parser constructed using such systems is essentially a DPDA; LR(0) grammar belongs to this family of DCFLs.

The symbol LR(0) stands for '*L*: left to right scan of the input, *R*: following rightmost reduction, and *0*: using zero symbols of look ahead from the input'. Look ahead means reading more than one token ahead of time, which has not been dealt with here.

Let us discuss some preliminary concepts related to LR(0) grammar.

### LR(0) Item

An LR(0) item of a grammar *G* is defined as a production of *G* with a dot at some position on the right-hand side of the production. For example, the production '$A \to XYZ$' in some grammar *G* generates four LR(0) items:

$$A \to \cdot\, XYZ$$
$$A \to X \cdot YZ$$
$$A \to XY \cdot Z$$
$$A \to XYZ\, \cdot$$

The production '$A \to \epsilon$' generates only one item, '$A \to \cdot$'.

An LR(0) item indicates the part of the production that is being read at a given point in the parsing process. For example, the first item in the example we just discussed indicates that we are expecting to read a string derivable from *XYZ* next on the input. In other words, the whole right-hand side is yet to be considered for parsing. The second item indicates that the parser has just completed reading a string derivable from *X* and is yet to read a string derivable from *YZ* from the input.

We can construct a *simple LR* (or SLR) parser using LR(0) grammar. The central idea is to construct some kind of a DFA from the LR(0) grammar and turn it into an *LR parsing table*, which can be used by the SLR parser as a look-up table to check the syntax. While constructing the DFA, we first require a collection of LR(0) items.

### Closure of LR(0) Item

If *I* is a set of items for a grammar *G*, then the set of items *closure* (*I*) is constructed from *I* by the following rules:

1. Every item in *I* is in closure (*I*).
2. If '$A \to \alpha \cdot B\beta$' is in closure (*I*) and '$B \to \gamma$' is a production, then add the item '$B \to \cdot\gamma$' to closure (*I*), if it is not already there. Here, *A* and *B* are non-terminals, while $\alpha$, $\beta$, and $\gamma$ are sentential forms.

For example, consider the following grammar:

$$\begin{aligned} E' &\to E \\ E &\to E + T \mid T \\ T &\to T * F \mid F \\ F &\to (E) \mid id \end{aligned} \tag{7.1}$$

If $I$ is the set consisting of only one item; such as $I = \{E' \rightarrow \cdot\, E\}$, then closure of $I$ can be given as:

$$\text{Closure } (I) = \{ [E' \rightarrow \cdot\, E], [E \rightarrow \cdot\, E + T], [E \rightarrow \cdot\, T], [T \rightarrow \cdot\, T * F], [T \rightarrow \cdot\, F], [F \rightarrow \cdot\, (E)], [F \rightarrow \cdot\, id] \}$$

The production '$E' \rightarrow \cdot\, E$' is in closure ($I$) by Rule 1.

Since there is a non-terminal $E$ immediately following a dot, by Rule 2, we add to closure ($I$), all productions of $E$ with a dot at the starting position on their respective right-hand sides.

Similarly, $T$ and $F$ appear immediately after the dot. Therefore, applying Rule 2 for $T$ and $F$ as well, we get the complete set of items in closure ($I$).

> ***Note***: If $G$ is a grammar with start symbol $S$, then $G'$—the *augmented grammar* for $G$—is $G$ with a new start symbol $S'$ and a production '$S' \rightarrow S$'. The grammar labelled 7.1 is an example of augmented grammar, as there is a production '$E' \rightarrow E$'. The purpose of augmenting the grammar is to accept the input by an empty stack. We observe from Table 7.1 that the input is accepted when the stack finally contains the start symbol $E$. Hence, if we wish to accept an empty stack, we must pop even the start symbol from the stack using the rule '$E' \rightarrow E$'.

### GOTO Function

If $I$ is a set of items and $X$ is a grammar symbol, then '$GOTO\ (I, X)$' is defined to be the closure of the set of all items $[A \rightarrow \alpha\, X \cdot\, \beta]$ such that $[A \rightarrow \alpha \cdot X\beta]$ is in $I$.

For example, for Grammar 7.1, if $I = \{[E' \rightarrow E\, \cdot], [E \rightarrow E \cdot + T]$, then $GOTO\ (I, +)$ consists of the following:

$$E \rightarrow E + \cdot\, T$$
$$T \rightarrow \cdot\, T * F$$
$$T \rightarrow \cdot\, F$$
$$F \rightarrow \cdot\, (E)$$
$$F \rightarrow \cdot\, id$$

The dot comes immediately before $T$ in the item '$E \rightarrow E + \cdot\, T$' obtained after moving on '+'. We have taken the closure of the item '$E \rightarrow E + \cdot\, T$' to arrive at the set $GOTO\ (I, +)$.

### Construction of LR(0) Sets-of-items

The algorithm to construct the canonical collection of sets-of-LR(0)-items for an augmented grammar $G'$ is as follows:

1. Start with $I$ = closure ($\{S' \rightarrow \cdot\, S\}$) and declare that as the '$I_0$'th set-of-items.

2. For each set-of-item in $I$ and each grammar symbol $X$, whether terminal or non-terminal, if $GOTO\ (I_0, X)$ is non-empty and is not in $I$, then add it to $I$; name it as $I_1$, and so on.
3. Repeat step 2 until no more sets-of-items can be added to $I$.

For example, for Grammar 7.1, we can write the following collection of sets-of-items:

$I_0$:
$E' \rightarrow \cdot E$
$E \rightarrow \cdot E + T$
$E \rightarrow \cdot T$
$T \rightarrow \cdot T * F$
$T \rightarrow \cdot F$
$F \rightarrow \cdot (E)$
$F \rightarrow \cdot id$

$I_1$:
$E' \rightarrow E \cdot$ $\quad GOTO\ (I_0, E)$
$E \rightarrow E \cdot + T$

$I_2$:
$E \rightarrow T \cdot$ $\quad GOTO\ (I_0, T)$
$T \rightarrow T \cdot * F$

$I_3$:
$T \rightarrow F \cdot$ $\quad GOTO\ (I_0, F)$

$I_4$:
$F \rightarrow (\cdot E)$ $\quad GOTO\ (I_0, ()$
$E \rightarrow \cdot E + T$
$E \rightarrow \cdot T$
$T \rightarrow \cdot T * F$
$T \rightarrow \cdot F$
$F \rightarrow \cdot (E)$
$F \rightarrow \cdot id$

$I_5$:
$F \rightarrow id \cdot$ $\quad GOTO\ (I_0, id)$

$I_6$:
$E \rightarrow E + \cdot T$ $\quad GOTO\ (I_1, +)$
$T \rightarrow \cdot T * F$
$T \rightarrow \cdot F$
$F \rightarrow \cdot (E)$
$F \rightarrow \cdot id$

$I_7$:

| | |
|---|---|
| $T \rightarrow T * \cdot F$ | $GOTO\ (I_2, *)$ |
| $F \rightarrow \cdot (E)$ | |
| $F \rightarrow \cdot id$ | |

$I_8$:

| | |
|---|---|
| $F \rightarrow (E \cdot)$ | $GOTO\ (I_4, E)$ |
| $E \rightarrow E \cdot + T$ | |

$I_9$:

| | |
|---|---|
| $E \rightarrow E + T \cdot$ | $GOTO\ (I_6, T)$ |
| $T \rightarrow T \cdot * F$ | |

$I_{10}$:

| | |
|---|---|
| $T \rightarrow T * F \cdot$ | $GOTO\ (I_7, F)$ |

$I_{11}$:

| | |
|---|---|
| $F \rightarrow (E) \cdot$ | $GOTO\ (I_8, ))$ |

The item $I_0$ is obtained using Rule 1 in the algorithm; $I_1$ is obtained from $I_0$, moving on the symbol $E$ as depicted by the dot. Similarly, items $I_2$, $I_3$, $I_4$, and $I_5$ are obtained from $I_0$ moving on symbols $T$, $F$, '(', and *id*, respectively.

The item $I_6$ is obtained using the function, $GOTO\ (I_1, +)$.

Similarly, $I_7 = GOTO\ (I_2, *)$ and $I_8 = GOTO\ (I_4, E)$.

There are multiple items that can be obtained from $I_4$, moving on symbols $T$, $F$, '(', and *id*, but these are already available as $I_2$, $I_3$, $I_4$, and $I_5$ respectively. Hence, these are not added again. Similar is the case for items $I_6$ and $I_7$, for a few symbols. Items $I_9$, $I_{10}$, and $I_{11}$ are obtained as $GOTO\ (I_6, T)$, $GOTO\ (I_7, F)$, and $GOTO\ [I_8, )\ ]$, respectively.

The process stops as one cannot add any more items into the sets-of-items collection already obtained. The DFA corresponding to this collection of sets-of-items is shown in Fig. 7.6.

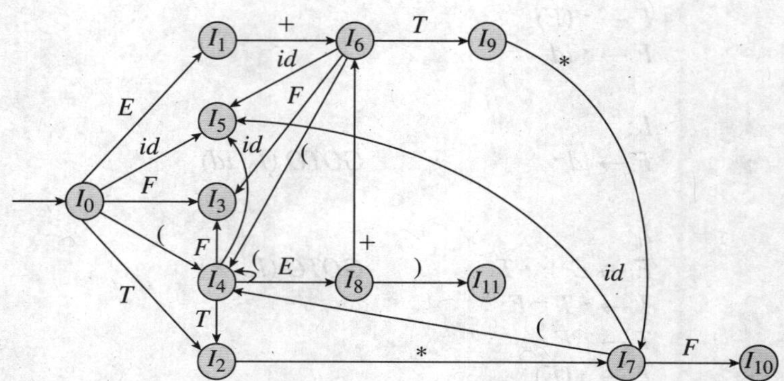


**Figure 7.6** DFA or *GOTO* function for collection of LR(0) sets-of-items

The *GOTO* function can be considered for showing the transitions for this type of DFA. If $I_1$ = *GOTO* ($I_0$, *X*), we show a transition labelled *X* from state $I_0$ to state $I_1$. Similarly, for this DFA, $I_0$ is the initial state and all states can be final states.

We further see that $I_7$ = *GOTO* ($I_2$, *) is represented by a transition labelled '*' from $I_2$ to $I_7$.

The collection of sets-of-items is more like a set of states, and the DFA explicitly depicts the information about the transitions. For example, $I_4$ makes transitions to $I_2$, $I_3$, $I_4$, and $I_5$ on symbols *T*, *F*, '(', and *id*, respectively. This is not so explicit from the collection of sets-of-items, but is made explicit in the DFA in Fig. 7.6.

## 7.5.2 SLR Parser

We have already seen that SLR stands for 'simple LR' parser, which uses the collection of sets-of-LR(0)-items. We can construct an SLR parsing table using the DFA in Fig. 7.6. The SLR parser is a table-driven parser, and hence relies only on the table look-up to make any parsing decision. It is thus much faster than the RDP, which uses recursive procedures for parsing. Use of recursion always has an impact on the execution time against simple table look-up.

For algorithmic construction of an SLR parser, we first need to understand a few basic concepts such as 'first' and 'follow' sets.

### *First*

If $\alpha$ is any sentential form, then 'first ($\alpha$)' is the set of terminals from which the strings derived from $\alpha$ starts. If $\alpha \overset{*}{\Rightarrow} \epsilon$, then $\epsilon$ is also in 'first ($\alpha$)'.

Rules for finding 'first (*X*)' are as follows:

1. If *X* is a terminal, then first $(X) = \{X\}$.
2. If *X* is a non-terminal and '$X \rightarrow a\alpha$' is a production, then add *a* to 'first (*X*)'. If there is a production of the form '$X \rightarrow \epsilon$', then add $\epsilon$ to 'first (*X*)'.
3. If '$X \rightarrow Y_1\ Y_2 \ldots Y_k$' is a production, then 'first (*X*)' contains the following:
   (a) All symbols in first ($Y_1$), if 'first ($Y_1$)' does not contain $\epsilon$.
   (b) If 'first ($Y_1$)' contains $\epsilon$, then 'first (*X*)' contains $\{\text{first } (Y_1) \cup \text{first } (Y_2)\} - \{\epsilon\}$, if 'first ($Y_2$)' does not contain '$\epsilon$'.
   (c) If all 'first ($Y_1$)', 'first ($Y_2$)', ..., 'first ($Y_{k-1}$)' contain $\epsilon$, and 'first ($Y_k$)' does not contain $\epsilon$, then first $(X) = [\text{first } (Y_1) \cup \text{first } (Y_2) \cup \ldots \cup \text{first } (Y_{k-1}) \cup \text{first } (Y_k)] - \{\epsilon\}$.
   (d) If 'first' of all '$Y_1$' to '$Y_k$' contains $\epsilon$, then 'first (*X*)' also contains $\epsilon$.

For example, let us consider Grammar 7.1.

$$E' \rightarrow E$$
$$E \rightarrow E + T \mid T$$
$$T \rightarrow T * F \mid F$$
$$F \rightarrow (E) \mid id$$

Let us find the set of 'first' for all the non-terminals in this grammar.

Consider the productions, '$E' \rightarrow E$', '$E \rightarrow T$', and '$T \rightarrow F$'. Using Rule 3 we can write:

$$\text{First } (E') = \text{first } (E) = \text{first } (T) = \text{first } (F)$$

Applying Rule 2 to the production rule '$F \to (E)$', we have:

$a = ($, and
$\alpha = E)$

Therefore, '(' is in 'first ($F$)'.

Similarly, applying Rule 2 to the production '$F \to id$', we have:

$a = id$, and
$\alpha = \epsilon$

Therefore, $id$ is in 'first ($F$)'.

Thus, first $(F) = \{(, id\}$

Therefore, first $(E')$ = first $(E)$
= first $(T)$
= first $(F)$
$= \{(, id\}$

***Follow***

'Follow ($A$)' for a non-terminal $A$ is the set of all terminals that can appear immediately to the right of $A$ in any sentential form in all the derivations possible using the given grammar. If $A$ appears to be a rightmost symbol in some sentential form, we then add \$ to 'follow ($A$)'.

The rules for finding the set 'follow' of a non-terminal are given here:

1. \$ is included in 'follow ($S$)', where $S$ is the start symbol.
2. If there is a production of the form '$A \to \alpha B\beta$', where $\beta \neq \epsilon$, then everything in 'first ($\beta$)', except $\epsilon$, is in 'follow ($B$)'.
3. If there is a production of the form '$A \to \alpha B$' or '$A \to \alpha B\beta$', where 'first ($\beta$)' contains $\epsilon$, then everything in 'follow ($A$)' is in 'follow ($B$)'.

Please note that both Rules 2 and 3 look for $B$ on the right-hand side of the grammar productions. Here, $B$ is assumed to be the non-terminal whose 'follow' set needs to be determined.

Rule 2 looks at any sentential form $\beta$, which does not derive $\epsilon$, and immediately follows $B$ in any derivation. This is used in case of strings derivable from $\beta$ and beginning with terminal symbols from 'first ($\beta$)', which immediately follow non-terminal $B$.

Rule 3 deals with the case when $B$ is the rightmost symbol on the right-hand side of any production or is immediately followed by $\beta$, which is capable of deriving $\epsilon$.

Consider a case in a derivation where we are going to replace $A$ on the right-hand side that has $B$ as the rightmost symbol. This means, whatever was following non-terminal $A$ earlier, now starts following $B$ because $B$ is the rightmost symbol of the replacement for $A$ in the derivation.

$$\Rightarrow \quad \ldots A \ldots \quad \uparrow$$
$$\Rightarrow \quad \ldots \alpha B \ldots, \quad \uparrow \quad A \to \alpha B$$

For example, let us consider Grammar 7.1 again and attempt to find 'follow' for all the non-terminals.

$E' \to E$
$E \to E + T \mid T$

$T \rightarrow T * F \mid F$
$F \rightarrow (E) \mid id$

Since $E'$ is the start symbol, by Rule 1 we have the following:

Follow ($E'$) = {\$}

Let us consider the next symbol $E$. To find 'follow ($E$)', we consider the following productions with $E$ on the right-hand side of these productions:

$E' \rightarrow E$
$E \rightarrow E + T$
$F \rightarrow (E)$

Let us apply Rules 2 and 3, whichever is applicable, to each of these productions.

We cannot apply Rule 2 to production '$E' \rightarrow E$', as $\beta$ does not exist, but we can apply Rule 3, using the production form, '$A \rightarrow \alpha B$', where,

$A = E'$
$B = E$
$\alpha = i\epsilon$

As per Rule 3, everything in 'follow ($E'$)' is now in 'follow ($E$)', that is, follow ($E$) = {\$}.

For the production '$E \rightarrow E + T$'' we can only apply Rule 2, using the production form '$A \rightarrow \alpha B\beta$', where,

$A = E$
$B = E$
$\alpha = \epsilon$
$\beta = + T$, which does not derive $\epsilon$

Hence, 'follow ($E$)' should contain 'first (+ $T$)', which is '+'.

Thus, we have follow ($E$) = {\$, +}.

Similarly, we apply Rule 2 to production '$F \rightarrow (E)$' using the production form '$A \rightarrow \alpha B\beta$', where,

$A = F$
$B = E$
$\alpha = ($
$\beta = )$

Therefore, as per the rule, 'follow ($E$)' contains 'first [)]'. Therefore, we now have follow ($E$) = {\$, +, )}.

Please note that we cannot apply Rule 3 to the productions '$E \rightarrow E + T$'' and '$F \rightarrow (E)$', as $\beta$ does not derive $\epsilon$. Thus, the final set for 'follow ($E$)' is as follows:

Follow ($E$) = {\$, +, )}

Similarly, using productions with $T$ on the right-hand side and applying Rules 2 and 3, whichever is applicable, we obtain 'follow ($T$)'.

From the rules, '$E \rightarrow E + T$' and '$E \rightarrow T$', we have, $B = T$ and $A = E$. In both cases, the form of the production is '$A \rightarrow \alpha B$', with different $\alpha$'s. Applying Rule 3 in both cases, we include everything in 'follow ($E$)' in 'follow ($T$)'. Therefore, follow ($T$) = {\$, +, )}.

From the rule '$T \rightarrow T * F$', using production form '$A \rightarrow \alpha B\beta$', where, $A = T$, $B = T$, $\alpha = \epsilon$, and $\beta = *F$, we have: follow ($T$) = {*}, by applying Rule 2.

Thus, combining these two findings, we have the final set as given here:

Follow ($T$) = {\$, +, ), *}

The non-terminal $F$ appears on the right-hand side of the productions, '$T \rightarrow T * F$' and '$T \rightarrow F$'. In both these cases, we can apply Rule 3 using the production form '$A \rightarrow \alpha B$', with $A = T$ and $B = F$. Though $\alpha$ is different in both cases, it does not impact the application of the rule. Thus, applying Rule 3 in both the cases, everything in 'follow ($T$) is included in 'follow ($F$)'. Therefore, follow ($F$) = {\$, +, ), *}. Thus, the final set for 'follow ($F$)' is:

Follow ($F$) = {\$, +, ), *}

Thus, 'follow' set for all the non-terminals is as given here:

Follow ($E'$) = {\$}
Follow ($E$) = {\$, +, )}
Follow ($T$) = follow ($F$) = {\$, + ,), *}

### Construction of SLR Parsing Table

An SLR parsing table consists of two parts: *ACTION* and *GOTO*, where the *ACTION* part consists of shift, reduce, or accept actions; and the *GOTO* part contains transitions from one state to another, mainly on non-terminal input symbols. Rows in the parsing table are labelled by states, while the columns are labelled either by terminals (in case of the *ACTION* part) or non-terminals (in case of the *GOTO* part).

> ***Note***: The *GOTO* function, as discussed earlier, is a generic transition function. It denotes transition on either a terminal or non-terminal input. In this context, *GOTO* is defined as part of the SLR parsing table and only denotes transition on non-terminal input symbols.

The following are the rules to construct an SLR parsing table:

1. If $[A \rightarrow \alpha \cdot a\beta]$ is in $I_i$ and *GOTO* $(I_i, a) = I_j$, then

   *ACTION* $(i, a)$ = 'shift $a$' and move to $j$', or
   *ACTION* $(i, a)$ = '$sj$'

   Here, $a$ is a terminal symbol.
2. If $[A \rightarrow \alpha \cdot]$ is in $I_i$, then for all terminal symbols $a$ in follow ($A$), we write:

   *ACTION* $(i, a)$ = 'reduce using rule $A \rightarrow \alpha$', or
   *ACTION* $(i, a)$ = '$rk$', where $k$ is the production rule number
3. If $[S' \rightarrow S\cdot]$ is in $I_i$, then

   *ACTION* $(i, \$)$ = 'accept'
4. If *GOTO* $(I_i, A) = I_j$, then

   *GOTO* $(i, A) = j$ where $A$ is any non-terminal

For example, let us consider Grammar 7.1 with productions numbered as follows:

0: $E' \rightarrow E$
1: $E \rightarrow E + T$
2: $E \rightarrow T$
3: $T \rightarrow T * F$
4: $T \rightarrow F$
5: $F \rightarrow ( E )$
6: $F \rightarrow id$

The SLR parsing table for the given LR(0) grammar is shown in Table 7.3. Here, we apply the rules for the collection of sets-of-items that we have already obtained. For simplicity, we consider the state labels as 0, 1, ..., 11, instead of $I_0$, $I_1$, ..., $I_{11}$.

**Table 7.3** SLR parsing table

| State | *ACTION* | | | | | | *GOTO* | | |
|---|---|---|---|---|---|---|---|---|---|
| | *id* | + | * | ( | ) | $ | *E* | *T* | *F* |
| 0 | *s*5 | — | — | *s*4 | — | — | 1 | 2 | 3 |
| 1 | — | *s*6 | — | — | — | Accept | — | — | — |
| 2 | — | *r*2 | *s*7 | — | *r*2 | *r*2 | — | — | — |
| 3 | — | *r*4 | *r*4 | — | *r*4 | *r*4 | — | — | — |
| 4 | *s*5 | — | — | *s*4 | — | — | 8 | 2 | 3 |
| 5 | — | *r*6 | *r*6 | — | *r*6 | *r*6 | — | — | — |
| 6 | *s*5 | — | — | *s*4 | — | — | — | 9 | 3 |
| 7 | *s*5 | — | — | *s*4 | — | — | — | — | 10 |
| 8 | — | *s*6 | — | — | *s*11 | — | — | — | — |
| 9 | — | *r*1 | *s*7 | — | *r*1 | *r*1 | — | — | — |
| 10 | — | *r*3 | *r*3 | — | *r*3 | *r*3 | — | — | — |
| 11 | — | *r*5 | *r*5 | — | *r*5 | *r*5 | — | — | — |

Let us consider state 0 and the transitions from state $I_0$ in the DFA shown in Fig. 7.6. The state $I_0$ goes to $I_1$ on input *E*; $I_2$ on input *T*; and $I_3$ on input *F*. Hence, we have these entries for state 0 in the *GOTO* part of the parsing table according to Rule 4.

Further, state $I_0$ in the DFA (refer to Fig. 7.6) makes a transition to state $I_5$ on input *id* and to state $I_4$ on input '('. Since *id* and '(' are terminals, by Rule 1, we place two entries, *s*5 and *s*4, in the *ACTION* part of the parsing table, for state 0.

We observe that the set-of-items for $I_1$ contains a special item $[E' \rightarrow E\ \cdot]$; hence, state 1, takes an 'accept' action on input $, as per Rule 3.

Let us consider state 2: There is only one transition from $I_2$ to $I_7$ on terminal '*'. Hence, we have the entry, *ACTION* (2, *) = *s*7, as shown in Table 7.3.

Similarly, the set-of-items for $I_2$ consists of the item '$[E \rightarrow T\ \cdot]$', which is of the form '$[A \rightarrow \alpha\ \cdot]$'. Hence, we can apply Rule 2 here. We have already computed 'follow (*E*)' = {$, +, )} in the previous section, and also, '$E \rightarrow T$' is rule number 2 as per our production rule numbering. Thus, for every symbol in 'follow (*E*)', that is, for every symbol *a* from the set {\$, +, )}, we can make an entry, *ACTION* (2, *a*) = *r*2. Here, *r*2 means reduce using rule number 2.

The following are the three entries for the three symbols from {\$, +, )}, as shown in Table 7.3.

*ACTION* [2, \$] = *r*2
*ACTION* [2, +] = *r*2
*ACTION* [2, )] = *r*2

The rest of the entries in Table 7.3 are also constructed in a similar fashion.

### *Working of SLR Parser*

Let us now see how an SLR parser works to check the syntax of an input string with the help of an SLR parsing table that we have generated.

The SLR parser, like other parsers, uses a stack for its actions.

The following are the actions of an SLR parser, if the state label on the top of the stack is *i* and the input symbol is *a*:

1. Start by shifting state label '0' onto the stack, indicating the initial state.
2. If *ACTION* (*i*, *a*) = *sj*, then push *a* first onto the stack and then push *j*.
3. If *ACTION* (*i*, *a*) = $r_j$, and the production numbered *j* is of the form '$A \rightarrow \alpha$', then pop everything out from the stack till it matches $\alpha$, and push the left-hand side *A* onto the stack. Let *k* be the state label on the stack below the newly-pushed symbol *A*; then push, *GOTO* (*k*, *A*) also onto the stack.
4. If *ACTION* (*i*, *a*) = accept, which indicates that the parsing process is complete, then declare the input string as syntactically correct.
5. If *ACTION* (*i*, *a*) is empty, that is, '–', then declare the input as syntactically incorrect.

For example, let us simulate the working of the SLR parser (Table 7.4) for the input string '*id* * *id* + *id*' using the parsing Table 7.3.

**Table 7.4** Working of SLR parser

| Stack | Input | Parser action |
|---|---|---|
| 0 | *id* * *id* + *id* \$ | Shift '0' initially |
| 0 *id* 5 | * *id* + *id* \$ | *ACTION* (0, *id*) = *s*5 |
| 0 *F* 3 | * *id* + *id* \$ | *ACTION* (5, *) = *r*6<br>*GOTO* (0, *F*) = 3 |
| 0 *T* 2 | * *id* + *id* \$ | *ACTION* (3, *) = *r*4<br>*GOTO* (0, *T*) = 2 |
| 0 *T* 2 * 7 | *id* + *id* \$ | *ACTION* (2, *) = *s*7 |
| 0 *T* 2 * 7 *id* 5 | + *id* \$ | *ACTION* (7, *id*) = *s*5 |
| 0 *T* 2 * 7 *F* 10 | + *id* \$ | *ACTION* (5, +) = *r*6<br>*GOTO* (7, *F*) = 10 |

| | | |
|---|---|---|
| 0 *T* 2 | + *id* $ | *ACTION* (10, +) = *r*3<br>*GOTO* (0, *T*) = 2 |
| 0 *E* 1 | + *id* $ | *ACTION* (2, +) = *r*2<br>*GOTO* (0, *E*) = 1 |
| 0 *E* 1 + 6 | *id* $ | *ACTION* (1, +) = *s*6 |
| 0 *E* 1 + 6 *id* 5 | $ | *ACTION* (6, *id*) = *s*5 |
| 0 *E* 1 + 6 *F* 3 | $ | *ACTION* (5, $) = *r*6<br>*GOTO* (6, *F*) = 3 |
| 0 *E* 1 + 6 *T* 9 | $ | *ACTION* (3, $) = *r*4<br>*GOTO* (6, *T*) = 9 |
| 0 *E* 1 | $ | *ACTION* (9, $) = *r*1<br>*GOTO* (0, *E*) = 1<br>'ACCEPT', because<br>*ACTION* (1, $) = 'accept' |

Thus, string '*id* * *id* + *id*' is accepted by the SLR parser.

### 7.5.3 LR(1) Grammar

LR(1) grammars use a *look-ahead* symbol, which is an additional symbol that is used to decide the state transition decisions such that conflicts are avoided. This additional symbol comes from the follow set for obvious reasons.

For finding the collection of sets-of-items for LR(1) grammars, the procedures 'closure' and '*GOTO*' are still required, similar to LR(0) grammars. The difference here is in the form of an item, which is specified as:

$$[A \rightarrow \alpha \cdot B\beta, a],$$

where, $a$ is the look-ahead (next probable input) symbol.

As the look-ahead symbol is included in every item, the reduction decisions, which are otherwise made for all symbols from the 'follow' set as in the SLR parser, are now restricted only to the probable next input symbol (in other words, to the probable subset of the 'follow' set only). Therefore, the decisions made by the parser using LR(1) grammar are more precise compared to those made by the SLR parser.

There is a slight change in finding the 'closure' in this grammar due to the change in form of the item.

For the aforementioned item, if there exists productions of the form '$B \rightarrow \gamma$', then we add '$[B \rightarrow \cdot\ \gamma]$' to the set-of-items. Here, we must also find the look-ahead symbol for '$[B \rightarrow \cdot\ \gamma]$'; it is obtained by 'first ($\beta a$)'.

Thus, the item to be added will be:

$$[B \rightarrow \cdot\ \gamma, \text{first } (\beta\ a)]$$

In the next section, we shall use an example to construct the canonical-LR parser that uses the collection of LR(1) sets-of-items.

***Construction of LR(1) Sets-of-items***

Let us consider the following augmented grammar, with $S'$ as the start symbol.

$0: S' \to S$
$1: S \to C\ C$
$2: C \to c\ C$
$3: C \to d$

We have:

First $(S)$ = first $(C) = \{c, d\}$.

The collection of sets-of-items is obtained using the same method as that for LR(0), except that the closure of every item includes the look-ahead computation as well.

To begin with, the item will be:

$[S' \to \cdot\ S, \$]$

The collection is:

| | |
|---|---|
| $I_0$: $S' \to \cdot\ S, \$$ | |
| $S \to \cdot\ C\ C, \$$ | match with $[A \to \alpha \cdot B\beta, a]$ |
| $C \to \cdot\ c\ C, c\ /\ d$ | $\beta = C, a = \$$ |
| $C \to \cdot\ d, c\ /\ d$ | first $(C\ \$)$ = first $(C) = \{c, d\}$ |

Item $I_0$ is obtained by taking the closure of $[S' \to \cdot S, \$]$.

$I_1$: $S' \to S\cdot, \$$

State $I_1$ is reached from $I_0$ moving on $S$.

| | |
|---|---|
| $I_2$: $S \to C \cdot C, \$$ | match with $[A \to \alpha \cdot B\beta, a]$ |
| $C \to \cdot\ c\ C, \$$ | $\beta = \epsilon, a = \$$ |
| $C \to \cdot\ d, \$$ | first $(\beta\ a) = \{\ \$\ \}$ |

State $I_2$ is reached from $I_0$ after making a transition on input $C$ and then taking a closure of the item $[S \to C \cdot C, \$]$.

| | |
|---|---|
| $I_3$: $C \to c \cdot C, c/d$ | match with $[A \to \alpha \cdot B\beta, a]$ |
| $C \to \cdot\ c\ C, c/d$ | $\beta = \epsilon, a = c$ or $d$ |
| $C \to \cdot\ d, c/d$ | first $(\beta\ a) = \{c, d\}$ |

State $I_3$ is reached from $I_0$ on input terminal $c$ and then taking a closure of $[C \to c \cdot C, c/d]$.

$I_4$: $C \to d\ \cdot, c/d$

State $I_4$ is reached from $I_0$ transiting on terminal symbol $d$.

$I_5$: $S \to C\ C\ \cdot, \$$

State $I_5$ is reached from $I_2$ on input non-terminal $C$. Similarly, state $I_6$ is reached from $I_2$ moving on the terminal symbol $c$ and then taking a closure of the item $[C \to c \cdot C, \$]$.

$I_6$: $C \rightarrow c \cdot C, \$$ match with $[A \rightarrow \alpha \cdot B\beta, a]$

$C \rightarrow \cdot c\, C, \$$ $\beta = \epsilon, a = \$$

$C \rightarrow \cdot d, \$$ first $(\beta\, a) = \{ \$ \}$

$I_7$: $C \rightarrow d \cdot , \$$

State $I_7$ is reached from $I_2$ on input symbol $d$.

$I_8$: $C \rightarrow c\, C \cdot, c/d$

State $I_8$ is reached from $I_3$ on input symbol $C$.

If we move from $I_3$ on input symbols $c$ or $d$, we get the same sets-of–items, which are already existing. For example, if we move on $c$ from $I_3$, we will again get $I_3$; similarly, if we move on $d$ we again get $I_4$.

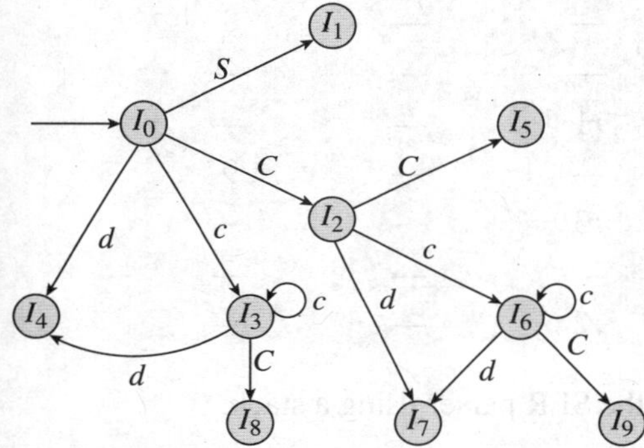


**Figure 7.7** DFA or *GOTO* graph for collection of LR(1) sets-of-items

We cannot move further from $I_4$ or $I_5$, as the entire right-hand side is already read, as indicated by the rightmost symbol, '·'.

$I_9$: $C \rightarrow c\, C \cdot , \$$

Moving from $I_6$ on $C$, we reach state $I_9$.

If we try to move on input symbols $c$ or $d$ from $I_6$, we again reach $I_6$ and $I_7$, respectively. We cannot transit further from $I_8$ and $I_9$. Thus, the collection of LR(1) sets-of-items is ready.

The *GOTO* graph or the DFA describing this collection of LR(1) sets-of-items is as shown in Fig. 7.7.

The state $I_0$ indicating the first set-of-LR(1)-items is the initial state, and all states can be final states.

This collection of sets-of-LR(1)-items is used to construct canonical-LR parsing table. An LR parser constructed using such a table table is called a *canonical LR parser*.

### 7.5.4 Canonical-LR Parser

The canonical-LR parsing table can be constructed using the following rules:

Assume that state $i$ of the parser is constructed from $I_i$ set-of-LR(1)-items.

The canonical-LR parsing table also contains two parts, '*ACTION*' and '*GOTO*', just as in the SLR parsing table.

The rules for constructing of the parsing table are as follows:

1. If $[A \rightarrow \alpha \cdot a\beta, b]$ is in $I_i$ and *GOTO* $(I_i, a) = I_j$, then

   *ACTION* $(i, a) =$ 'shift $a$ and move to $j$', or '$sj$'
2. If $[A \rightarrow \alpha \cdot, a]$ is in $I_i$, then

   *ACTION* $(i, a) =$ 'reduce using rule $A \rightarrow \alpha$' or '$rk$',

   where $k$ is the production rule number
3. If $[S' \rightarrow S \cdot, \$]$ is in $I_i$, then

   *ACTION* $(i, \$) =$ 'accept'

4. If *GOTO* $(I_i, A) = I_j$, then

   *GOTO* $(i, A) = j$

The canonical-LR parsing table for the collection of sets-of-LR(1)-items is given in Table 7.5.

**Table 7.5** Canonical-LR parsing table

| State | *ACTION* | | | *GOTO* | |
|---|---|---|---|---|---|
| | *c* | *d* | $ | *S* | *C* |
| 0 | *s*3 | *s*4 | — | 1 | 2 |
| 1 | — | — | Accept | — | — |
| 2 | *s*6 | *s*7 | — | — | 5 |
| 3 | *s*3 | *s*4 | — | — | 8 |
| 4 | *r*3 | *r*3 | — | — | — |
| 5 | — | — | *r*1 | — | — |
| 6 | *s*6 | *s*7 | — | — | 9 |
| 7 | — | — | *r*3 | — | — |
| 8 | *r*2 | *r*2 | — | — | — |
| 9 | — | — | *r*2 | — | — |

Parsing actions are taken the same way as the SLR parser using a stack.

***Note***: We can see from Rule 2 that reduce actions are taken only on the look-ahead symbol and not on the entire 'follow' set—the set of look-ahead symbols is always a subset of the 'follow' set. This actually is a major differentiator between SLR and canonical-LR parsers. The SLR parser at times generates conflicts, which can be resolved using a look-ahead. This is illustrated in the following examples.

**Example 7.1** Construct an SLR parsing table for the following grammar:

$0: S' \to S$
$1: S \to L = R$
$2: S \to R$
$3: L \to *R$
$4: L \to id$
$5: R \to L$

***Solution*** We need to find the 'first' and 'follow' sets for all the non-terminals first.

First $(S')$ = first $(S)$ = first $(L)$ = first $(R)$ = $\{*, id\}$

Follow $(S')$ contains \$ by Rule 1 for finding 'follow' discussed earlier.

Using production '$S' \to S$', which is the only production with $S$ on the right-hand side of the production, and applying Rule 3 for finding 'follow', we get:

Follow $(S)$ = Follow $(S')$ = $\{\$\}$

Let us find 'follow ($L$)' now.

Consider the productions, '$S \to L = R$' and '$R \to L$', where '$L$' exists on the right-hand side.

For the production '$S \to L = R$', if we apply Rule 2 for finding 'follow', we get '$A \to \alpha B\beta$', where $A = S$, $\alpha = \epsilon$, $B = L$, and $\beta$ is equal to '$=R$'. Therefore, 'follow ($L$)' contains first ($=R$), which is '$=$'.

For the production '$R \to L$', applying Rule 3 for finding 'follow', we have, everything in 'follow ($R$)' in 'follow ($L$)'. However, we are yet to find 'follow ($R$)'.

To find follow ($R$), we need to consider three productions, which are '$S \to L = R$', '$S \to R$', and '$L \to *R$'.

From the productions '$S \to L = R$' and '$S \to R$', which match the pattern '$A \to \alpha B$', we apply Rule 3 for finding 'follow'. Thus, 'follow ($R$)' contains everything in 'follow ($S$)', which is \$.

Applying Rule 3 to the production '$L \to * R$', 'follow (R)' also contains '$=$'. Thus, finally we have:

$$\text{Follow } (R) = \text{follow } (L) = \{=, \$\}$$

Let us now construct the collection of LR(0) sets-of-items:

$I_0$: $S' \to \cdot S$
$S \to \cdot L = R$
$S \to \cdot R$
$L \to \cdot * R$
$L \to \cdot id$
$R \to \cdot L$

$I_1$: $S' \to S \cdot$ — $GOTO\ (I_0, S)$

$I_2$: $S \to L \cdot = R$ — $GOTO\ (I_0, L)$
$R \to L \cdot$

$I_3$: $S \to R \cdot$ — $GOTO\ (I_0, R)$

$I_4$: $L \to * \cdot R$ — $GOTO\ (I_0, *)$
$R \to \cdot L$
$L \to \cdot * R$
$L \to \cdot id$

$I_5$: $L \to id \cdot$ — $GOTO\ (I_0, id)$

$I_6$: $S \to L = \cdot R$ — $GOTO\ (I_2, =)$
$R \to \cdot L$
$L \to \cdot * R$
$L \to \cdot \text{Id}$

$I_7$: $L \to * R \cdot$ — $GOTO\ (I_4, R)$

$I_8$: $R \to L \cdot$ — $GOTO\ (I_4, L)$

$I_9$: $S \to L = R \cdot$ — $GOTO\ (I_6, R)$

Let us construct the parsing table now using the construction algorithm. Refer to Table 7.6.

**Table 7.6** SLR parsing table with conflicts

| State | ACTION | | | | GOTO | | |
|---|---|---|---|---|---|---|---|
| | *id* | = | * | $ | *S* | *L* | *R* |
| 0 | *s*5 | — | *s*4 | — | 1 | 2 | 3 |
| 1 | — | — | — | Accept | — | — | — |
| 2 | — | *s*6, *r*5 | — | *r*5 | — | — | — |
| 3 | — | — | — | *r*2 | — | — | — |
| 4 | *s*5 | — | *s*4 | — | — | 8 | 7 |
| 5 | — | *r*4 | — | *r*4 | — | — | — |
| 6 | *s*5 | — | *s*4 | — | — | 8 | 9 |
| 7 | — | *r*3 | — | *r*3 | — | — | — |
| 8 | — | *r*5 | — | *r*5 | — | — | — |
| 9 | — | — | — | *r*1 | — | — | — |

We see from Table 7.6 that there is a *shift-reduce conflict* for the entry *ACTION* (2, =). This makes the parser non-deterministic, and hence, is not useful unless we get rid of the conflict. When we get such multiple entries in the parsing table, it is an indication that the grammar is not LR(0) grammar.

---

**Example 7.2** Construct a canonical-LR parsing table for the following grammar:

$0: S' \to S$
$1: S \to L = R$
$2: S \to R$
$3: L \to *R$
$4: L \to id$
$5: R \to L$

***Solution*** Let us now construct the collection of LR(1) sets-of-items as follows:

$I_0: S' \to \cdot\, S, \$$

| | |
|---|---|
| $S \to \cdot\, L = R, \$$ | match with $[A \to \alpha \cdot B\beta, a]$ |
| $L \to \cdot * R, =$ | $\alpha = \epsilon, \beta =$ '$= R$', $a = \$$ |
| $L \to \cdot\, id, =$ | first $(\beta\, a) = \{=\}$ |
| $S \to \cdot\, R, \$$ | match with $[A \to \alpha \cdot B\beta, a]$ |
| $R \to \cdot\, L, \$$ | $\alpha = \epsilon, \beta = \epsilon; a = \$$ |
| | first $(\beta\, a) = \{\$\}$ |

$I_1: S' \to S\, \cdot, \$$     *GOTO* $(I_0, S)$

| | |
|---|---|
| $I_2$: $S \rightarrow L \cdot = R, \$$ | *GOTO* $(I_0, L)$ |
| $R \rightarrow L \cdot, \$$ | |
| $I_3$: $S \rightarrow R \cdot, \$$ | *GOTO* $(I_0, R)$ |
| $I_4$: $L \rightarrow * \cdot R, =$ | *GOTO* $(I_0, *)$ |
| $R \rightarrow \cdot L, =$ | match with $[A \rightarrow \alpha \cdot B\beta, a]$ |
| $L \rightarrow \cdot * R, =$ | $\alpha = \epsilon, \beta = \epsilon, a =$ '=' |
| $L \rightarrow \cdot\ id, =$ | first $(\beta\ a) = \{=\}$ |
| $I_5$: $L \rightarrow id \cdot, =$ | *GOTO* $(I_0, id)$ |
| $I_6$: $S \rightarrow L = \cdot R, \$$ | *GOTO* $(I_2, =)$ |
| $R \rightarrow \cdot L, \$$ | match with $[A \rightarrow \alpha \cdot B\beta, a]$ |
| $L \rightarrow \cdot * R, \$$ | $\alpha = \epsilon, \beta = \epsilon, a = \$$ |
| $L \rightarrow \cdot\ id, \$$ | first $(\beta\ a) = \{\$\}$ |
| $I_7$: $L \rightarrow * R \cdot, =$ | *GOTO* $(I_4, R)$ |
| $I_8$: $R \rightarrow L \cdot, =$ | *GOTO* $(I_4, L)$ |
| $I_9$: $S \rightarrow L = R \cdot \$$ | *GOTO* $(I_6, R)$ |
| $I_{10}$: $R \rightarrow L \cdot, \$$ | *GOTO* $(I_6, L)$ |
| $I_{11}$: $L \rightarrow * \cdot R, \$$ | *GOTO* $(I_6, *)$ |
| $R \rightarrow \cdot L, \$$ | match with $[A \rightarrow \alpha \cdot B\beta, a]$ |
| $L \rightarrow \cdot * R, \$$ | $\alpha = \epsilon, \beta = \epsilon, a = \$$ |
| $L \rightarrow \cdot\ id, \$$ | first $(\beta\ a) = \{\$\}$ |
| $I_{12}$: $L \rightarrow id \cdot, \$$ | *GOTO* $(I_6, id)$ |
| $I_{13}$: $L \rightarrow * R \cdot, \$$ | *GOTO* $(I_{11}, R)$ |
| $I_{14}$: $R \rightarrow L \cdot, \$$ | *GOTO* $(I_{11}, L)$ |

***Note***: We see that the number of states in a canonical-LR parser is more than the number of states in an SLR parser.

Let us now build the canonical-LR parsing table to see whether or not the shift-reduce conflict problem— that we have seen in the previous example—has been solved (refer to Table 7.7).

We see from Table 7.7 that the shift-reduce conflict we saw earlier in Table 7.5 is resolved with the help of the look-ahead symbol.

We see that in Table 7.6, state $I_2$ has the conflict—whether to shift '=' onto the stack or reduce by rule number 6, which is '$R \rightarrow L$'. The conflict arises because both the symbols $\{=, \$\}$ were included in 'follow ($R$)'. Table 7.7 uses a look-ahead symbol from the subset of the 'follow' set. It uses 'shift =' for the symbol '=', while the reduce entry is only meant for the symbol \$. The conflict is thus resolved and the result is a more precise parser. However, the overall number of states in the canonical-LR parser is much more than the SLR parser.

**Table 7.7** Canonical-LR parsing table without conflicts

| State | ACTION | | | | GOTO | | |
|---|---|---|---|---|---|---|---|
| | *id* | = | * | $ | *S* | *L* | *R* |
| 0 | *s*5 | — | *s*4 | — | 1 | 2 | 3 |
| 1 | — | — | — | Accept | — | — | — |
| 2 | — | *s*6 | — | *r*5 | — | — | — |
| 3 | — | — | — | *r*2 | — | — | — |
| 4 | *s*5 | — | *s*4 | — | — | 8 | 7 |
| 5 | — | *r*4 | — | — | — | — | — |
| 6 | *s*12 | — | *s*11 | — | — | 10 | 9 |
| 7 | — | *r*3 | — | — | — | — | — |
| 8 | — | *r*5 | — | — | — | — | — |
| 9 | — | — | — | *r*1 | — | — | — |
| 10 | — | — | — | *r*5 | — | — | — |
| 11 | *s*12 | — | *s*11 | — | — | 14 | 13 |
| 12 | — | — | — | *r*4 | — | — | — |
| 13 | — | — | — | *r*3 | — | — | — |
| 14 | — | — | — | *r*5 | — | — | — |

Hence, a new type of parser called the LALR parser is introduced in the next section, which has a comparable number of states to the SLR parser and uses look-ahead, as in the canonical-LR parser.

### 7.5.5 LALR Parser

LALR is expanded as 'look-ahead LR' parser and is very commonly used in compiler construction. It requires much lesser space to store the parsing table and is equally capable of resolving conflict using look-ahead.

Let us consider the canonical-LR parsing table (refer to Table 7.5) we have seen in the previous section. The collection of LALR sets-of-items combines the sets of LR(1) items, which differ only in the look-ahead and not in the behaviour, so as to reduce the overall number of states involved. If we can thus construct the reduced parsing table, then the grammar is called LALR(1) *grammar*.

For example, the LR(1) item sets in the previous section, $I_3$ and $I_6$ can be combined as follows into $I_{36}$:

$$I_{36}: C \to c \cdot C, c/d/\$$$
$$C \to \cdot c\ C, c/d/\$$$
$$C \to \cdot d, c/d/\$$$

Similarly, $I_4$ and $I_7$ can be combined into $I_{47}$ as:

$$I_{47}: C \to d \cdot , c/d/\$$$

States $I_8$ and $I_9$ can also be combined into $I_{89}$ as:

$$I_{89}: C \rightarrow c\ C \cdot,\ c/d/\$$$

Thus, the LALR parsing table can be drawn using the reduced number of states as shown in Table 7.8.

**Table 7.8** LALR parsing table

| State | *ACTION* | | | *GOTO* | |
|---|---|---|---|---|---|
| | *c* | *d* | \$ | *S* | *C* |
| 0 | *s*36 | *s*47 | — | 1 | 2 |
| 1 | — | — | Accept | — | — |
| 2 | *s*36 | *s*47 | — | — | 5 |
| 36 | *s*36 | *s*47 | — | — | 89 |
| 47 | *r*3 | *r*3 | *r*3 | — | — |
| 5 | — | — | *r*1 | — | — |
| 89 | *r*2 | *r*2 | *r*2 | — | — |

We see that we almost got rid of three states from the earlier canonical-LR table.

***Note***: The LALR parser takes more number of parsing steps than the canonical-LR parser to declare a given input as syntactically incorrect, but takes exactly the same number of steps for any input acceptance. Since acceptance is what matters in compilers, where the stress is on further processing and machine-code generation, the LALR is considered the optimum type of parser and hence is used very commonly.

## SUMMARY

In compiler construction, the first phase is lexical analysis, which processes the source input program and identifies the valid words (or tokens) from it. Parsing is the *second phase of the compiler* construction process. A parser is a program, which groups the tokens that are received from the lexical analyser to formulate statements, using a context-free grammar (CFG) as reference. If a statement can be formulated (or constructed) from the given stream of tokens as per the reference CFG, then the stream of tokens and hence, the source input program is considered to be syntactically correct. If no statement can be formulated as per the reference CFG, then the source input program is considered syntactically incorrect, and errors are generated.

A parser is a program that is *deterministic* in nature, and ambiguity of a grammar introduces non-determinism. Hence, ambiguous grammars are not suitable for parsing—we must first remove the ambiguity and then use the modified unambiguous grammar for parsing.

A parser tries to derive the statement using the grammar; if it can derive the statement, the statement is considered to be syntactically correct; else, it is considered to be incorrect.

Parsers are classified as *top-down parsers* and *bottom-up* (or *shift-reduce*) *parsers*. Both these techniques are fundamentally different from each other.

As we know, derivation involves construction of a derivation tree (or parse tree). The *top-down parser* begins from the start symbol, which happens to be the root node (*top*) of the parse tree, and works its way to the terminals, which are the leaves of the derivation tree representing bottom (*down*) of the tree. The top-down parser uses *leftmost derivation* for reconstructing a statement. As we are aware, leftmost derivation generates the symbols in the same order as they are read from the input token stream, that is, from left to right.

A top-down parser may suffer from multiple problems such as *backtracking* or *incorrect parsing decisions*, if it follows the same production sequence as received from the CFG. Backtracking is more like a redo of the decision making by applying the next available rule, which continues till the parser reaches the symbol matching the input token. This may cause delays.

The solution to such problems is to read the input token beforehand, and then apply the rule whose right-hand side begins with the same symbol as the input token. To simplify this process, the production rule must start with a terminal symbol, which means, the grammar must be expressed in Greibach normal form (GNF). At times, there might be multiple rules that start with the same terminal symbol. In such cases *left-factoring* is used. Left-factoring takes out a common part from the multiple production rules and introduces a new non-terminal to take care of the remaining part of the production rule.

Another problem that might occur during top-down parsing is *left recursion*. A grammar is said to be left-recursive if there exists a non-terminal $A$, such that some derivation from $A$ yields a sentential form $A\,\alpha$ for some $\alpha$, that is, $A \stackrel{+}{\Rightarrow} A\,\alpha$. If there is a left-recursive pair of productions of the form:

$$A \to A\,\alpha \mid \beta,$$

where, $\beta$ does not begin with $A$, then we can get rid of these productions by introducing the following new set of productions to remove left-recursion:

$$A \to \beta\, A'$$
$$A' \to \alpha\, A' \mid \epsilon$$

A *recursive descent parser* (RDP) is a type of top-down parser that needs no backtracking. This parser makes use of recursive procedures to validate the input for correctness. It does not require backtracking since every procedure checks the input token before taking any action; this is required to minimize the delay caused due to backtracking. Thus, the solution to the backtracking problem is in-built in this type of top-down parser.

Every parser works as a DPDA. Therefore, every parser is bound to use a stack either directly or indirectly. An RDP uses the stack indirectly, as it needs to call multiple recursive procedures for making parsing decisions.

A *bottom-up parser*, as the name suggests, constructs the parse tree from leaves to the root (start symbol) of the grammar. It is also called a *shift-reduce* (SR) parser as it consumes the statement to be parsed and attempts to reduce it to the start symbol. If a given statement gets reduced to the start symbol, the statement is considered to be syntactically correct; else, it is considered to be incorrect. The behaviour of this parser is exactly the reverse of the top-down parser; it uses the rightmost derivation in the reverse order, which is also called *rightmost reduction* or *canonical reduction*.

Reaching from one sentential form to the previous in the reduction process requires a production of the form '$A \to \alpha$' with the right-hand side as $\alpha$, which gets reduced to the left-hand side symbol, $A$. The symbol that must be reduced is called the *handle*. In order to perform the reduction, at every step, the handle needs to be identified. A handle is always the right-hand side of some production. This process of identifying a handle at every step and reducing it appropriately to reach a start symbol eventually is known as *handle pruning*.

A bottom-up (or shift-reduce) parser also makes use of a stack for the handle pruning process. The 'shift' operation thus means shifting a symbol onto the stack from the token stream. Reduction using the production rule '$A \to \alpha$' means popping out the handle $\alpha$ from the stack and pushing $A$ instead.

An *operator precedence parser* is a type of shift-reduce parser, which handles a small class of parsers that use the precedence and associative relations among the operators to make parsing decisions.

There are a few types of bottom-up parsers called LR-parsers, which are efficient parsers as they are table-driven. These parsers use table lookup to perform parsing actions, and are hence much faster compared to RDP.

An *SLR parser* uses *LR(0) grammar*, a special type of DCFL, where LR(0) stands for the following: '*L*: left to right scan of the input, *R*: following a rightmost reduction, and *0*: using zero symbols of look-ahead from the input'; and SLR stands for 'simple LR' parser, which uses a collection of sets-of-LR(0)-items.

The *LR(0) item* of a grammar G is defined as a production of G with a dot at some position on the right-hand side of the production. For example, the production '$A \rightarrow XYZ$' in some grammar G generates four items:

$A \rightarrow \cdot XYZ$
$A \rightarrow X \cdot YZ$
$A \rightarrow XY \cdot Z$
$A \rightarrow XYZ \cdot$

The production '$A \rightarrow \epsilon$' generates only one item, '$A \rightarrow \cdot$'.

If $I$ is a set of items for a grammar G, then the set of items in *closure* ($I$) is constructed from $I$ using the following rules:

1. Every item in $I$ is in closure ($I$)
2. If '$A \rightarrow \alpha \cdot B\beta$' is in closure ($I$) and '$B \rightarrow \gamma$' is a production, then add the item '$B \rightarrow \cdot \gamma$' to closure ($I$), if it is not already there. Here, $A$ and $B$ are non-terminals, while $\alpha$, $\beta$, and $\gamma$ are sentential forms.

If $I$ is a set of items and $X$ is a grammar symbol, then *GOTO* ($I$, $X$) is defined as the closure of the set of all items [$A \rightarrow \alpha X \cdot \beta$], such that [$A \rightarrow \alpha \cdot X\beta$] is in $I$.

The algorithm to construct the canonical *collection of sets-of-LR(0)-items* for an augmented grammar G' is as follows:

1. Start with $I$ = closure ({$S' \rightarrow \cdot S$}) and declare that as '$I_0$'th set-of-items.
2. For each set-of-item in $I$ and each grammar symbol $X$, whether terminal or non-terminal, if *GOTO* ($I_0$, $X$) is non-empty and not in $I$, then add it to $I$; and name it as $I_1$, and so on.
3. Repeat Step 2 until no more sets-of-items can be added to $I$.

The *SLR parsing table* can be constructed from the collection of sets-of-LR(0)-items using the following rules:

1. If [$A \rightarrow \alpha \cdot a\beta$] is in $I_i$, and *GOTO* ($I_i$, $a$) = $I_j$, then
   *ACTION* ($i$, $a$) = 'shift $a$ and move to $j$', or
   *ACTION* ($i$, $a$) = '$sj$'
   Here, $a$ is a terminal symbol.
2. If [$A \rightarrow \alpha \cdot$] is in $I_i$, then for all terminal symbols $a$ in follow ($A$), we write:
   *ACTION* ($i$, $a$) = 'reduce using rule $A \rightarrow \alpha$', or
   *ACTION* ($i$, $a$) = '$rk$', where $k$ is the production rule number
3. If [$S' \rightarrow S \cdot$] is in $I_i$, then
   *ACTION* ($i$, \$) = 'accept'
4. If *GOTO* ($I_i$, $A$) = $I_j$, then
   *GOTO* ($i$, $A$) = $j$, where $A$ is any non-terminal

'*First (X)*' is the set of terminal symbols with which the strings derivable from $X$ begins; '*follow (X)*' is the set of all terminal symbols that immediately follow $X$ in any derivation for the given grammar.

Grammars that use a *look-ahead* symbol are called *LR(1) grammars*. The look-ahead is an additional symbol that is used to decide the state transitions such that no conflicts arise. Evidently, this additional symbol comes from the follow set. For finding the collection of sets-of-items for LR(1) grammars, the procedures 'closure' and '*GOTO*' are still required just as in LR(0) grammars. The difference here is in the form of an *LR(1) item*, which is specified as:

[$A \rightarrow \alpha \cdot B\beta, a$],

where, $a$ is the look-ahead (next probable input) symbol. As the look-ahead symbol is included in every item, the reduction decisions, which were otherwise made for all symbols from the follow set as in an SLR parser, are now restricted only to the next probable input symbol; in other words, to the probable subset of the follow set. Therefore, the decisions made by the parser that uses LR(1) grammar are more precise compared to the SLR parser.

There is a slight change in finding the '*closure*' now due to change in form of the item. For the item, [$A \rightarrow \alpha \cdot B\beta, a$], if there exist productions of the form '$B \rightarrow \gamma$', then we add '[$B \rightarrow \cdot \gamma$]' to the set-of-items. Here, we also need to find the look-ahead symbol for '[$B \rightarrow \cdot \gamma$]', and it is obtained by 'first ($\beta a$)'. Thus, the item to be added will be [$B \rightarrow \cdot \gamma$, first ($\beta$ $a$)]. The *collection of LR(1) sets-of-items* is obtained using the same method that was used for collection of LR(0) sets-of-items, except that the closure of every item includes the look-ahead computation as well.

A *canonical-LR parser* uses the parsing table generated from the collection of LR(1) sets-of-items. The canonical-LR parsing table is constructed using the following rules:

1. If $[A \to \alpha \cdot a\beta, b]$ is in $I_i$ and $GOTO\ (I_i, a) = I_j$, then

   $ACTION\ (i, a)$ = 'shift $a$ and move to $j$', or '$sj$'

2. If $[A \to \alpha\cdot, a]$ is in $I_i$, then

   $ACTION\ (i, a)$ = 'reduce using rule $A \to \alpha$', or '$rk$',

   where $k$ is the production rule number

3. If $[S' \to S\cdot, \$]$ is in $I_i$, then

   $ACTION\ (i, \$)$ = 'accept'

4. If $GOTO\ (I_i, A) = I_j$, then

   $GOTO\ (i, A) = j$

The SLR parser at times generates conflicts, which can be resolved using a look-ahead symbol as in a canonical-LR parser, though the number of overall states in the canonical-LR parser is more than the SLR parser. Hence, a new type of parser called the *LALR parser* is introduced; it has a comparable number of states as in the SLR parser and uses look-ahead as in the canonical-LR parser.

The collection of LALR sets-of-items is a combination of the sets-of-LR(1)-items, which differ only in the look-ahead, and not in the behaviour, so as to reduce the overall number of states required. If we can construct the reduced form parsing table in this way, then the grammar is called *LALR(1) grammar*.

## EXERCISES

This section lists a few unsolved problems to help the readers understand the topic better and practise a few examples related to the parsing techniques.

### Objective Questions

(U) 7.1 Which of the following statements is true?
  (a) From any CFG, we can construct an SLR parser.
  (b) Ordering of productions is important while building a top-down parser.
  (c) A top-down parser is less precise than a bottom-up parsers.
  (d) An LALR parser generally has fewer states than the equivalent canonical-LR parser.

(U) 7.2 If $A$ is a top-down parser and $B$ is a bottom-up parser, which of the following statements is false?
  (a) $A$ regenerates the string to be parsed, beginning with the start symbol of the grammar.
  (b) $B$ reduces the input string to the start symbol of the grammar.
  (c) $A$ uses canonical reduction to check the syntactic errors.
  (d) $B$ uses canonical reduction to reach the start symbol.

(U) 7.3 'Left recursion sends the top-down parser into an infinite loop while parsing the input string.' Is this statement true or false?

(U) 7.4 Which of the following statements are true?
  $S1$: Left recursion is a major problem in top-down parsing and needs to be removed first.
  $S2$: Backtracking makes the bottom-up parser delay the input processing.
  $S3$: SLR parser has lesser number of states than canonical-LR parser.
  $S4$: Canonical-LR parser is more powerful than LALR parser.
  (a) $S1$ and $S2$
  (b) $S1$ only
  (c) $S2$ only
  (d) $S1$ and $S3$
  (e) $S4$ only
  (f) $S3$ only
  (g) None of these
  (h) All of these

(U) 7.5 'Ambiguous grammar can be used as is for building a parser.' Is this statement true or false?

(R) 7.6 Rightmost reduction is also known as ___________.

(U) 7.7 'An LALR parser has a comparable number of states to the SLR parser.' Is this statement true or false?

(L) 7.8 'An LALR parser is less efficient than a canonical-LR parser when it comes to rejecting the invalid input.' Is this statement true or false?

## Review Questions

(U) 7.1 Explain the applications of leftmost and rightmost derivations in parsing.

(A) 7.2 Construct the LALR parsing table for the following grammar:

$D \rightarrow L : T$
$L \rightarrow L, id \mid id$
$T \rightarrow \text{int} \mid \text{real}$

Simulate the LALR parser actions for the acceptance of the string '$a, b, c$ : int'.

(L) 7.3 Differentiate between top-down and bottom-up parsers.

(U) 7.4 Write a short note on recursive descent parser.

(L) 7.5 Explain, giving reasons, why leftmost derivation cannot be applied in shift-reduce parsing.

(A) 7.6 Construct the LALR parsing table for the following grammar:

0: $S' \rightarrow S$
1: $S \rightarrow L = R$
2: $S \rightarrow R$
3: $L \rightarrow * R$
4: $L \rightarrow id$
5: $R \rightarrow L$

(U) 7.7 Explain the concept of 'first' and 'follow' sets using suitable examples. In addition discuss the rules to compute 'first' and 'follow'.

(A) 7.8 Find 'first' and 'follow' sets for the non-terminals $S$ and $C$ for the following grammar:

$S \rightarrow i\,C\,t\,S\,e\,S \mid i\,C\,t\,S \mid a$
$C \rightarrow b$

State whether or not the given grammar is suitable for parsing.

(A) 7.9 Prepare the following grammar for top-down parsing:

$E \rightarrow E + E \mid E - E \mid E * E \mid E / E \mid E \wedge E \mid (E) \mid id$

***Hint***: Remove ambiguity, remove left recursion, use left-factoring, if required.

(U) 7.10 Discuss the problems that may occur while constructing the top-down parser and their solutions.

(U) 7.11 Explain why canonical reduction is used in bottom-up parsing.

(U) 7.12 Explain the steps required to construct the SLR parsing table.

(U) 7.13 Discuss the pros and cons of an RDP.

(U) 7.14 Explain why ambiguity is a trouble while parsing.

(U) 7.15 Explain 'backtracking' in the context of top-down parsing. Give suitable examples wherever required.

**Answers to Objective Questions**

7.1. (d) 7.2. (c) 7.3. True 7.4. (d) 7.5. False 7.6. canonical reduction 7.7. True
7.8. True

# 8 Post Machine

## LEARNING OBJECTIVES

After completing this chapter, the reader will be able to understand the following:

- Introduction to Post machine and its finite control model
- Pictorial representation of Post machine
- Comparison of powers of pushdown stack-memory machine (PDM) and Post machine (PM)
- Comparison of powers of finite state machine (FSM) and Post machine (PM)
- Equivalence of Post machine (PM) and Turing machine (TM)

## 8.1 INTRODUCTION

In Chapter 6, we have seen the elements and working of a pushdown stack-memory machine (PDM). The PDM uses a stack as an external memory, which is an improvement over the finite state machine (FSM). We also know that the power of the PDM is intermediate between the FSM and the Turing machine (TM).

There is one more machine comparable to the TM, which is called the Post machine (PM). This machine can accept the set of languages accepted by the FSM, PDM, as well as the TM. The major difference between the PDM and the PM, apart from the fact that the latter is more powerful, is that the PM uses queue data structure as memory, while the PDM uses external stack.

The power of the PM is equivalent to that of the TM; the only difference is in the representation.

## 8.2 ELEMENTS OF POST MACHINE

A PM is collectively defined by the following elements:

1. A tape, which is bounded on one end and unbounded (or infinite) on the other. Initially, the input string is written onto the tape, using a special character '#' to indicate the end; the rest of the tape is blank ($\not{b}$)

2. A finite set of allowable tape symbols ($\Gamma$) including '#' and blank character ƀ
3. A finite input alphabet $\Sigma$, which is a subset of the set of allowable tape symbols, that is, $\Sigma \subseteq \Gamma$
4. A start (or initial) state
5. Halt states: 'accept' and 'reject'
6. A non-branching state: 'add'
7. A branching state: 'read'
8. A tape implemented as a queue data structure

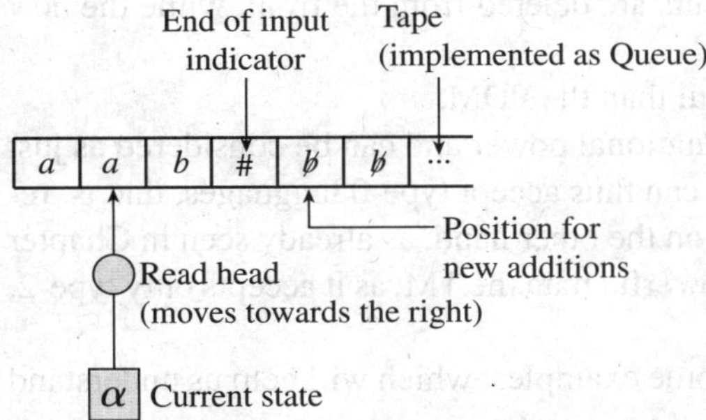


**Figure 8.1** Finite control representation for PM

Thus, in a PM the input is written onto its tape; the machine reads the tape symbols and, if necessary, adds symbols to the end of the input string (rear). This means that the PM can write symbols onto its tape just as the TM does. However, the major difference between the TM and the PM is that the head of the PM is allowed to move towards the right only. It cannot move towards the left, or remain in the same position like in the TM (refer to Fig. 8.1).

***Note***: Though the head of the PM can only move in one direction; it can add symbols to the rear of the tape. This means that the mechanism of moving to the right till the end of the input, adding symbols to the end, and coming back to read the next input symbol, is kept implicit. Addition of the symbol is thus implemented as a subroutine called 'add'. However, we know that internally, this requires moving in both the directions. Hence, the PM is simply an alternative visualization of the TM that implements its tape as a queue of symbols.

## 8.3 PUSHDOWN STACK-MEMORY MACHINE VS POST MACHINE

As we have already discussed, the PM uses queue data structure, while the PDM uses stack data structure as its external memory. Since the stack is external to the PDM, the stack and tape are two distinct entities. On the other hand, the PM uses its tape as queue, and can add new symbols at the end of the input string, which is indicated by the '#' symbol; hence, in a PM, the tape and queue are not distinct entities—the tape is implemented as its queue. Essentially, the PM consumes its own output (symbols added to the queue) as an input for use a later instance just as a TM does. The PDM, however, cannot consume the stack as an input, as it is external to its tape.

Since the PM uses its tape as queue, it has the ability to add symbols to the tape while executing. This means that the PM can write symbols onto its tape. On the other hand, the PDM cannot write anything onto its tape; it can only read from the tape, because it has access to an external stack for storing symbols. The PDM, thus, has a read head only, whereas, the PM has a read/write head.

In the PM, the head is perceived to read from left to right and traverse only in one direction. However, in reality, the addition of more symbols to the rear of the tape is kept implicit.

This means that the head can traverse to the extreme right till end of input (#) is received, add some symbols, and traverse back from right to left to point to the new symbol that is to be read from the tape. Thus, the head of the PM head can move in any direction in reality, while the head of the PDM can only move from left to right. The only restriction the PM has is that it is not allowed to read the symbols, which are already read. The symbols that are read are considered as deleted, as the tape is implemented as a queue—first-in-first-out (FIFO)—data structure. In queue, the elements are deleted from the front, while the new elements are added at the rear.

Thus, we see that the PM is more powerful than the PDM.

The PM is equivalent to the TM in computational power and can be considered as just another implementation of the TM. The PM can thus accept type-0 languages, that is, recursively enumerable languages. The PDM, on the other hand, as already seen in Chapter 6, is more powerful than the FSM, but less powerful than the TM, as it accepts only type-2, that is, context-free languages (CFLs).

In the subsequent sections, we shall see some examples, which will help us understand this better.

## 8.4 PICTORIAL REPRESENTATION OF POST MACHINE ELEMENTS

We can represent the PM with the help of a flow-chart-like notation similar to the PDM. The pictorial representation of the different PM elements is shown in Fig. 8.2.

We see that the start block denotes the initial state of the PM, that is, the entry point.

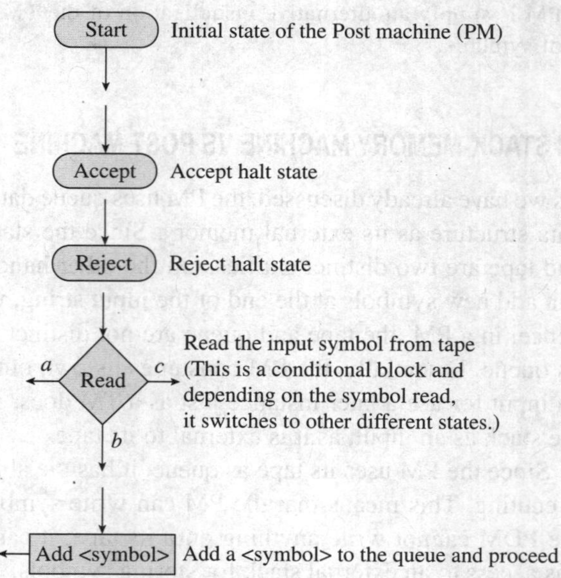


**Figure 8.2** Pictorial representation of PM elements

The 'accept' and 'reject' blocks respectively represent the accept halt and reject halt states, depending on whether the machine has accepted or rejected the input string.

The 'read' block is a conditional block, and, depending on the symbol read, the machine makes transitions to different states.

The'add' block is a process block and must be provided along with a symbol. This symbol gets added to the end of the queue, that is, after the '#' symbol. The add block is more like a subroutine, as discussed earlier, which abstracts the following steps—move to the right to detect the end of input (#); write the symbol to be added onto the tape at the rear; and move towards the left to point to the next symbol that is to be read. The add block simply abstracts the head movement in the direction—from right to left, though it seems that the head of the PM can only move in one direction, that is from left to right.

## 8.5 FINITE STATE MACHINE VS POST MACHINE

As we know, the FSM can only accept regular languages (or type-3 languages). Regular languages are thus acceptable by machines such as the FSM, which does not have a memory. The same set of regular languages can also be accepted using the PM. However, the PM is more powerful than the FSM, as the former has infinite memory in the form of its unbounded tape. The PM can remember any large string of symbols with the help of the internal queue (tape), which is a first-in-first-out (FIFO) type of data structure. Anyway, the queue (or memory) is not required for accepting or recognizing any regular language.

Thus, we see that the PM, being equivalent to the TM, is much powerful machine than the FSM.

Let us discuss some examples of PMs that accept regular languages.

---

**Example 8.1** Construct a PM that recognizes the language accepted by the DFA shown in Fig. 8.3.

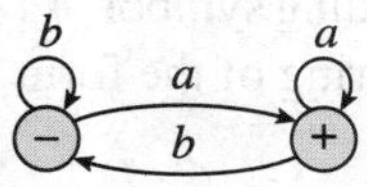

**Figure 8.3** An example DFA

***Solution*** The PM equivalent to DFA in Fig. 8.3 can be constructed as shown in Fig. 8.4.

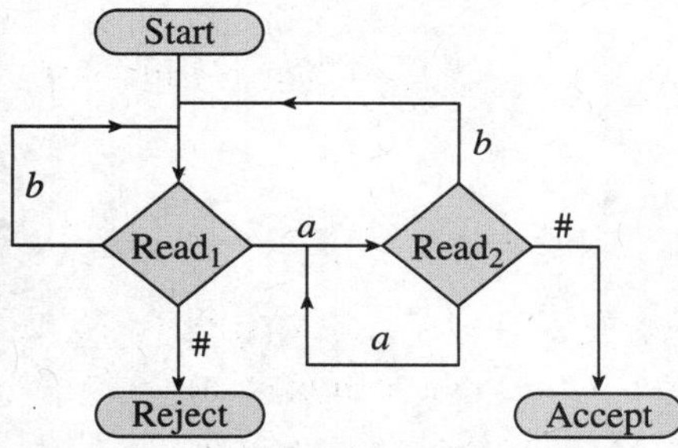

**Figure 8.4** PM equivalent to DFA in Fig. 8.3

We see that state $Read_1$ is analogous to the initial state of the given DFA, and state $Read_2$ is analogous to the final state of the given DFA. The only difference is that acceptance and rejection are clearly specified in the PM, which is not made explicit in the given DFA.

In state $Read_1$, the PM consumes any number of $b$'s and does not change the state till it reads the symbol $a$. Upon reading $a$, it makes a transition to state $Read_2$. In this state, the PM keeps consuming the $a$'s till it reads symbol $b$. Upon reading $b$, it makes a transition back to state $Read_1$. If the end of input indicator '#' is received in the final state, that is, $Read_2$, then the input is accepted; else, it is rejected.

> ***Note***: The DFA shown in Fig. 8.3 and the PM in Fig. 8.4 are equivalent machines, since they accept the same language. In this example, the PM does not use queue to store anything, as the language being accepted is regular. As we know, regular languages are accepted by the DFA, as they require no memory. Thus, Fig. 8.4 is more like a DFA expressed in the form of a PM. Further, if we compare the PM in Fig. 8.4 with the PDA in Fig. 6.4 (refer to Chapter 6, Section 6.4.1), we observe that they are the same. This is because neither of the two machines have used a stack or a queue, while accepting the given regular language. We can also say that, the diagrams drawn in Fig. 8.4 and Fig. 6.3 are only DFAs that are represented using the pictorial representation scheme.

Obviously, if we delete stack from the PDA and queue from the PM, we will get the machine without an external memory, which is nothing but the FA.

---

**Example 8.2** Construct a PM that accepts the following language:

$$L = \{a^n\, b^m \mid n \geq 0, m \geq 0\}$$

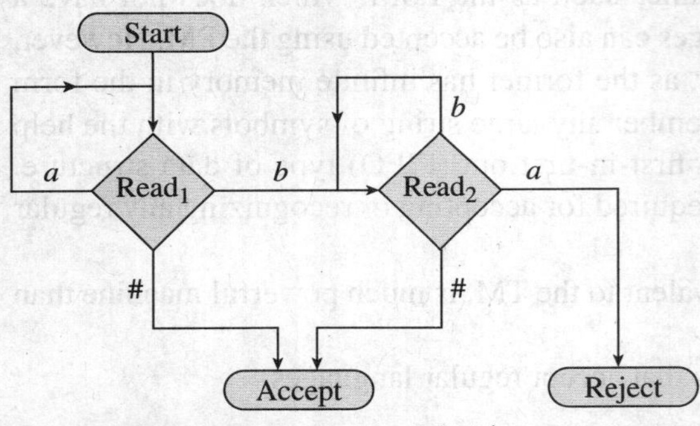


**Figure 8.5** PM accepting $\{a^n\, b^m \mid n, m \geq 0\}$

***Solution*** We see that the given language is a regular language and can be represented by the regular expression $a^* \cdot b^*$. The language contains all the strings with any number of $a$'s, followed by any number of $b$'s. Thus, the PM that accepts the given language is a simple machine that does not require memory, as shown in Fig. 8.5.

We see from Fig. 8.5 that the PM also accepts the minimal length string—for $n = 0$, $m = 0$, which is nothing but an empty string. An empty string is accepted by the machine when it reads '#' in the state $Read_1$. This state consumes all the $a$'s before it transits to state $Read_2$ on reading symbol $b$. State $Read_2$ consumes all the remaining $b$'s before it accepts the string on reading symbol '#'.

If $a$ follows $b$ in the input, then the PM rejects the input string, as the string of the form $a^n b^m$ cannot have a $b$ followed by an $a$.

### *Simulation*

1. Let us simulate the acceptance of the string '*aab*'.

| Current state | Tape and head position |
|---|---|
| Start | $a\ a\ b\ \#\ \not b\ \not b\ \ldots$ |
| | $\uparrow$ (under first $a$) |
| $\downarrow$ | |
| $Read_1$ | $a\ a\ b\ \#\ \not b\ \not b\ \ldots$ |
| | $\uparrow$ (under second $a$) |
| $a \downarrow$ | |
| $Read_1$ | $a\ a\ b\ \#\ \not b\ \not b\ \ldots$ |
| | $\uparrow$ (under $b$) |
| $a \downarrow$ | |
| $Read_1$ | $a\ a\ b\ \#\ \not b\ \not b\ \ldots$ |
| | $\uparrow$ (under $\#$) |
| $b \downarrow$ | |
| $Read_2$ | $a\ a\ b\ \#\ \not b\ \not b\ \ldots$ |
| | $\uparrow$ (under first $\not b$) |
| $\# \downarrow$ | |
| Accept | |

2. Let us simulate the working of the machine for the input string '*b*' (i.e., for $n = 0$ and $m = 1$).

| Current state | Tape and head position |
|---|---|
| Start | *b* # ƀ ƀ … |
| ↓ | ↑ (at *b*) |
| *Read*$_1$ | *b* # ƀ ƀ … |
| *b* ↓ | ↑ (at #) |
| *Read*$_2$ | *b* # ƀ ƀ … |
| # ↓ | ↑ (at first ƀ) |
| Accept | |

3. Let us simulate the rejection of the string '*aba*'.

| Current state | Tape and head position |
|---|---|
| Start | *a b a* # ƀ ƀ … |
| ↓ | ↑ (at first *a*) |
| *Read*$_1$ | *a b a* # ƀ ƀ … |
| *a* ↓ | ↑ (at *b*) |
| *Read*$_1$ | *a b a* # ƀ ƀ … |
| *b* ↓ | ↑ (at second *a*) |
| *Read*$_2$ | *a b a* # ƀ ƀ … |
| *a* ↓ | ↑ (at #) |
| Reject | |

## 8.6 PM ACCEPTING CFLs

As already mentioned, the PM can accept all regular languages that are accepted by any FSM. However, since the PM has *unlimited memory* in the form of queue, it can be used to remember arbitrarily long strings of symbols. Hence, it can also solve problems such as checking if the given parentheses are well-formed, and accept most CFLs.

**Example 8.3** Construct a PM that recognizes the following CFL:

$$L = \{a^n b^n \mid n \geq 0\}$$

***Solution*** We can check using the pumping lemma, whether or not the given language *L* is a regular language, and hence, whether or not we can have an FA that recognizes it. We require a machine, which is capable of remembering the string of *a*'s so that they can be compared with the string of *b*'s to check if the number of *a*'s and *b*'s are equal. Recall that in Chapter 6 (refer to Section 6.5), we already have solved this problem using PDA, which uses stack data structure. Let us now construct a PM, which uses its tape as a queue data structure, for remembering arbitrarily long strings.

We further know that the PM can write onto its tape in a restricted fashion—it can only add more symbols to the end of the input string and cannot overwrite or delete the previous contents as the TM does.

**Algorithm**

1. After reading the string of $a$'s, skip the first $a$ and add all the remaining $a$'s to the queue. Similarly, skip the first $b$ and add the remaining $b$'s to the queue.
2. While reading, if you get '#', representing the end of the input, then add '#' to the end of newly added string of $a$'s and $b$'s, which will be in the form:

$$a^1 a^2 \dots a^{n-1} b^1 b^2 \dots b^{n-1}$$

3. Thus, we are deleting one $a$ and one $b$ to compare or match the number of $a$'s with $b$'s, as we want to check equality of the number of $a$'s and $b$'s.
4. Repeat the aforementioned procedure for the newly added string with $(n - 1)$ number of $a$'s and $(n - 1)$ number of $b$'s. Keep cancelling one $a$ and one $b$ each time. If the number of $a$'s is equal to the number of $b$'s, then all of them will be finally exhausted.

The PM following this algorithm is as shown in Fig. 8.6.

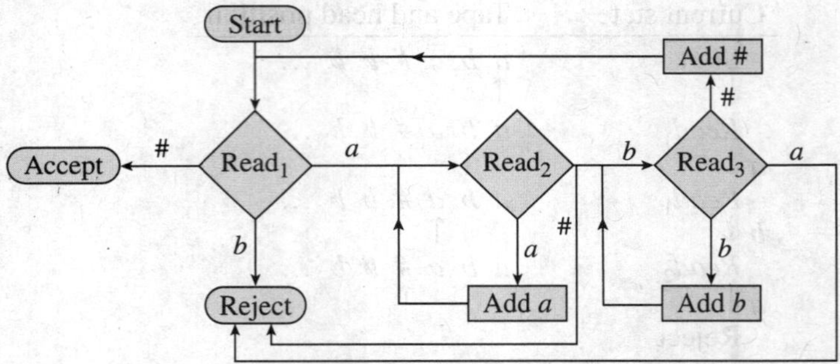


**Figure 8.6** PM that accepts $\{a^n b^n \mid n \geq 0\}$

The various decision boxes function as follows:

*Read*$_1$: Skip one $a$.
If # is read, then go to 'Accept'.
If $b$ is a starting symbol, then go to 'Reject'.
*Read*$_2$: Add all remaining $a$'s to the queue.
Skip one $b$.
*Read*$_3$: Add remaining $b$'s to the queue.
If '#' is read, then add '#' to the queue and repeat.
If $a$ follows $b$ in the input string, then go to 'Reject'.

We see that state *Read*$_1$ is associated with three different functions: It reads the first $a$ and moves to state *Read*$_2$ without adding it to the queue. Thus, it skips the first $a$ read. On reading '#' from the input tape, it accepts the input. Thus, it also accepts an empty input with zero number of $a$'s and zero number of $b$'s (i.e., $n = 0$), along with the correct input for $n > 0$.

If state *Read*$_1$ reads $b$ first, it rejects the input, because a string of the form $a^n b^n$ cannot start with $b$.

State *Read*$_2$ skips the first $b$ to match with the $a$ skipped by *Read*$_1$. It queues the remaining $a$'s to be processed later.

State *Read*$_3$ is also associated with three different functionalities, depending on the input symbol read. It adds the remaining $b$'s to the queue for later processing. If it reads

'#', then it adds '#' (end marker to the newly added string) to the queue. On reading *a*, it rejects the input because in a string of the form $a^n b^n$, *a* cannot follow *b*.

### *Simulation*

1. Let us simulate the acceptance of the string '*aabb*'.

| Current state | Tape as queue with head |
|---|---|
| Start | $a\ a\ b\ b\ \#\ \not{b}\ \not{b}\ \ldots$ |
| ↓ | $\uparrow$ |
| $Read_1$ | $a\ a\ b\ b\ \#\ \not{b}\ \not{b}\ \ldots$ |
| *a* ↓ | $\phantom{a\ }\uparrow$ |
| | (skip one *a*) |
| $Read_2$ | $a\ a\ b\ b\ \#\ \not{b}\ \not{b}\ \ldots$ |
| *a* ↓ | $\phantom{a\ a\ }\uparrow$ |
| Add *a* | $a\ a\ b\ b\ \#\ a\ \not{b}\ \ldots$ |
| ↓ | $\phantom{a\ a\ }\uparrow$ |
| | (add remaining *a* to the queue) |
| $Read_2$ | $a\ a\ b\ b\ \#\ a\ \not{b}\ \ldots$ |
| *b* ↓ | $\phantom{a\ a\ b\ }\uparrow$ |
| | (skip one *b*) |
| $Read_3$ | $a\ a\ b\ b\ \#\ a\ \not{b}\ \ldots$ |
| *b* ↓ | $\phantom{a\ a\ b\ b\ }\uparrow$ |
| Add *b* | $a\ a\ b\ b\ \#\ a\ b\ \not{b}\ \ldots$ |
| ↓ | $\phantom{a\ a\ b\ b\ }\uparrow$ |
| | (add remaining *b* to the queue) |
| $Read_3$ | $a\ a\ b\ b\ \#\ a\ b\ \not{b}\ \ldots$ |
| # ↓ | $\phantom{a\ a\ b\ b\ \#\ }\uparrow$ |
| Add # | $a\ a\ b\ b\ \#\ a\ b\ \#\ \not{b}\ \ldots$ |
| ↓ | $\phantom{a\ a\ b\ b\ \#\ }\uparrow$ |
| | (add # to the queue) |
| | (repeat the procedure for the newly added string) |
| $Read_1$ | $a\ a\ b\ b\ \#\ a\ b\ \#\ \not{b}\ \ldots$ |
| *a* ↓ | $\phantom{a\ a\ b\ b\ \#\ a\ }\uparrow$ |
| | (skip one *a*) |
| $Read_2$ | $a\ a\ b\ b\ \#\ a\ b\ \#\ \not{b}\ \ldots$ |
| *b* ↓ | $\phantom{a\ a\ b\ b\ \#\ a\ b\ }\uparrow$ |
| | (skip one *b*) |
| $Read_3$ | $a\ a\ b\ b\ \#\ a\ b\ \#\ \not{b}\ \ldots$ |
| # ↓ | $\phantom{a\ a\ b\ b\ \#\ a\ b\ }\uparrow$ |
| Add # | $a\ a\ b\ b\ \#\ a\ b\ \#\ \#\ \not{b}\ \ldots$ |
| ↓ | $\phantom{a\ a\ b\ b\ \#\ a\ b\ \#\ }\uparrow$ |
| | (add '#' to the queue) |
| | (repeat the procedure for the newly added string) |
| $Read_1$ | $a\ a\ b\ b\ \#\ a\ b\ \#\ \#\ \not{b}\ \ldots$ |
| # ↓ | $\phantom{a\ a\ b\ b\ \#\ a\ b\ \#\ \#\ }\uparrow$ |
| Accept | |

> ***Note***: The arrows on the left-hand side indicate the transitions from one state to another on reading some symbol. All the states are shown in *italics*. Add is not a state but a process and hence is not in italics.

2. Let us simulate the rejection of the input string '*aab*'.

| Current state | Tape as queue with head |
|---|---|
| Start | *a a b* # ƀ ƀ … |
| ↓ | ↑ |
| *Read*$_1$ | *a a b* # ƀ ƀ … |
| *a* ↓ |     ↑ |
| | (skip one *a*) |
| *Read*$_2$ | *a a b* # ƀ ƀ … |
| *a* ↓ |         ↑ |
| Add *a* | *a a b* # *a* ƀ … |
| ↓ |         ↑ |
| | (add the remaining *a* to the queue) |
| *Read*$_2$ | *a a b* # *a* ƀ … |
| *b* ↓ |             ↑ |
| | (skip one *b*) |
| *Read*$_3$ | *a a b* # *a* ƀ … |
| # ↓ |                 ↑ |
| Add # | *a a b* # *a* # ƀ … |
| ↓ |                 ↑ |
| | (repeat the procedure for the newly added string) |
| *Read*$_1$ | *a a b* # *a* # ƀ … |
| *a* ↓ |                     ↑ |
| *Read*$_2$ | *a a b* # *a* # ƀ … |
| # ↓ |                         ↑ |
| Reject | |

3. Simulation of rejection of the input string '*abb*':

| Current state | Tape as queue with head |
|---|---|
| Start | *a b b* # ƀ ƀ … |
| ↓ | ↑ |
| *Read*$_1$ | *a b b* # ƀ ƀ … |
| *a* ↓ |     ↑ |
| | (skip one *a*) |
| *Read*$_2$ | *a b b* # ƀ ƀ … |
| *b* ↓ |         ↑ |
| | (skip one *b*) |
| *Read*$_3$ | *a b b* # ƀ ƀ … |
| *b* ↓ |             ↑ |
| Add *b* | *a b b* # *b* ƀ … |
| ↓ |             ↑ |

| | |
|---|---|
| | (add the remaining $b$ to the queue) |
| $Read_3$ | $a\ b\ b\ \#\ b\ \not b\ \ldots$ |
| $\#\downarrow$ | $\uparrow$ |
| Add # | $a\ b\ b\ \#\ b\ \#\ \not b\ \ldots$ |
| $\downarrow$ | $\uparrow$ |
| | (add '#' to the queue) |
| | (repeat the procedure for the newly added string) |
| $Read_1$ | $a\ b\ b\ \#\ b\ \#\ \not b\ \ldots$ |
| $b\downarrow$ | $\uparrow$ |
| Reject | |

4. Let us simulate the rejection of the string '*aba*'.

| Current state | Tape as queue with head |
|---|---|
| Start | $a\ b\ a\ \#\ \not b\ \not b\ \ldots$ |
| $\downarrow$ | $\uparrow$ |
| $Read_1$ | $a\ b\ a\ \#\ \not b\ \not b\ \ldots$ |
| $a\downarrow$ | $\uparrow$ |
| | (skip one $a$) |
| $Read_2$ | $a\ b\ a\ \#\ \not b\ \not b\ \ldots$ |
| $b\downarrow$ | $\uparrow$ |
| | (skip one $b$) |
| $Read_3$ | $a\ b\ a\ \#\ \not b\ \not b\ \ldots$ |
| $a\downarrow$ | $\uparrow$ |
| Reject | |

---

**Example 8.4** Design a PM that checks if the given string contains well-formed parentheses.

***Solution*** As we know, every string of well-formed parentheses should start with a '(' and should end with a ')'. Let us apply a similar logic as that in the previous example (Example 8.3).

**Algorithm**

When the machine reads an opening parenthesis '(', it skips the first one and adds the remaining opening parentheses '(' to the queue. Similarly, when it reads a closing parenthesis ')', it skips the first one and adds the remaining to the queue. Thus, the machine matches and deletes each opening parenthesis with one closing parenthesis. This process is repeated until there are no more symbols in the queue. The required PM is constructed as shown in Fig. 8.7.

Every state is associated with some functionality, which is stated as follows:

$Read_1$: Skip one '('.
If string starts with ')', then go to 'Reject'.
If symbol read is '#', then go to 'Accept'.

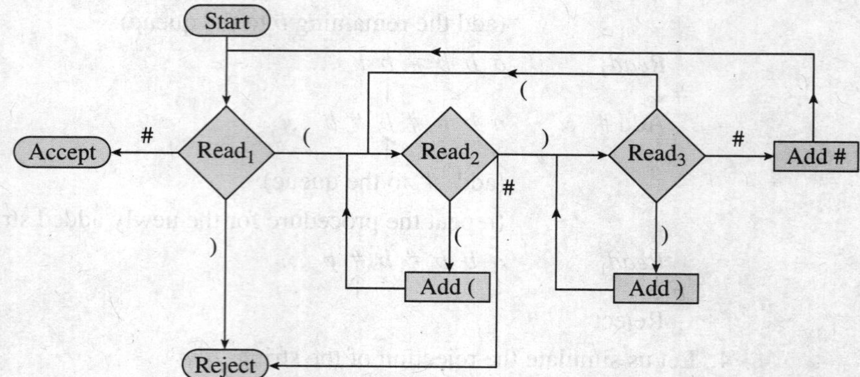


**Figure 8.7** PM that checks for well-formed parentheses

*Read*$_2$: Add the remaining '('s.
Skip one ')'.
If the symbol read is '#', then go to 'Reject'.

*Read*$_3$: Add the remaining ')'s.
Skip one '('.
If symbol read is '#, then add '#' to the queue and repeat the procedure.

***Simulation***

1. Let us trace the acceptance of the string '( ( ) ) ( )'.

| Current state | Tape as queue and head |
|---|---|
| Start | ( ( ) ) ( ) # $\not{b}$ $\not{b}$ … |
| ↓ | ↑ |
| *Read*$_1$ | ( ( ) ) ( ) # $\not{b}$ $\not{b}$ … |
| ( ↓ | ↑ |
| | [skip one '(' ] |
| *Read*$_2$ | ( ( ) ) ( ) # $\not{b}$ $\not{b}$ … |
| ( ↓ | ↑ |
| Add ( | ( ( ) ) ( ) # ( $\not{b}$ … |
| ↓ | ↑ |
| | [add the remaining ('*s* to the queue] |
| *Read*$_2$ | ( ( ) ) ( ) # ( $\not{b}$ … |
| ) ↓ | ↑ |
| | [skip one ')'] |
| *Read*$_3$ | ( ( ) ) ( ) # ( $\not{b}$ … |
| ) ↓ | ↑ |
| Add ) | ( ( ) ) ( ) # ( ) $\not{b}$ … |
| ↓ | ↑ |
| | [add the remaining )'s to the queue] |
| *Read*$_3$ | ( ( ) ) ( ) # ( ) $\not{b}$ … |
| ( ↓ | ↑ |

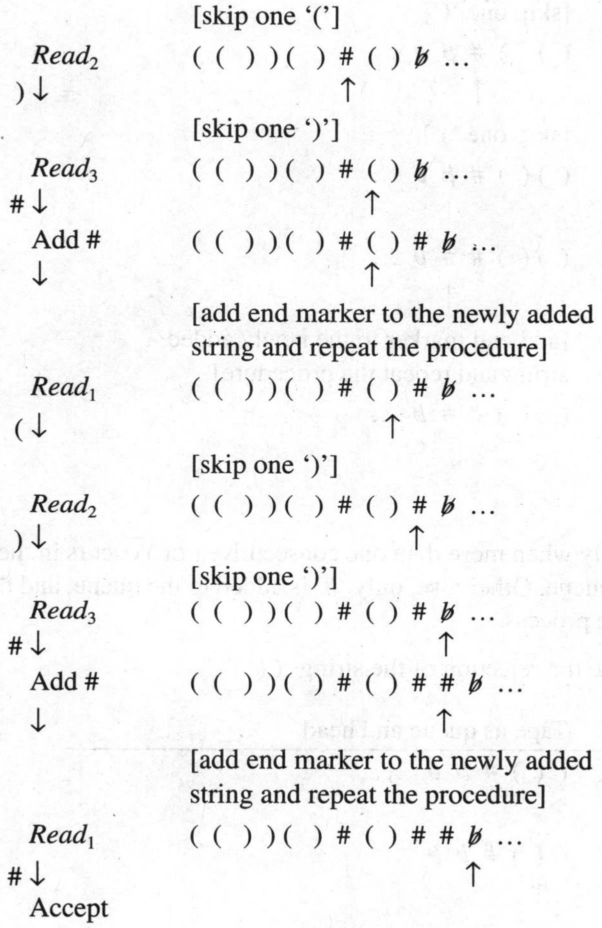

| | |
|---|---|
| | [skip one '('] |
| *Read*$_2$ | ( ( ) ) ( ) # ( ) b̸ … |
| ) ↓ | ↑ |
| | [skip one ')'] |
| *Read*$_3$ | ( ( ) ) ( ) # ( ) b̸ … |
| # ↓ | ↑ |
| Add # | ( ( ) ) ( ) # ( ) # b̸ … |
| ↓ | ↑ |
| | [add end marker to the newly added string and repeat the procedure] |
| *Read*$_1$ | ( ( ) ) ( ) # ( ) # b̸ … |
| ( ↓ | ↑ |
| | [skip one ')'] |
| *Read*$_2$ | ( ( ) ) ( ) # ( ) # b̸ … |
| ) ↓ | ↑ |
| | [skip one ')'] |
| *Read*$_3$ | ( ( ) ) ( ) # ( ) # b̸ … |
| # ↓ | ↑ |
| Add # | ( ( ) ) ( ) # ( ) # # b̸ … |
| ↓ | ↑ |
| | [add end marker to the newly added string and repeat the procedure] |
| *Read*$_1$ | ( ( ) ) ( ) # ( ) # # b̸ … |
| # ↓ | ↑ |
| Accept | |

2. Let us simulate the acceptance of the string '( ) ( )'.

| Current state | Tape as queue and head |
|---|---|
| Start | ( ) ( ) # b̸ b̸ … |
| ↓ | ↑ |
| *Read*$_1$ | ( ) ( ) # b̸ b̸ … |
| ( ↓ | ↑ |
| | [skip one '('] |
| *Read*$_2$ | ( ) ( ) # b̸ b̸ … |
| ) ↓ | ↑ |
| | [skip one ')'] |
| *Read*$_3$ | ( ) ( ) # b̸ b̸ … |
| ( ↓ | ↑ |

| | |
|---|---|
| | [skip one '('] |
| *Read*$_2$ | ( ) ( ) # ƀ ƀ … |
| ) ↓ | ↑ |
| | [skip one ')'] |
| *Read*$_3$ | ( ) ( ) # ƀ ƀ … |
| # ↓ | ↑ |
| Add # | ( ) ( ) # # ƀ … |
| ↓ | ↑ |
| | [add end marker to the newly added string and repeat the procedure] |
| *Read*$_1$ | ( ) ( ) # # ƀ … |
| # ↓ | ↑ |
| Accept | |

We see that only when more than one consecutive ( or ) occurs in the input string, they get added to the queue. Otherwise, only '#' is added to the queue, and the rest of the pairs are skipped in the process.

3. Let us simulate the rejection of the string '( ( )'.

| Current state | Tape as queue and head |
|---|---|
| Start | ( ( ) # ƀ ƀ … |
| ↓ | ↑ |
| *Read*$_1$ | ( ( ) # ƀ ƀ … |
| ( ↓ | ↑ |
| | [skip one '('] |
| *Read*$_2$ | ( ( ) # ƀ ƀ … |
| ( ↓ | ↑ |
| Add ( | ( ( ) # ( ƀ … |
| ↓ | ↑ |
| | [add remaining '(' to the queue] |
| *Read*$_2$ | ( ( ) # ( ƀ … |
| ) ↓ | ↑ |
| | [skip one ')'] |
| *Read*$_3$ | ( ( ) # ( ƀ … |
| # ↓ | ↑ |
| Add # | ( ( ) # ( # ƀ … |
| ↓ | ↑ |

| | |
|---|---|
| | [add end marker to the newly added string and repeat the procedure] |
| $Read_1$ | ( ( ) # ( # ƀ … |
| ( ↓ | ↑ |
| | [skip one '('] |
| $Read_2$ | ( ( ) # ( # ƀ … |
| # ↓ | ↑ |
| Reject | |

In the given string '( ( )', one ')' is less; so the string is not well-formed, and is hence, rejected.

4. Let us trace the rejection of the string '( ) )'. This string has one less opening parenthesis '('.

| Current state | Tape as queue and head |
|---|---|
| Start | ( ) ) # ƀ ƀ … |
| ↓ | ↑ |
| $Read_1$ | ( ) ) # ƀ ƀ … |
| ( ↓ | ↑ |
| | [skip one '('] |
| $Read_2$ | ( ) ) # ƀ ƀ … |
| ) ↓ | ↑ |
| | [skip one ')'] |
| $Read_3$ | ( ) ) # ƀ ƀ … |
| ) ↓ | ↑ |
| Add ) | ( ) ) # ) ƀ … |
| ↓ | ↑ |
| | [add remaining '(' to the queue] |
| $Read_3$ | ( ) ) # ) ƀ … |
| # ↓ | ↑ |
| Add # | ( ( ) # ) # ƀ … |
| ↓ | ↑ |
| | [add end marker to the newly added string and repeat the procedure] |
| $Read_1$ | ( ( ) # ) # ƀ … |
| ) ↓ | ↑ |
| Reject | |

5. An empty input, that is, string with length zero, is a special case of the input that is well-formed. Let us trace the acceptance of the empty string. In this case, the tape will contain only '#', the end marker, as the start symbol; the tape head initially points to it.

| Current state | Tape as queue and head |
|---|---|
| Start | # ƀ ƀ ... |
| ↓ | ↑ |
| | (empty input) |
| $Read_1$ | # ƀ ƀ ... |
| # ↓ | ↑ |
| Accept | |

Thus, the empty string $\epsilon$ is also considered to be well-formed and is accepted by the PM in Fig. 8.7.

> ***Note***: As we have already discussed in Chapter 6, the context-free grammar (CFG) for this language—with strings of well-formed parentheses—can be defined as follows:
>
> $$S \to (S)\, S \mid \epsilon$$
>
> We see that $\epsilon$ can be derived from the start symbol $S$. Hence, the PM also accepts CFLs.

Similarly, we have seen that the PM in Example 8.3 accepted the language, $L = \{a^n\, b^n \mid n \geq 0\}$, which is also a context-free language; the CFG for this can be written as:

$$S \to a\, S\, b \mid \epsilon$$

Thus, we have demonstrated that PMs can accept regular languages as well as CFLs. Let us now discuss more complex examples.

## 8.7 NON-DETERMINISTIC POST MACHINE

A *non-deterministic PM* (NPM), after reading a single symbol, makes a transition to any of the multiple possible next states. The NPM is thus a possibilistic machine; and unless executed, one cannot really predict the behaviour of such machines. Let us illustrate this concept through the following example.

**Example 8.5** Design a PM to accept palindrome strings over the alphabet, $\Sigma = \{a, b\}$.

***Solution*** We can design a non-deterministic PM (NPM) for this problem. Each time, we check for the starting and ending symbols of the input string. If these are equal, then the algorithm proceeds with the rest of the symbols; else, an error is produced.

Recall that in Chapter 6 (refer to Section 6.6, Example 6.6) we have already constructed an NPDA for the same language.

**Algorithm**

As the input string is defined over $\Sigma = \{a, b\}$, it can either start with symbol $a$ or with symbol $b$. If it starts with $a$, then it should end in $a$, in order to be a palindrome string.

Similarly, if it starts with $b$, it should end in $b$. The algorithm steps can be stated as follows:

1. Skip the first symbol, which is to be matched with the ending symbol, and add all the intermediate symbols to the queue.
2. Check the last symbol; if it is same as the first symbol, skip it as well.
3. Repeat the procedure for the newly added intermediate symbols till you get a string with zero symbols.

For example, consider the string '*aabbaa*'. In the first iteration, the first and last *a*'s are cancelled, and the remaining intermediate characters, that is, '*abba*', are added to the queue. In the second iteration, again the first and last *a*'s are cancelled and the remaining string, that is, '*bb*', is added to the queue. In the next iteration, the string '*bb*' is also cancelled, leaving an empty string. Finally, the machine accepts it as a palindrome string.

The NPM is constructed as shown in Fig. 8.8. We see from the figure that $Read_1$ makes a transition to $Read_2$ and $Read_4$, based on whether the beginning symbol is $a$ or $b$, respectively. State $Read_6$ is reached only when there is a single symbol in the string—typically, a scenario for odd-length palindromes. Let us simulate the working of the PM to understand it better.

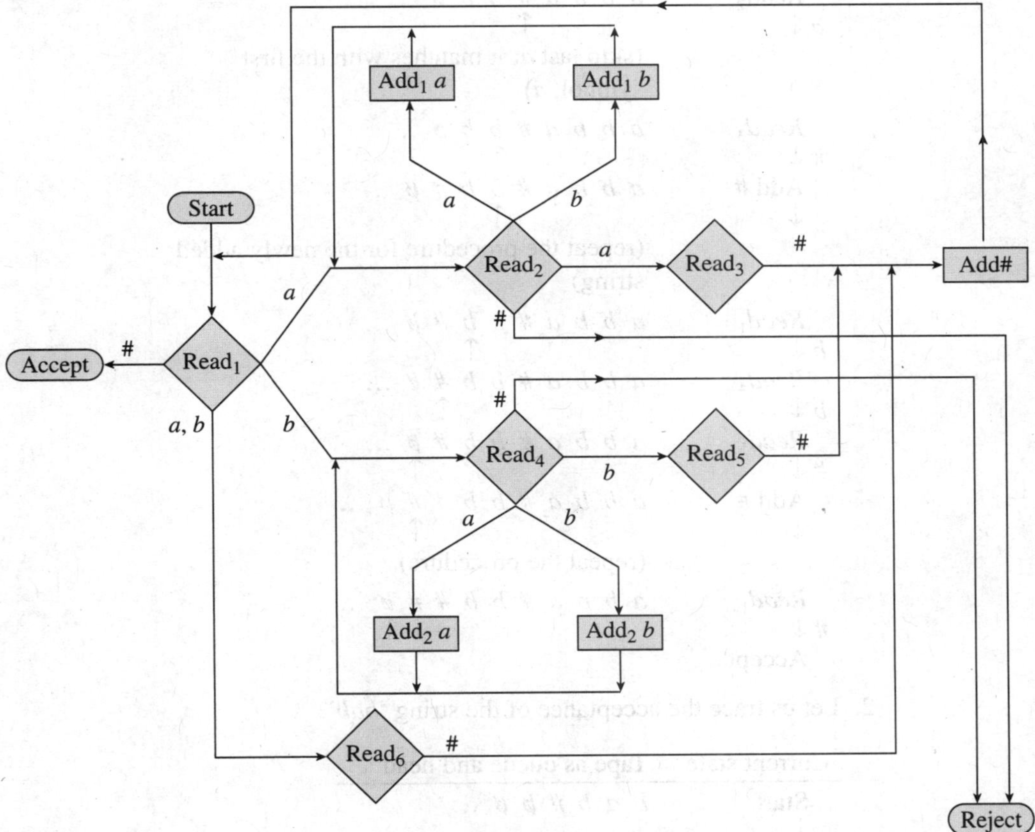


**Figure 8.8** NPM that accepts palindrome strings over $\Sigma = (a, b)$

### *Simulation*

1. Let us trace the acceptance of the input string '*abba*'.

| Current state | Tape as queue and head |
|---|---|
| Start | $a\ b\ b\ a\ \#\ \not{b}\ \not{b}\ \not{b}$ … |
| ↓ | ↑ |
| *Read*$_1$ | $a\ b\ b\ a\ \#\ \not{b}\ \not{b}\ \not{b}$ … |
| $a$ ↓ | ↑ |
| | (skip first $a$) |
| *Read*$_2$ | $a\ b\ b\ a\ \#\ \not{b}\ \not{b}$ … |
| $b$ ↓ | ↑ |
| Add$_1$ $b$ | $a\ b\ b\ a\ \#\ b\ \not{b}$ … |
| ↓ | ↑ |
| *Read*$_2$ | $a\ b\ b\ a\ \#\ b\ \not{b}$ … |
| $b$ ↓ | ↑ |
| Add$_1$ $b$ | $a\ b\ b\ a\ \#\ b\ b\ \not{b}$ … |
| ↓ | ↑ |
| | (add the remaining intermediate string '*bb*') |
| *Read*$_2$ | $a\ b\ b\ a\ \#\ b\ b\ \not{b}$ … |
| $a$ ↓ | ↑ |
| | (skip last $a$; it matches with the first symbol, $a$) |
| *Read*$_3$ | $a\ b\ b\ a\ \#\ b\ b\ \not{b}$ … |
| # ↓ | ↑ |
| Add # | $a\ b\ b\ a\ \#\ b\ b\ \#\ \not{b}$ … |
| ↓ | ↑ |
| | (repeat the procedure for the newly added string) |
| *Read*$_1$ | $a\ b\ b\ a\ \#\ b\ b\ \#\ \not{b}$ … |
| $b$ ↓ | ↑ |
| *Read*$_4$ | $a\ b\ b\ a\ \#\ b\ b\ \#\ \not{b}$ … |
| $b$ ↓ | ↑ |
| *Read*$_5$ | $a\ b\ b\ a\ \#\ b\ b\ \#\ \not{b}$ … |
| # ↓ | ↑ |
| Add # | $a\ b\ b\ a\ \#\ b\ b\ \#\ \#\ \not{b}$ … |
| ↓ | ↑ |
| | (repeat the procedure) |
| *Read*$_1$ | $a\ b\ b\ a\ \#\ b\ b\ \#\ \#\ \not{b}$ … |
| # ↓ | ↑ |
| Accept | |

2. Let us trace the acceptance of the string '*bab*'.

| Current state | Tape as queue and head |
|---|---|
| Start | $b\ a\ b\ \#\ \not{b}\ \not{b}$ … |
| ↓ | ↑ |
| *Read*$_1$ | $b\ a\ b\ \#\ \not{b}\ \not{b}$ … |
| $b$ ↓ | ↑ |

```
                (skip starting b)
   Read4        b a b # ƀ ƀ ...
a ↓                 ↑
   Add2 a       b a b # a ƀ ...
  ↓                 ↑
   Read4        b a b # a ƀ ...
b ↓                   ↑
                (skip last b)
   Read5        b a b # a ƀ ...
# ↓                     ↑
   Add #        b a b # a # ƀ ...
  ↓                     ↑
                (repeat the procedure)
   Read1        b a b # a # ƀ ...
a ↓                       ↑
   Read6        b a b # a # ƀ ...
# ↓                         ↑
   Add #        b a b # a # # ƀ ...
  ↓                         ↑
   Read1        b a b # a # # ƀ ...
# ↓                           ↑
   Accept
```

3. Let us simulate the acceptance of the string '$b$'.

```
Current state   Tape as queue and head
---------------------------------------
   Start        b # ƀ ƀ ...
  ↓             ↑
   Read1        b # ƀ ƀ ...
b ↓               ↑
   Read6        b # ƀ ƀ ...
# ↓                 ↑
   Add #        b # # ƀ ...
  ↓                 ↑
   Read1        b # # ƀ ...
# ↓                   ↑
   Accept
```

4. Let us trace the rejection of the string '$abaa$'.

```
Current state   Tape as queue and head
---------------------------------------
   Start        a b a a # ƀ ƀ ...
  ↓             ↑
   Read1        a b a a # ƀ ƀ ...
a ↓               ↑
                (skip the first a)
   Read2        a b a a # ƀ ƀ ...
b ↓                 ↑
   Add1 b       a b a a # b ƀ ...
  ↓                 ↑
```

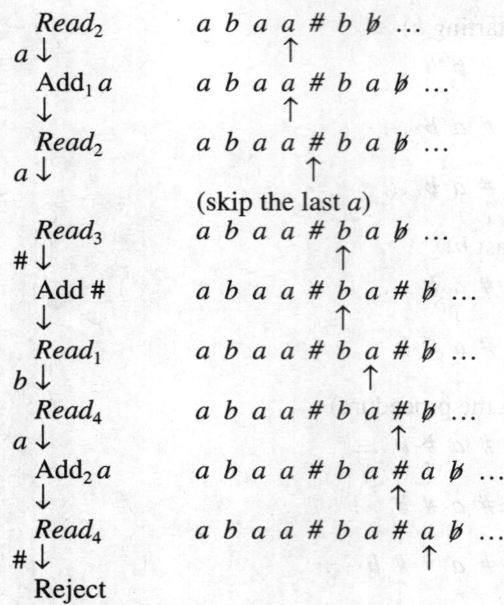

> ***Note***: Observe that the aforementioned PM is non-deterministic. In every non-deterministic machine, there are multiple possible paths for every input string, beginning with the start state. If the input is valid, then out of these possible paths only one leads to acceptance of the string, while the others lead to rejection of the string. Such a machine is called a *possibilistic machine*.

## 8.8 POST MACHINE ACCEPTING NON-CFLs

In the previous section, we constructed PMs that accept regular languages and CFLs such as, $\{a^n b^n \mid n \geq 0\}$ and well-formed parentheses. In this section, let us demonstrate through some complex examples that PMs also accept non-CFLs. We also demonstrate that the PM can solve complex problems such as multiplication, proving that the PM is equivalent in power to the TM.

**Example 8.6** Construct a PM that accepts the following language:

$$L_1 = \{a^n b^n a^n \mid n \geq 0\}$$

***Solution*** The given language is not a CFL. Therefore, we cannot write a CFG for this language; we also cannot construct a PDA, because they accept only CFLs. However, we can construct a PM that accepts the given language $L_1 = \{a^n b^n a^n \mid n \geq 0\}$, as shown in Fig. 8.9.

We see that state $Read_1$ skips one $a$ and makes a transition to state $Read_2$, which adds the remaining $a$'s to the queue till it reads the first $b$. State $Read_2$ skips the first $b$ to match with the skipped $a$ and makes a transition to state $Read_3$. State $Read_3$ adds the remaining

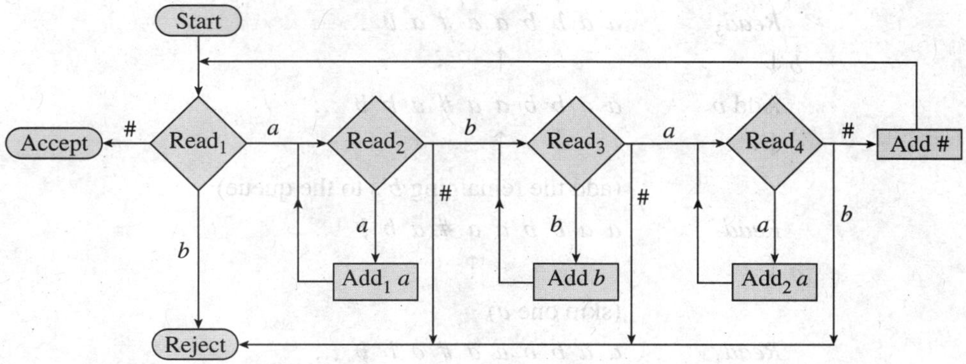

Figure 8.9 PM that accepts $\{a^n b^n a^n \mid n \geq 0\}$

$b$'s to the queue and makes a transition to state $Read_4$ on reading symbol $a$, which is not added to the queue; thus, it is skipped to match the symbols skipped earlier. State $Read_4$ adds the remaining $a$'s to the queue till it reads the end of input '#'. Then, it adds '#' to the queue and repeats the process on the remaining string with three symbols less than the original. This goes on till the remaining string is empty, that is, till symbol '#' is received in state $Read_1$. State $Read_1$, on reading '#'s, accepts the string.

Thus though the given language $L_1$ is not a CFL, there exists a PM that can accept the language. Thus, a PM accepts CFLs as well as non-CFLs. Hence, we conclude that *the PM is more powerful than the PDA*, and the set of languages accepted by the PDA is a subset of the set of languages accepted by a PM.

### *Simulation*

Let us trace the acceptance of the string '*aabbaa*'.

| Current state | Tape as queue and head |
|---|---|
| Start | $a\ a\ b\ b\ a\ a\ \#\ \not b\ \not b\ \ldots$ |
| $\downarrow$ | $\uparrow$ (under 1st symbol) |
| $Read_1$ | $a\ a\ b\ b\ a\ a\ \#\ \not b\ \not b\ \ldots$ |
| $a\downarrow$ | $\uparrow$ (under 2nd symbol) |
| | (skip one $a$) |
| $Read_2$ | $a\ a\ b\ b\ a\ a\ \#\ \not b\ \not b\ \ldots$ |
| $a\downarrow$ | $\uparrow$ (under 3rd symbol) |
| $\text{Add}_1\ a$ | $a\ a\ b\ b\ a\ a\ \#\ a\ \not b\ \ldots$ |
| $\downarrow$ | $\uparrow$ (under 3rd symbol) |
| | (add the remaining $a$'s to the queue) |
| $Read_2$ | $a\ a\ b\ b\ a\ a\ \#\ a\ \not b\ \ldots$ |
| $b\downarrow$ | $\uparrow$ (under 4th symbol) |
| | (skip one $b$) |

$Read_3$ $\quad a\ a\ b\ b\ a\ a\ \#\ a\ \not b\ \ldots$

$b \downarrow$ $\quad \uparrow$

Add $b$ $\quad a\ a\ b\ b\ a\ a\ \#\ a\ b\ \not b\ \ldots$

$\downarrow$ $\quad \uparrow$

(add the remaining $b$'s to the queue)

$Read_3$ $\quad a\ a\ b\ b\ a\ a\ \#\ a\ b\ \not b\ \ldots$

$a \downarrow$ $\quad \uparrow$

(skip one $a$)

$Read_4$ $\quad a\ a\ b\ b\ a\ a\ \#\ a\ b\ \not b\ \ldots$

$a \downarrow$ $\quad \uparrow$

Add$_2$ $a$ $\quad a\ a\ b\ b\ a\ a\ \#\ a\ b\ a\ \not b\ \ldots$

$\downarrow$ $\quad \uparrow$

(add the remaining $a$'s to the queue)

$Read_4$ $\quad a\ a\ b\ b\ a\ a\ \#\ a\ b\ a\ \not b\ \ldots$

$\# \downarrow$ $\quad \uparrow$

Add # $\quad a\ a\ b\ b\ a\ a\ \#\ a\ b\ a\ \#\ \not b\ \ldots$

$\downarrow$ $\quad \uparrow$

(repeat the procedure)

$Read_1$ $\quad a\ a\ b\ b\ a\ a\ \#\ a\ b\ a\ \#\ \not b\ \ldots$

$a \downarrow$ $\quad \uparrow$

(skip one $a$)

$Read_2$ $\quad a\ a\ b\ b\ a\ a\ \#\ a\ b\ a\ \#\ \not b\ \ldots$

$b \downarrow$ $\quad \uparrow$

(skip one $b$)

$Read_3$ $\quad a\ a\ b\ b\ a\ a\ \#\ a\ b\ a\ \#\ \not b\ \ldots$

$a \downarrow$ $\quad \uparrow$

(skip one $a$)

$Read_4$ $\quad a\ a\ b\ b\ a\ a\ \#\ a\ b\ a\ \#\ \not b\ \ldots$

$\# \downarrow$ $\quad \uparrow$

Add # $\quad a\ a\ b\ b\ a\ a\ \#\ a\ b\ a\ \#\ \#\ \not b\ \ldots$

$\downarrow$ $\quad \uparrow$

$Read_1$ $\quad a\ a\ b\ b\ a\ a\ \#\ a\ b\ a\ \#\ \#\ \not b\ \ldots$

$\# \downarrow$ $\quad \uparrow$

Accept

The procedure we have used for this problem is very similar to the procedure used in Example 8.3 (Section 8.6) for accepting the language, $\{a^n\, b^n \mid n \geq 0\}$.

Thus, we see that the PM accepts a larger class of languages than the PDA. Therefore, the PM is far more powerful than the PDA and is comparable to the TM. In fact, we can show that the PM and the TM have equal power. Let us demonstrate this with the help of another complex example.

---

**Example 8.7** Construct a PM that multiplies two unary numbers.

***Solution*** Recall that we have already solved this problem using the TM (refer to Chapter 4, Section 4.6, Example 4.10), in which multiplication was achieved through repetitive addition. Here, we are going to apply a similar approach, though the algorithm is slightly different because of the usage of the queue data structure for memory. The PM performing the multiplication of the two unary numbers can be designed as shown in the Fig. 8.10.

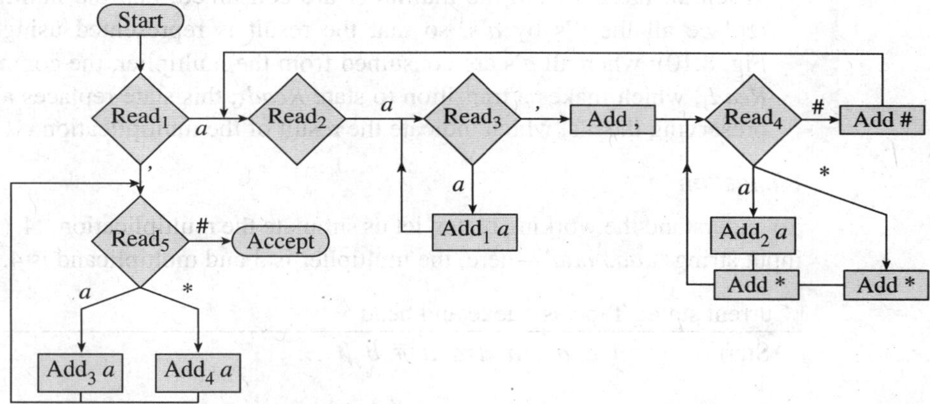


**Figure 8.10** PM that multiplies two unary numbers

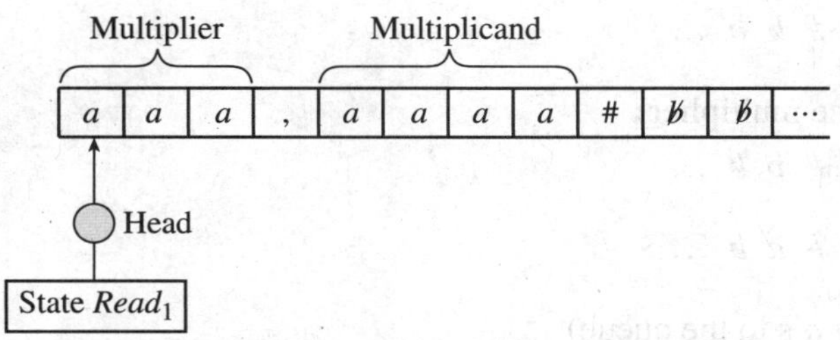


**Figure 8.11** Initial configuration

Let us consider the initial configuration of the PM as shown in Fig. 8.11.

The multiplier is written first onto the tape, followed by the multiplicand; the two numbers are separated by a comma. The unary representation of the numbers in made using the symbol *a*. Figure 8.11 shows a sample multiplier and multiplicand; the required PM can accept any positive integers.

**Algorithm**

1. Ignore the first *a* in the multiplier. We know that in multiplication, the multiplicand is added to itself, multiplier number of times. Since in the case of the PM, there is no separate result area defined as in the TM, the multiplicand is assumed to be expanded as the result. This means that it is already once present in the result; to accommodate this, the multiplier is reduced by one—by ignoring the first *a* from the multiplier. We see that in Fig. 8.10, state $Read_1$, on reading input symbol *a*, moves to state $Read_2$, ignoring the *a* that is read.

2. Add the remaining *a*'s from the multiplier as they are to the queue. In Fig. 8.10, we see that state $Read_2$ moves to $Read_3$ on reading *a,* thus reducing the multiplier by one. State $Read_3$ adds the remaining *a*'s from the multiplier to the queue. It also preserves the separator symbol comma on the queue before moving to state $Read_4$.
3. For every *a* in the multiplicand, add two symbols to the queue, *a* and '*'. This is to indicate the addition. The multiplicand is expanded as a result of repetitive addition; so for every iteration, a new symbol '*' is used to preserve the original multiplicand—the symbol *a* from the multiplicand is added as it is, and the additional symbol '*' is added to indicate repetitive addition. During further iterations, if the symbol read is '*', it is preserved as is. This is represented in Fig. 8.10 as transitions from state $Read_4$.
4. If the end of input symbol '#' is received, then add it to the queue, and the process is repeated for the newly added symbols.
5. When all the *a*'s from the multiplier are consumed, i.e., the multiplication is done, replace all the *'s by *a*'s, so that the result is represented using all *a*'s (refer to Fig. 8.10); when all *a*'s are consumed from the multiplier, the comma is read in state $Read_1$, which makes a transition to state $Read_5$; this state replaces all *'s by *a*'s, thus preserving the *a*'s, which indicate the result of the multiplication.

***Simulation***

To understand the working better, let us simulate the multiplication, '4 * 3', that is, for the input string '*aaa,aaaa*'—here, the multiplier is 3 and multiplicand is 4.

```
Current state   Tape as queue and head
-------------------------------------------------------------
  Start         a a a , a a a a # ƀ ƀ ...
  ↓             ↑
  Read1         a a a , a a a a # ƀ ƀ ...
a ↓               ↑
                (ignore one a from the multiplier)
  Read2         a a a , a a a a # ƀ ƀ ...
a ↓                 ↑
                (skip one a from the multiplier)
  Read3         a a a , a a a a # ƀ ƀ ...
a ↓                   ↑
  Add1 a        a a a , a a a a # a ƀ ...
  ↓                   ↑
                (add the remaining a's to the queue)
  Read3         a a a , a a a a # ƀ ƀ ...
, ↓                     ↑
  Add,          a a a , a a a a # a , ƀ ...
  ↓                     ↑
                (add a comma to the queue)
  Read4         a a a , a a a a # a , ƀ ...
a ↓                       ↑
  Add2 a        a a a , a a a a # a , a ƀ ...
  ↓                       ↑
```

```
 Add *        a a a , a a a a # a , a * b̸ ...
 ↓                      ↑
              (for every a in the multiplier, add a followed by *)
 Read_4       a a a , a a a a # a , a * b̸ ...
a↓                        ↑
 Add_2 a      a a a , a a a a # a , a * a b̸ ...
 ↓                        ↑
 Add *        a a a , a a a a # a , a * a * b̸ ...
 ↓                        ↑
              (for every a in the multiplier, add a followed by *)
 Read_4       a a a , a a a a # a , a * a * b̸ ...
a↓                          ↑
 Add_2 a      a a a , a a a a # a , a * a * a b̸ ...
 ↓                          ↑
 Add *        a a a , a a a a # a , a * a * a * b̸ ...
 ↓                          ↑
              (for another a in the multiplier, add a followed by *)
 Read_4       a a a , a a a a # a , a * a * a * b̸ ...
a↓                            ↑
 Add_2 a      a a a , a a a a # a , a * a * a * a b̸ ...
 ↓                            ↑
 Add *        a a a , a a a a # a , a * a * a * a * b̸ ...
 ↓                            ↑
              (for every a in the multiplier, add a followed by *)
 Read_4       a a a , a a a a # a , a * a * a * a * b̸ ...
#↓                              ↑
 Add #        a a a , a a a a # a , a * a * a * a * # b̸ ...
 ↓                              ↑
              (repeat the procedure)
 Read_2       a a a , a a a a # a , a * a * a * a * # b̸ ...
a↓                              ↑
              (skip one a from the multiplier)
 Read_3       a a a , a a a a # a , a * a * a * a * # b̸ ...
,↓                                ↑
 Add ,        a a a , a a a a # a , a * a * a * a * # , b̸ ...
 ↓                                ↑
              (add a comma to the queue)
 Read_4       a a a , a a a a # a , a * a * a * a * # , b̸ ...
a↓                                    ↑
 Add_2 a      a a a , a a a a # a , a * a * a * a * # , a b̸ ...
 ↓                                    ↑
 Add *        a a a , a a a a # a , a * a * a * a * # , a * b̸ ...
 ↓                                    ↑
              (for every a in the multiplier, add a followed by *)
 Read_4       a a a , a a a a # a , a * a * a * a * # , a * b̸ ...
*↓                                      ↑
```

Add * a a a , a a a a # a , a * a * a * a * # , a * * ƀ …
↓ ↑

(for every *, add *)

$Read_4$ a a a , a a a a # a , a * a * a * a * # , a * * ƀ …
a ↓ ↑

$Add_2$ *a* a a a , a a a a # a , a * a * a * a * # , a * * a ƀ …
↓ ↑

Add * a a a , a a a a # a , a * a * a * a * # , a * * a * ƀ …
↓ ↑

(for every *a* in the multiplier, add *a* followed by *)

$Read_4$ a a a , a a a a # a , a * a * a * a * # , a * * a * ƀ …
* ↓ ↑

Add * a a a , a a a a # a , a * a * a * a * # , a * * a * * ƀ …
↓ ↑

(for every *, add *)

$Read_4$ a a a , a a a a # a , a * a * a * a * # , a * * a * * ƀ …
a ↓ ↑

$Add_2$ *a* a a a , a a a a # a , a * a * a * a * # , a * * a * * a ƀ …
↓ ↑

Add * a a a , a a a a # a , a * a * a * a * # , a * * a * * a * ƀ …
↓ ↑

(for every *a* in the multiplier, add *a* followed by *)

$Read_4$ a a a , a a a a # a , a * a * a * a * # , a * * a * * a * ƀ …
* ↓ ↑

Add * a a a , a a a a # a , a * a * a * a * # , a * * a * * a * * ƀ …
↓ ↑

(for every *, add *)

$Read_4$ a a a , a a a a # a , a * a * a * a * # , a * * a * * a * * ƀ …
a ↓ ↑

$Add_2$ *a* a a a , a a a a # a , a * a * a * a * # , a * * a * * a * * a ƀ …
↓ ↑

Add * a a a , a a a a # a , a * a * a * a * # , a * * a * * a * * a * ƀ …
↓ ↑

(for every *a* in the multiplier, add *a* followed by *)

$Read_4$ a a a , a a a a # a , a * a * a * a * # , a * * a * * a * * a * ƀ …
* ↓ ↑

Add * a a a , a a a a # a , a * a * a * a * # , a * * a * * a * * a * * ƀ …
↓ ↑

(for every *, add *)

$Read_4$ a a a , a a a a # a , a * a * a * a * # , a * * a * * a * * a * * ƀ …
# ↓ ↑

Add # a a a , a a a a # a , a * a * a * a * # , a * * a * * a * * a * * # ƀ …
↓ ↑

(repeat the procedure)

$Read_1$ a a a , a a a a # a , a * a * a * a * # , a * * a * * a * * a * * # ƀ …
, ↓ ↑

(comma is received in *Read*$_1$; this means multiplication is complete. We now need to replace every '*' by *a* to get the final answer. Let us write the input string in a simplified form as follows—since all the symbols to the left of the head pointer are always deleted, they cannot be accessed.)

```
          ... # , a * * a * * a * * a * * # b̸ ...
                  ↑
Read5     ... # , a * * a * * a * * a * * # b̸ ...
a ↓                 ↑
Add a     ... # , a * * a * * a * * a * * # a b̸ ...
↓                   ↑
Read5     ... # , a * * a * * a * * a * * # b̸ ...
* ↓                   ↑
Add a     ... # , a * * a * * a * * a * * # a a b̸ ...
↓                     ↑
Read5     ... # , a * * a * * a * * a * * # a a b̸ ...
* ↓                     ↑
Add a     ... # , a * * a * * a * * a * * # a a a b̸ ...
↓                       ↑
Read5     ... # , a * * a * * a * * a * * # a a a b̸ ...
a ↓                       ↑
Add a     ... # , a * * a * * a * * a * * # a a a a b̸ ...
↓                         ↑
Read5     ... # , a * * a * * a * * a * * # a a a a b̸ ...
* ↓                         ↑
Add a     ... # , a * * a * * a * * a * * # a a a a a b̸ ...
↓                           ↑
Read5     ... # , a * * a * * a * * a * * # a a a a a b̸ ...
* ↓                           ↑
Add a     ... # , a * * a * * a * * a * * # a a a a a a b̸ ...
↓                             ↑
Read5     ... # , a * * a * * a * * a * * # a a a a a a b̸ ...
a ↓                             ↑
Add a     ... # , a * * a * * a * * a * * # a a a a a a a b̸ ...
↓                               ↑
Read5     ... # , a * * a * * a * * a * * # a a a a a a a b̸ ...
* ↓                             ↑
Add a     ... # , a * * a * * a * * a * * # a a a a a a a a b̸ ...
↓                                 ↑
Read5     ... # , a * * a * * a * * a * * # a a a a a a a a b̸ ...
* ↓                               ↑
Add a     ... # , a * * a * * a * * a * * # a a a a a a a a a b̸ ...
↓                                 ↑
Read5     ... # , a * * a * * a * * a * * # a a a a a a a a a b̸ ...
a ↓                                 ↑
Add a     ... # , a * * a * * a * * a * * # a a a a a a a a a a b̸ ...
↓                                   ↑
Read5     ... # , a * * a * * a * * a * * # a a a a a a a a a a b̸ ...
* ↓                                   ↑
```

```
Add a      ... # , a * * a * * a * * a * * # a a a a a a a a a a a b̸ ...
↓                                      ↑
Read5      ... # , a * * a * * a * * a * * # a a a a a a a a a a a b̸ ...
* ↓                                        ↑
Add a      ... # , a * * a * * a * * a * * # a a a a a a a a a a a a b̸ ...
↓                                          ↑
Read5      ... # , a * * a * * a * * a * * # a a a a a a a a a a a a b̸ ...
# ↓                                          ↑
Accept                                         ──► Result of multiplication
```

Hence, multiplication of two unary numbers is achieved through repetitive addition. This requires storing the intermediate result as a part of the multiplicand with the help of the special symbol '*'.

Therefore, we see that the PM can perform a complex operation that cannot be achieved using PDA, which has a single stack. Thus, the PM is equivalent to the TM; the only difference between the two is the representation.

---

## SUMMARY

The Post machine (PM) is equivalent in power with the Turing machine (TM). The only difference between the two is in the representation. In a PM, the input is written onto its tape; the tape reads the symbols and, if necessary, adds symbols to the end of the input string (rear). The PM, thus, uses the tape as an infinite queue.

Though the head of the PM can only move in one direction (from left to right), it can add symbols to the rear of the tape. This means that the mechanism for moving to the right till the end of input, adding symbols to the end, and coming back to the next input symbol to be read is kept implicit. The addition of symbols is implemented as a subroutine called 'add'. Hence, we see that internally, the tape head of the PM moves in both directions—it goes to the right end of the tape, adds symbols, and comes back again. Therefore, a PM is simply an alternative visualization of a TM that implements tape as a queue of symbols.

The PM is collectively defined by the following elements:

1. A tape, which is bounded on one end and unbounded (or infinite) on the other. Initially, the input string is written onto the tape, ending with a special character '#'; the rest of the tape is blank (b̸)
2. A finite set of allowable tape symbols ($\Gamma$), including '#' and blank character b̸
3. A finite input alphabet $\Sigma$, which is the subset of the set of allowable tape symbols, $\Sigma \subset \Gamma$
4. A start (or initial) state
5. Halt states: accept and reject
6. A non-branching state: add
7. A branching state: read
8. A tape, implemented as a queue data structure

The PM is also represented with the help of a flowchart-like notation, similar to a pushdown stack-memory machine (PDM),

As the PM uses its tape as a queue, it has the ability to add symbols to the tape while executing. This means that the PM can write symbols onto its tape, which is an improvement over the PDM, which cannot write anything onto its tape—it can only read from the tape, because it has access to an external stack for storing symbols. The PDM, thus, has only a read head, while the PM has a read/write head. In a PM, the tape and queue are not distinct entities; the tape is implemented as its queue. Essentially, the PM can consume its own output (symbols added to the queue) as its input for later use, like a TM. On the other hand, the PDM cannot consume its stack as input, as it is external to its tape. Thus, the PM is more powerful than the PDM.

A finite state machine (FSM) can accept only regular languages (or type-3 languages), since it does not have memory. The same set of regular languages can also be accepted by the PM. However, the PM is more powerful than the former as it has infinite memory in the form of its unbounded tape. Hence, the PM can remember any large string of symbols with the help of the internal queue (tape), which is a first-in-first-out (FIFO) kind of structure; though, however, queue (or memory) is not required for accepting or recognizing the regular languages.

The PM is equivalent to the TM in computation power, and can be considered as just another implementation of the TM. Thus, the PM can also accept type-0 languages, that is, recursively enumerable languages. On the other hand, though the PDM is more powerful than the FSM, it is less powerful than the TM; the PDM accepts only type-2, that is, context-free languages.

## EXERCISES

This section lists a few unsolved problems to help the readers understand the topic better and practise examples related to the Post machine (PM).

### Objective Questions

(U) 8.1 Which of the following statements is false?
(a) PM is more powerful than finite state machine (FSM).
(b) PM cannot accept recursively enumerable languages.
(c) PM accepts type-0 languages.
(d) Pushdown stack-memory machine uses stack to accept type-2 languages.

(L) 8.2 If $A$ is a class of problems solved by PMs, $B$ is a class of problems solved by TMs, and $C$ is a class of problems solved by pushdown automata, then which of the following statements is false?
(a) $A$ is a subset of $B$.
(b) $B$ is a subset of $A$.
(c) $C$ is a subset of both $A$ and $B$.
(d) $A$ and $B$ are different sets with a possible overlap.

(L) 8.3 'The PM is equivalent in power to the TM.' Is this statement true or false?

(U) 8.4 Which of the following statements are true?
$S1$: It is possible to design an FSM that accepts well-formed parentheses.
$S2$: The language consisting of all palindrome strings over $\{0, 1\}$ is a type-0 language.
$S3$: The PM can perform division of two unary numbers.
$S4$: PMs cannot solve every problem that is solvable by TMs.
(a) $S1$ and $S2$
(b) $S1$ only
(c) $S2$ only
(d) $S2$ and $S3$
(e) $S4$ only
(f) $S3$ only
(g) None of these
(h) All of these

(U) 8.5 'The PM is equivalent in power to the pushdown stack-memory machine except for the fact that it uses a queue instead of a stack.' Is this statement true or false?

(U) 8.6 The PM is equivalent in power to the ___________.

(U) 8.7 'The PM is equivalent in power to the pushdown automata.' Is this statement true or false?

(U) 8.8 The PM is more powerful than the ___________ machine.

### Review Questions

(U) 8.1 Write a short note on PMs.

(L) 8.2 Compare TM, PDM, FSM, and PM (definition is not required).

Ⓤ 8.3 Write a short note on the power of PMs.

Ⓛ 8.4 Show that a PM has more power than a PDA.

Ⓤ 8.5 What are the different elements of a PM?

Ⓒ 8.6 Design a PM to check if the given parentheses are well formed. Simulate it with the help of a suitable example.

Ⓒ 8.7 Design a PM to accept palindrome strings over the alphabet $\Sigma = \{x, y\}$. Simulate its working with the help of a suitable example.

Ⓒ 8.8 Design PMs that accept the following languages:
(a) $L = \{a^n b^n c^n \mid n \geq 0\}$
(b) $L = \{a^n b^n \mid n \geq 0\}$

Ⓒ 8.9 Design a PM that accepts the strings of $a$'s and $b$'s having odd length, with $a$ as the middle element.

Ⓒ 8.10 Design a PM that accepts the language described by the following grammar:
$G = (\{S, A\}, \{0, 1\}, P, S)$, where $P$ consists of:
$S \rightarrow 0\,A\,S \mid 0$
$A \rightarrow S\,1\,A \mid S\,S \mid 1\,0$

Ⓒ 8.11 Design a PM that accepts the language described by the following grammar:
$S \rightarrow A\,B\,A$
$A \rightarrow a\,A \mid \epsilon$
$B \rightarrow b\,B \mid \epsilon$
Comment on the type of language.

Ⓒ 8.12 Design a PM the accepts the language $L$, over $\Sigma = \{a, b\}$, such that $L$ contains words in which the letter $b$ does not appear consecutively three times.

**Answers to Objective Questions**

8.1. (b) 8.2. (d) 8.3. True 8.4. (d) 8.5. False 8.6. Turing machine 8.7. False
8.8. finite state

# Undecidability

## LEARNING OBJECTIVES

After completing this chapter, the reader will be able to understand the following:

- Revision of recursive and recursively enumerable languages
- Some important properties of recursive and recursively enumerable languages
- Decidable versus undecidable problems
- Non-recursively enumerable language and diagonalization language
- Gödel encoding for Turing machines (TMs)
- Undecidability and halting problem
- Some undecidable problems regarding TMs and context-free grammars (CFGs)
- Ackermann's function, universal language, reducibility, Rice's theorem, Post's correspondence problem, Greibach's theorem, and Hilbert's problem

## 9.1 INTRODUCTION

We have seen in Chapter 4 that a Turing machine (TM) is an idealistic machine with no limitations on the memory size. However, there are certain problems that no TM can solve—we may recall that the halting problem is an unsolvable problem.

The problems that can be solved by a TM can be divided into two classes. Firstly, there are problems during which the TM always halts whether or not it accepts the input; and secondly, there are problems during which the TM halts only when it accepts the input (else, it may run forever).

This chapter deals with a certain class of problems, called undecidable problems, for which it is impossible to construct a single algorithm (or TM) that always leads to correctness.

## 9.2 RECURSIVE AND RECURSIVELY ENUMERABLE LANGUAGES

We have already discussed these languages in Chapter 4 (refer to Section 4.15). Let us briefly revise the concepts here as we require them to discuss undecidability.

A language $L$ is said to be *recursive*, if $L = L(M)$ for some TM $M$, such that:

1. If $w$ is in $L$, then $M$ accepts $w$, and therefore, halts.
2. If $w$ is not in $L$, then $M$ eventually halts without accepting $w$.

Such a TM, which always halts whether or not the input string is acceptable, corresponds to our intuitive notion of an algorithm—a well-defined sequence of operations that always halts and produces an answer. If a recursive language is considered as a problem, then this type of problem is called a *decidable* problem; on the other hand, a non-recursive language is called an *undecidable* problem.

A language $L$ is said to be *recursively enumerable (RE)*, if $L = L(M)$ for some TM $M$, such that:

1. If $w$ is in $L$, then $M$ accepts $w$, and therefore, halts.
2. If $w$ is not in $L$, then $M$ may or may not halt.

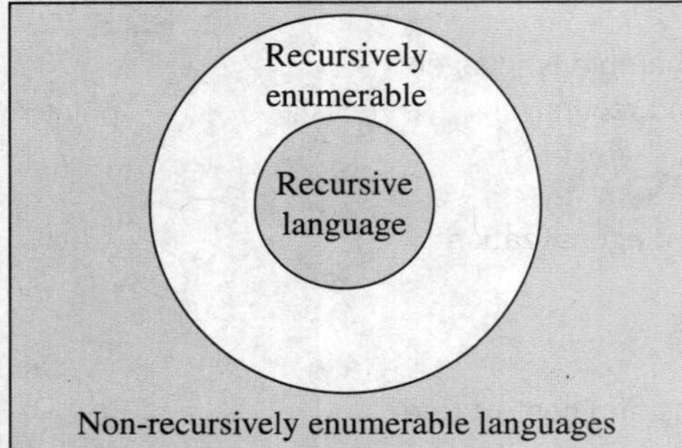


**Figure 9.1** Recursive and recursively enumerable languages

Recursively enumerable languages are partial recursive functions that are semi-solvable, whereas recursive languages are total recursive functions that are completely solvable. Thus, every recursive language is recursively enumerable, but the converse is not true. Recursive languages are a proper subset of RE languages (refer to Fig. 9.1).

As we know, recursive languages are decidable, while undecidable problems can be further categorized into two classes:

1. Recursively enumerable languages: For such languages, the TM may or may not halt on all inputs, that is, they are partially-solvable problems.
2. Non-recursively enumerable languages: For such languages, it is not possible to construct a TM, that is, they are unsolvable problems.

***Note***: In all our discussions, the word 'recursive' should be taken as a synonym for 'decidable'. The term 'recursive' has a historic background of how the theory of computation evolved. This history is not covered here.

### 9.2.1 Some Important Results

We need to be familiar with a few important results regarding recursive and recursively enumerable languages. Let us consider the complement operation.

Here, we shall show that the recursive languages are closed under the complement operation. We know that every recursive language is also RE. We shall prove that if a language $L$ is RE but $\bar{L}$ (complement of $L$) is not RE, then $L$ cannot be recursive.

For this, let us first prove the important closure property of recursive languages–$\overline{M}$ they are *closed under complement*. This means that if $L$ is a recursive language, then $\bar{L}$ is also a recursive language.

**Theorem 9.1**

If $L$ is a recursive language, then $\bar{L}$ is also a recursive language.

*Proof*

Let $L = L(M)$ for some TM $M$ that always halts. Then, $\bar{L}$ is the complement of $L$ such that:

If $w$ is in $L$, then $w$ is surely not in $\bar{L}$ and vice versa.

We can construct a TM, $\overline{M}$ such that $\bar{L} = L(\overline{M})$, as shown in Fig. 9.2.

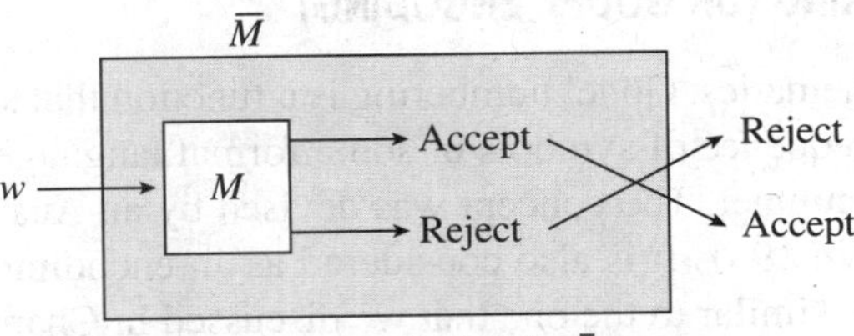


**Figure 9.2** TM for $\bar{L}$

We see from Fig. 9.2 that $\overline{M}$ can be constructed from $M$ by just reversing the 'accept' and 'reject' halt states. Thus, $\overline{M}$ is guaranteed to halt on any input; so, $\bar{L}$ is also a recursive language. Therefore, we conclude that *all recursive languages are closed under complement operation.*

Similarly, another important result about recursive and RE languages that we need to prove is that if both $L$ and $\bar{L}$ are RE, then $L$ is recursive. Hence from Theorem 9.1, $\bar{L}$ is also recursive.

**Theorem 9.2**

If a language $L$ and its complement $\bar{L}$ are recursively enumerable languages, then $L$ is a recursive language.

*Proof*

Let us assume that $L = L(M_1)$ and $\bar{L} = L(\overline{M}_1)$, and $M_1$ halts on any input $w$ belonging to $L$ and may loop if $w$ does not belong to $L$. Similarly, $\overline{M}_1$ halts on any input $w$ that belongs to $\bar{L}$ and may loop if $w$ does not belong to $\bar{L}$.

We can construct another TM $M_2$ using $M_1$ and $\overline{M}_1$, as shown in Fig. 9.3.

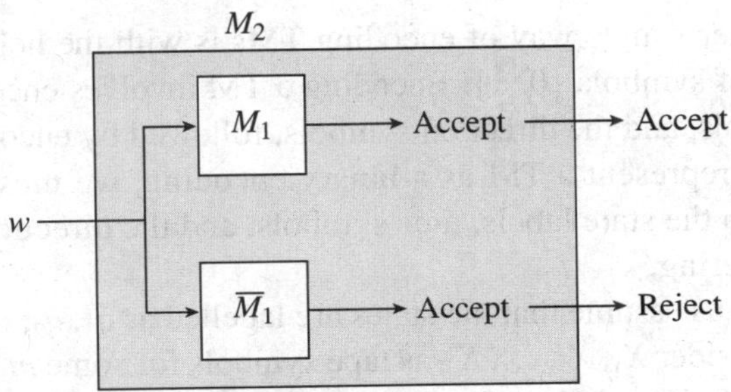


**Figure 9.3** A TM simulating two TMs that accept an RE language and its complement

Since both $L$ and $\bar{L}$ are RE languages, we know that $M_1$ and $\overline{M}_1$ halt on acceptance.

We observe from Fig. 9.3 that if $w$ is in $L$, then $M_1$ eventually accepts it and halts; similarly, $M_2$, the newly-constructed TM also accepts it and halts. If $w$ is not in $L$, then it must be in the complement of $L$, which is $\bar{L}$. Therefore, $\bar{M}_1$ eventually accepts it and halts; in this case, $M_2$ rejects the input and halts.

Thus, $M_2$ halts on all the inputs, and $L(M_2) = L = L(M_1)$. Therefore, we conclude that $L$ is a recursive language; and hence, from Theorem 9.1, $\bar{L}$ is also a recursive language.

## 9.3 GÖDEL NUMBERING (OR GÖDEL ENCODING)

In mathematics, Gödel numbering is a function that assigns to each symbol, and hence, to every sequence of symbols of some formal language, a unique natural number called its Gödel number. The concept was devised by an Austrian American mathematician, Kurt Gödel, in 1931. It is also considered as an encoding in which a number is assigned to a symbol, similar to the one that we discussed in Chapter 4 (refer to Section 4.9).

In his proposed encoding, Gödel first assigned a unique natural number to each basic symbol. Encoding of an entire sequence of symbols is obtained as the product of the first $n$ primes raised to their corresponding values in the sequence. For example, given a sequence ($x1$, $x2$, …, $xn$) of numbers, its encoding can be written as, '$2^{x1} . 3^{x2} . 5^{x3} .... p_n^{xn}$'. Note that, '$x1$', '$x2$', and so on, are the encoding of the individual symbols, and '2', '3', '5', …, '$p_n$' are the first $n$ primes.

Any encoded number obtained in this way can be uniquely expressed in terms of its prime factors. Hence, it is possible to recover the original sequence from it. Gödel numbering is based on the number theory. In number theory, the fundamental theorem of arithmetic (or the unique-prime-factorization theorem) states that any integer greater than '1' can be written as a unique product of prime numbers.

For example:

$$10 = 1^1 \times 2^1 \times 5^1$$
$$24 = 1 \times 2 \times 2 \times 2 \times 3 = 1^1 \times 2^3 \times 3^1$$
$$15 = 1^1 \times 3^1 \times 5^1$$

### 9.3.1 Encoding of Turing Machines

Another simple way of encoding TMs is with the help of binary codes, that is, with the help of symbols {0, 1}. Encoding a TM involves encoding the state symbols, input tape symbols, and the direction symbols, followed by encoding the entire functional matrix.

To represent a TM as a binary encoding, we must first assign unique natural numbers to the state labels, tape symbols, and the direction symbols $\{L, R, N\}$ as per Gödel numbering.

Let us assume that the states are labelled as $q_1, q_2, \ldots, q_k$ for some $k > 0$. Similarly, let us consider $X_1, X_2, \ldots, X_m$ as tape symbols for some $m > 0$; and let us represent the directions, $L$, $R$, and $N$, as $D_1$, $D_2$, and $D_3$, respectively.

After encoding all the aforementioned symbols, we need to encode the functional matrix, $\delta$. If a transition from the functional matrix is represented as the following quintuple:

$$\delta\,(q_i, X_j) = (q_k, X_l, D_m),$$

where *i*, *j*, *k*, *l*, and *m* are integers, then we can encode it as:

$$0^i\,1\,0^j\,1\,0^k\,1\,0^l\,1\,0^m$$

Note that the value of *i*, *j*, *k*, *l*, and *m* is at least 1, and hence, there are no two consecutive 1's in the encoded string. In the binary encoding of the transition symbol, '1' acts as a separator between the five entities that represent the transition.

The encoding of the functional matrix can now be obtained from the individual transition encodings. We need to represent the functional matrix in a linear fashion—using column-major or row-major method—as discussed in Chapter 4, Section 4.9. Assume that we impose some ordering on the transitions in this way. The functional matrix encoding can then be obtained from the transition encodings separated by a pair of 1's as

$$C_1 \ 11 \ C_2 \ 11 \ldots C_{n-1} \ 11 \ C_n,$$

where, $C_i$ is the code for the *i*th transition from the functional matrix $\delta$ considered linearly.

Let us consider the following example TM.

$$M = \{(q_1, q_2, q_3), (0, 1), (0, 1, B), \delta, q_1, B, (q_2)\},$$

where, $\delta$ consists of the following transitions:

$$\delta(q_1, 1) = (q_3, 0, R) \qquad \delta(q_3, 1) = (q_2, 0, R)$$
$$\delta(q_3, 0) = (q_1, 1, R) \qquad \delta(q_3, B) = (q_3, 1, L)$$

The following are the codes for each of the aforementioned transitions respectively:

$$C_1 = 0^1\,1\,0^2\,1\,0^3\,1\,0^1\,1\,0^2 = 0\ 1\ 00\ 1\ 000\ 1\ 0\ 1\ 00$$
$$C_2 = 0^3\,1\,0^1\,1\,0^1\,1\,0^2\,1\,0^2 = 000\ 1\ 0\ 1\ 0\ 1\ 00\ 1\ 00$$
$$C_3 = 0^3\,1\,0^2\,1\,0^2\,1\,0^1\,1\,0^2 = 000\ 1\ 00\ 1\ 00\ 1\ 0\ 1\ 00$$
$$C_4 = 0^3\,1\,0^3\,1\,0^3\,1\,0^2\,1\,0^1 = 000\ 1\ 000\ 1\ 000\ 1\ 00\ 1\ 0$$

Here, $q_1$, $q_2$, and $q_3$ are assigned the unique natural numbers 1, 2, and 3 respectively. Similarly, the tape symbols 0, 1, and *B* (blank) are assigned natural numbers 1, 2, and 3 respectively. The direction symbols *L* and *R* are assigned natural numbers 1 and 2 respectively.

The code for the entire TM, that is, the code for the entire functional matrix $\delta$ is given by

$$C_1 \ 11 \ C_2 \ 11 \ C_3 \ 11 \ C_4,$$

which is as follows:

0 1 00 1 000 1 0 1 00 11 000 1 0 1 0 1 00 1 00 11 000 1 00 1 00
1 0 1 00 11 000 1 000 1 000 1 00 1 0

There can be many different encoding techniques for a TM; the one discussed here is just a sample for illustration.

## 9.4 NON-RECURSIVELY ENUMERABLE LANGUAGES

As discussed earlier, non-recursively enumerable languages represent the class of undecidable/unsolvable problems.

Consider a language $L$ consisting of pairs of the form $(M, w)$ where, $M$ is any TM and $w$ is any string that is accepted by $M$. The language $L$ represents a more generic undecidable problem: 'Does this TM accept this input?'

### 9.4.1 Diagonalization Language

*Diagonalization language* $L_d$ is the language defined as $\{w_i \mid w_i \notin L(M_i)\}$. It is the set of strings $w_i$ such that $w_i$ does not belong to the language accepted by any TM $M_i$. Thus, $L_d$ consists of all the strings $w$ such that any TM $M$ does not accept the input $w$.

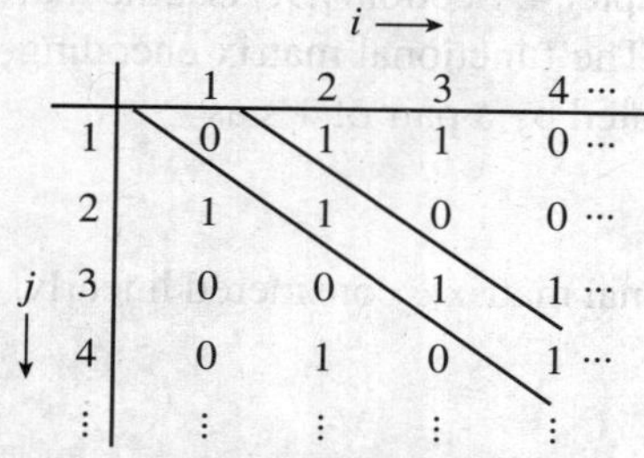

| | 1 | 2 | 3 | 4 ... |
|---|---|---|---|---|
| 1 | 0 | 1 | 1 | 0 ... |
| 2 | 1 | 1 | 0 | 0 ... |
| 3 | 0 | 0 | 1 | 1 ... |
| 4 | 0 | 1 | 0 | 1 ... |
| ⋮ | ⋮ | ⋮ | ⋮ | ⋮ |

**Figure 9.4** Imaginary table showing acceptance of words by TMs

Let us imagine an infinite table that tells us for all values of $i$ and $j$, if $w_i$ is in $L(M_j)$. Figure 9.4 shows such a table. All the columns contain the variable $i$ and indicate the input strings, while the rows contain the variable $j$ and represent the TMs. It is assumed that such an infinite table consists of all possible TMs and all possible languages accepted by these TMs, that is, all possible recursively enumerable languages.

If an entry in the table is 0, it indicates that $w_i$ is not in $L(M_j)$; and if the entry is 1, it indicates that $w_i$ is in $L(M_j)$. We may consider every row as the characteristic vector for the language $L(M_j)$.

The diagonal values of the table, where $i = j$, indicate whether or not $M_j$ accepts $w_i$. To construct the diagonalization language $L_d$, we complement the characteristic vector for the diagonal elements. The complemented diagonal vector for Fig. 9.4 can be written as '1 0 0 0 ...', since the diagonal vector is '0 1 1 1 ...'. The act of complementing the diagonal elements to construct the characteristic vector of a language that cannot be the language that already appears in any row is called *diagonalization*. This is the reason why $L_d$ is called diagonalization language.

Thus, $L_d$ is obtained by complementing the diagonal elements and is not already there in the matrix. This means that after taking the diagonal elements and complementing them, we get a new language every time, which is not there in the matrix.

### 9.4.2 $L_d$ Not Recursively Enumerable

Let us now prove that $L_d$ is not recursively enumerable. This means that there is no TM that accepts $L_d$.

**Theorem 9.3**

$L_d$ is not recursively enumerable.

*Proof*

Let us prove this by contradiction.

We begin with the assumption that there exists a TM, $M$ such that $L_d = L(M)$. The infinite table in Fig. 9.4 includes all the possible TMs and all the possible languages accepted by these TMs. Thus, TM $M$ must also be included therein, say as $M_j$.

If $w_i$ is in $L_d$, then $M_j$ accepts $w_i$. However, $w_i$ is not in $L_d$ because by definition, $L_d$ contains only those $w_i$ that are accepted by $M_j$.

Similarly, if $w_i$ is not in $L_d$, then $M_j$ does not accept it. Thus, by definition, $w_i$ is in $L_d$.

This is a contradiction. Therefore, our assumption that a TM $M$ exists such that $L(M) = L_d$ is wrong.

Hence, $L_d$ is not acceptable by any TM. Therefore, $L_d$ is not a recursively enumerable language.

Therefore, the problem represented by the diagonalization language is an undecidable problem, and no TM can solve it.

## 9.5 UNIVERSAL LANGUAGE

The language accepted by a universal Turing machine (UTM) is called *universal language* ($L_u$). It is defined as follows:

$L_u = L(U)$, where $U$ is the UTM, and $L_u$ is recursively enumerable (RE) but not recursive, due to the fact that a UTM exists. Further, $L_u = \bar{L}_d$; that is, $L_u$ is the complement of the diagonalization language $L_d$, which is not an RE language. Since $L_u$ is non-recursive, it is included in the undecidable category of problems.

Thus $L_u$, is similar to the halting problem of a TM, that is, the language is RE but not recursive. We can define the $H(M)$ for a TM $M$ as the set of inputs $w$ such that $M$ halts given input $w$, regardless of whether or not $M$ accepts $w$.

Then the halting problem is the set of pairs $(M, w)$ such that $w$ is in $H(M)$. Thus, the halting problem gets reduced to $L_u$, which is RE but not recursive.

## 9.6 REDUCIBILITY AND UNDECIDABLE PROBLEMS

Reduction of a given problem to a known problem helps us decide what type of problem it is. If we have an algorithm to convert instances of problem $P_1$ to instances of problem $P_2$ that have the same answer, then we say that $P_1$ is reduced to $P_2$. We can also say that $P_2$ is as hard as $P_1$. Thus, if $P_1$ is not recursive, then $P_2$ cannot be recursive; and if $P_2$ is not RE, then $P_1$ also cannot be RE. Similarly, if $P_1$ is undecidable, so is $P_2$.

To illustrate this, let us consider two languages $L_e$ and $L_{ne}$, where $L_e$ consists of all coded TMs—such as those in Fig. 9.4—whose language is empty, that is, $L(M_i) = \phi$.

On the other hand, if $L(M_i)$ is not empty, then $M_i$ is in $L_{ne}$. Therefore we have:

$$L_e = \{M_i \mid L(M_i) = \phi\}$$
$$L_{ne} = \{M_i \mid L(M_i) \neq \phi\}$$

Thus, we see that $L_e$ and $L_{ne}$ are complements of each other; and while $L_{ne}$ is a recursively enumerable language, though not recursive, $L_e$ is not an RE language.

To show that $L_{ne}$ is RE, we need to construct a TM $M$ that accepts $L_{ne}$.

We can reduce $L_u$ to $L_{ne}$. TM $M$ can be considered as a variant of the UTM, which takes the TM $M_i$ as input. This TM $M$ then tests whether $M_i$ accepts $w$ by simulating $M_i$ (same as UTM). If $M_i$ accepts $w$, then $M$ accepts the input, which is $M_i$; and if $M_i$ loops, so does $M$ (refer to Fig. 9.5).

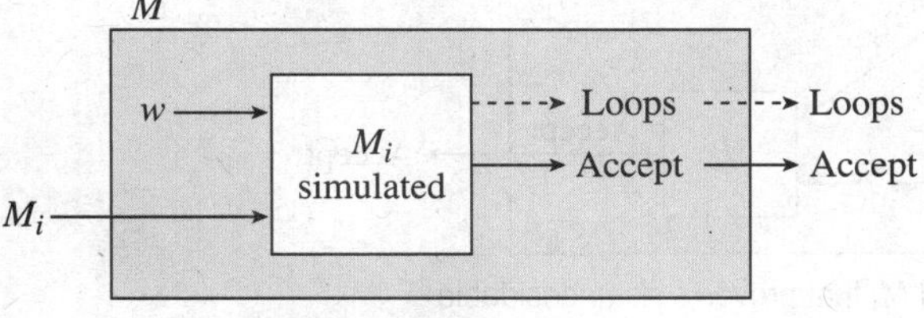

**Figure 9.5** TM $M$ that simulates $M_i$

It can be easily seen from Fig. 9.5 that if $M_i$ accepts $w$, then $M$ accepts $M_i$; else, it loops forever. Hence, the language $L_{ne}$ is RE, but not recursive.

Since $L_e$ and $L_{ne}$ are complements of each other, and $L_{ne}$ is RE but not recursive, by Theorem 9.2, we conclude the $L_e$ is not an RE language .

Thus, we see that both $L_e$ and $L_{ne}$ are undecidable. There are many other undecidable problems for TMs. Some of them are listed as follows:

- To decide whether or not the language accepted by a TM is finite
- To decide whether or not the language accepted by a TM is regular
- To decide whether or not the language accepted by a TM is context-free
- To decide whether or not the language accepted by a TM is empty

## 9.7 RICE'S THEOREM

A property of RE languages forms a set of RE languages. Thus, if being a regular language is the property of the RE language, then it forms a set of all regular languages. A property of RE languages is said to be *trivial* if it is empty (i.e., not satisfied by any RE language), or if it is satisfied by all RE languages. Otherwise, it is said to be *non-trivial*. Note that the empty property is not the same as an empty language.

We cannot recognize a set of languages using a TM. The reason is that languages that are members of the set defined by a property, may be infinite and cannot be represented using strings of finite length, which needs to be the input to a TM. Instead, we need to construct a TM that recognizes the TMs, which in turn accept these individual languages. Every TM can be coded into a binary string of finite length, as discussed in Section 9.3.1. Thus, if $P$ is a property of RE languages, then the language $L_p$ is the set of codes of TMs $M_i$ such that $L(M_i)$ is in $P$. We can construct a TM that recognizes $L_p$.

**Statement of Rice's theorem** Every non-trivial property of an RE language is undecidable.

*Proof*

To prove Rice's theorem, we need to show that $L_p$ is undecidable for a non-trivial property $P$. We shall proceed by reducing $L_u$ to $L_p$. As we know, if $L_u$ is undecidable, so is $L_p$. To demonstrate this reduction, we construct a TM $M_1$, as shown in Fig. 9.6.

The construction of $M_1$ is such that if $M$ does not accept $w$, then $L(M_1) = \phi$; if $M$ accepts $w$, then $L(M_1) = L_p$. This construction is shown in Fig. 9.6.

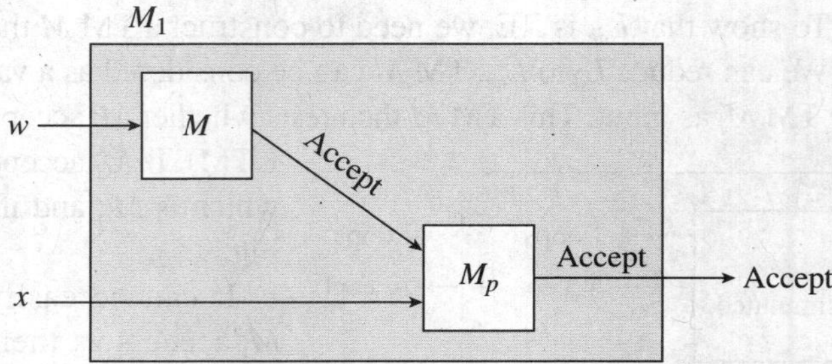


**Figure 9.6** TM $M_1$ that proves $L_p$ is undecidable

On input $(M, w)$, we create a (description of a) TM $M_1$ as follows:

1. On input $x$, let the TM $M$ run on the string $w$ until it accepts (if it does not accept, $M_1$ will run forever) the string.
2. Next, run $M_p$ on $x$. Accept it if and only if $M_p$ does.

Note that $M_1$ accepts the same language as $M_p$ if $M$ accepts $w$; $M_1$ accepts the empty language if $M$ does not accept $w$.

Thus, if $M$ accepts $w$, the TM $M_1$ has the property $P$; else, it does not have it. This turns $M_1$ into $M_p$ if and only if $(M, w)$ is in $L_u$. Hence, $L_u$ is reduced to $L_p$. This proves that the property $P$ is undecidable just like $L_u$.

The essence of the Rice's theorem is that any problem, which requires determining a property of the language recognized by a given TM, is undecidable. The only exceptions are the trivial properties that are always either true or false.

Rice's theorem can also be stated as follows:

**Alternate statement** Let $C$ be a set of languages (with a certain property, $P$). Consider the language $L_C$, which is defined as follows:

$$L_C = \{M \mid L(M) \in C\}$$

Then, either $L_C$ is empty (trivial), or it contains the descriptions of all TMs that are trivial, or it is undecidable (non-trivial).

This is analogous to asking—in a software testing problem—whether a given program computes a function $x$; or in TM terminology, asking whether the language accepted by the TM $M$ is $L$.

We now know that these problems are undecidable and this is exactly what is stated in Rice's theorem.

## 9.8 POST'S CORRESPONDENCE PROBLEM

We have already discussed Post's correspondence problem (PCP) in Chapter 4 (Sec-tion 4.18), which is an undecidable problem. This problem can be reduced to $L_u$, which is undecidable. Given a pair $(M, w)$, we construct an instance $(A, B)$ of the PCP such that TM $M$ accepts input $w$ if and only if $(A, B)$ has a solution. Thus PCP is also an undecidable problem.

## 9.9 UNDECIDABLE PROBLEMS FOR CONTEXT-FREE GRAMMARS

There are many problems about CFGs that are undecidable, including whether or not the intersection of two context-free languages (CFLs) is empty, the given grammar is ambiguous, and so on.

Let us consider the problem to decide whether the intersection, $L(G_1) \cap L(G_2)$, where $G_1$ and $G_2$ are CFGs, is empty or not.

**Theorem 9.4**

It is undecidable for arbitrary CFGs $G_1$ and $G_2$ whether $L(G_1) \cap L(G_2) = \phi$.

*Proof*

Assume that we can construct a TM $M$ such that $L(G_1) \cap L(G_2)$ is a valid set of computations of $M$. If there is an algorithm $A$ to check whether the intersection of two CFLs is empty, we can construct an algorithm $B$ to check whether $L(M) = \phi$. If the intersection is empty, then $L(M) = \phi$, that is, there are no valid computations for TM $M$. Since the language $L_e$ is undecidable, the problem of intersection of two CFLs gets reduced to $L_e$ and is also undecidable.

Other undecidable problems with CFGs include the following:

1. Deciding for any arbitrary CFG, $G$ whether $L(G) = \Sigma^*$
2. If $G_1$ and $G_2$ are CFGs and $R$ is an arbitrary regular set, it is undecidable to show that:
   (a) $L(G_1) = L(G_2)$
   (b) $L(G_1) \subseteq L(G_2)$
   (c) $L(G_1) = R$
   (d) $R \subseteq L(G_1)$
   (e) $L(G_1) \cap L(G_2)$ is a CFL
   (f) $L(G_1)$ is ambiguous (or unambiguous)

## 9.10 GREIBACH'S THEOREM

This theorem is analogous to Rice's theorem in the case of CFLs.

**Statement of Greibach's theorem** Let $\sigma$ be a countable family of languages that is effectively closed under union and concatenation with regular languages. Let us assume that the problem $L = \Sigma^*$ is undecidable for $L \in \sigma$ and any given sufficiently large alphabet $\Sigma$. Let $P$ be any non-trivial property of languages that is true for regular languages such that if $P(L)$ holds, then $P(L/a)$ also holds for any symbol $a$. Then, $P$ is undecidable for $\sigma$.

*Proof*

Let us first understand the meaning of $L/w$.

Given any language, $L \subseteq \Sigma^*$, and any string, $w \in \Sigma^*$, we define $L/w$ as:

$$L/w = \{u \in \Sigma^* \mid uw \in L\}$$

The simplified definition using $w = a$ is:

If $P$ is the property of $L$, then it is preserved under symbol $a$. This means that:

$$L/a = \{u \mid ua \in L\}$$

Since $P$ is a non-trivial property for $\sigma$, there is some $L_0 \in \sigma$ such that $P(L_0)$ is false. Let $\Sigma$ be large enough such that $L_0 \subseteq \Sigma^*$, and the problem $L = \Sigma^*$ is undecidable for $L \in \sigma$.

We shall show that given any $L \in \sigma$, for $L \subseteq \Sigma^*$, we can construct a language $L_1 \in \sigma$, such that $L = \Sigma^*$, iff $P(L_1)$ holds. Thus, the problem $L = \Sigma^*$ for $L \in \sigma$ reduces to property $P$ for $\sigma$; and since for $\Sigma$ that is big enough, the first problem is undecidable, so is the second.

Now, for any language $L \in \sigma$, with $L \subseteq \Sigma^*$

Let $L_1 = L_0 \,.\, \Sigma^* \cup \Sigma^* \,.\, L$

Since $\sigma$ is effectively closed under union and concatenation with regular languages, we have:

$$L_1 \in \sigma$$

If $L = \Sigma^*$, then $L_1 = \Sigma^*.\ \Sigma^*$, which is a regular language, and thus $P(L_1)$ holds, since $P$ holds for the regular languages.

Conversely, we would like to prove that if $L \neq \Sigma^*$, then $P(L_1)$ is false.

Since $L \neq \Sigma^*$, there is some $w \notin L$ such that:

$$L_1/w = L_0$$

Since $P$ is preserved under the quotient by a single letter, by a trivial induction, we can say that if $P(L_1)$ holds, then $P(L_0)$ also holds. However, $P(L_0)$ is false; hence, $P(L_1)$ must also be false.

Thus, we have proved that $L = \Sigma^*$, iff $P(L_1)$ holds, as claimed.

Greibach's theorem can be used to prove that many problems related to CFGs are undecidable.

For example, let us consider the problem that checks whether or not an arbitrary CFG $G$, $L(G)$ is regular. We know that CFLs are closed under concatenation and union with regular sets. Let $P$ be the property that $L$ is regular. Since $P$ is a non-trivial property for CFLs, by Greibach's theorem, the problem of whether or not the CFL is regular is undecidable.

Similarly, it can be shown that inherent ambiguity of CFLs is an undecidable problem.

## 9.11 HILBERT'S PROBLEM

Entscheidungsproblem is the German word for 'decision problem' and was a challenge posed by David Hilbert in 1928. It can be viewed as asking for an algorithm to decide whether a given predicate is provable from the axioms using the rules of logic. Turing published his most important paper in 1936—'On Computable Numbers, with an Application to the Entscheidungsproblem'. In this paper, he introduced what later became known as the TM—a machine capable of performing any mathematical function if it can be expressed as an algorithm (a set of instructions for the machine to follow). However, there are multiple other problems stated by Hilbert that are undecidable. One such problem is known as Hilbert's tenth problem, which topped the list of Hilbert's problems in 1900.

**Statement of Hilbert's Tenth Problem** Given a Diophantine equation with any number of unknown quantities and with rational integral numerical coefficients, devise a process according to which it can be determined in a finite number of operations whether the equation is solvable in rational integers.

This problem calls for an algorithm to determine whether or not a given Diophantine equation has any integer solutions.

Diophantine equations are equations expressed entirely in terms of integers and operations on integers, whose unknowns also have to be solved for integers, $I = \{\ldots, -3, -2, -1, 0, 1, 2, 3, \ldots\}$. The term 'rational integers' from the problem statement simply refers to integers that are either positive, negative, or zero.

A Diophantine equation is an equation of the form:

$$p(x_1, x_2, x_3, \ldots, x_n) = 0,$$

where $p$ is a polynomial with integer coefficients.

Thus, Hilbert was asking for a general algorithm to decide whether a given polynomial Diophantine equation with integer coefficients has a solution in integers.

This problem was eventually solved in the negative in 1970 by a young Russian mathematician, Yuri Matiyasevich. It was later proved to be undecidable by the work of Davis, Putnam, Robinson, and Matiyasevich. Thus, Hilbert's tenth problem is just one among a host of decision problems that have been settled in one way or the other, and lie on the borderline of logic, mathematics, and computer science. Hence, it is considered significant.

**Theorem 9.5**

Hilbert's tenth problem is unsolvable.

*Proof*

Let us assume that we have an algorithm (or a TM) to decide whether a Diophantine equation of the form, $p(x_1, x_2, x_3, \ldots, x_n) = 0$, has integer solutions. To achieve this, we need to feed $n$ integers to such an algorithm, which will then try to solve the polynomial $p$ and check whether it has integer solutions. Note that we can arrange the set of integers into a set of $n$-tuples using some intuitive ordering so that we know what $n$ integers to feed to the algorithm at every execution. We see that such a set of $n$-tuples is a recursively enumerable set and, of course, infinite. This is because one can arrange all possible tuples of unknowns values in a sequence and then for a given value of the parameter(s), test these tuples, one by one, to see whether they are solutions to the corresponding equation.

Such an algorithm or TM can return a result if there is a solution to the polynomial, but may loop forever if there exists no solution—that is, no $n$-tuple from the set of tuples is a solution; it may simply keep consuming the tuples and continue forever.

We can reduce this problem to the halting problem by assuming another TM that can simulate the TM that tries to solve the polynomial, and halts with an 'accept' message when there is a solution, and with a 'reject' message when the simulated TM loops. As we know, the halting problem is unsolvable. Hence, Hilbert's tenth problem is also unsolvable.

## 9.12 ACKERMANN'S FUNCTION

In computability theory, the Ackermann function, named after Wilhelm Ackermann, is one of the simplest and earliest discovered examples of a total recursive function.

The original Ackermann's function had three non-negative arguments; many authors modified it to suit various purposes. The most common version of the Ackermann's function has two arguments. The *Ackermann-Péter function* is defined as follows for non-negative integers $m$ and $n$:

$$A(m, n) = \begin{cases} n + 1 & \text{if } m = 0 \\ A(m - 1, 1) & \text{if } m > 0 \text{ and } n = 0 \\ A[(m - 1, A(m, n - 1)] & \text{if } m > 0 \text{ and } n > 0 \end{cases}$$

From the definition, we observe the following:

1. The value of the function grows rapidly, even for small inputs.
2. It is not very obvious from the definition that the evaluation of the function always terminates.
3. Either the value of $m$ decreases, or the value of $n$ decreases and the value of $m$ remains the same.
4. Whenever $n$ reaches 0, the value of $m$ decreases and eventually reaches 0 as well.

Thus, though recursive, the Ackermann's function exhibits bounded recursion, and hence, is a total computable function.

Let us see an illustration of the evaluation of Ackermann's function for small inputs.

$$\begin{aligned}A(1, 2) &= A[0, A(1, 1)]\\ &= A\{0, A[0, A(1, 0)]\}\\ &= A\{0, A[0, A(0, 1)]\}\\ &= A[0, A(0, 2)]\\ &= A(0, 3)\\ &= 4\end{aligned}$$

If we try to evaluate the Ackermann's function even on small inputs such as $A(4, 2)$, the value is very high, with many decimal digits. It grows faster than the exponential function. Table 9.1 gives a rough idea of the evaluation of the function.

Ackermann's function is a classic recursive example in computer science, whose value grows at a rapid pace, but is still totally computable.

**Table 9.1** Rapid growth of Ackermann's function even for small values of $m$ and $n$

| $A(m, n)$ | $n = 0$ | $n = 1$ | $n = 2$ | $n = 3$ | $n = 4$ | $n = 5$ |
|---|---|---|---|---|---|---|
| $m = 0$ | 1 | 2 | 3 | 4 | 5 | 6 |
| $m = 1$ | 2 | 3 | 4 | 5 | 6 | 7 |
| $m = 2$ | 3 | 5 | 7 | 9 | 11 | 13 |
| $m = 3$ | 5 | 13 | 29 | 61 | 125 | 253 |
| $m = 4$ | 13 | 65533 | $2^{265536} - 3$ | $2^{265536} - 3$ | $A(3, 2^{265536} - 3)$ | $A(3, A(4, 4))$ |

Ackermann's original three-argument function for non-negative integers $m$, $n$, and $p$, is defined recursively as follows:

$$\phi(m, n, p) = \begin{cases} \phi(m, n, 0) = m + n & \\ \phi(m, 0, 1) = 0 & \\ \phi(m, 0, 2) = 1 & \\ \phi(m, 0, p) = m & \text{for } p > 2\\ \phi[m, \phi\,(m, n-1, p), p-1] & \text{for } n > 0 \text{ and } p > 0\end{cases}$$

We shall talk about Ackermann's function once again while discussing algorithm complexity in Chapter 10. The intent of discussing it here is to introduce a totally computable, completely decidable problem that cannot be solved merely using simple loops with predefined upper limits. This function is one of the examples of totally computable but non-primitive recursive functions.

## SUMMARY

A language $L$ is said to be *recursive*, if $L = L(M)$ for some TM $M$ such that:

1. If $w$ is in $L$, then $M$ accepts $w$, and therefore, halts.
2. If $w$ is not in $L$, then $M$ eventually halts without accepting $w$.

A language $L$ is said to be *recursively enumerable* if $L = L(M)$ for some TM $M$ such that:

1. If $w$ is in $L$, then $M$ accepts $w$, and therefore, halts.
2. If $w$ is not in $L$, then $M$ may or may not halt.

If a recursive language is considered as a problem, then this type of problem is called a *decidable* problem; on the other hand, a non-recursive language is called an *undecidable* problem.

Recursively enumerable languages are partial recursive functions that are semi-solvable, whereas recursive languages are total recursive functions that are completely solvable. Thus, every recursive language is recursively enumerable, but the converse is not true.

As we know, recursive languages are decidable while undecidable problems can be further categorized into two classes:

1. Recursively enumerable (RE) languages: For such languages, the TM may or may not halt on all inputs, that is, they are partially-solvable problems.
2. Non-recursively enumerable languages: For such languages, it is not possible to construct a TM, that is, they are unsolvable problems.

Recursive languages are *closed under complement operation*. This means that if $L$ is a recursive language, then its complement $\bar{L}$ is also a recursive language. Further, if a language $L$ and its complement $\bar{L}$ are recursively enumerable languages, then $L$ is a recursive language.

Gödel numbering is a function that assigns to each symbol, and hence to every sequence of symbols of some formal language, a unique natural number, called its Gödel number. In his proposed encoding, Gödel first assigned a unique natural number to each basic symbol. Encoding of an entire sequence of symbols is obtained as the product of the first $n$ primes raised to their corresponding values in the sequence. For example, given a sequence ($x1$, $x2$, ..., $xn$) of numbers, its encoding can be written as, $2^{x1} \cdot 3^{x2} \cdot 5^{x3} \cdot \ldots p_n^{xn}$ · Note that, $x1$, $x2$, and so on, are the encoding of the individual symbols, and 2, 3, 5, ..., $p_n$ are the first $n$ primes.

TMs can be encoded, based on the Gödel numbering, after assigning unique numbers to the state symbols, direction symbols, and tape symbols.

Diagonalization language $L_d$ is the language $\{w_i \mid w_i \notin L(M_i)\}$, which means that it is the set of strings $w_i$ such that $w_i$ does not belong to the language accepted by any TM $M_i$. Since $L_d$ is not recursively enumerable, it is undecidable.

The language accepted by a universal Turing machine (UTM) is called *universal language* ($L_u$), which is defined as $L_u = L(U)$, where $U$ is the UTM. Note that $L_u$ is recursively enumerable but not recursive due to the fact that the UTM exists. Further, $L_u = \bar{L}_d$, that is, it is a complement of the diagonalization language $L_d$, which is a non-RE language. Since $L_u$ is non-recursive, it is included in the undecidable category of problems.

Reduction of a given problem to a known problem helps us decide what type of problem it is. If we have an algorithm to convert instances of problem $P_1$ to the instances of a problem $P_2$ that has the same answer, then we say that $P_1$ is reduced to $P_2$. We can also say that $P_2$ is as hard as $P_1$.

There are many other undecidable problems for TMs. Some of them can be listed as follows:

1. To decide whether or not the language accepted by a TM is finite
2. To decide whether or not the language accepted by a TM is regular
3. To decide whether or not the language accepted by a TM is a context-free language
4. To decide whether or not the language accepted by a TM is empty

Further, there are many undecidable problems for CFGs as well. Greibach's theorem can be used to prove that many problems related to CFGs are undecidable. Some of them can be listed as follows:

1. Deciding for any arbitrary CFG, $G$ whether $L(G) = \Sigma^*$

2. If $G_1$ and $G_2$ are CFGs, and $R$ is an arbitrary regular set, it is undecidable to show that:
   (a) $L(G_1) \cap L(G_2) = \phi$
   (b) $L(G_1) = L(G_2)$
   (c) $L(G_1) \subseteq L(G_2)$
   (d) $L(G_1) = R$
   (e) $R \subseteq L(G_1)$
   (f) $L(G_1) \cap L(G_2)$ is a CFL
   (g) $L(G_1)$ is ambiguous (or unambiguous)

According to Rice's theorem, every non-trivial property of the RE languages is undecidable. The essence of Rice's theorem is that any problem which requires determining a property of the language recognized by a given TM, is undecidable. The only exceptions are the trivial properties that are either always true or false.

Hilbert's tenth problem asks for a general algorithm to decide whether a given polynomial Diophantine equation with integer coefficients having a solution in integers is unsolvable.

Ackermann's function is a totally computable, completely decidable problem that cannot be solved merely by using simple loops with pre-defined upper limits. It is one of the examples of totally computable but non-primitive recursive functions. Ackermann's function, when evaluated, grows even more rapidly than the exponential function.

## EXERCISES

This section lists a few unsolved problems to help the readers understand the topic better and practise examples related to undecidability.

### Objective Questions

(U) 9.1 Which of the following statements is false?
   (a) $L_u$ is the complement of $L_d$.
   (b) $L_d$ is decidable.
   (c) Recursive languages are closed under the complement operation.
   (d) RE languages are undecidable.

(U) 9.2 If $A$ is a class of problems solved by a TM that always halts and $B$ is a class of problems solved by TMs that may not halt for an invalid input, then, which of the following statements is false?
   (a) $A$ is a recursive language.
   (b) $B$ is a recursively enumerable language.
   (c) $B$ is undecidable.
   (d) $A$ is undecidable.

(U) 9.3 'The set of all recursive languages is a subset of the set of all recursively enumerable languages.' Is this statement true or false?

(U) 9.4 Which of the following statements are true?
   $S1$: Hilbert's tenth problem is solvable.
   $S2$: Rice's theorem is used to prove some undecidable problems for TMs.
   $S3$: Ackermann's function is a solvable problem.
   $S4$: Recursively enumerable languages are closed under complementation.
   (a) $S1$ and S2
   (b) $S1$ only
   (c) $S2$ only
   (d) $S2$ and $S3$
   (e) $S4$ only
   (f) $S3$ only
   (g) None of these
   (h) All of these

(U) 9.5 For any two arbitrary CFGs, $G1$ and $G2$, $L(G_1) \cap L(G_2)$ is a CFL. Is this statement true or false?

(U) 9.6 Recursively enumerable languages are equivalent to the class of __________ functions.

### Review Questions

(U) 9.1 Write a short note on Rice's theorem.

(U) 9.2 What are the different properties of recursive and recursively enumerable languages?

Ⓤ 9.3 Write a short note on Hilbert's tenth problem.

Ⓤ 9.4 What is diagonalization? Use diagonalization to show that the halting problem is unsolvable.

Ⓛ 9.5 Show that if $L$ is a recursive language, then $L_d$ is also a recursive language.

Ⓛ 9.6 Show that the diagonalization language $L_d$ is not recursively enumerable.

Ⓛ 9.7 Prove that if a language $L$ and its complement $\bar{L}$ are recursively enumerable, then $L$ is a recursive language.

Ⓤ 9.8 State the undecidable problems for TMs.

Ⓤ 9.9 State how Greibach's theorem can be used to prove that many problems related to CFGs are undecidable. List a few undecidable problems for CFGs.

Ⓤ 9.10 What is Ackermann's function? State its significance.

Ⓤ 9.11 Show that Post's correspondence problem is undecidable.

Ⓤ 9.12 Write a short note on Gödel numbering.

**Answers to Objective Questions**

9.1 (b) 9.2 (d) 9.3 True 9.4 (d) 9.5 False 9.6 partial recursive

# Complexity and Classification of Problems

**LEARNING OBJECTIVES**

After completing this chapter, the reader will be able to understand the following:

- Complexity of a problem
- Mathematical notations for complexity measure
- Time and space complexity
- Non-deterministic algorithm
- Problem classification: P-type vs NP-type
- Satisfiability problem
- NP-hard and NP-complete problems
- Cook's theorem

## 10.1 INTRODUCTION

Until now, we have solved problems using different algorithmic machines, such as Turing machines and pushdown stack-memory machines. Let us now make an attempt to analyse these and other problems.

Analysing a problem requires determining the operations it is composed of, and their relative costs in terms of time and space. These operations may include simple arithmetic operations such as addition, subtraction, multiplication, and division, or other more complex operations, such as floating-point arithmetic and comparisons. Majority of the simple operations typically take no more than a fixed amount of time, and we can say that their processing time is bounded by a constant. However, this is not true for all operations. For example, the problem of comparison of two-character strings may differ every time depending on the length of the string. Let us discuss the complexity measures for a problem and the classification of the problems based on their complexity measures.

## 10.2 COMPLEXITY OF A PROBLEM

Usually, the complexity of a problem (or a program) is measured in terms of the computing time required and/or the storage (or space) requirement of the problem.

Two parameters are required for computing the time complexity of a problem (or a program). The frequency count of each operation (or statement), that is, the number of times each operation is performed (or statement is executed) and the time taken for one computation. The total time required to solve the problem is the product of these two parameters.

Usually, time complexity analysis limits itself to finding the frequency count of each statement. The order of magnitude of the complexity of a problem refers to the sum of the frequencies of its constituent operations/statements.

### 10.2.1 Mathematical Notations for Time Complexity Measure

There are several mathematical notations, which are very useful in complexity analysis; with the help of these notations, complexity analysis concentrates on determining the order of magnitude of the frequency of execution of a problem, rather than worrying about the machine dependencies.

#### *Big-O Notation*

Big-O notation is used to express an upper bound of the computing time.

**Definition** $f(n) = O[g(n)]$ (read as '$f$ of $n$ equals big-O of $g$ of $n$') if and only if there exist two positive constants $c$ and $n_0$ such that $|f(n)| \le c\,|g(n)|$ for all $n \ge n_0$.

A problem for which we are determining the computing time, that is, $f(n)$, is said to have computing time $O[g(n)]$. This means that for increasing values of $n$, the resulting time will always be less than some constant time, $|g(n)|$.

To find the order of magnitude of the computing time—$f(n)$—of a problem, we try to obtain the smallest $g(n)$ such that, $f(n) = O[g(n)]$.

For example, for the polynomial:

$$P(x) = a_0 + a_1 x + a_2 x^2 + \cdots + a_k x^k,$$

the order of magnitude is equal to $O(x^k)$.

If there are two problems, whose computing times are $O(n)$ and $O(n^2)$ respectively, and both are performing the same task, on $n$ inputs, then the problem having computing time $O(n)$ is superior and faster compared to the problem with computing time $O(n^2)$.

The most common computing times for many problems are: $O(1)$, $O(\log n)$, $O(n)$, $O(n \log n)$, $O(n^2)$, $O(n^3)$, and $O(2^n)$. These can be mapped against the number of inputs $n$, as shown in Fig. 10.1.

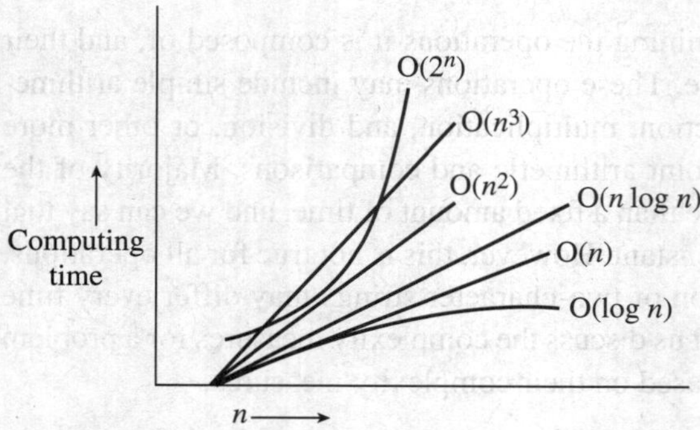


**Figure 10.1** Computing time comparisons (growth rates)

We see that $O(1)$ is not shown in Fig. 10.1 as it is bounded by a constant; it is the fixed time required for the basic operations. The relationships between the different computing times can be seen as follows:

$$O(1) < O(\log n) < O(n) < O(n \log n) < O(n^2) < O(n^3) < O(2^n)$$

A problem whose computing time is $O(2^n)$ requires exponential time; this can be seen from Fig. 10.1, which shows a parabolic curve. The computing time for such problems increases exponentially with increasing value of $n$.

We have earlier seen that the Ackermann's function $A(m, n)$—refer to Chapter 9, Section 9.12—has much more complexity than $O(2^n)$; the value of the function increases rapidly with growing values of $m$ and $n$ as demonstrated in Chapter 9 (refer to Table 9.1).

Hence, it is very clear from the definition of big-O notation that it is used to express an upper bound of the computing time. If we wish to find a function which is a lower bound on the computing time, there is another notation known as the $\Omega$-notation (omega-notation).

### *Little-o Notation*

The little-o notation is defined the same way as the big-O notation, except that the computing time $f(n)$ of a problem is less than $g(n)$; as against that of big-O notation, which states that the computing time $f(n)$ of a problem is no larger than $g(n)$.

**Definition** $f(n) = o[g(n)]$, (reads as '$f$ of $n$ equals little-o of $g$ of $n$') if and only if there exist two positive constants $c$ and $n_0$ such that $|f(n)| < c|g(n)|$ for all $n \geq n_0$.

Little-o notation always represents a slightly greater complexity than the actual complexity of the problem.

### *Omega (Ω) Notation*

As mentioned earlier, omega ($\Omega$) notation is used to express a lower bound of the computing time.

**Definition** $f(n) = \Omega[g(n)]$, (read as '$f$ of $n$ equals omega of $g$ of $n$') if and only if there exist positive constants $c$ and $n_0$ such that for all $n > n_0$, $|f(n)| \geq c|g(n)|$

To explain the aforementioned notations further, let us consider a problem that searches for one number out of a given set of $n$ numbers. In the best case, we might find the number on the first comparison, which means $\Omega(1)$ is the computing time. In the worst case, we might need to look for all the $n$ numbers, and the computing time is $\Omega(n)$.

### *Theta (θ) Notation*

In some cases $g(n)$ represents both lower and upper bounds on the computing time $f(n)$. In such cases, theta ($\theta$) notation is used.

**Definition** $f(n) = \theta[g(n)]$ if and only if there exist positive constants $c_1$, $c_2$, and $n_0$ such that for all $n > n_0$, $c_1|g(n)| \leq |f(n)| \leq c_2|g(n)$.

In such a case, $f$ and $g$ are said to have a proportional growth rate or proportional order of magnitude.

Let us consider a problem of finding the maximum of a given set of $n$ elements. The best and the worst case times for this problem are $\Omega(n)$ and $O(n)$ respectively, as we need to read all $n$ elements and determine the maximum. For such a problem, where the worst and best case complexities are the same, we say that its computing time is $\theta(n)$.

### 10.2.2 Time and Space Complexity of a Turing Machine

In the previous section, we have seen the different notations used to represent the time complexity of a problem at hand. Space complexity is a measure of storage required for a problem.

In terms of a Turing machine (TM), the time complexity $T$ is denoted as follows:

$$\tau_T(n) = \text{maximum number of moves } T \text{ can make on any input string of length } n$$

If for a given input string, $T$ loops forever, then the time complexity is undefined.

Similarly, a space complexity of a TM $T$ is denoted as:

$$S_T(n) = \text{maximum number of tape cells used by } T \text{ while working with any input string of length } n$$

If on some input, $T$ loops forever and causes an infinite number of tape cells to be used, then $S_T(n)$ is undefined.

## 10.3 CLASSIFICATION OF PROBLEMS

Many of the problems that we know are broadly classified into two main categories: polynomial time (P) problems and non-polynomial time (NP) problems. Actually, NP is the term used for 'non-deterministically polynomial'. We shall clarify the meaning of this term later.

A problem, whose solution can be given by a polynomial time algorithm, which means that the function $f(n)$ representing the computing time is a polynomial, then the problem is called a *P-type* problem. If there is no polynomial time algorithm to solve a problem, then the problem is classified as *NP-type* problem.

There are many problems, which can be classified into these classes depending upon whether their computing time is a polynomial of a small degree or a greater degree. For example, if the computing time of a problem is of the order $O(\log n)$, $O(n)$, $O(n \log n)$, $O(n^2)$, and so on, then these problems belong to the first cluster. The second group consists of problems, whose best-known algorithms have their complexities denoted by a non-polynomial. For example, a typical computing time for these types of problems is $O(n^2 2^n)$, $O(2^{n/2})$, and so on. The problems belonging to the second group require a large amount of computing time.

### 10.3.1 Non-deterministic Algorithm

For a *deterministic* solution, the result of every operation is uniquely defined and predictable. If we allow an algorithm to contain operations, whose result is not uniquely determined but is limited to a finite set of possibilities, then such an algorithm is said to be *non-deterministic*.

For example, let us consider the problem of searching for an element $x$ from a given set of elements. We need to obtain an index $i$ of the collection $A$ of $n$ elements ($n \geq 1$), such that $A(i) = x$, if $x$ is an element existing in that collection, or $i = 0$ if $x$ is not in $A$.

A non-deterministic algorithm for this problem can be written as follows:

```
i = choose (n);
if (A[i] = x)
    printf ('%d', i);    // success
printf('0') ;            // failure
```

Here, 'choose (n)' is a procedure assumed, which randomly chooses one element of the given $n$ elements. A zero is printed if $x$ does not belong to the set of elements.

The aforementioned algorithm is of non-deterministic complexity, O(1). This is because, there is only one way to achieve success, and the algorithm is possibilistic. The complexity of a deterministic algorithm for the same problem is $\Omega(n)$.

A deterministic interpretation of the aforementioned non-deterministic algorithm can be made by allowing unbounded parallel operations. This means that many instances of the same operations execute at the same time (*multitasking*). The first successful copy terminates all other copies, while the failure in an operation terminates only that operation. This clearly explains the reason why the complexity of the given non-deterministic algorithm is O(1). The main concern is to restrict ourselves to non-deterministic algorithms, which yield a unique output.

The time required by a non-deterministic algorithm for a given input is the minimum number of steps required to reach a successful completion if there is a sequence of choices leading to such a completion. In general, the complexity of a non-deterministic algorithm is $O[f(n)]$, if for all inputs of size $n$—such that $n \geq n_0$—that result in a successful completion, the time required is at most '$c \cdot f(n)$', for some constants $c$ and $n_0$.

The fact to be noted here is that it is very easy to obtain polynomial time non-deterministic algorithms for many problems that can be deterministically solved in exponential time.

### 10.3.2 Satisfiability

Before discussing satisfiability, let us first discuss the concept of a propositional formula in mathematical logic theory.

#### *Propositional Formula*

Let $x_1, x_2, \ldots$ denote Boolean variables, that is, variables whose values are either true or false. Let $\bar{x}$ denote the negation of $x$. This means that if $x$ is true, $\bar{x}$ is false and vice versa.

A *formula* in propositional calculus is an expression that can be constructed using variables, their negations, and the operators, $\bigwedge$ (and) and $\bigvee$ (or). For example, $(x_1 \bigvee x_2)$ and $(\bar{x}_2 \bigwedge x_3) \bigvee (x_4 \bigvee \bar{x}_1)$ are formulae.

A formula is said to be in conjunctive normal form (CNF), if it can be represented as:

$$e_1 \bigwedge e_2 \bigwedge \ldots \bigwedge e_n,$$

where $e_1, e_2, \ldots, e_n$ are sub-formulae that are represented using variables, their negations, and the $\bigvee$ (or) operator. For example, the formula $(x_1 \bigvee x_2) \bigwedge (x_3 \bigvee x_4)$ is in CNF.

A formula is said to be in disjunctive normal form (DNF), if it can be represented as:

$$e_1 \bigvee e_2 \bigvee \ldots \bigvee e_n,$$

where $e_1, e_2, \ldots, e_n$ are sub-formulae, which are further represented using variables, their negations, and the $\bigwedge$ (and) operator. For example, the formula $(x_1 \bigwedge x_2) \bigvee (\bar{x}_1 \bigwedge x_3)$ is in DNF.

### *Satisfiability Problem*

The *satisfiability problem* (often written in all capitals, or abbreviated as SAT) is to determine if a given propositional formula is true for some assignment of truth values to the variables in the formula. In other words, satisfiability is the problem of determining if the variables in a given Boolean formula can be assigned in such a way as to make the formula evaluate to true.

CNF-satisfiability is the satisfiability problem for CNF formulae; similarly DNF-satisfiability is the satisfiability problem related to the DNF formulae.

A formula is said to be *satisfiable* if it is possible to find truth assignments to its variables that make the formula true. For example, the formula $(a \wedge b)$ is satisfiable because we can find the values $a$ = true and $b$ = true, which make $(a \wedge b)$ = true.

A formula is said to be *valid* if all truth values of its variables make the formula true. This is also termed as *tautology* in mathematical logic.

A formula is said to be *unsatisfiable* if none of the truth assignments of its variables make the formula true. This is also termed as *contradiction* in mathematical logic.

A formula is said to be *invalid* if some such truth assignments to its variables make the formula false.

The worst-case complexity of a deterministic algorithm to find the satisfiability of a given formula of $n$ variables is $O(2^n)$. There are $2^n$ possible assignments of truth values to $n$ variables, and one can verify whether the formula is true for these assignments.

The deterministic algorithm for the satisfiability problem requires exponential time. The problem is very important in complexity theory and is considered as the boundary between P-type and NP-type problems. It is also considered to be useful in defining the NP-complete and NP-hard problems (discussed in the next section).

It is easy to obtain a polynomial time non-deterministic algorithm that terminates successfully if and only if a given propositional formula of $n$ variables is satisfiable. Such an algorithm, thus, chooses non-deterministically one of the $2^n$ possible assignments of truth values to $n$ variables and can verify that the formula is true for that assignment. The time required by the non-deterministic algorithm to choose the value of $n$ variables and the time required to deterministically evaluate the formula for that set of values is $O(n)$. This time is thus proportional to the length of the formula.

## 10.3.3 P-type and NP-type Problems

As we know, an algorithm $A$ is of polynomial complexity if there exists a polynomial $p(n)$ such that the computing time of $A$ is $O[p(n)]$ for every input of size $n$.

We know that $P$ is the set of all decision problems solvable by a deterministic algorithm in polynomial time, and $NP$ is the set of all decision problems solvable by a non-deterministic algorithm in polynomial time.

Since deterministic algorithms are only a special case of non-deterministic algorithms, we can write:

$$[P] \subseteq [NP]$$

P-type problems are also known as efficiently solvable or *tractable* problems, while NP-type problems are also known as *intractable* problems.

### NP-hard and NP-complete Problems

Let $A_1$ and $A_2$ be problems such that $A_1$ *reduces* to $A_2$ (written as $A_1 \propto A_2$) if and only if it is possible to solve $A_1$ using a deterministic polynomial time algorithm that uses a deterministic algorithm to solve $A_2$ in polynomial time.

This implies that if we have a polynomial time algorithm for $A_2$, then we can solve $A_1$ in polynomial time.

A problem $A$ is said to be NP-hard if and only if the satisfiability problem reduces to $A$.

A problem $A$ is said to be NP-complete if and only if $A$ is NP-hard and $A \in [NP]$.

Hence, to show that an NP-hard problem is NP-complete, we just have to determine a polynomial time non-deterministic algorithm for that problem.

There are many NP-hard problems, which are not NP-complete.

> ***Note***: Two problems $A_1$ and $A_2$ are said to be polynomially equivalent if and only if $(A_1 \propto A_2)$ and $(A_2 \propto A_1)$. In order to show that a problem $A_2$ is NP-hard, it is sufficient to show that $(A_1 \propto A_2)$, where $A_1$ is some problem already known to be NP-hard. Since $\propto$ is a transitive relation, it follows that if (satisfiability $\propto A_1$) and $(A_1 \propto A_2)$, then (satisfiability $\propto A_2$).

### Cook's Theorem

The Cook–Levin theorem, also known as Cook's theorem, is named after Stephen Cook and Leonid Levin.

**Statement** The Boolean satisfiability problem is NP-complete.

Cook's theorem is evident from the explanation given in Section 10.3.2. We can write a non-deterministic algorithm to solve the satisfiability problem.

Any problem in [*NP*] can be reduced in polynomial time by a deterministic algorithm (or TM) to the problem of determining whether a Boolean formula is satisfiable. The question of whether such an algorithm exists is called the '*P* versus *NP* problem', and is widely considered to be the most important unsolved problem in theoretical computer science.

An important consequence of the theorem is that if there is a deterministic polynomial time algorithm for solving Boolean satisfiability, then there exists a deterministic polynomial time algorithm for solving all problems in [*NP*].

### Halting Problem

Consider the example of the halting problem that we have discussed in Chapter 4. The halting problem is to determine for an arbitrary deterministic algorithm $A$ and an input $I$, whether algorithm $A$ with input $I$ ever terminates or enters into an infinite loop. It is well known that this problem is undecidable, and hence, unsolvable. There exists no algorithm of any complexity to solve this problem. Therefore, it cannot belong to the class [*NP*].

To show that the satisfiability problem reduces to the halting problem, we simply construct an algorithm $A$, whose input is a propositional formula $E$. If $E$ has $n$ variables, then $A$ tries out all the $2^n$ possible truth assignments and verifies if $E$ is satisfiable. If $E$ is satisfiable, $A$ terminates; if $E$ is not satisfiable, then $A$ enters into an infinite loop. This means that $A$ halts on input $E$ if and only if $E$ is satisfiable. Thus, we can now say that the satisfiability problem reduces to the halting problem.

If we had a polynomial time algorithm for the halting problem, then we could solve the satisfiability problem in polynomial time. Thus, though the satisfiability problem reduces to the halting problem, it does not belong to the [*NP*] class of problems, as no algorithm can solve it. Hence, the halting problem is an NP-hard problem.

## SUMMARY

The complexity of a problem (or a program) is measured in terms of the computing time required by the problem and/or the storage (or space) requirement of the problem.

Two parameters are required for computing the time complexity of a problem (or a program): the frequency count of each operation (or statement), that is, the number of times the operation is performed (or the statement gets executed), and the time required for one computation. The product of these two parameters is the total time required for computing.

There are several mathematical notations, which are very useful in complexity analysis:

1. *Big-O* notation is used to express an upper bound of the computing time.
2. *Little-o* notation, which always represents a slightly greater complexity than the actual complexity of the problem, is similar to the big-O notation.
3. *Omega* (Ω) notation is used to express a lower bound of the computing time.
4. *Theta* (θ) notation is used in cases where both lower and upper bounds on the computing time are equal.

The time complexity of a Turing machine (TM) $T$ is denoted as given here:

$\tau_T(n)$ = maximum number of moves $T$ can make on any input string of length $n$

If for a given input string, $T$ loops forever, then the time complexity is undefined.

Similarly, a space complexity of a TM $T$ is denoted as:

$S_T(n)$ = maximum number of tape cells used by $T$ while working with any input string of length $n$

If, on some input, $T$ loops forever and causes an infinite number of tape cells to be used, then $S_T(n)$ is undefined.

A problem, whose solution can be given by a polynomial time algorithm, which means that the function $f(n)$ representing the computing time of a problem is a polynomial, is called a P-type problem. If there is no polynomial time algorithm to solve a problem, then the problem is called an NP-type problem. P-type problems are also known as efficiently solvable or *tractable* problems. NP-type problems are also known as *intractable* problems.

Problems are classified as either P-type or NP-type, depending upon whether their computing time is a polynomial of a small degree or a greater degree. For example, If the computing time of a problem is of the order $O(\log n)$, $O(n)$, $O(n \log n)$, $O(n^2)$, and so on, then these problems belong to the first group. The second group consists of problems, whose best-known algorithms have their complexities denoted by a non-polynomial. For example, the typical computing time for such problems is $O(n^2 2^n)$, $O(2^{n/2})$, and so on. The problems belonging to the second group require a large amount of computing time.

The complexity of the Ackermann's function, $A(m, n)$ is much more than even exponential time complexity, that is, much more than $O(2^n)$; the value of the function increases rapidly with growing values of $m$ and $n$.

For a deterministic solution, the result of every operation is uniquely defined and predictable. If we allow an algorithm to contain operations, whose result is not uniquely determined but is limited to a finite set of possibilities, then such an algorithm is said to be non-deterministic. A deterministic interpretation of such non-deterministic algorithm can be made by allowing unbounded parallel operations. This means, many instances of the same operations execute at the same time (*multitasking*). It is very easy to obtain polynomial time non-deterministic algorithms for many problems that can be deterministically solved in exponential time.

A *formula* in propositional calculus is an expression that can be constructed using variables, their negations, and the operators, $\wedge$ (and) and $\vee$ (or). For example, $(x_1 \vee x_2)$ and $(\bar{x}_2 \wedge x_3) \vee (x_4 \vee \bar{x}_1)$ are formulae.

The *satisfiability problem* is to determine if a given propositional formula is true for some assignment of truth values to the variables in the formula. In other words, satisfiability is the problem of determining if the variables of a given Boolean formula can be assigned in such a way as to make the formula evaluate to true. A deterministic algorithm to determine the satisfiability of a given formula of $n$ variables has the worst-case complexity $O(2^n)$. There are $2^n$ possible assignments of truth values to $n$ variables, and one can verify whether the formula is true for these assignments. Thus, satisfiability problem has an exponential time deterministic algorithm. The time required by the non-deterministic algorithm to choose the value of $n$ variables and the time required to deterministically evaluate the formula for that set of values is $O(n)$.

Let $A_1$ and $A_2$ be problems such that $A_1$ *reduces* to $A_2$ (written as $A_1 \propto A_2$) if and only if it is possible to solve $A_1$ using a deterministic polynomial time algorithm, which uses a deterministic algorithm to solve $A_2$.

A problem $A$ is said to be NP-hard if and only if the satisfiability problem reduces to $A$. A problem $A$ is said to be NP-complete if and only if $A$ is NP-hard and $A \in$ [NP]. It can be shown that the halting problem is an NP-hard problem.

## EXERCISES

This section lists a few unsolved problems to help the readers understand the topic better and practise examples related to complexity and classification of problems.

### Objective Questions

(U) 10.1 Which of the following statements is true?
- (a) Satisfiability problem is a P-type problem.
- (b) Satisfiability problem has exponential time complexity.
- (c) NP-complete problems are NP-hard.
- (d) Ackermann's function is NP-hard.

(U) 10.2 If $A$ is a P-type problem solved by a TM, and $B$ is an NP-type problem solved by a TM, then which of the following statements is false?
- (a) $A$ may be a recursive language.
- (b) $B$ may be a recursively enumerable language.
- (c) $B$ may be undecidable.
- (d) $A$ may be undecidable.
- (e) $B$ cannot be solved by a non-deterministic TM of polynomial time complexity.

(U) 10.3 'A formula is said to be unsatisfiable if none of the truth assignments of its variables make the formula true.' Is this statement true or false?

(U) 10.4 Which of the following statements are false?
- $S1$: Satisfiability problem is solvable.
- $S2$: As per Cook's theorem halting problem is NP-complete.
- $S3$: Ackermann's function is NP-hard.
- $S4$: Intractable problems have non-polynomial time complexity.

(a) $S1$ and $S2$
(b) $S1$ only
(c) $S2$ only
(d) $S2$ and $S3$
(e) $S4$ only
(f) $S3$ only
(g) None of these
(h) All of these

Ⓤ 10.5 'All P-type problems are tractable.' Is this statement true or false?

Ⓤ 10.6 Boolean satisfiability is an NP-________ problem.

## Review Questions

Ⓤ 10.1 Write a short note on P-type and NP-type problems.

Ⓡ 10.2 Define the following terms:
(a) NP-complete problem
(b) Intractable problem

Ⓤ 10.3 What is a non-deterministic algorithm? Explain with the help of an example.

Ⓤ 10.4 Explain Cook's theorem.

Ⓤ 10.5 What is a satisfiability problem?

Ⓤ 10.6 Write a short note on time complexity and different complexity notations.

Ⓤ 10.7 How is the time and space complexity of a TM measured?

Ⓤ 10.8 What are conjunctive normal form and disjunctive normal form?

Ⓤ 10.9 Explain the terms: valid/invalid formula and satisfiable/unsatisfiable formula.

Ⓤ 10.10 What is Ackermann's function? Comment on the time complexity of the Ackermann's function.

Ⓤ 10.11 Explain NP-hard and NP-complete problems with the help of suitable examples.

**Answers to Objective Questions**

10.1 (b) 10.2 (e) 10.3 True 10.4 (d) 10.5 True 10.6 complete

# Production Systems

**LEARNING OBJECTIVES**

After completing this chapter, the reader will be able to understand the following:

- Production systems
- Post–Markov–Thue (PMT) production system
- Post canonical system
- Post normal form
- Turing machine's (TM) interpretation as a PMT system
- Finite state machine's interpretation as a PMT system
- Markov algorithm
- Equivalence of Markov algorithm and TM
- Labelled Markov algorithm

## 11.1 INTRODUCTION

In Chapter 4, we have learnt how to obtain algorithmic solutions for many complex problems such as checking if a given set of parentheses are well-formed, and multiplying two unary numbers, which are implemented as Turing machines (TMs). From the TM simulations discussed in Chapter 4, we know that the TM is a symbol manipulation system.

In this chapter, we shall discuss another symbol manipulation system, known as the *productions system*, which does the same job as a TM and can be formalized as a finite set of productions.

Post, Markov, and Thue are the three scientists who have devised the formalism of a production system, which defines an algorithm as a set of rules that transform a given initial string of symbols from a given alphabet set Σ into another string of symbols over the same alphabet. The initial string of symbols, which gets transformed into a new string, is called as an *axiom*—this is analogous to the initial configuration of a TM.

A productions system, as we have discussed, is a symbol manipulation system; this means that it manipulates the axioms to convert them into a new string over the same alphabet, using some sequence of production rules from a set of rules (similar to the rules for grammars) that formally define the algorithm. We write the algorithm in the form of a functional matrix (FM) of a TM, which, as we have seen, is also based on symbol manipulation and movement of the read/write head.

## 11.2 POST–MARKOV–THUE SYSTEM

The Post–Markov–Thue (PMT) system is named after the scientists who formalized it. Every PMT production system consists of the following:

1. An alphabet, $\Sigma$
2. A set of axioms (initial strings), $A$
3. A finite set of rules or productions $P$ to derive new strings over the same alphabet $\Sigma$ from the axioms in $A$

The rules or productions, which define an algorithm using symbol manipulation techniques, are also called *rewrite rules* or *symbol replacement rules*.

For a production rule of the form '$\alpha \to \beta$', the left-hand side, that is, $\alpha$, is called the *antecedent* and the right-hand side, that is, $\beta$, is called the *consequent*.

Let us discuss an example to illustrate the PMT.

---

**Example 11.1** Consider the alphabet $\Sigma$ with only one symbol: $\Sigma = \{1\}$. The other sets—set $P$ of productions and set $A$ of axioms also consist of one element each and are defined as follows:

$$P = \{\alpha \to \alpha\, 11\}$$
$$A = \{11\}$$

Find the set of strings generated by the PMT system.

***Solution*** There is only one axiom or initial string, which is '11'; this is the minimum length string generated without applying any further rule.

If we start with the string '11', and apply the rule '$\alpha \to \alpha$ 11' once, we get:

1 1 (axiom or initial string)
1 1 1 1 (by applying rule $\alpha \to \alpha$ 11)

Thus, '1111' is the generated string.

Similarly, if we apply the rule twice, then we get the string '111111', as follows:

1 1 (axiom)
1 1 1 1 (by applying rule $\alpha \to \alpha$ 11)
1 1 1 1 1 1 (by applying rule $\alpha \to \alpha$ 11)

Thus, we can say that, the example production system generates the following set of strings:

$$\{11, 1111, 111111, \ldots\}$$

This is the set of all even numbers (excluding zero) represented in unary format, using the symbol '1'.

---

*Note*: For this example, if we change the axiom from '11' to '1', that is, if $A = \{1\}$, then the set of generated strings will be:

$$\{1, 111, 11111, \ldots\}$$

This is the set of all odd numbers represented using unary format over the alphabet $\Sigma = \{1\}$. Now, if we consider the set of axioms for the same production system as, $A = \{1, 11\}$ then, the set of generated strings will be,

$$\{1, 11, 111, 1111, 11111, 111111, \ldots\}$$

This is the set of all numbers in unary format, excluding zero.

From Example 11.1, we see that if $P$ (set of rules) and $\Sigma$ (alphabet) are same, and if we change the axioms, we can derive different sets of strings over the same alphabet $\Sigma$. Thus, the axioms play an important role in the derivation or generation process for the PMT system. This is similar to a TM, where the initial configuration decides the end result and the fact that the algorithm (or functional matrix) cannot be written without deciding the initial configuration of the TM.

### 11.2.1 Formal Definition

A Post–Markov–Thue (PMT) production system is formally defined as a quadruple:

$$T = (\Sigma, \Sigma^*, A, P),$$

where,

$\Sigma$: Finite and non-empty alphabet

$\Sigma^*$: Set of all words over $\Sigma$

$A$: Set of axioms over $\Sigma$, i.e., $A \subseteq \Sigma^*$

$P$: Finite set of rules of the form '$\alpha\, x\, \beta \rightarrow \alpha\, y\, \beta$', where $x, y \subseteq \Sigma^*$ and $\alpha, \beta$ are the syntactic variables over $\Sigma^*$ ($\alpha$ and $\beta$ may also be null strings)

The rules, '$\alpha\, x\, \beta \rightarrow \alpha\, y\, \beta$' can be interpreted as some occurrence of $x$ in $\alpha\, x\, \beta$ being replaced by $y$, giving $\alpha\, y\, \beta$. These rules are similar to the productions we have discussed in Chapter 5.

### 11.2.2 Examples

Let us discuss some more examples of PMT systems.

---

**Example 11.2** Write the PMT system that generates palindromes over $\{0, 1, 2\}$.

***Solution*** The alphabet $\Sigma$ is given as: $\Sigma = \{0, 1, 2\}$.

For generating palindrome strings, the rules can be written as:

$$\left.\begin{array}{l} \alpha \rightarrow 0\,\alpha\,0 \\ \alpha \rightarrow 1\,\alpha\,1 \\ \alpha \rightarrow 2\,\alpha\,2 \end{array}\right\} \quad \begin{array}{l} \text{set of rules} \\ \\ P \end{array}$$

As it is necessary to generate odd as well as even length palindromes, the set of axioms should be:

$$A = \{0, 1, 2, 00, 11, 22\}$$

The axioms are also considered as a part of the generated string set. Hence, the least length palindrome, which can be generated using the aforementioned system, is '0', '1', or '2'; their length is one. The system may start with any of the axioms, and does not apply any of the rules; hence, the axioms will be treated as the generated strings.

Let us check whether this system can generate the string '10101'.

| | |
|---|---|
| 1 | (starting string or axiom) |
| 0 1 0 | (applying rule $\alpha \to 0\ \alpha\ 0$) |
| 1 0 1 0 1 | (applying rule $\alpha \to 1\ \alpha\ 1$) |

Let us also check the generation of the string '2222'.

| | |
|---|---|
| 2 2 | (axiom to start with) |
| 2 2 2 2 | (applying rule $\alpha \to 2\ \alpha\ 2$) |

Thus, this PMT system can generate all possible non-empty palindromes over $\Sigma = \{0, 1, 2\}$, as follows:

$$\{0, 1, 2, 00, 11, 22, 000, 010, 020, 010, \ldots\}$$

---

**Example 11.3** Show that the following PMT system $T$ can generate the string '*bbbba*':

$T = (\Sigma, \Sigma^*, A, P)$, where,
$\Sigma = \{a, b\}$
$A = \{a, b\}$
$P = \{a \to aa;\ a \to ab;\ b \to bb;\ b \to ba\}$

***Solution*** As we want to derive the string '*bbbba*', which starts with symbol *b*, we should start the generation with the axiom *b* instead of *a*, based on the rules we have:

| | |
|---|---|
| $b$ | (axiom 2) |
| $b\ a$ | (rule $b \to ba$) |
| $b\ b\ a$ | (rule $b \to bb$) |
| $b\ b\ b\ a$ | (rule $b \to bb$) |
| $b\ b\ b\ b\ a$ | (rule $b \to bb$) |

Thus, the string '*bbbba*' can be generated using the given PMT production system. The same can also be generated as follows:

| | |
|---|---|
| $b$ | (axiom 2) |
| $b\ b$ | (rule $b \to bb$) |
| $b\ b\ b$ | (rule $b \to bb$) |
| $b\ b\ b\ b$ | (rule $b \to bb$) |
| $b\ b\ b\ b\ a$ | (rule $b \to ba$) |

---

**Example 11.4** Design a PMT system, which can generate well-formed parentheses.

***Solution*** The alphabet $\Sigma$ for the required PMT is:

$$\Sigma = \{(, )\}$$

Only one axiom can be considered, as follows:

$A = \{ ( ) \}$

The rule set $P$ consists of the following rules:

$\alpha \rightarrow (\alpha)$ (rule 1)
$\alpha \rightarrow \alpha\, \alpha$ (rule 2)
$\beta\, (\ )\, \gamma \rightarrow \beta\gamma$ (rule 3)

Let us check whether we can derive string '( ( ) ( ( ) ) )' using the aforementioned rules.

( ) (axiom)
( ( ) ) (using rule 1)
( ( ) ) ( ( ) ) (using rule 2)
( ( ( ) ) ( ( ) ) ) (using rule 1)

$\underbrace{(}_{\beta}\ \ (\ )\ \ \underbrace{(\ (\ )\ )\ )}_{\gamma}$

( ( ) ( ( ) ) ) (using rule 3)

---

**Example 11.5** Find the PMT system for the language:

$L = \{0^n\, 1^n \mid n > 0\}$

***Solution*** The required PMT system can be defined as follows:

$T = (\Sigma, \Sigma^*, A, P)$,

where,

$\Sigma = \{0, 1\}$
$A = \{01\}$
$P = \{\alpha \rightarrow 0\, \alpha\, 1\}$

Let us derive the string '000111' using the production rules in $P$.

0 1 (axiom)
0 0 1 1 (rule $\alpha \rightarrow 0\, \alpha\, 1$)
0 0 0 1 1 1 (rule $\alpha \rightarrow 0\, \alpha\, 1$)

---

**Example 11.6** Find the PMT system which generates strings having equal number of 0's and 1's.

***Solution*** Consider the alphabet $\Sigma = \{0, 1\}$. The set of axioms can be considered as:

$A = \{01, 10\}$

The production rules can be given as:

1. $\alpha \rightarrow \alpha\, 01$
2. $\alpha \rightarrow \alpha\, 10$
3. $\alpha \rightarrow 10\, \alpha$
4. $\alpha \rightarrow 01\, \alpha$
5. $\alpha \rightarrow 0\, \alpha\, 1$

6. $\alpha \rightarrow 1\,\alpha\,0$
7. $\alpha \rightarrow \alpha\,\alpha$
8. $\alpha\,01\,\beta \rightarrow \alpha\,10\,\beta$
9. $\alpha\,10\,\beta \rightarrow \alpha\,01\,\beta$

Let us try to generate the string '0001110110' using the production rules in *P*.

| | |
|---|---|
| 0 1 | (axiom) |
| 0 0 1 1 | (rule 5) |
| 0 0 0 1 1 1 | (rule 5) |
| 0 0 0 1 1 1 0 1 | (rule 1) |
| 0 0 0 1 1 1 0 1 1 0 | (rule 2) |

Let us also try to generate the string '00111100'. Let us start with the axiom '01'.

| | |
|---|---|
| 0 1 | (axiom) |
| 0 0 1 1 | (rule 5) |
| 0 0 1 1 1 0 | (rule 2) |
| $\underbrace{0\,0\,1\,1\,1}_{\alpha}\,0\,1\,\underbrace{0}_{\beta}$ | (rule 2) |
| 0 0 1 1 1 1 0 0 | (rule 8) |

## 11.3 POST CANONICAL SYSTEM

In a PMT system, if the productions in the rule set *P* contains only constant strings over $\Sigma$, then that PMT system is called a Post canonical system (PCS).

In order to generate the class of rich and useful theorems, or *rich class of languages*, the input alphabet $\Sigma$ is not sufficient, and has to be extended to $\Sigma'$, which includes additional or auxiliary symbols. These additional symbols participate in the generation of the required string. However, the generated string only contains symbols from the original alphabet $\Sigma$.

**Example 11.7** Consider the following PCS that generates all prime numbers represented in unary form:

| | |
|---|---|
| $\Sigma = \{1\}$ | original alphabet |
| $\Sigma' = \{1, A, B, C, D\}$ | extended alphabet with auxiliary symbols, viz. *A*, *B*, *C*, and *D* |
| $A = \{A111, 11\}$ | axioms |

The set of productions *P* is given as:

1. $A\,\alpha' \rightarrow A\,\alpha\,1$
2. $A\,\alpha\,1 \rightarrow C\,\alpha\,D\,B\,\alpha\,1$
3. $\alpha_1\,1\,D\,\alpha_2\,1 \rightarrow 1\,\alpha_1\,D\,1\,\alpha_2$
4. $\alpha_1\,C\,D\,\alpha_2\,1 \rightarrow C\,\alpha_1\,D\,\alpha_2\,1$
5. $\alpha_2\,C\,\alpha_2\,1\,D\,\alpha_3\,B \rightarrow C\,\alpha_1\,\alpha_2\,D\,B\,\alpha_3$
6. $1\,1\,C\,D\,\alpha\,B\,1 \rightarrow \alpha\,1$

Show the derivation of the string '111'.

***Solution*** Let us begin with the axiom '$A111$'.

$$\begin{array}{ll} A\,\underbrace{1\;1}_{\alpha}\;1 & \text{(Axiom)} \\ \underbrace{C\;1}_{\alpha_1}\;1\;D\;\underbrace{B\;1}_{\alpha_2}\;1\;1 & \text{(using rule 2 with } \alpha = 11) \\ \underbrace{1\;C}_{\alpha_1}\;1\;D\;\underbrace{1\;B}_{\alpha_2}\;1\;1 & \text{(using rule 3 with } \alpha_1 = C1 \text{ and } \alpha_2 = B11) \\ 1\;1\;C\;D\;\underbrace{1\;1}_{\alpha}\;B\;1 & \text{(using rule 3 with } \alpha_1 = 1C \text{ and } \alpha_2 = 1B1) \\ 1\;1\;1 & \text{(using rule 6 with } \alpha = 11) \end{array}$$

***Note***: With the help of the additional auxiliary symbols from an extended alphabet $\Sigma'$, the PCS system can generate a richer class of languages than the usual PMT system.

## 11.4 POST NORMAL FORM

The Post normal form (PNF) theorem states that any formal system can be reduced to a PCS with a single axiom, and simple productions of the form:

$$x\,\alpha \rightarrow \alpha\, y,$$

where $x, y \subseteq \Sigma^*$, and $\alpha$ is a syntactic variable over $\Sigma^*$.

The reduced production form thus obtained from a given PCS is called a PNF.

To obtain a PNF, which is the reduced form of a given PCS having only one axiom, we use an auxiliary alphabet. The PNF thus obtained is also known as the *canonical extension* of the original PCS.

## 11.5 PMT SYSTEM AND TURING MACHINE

Any TM can be interpreted as a PMT system using the following analogy:

Alphabet $\Sigma$: $S \cup I$, where $S$ is the set of states being treated as the set of auxiliary symbols, and $I$ is the tape alphabet

Set of axioms $A$: Initial configuration of the TM

Set of productions $P$: Functional matrix of the TM

It is very logical to consider the initial configuration with the input string as the axiom, because it is the axiom that is transformed into the new string, just as the TM modifies the given input string to produce the output string.

As discussed in Chapter 4 (refer to Section 4.4 on instantaneous description), let us suppose for a given TM:

$$\delta\,(\alpha, a) = (b, \beta, R)$$

This indicates that if the TM reads symbol $a$ while in state $\alpha$, it replaces that $a$ by another symbol $b$, changes the state to $\beta$, and moves the head one position to the right.

The instantaneous description (ID) for this move can be shown as follows:

If the current ID is '$p\,c\,\alpha\,a\,b\,q$', then after the transition, the next ID will be '$p\,c\,b\,\beta\,b\,q$'.

$$p\,c\,\alpha\,a\,b\,q \vdash_{M} p\,c\,b\,\beta\,b\,q$$

The same can be represented as the following production rule:

$$p\,c\,\alpha\,a\,b\,q \rightarrow p\,c\,b\,\beta\,b\,q$$

The reason for writing '$b\beta$' in place of '$\alpha\,a$' is to indicate that the head moves one position in the right direction after reading symbol 'a' which is replaced to 'b' while the state is changed to '$\beta$'.

Similarly, the functional matrix entry:

$$\delta\,(\alpha, a) = (b, \beta, L),$$

can be represented as the following production rule, for the string '$p\,c\,\alpha\,a\,b\,q$':

$$p\,c\,\alpha\,a\,b\,q \rightarrow p\,\beta\,c\,b\,b\,q$$

Thus, the functional matrix of a TM can be represented as a finite set of productions, and therefore, we can say that for every TM there exists a PMT system, which is equivalent to it.

## 11.6 POST–MARKOV–THUE SYSTEM AND FINITE STATE MACHINE

Every finite state machine (FSM) can be identified as a PMT system using the following analogy:

Alphabet $\Sigma$: $S \cup I$, where $S$ is the set of states being treated as the set of auxiliary symbols, and $I$ is the input alphabet

Set of axioms $A$ : Initial state

Set of productions $P$: State transition table of the FSM

If there is a transition from state $\alpha$ to state $\beta$ on reading symbol $a$ for a given FSM, then the transition can be represented as a production for the equivalent PMT system: $\alpha \rightarrow a\,\beta$

If $\alpha$ is a final state, then we introduce a production: $\alpha \rightarrow \epsilon$, to the production list for the equivalent PMT system.

---

**Example 11.8** Consider the DFA in Fig. 11.1. Construct an equivalent PMT system.

***Solution*** For the given DFA, we have

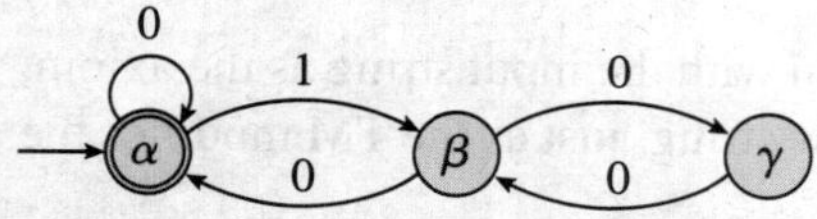


**Figure 11.1** DFA for Example 11.8

$$S = \{\alpha, \beta, \gamma\}, \text{ and}$$
$$I = \{0, 1\}$$

For the equivalent PMT system that generates the language accepted by the given DFA, the input alphabet $\Sigma$ and the set of axioms $A$ are given as:

$$\Sigma = S \cup I$$
$$= \{0, 1, \alpha, \beta, \gamma\}, \text{ and}$$
$$A = \{\alpha\}$$

The following productions can now be written from the transitions:

$\alpha \rightarrow 0\,\alpha$
$\alpha \rightarrow 1\,\beta$
$\alpha \rightarrow \epsilon$ (because $\alpha$ is a final state)
$\beta \rightarrow 0\,\alpha$
$\beta \rightarrow 0\,\gamma$
$\gamma \rightarrow 0\,\beta$

***Note***: Observe that these productions are similar to right-linear grammar (refer to Chapter 5).

---

**Example 11.9** Define a PMT that generates the language represented by the regular expression, 0* · 1* · 2*.

***Solution*** The DFA that accepts the language represented by the given regular expression, 0* · 1* · 2*, can be constructed as shown in Fig. 11.2 (refer to Chapter 3, Fig. 3.11b).

For the DFA in Fig. 11.2, we have:

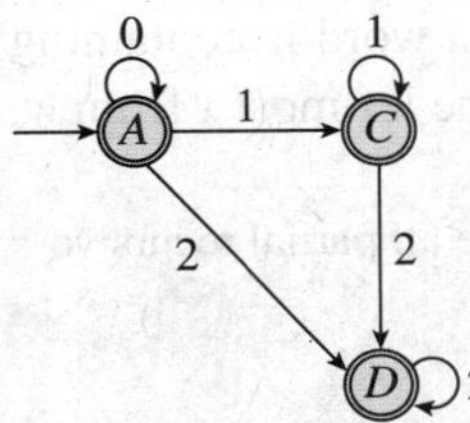

**Figure 11.2** DFA for 0* · 1* · 2*

$S = \{A, C, D\}$, and
$I = \{0, 1, 2\}$

For the equivalent PMT system, we have:

$$\Sigma = S \cup I$$
$$= \{0, 1, 2, A, C, D\}$$
$$A = \{A\}$$

The set of productions $P$ is given as follows:

1. $A \rightarrow 0\,A$
2. $A \rightarrow 1\,C$
3. $A \rightarrow \epsilon$ (since $A$ is a final state)
4. $A \rightarrow 2\,D$
5. $C \rightarrow 1\,C$
6. $C \rightarrow \epsilon$ (since $C$ is a final state)
7. $C \rightarrow 2\,D$
8. $D \rightarrow 2\,D$
9. $D \rightarrow \epsilon$ (since $D$ is a final state)

Let us generate the string '00122' using the equivalent PMT system:

| | |
|---|---|
| $A$ | (axiom) |
| $0\,A$ | (using rule 1) |
| $0\,0\,A$ | (using rule 1) |
| $0\,0\,1\,C$ | (using rule 2) |
| $0\,0\,1\,2\,D$ | (using rule 7) |
| $0\,0\,1\,2\,2\,D$ | (using rule 8) |
| $0\,0\,1\,2\,2$ | (using rule 9) |

---

## 11.7 MARKOV ALGORITHM

In theoretical computer science, a Markov algorithm is a symbol manipulation system or string rewriting system that uses grammar-like rules to operate on strings of symbols. Markov algorithms are Turing-complete, which means that they are suitable as a general model of computation and can represent any mathematical expression from its simple notation. Markov algorithms are named after the mathematician Andrey Markov, Jr. Markov algorithm is defined in the following subsection.

### 11.7.1 Formal Definition

Markov algorithm is a PMT system with the following features:

1. All the productions from the set of productions $P$ are assigned indices or numbers (1, 2, 3, ...). This means that $P$ contains an ordered production list.
2. A production of the form $\alpha\ x\ \beta \rightarrow \bullet$ is considered as a 'stop' indicator. No other production is applied after the application of this type of production.
3. If more than one production can be applied to derive the string $w_2$ from a string $w_1$, then the production with the lowest number (or index) is applied.
4. If a production, whose left-hand side is '$\alpha\ x\ \beta$', is applicable to a word $w$ containing more than one occurrence of $x$, then the production is applied to the leftmost $x$ from $w$.

***Note***: Markov algorithm has the same power as a TM, which can compute all partial recursive functions (refer to Chapter 4, Section 4.16.2).

The following algorithm is used while applying the productions to a given string over an alphabet $\Sigma$ to derive a new string over the same alphabet $\Sigma$:

1. Search for the first applicable production for the given string and apply it to the leftmost occurrence of a particular sub-string from the given string.
2. If the applied production is of the form '$\alpha\ x\ \beta \rightarrow \bullet$', that is, the stop production, then terminate the process after applying this final production and declare the resultant string as the required final string.
3. If the production applied is not a stop production, go to the first step and repeat the process.
4. If, after searching, no appropriate rule or production can be found, which is applicable, then stop the process.

### 11.7.2 Examples

Let us discuss some examples of Markov algorithm to help understand the concept better.

---

**Example 11.10** Let $\Sigma = \{a, b, c, d\}$. Write the Markov algorithm, which can remove the first $d$ and every symbol which follows it in the given string from $\Sigma^*$.

***Solution*** Whenever the machine reads the first $d$, it removes all the letters from $\{a, b, c, d\}$, which immediately follow the $d$.

Hence, if $d$ is the last symbol of the string, the machine deletes it and stops.

To apply this method, let us assume that whenever we get a sub-string of the form '*dp*', where $p = \{a, b, c, d\}$, we should replace it by *d*. Finally, *d* can be replaced by a '•', which indicates the 'stop' action.

The productions can therefore be written as:

1. $d\,a \rightarrow d$
2. $d\,b \rightarrow d$
3. $d\,c \rightarrow d$
4. $d\,d \rightarrow d$
5. $d \rightarrow \bullet$ (stop)

Let us simulate the working of this Markov algorithm for the input string '*aabdcbdda*'.

$a\ a\ b\ \underline{d\ c}\ b\ d\ d\ a$ (initial string)
↓
$a\ a\ b\ \underline{d\ b}\ d\ d\ a$ (applying rule 3)
↓
$a\ a\ b\ \underline{d\ d}\ d\ a$ (applying rule 2)
↓
$a\ a\ b\ \underline{d\ d}\ a$ (applying rule 4)
↓
$a\ a\ b\ \underline{d\ a}$ (applying rule 4)
↓
$a\ a\ b\ \underline{d}$ (applying rule 1)
↓
$a\ a\ b\ \bullet$ (stop) (applying rule 5)

Thus, '*aab*' is the final string after removing the first *d* and all letters following it.

---

**Example 11.11** Write the Markov algorithm to find the 1's complement of a given binary number.

***Solution*** To find the 1's complement of the given binary number, we replace each '1' by '0' and each '0' by '1'. The Markov algorithm can be written as follows:

1. $S \rightarrow \alpha\, S$
2. $\alpha\, 0 \rightarrow 1\, \alpha$
3. $\alpha\, 1 \rightarrow 0\, \alpha$
4. $\alpha \rightarrow \bullet$ (stop)

Let us simulate the working of this algorithm for the binary number '101001'.

$1\ 0\ 1\ 0\ 0\ 1$ (initial string)
↓
$\underline{\alpha\ 1}\ 0\ 1\ 0\ 0\ 1$ (applying rule 1)
↓
$0\ \underline{\alpha\ 0}\ 1\ 0\ 0\ 1$ (applying rule 3)
↓
$0\ 1\ \underline{\alpha\ 1}\ 0\ 0\ 1$ (applying rule 2)
↓
$0\ 1\ 0\ \underline{\alpha\ 0}\ 0\ 1$ (applying rule 3)
↓

$$
\begin{array}{ll}
0\ 1\ 0\ 1\ \underline{\alpha\ 0}\ 1 & \text{(applying rule 2)} \\
\downarrow & \\
0\ 1\ 0\ 1\ 1\ \underline{\alpha\ 1} & \text{(applying rule 2)} \\
\downarrow & \\
0\ 1\ 0\ 1\ 1\ 0\ \underline{\alpha} & \text{(applying rule 3)} \\
\downarrow & \\
0\ 1\ 0\ 1\ 1\ 0\ \bullet\ \text{(stop)} & \text{(applying rule 4)}
\end{array}
$$

Thus, we see that the final string, '010110', is the 1's complement of the given input binary number '101001'.

---

**Example 11.12** Let $\Sigma = \{a, b, c\}$ be the alphabet, and $\Sigma' = \{\alpha, \beta\}$ be the auxiliary alphabet. Write the Markov algorithm for duplicating the string in $\Sigma^*$.

***Solution*** Markov algorithm for duplicating the input string over $\Sigma$ can be written as follows:

1. $S \rightarrow \alpha\, S$
2. $\alpha\, w \rightarrow w\, \beta\, w\, \alpha$ $\quad (w \subseteq \Sigma)$
3. $\beta\, w_1\, w_2 \rightarrow w_2 \beta\, w_1$ $\quad (w_1, w_2 \subseteq \Sigma)$
4. $\beta \rightarrow \epsilon$ $\quad$ (empty string)
5. $\alpha \rightarrow \bullet$ $\quad$ (stop)

Consider the input string '*abc*'. Let us simulate the working of this algorithm for this input string.

$$
\begin{array}{ll}
a\ b\ c & \text{(initial string)} \\
\downarrow & \\
\underline{\alpha\ a}\ b\ c & \text{(applying rule 1)} \\
\downarrow & \\
a\ \beta\ a\ \underline{\alpha\ b}\ c & \text{(applying rule 2 for } w = a) \\
\downarrow & \\
a\ \beta\ a\ b\ \beta\ b\ \underline{\alpha\ c} & \text{(applying rule 2 for } w = b) \\
\downarrow & \\
a\ \underline{\beta\ a\ b}\ \beta\ b\ c\ \beta\ c\ \alpha & \text{(applying rule 2 for } w = c) \\
\downarrow & \\
a\ b\ \beta\ a\ \underline{\beta\ b\ c}\ \beta\ c\ \alpha & \text{(applying rule 3 for } w_1 = a, w_2 = b) \\
\downarrow & \\
a\ b\ \underline{\beta\ a\ c}\ \beta\ b\ \beta\ c\ \alpha & \text{(applying rule 3 for } w_1 = b, w_2 = c) \\
\downarrow & \\
a\ b\ c\ \underline{\beta}\ a\ \beta\ b\ \beta\ c\ \alpha & \text{(applying rule 3 for } w_1 = a, w_2 = c) \\
\downarrow & \\
a\ b\ c\ a\ \underline{\beta}\ b\ \beta\ c\ \alpha & \text{(applying rule 4)} \\
\downarrow & \\
a\ b\ c\ a\ b\ \underline{\beta}\ c\ \alpha & \text{(applying rule 4)} \\
\downarrow & \\
a\ b\ c\ a\ b\ c\ \underline{\alpha} & \text{(applying rule 4)} \\
\downarrow & \\
a\ b\ c\ a\ b\ c\ \bullet\ \text{(stop)} & \text{(applying rule 5)}
\end{array}
$$

Thus, the initial string '*abc*' gets duplicated as '*abcabc*' using the aforementioned Markov algorithm.

> *Note*: Observe that these productions are similar to type-0 grammar (refer to Chapter 5, Section 5.11.1).

**Example 11.13** Write the Markov algorithm for the addition of two unary numbers.

***Solution*** Let us represent the numbers to be added using unary format with symbol '1'. Thus, the alphabet set contains $\Sigma = \{1\}$.

Consider the auxiliary alphabet set as $\Sigma' = \{+, a, b\}$.

The addition of two unary numbers is just writing one number after the other (appending), as we have seen in the case of the TM (refer to Chapter 4, Example 4.9). The production rules can be written as:

1. $S \to a\, S$
2. $a\, 1 \to 1\, a$
3. $a + \to b$
4. $b\, 1 \to 1\, b$
5. $b \to \bullet$ (stop)

Let us consider the numbers 2 and 3 for addition. Their unary equivalents are '11' and '111' respectively.

| | |
|---|---|
| 1 1 + 1 1 1 | (initial string) |
| ↓ | |
| $\underline{a\,1}$ 1 + 1 1 1 | (using rule 1) |
| ↓ | |
| 1 $\underline{a\,1}$ + 1 1 1 | (using rule 2) |
| ↓ | |
| 1 1 $\underline{a\,+}$ 1 1 1 | (using rule 2) |
| ↓ | |
| 1 1 $\underline{b\,1}$ 1 1 | (using rule 3) |
| ↓ | |
| 1 1 1 $\underline{b\,1}$ 1 | (using rule 4) |
| ↓ | |
| 1 1 1 1 $\underline{b\,1}$ | (using rule 4) |
| ↓ | |
| 1 1 1 1 1 $\underline{b}$ | (using rule 4) |
| ↓ | |
| 1 1 1 1 1 $\bullet$ (stop) | (using rule 5) |

Thus, the result of the addition of 2 and 3 is 5, which is represented in unary format as '11111'.

**Example 11.14** Write the Markov algorithm to find the 2's complement of a given binary number.

***Solution*** For binary numbers $\Sigma$ can be defined as $\Sigma = \{0, 1\}$.

We have already discussed the method to obtain the 2's complement of a given binary number while discussing TM (refer to Chapter 4, Example 4.3). The method is as follows:

1. Start from the right end of the binary number and keep moving left till you read the first '1'.
2. Every '0' that you read after this first '1' is replaced by '1', while moving left.
3. Every '1' that you read after this first '1' is replaced by '0', while moving left.
4. When you reach the left end of the given binary number, stop.

The required Markov algorithm is written as:

1. $S \to S\,\alpha$
2. $0\,\alpha \to \alpha\,0$
3. $1\,\alpha \to \beta\,1$
4. $0\,\beta \to \beta\,1$
5. $1\,\beta \to \beta\,0$
6. $\beta \to \bullet$ (stop)

Let us simulate the working of this algorithm for the input binary string '101100'.

$1\;0\;1\;1\;0\;0$ (initial string)
$\downarrow$
$1\;0\;1\;1\;0\;\underline{0\;\alpha}$ (using rule 1)
$\downarrow$
$1\;0\;1\;1\;\underline{0\;\alpha}\;0$ (using rule 2)
$\downarrow$
$1\;0\;1\;\underline{1\;\alpha}\;0\;0$ (using rule 2)
$\downarrow$
$1\;0\;\underline{1\;\beta}\;1\;0\;0$ (using rule 3)
$\downarrow$
$1\;\underline{0\;\beta}\;0\;1\;0\;0$ (using rule 5)
$\downarrow$
$\underline{1\;\beta}\;1\;0\;1\;0\;0$ (using rule 4)
$\downarrow$
$\beta\;0\;1\;0\;1\;0\;0$ (using rule 5)
$\downarrow$
$\bullet\;0\;1\;0\;1\;0\;0$ (stop) (using rule 6)

Thus, we have obtained the 2's complement as '010100' for the given binary number '101100'.

---

**Example 11.15** Write the Markov algorithm for the multiplication of two unary numbers.

***Solution*** Let us assume that the numbers are represented using unary format over $\Sigma = \{1\}$. Further, let us consider the auxiliary alphabet as:

$\Sigma' = \{*, a, b, c\}$, where, $a$ and $b$ are any strings from $\Sigma^*$.

The productions can be written as:

1. $(a * b1) \to (a * b) + a$
2. $(a * \epsilon) \to \epsilon$
3. $\epsilon + a \to a$

4. $a + b \rightarrow a\,b$
5. $a \rightarrow a\,c$
6. $c \rightarrow \bullet$ (stop)

Let us simulate the working of this algorithm for the multiplication of '111' and '11'.

$$(\underbrace{1\ 1\ 1}_{a} \times \underbrace{1}_{b}\ 1) \quad \text{(initial string)}$$
$$\downarrow$$
$$(\underbrace{1\ 1\ 1}_{a} \times 1) + 1\ 1\ 1 \quad \text{(applying rule 1 for } a = 1\,1\,1, b = 1)$$
$$\downarrow$$
$$(\underbrace{1\ 1\ 1}_{a} \times \epsilon) + 1\ 1\ 1 + 1\ 1\ 1 \quad \text{(applying rule 1 for } a = 1\,1\,1, b = \epsilon)$$
$$\downarrow$$
$$\epsilon + 1\ \underbrace{1\ 1}_{a} + 1\ 1\ 1 \quad \text{(applying rule 2 for } a = 1\,1\,1)$$
$$\downarrow$$
$$\underbrace{1\ 1\ 1}_{a} + \underbrace{1\ 1\ 1}_{b} \quad \text{(applying rule 3 for } a = 1\,1\,1)$$
$$\downarrow$$
$$1\ 1\ 1\ 1\ 1\ 1 \quad \text{(applying rule 4 for } a = 1\,1\,1, b = 1\,1\,1)$$
$$\downarrow$$
$$1\ 1\ 1\ 1\ 1\ 1\ c \quad \text{(applying rule 5 for } a = 1\,1\,1\,1\,1\,1)$$
$$\downarrow$$
$$1\ 1\ 1\ 1\ 1\ 1 \bullet \text{(stop)} \quad \text{(applying rule 6)}$$

---

**Example 11.16** Write the Markov algorithm to find the GCD of two given numbers.

***Solution*** We have:

$\Sigma = \{0, 1, 2, 3, 4, 5, 6, 7, 8, 9\}$, and
$\Sigma' = \{a, m, n, r, c\}$,

where $a$, $m$, $n$, and $r$ are integers over $\Sigma$.

The productions are given as:

1. $(a, 0) \rightarrow (a)\, c$
2. $(m, n) \rightarrow (n, r)$ (where $r = m \bmod n$, and $m > n$)
3. $c \rightarrow \bullet$ (stop)

Let us simulate the working of this algorithm for $m = 77$ and $n = 44$:

(77, 44) (initial pair)
$\downarrow$
(44, 33) (using rule 2 for $m = 77$, $n = 44$)
$\downarrow$

(33, 11) (using rule 2 for $m = 44$, $n = 33$)
↓
(11, 0) (using rule 2 for $m = 33$, $n = 11$)
↓
(11) $c$ (using rule 1 for $a = 11$)
↓
(11) • (stop) (using rule 1 for $a = 11$)

Thus, the GCD of 77 and 44 is 11.

---

**Example 11.17** Design a Markov algorithm for subtraction of one number from the other.

***Solution*** Let us assume that the numbers are represented in unary format over $\Sigma = \{1\}$, and the auxiliary alphabet $\Sigma'$ is defined as:

$\Sigma' = \{-, a, b\}$, where $a$ and $b$ are strings over $\Sigma$.

The productions are:

1. $a\,1 - b\,1 \rightarrow a - b$ (where $a > b$)
2. $a - \epsilon \rightarrow a\,c$
3. $c \rightarrow \bullet$ (stop)

Let us simulate the working of this algorithm for subtracting the unary number '11' (i.e., 2) from the unary number '1111' (i.e., 4).

$\underbrace{1\ 1\ 1}_{a}\ 1 - \underbrace{1}_{b}\ 1$ (initial string)
↓
$\underbrace{1\ 1}_{a}\ 1 - 1$ (using rule 1 for $a = 1\ 1\ 1$, $b = 1$)
↓
$\underbrace{1\ 1}_{a} - \epsilon$ (using rule 1 for $a = 1\ 1$, $b = \epsilon$)
↓ (using rule 2 for $a = 1\ 1$)
$1\ 1\ c$
↓
$1\ 1\ \bullet$ (stop) (using rule 3)

Thus, the result of '4 – 2' is '2', which is represented in unary format as '11'.

---

**Example 11.18** Design a Markov algorithm for reversing a given string over $\Sigma = \{a, b, c, d\}$.

***Solution*** The productions can be stated as:

1. $\sigma \rightarrow \alpha\,\sigma$
2. $\alpha\,s\,t \rightarrow t\,\alpha\,s$ (where, $t \neq \epsilon$ and $s \in \Sigma$)
3. $\alpha\,\alpha \rightarrow \beta$
4. $\beta\,s \rightarrow s\,\beta$
5. $\beta\,\alpha \rightarrow \beta$
6. $\beta \rightarrow \bullet$ (stop)

Let us simulate the working of this algorithm for the string '*abcd*'.

| | |
|---|---|
| $a\ b\ c\ d$ | (initial string) |
| $\downarrow$ | |
| $\alpha\ a\ b\ c\ d$ | (using rule 1 for $\sigma = abcd$) |
| $\downarrow$ | |
| $b\ c\ d\ \alpha\ a$ | (using rule 2 for $s = a, t = bcd$) |
| $\downarrow$ | |
| $\alpha\ b\ c\ d\ \alpha\ a$ | (using rule 1 for $\sigma = bcd\alpha a$) |
| $\downarrow$ | |
| $c\ d\ \alpha\ b\ \alpha\ a$ | (using rule 2 for $s = b, t = cd$) |
| $\downarrow$ | |
| $\alpha\ c\ d\ \alpha\ b\ \alpha\ a$ | (using rule 1 for $\sigma = cd\alpha b\alpha a$) |
| $\downarrow$ | |
| $d\ \alpha\ c\ \alpha\ b\ \alpha\ a$ | (using rule 2 for $s = c, t = d$) |
| $\downarrow$ | |
| $\alpha\ d\ \alpha\ c\ \alpha\ b\ \alpha\ a$ | (using rule 1 for $\sigma = d\alpha c\alpha b\alpha a$) |
| $\downarrow$ | |
| $\underline{\alpha\ \alpha}\ d\ \alpha\ c\ \alpha\ b\ \alpha\ a$ | (using rule 1 for $\sigma = \alpha d\alpha c\alpha b\alpha a$) |
| $\downarrow$ | |
| $\underline{\beta\ d}\ \alpha\ c\ \alpha\ b\ \alpha\ a$ | (using rule 3) |
| $\downarrow$ | |
| $d\ \underline{\beta\ \alpha}\ c\ \alpha\ b\ \alpha\ a$ | (using rule 4 for $s = d$) |
| $\downarrow$ | |
| $d\ \beta\ c\ \alpha\ b\ \alpha\ a$ | (using rule 5) |
| $\downarrow$ | |
| $d\ c\ \underline{\beta\ \alpha}\ b\ \alpha\ a$ | (using rule 4 for $s = c$) |
| $\downarrow$ | |
| $d\ c\ \underline{\beta\ b}\ \alpha\ a$ | (using rule 5) |
| $\downarrow$ | |
| $d\ c\ b\ \underline{\beta\ \alpha}\ a$ | (using rule 4 for $s = b$) |
| $\downarrow$ | |
| $d\ c\ b\ \underline{\beta\ \alpha}$ | (using rule 5) |
| $\downarrow$ | |
| $d\ c\ b\ \underline{a\ \beta}$ | (using rule 4 for $s = a$) |
| $\downarrow$ | |
| $d\ c\ b\ a\ \bullet$ (stop) | (using rule 6) |

***Note***: Almost all the examples we have solved here can also be solved using a TM, as seen in Chapter 4. Hence, Markov algorithm is an equivalent model of computation as the TM.

## 11.8 LABELLED MARKOV ALGORITHM

We have seen that in case of the Markov algorithm, we need to search for a production rule, which is applicable at each stage, while generating a new string from a given input string.

On the other hand, in labelled Markov algorithm (LMA), it is possible to assign labels—usually their respective indices—to different productions. Further, each production specifies a go-to statement, indicating the next production rule that needs to be applied. With the help of these labels and the go-to statements, the search required at every stage can be avoided, and hence, the execution is comparatively much faster.

### 11.8.1 Formal Definition

An LMA over an alphabet $\Sigma \cup \Sigma'$ is a non-empty ordered list of productions of the form:

1: $x_1 \rightarrow y_1 / a_1$
2: $x_2 \rightarrow y_2 / a_2$
⋮
$n$: $x_n \rightarrow y_n / a_n$

The numbers to the left of the colon (:) are the labels, and the $a_i$'s, for $i = 1, 2, \ldots, n$ are also numbers from the set $\{1, 2, \ldots, n\}$ indicating the go-to statements that specify the production label (number), which needs to be applied next.

For example, if $x_i$ is any sub-string of string $w$, which can be replaced by $y_i$ using production '$i$: $x_i \rightarrow y_i / a_i$', then after replacement the next production rule to be applied is $a_i$. Further, if the production with label $a_i = j$ is not applicable, then the $(j + 1)^{\text{th}}$ production is applied.

### 11.8.2 Examples

Let us now discuss some examples of labelled Markov algorithm that will help understand the concept better.

---

**Example 11.19** Design LMA which writes '2' at the right end of any word, $w \subseteq \Sigma^*$, where $\Sigma = \{1, 2\}$.

***Solution*** Let us consider the auxiliary alphabet $\Sigma'$ as:

$$\Sigma' = \{\alpha, \sigma\}.$$

The productions or statements are given as follows:

1: $\sigma \rightarrow \alpha\, \sigma / 2$
2: $\alpha\, 1 \rightarrow 1\, \alpha / 2$
3: $\alpha\, 2 \rightarrow 2\, \alpha / 2$
4: $\alpha \rightarrow 2 / 5$

Let us simulate the working of this LMA for the string '121'.

$1\ 2\ 1$ (initial string)

At this stage we can apply rule 1, which writes $\alpha$ before the string and goes to rule 2. After applying rule 1, we get

$\underline{\alpha\ 1}\ 2\ 1$

Now, rule 2 can be applied; it replaces '$\alpha 1$' by '$1\alpha$', and goes to rule 2. After applying this, we get

$1\ \underline{\alpha\ 2}\ 1$

We now apply rule 2 to the sub-string '$\alpha$ 2'; however, rule 2 assumes left-hand side as '$\alpha$ 1' and is hence not applicable. Therefore, we apply rule '2 + 1', that is, rule 3. After applying rule 3, we get

$1\ 2\ \underline{\alpha\ 1}$

Rule 3 also takes the next step to rule 2. Applying rule 2, we get

$1\ 2\ 1\ \underline{\alpha}$

As per the algorithm, if the production with label $a_i = j$ is not applicable, then the $(j + 1)$th production is applied. One can see that neither rule 2 nor rule 3 is applicable here. At this stage, we can apply rule 4, which replaces $\alpha$ by 2, and moves to rule 5, that is, stops.

After applying rule 4, we get

$1\ 2\ 1\ 2$

Thus, the algorithm has written '2' after '1 2 1' to generate a new string '1 2 1 2'.

---

**Example 11.20** Consider the LMA over

$\Sigma = \{a, b\}$, and
$\Sigma' = \{\alpha, \beta\}$,

having the following set of productions:

1: $\epsilon \to \alpha / 2$
2: $\alpha\, s \to s\, \beta\, s\, \alpha / 2$ (where $s \in \Sigma$)
3: $\alpha \to \epsilon / 4$
4: $s\, t\, \beta \to t\, \beta\, s / 4$ (where $s, t \in \Sigma$)
5: $\beta \to \epsilon / 5$

Find the function of this algorithm.

***Solution*** Let us consider an input string '*aba*' $\subseteq \Sigma^*$, and simulate the working of the given algorithm for this string.

$a\ b\ a$ (initial string)
$\downarrow$
$\underline{\alpha\ a}\ b\ a$ (using rule 1, go to rule 2)
$\downarrow$
$a\ \beta\ a\ \underline{\alpha\ b}\ a$ (using rule 2 for $s = a$, go to rule 2)
$\downarrow$
$a\ \beta\ a\ b\ \beta\ b\ \underline{\alpha\ a}$ (using rule 2 for $s = b$, go to rule 2)
$\downarrow$
$a\ \beta\ a\ b\ \beta\ b\ a\ \beta\ a\ \alpha$ (using rule 2 for $s = a$, go to rule 2)

As '$\alpha\, s$' is not a sub-string of '$a\, \beta\, a\, b\, \beta\, b\, a\, \beta\, a\, \alpha$' therefore, we cannot apply rule 2. Hence, we need to apply rule $(2 + 1)$, that is, rule 3.

$a\ \beta\ \underline{a\ b\ \beta}\ b\ a\ \beta\ a$ (using rule 3, go to rule 4)
$\downarrow$
$a\ \beta\ b\ \beta\ a\ \underline{b\ a\ \beta}\ a$ (using rule 4 for $s = a$ and $t = b$, go to rule 4)
$\downarrow$
$a\ \beta\ b\ \beta\ \underline{a\ a\ \beta}\ b\ a$ (using rule 4 for $s = b$ and $t = a$, go to rule 4)
$\downarrow$
$a\ \underline{\beta}\ b\ \beta\ a\ \beta\ a\ b\ a$ (using rule 4 for $s = a$ and $t = a$, go to rule 4)

Since there is no sub-string of the form '$s\ t\ \beta$'; therefore, rule 4 cannot be applied. Hence, we apply rule 5.

$a\ b\ \underline{\beta}\ a\ \beta\ a\ b\ a$ (using rule 5 for leftmost occurrence of $\beta$)
$\downarrow$
$a\ b\ a\ \underline{\beta}\ a\ b\ a$ (using rule 5 for leftmost occurrence of $\beta$)
$\downarrow$
$a\ b\ a\ a\ b\ a$ (stop) (using rule 5; as there is no further occurrence of $\beta$, it stops)

We see that the given LMA has converted the original string '*aba*' to a new string '*abaaba*' over $\Sigma$. Thus, we can say that this algorithm duplicates any input string over $\Sigma = \{a, b\}$.

## SUMMARY

There exists a symbol manipulation system, termed as *productions system*, which does the same job as a Turing machine (TM) and can be formalized as a finite set of productions. Post, Markov, and Thue are the three scientists, who devised the formalism of a production system (Post–Markov–Thue system); it defines an algorithm as a set of rules that transform a given initial string of symbols from a given alphabet set $\Sigma$ into another string of symbols over the same alphabet. The initial string of symbols, which gets transformed into a new string is called an *axiom*; it is analogous to the initial configuration of a TM.

A *Post–Markov–Thue system* or in short, a *PMT* system consists of the following:

1. An alphabet, $\Sigma$
2. A set of axioms (initial strings), *A*
3. A finite set of rules or productions *P* to derive new strings over the same alphabet $\Sigma$ from the axioms in *A*

These rules or productions, which define an algorithm using symbol manipulation techniques, are also called *rewrite rules* or *symbol replacement rules*.

A PMT production system is formally defined as a quadruple:

$$T = (\Sigma, \Sigma^*, A, P),$$

where:

$\Sigma$: Finite and non-empty alphabet
$\Sigma^*$: Set of all words over $\Sigma$
*A*: Set of axioms over $\Sigma$, i.e., $A \subseteq \Sigma^*$
*P*: Finite set of rules of the form: '$\alpha\ x\ \beta \rightarrow \alpha\ y\ \beta$', where $x, y \subseteq \Sigma^*$ and $\alpha, \beta$ are the syntactic variables over $\Sigma^*$; ($\alpha$ and $\beta$ may be null strings)

The rules of the form '$\alpha\ x\ \beta \rightarrow \alpha\ y\ \beta$' can be interpreted as some occurrence of *x* in '$\alpha\ x\ \beta$' being replaced by *y*, giving '$\alpha\ y\ \beta$'.

In a PMT system, if the productions in the rule set *P* contain only constant strings over $\Sigma$, then that PMT system is called a *Post Canonical System (PCS)*. In order to generate the class of rich and useful theorems, or *rich class of languages*, the input alphabet, $\Sigma$, is not sufficient and has to be extended to $\Sigma'$ that includes additional or auxiliary symbols.

The *post normal form (PNF)* theorem states that any formal system can be reduced to a PCS with a single axiom and simple productions of the form:

$$x\ \alpha \rightarrow \alpha\ y,$$

where $x, y \subseteq \Sigma^*$ and $\alpha$ is a syntactic variable over $\Sigma^*$.

Any TM can be interpreted as a PMT system using the following analogy:

Alphabet $\Sigma$: $S \cup I$, where *S* is the set of states being treated as the set of auxiliary symbols, and *I* is the tape alphabet

Set of axioms *A*: Initial configuration of the TM

Set of productions *P*: Functional matrix of the TM

It is very logical to consider the initial configuration with the input string as the axiom, because it is the axiom that is transformed into the new string, just as the TM modifies the given input string to produce the output string.

Similarly, every finite state machine (FSM) can be identified as a PMT system using the following analogy:

Alphabet $\Sigma$: $S \cup I$, where $S$ is the set of states being treated as the set of auxiliary symbols, and $I$ is the input alphabet

Set of axioms $A$: Initial state of the FSM

Set of productions $P$: State transition table of the FSM

For example, if there is a transition from state $\alpha$ to state $\beta$ on reading symbol $a$ for a given FSM, then the transition can be represented as a production for the equivalent PMT system:

$\alpha \rightarrow a\,\beta$

*Markov algorithm* is a PMT system with the following features:

1. All the productions from the set of productions $P$ are assigned indices or numbers (1, 2, 3, ...). This means that $P$ contains an ordered production list.
2. A production of the form: $\alpha\, x\, \beta \rightarrow \bullet$ is considered as a stop indicator. No other production is applied after the application of this type of production.
3. If more than one production can be applied to derive the string $w_2$ from a string $w_1$, then the production with the lowest number (or index) is applied.
4. If a production, whose left-hand side is '$\alpha\, x\, \beta$', is applicable to a word $w$ containing more than one occurrence of $x$, then the production is applied to the leftmost $x$ from $w$.

Markov algorithm has the same power as a TM, which can compute all partial recursive functions. Hence, Markov algorithm is an equivalent model of computation as the TM.

In a *labelled Markov algorithm* (LMA), it is possible to assign labels to different productions. These labels are usually their respective indices. Further, each production specifies a go-to statement, indicating the next production rule to be applied. With the help of these labels and the go-to statements, the searching required at each stage can be avoided and hence, the execution is comparatively much faster than the Markov algorithm.

An LMA over an alphabet $\Sigma \cup \Sigma'$ is a non-empty ordered list of productions of the form:

$$\begin{aligned} 1&: x_1 \rightarrow y_1 \,/\, a_1 \\ 2&: x_2 \rightarrow y_2 \,/\, a_2 \\ &\vdots \\ n&: x_n \rightarrow y_n \,/\, a_n \end{aligned}$$

The numbers to the left of the colon (:) are the labels and the $a_i$'s, for $i = 1, 2, \ldots, n$ are also numbers from the set {1, 2, ..., $n$}, indicating the go-to statements that specify the production label (number), which needs to be applied next.

For example, if $x_i$ is any sub-string of string $w$, which can be replaced by $y_i$ using production '$i$: $x_i \rightarrow y_i / a_i$', then after replacement the next production rule to be applied is $a_i$. Further, if the production with label $a_i = j$ is not applicable, then the $(j + 1)$th production is applied.

## EXERCISES

This section lists a few unsolved problems to help the readers understand the topic better and practise a few examples related to production systems.

### Objective Questions

(U) 11.1 Which of the following statements is true?
- (a) TMs are more powerful than Markov algorithms.
- (b) Markov algorithm is an equivalent model of computation as the TM.
- (c) Markov algorithm cannot compute partial recursive functions.
- (d) Labelled Markov algorithm is computationally more powerful than the TM.

(U) 11.2 If $A$ is a function computed by a TM, and $B$ is a function computed by a Markov algorithm, then which of the following statements is false?
- (a) $A$ may be a recursive language.

(b) $B$ may be a recursively enumerable language.

(c) $A$ and $B$ are both partial recursive functions.

(d) $A$ cannot be computed using Markov algorithm.

(U) 11.3 'A production system is a symbol manipulation system alike the TM.' Is this statement true or false?

(U) 11.4 Which of the following statements are false?

$S1$: LMA is equivalent to TM

$S2$: Any function computable by Markov algorithm is undecidable

$S3$: LMA is slower in computation than the Markov algorithm

$S4$: Every FSM can be converted to an equivalent PMT system

(a) $S1$ and $S2$
(b) $S1$ only
(c) $S2$ only
(d) $S2$ and $S3$
(e) $S4$ only
(f) $S3$ only
(g) None of these
(h) All of these

(U) 11.5 'A production system defines an algorithm as a set of rules that transform a given initial string of symbols from a given alphabet set $\Sigma$ into another string of symbols over the same alphabet set.' Is this statement true or false?

(R) 11.6 LMA stands for ________.

(R) 11.7 PMT stands for ________.

## Review Questions

(U) 11.1 Write a Markov algorithm to find the 1's complement of a given binary number.

(U) 11.2 Explain the post canonical system.

(U) 11.3 Describe the PMT system with the help of suitable examples.

(C) 11.4 Write a Markov algorithm to find the 2's complement of a given binary number.

(C) 11.5 Write the PMT system for generating palindromes over {1, 2, 3}.

(U) 11.6 Write a short note on production systems.

(L) 11.7 Define the PMT system. Give the pros and cons of a PMT system with respect to its capability.

(C) 11.8 Let $\Sigma = \{a, b, c, d\}$. Construct the Markov algorithm that removes the first '$c$' and every symbol following it from any string over $\Sigma^*$.

(U) 11.9 Write a short note on the pros and cons of the PMT system.

(C) 11.10 Design a Markov algorithm to generate an odd/even parity bit for a string of 1's and 0's.

***Hint:*** A parity bit is a bit that is added to ensure that the number of bits having value one in a set of bits is even or odd. An even parity bit will be set to '1' if the number of 1's + 1 is even; otherwise, it is set to '0'. For example, a 7-bit binary number '1010001 (3)' is written as an 8-bit number with even parity, which is '11010001 (4)'. Similarly, the number '1101001 (4)' is written with even parity as '01101001 (4)'. An odd parity bit will be set to '1' if the number of 1's + 1 is odd; otherwise, it is set to '0'. For example, a 7-bit binary number '1010001 (3)' is written as an 8-bit number with odd parity, which is '01010001 (3)'. Similarly, the number '1101001 (4)' is written with even parity as '11101001 (5)'.

(C) 11.11 Give the PMT system for generating the language represented by 0*.1*.2*.

(C) 11.12 Write the Markov algorithm to find the GCD of two decimal numbers.

(C) 11.13 Give the formal definition of the production system. What is the production system for an even palindrome defined over $\Sigma = \{0, 1, 2\}$?

(C) 11.14 Give the production system for:

(a) Palindromes over $\Sigma = \{a, b, c\}$

(b) Strings of $a$, $b$, and $c$ that always end with $c$ over $\Sigma = \{a, b, c\}$

(U) 11.15 Write a short note on labelled Markov algorithm.

(L) 11.16 Explain the correspondence among FSM and PMT systems using appropriate examples.

(L) 11.17 'Markov algorithm is equivalent to the TM', justify the statement with the help of examples.

**Answers to Objective Questions**

11.1 (b) 11.2 (d) 11.3 True 11.4 (d) 11.5 True 11.6 labelled Markov algorithm
11.7 Post–Markov–Thue

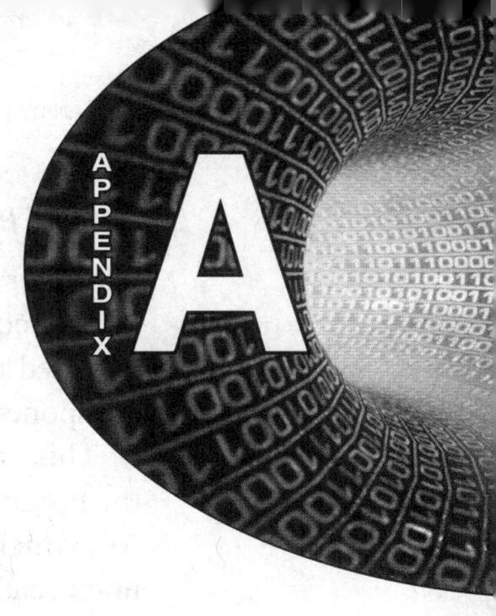


# Implementations

## A.1 INTRODUCTION

In this book, we have discussed the theory related to many practical aspects of computations, namely problem solvability, language acceptance/rejection, and so on. We shall now discuss the practical implementations of these concepts, especially those related to regular languages.

In this appendix, we are going to discuss the implementations for obtaining non-deterministic finite automata (NFA)/deterministic finite automata (DFA) equivalents of input regular expressions, converting right-linear regular grammar to the equivalent left-linear regular grammar, and obtaining the finite automata (FA) that accept the language generated by a given regular grammar. For this, we shall use the high-level programming language, 'C'.

## A.2 CONVERSION FROM REGULAR EXPRESSIONS TO FINITE AUTOMATA

Recall the methods (algorithms) we discussed in Chapter 3 (refer to Fig. 3.7) for converting a given regular expression to a finite automaton (FA). In this section, we shall consider the following path for the implementation; the representation for the same is shown in Fig. A.1.

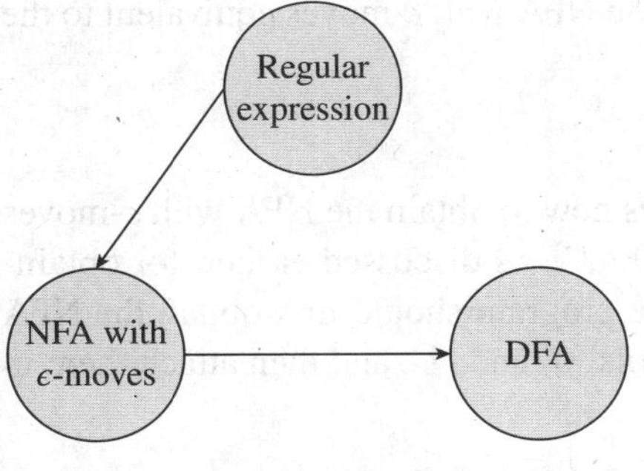

**Figure A.1** Conversion from regular expression to FA

Initially, we shall discuss the generation of an equivalent NFA with $\epsilon$-moves from the input regular expression. Thereafter, we shall derive the equivalent DFA formation.

### A.2.1 Representing Regular Expressions

Let us limit ourselves to the alphabet $\Sigma = \{a, b\}$, that is, an alphabet consisting of only two symbols. The input regular expression represents the regular language over the alphabet $\Sigma$. Further, let us consider three regular expression constructs, namely, '+' (parallel paths), '·' (concatenation), and '*' (Kleene closure). Expressions may also contain parentheses—'(' and ')'—wherever necessary. Some valid examples for regular expressions are $(a^* + b^*)$, $(a + b \cdot b)^*$, and $(a + b \cdot a^*)$.

For the 'C' implementation, we consider these regular expressions as character strings.

### A.2.2 Need for Postfix Conversion of Regular Expressions

We have discussed the rules for constructing NFA with $\epsilon$-moves from a given regular expression in Chapter 3 (refer to Fig. 3.3). The postfix form of the expressions allows us to construct the operand NFAs first before we connect them based on the operators into a bigger NFA.

### *Parallel Paths*

Consider Fig. 3.3(a) in Chapter 3. For obtaining the NFA component equivalent to '0 + 1', we require two individual components representing '0' and '1'. These components are attached using $\epsilon$-transitions, with the help of two new states at both the ends to get the component representing '0 + 1'.

This process is easier if we have the postfix equivalent to '0 + 1', that is, '0 1 +', so that the program can read the first character '0' and prepare the NFA components representing '0', which include two states that are connected by a transition on symbol '0'. Similarly, upon reading the second symbol '1', the program can prepare the NFA components representing the transition on symbol '1'.

When the program reads '+', it joins the two components for '0' and '1', which are already constructed in the form of parallel paths. This process is explained in Fig. A.2.

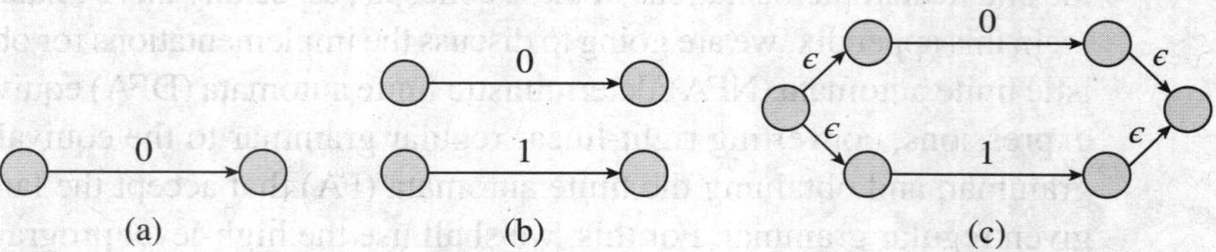


**Figure A.2** Construction of NFA with $\epsilon$-moves using postfix equivalent of input regular expression (a) After reading '0' from postfix equivalent '01+' (b) After reading '1' from postfix equivalent '01+' (c) After reading '+' from postfix equivalent '01+'

Thus, the postfix equivalent of the input regular expression makes the construction of the NFA with $\epsilon$-moves simpler and mechanical. Such postfix strings place the operands before the operators so that the program can first construct the equivalent NFA components and process them on reading the operators. Thus, the NFA with $\epsilon$-moves equivalent to the given regular expression is built.

### *Series Connection*

Consider Fig. 3.3(b) in Chapter 3. The figure shows how to obtain the NFA with $\epsilon$-moves component equivalent to the regular expression '0 · 1'. As discussed earlier, for obtaining the NFA equivalent to the series operation, the program should first obtain the NFA components corresponding to the individual symbols '0' and '1', and then attach them in series, as shown in Fig. A.3.

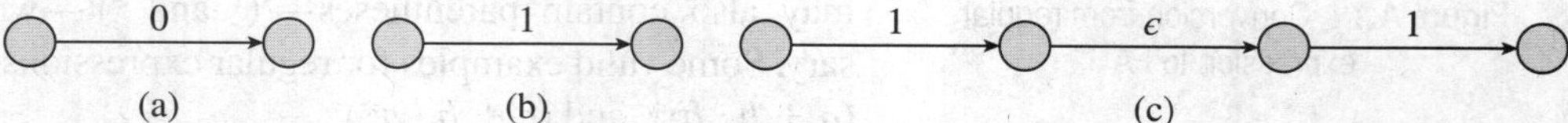


**Figure A.3** Need for postfix equivalent of input regular expression (a) After reading '0' from postfix equivalent '01·' (b) After reading '1' from postfix equivalent '01·' (c) After reading '·' from postfix equivalent '01·'

### *Kleene Closure*

We have seen that it is necessary to obtain the postfix equivalent form of a given regular expression before we begin constructing the equivalent NFA with $\epsilon$-moves. Figure A.4 demonstrates the construction process for NFA with $\epsilon$-moves for '0*'. As one can see '0*'

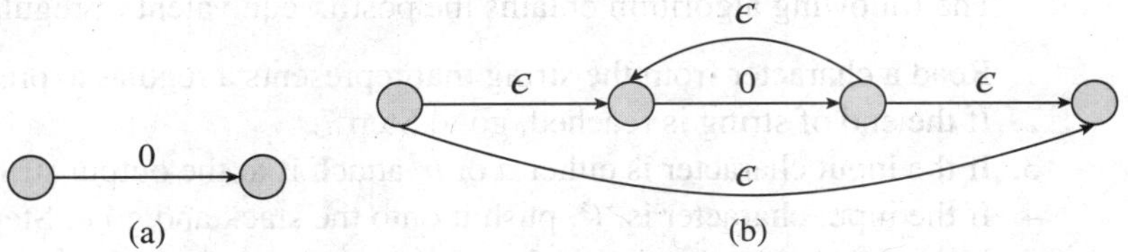


**Figure A.4** Construction of NFA with $\epsilon$-moves using postfix equivalent of input regular expression (a) After reading '0' from the expression '0*' (b) After reading '*' from '0*'

is the postfix form of itself. If the expression had been '(0+1)*', then the postfix form would have been '01+ *'.

## A.2.3 Obtaining Postfix Equivalent of Regular Expressions

We have already discussed in Section A.2.1 that our implementation will consider regular expressions over the alphabet set, $\Sigma = \{a, b\}$, which may or may not have parentheses expressed in infix form. Infix notation is the common formula notation, in which operators are written between the operands they act on. For example, '0+1', '0 · 1', and so on. In infix notation, unlike postfix notation, parentheses surrounding groups of operands and operators are necessary to indicate the intended order in which operations are to be performed. For example, '(0+1) · 0'. In the absence of parentheses, operator precedence rules determine the order of operations. For example, '0+1 · 0' is not same as '(0+1) · 0'.

The postfix form of the expression puts the operands first, before the operators that help us build the NFA easily. In order to obtain the postfix equivalent form of a given infix form of a regular expression, we must know the relative priorities of the operators, '+' (parallel paths), '·' (series), and '*' (closure). We have seen earlier that '*' has the highest priority, followed by '·', while '+' has the lowest priority among the three operators.

This can be explained with the help of the following examples:

1. Let us consider, a regular expression, '$a + b \cdot b$'. In this expression, we perform the '+' operation on $a$ and '$b \cdot b$'; and not the '·' operation on '$a + b$' and $b$. This is because the '+' operator has lower priority compared to the '·' operator. Hence, we may also write the given regular expression as '$a + (b \cdot b)$'.

   We may use parentheses to change the order of the operations. The expression '$(a + b) \cdot b$' uses a different order of operations—the operation, '+', within the parentheses, is performed first. We also know that $a + b \cdot b \neq (a + b) \cdot b$
2. Let us consider the regular expression, '$a^* \cdot b^*$'. In this expression, '$a^*$' and '$b^*$' are individually processed first and then concatenated using the '·' operation. This is because the '·' operation has lower priority compared to the '*' operation. Hence, $a^* \cdot b^* = (a^*) \cdot (b^*)$.

### *Algorithm for Obtaining Postfix Equivalent of Regular Expressions*

The algorithm considers the input expression as a character string, and works on expressions with or without parentheses; it uses a stack to perform the required function.

The following algorithm obtains the postfix equivalent of regular expressions:

1. Read a character from the string that represents a regular expression.
2. If the end of string is reached, go to Step 7.
3. If the input character is either $a$ or $b$, attach it to the output string.
4. If the input character is '(', push it onto the stack and go to Step 1.
5. If the input character is ')', then pop everything from the stack till you get '(' on the stack and attach it to the output string. Go to Step 1.
6. If the character currently read is either '+', '·', or '*', then:
   (a) If '(priority of incoming symbol) > (priority of in-stack symbol)', then push the character onto the stack and go to Step 1. Here the incoming symbol is either '+', '·', or, '*'.
   (b) Else, if '(priority of incoming symbol) < (priority of in-stack symbol)', then pop characters one by one from the stack and attach to the output string till the priority of the incoming symbol becomes greater than the priority of the in-stack symbol. Then push the incoming character onto the stack and go to Step 1.
7. If the stack is not empty, then pop characters one by one and keep on attaching them to the output string. When the stack becomes empty, stop.

### *Stack Implementation*

Program A.1 describes the generic stack implementation as a header file 'STACK.h', which can be used while implementing the infix to postfix conversion described in the algorithm discussed in the previous section.

**Program A.1** Stack implementation

```
// ------ STACK.h
// This header file provides the generic stack implementation.
// This stack can be used for any type of element, including
// 'int', 'char', a 'pointer' to a 'structure', and so on.
void *stack[STACK_SIZE];
int top;
void initialize()                    // Initialize the stack to an empty state.
{
    top = 0;
}

void push(void *element) // Push the element onto the stack if the stack is not full.
{
    if(!stackfull())
      stack[top++] = element;
    else
    {
        printf("Stack full");
        exit(-1);
    }
```

```
}

void* pop()                   //     Pop and return the popped element from
                              //     the stack, if the stack is not empty.
{
     if(!stackempty())
          return(stack[--top]);
     else
     {
          printf("Stack empty");
          exit(-1);
     }
}

int stackfull()                   //    Returns '1' if stack is full else returns '0'.
{
     if(top == STACK_SIZE)
          return 1;
     else
          return 0;
}

int stackempty()                  //    Returns '1' if stack is empty, else returns '0'.
{
     if (top == 0)
          return 1;
     else
          return 0;
}
// ------ End of STACK.h
```

Program A.1 is a collection of five function implementations, namely 'push', 'pop' 'stackempty', 'stackfull', and 'initialize'.

The 'initialize' function initializes the top of the stack to zero, that is, it initializes the stack to its empty state.

The 'stackfull' function checks if the stack is full and prevents the program from pushing an element onto the stack if it is full.

Similarly, the 'stackempty' function checks if the stack is empty and prevents the program from popping an element if it is empty.

We see that the header file 'STACK.h' provides the generic stack implementation. The same stack implementation can be used for a variety of elements, including integers, characters, and pointers to structures, without changing the code; hence, it is said to be generic. The program is implemented as an 'array of void pointers'. Therefore, while pushing and popping different types of elements, the program has to perform 'typecasting'.

For example, to push an integer, 'element', we use:

```
push((void *) element));
```

Here, (void *) is a typecast operator, which converts the integer, 'element', to 'pointer to void' type. Similarly, while popping, we use

```
element = (int) pop();
```

### *Implementation of Algorithm (Infix to Postfix Conversion)*

Program A.2 provides the 'C' implementation for the algorithm described in the section on the algorithm for obtaining postfix equivalent of regular expressions. The program execution provides as output, the postfix equivalent of the input regular expression (in infix form), which is represented as character string.

Program A.2 denoted by the header file 'IN_POST.h' contains three function implementations, namely 'infix_to_postfix', 'check_priority', and 'priority'.

**Program A.2** Infix to postfix conversion for regular expressions over {*a*, *b*} represented as strings

```
// ------ IN_POST.h
// This header file deals with the conversion of an infix expression to its
// equivalent postfix expression.
#include "STACK.h"          // Required for maintaining the stack of character
                            // elements.

// The following procedure takes the input infix expression in 'input_string' and
// returns the equivalent postfix expression in 'output_string'. The expression
// should be over an alphabet {a, b} with or without parentheses and the allowed
// operators are {'+', '.', '*'}.

void infix_to_postfix(char* input_string, char* output_string)
{
      int check_priority(char c);
      int i = 0, j = 0;
      char c;

      while (input_string[i] != '\0')
      {
            switch (input_string[i])
            {
                  case 'a' :
                  case 'b' :   output_string[j++] = input_string[i];
                               break;
                  case '(' :   push((void *)(input_string + i));
                               break;
                  case ')' :   c = *(char *)pop();
                                   while (c != '(')
                                   {
                                         output_string[j++] = c;
                                         c = *(char *)pop();
                                   }
                                   break;
                  case '+' :
                  case '.' :
```

```
            case '*' :  if (check_priority(input_string[i]))
                                push ((void*)(input_string + i)) ;
                        else
                        {
                                while (!check_priority(input_string[i]))
                                output_string [j++] = *(char *)pop();
                                push ((void *)(input_string + i));
                        }
                        break;
            default   :  printf("Invalid expression");
                        exit(-1);
                        break;
            }
            i++;
    }
    while (!stackempty())
            output_string [j++] = *(char *)pop();
    output_string [j++] = '\0';
}
// The following function checks the incoming priority with the in-stack priority.
// It returns '1' if incoming priority > in-stack priority, else it returns '0'.
int check_priority (char c)
{
    int priority (char c) ;
    if (top == 0)          // If it is the first element to be pushed.
            return 1;
    if (priority(c) > priority(*(char *)stack[top - 1]))
            return 1;
    else
            return 0;
}

// The following function returns the priority associated with every operator,
// as well as with '('.

int priority (char  c)
{
    switch (c)
    {
            case '(' : return 0;
            case '+' : return 1;
            case '.' : return 2;
            case '*' : return 3;
    }
}
//_------ End of IN_POST.h
```

The function 'priority' returns the priority value associated with each of the operators '+', '·', and '*'. It also associates the lowest priority to '(', so that it gets pushed every time it occurs.

The function 'check_priority' compares the priority of the incoming symbol with the priority of the in-stack symbol. It returns '1' if the incoming symbol has higher priority compared to the topmost symbol in the stack; otherwise, it returns '0'.

The main function, 'infix_to_postfix', deals with the actual conversion. It uses more than two function implementations as per the requirement of the algorithm. It accepts the input infix expression with the help of the 'input_string' parameter, and returns its postfix equivalent in the 'output_string' parameter.

### *Simulation of Algorithm (Infix to Postfix Conversion)*

1. Consider the regular expression '$(a + b \cdot b)^*$'. Let us simulate the working of Program A.2 to find the equivalent postfix expression of the given regular expression, which is in its infix form. The '\$' symbol in Table A.1 indicates the bottom of the stack and '\0' indicates the end of the input string.

**Table A.1** Simulation of algorithm

| Stack contents | Input string | Action | Output string |
|---|---|---|---|
| \$ | $( a + b \cdot b ) *$ \0<br>↑ (at '(') | | — |
| \$ ( | $( a + b \cdot b ) *$ \0<br>↑ (at $a$) | Push '(' | — |
| \$ ( | $( a + b \cdot b ) *$ \0<br>↑ (at '+') | Attach $a$ to the output string directly | $a$ |
| \$ ( + | $( a + b \cdot b ) *$ \0<br>↑ (at $b$) | Push '+', since priority ('+') > priority ['('] | $a$ |
| \$ ( + | $( a + b \cdot b ) *$ \0<br>↑ (at '·') | Attach $b$ to the output string directly | $a\ b$ |
| \$ ( + · | $( a + b \cdot b ) *$ \0<br>↑ (at $b$) | Push '·', since priority ('·') > priority ('+') | $a\ b$ |
| \$ ( + · | $( a + b \cdot b ) *$ \0<br>↑ (at ')') | Attach $b$ to the output string directly | $a\,b\,b$ |
| \$ | $( a + b \cdot b ) *$ \0<br>↑ (at '*') | Pop everything till you get '(' and attach to the output string | $a\,b\,b\ \cdot +$ |
| \$ * | $( a + b \cdot b ) *$ \0<br>↑ (at \0) | Push '*' as the stack is empty | $a\,b\,b\ \cdot +$ |
| \$ | $( a + b \cdot b ) *$ \0 | String ends; therefore, if the stack is not empty, pop the characters one by one and attach them to the output string till the stack becomes empty, then stop | $a\,b\,b\ \cdot + *$ |

Thus, the postfix equivalent of the input regular expression, '$(a + b \cdot b)$ *', is '$a\,b\,b\ \cdot + *$', which can now be used to construct the required NFA with $\epsilon$-moves.

2. Consider the regular expression '$a* \cdot b*$'. Let us stimulate the working of Program A.2 (in Table A.2) to find its equivalent postfix expression. We represent the given expression as a string, that is, '$a * \cdot b *$', just as in the previous simulation.

**Table A.2** Simulation of program A.2

| Stack contents | Input string | Action | Output string |
|---|---|---|---|
| \$ | $a * \cdot b *$ \0 ↑ (at $a$) | | — |
| \$ | $a * \cdot b *$ \0 ↑ (at $*$) | Attach $a$ to the output string directly | $a$ |
| \$ * | $a * \cdot b *$ \0 ↑ (at $\cdot$) | Push '*' onto the stack as the stack is empty | $a$ |
| \$ · | $a * \cdot b *$ \0 ↑ (at $b$) | Since priority ('·') < priority ('*'), pop '*' and attach it to output string; then push '·' onto the stack | $a *$ |
| \$ · | $a * \cdot b *$ \0 ↑ (at $*$) | Attach '$b$' to the output string directly | $a * b$ |
| \$ · * | $a * \cdot b *$ \0 ↑ (at \0) | Since priority ('·') < priority ('*'), push '*' onto the stack | $a * b$ |
| \$ | $a * \cdot b *$ \0 | Since the string ends, pop everything and attach it to the output string | $a * b * \cdot$ |

Thus, the postfix equivalent of the input regular expression '$a* \cdot b*$' is '$a * b * \cdot$'. This can now be used to construct the required NFA with $\epsilon$-moves.

### A.2.4 Construction of NFA with $\epsilon$-moves

We have discussed in Section A.2.2, the construction of an NFA with $\epsilon$-moves using the postfix form of an input regular expression. We also discussed how it makes the construction process simpler—we get the symbols before the operator constructs. During implementation, we generate the state transition table for the required NFA with $\epsilon$-moves. This implementation uses the stack data structure to store intermediate state numbers, which can be popped to perform operations, whenever an operator ('+', '·', or '*') is read as the input symbol.

***Algorithm for Constructing NFA with $\epsilon$-moves***

**Input:** Postfix equivalent of the input regular expression
**Output:** State transition table for equivalent NFA with $\epsilon$-moves

The following is the required algorithm:

1. Read a character from the input string (postfix equivalent of input regular expression).
2. If end of input string is detected, go to Step 7.
3. If the input character is either $a$ or $b$, then introduce two new states into the required state transition table, with transition on the respective input (the symbol read) from one state to another. The states should be labelled using consecutive numbers (this is obtained using the 'current_state_number' function, which gives information regarding the number of the next state).
   (a) Push both these state numbers onto the stack. These states represent the first and last states of the newly-created NFA component for the respective symbol.
   (b) Go to Step 1.
4. If the input character is '·', that is, concatenation or series connection, then we require two NFA components that we can join using an $\epsilon$-transition. Pop four state numbers from the stack, indicating the first and last states of the two NFA components. Introduce an $\epsilon$-transition from the last state of the first component to the first state of the second component.
   (a) This concatenation converts the two components into a single concatenated component (refer to Fig. A.3). Push the state numbers of the first and last states of this newly-generated component onto the stack.
   (b) Go to Step 1.
5. Similarly, if the input character is '+', that is, parallel paths, we require two NFA components to join as parallel paths with the help of $\epsilon$-transitions. Pop four state numbers, indicating the first and last states of the two NFA components that need to be placed parallel to each other.
   (a) Introduce two new states in the state transition table with consecutive state numbers (this is obtained using the 'current_state_number' function). The first state has two $\epsilon$-transitions to the first states of the two NFA components.
   (b) Introduce two more $\epsilon$-transitions, one each from the last state of the two NFA components to the second new state. This parallel path operation converts the two NFA components into a single component (refer to Fig. A.2).
   (c) Push the state numbers of the first and last states of this newly-generated component onto the stack.
   (d) Go to Step 1.
6. If the input character is '*', that is, closure, then we require a single component for which the closure is to be obtained.
   (a) Pop two state numbers indicating the first and last states of the NFA component.
   (b) Introduce two new states with consecutive state numbers and four $\epsilon$-transitions to obtain the closure (refer to Fig. A.4). These two new states are the first and the last states of the newly-generated component after the closure operation.
   (c) Push their state numbers onto the stack.
   (d) Go to Step 1.
7. When the input string (regular expression in postfix form) ends, the stack contains two state numbers. Pop the topmost state number and declare that as the final state of the required NFA with $\epsilon$-transitions.

8. Pop the remaining state number and declare it as the initial state of the required NFA.
9. Halt with the stack empty status.

### *Implementation of Algorithm (State Transition Table for NFA with $\epsilon$-moves)*

Program A.3 is the 'C' implementation of the algorithm discussed in the previous section. It takes the postfix form of the regular expression, which is represented as a string, as input and generates the state transition table for the equivalent NFA with $\epsilon$-moves.

**Program A.3** Generation of state transition table for NFA with $\epsilon$-moves

```
// ------ RE_NFA.h

// This header file deals with the construction of an equivalent NFA with epsilon-
// moves from the given regular expression. It generates the state transition table
// for the NFA with epsilon-moves.

#include <conio.h>
#include "IN_POST.h" //   Required for finding the postfix equivalent of given regular
                     //   expression.

// For the NFA with epsilon-moves, from every state there will be either
// 1>one transition on 'a' or
// 2>one transition on 'b' or
// 3>one transition on 'epsilon' or
// 4>at most two transitions on 'epsilon' to other states
Struct nfa_state
{
     int transition_on_a;
     int transition_on_b;
     int first_transition_on_epsilon;
     int second_transition_on_epsilon;
     char state_type;
};
struct nfa_state nfa_state_table[TABLE_SIZE];
int current_state_number = 0, initial_state, final_state;

// The following procedure initializes all transitions in the state transition table
// for NFA with epsilon-moves to '-1' and initially, marks all states as non-final
// states, i.e., 'state_type' = 'n'.

void initialize_nfa_state_table()
{
     int i;
     for ( i = 0; i < TABLE_SIZE; i++)
     {
          nfa_state_table[i].transition_on_a = -1;
          nfa_state_table[i].transition_on_b = -1;
          nfa_state_table[i].first_transition_on_epsilon = -1;
          nfa_state_table[i].second_transition_on_epsilon = -1;
```

```
            nfa_state_table[i].state_type = 'n';
        }
    }

// Input to the following procedure is the postfix equivalent of the input regular
// expression, which is obtained in "IN_POST.h" as 'output_string'. Hence, the same
// name is carried here to the parameter. This procedure constructs the state
// transition table for the equivalent NFA with epsilon-moves.

void construct_NFA(char* output_string)
{
        void NFA_for_symbol (char c);
        void concatenation();
        void parallel_paths();
        void closure();

        int i  = 0;
        while (output_string[i] != '\0')
        {
            switch (output_string[i])
            {
                case 'a'     :
                case 'b'     :   NFA_for_symbol(output_string[i]);
                                 break;
                case '.'     :   concatenation();
                                 break;
                case '+'     :   parallel_paths();
                                 break;
                case '*'     :   closure();
                                 break;
            }
            i++ ;
        }

        final_state = (int)pop();
        nfa_state_table[final_state].state_type = 'f';
        initial_state = (int)pop();
        nfa_state_table [initital_state].state_type = 'i';
}

// The following procedure creates a minimal NFA with only two states, with
// transition from one state to the other on the input symbol 'a' or 'b'.

void NFA_for_symbol(char c)
{
        push((void *)current_state_number);
        push((void *)(current_state_number + 1));
        if (C == 'a')
            nfa_state_table[current_state_number].transition_on_a
                                = current_state_number + 1;
        else if (c == 'b')
```

```
        nfa_state_table [current_state_number].transition_on_b
                        = current_state_number + 1;

        current_state_number += 2;
}

// Procedure for connecting two NFA segments with epsilon transition from 'last'
// state of first to the 'first' state of the second. The procedure handles the
// 'series' operation in the construction of NFA with epsilon-moves.

void concatenation()
{
     int first1, first2, last1, last2;

     last2 = (int) pop(); // Operand2 appears on top of the stack.
     first2 = (int) pop();
     last1 = (int) pop();
     first1 = (int) pop();

     nfa_state_table[last1].first_transition_on_epsilon = first2;

     push((void *) first1);
     push((void *) last2);
}

// The following procedure introduces two 'parallel paths' in the construction of NFA
// with epsilon-moves. While doing this, it has to introduce two additional states, one
// which transits to the starting states of the two NFA segments on epsilon
// transitions and the other, which is reached from the ending states of these NFA
// segments on epsilon transition.

void parallel_paths()
{
     int first1, first2, last1, last2;
     last2 = (int) pop(); // Operand2 appears on top of the stack.
     first2 = (int) pop();
     last1 = (int) pop();
     first1 = (int) pop();

     push((void *) current_state_number);
     push((void *) (current_state_number + 1));

     nfa_state_table[current_state_number].first_transition_on_epsilon = first1;
     nfa_state_table[current_state_number].second_transition_on_epsilon = first2;
     nfa_state_table[last1].first_transition_on_epsilon
                          = current_state_number + 1;
     nfa_state_table [last2].first_transition_on_epsilon
                          = current_state_number + 1;

     current_state_number += 2;
```

```
}

// The following procedure performs the 'closure' operation during the construction of
// NFA with epsilon-moves. According to the rules for construction, it also
// introduces two additional states.
void closure()
{
    int first, last;

    last = (int) pop();
    first = (int) pop();

    push ((void *) current_state_number);
    push ((void *) (current_state_number + 1));
    nfa_state_table[current_state_number]
         .first_transition_on_epsilon = first;
    nfa_state_table[current_state_number]
         .second_transition_on_epsilon = current_state_number + 1;
    nfa_state_table[last].first_transition_on_epsilon = first;
    nfa_state_table[last].second_transition_on_epsilon
                                   = current_state_number + 1;
    current_state_number += 2;
}

// The following procedure displays the above-constructed state transition table for
// the equivalent NFA with epsilon-moves.
void display_NFA_state_table()
{
    int i;
    clrscr();
    printf("State transition table for NFA with epsilon-moves
              : \n\n");
    printf(" state a b epsilon\n");
    printf("______________________________\n\n");
    for (i = 0; i < current_state_number; i++)
    {
         if (nfa_state_table[i].state_type == 'n')
            printf("  %d     ", i);
         // initial state is indicated with a pointed arrow
         else if (nfa_state_table[i].state_type == 'i')
            printf("-. %d    ", i);
         // final state is indicated with a '*'
         else if (nfa_state_table [i].state_type == 'f')
            printf(" *  %d    ", i);

         if (nfa_state_table[i].transition_on_a != -1)
            printf("(%d)", nfa_state_table[i].transition_on_a);
         else
            printf("   -   "); // '-1' indicates no transition
```

```
            if (nfa_state_table[i].transition_on_b != -1)
               printf(" (%d)", nfa_state_table[i]. transition_on_b);
            else
               printf("   -   " ); // '-1' indicates no transition
            if (nfa_state_table[i].first_transition_on_epsilon != -1)
            {
               printf("{ %d ", nfa_state_table [i]
                           .first_transition_on_epsilon);
               if (nfa_state_table[i]
                           .second_transition_on_epsilon != -1)
               printf(", %d)\n", nfa_state_table [i]
                           .second_transition_on_epsilon) ;
               else
                           printf("}\n");
            }
            else
               printf("    -     \n");
        }
        printf("\n\n\n\n");
        printf(" ->    :  Initial state\n\n");
        printf("   *   : Final state");
}
// ------ End of RE_NFA.h
```

Program A.3, denoted by the file 'RE_NFA.h', contains six function implementations. For NFA with $\epsilon$-moves, from every state we can have any of the following:

1. One transition on $a$
2. One transition on $b$
3. One $\epsilon$-transition
4. Two $\epsilon$-transitions to some other state

The program provides the structure for an NFA state with four fields for recording these transitions and one 'state_type' field, which indicates whether the state is final, initial, or intermediate (non-final). The program also provides separate function implementations for all operations—concatenation, parallel paths, and closure—and displays the generated state transition table of the NFA.

### *Simulation of Algorithm (State Transition Table for NFA with $\epsilon$-moves)*

Let us consider the regular expression, '$( a + b \cdot b )^*$'. We have seen that its postfix equivalent form is '$a\, b\, b \cdot + *$', when represented as a string. Let us simulate the working of Program A.3 for this postfix expression.

Initially, 'current_state_number' is assigned the value 0, indicating that the initial state number is '0'. When the program reads the first character, which is $a$, it introduces two new states having state numbers '0' and '1', with transition on $a$ from state '0' to state '1'. The program pushes the state numbers '0' and '1' onto the stack and the 'current_state_number' is incremented by two. The value of 'current_state_number' is now 2, and indicates the label for the next new state. Figure A.5(a) shows the status of the stack as well as the state transition table of the NFA after reading the first character, that is, *a*.

Now, from the string '*a b b* · + *', the program reads the second character, *b*. This time also it performs similar actions—it introduces two new states '2' and '3' with transition on *b* from state '2' to state '3'.

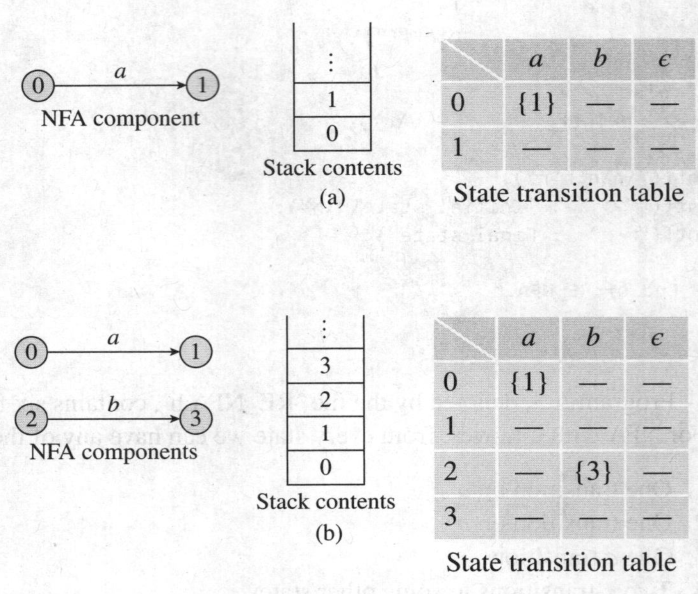


| | a | b | ϵ |
|---|---|---|---|
| 0 | {1} | — | — |
| 1 | — | — | — |

| | a | b | ϵ |
|---|---|---|---|
| 0 | {1} | — | — |
| 1 | — | — | — |
| 2 | — | {3} | — |
| 3 | — | — | — |

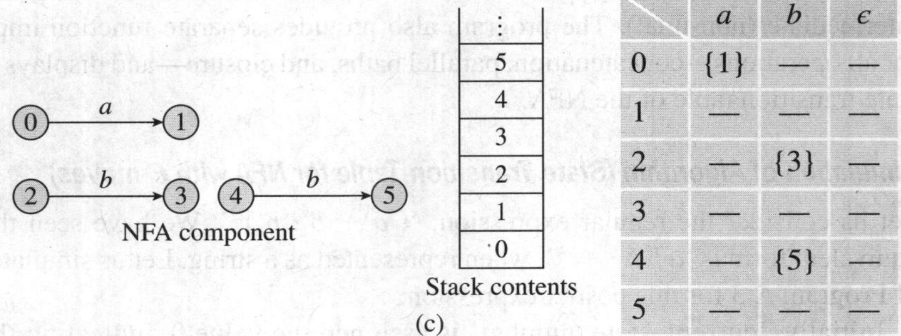


| | a | b | ϵ |
|---|---|---|---|
| 0 | {1} | — | — |
| 1 | — | — | — |
| 2 | — | {3} | — |
| 3 | — | — | — |
| 4 | — | {5} | — |
| 5 | — | — | — |

**Figure A.5** Construction of NFA with $\epsilon$-moves (a) After reading the first character, *a*, from '*a b b* · + *' (b) After reading the second character, *b*, from '*a b b* · + *' (c) After reading the third character, *b*, from '*a b b* · + *'

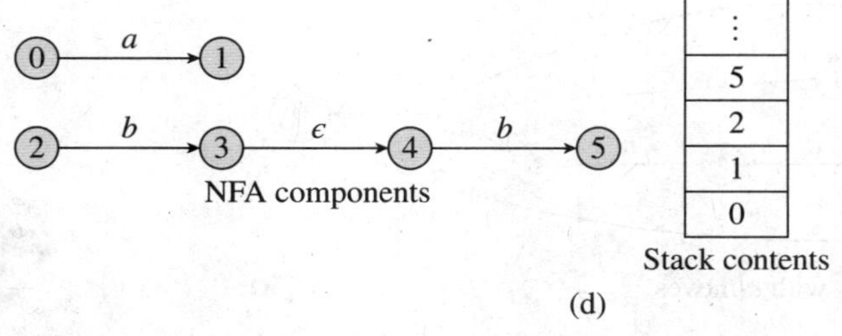


| | $a$ | $b$ | $\epsilon$ |
|---|---|---|---|
| 0 | {1} | — | — |
| 1 | — | — | — |
| 2 | — | {3} | — |
| 3 | — | — | {4} |
| 4 | — | {5} | — |
| 5 | — | — | — |

State transition table

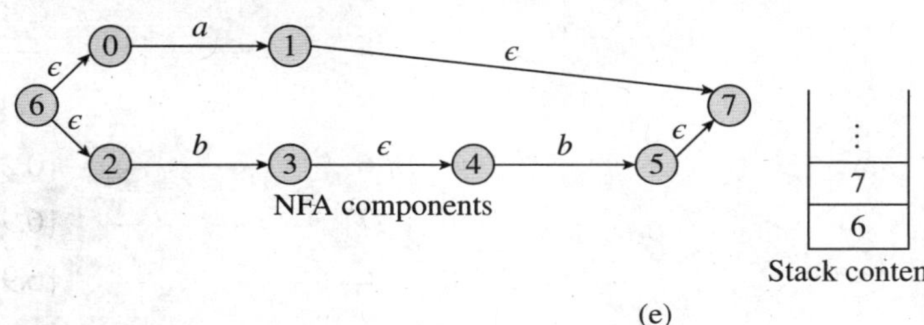


| | $a$ | $b$ | $\epsilon$ |
|---|---|---|---|
| 0 | {1} | — | — |
| 1 | — | — | {7} |
| 2 | — | {3} | — |
| 3 | — | — | {4} |
| 4 | — | {5} | — |
| 5 | — | — | {7} |
| 6 | — | — | {0.2} |
| 7 | — | — | — |

State transition table

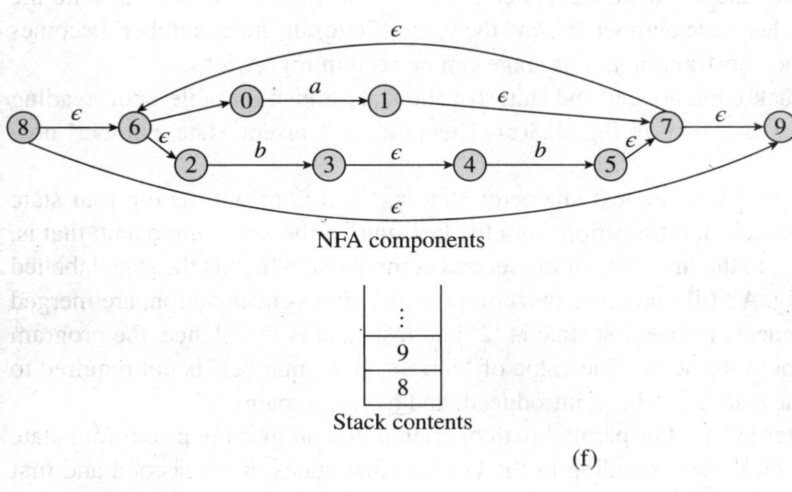


| | $a$ | $b$ | $\epsilon$ |
|---|---|---|---|
| 0 | {1} | — | — |
| 1 | — | — | {7} |
| 2 | — | {3} | — |
| 3 | — | — | {4} |
| 4 | — | {5} | — |
| 5 | — | — | {7} |
| 6 | — | — | {0.2} |
| 7 | — | — | {6.9} |
| 8 | — | — | {6.9} |
| 9 | — | — | — |

State transition table

**Figure A.5** (*Continued*) (d) After reading the fourth character, '.', from '$a\ b\ b \cdot + *$' (e) After reading the fifth character '+' from '$a\ b\ b \cdot + *$' (f) After reading the last character '*' from '$a\ b\ b \cdot + *$'

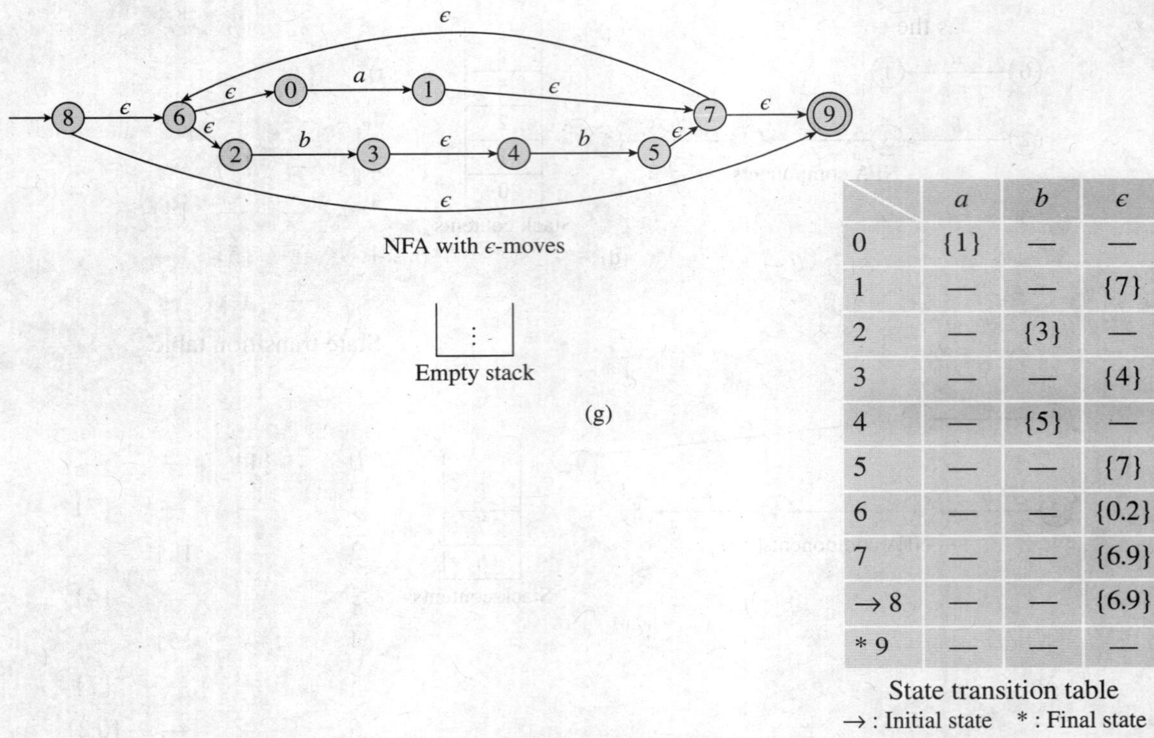


| | $a$ | $b$ | $\epsilon$ |
|---|---|---|---|
| 0 | {1} | — | — |
| 1 | — | — | {7} |
| 2 | — | {3} | — |
| 3 | — | — | {4} |
| 4 | — | {5} | — |
| 5 | — | — | {7} |
| 6 | — | — | {0.2} |
| 7 | — | — | {6.9} |
| → 8 | — | — | {6.9} |
| * 9 | — | — | — |

**Figure A.5** (*Continued*) (g) After reading the entire string '*a b b* · + *'

It pushes the start state of this new NFA component, that is, state number '2' onto the stack along with the last state number '3', and the value of current_state_number' becomes '4'. The status of the construction at this stage can be seen in Fig. A.5(b).

Similarly, the stack contents and the status of the state transition table upon reading the third character *b*, is shown in Fig. A.5(c). The value of 'current_state_number' now becomes '6'.

When the program reads the next character, that is, '·', it pops out the top four state numbers, and introduces an $\epsilon$-transition from the last state of the first component, that is, the state labelled '3', to the first state of the second component, which is the state labelled '4'. We see from Fig. A.5(d) that these two components, after concatenation, are merged into a single component, whose first state is '2' and last state is '5'. Hence, the program inserts '2' and '5' onto the stack. The value of 'current_state_number' is not required to be modified as no new state has been introduced, and hence, remains '6'.

The next character is '+'. For parallel path operation, the program pops out four state numbers from the stack corresponding to the last and first states of the second and first NFA components respectively, as they are required for the operation. Next, it introduces two new states '6' and '7' and four $\epsilon$-transitions: from '6' to '0'; from '6' to '2'; from '1' to '7'; and from '5' to '7', as shown in Fig. A.5(e). After performing the parallel path operation, the program generates only one component with '6' as the starting state and

'7' as the ending state. It also pushes '6' and '7' onto the stack. Since two new states are introduced, the value of 'current_state_number' is incremented to 8.

Finally, the program reads the last character '*', that is, the closure operator. It pops two state numbers from the stack—'7', which is the ending state, and '6', which is the start state of the component for which the closure is to be obtained. It introduces two new states '8' and '9', and four $\epsilon$-transitions: from '8' to '6'; from '8' to '9'; from '7' to '6'; and from '7' to '9'. The NFA component after the closure operation is shown in Fig. A.5(f) with '8' as the start state and '9' as the ending state. The program pushes '8' and '9' onto the stack and increments the value of 'current_state_number' to '10', since two new states have been introduced.

The program then detects the end of the string. Hence, it pops the state number '9' from the stack and marks it as the final state. It then pops state number '8' and declares it as the initial state of the NFA with $\epsilon$-moves; this leaves the stack empty. The program then displays the state transition table for the NFA with $\epsilon$-moves, which is equivalent to the input regular expression, as shown in Fig. A.5(g).

### A.2.5 Construction of DFA

Now the final step is to obtain a DFA equivalent to the NFA with $\epsilon$-moves generated in the previous section. For this, we shall use the method discussed in Chapter 2 (refer to Section 2.9.2). In this method, the DFA is directly constructed from the given NFA with $\epsilon$-moves, without constructing the NFA without $\epsilon$-moves.

The method collects all reachable states from a given state. Reachable states are the states '$q$' to which there exists at least one path from the current state, labelled by '$\epsilon$'; in other words, the set of reachable states of a given state is the collection of all states '$q$', which are at zero distance from the given state.

#### *Algorithm for Construction of DFA*

**Input:** State transition table of NFA with $\epsilon$-moves
**Output:** State transition table of the equivalent DFA

The following is the required algorithm:

1. Consider the initial state of the NFA with $\epsilon$-moves as the initial state of the equivalent DFA.
2. Collect all reachable states from the current state.
3. Consider all reachable states and find a transition on $a$ and $b$ from the current state.
4. Obtain the next state for the transition on $a$ from the current state. The label for this new state may contain one or more state numbers, depending on whether the current state makes a transition to a single state, or more than one state, on input $a$.
5. Check whether this next state is already present in the state transition table for the DFA or not.
   (a) If already present, just introduce a transition on $a$ from the current state to this state in the table.
   (b) If the next state is not already present, then introduce the next state as a new state in the state transition table of the DFA with the next consecutive state number; and introduce a transition on $a$ from the current state to this new state.

6. Repeat steps 4 and 5 for obtaining transition on symbol *b*.
7. Check whether or not there is any new state in the state transition table of the DFA. If yes, make that next consecutive new state as the current state and go to Step 2.
8. If no new state is left for processing (i.e., for finding transitions) in the state transition table of the DFA, then halt.

### *Implementation of Algorithm (DFA Construction)*

Program A.4 is the 'C' implementation for the algorithm discussed in the previous section for obtaining the equivalent state transition table of the DFA from the input state transition table of the NFA with $\epsilon$-moves.

**Program A.4** Construction of the DFA

```
// ------ RE_DFA.c

// This program deals with the construction of an equivalent
// DFA from the given regular expression.

#include "RE_NFA.h" // Required for obtaining equivalent NFA with epsilon-moves
// from given regular expression. While obtaining DFA from NFA with epsilon-moves,
// the state 'label' may contain multiple symbols. 'Reachable_states' are the states,
// which are at zero distance (paths labelled by 'epsilon') from the current state.

Struct dfa_state
{
     int label[LABEL_LENGTH];
     int reachable_states[REACHABLE_STATE_COUNT];
     int transition_on_a;
     int transition_on_b;
     char state_type;
};
struct dfa_state dfa_state_table[TABLE_SIZE];

void main(void)
{
     void initialize_dfa_state_table();
     void construct_DFA();

     char *input_string, *output_string;

     clrscr();
     printf("Enter the regular expression :    ");
     gets(input_string);

     initialize();              // Defined in "STACK.h".
     infix_to_postfix(input_string, output_string); // Defined in "IN_POST.h".
     printf("\n\nPostfix form of the input expression is : %s", output_string);
     getch();
     initialize();                  // Defined in "STACK.h".
```

```
    initialize_nfa_state_table();   // Defined in "RE_NFA.h".
    construct_NFA(output_string);   // Defined in "RE_NFA.h".
    display_NFA_state_table();      // Defined in "RE_NFA.h".
    getch();

    clrscr();
    initialize();                   // Defined in 'STACK.h'.
    initialize_dfa_state_table();
    construct_DFA();
    getch();
}

// The following procedure initializes all labels, reachable_states, and transitions
// to '-1' in the state transition table for the DFA, and initially marks all states as
// non-final states, i.e., 'state_type' = 'n'.

void initialize_dfa_state_table ()
{
    int i, j;

    for (i = 0; i < TABLE_SIZE; i++)
    {
        for (j = 0; j < LABEL_LENGTH; j++)
            dfa_state_table[i].label[j] = -1;
        for (j = 0; j < REACHABLE_STATE_COUNT; j++)
            dfa_state_table [i].reachable_states [j] = -1;

        dfa_state_table[i].transition_on_a = -1;
        dfa_state_table[i].transition_on_b = -1;
        dfa_state_table[i].state_type = 'n';
    }
}

// The following procedure constructs the state transition table for the equivalent
// DFA from the input NFA with epsilon-moves.
void construct_DFA ()
{
    void reachable_state_collection(int label[], int reachable_states[], int index);
    void find_transition(int label[], int i, int flag);
    int search_state (int label[], int j);
    void display_DFA_state_table (int j);

    int i = 0, j = 1;
    dfa_state_table[0].label[0] = initial_state;

    while (dfa_state_table[i].label[0]!= -1)
    {
        int a, label[LABEL_LENGTH];
        reachable_state_collection(dfa_state_table[i].label,
```

```
                dfa_state_table[i].reachable_states, i);

            find_transition(label, i, 0); // 0 ==> transition on 'a'.
            if (label[0] != -1)
            {
                a = search_state(label, j);
                if ( a != -1 )
                            dfa_state_table[i].transition_on_a = a;
                else
                {
                            int k;
                            for (k = 0; k < LABEL_LENGTH; k++)
                                dfa_state_table[j].label[k] = label[k];
                            dfa_state_table[i].transition_on_a = j;
                            j++;
                }
            }
            find_transition(label, i, 1); //1 ==> transition on 'b'.

            if (label[0] != -1)
            {
                a = search_state(label, j);

                if (a != -1)
                 dfa_state_table[i].transition_on_b = a;
                else
                {
                            int k;
                            for (k = 0; k < 10; k++)
                                dfa_state_table[j].label[k] = label[k];
                            dfa_state_table[i].transition_on_b = j;
                            j++;
                }
            }
            i++;
        }

        display_DFA_state_table(j);
}

// The following procedure collects all the reachable states for
// the current state, i.e., it collects the states at
// zero distance (paths labelled by 'epsilon') from the
// current state.

void reachable_state_collection (int label[], int reachable_states[], int index)
{
        int i = 0, j, k;

        while {label[i] != -1)
        {
```

```
            j = 0;
            if (nfa_state_table[label[i])
                            .first_transition_on_epsilon != -1)
            {
               reachable_states[j] = nfa_state_table[label[i])
                                    .first_transition_on_epsilon;
               if (reachable_states[j] == final_state)
                            dfa_state_table[index].state_type = 'f';
               j++;
            }

            if (nfa_state_table[label[i]]
                                    .second_transition_on_epsilon != -1)
            {
               reachable_states[j] = nfa_state_table[label[i]]
                                    .second_transition_on_epsilon;
               if (reachable_states[j] == final_state)
                             dfa_state_table[index].state_type = 'f')
               j++;
            }

            k = 0;
            while (reachable_states[k] != -1)
            {
               int temp = reachable_states[k];
               if (nfa_state_table[temp]
                                  .first_transition_on_epsilon != -1)
               {
                            reachable_states[j] = nfa_state_table[temp]
                                   .first_transition_on_epsilon;
                            if (reachable_states[j] == final_state)
                                   dfa_state_table[index].state_type = 'f';
                            j++;
               }
               if (nfa_state_table [temp]
                                  .second_transition_on_epsilon != -1)
               {
                            reachable_states[j] = nfa_state_table[temp]
                                  .second_transition_on_epsilon ;
                            if ( reachable_states[j] == final_state )
                                    dfa_state_table[index].state_type = 'f';
                            j++;
               }
               k++;
            }
            i++;
       }
  }

  // The following procedure determines the next state of the transition from the
  // current state on input symbol 'a' or 'b'; 'flag' value '0' indicates that the next
```

```
// state for transition on 'a' is to be obtained; 'flag' value '1' indicates that the
// next state for transition on 'b' is to be obtained.
void find_transition(int label[], int i, int flag)
{
      int j, temp, k = 0;

      for (j = 0; j < 10; j++)
            label [ j ] = -1;

            switch (flag)
            {
               case 0:
               {
                           j = 0;
                           while (dfa_state_table[i]
                                             .reachable_states[j] != -1)
                               {
                                   temp = dfa_state_table[i]
                                             .reachable_states[j];
                                   if (nfa_state_table[temp]
                                             .transition_on_a != -1)
                                   {
                                     label[k] = nfa_state_table[temp]
                                                      .transition_on_a;
                                     k++;
                                   }
                                   j++;
                           }
                           break;
               }
               case 1:
               {
                  j = 0;
                  while (dfa_state_table[i].reachable_states[j] != -1)
               {
                           temp = dfa_state_tabel[i]
                                  .reachable_states[j];
                           if (nfa_state_table[temp].transition_on_b != -1)
                           {
                               label[k] = nfa_state_table[temp]
                                             .transition_on_b;
                               k++;
                           }
                           j++;
               }
               break;
            }
      }
}

// The following procedure checks whether the state specified by 'label' already
```

```
// exists or not. If it already exists, it returns the state number from the state
// transition table; else it returns '-1', indicating that the state does not exist
// and must be created.

int search_state(int label[], int j)
{
      int i, flag, k;
      for (i = 0, i < j; i++)
      {
            for (k = 0; k < LABEL_LENGTH; k++)
            {
               if (label[k] == dfa_state_tabel[i].label[k])
                          flag = 1;
                  else
                  {
                          flag = 0;
                          break;
                  }
            }

            if (flag == 1)
                 return(i);

      }
      return (-1);
}

// The following procedure displays the state transition table for the equivalent DFA.
void display_DFA_state_table(int j)
{
      int i;
      clrscr();
      printf ("State transition table for the resultant DFA:\n\n");
      printf ("  State a  b  \n");
      printf ("________________________\n\n");

      for (i = 0; i < j; i++)
      {
            if (i == 0)
               printf ("->");
            if (dfa_state_table[i].state_type == 'n')
               printf ("\t%d    ",  i);
            else if (dfa_state_tabel[i].state_type == 'f')
               printf ("*\t%d   ",  i);
            if (dfa_state_table [i].transition_on_a != -1)
               printf ("(%d)",dfa_state_tabel[i].transition_on_a);
            else
               printf ("  -                    ");
            if (dfa_state_table[i].transition_on_b != -1)
               printf ("{%d}\n",dfa_state_table[i].transition_on_b);
```

```
        else
            printf ("  -\n");
    }

    printf ( "\n\n\n\n" )  ;
    printf ( " ->  :     Initial state\n\n" ) ;
    printf ( "  *        :   Final state" ) ;
}

// ------ End of RE_DFA.c
```

The name of this program file is 'RE_DFA.c'. The file contains many function implementations, out of which 'construct_DFA' is the main function, as it deals with the process of building the state transition table for the DFA. For the construction, this function relies on other functions, as mentioned here:

1. 'reachable_state_collection', which searches for the reachable states from the current state;
2. 'find_transition', which finds the next state for the transitions on either *a* or *b* from the current state; and
3. 'search_state', which checks whether a given state already exists or not.

After generating the state transition table for the equivalent DFA, the program also displays the table in a proper format.

### *Simulation of Algorithm (DFA Construction)*

Let us simulate the working of Program A.4 for the NFA with $\epsilon$-moves constructed in the previous simulation (refer to Fig. A.5g).

We shall begin with the initial state '8' of the NFA (see Table A.3) with $\epsilon$-moves that we have constructed earlier. This state becomes the initial state (state '0') of the resultant DFA.

**Table A.3** DFA construction for Program A.4

| State no. | State label | Reachable states | Transition on *a* | Transition on *b* | State type |
|---|---|---|---|---|---|
| 0 | 8 | 6, 9, 0, 2 | 1 | 2 | Final |
| (State '0' of the resultant DFA is a final state because the final state of the NFA, i.e., '9' is reachable from this DFA state) | | | | | |
| 1 | 1 | 7, 6, 9, 0, 2 | 1 | 2 | Final |
| (Similarly, this state is also a final state of the resultant DFA) | | | | | |
| 2 | 3 | 4 | — | 3 | Non-final |
| 3 | 5 | 7, 6, 9, 0, 2 | 1 | 2 | Final |
| (Similarly, this is also a final state of the resultant DFA) | | | | | |

The program first considers the initial state '8' of the given NFA with $\epsilon$-moves and labels it as state '0' for the resultant DFA. It then calculates the reachable states from this state. We see from the state transition table for the NFA (refer to Fig. A.5g) that from state '8' there are transitions to states '6' and '9' on symbol '$\epsilon$'. Therefore, these states are reachable from '8'. Similarly, from state '6', the states '0' and '2' are reachable. Therefore, they are also reachable from '8'. Thus, the program considers {6, 9, 0, 2} as the set of reachable states from state '0' of the equivalent DFA. These reachable states are now used to find the transitions on $a$ and $b$.

Out of '6', '9', '0', and '2' only '0' makes a transition to '1' on reading $a$. The state with label '1' does not exist in the DFA table; therefore, state '1' with label '1' is added to the state transition table of the DFA. Similarly, on reading $b$ we obtain a new DFA state '2' with label '3'. For these new states, the program repeats the same process of finding reachable states and transitions.

The program halts with only four states in the DFA table. The transition graph and state transition table for the DFA are shown in Fig. A.6.

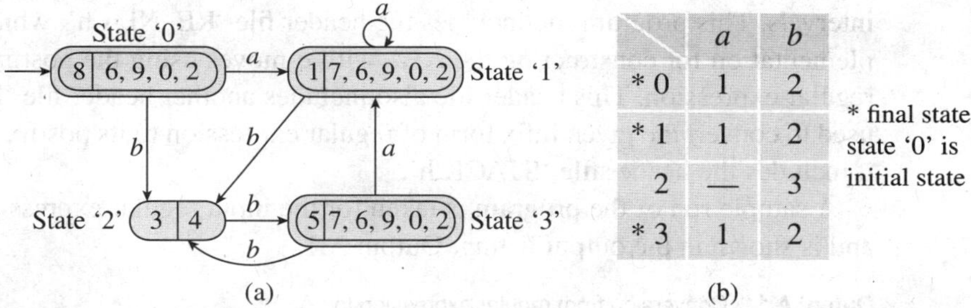


| | $a$ | $b$ |
|---|---|---|
| * 0 | 1 | 2 |
| * 1 | 1 | 2 |
| 2 | — | 3 |
| * 3 | 1 | 2 |

**Figure A.6** Resultant DFA (a) Transition graph of DFA (b) State transition table of DFA

## A.2.6 Program Execution (Conversion from Regular Expression to DFA)

For constructing a DFA equivalent to a given regular expression, we have broken the problem statement into four modules and executed them in sequence; this is depicted in Fig. A.7.

Out of the four modules, the 'stack implementation' module is a supporting module required by the 'postfix conversion' module as well as by the 'NFA with $\epsilon$-moves construction' module.

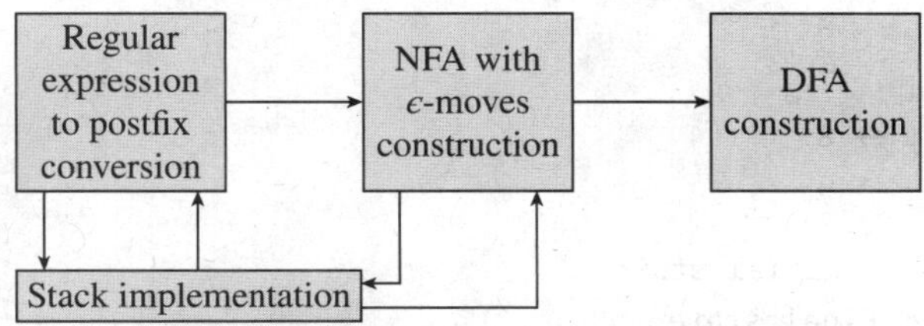


**Figure A.7** Program building blocks (RE to DFA conversion)

We have seen four program files for all these four modules. These are shown in Table A.4.

**Table A.4** Program files for modules in Fig. A.7

| Module | Program file name |
|---|---|
| Stack implementation | 'STACK.h' |
| Infix to postfix conversion for given regular expression | 'IN_POST.h' |
| Regular expression (postfix form) to NFA with $\epsilon$-moves conversion | 'RE_NFA.h' |
| NFA with $\epsilon$-moves to DFA conversion | 'RE_DFA.c' |

'RE_DFA.c' is the main program that is executed for getting the output DFA. It takes care of reading the input regular expression and initiating different functions at specific intervals. This program file includes the header file 'RE_NFA.h', which includes the implementation for constructing the NFA with $\epsilon$-moves using the postfix form of the input regular expression. This header file also includes another header file 'IN_POST.h' that is used to convert the given infix form of regular expression to its postfix equivalent; for that it includes the header file 'STACK.h'.

A sample run of the program is taken for the input regular expression '$( a + b \cdot b )^*$' and is shown in the output listing, Output A.1.

**Output A.1** Conversion from regular expression to FA

```
Enter the regular expression: (a+b·b)*
Postfix form of the input expression is: abb·+*
State transition table for NFA with epsilon-moves:

      State         a            b            epsilon
    ------------------------------------------------------
        0         { 1 }          -               -
        1           -            -             { 7 }
        2           -          { 3 }             -
        3           -            -             { 4 }
        4           -          { 5 }             -
        5           -            -             { 7 }
        6           -            -           { 0 , 2 }
        7           -            -           { 6  , 9 }
      → 8           -            -           { 6 , 9 }
      * 9           -            -               -

  → : Initial state
  * : Final state
```

```
State transition table for resultant DFA:
   State              a              b
-----------------------------------------
 → * 0              { 1 }          { 2 }
   * 1              { 1 }          { 2 }
     2                -            { 3 }
   * 3              { 1 }          { 2 }

→ : Initial state
* : Final state
```

## A.3 CONVERSION FROM REGULAR GRAMMAR TO FINITE AUTOMATA

As we know, regular grammar generates regular language. We can design a finite automaton (FA), which can accept a regular language generated by any regular grammar. Further, we have seen in Chapter 5 (refer to Section 5.11.4) that regular grammar is classified as right-linear grammar and left-linear grammar. In this section, we construct an FA that accepts the language generated by an input right-linear grammar.

Since it is possible to convert a given left-linear grammar to its equivalent right-linear grammar (refer to Chapter 5, Section 5.12.2), we may also construct an FA that accepts a language generated by a left-linear grammar. However, the conversion code for this is left to the reader.

In the next section, we shall discuss the conversion method for obtaining an equivalent left-linear grammar from a given right-linear grammar. The reader may refer to this implementation and write a similar conversion method for obtaining an equivalent right-linear grammar from a given left-linear grammar.

### A.3.1 Representation

For implementing the construction of the FA, the input is going to be a right-linear grammar. As we know, right-linear grammar consists of a set of productions of the form given here:

$$A \to w\,B,\ A \to w, \text{ or } A \to \epsilon,$$

where $A$ and $B$ are non-terminals and $w$ is any string of terminals.

For our implementation, we shall only consider the following types of productions:

$$A \to w\,B, \text{ or } A \to w,$$

where $A$ and $B$ are non-terminals, and $w$ is any single terminal and can either be $a$ or $b$. This means that $w \in \Sigma$, where, $\Sigma = \{a, b\}$. Thus, the input right-linear grammar generates a regular language over the alphabet $\Sigma = \{a, b\}$.

Let us consider the following example grammar over the given alphabet:

$$S \to b\,B$$
$$B \to b\,C \mid a\,B \mid b\,B \mid b$$
$$C \to a$$

The aforementioned grammar is a simplified form of the following set of productions:

$$S \rightarrow b\,B$$
$$B \rightarrow b\,C$$
$$B \rightarrow a\,B$$
$$B \rightarrow b\,B$$
$$B \rightarrow b$$
$$C \rightarrow a$$

This grammar can now be represented in matrix form with each row representing a production as shown in Fig. A.8. The start symbol is stored at the position (0, 0) in the matrix.

### A.3.2 Grammar Input

Program A.5 provides the implementation of the input function for the right-linear grammar. The grammar is represented as a two-dimensional array (matrix) of characters, as shown in Fig. A.8.

**Program A.5** Procedure to input right-linear grammar

```
// ------ GRAMMAR.h

// This header defines how to input the right-linear grammar.

int n;
char grammar[MAX_PRODUCTION_COUNT][MAX_PRODUCTION_LENGTH];
// Productions stored in a matrix form.

// The following is the procedure to input the right-linear grammar.

void input()
{
    int i, j;
    char c;
    printf ("Enter the number of production rules: ");
    scanf ("%d", &n);
    printf ("\nProduction rules :\n");
    flushall();
    gotoxy( 1, 7 );
    for (i = 0; i < n; i++)
    {
        c = getchar ();
        flushall();
        if (c != '\n')
        {
           gotoxy (3 , 7 + i);
           printf (" -> ");
        }
```

```
            j = 0;
            while (c != '\n')
            {
                grammar[i][j] = c;
                j++;
                c = getchar();
            }
            grammar[i][j] = '\0' ;
        }
}
// ------ END of GRAMMAR.h
```

| | | | |
|---|---|---|---|
| *S* | *b* | *B* | \0 |
| *B* | *b* | *C* | \0 |
| *B* | *a* | *B* | \0 |
| *B* | *b* | *B* | \0 |
| *B* | *b* | \0 | |
| *C* | *a* | \0 | |

**Figure A.8** Grammar stored in matrix form

The header file 'GRAMMAR.h' includes one function named 'input', which takes the input—the right-linear grammar—from the user and stores it in the form of a matrix as shown in Fig. A.8.

### A.3.3 Construction of NFA from Right-linear Grammar

From the input right-linear grammar, we can directly construct an NFA. Suppose, there is a production of the form, '$A \rightarrow a\ B$', then we obtain the NFA component having two states labelled *A* and *B*, and show the transition from *A* to *B* on terminal symbol *a*.

#### *Algorithm*

We see from Fig. A.8 that if a production is of the form '$A \rightarrow a\ B$', then the row in the matrix contains three characters; and if the production is of the form '$A \rightarrow a$', then the row in the matrix representing the production contains only two characters.

The algorithm for NFA construction can be stated as follows:

1. Declare state '0' in the state transition table as the final state by assigning label '#'.
2. Consider state '1' as the initial state and label it with the start symbol of the grammar, which is stored at position (0, 0) in the matrix.
3. For the current production rule, read the non-terminal symbol, for example, $S_1$, on the left-hand side (initially, the first production, whose left-hand side is the start symbol).
4. Search the state transition table to check whether there is a state labelled by this non-terminal symbol. If it is not there in the state transition table of the NFA, then add it to the table.
5. Check the production type—whether it is of the form '$A \rightarrow a\ B$' or '$A \rightarrow a$'.
   (a) If production is of the form '$A \rightarrow a\ B$', then search the table for a state labelled, say $S_2$. If it is not there, then add it to the table, and introduce a transition from $S_1$ to $S_2$ on input *a*.
   (b) If production is of the form '$A \rightarrow a$', then $S_2$ should be the final state, that is, state '0'. Then, introduce a transition from $S_1$ to the final state on symbol *a*.

6. Make the next production as the current production and go to step 3. If there is no new production left for processing, then stop.

### *Implementation of Algorithm (NFA Construction)*

Program A.6 provides the implementation for the construction of the NFA from the input right-linear grammar.

**Program A.6** Construction of NFA from the input right-linear grammar

```
// ------ RG_NFA.h

// This header file deals with the construction of an equivalent NFA from the given
// right-linear grammar. For an NFA, there may be more than one transition on 'a'
// as well as on 'b'.

struct nfa_state
{
      char state_label;
      int transition_on_a[MAX_NO_OF_TRANSITIONS];
      int transition_on_b[MAX_NO_OF_TRANSITIONS];
      char state_type;
};

struct nfa_state nfa_state_table [TABLE_SIZE];
int state_count; // Number of states for constructed NFA.

// Initialize all transitions to '-1' and mark initially all states as non-final
// states, i.e., state_type = 'n'.

void initialize_nfa_state_table(struct nfa_state dummy_table[])
{
      int i, j;
      for (i = 0 ; i < TABLE_SIZE; i++)
      {
            for (j = 0; j < 10; j++)
            {
               dummy_table[i].transition_on_a[j] = -1;
               dummy_table[i].transition_on_b[j] = -1;
            }
            dummy_table [i].state_type = 'n';
      }
}

// The following procedure constructs a state transition table for the equivalent
// NFA from the input right-linear grammar.
void construct_NFA()
{
      int search_table(char symbol, int j);
      int i, j, k, state_1, state_2;
```

```
    j = 0;
    nfa_state_table[j].state_label = '#';        // Final state
    nfa_state_table[j].state_type = 'f';

    j++;
    nfa_state_table[j].state_label = grammar [0][0]; // Initial state
    nfa_state_table[j].state_type = 'i';

    j++;
    i = 0;

    do
    {
         state_1 = search_table(grammar[i][0], j);
         if (grammar[ i ][ 2 ] != '\0')
         {
            state_2 = search_table(grammar[i][2], j);
            if  (state_2 == -1);
            {
                nfa_state_table[j].state_label = grammar[i][2];
                state_2 = j;
                j++;
            }
         }
         else
            state_2 = 0;

         switch (grammar [i][1])
         {
            case 'a':
            {
                    k = 0;
                    while (nfa_state_table[state_1].transition_on_a [k] != -1)
                         k++;
                    nfa_state_table [state_1].transition_on_a[k] = state_2;
                    break;
            }

            case 'b':
            {
                    k = 0;
                    while (nfa_state_table[state_1] .transition_on_b [k] != -1)
                         k++;
                    nfa_state_table [state_1].transition_on_b[k] = state_2;
                    break;
            }
         }
         i++;
    } while (i ! = n);
    state_count = j;    // Total number of states for the constructed NFA.
}
```

```
// The following procedure checks whether or not the state with label <symbol>
// already exists. If it already exists, then its state number is returned in the
// table; else it returns '-1', indicating that it is not present and needs to
// be created.
int search_table (char symbol, int j)
{
      int i = 0;

      while (i < j)
      {
            if (nfa_state_table[i].state_label == symbol)
                return(i);
            else
                i++;
      }
      return(-1);
}
//_------ END of RG_NFA.h
```

The header file 'RG_NFA.h' contains three function implementations, out of which one is the initialization procedure. The major function in this program is 'construct_NFA', which actually deals with the NFA construction according to the algorithm we discussed in the previous section. The 'search_table' function searches for a state with a particular label in the generated state transition table and returns the state number if the state is found; else it returns '$-1$', indicating no such state is present at that stage in the existing state transition table.

### *Simulation of Algorithm for NFA Construction*

Let us simulate the working of Program A.6 for the following right-linear grammar:

0. $S \rightarrow a\,A$
1. $S \rightarrow b\,B$
2. $A \rightarrow a\,C$
3. $A \rightarrow b\,A$
4. $A \rightarrow a$
5. $B \rightarrow b\,B$
6. $B \rightarrow b\,A$
7. $B \rightarrow b$
8. $C \rightarrow a$
9. $C \rightarrow a\,A$

Observe that the productions are numbered from '0' to '9'. Initially, the program creates two states—state '0', which is the final state of the resultant NFA, labelled as '#'; and state '1', which is the initial state and labelled by the start symbol, that is, $S$ for the example grammar (refer to Fig. A.9a).

When the program processes the production '0', that is, production '$S \rightarrow a\,A$', it introduces a new state '2' labelled as '$A$', along with a transition from state '1' to state '2' on symbol $a$ (refer to Fig. A.9b).

On reading the next production, that is, production '1', which is '$S \rightarrow b\,B$', the program adds a new state '3' labelled as '$B$' and introduces a transition from state '1' to state '3' on symbol $b$. This is shown in Fig. A.9(c).

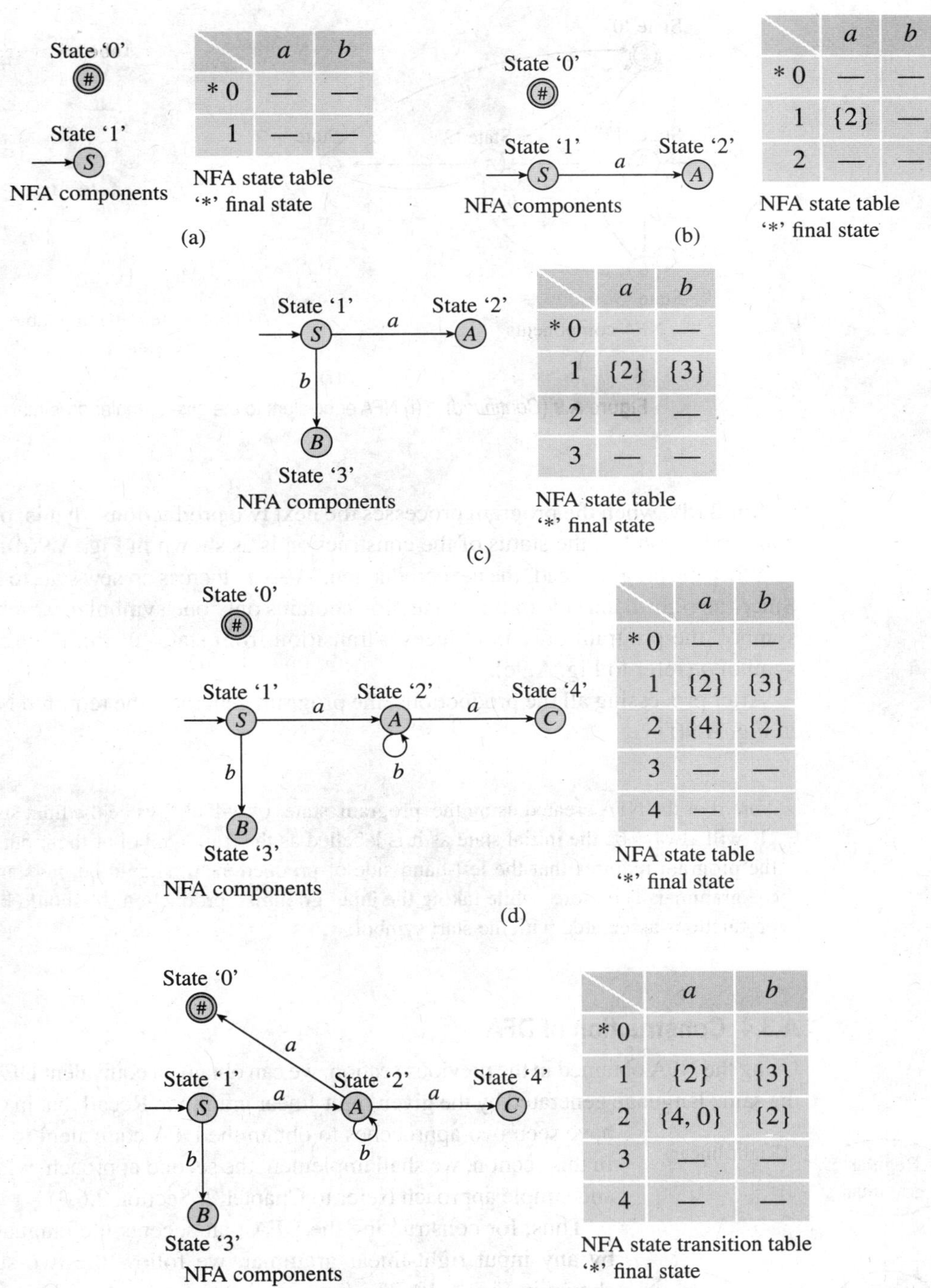


| | a | b |
|---|---|---|
| * 0 | — | — |
| 1 | — | — |

| | a | b |
|---|---|---|
| * 0 | — | — |
| 1 | {2} | — |
| 2 | — | — |

| | a | b |
|---|---|---|
| * 0 | — | — |
| 1 | {2} | {3} |
| 2 | — | — |
| 3 | — | — |

| | a | b |
|---|---|---|
| * 0 | — | — |
| 1 | {2} | {3} |
| 2 | {4} | {2} |
| 3 | — | — |
| 4 | — | — |

| | a | b |
|---|---|---|
| * 0 | — | — |
| 1 | {2} | {3} |
| 2 | {4, 0} | {2} |
| 3 | — | — |
| 4 | — | — |

**Figure A.9** NFA Construction (a) Initial status (b) After processing production '0' (c) After processing production '1' (d) After processing productions '0' to '3' (e) After processing production '4'

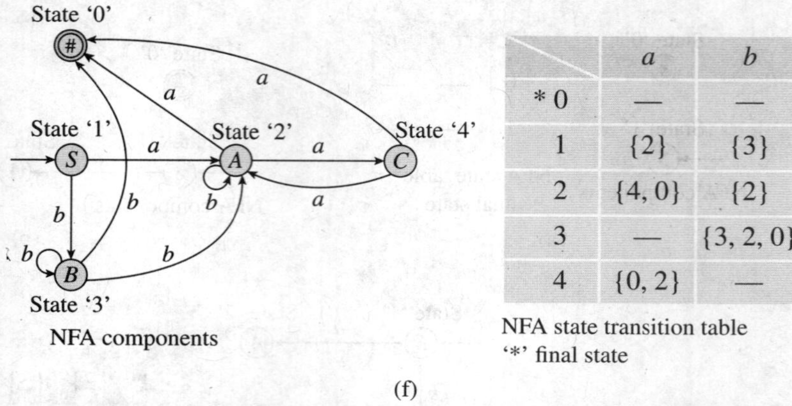


|  | $a$ | $b$ |
|---|---|---|
| * 0 | — | — |
| 1 | {2} | {3} |
| 2 | {4, 0} | {2} |
| 3 | — | {3, 2, 0} |
| 4 | {0, 2} | — |

NFA state transition table
'*' final state

(f)

**Figure A.9** (*Continued*) (f) NFA equivalent to the given regular grammar

Similarly, when the program processes the next two productions, that is, production '2' and production '3', the status of the construction is as shown in Fig. A.9(d).

When the program reads the next production, '$A \rightarrow a$', there is no new state to be introduced. Since the right-hand side of the production contains only one symbol $a$, which is a terminal symbol, the program only introduces a transition from state '2' to the final state on the symbol $a$ (refer to Fig. A.9e).

After processing all the productions, the program generates the required NFA as shown in Fig. A.9(f).

> ***Note***: For the NFA created using the program, state '0' will always be the final state and state '1' will always be the initial state as it is labelled as the start symbol of the input grammar—the program requires that the left-hand side of production '0' should be the start symbol of the grammar. Therefore, while taking the input grammar, production '0' should be one of the productions associated with the start symbol.

### A.3.4 Construction of DFA

Using the NFA obtained in the previous section, we can obtain an equivalent DFA that accepts the same language generated by the given right-linear grammar. Recall that in Chapter 2, we have seen two approaches to obtain the DFA equivalent to a given NFA. In this section, we shall implement the second approach, which is a direct and simple approach (refer to Chapter 2, Section 2.6.3).

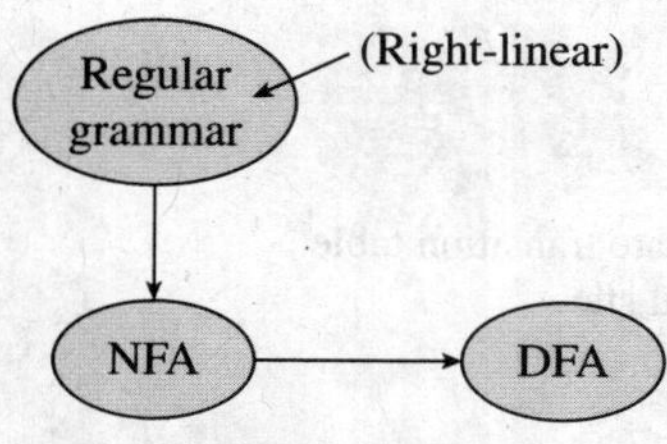


**Figure A.10** Conversion from regular grammar to FA

Thus, for constructing the DFA that accepts the language generated by any input right-linear grammar, we follow the two-step approach shown in Fig. A.10. The first step is to construct the NFA equivalent to the input right-linear grammar (as we did in the previous section) and the second step is to convert this NFA to its equivalent DFA (which we are going to discuss in this section).

### Algorithm (NFA to DFA Conversion)

The following algorithm obtains a DFA equivalent to the given NFA.

1. Create state '0' for the resultant DFA. Mark it as the initial state. Its label is the state number for the initial state of the given input NFA, that is, '1'. As discussed in the section on simulation of algorithm for NFA construction, state '1' is the initial state of the given NFA.
2. Consider state '0' as the current state.
3. Find the label for the transition from the current state to the next state on symbol *a*. This label may contain multiple state numbers depending on the fact that one NFA state might make more than one transition on the same symbol.
4. Search the state transition table of the DFA for a state with this label.
   (a) If the state is already present in the table, then add only the transition on symbol *a* from the current state to this state with the required label.
   (b) If it does not already exist, then create a new state with the required label; next, introduce a transition from the current state to this new state on symbol *a*.
   (c) If the label for this new state contains the state number for the final state of the input NFA, then mark this new state as the final state of the DFA.
5. Repeat steps 3 and 4 to find the transition on the second symbol *b*.
6. Make the next available state from the state transition table of the DFA as the current state and go to Step 3.
7. If there is no new state left (i.e, all transitions are processed), then stop.

### Implementation of Algorithm (NFA to DFA Conversion)

Program A.7 provides the implementation for the algorithm discussed in the previous section. It reads the state transition table of the NFA as input, obtains the equivalent state transition table for the required DFA, and displays it.

**Program A.7** Construction of DFA

```
// ------ RG_DFA.c

// This program constructs an equivalent DFA from the input right-linear grammar.

#include <stdio.h>
#include <conio.h>

#include "GRAMMAR.h" // Required to input the right-linear grammar.
#include "RG_NFA.h"  // Required for obtaining the NFA from the input right-linear
                     // grammar.
//    While obtaining the DFA from the NFA state, 'label' may
//    contain many symbols.
Struct dfa_state
{
      int label[LABEL_LENGTH];
      int transition_on_a;
      int transition_on_b;
      char state_type;
};
```

```
struct dfa_state  dfa_state_table[TABLE_SIZE];

void main(void)
{
      void initialize_dfa_state_table();
      void NFA_to_DFA();
      clrscr();
      printf("Right linear grammar to FA conversion:\n\n");
      input();                    // Defined in "GRAMMAR.h".
      initialize_nfa_state_table(nfa_state_table); // Defined in "RG_NFA.h".
      construct_NFA();                             // Defined in "RG_NFA.h".

      initialize_dfa_state_table();
      NFA_to_DFA();
      getch();
}

// The following procedure initializes all labels and transitions to '-1'. It also
// initializes all states as non-final states, i.e., state_type = 'n' for the state
// transition table of the required DFA.

void initialize_dfa_state_table()
{
      int i, j;
      for (i = 0; i < TABLE_SIZE; i++)
      {
            for (j = 0; j < LABEL_LENGTH; j++)
                dfa_state_table[i].label[j] = -1;
            dfa_state_table[i].transition_on_a = -1;
            dfa_state_table[i].transition_on_b = -1;
            dfa_state_table[i].state_type = 'n';
      }
}

// The following procedure constructs the state transition table for the DFA equivalent
// to the state transition table of the input NFA

void NFA_to_DFA()
{
      void find_transition(int label[], int i, int flag);
      int search_state(int label [], int j);
      void display_DFA_state_table(int j );

      int initial_state = 1, final_state = 0;
      int i = 0, j = 1;

      dfa_state_table[0].label[0] = initial_state;
      while (dfa_state_table[i].label[0] != -1)
      {
            int a, label[LABEL_LENGTH];
            find_transition(label, i, 0); // '0' ==> transition on 'a'
            if (label[0] != -1)
```

```
            {
                    a = search_state(label, j);
                    if (a != -1)
                            dfa_state_table[i].transition_on_a = a;
                    else
                    {
                            int k;
                            for (k = 0; k < LABEL_LENGTH; k++)
                            {
                                dfa_state_table[j].label[k] = label[k];
                                if (label[k] == final_state)
                                    dfa_state_table[j].state_type = 'f';
                            }
                            dfa_state_table[i].transition_on_a = j;
                            j++;
                    }
            }

            find_transition(label, i, 1); // '1' ==> transition on 'b'

            if (label[0] != -1)
            {
                a = search_state(label, j);
                if (a != -1)
                        dfa_state_table[i].transition_on_b = a;
                else
                {
                        int k;
                        for (k = 0; k < LABEL_LENGTH; k++)
                        {
                            dfa_state_tabel[j].label[k] = label[k];
                            if (label[k] == final_state)
                               dfa_state_tabel[j].state_type = 'f';
                        }
                        dfa_state_table[i].transition_on_b = j;
                        j++;
                }
            }
            i++;
    }
    display_DFA_state_table(j);
}

// The following procedure determines the next state of the transition from the
// current state on the input symbol 'a' or 'b'. If 'flag' value is '0' it indicates
// that the next state to be obtained is for the transition on symbol 'a', and if 'flag'
// value is '1' it indicates that the next state to be obtained is for the transition
// on symbol 'b'.
void find_transition(int label [], int i, int flag)
{
```

```
int is_already_present(int label[], int k, int element);
int j, temp, k = 0, m;
for (j = 0; j < 10; j++)
     label[j] = -1;

switch (flag)
{
      case 0:
      {
         j = 0;
         while (dfa_state_table[i].label[j] != -1)
         {
             temp = dfa_state_table[i].label[j];
             m = 0;
             while (nfa_state_table[temp].transition_on_a [m] != -1)
             {
                       if ( is_already_present (label, k, nfa_state_table[temp]
                              .transition_on_a [m]; == 0)
                       {
                              label[k] = nfa_state_table[temp].transition_on_a[m];
                              k++;
                       }
                       m++;
             }
             j++;
         }
         break;
      }

      case 1:
      {
         j = 0;
         while (dfa_state_table[i].label[j] != -1)
         {
             temp = dfa_state_tabel[i].label[j];
             m = 0;
             while (nfa_state_table[temp].transition_on_b [m] != -1)
             {
                       if (is_already_present(label, k, nfa_state_table[temp]
                              .transition_on_b[m]) == 0)
                       {
                           label[k] = nfa_state_tabel[temp].transition_on_b[m] ;
                           k++;
                        }
                        m++;
             }
             j++;
         }
         break;
      }
```

```
        }
    }

    // The following procedure avoids re-entering of 'element' into the label. It returns
    // '1' if 'element' is already a part of the label. Else it returns '0'.
    int is_already_present(int label [], int k, int element)
    {
        int i = 0;
        while (i < k)
        {
            if (label[i] == element)
                return(1);
            i++;
        }
        return(0);
    }

    // The following procedure checks if the given state that is specified by 'label'
    // already exists in the table or not. If it already exists, then the procedure returns
    // the state number in the state transition table. Else it returns '-1', indicating that
    // the state does not exist and needs to be created.

    int search_state(int label[], int j)
    {
        int i, flag, k;

        for (i = 0; i < j; i++)
        {
            for (k = 0; k < LABEL_LENGTH; k++)
            {
                if (label[k] == dfa_state_table[i].label[k])
                    flag = 1;
                else
                {
                    flag = 0;
                    break;
                }
            }

            if (flag == 1)
                return(i);
        }

        return (-1);
    }

    // The following procedure displays the state transition table for the resultant DFA.
    void display_DFA_state_table (int j)
    {
        int i;
        clrscr();
```

```
        printf("State transition table for resultant DFA :\n\n");
        printf("   State  a b \n" );
        printf("____________________\n\n" );
        for (i = 0; i < j; i++)
        {
             if (i == 0)
                printf ("->") ;
             if (dfa_state_table[i].state_type == 'n')
                printf("\t%d         ", i);
             else if(dfa_state_table[i].state_type == 'f')
                printf ("*\t%d       ", i);
             if (dfa_state_table[i].transition_on_a != -1)
                printf("(%d)", dfa_state_table[i].transition_on_a);
             else
                printf("     -        ");
             if (dfa_state_tabel[i].transition_on_b != -1)
                printf("(%d)\n",dfa_state_table[i].transition_on_b);
             else
                printf("        -\n" );
        }

        printf ( "\n\n\n\n" ) ;
        printf ( " ->                 :  Initial state\n\n" ) ;
        printf ( "                     *   :  Final state" ) ;
}
// ------ END of RG_DFA.c
```

The program file 'RG_DFA.c' provides many procedures and functions. Out of these, the procedure 'NFA_to_DFA' performs the major role of converting the NFA to its equivalent DFA. It is implemented according to steps in the algorithm in the previous section. Other procedures and functions perform the supporting role. For example, the 'find_transition' procedure finds the label for the next state for the transitions on *a* and *b* from the current state. The 'is_already_present' function avoids re-insertion of a state number into the label. The 'search_state' function searches for a particular state with a specified label in the state transition table of the DFA and returns the state number, if it already exists; else it returns '$-1$', indicating that a new state with this label must be created. Finally, the 'display_DFA_state_table' procedure displays the state transition table of the resultant DFA.

### *Simulation of Algorithm (NFA to DFA Conversion)*

Let us simulate the working of Program A.7 for the NFA obtained in Fig. A.9(f).

We see that the initial state of the NFA in the figure is state '1'; therefore, '1' is the label of state '0' (initial state) of the resultant DFA. Since, state '1' of the NFA transits to state '2' on input *a* and to state '3' on input *b*, '2' and '3' are labels for state '1' and state '2' of the resultant DFA, as shown in Fig. A.11(a).

The program now considers the next state, that is, state '1', as the current state in the state transition table for the required DFA. The label for this state is '2', as shown in Fig. A.11(a).

State '2' of the given NFA makes transition to {4, 0} on symbol *a*; therefore, the program creates a new state, state '3' for 4 and 0, and shows the transition from state '1' to state '3' of the DFA on symbol *a*. Similarly, state '2' of the NFA makes a transition to itself on symbol *b*. Hence, the program does not create a new state; it only adds a transition from state '1' to itself on the symbol *b*. Figure A.11(b) shows the construction of the DFA at this stage. Since state '3' includes '0'—the state number for the final state of the given NFA—it is marked as a final state.

The construction of the DFA after processing the transitions on symbols *a* and *b* from states '2' and '3', is shown in Fig. A.11(c). Since in the NFA, state '3' goes to {3, 2, 0} on input symbol *b*, state '3' in the equivalent DFA makes a transition to a new state '4',

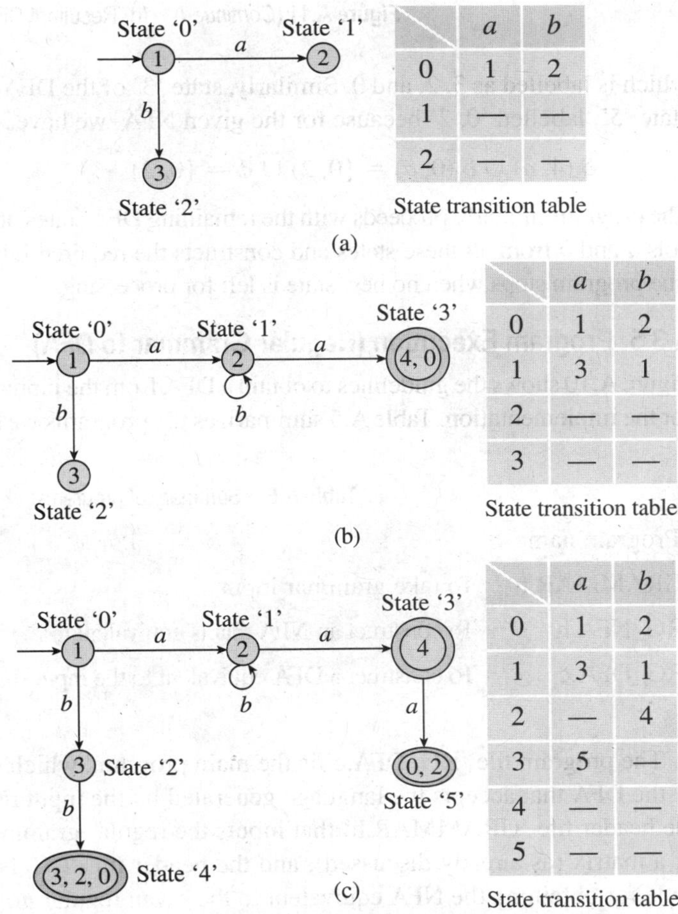


| | a | b |
|---|---|---|
| 0 | 1 | 2 |
| 1 | — | — |
| 2 | — | — |

| | a | b |
|---|---|---|
| 0 | 1 | 2 |
| 1 | 3 | 1 |
| 2 | — | — |
| 3 | — | — |

| | a | b |
|---|---|---|
| 0 | 1 | 2 |
| 1 | 3 | 1 |
| 2 | — | 4 |
| 3 | 5 | — |
| 4 | — | — |
| 5 | — | — |

**Figure A.11** Construction of an equivalent DFA from the given NFA (a) After processing state '0' of the DFA (b) After processing state '1' of the DFA (c) After processing state '2' and state '3'

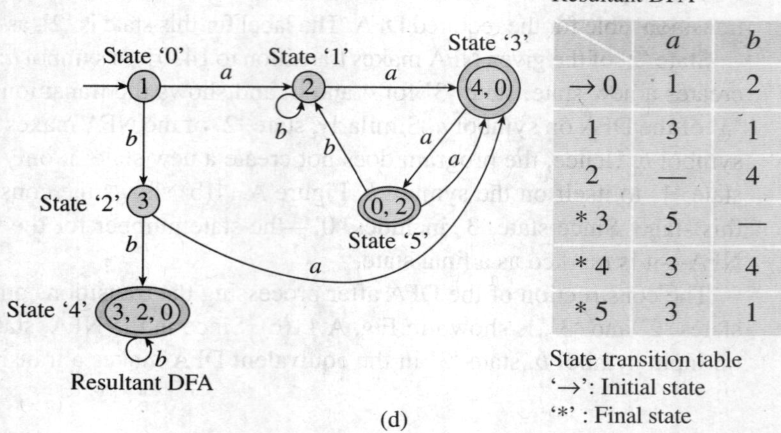


| | $a$ | $b$ |
|---|---|---|
| → 0 | 1 | 2 |
| 1 | 3 | 1 |
| 2 | — | 4 |
| * 3 | 5 | — |
| * 4 | 3 | 4 |
| * 5 | 3 | 1 |

**Figure A.11** (*Continued*) (d) Resultant DFA

which is labelled as 3, 2, and 0. Similarly, state '3' of the DFA makes a transition to a new state '5', labelled '0, 2' because for the given NFA, we have:

$$\delta\,(4, a) \cup \delta\,(0, a) = \{0, 2) \cup \phi = \{0, 2\}$$

The program similarly proceeds with the remaining DFA states; it finds the transitions on symbols $a$ and $b$ from all these states and constructs the required DFA as shown in Fig. A.11(d). The program stops when no new state is left for processing.

### A.3.5 Program Execution (Regular Grammar to DFA)

Figure A.10 shows the guidelines to obtain a DFA from the input regular grammar considered for the implementation. Table A.5 summarizes the programs we have seen and their purpose.

**Table A.5** Summary of programs

| Program name | Purpose |
|---|---|
| GRAMMAR.h | To take grammar input |
| RG_NFA.h | To construct an NFA that is equivalent to the input right-linear grammar |
| RG_DFA.c | To construct a DFA equivalent to the input right-linear grammar |

The program file 'RG_DFA.c' is the main program, which deals with the construction of the DFA that accepts the language generated by the input regular grammar. It includes the header file 'GRAMMAR.h' that inputs the regular grammar and stores it in the form of a matrix (as already discussed), and the header file 'RG_NFA.h', which provides the code for obtaining the NFA equivalent to the given regular grammar.

Thus, with the help of these header files, the program 'RG_DFA.c' constructs the resultant state transition table for the DFA, which is equivalent to the input right-liner grammar, and displays it as well.

After compiling this program, the output will be as shown in Output A.2, for the input grammar we have taken in the previous sample.

**Output A.2** Construction of DFA from given NFA

```
Right-linear grammar to FA conversion:
Enter the number of production rules:   10
Production rules:
S       ->          aA
S       ->          bB
A       ->          aC
A       ->          bA
A       ->          a
B       ->          bB
B       ->          bA
B       ->          b
C       ->          a
C       ->          aA
State transition table for the resultant DFA:

              State         A          b
------------------------------------------
    ->          0         ( 1 )      ( 2 )
                1         ( 3 )      ( 1 )
                2           -        ( 4 )
     *          3         ( 5 )        -
     *          4         ( 3 )      ( 4 )
     *          5         ( 3 )      ( 1 )

->  :  Initial state
*   :  Final state
```

## A.4 CONVERSION OF RIGHT-LINEAR GRAMMAR TO LEFT-LINEAR GRAMMAR

In Chapter 5 (refer to Section 5.12.1), we discussed the method to obtain an equivalent left-linear grammar from a given right-linear grammar. The process is shown in Fig. A.12, which is described as follows:

1. Represent the given right-linear grammar using a transition graph (TG) or state transition table.
2. Reverse the directions of all the transitions and interchange the positions of initial and final states.
3. From this changed TG or state transition table, write the equivalent left-linear grammar.

In other words, we begin by constructing an NFA that is equivalent to the input right-linear grammar. We then reverse the transitions and interchange the positions of the initial and final states of this NFA. Using this NFA, we rewrite the left-linear grammar (refer to Fig. A.13).

Now let us compare Fig. A.10, which describes the process of constructing a DFA equivalent to the given right-linear grammar, with Fig. A.13. We observe that the first part—obtaining an equivalent NFA using the given right-linear grammar—is the same.

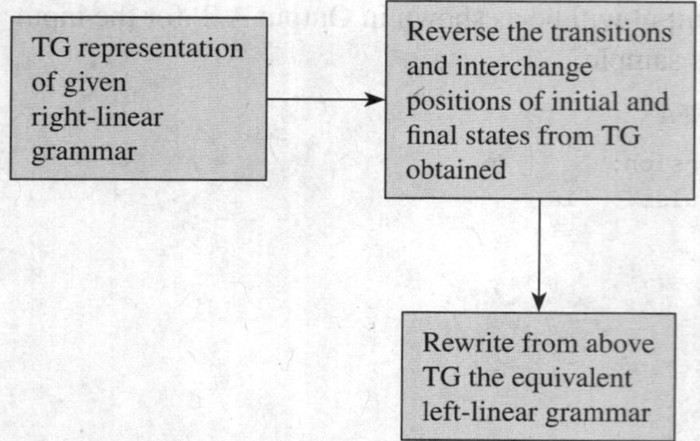


**Figure A.12** Process of obtaining left-linear grammar equivalent to given right-linear grammar

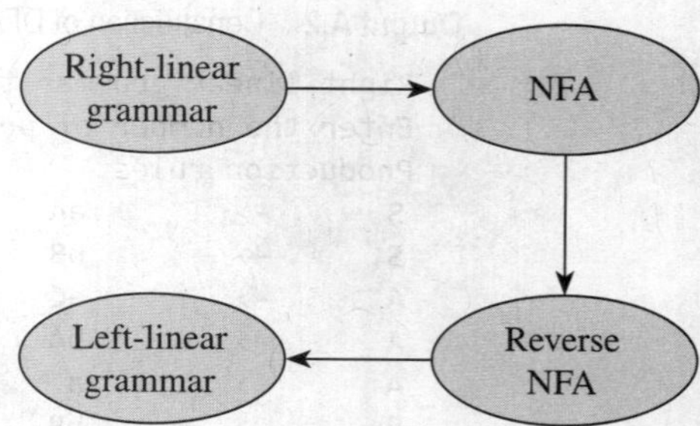


**Figure A.13** Conversion of right-linear grammar to equivalent left-linear grammar

Therefore, in the implementation, the grammar representation and the NFA construction algorithms do not change. Hence, we can reuse the header files 'GRAMMAR.h' and 'RE_NFA.h', which deal with grammar input and NFA construction respectively.

In this section, we can therefore restrict ourselves to reversing the NFA and formulating the left-linear grammar using the state transition table of the reversed NFA.

The algorithm for converting right-linear grammar to its equivalent left-linear grammar is the same as the one discussed in Chapter 5 (refer to Section 5.12.1).

### A.4.1 Implementation of the Algorithm (Right-linear to Left-linear Conversion)

Program A.8 provides the 'C' implementation of the required algorithm.

**Program A.8** Conversion of right-linear grammar to its equivalent left-linear grammar

```
// ------ CR_TO_CL.c

// This program obtains an equivalent left-linear grammar from the given right-linear
// grammar.
#include <stdio.h>
#include <conio.h>
#include "GRAMMAR.h" //Required to input the right-linear grammar.
#include "RG_NFA.h"        //Required for obtaining the NFA from the input right-
                           //linear grammar.
// State transition table for the NFA after interchanging initial and final states and
// reversing the direction of the transitions.
struct nfa_state reverse_nfa_table[TABLE_SIZE];
void main(void)
{
     void reverse();
     void print_Left_Linear_Grammar();
     clrscr();
```

```
    printf("Conversion of right-linear grammar to left-linear
           grammar:\n\n");
    input();                              // Defined in "GRAMMAR.h".

    initialize_nfa_state_table(nfa_state_table); // Defined in "RG_NFA.h".
    construct_NFA();                             // Defined in "RG_NFA.h".

    initialize_nfa_state_table(reverse_nfa_table); // Defined in "RG_NFA.h".
    reverse();
    clrscr();
    print_Left_Linear_Grammar();
    getch () ;
}

// The following procedure interchanges initial and final state positions and reverses
// the directions of all the transitions in the NFA obtained from the right-linear
// grammar. After reversing, the new NFA can be used to write the equivalent
// left-linear grammar.
void reverse ()
{
     void copy_labels();
     int i = 1, j, k, state;
     copy_labels();
     //    Reverse the transitions.
     while (i < state_count)
     {
          j = 0;
          while (nfa_state_table[i].transition_on_a[j] != -1)
          {
             state = nfa_state_table[i].transition_on_a[j];
             k = 0;
             while (reverse_nfa_table[state].transition_on_a [k] !=  -1)
                  k++;
             reverse_nfa_table[state].transition_on_a[k] = i;
             j++;
          }
          j = 0;
          while (nfa_state_table[i].transition_on_b [j] != -1)
          {
             state = nfa_state_table[i].transition_on_b[j];
             k = 0;
             while (reverse_nfa_table[state].transition_on_b[k] != -1)
             k++;
             reverse_nfa_table[state].transition_on_b[k] = i;
             j++;
          }
          i++;
     }
}
```

```
// The following procedure copies the labels from the state transition table of the
// NFA obtained from the right-linear grammar into the state transition table for the
// NFA after 'reverse' process.
void copy_labels ()
{
      int i = 2;
      while (i < state_count)
      {
            reverse_nfa_table[i].state_label = nfa_state_table[i].state_label;

            reverse_nfa_table[i].state_type = nfa_state_table[i].state_type;
            i++;
      }
      // Interchange initial and final states.
      reverse_nfa_table[0].state_label = nfa_state_table[1].state_label;
      reverse_nfa_table[0].state_type = 'i';

      reverse_nfa_table[1].state_label = nfa_state_table[0].state_label;
      reverse_nfa_table[1].state_type = 'f';
}

// The following procedure displays the left-linear grammar equivalent to given
// right-linear grammar using the state transition table of the new NFA obtained
// using 'reverse' process.
Void print_Left_Linear_Grammar()
{
      int i = 0, j, state;
      printf ("\n\nThe equivalent left-linear grammar is : \n\n");
      while (i < state_count)
      {
            j = 0;
            while (reverse_nfa_table[i].transition_on_a[j] != -1)
            {
               state = reverse_nfa_table[i].transition_on_a[j];
               printf("%c", reverse_nfa_table[i].state_label);
               printf("     ->    ");
               if (reverse_nfa_table[state].state_label != "#")
                    printf ("%c", reverse_nfa_table[state].state_label);
               printf("a");
               printf("\n");
               j++;
            }

            j = 0;
            while (reverse_nfa_table[i].transition_on_b[j] != -1)
            {
               state = reverse_nfa_table[i].transition_on_b[j];
               printf ("%c", reverse_nfa_table[i].state_label);
               printf ("   ->  ");
```

```
            if (reverse_nfa_table[state].state_label != "#")
            printf ("%c", reverse_nfa_table[state].state_label);
            printf("b");
            printf("\n");
            j++;
        }
        i++;
    }
}
// ------ End of CR_TO_CL.c
```

The program file 'CR_TO_CL.c' includes three function implementations the 'copy_labels' function copies the NFA states from its state transition table to the state transition table of another NFA named 'reverse_nfa_table'. The 'reverse' procedure deals with reversing the directions of the transitions and interchanging the positions of the initial and the final states for the NFA obtained from the right-linear grammar. The procedure 'print_Left_Linear_Grammar' does the job of re-writing the grammar from the state transition table obtained after reversing.

### A.4.2 Simulation of Algorithm

Let us simulate the working of the program for the following grammar:

0. $S \to a\,A$
1. $S \to b\,B$
2. $A \to a\,C$
3. $A \to b\,A$
4. $A \to a$
5. $B \to b\,B$
6. $B \to b\,A$
7. $B \to b$
8. $C \to a$
9. $C \to a\,A$

We observe that this is the same right-linear grammar we converted to NFA, in Fig. A.9(f).

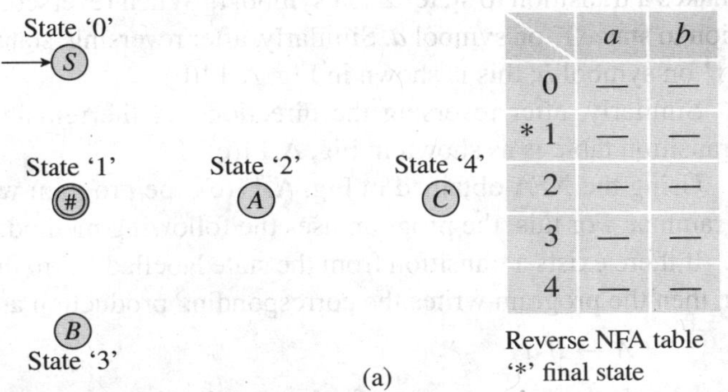


| | a | b |
|---|---|---|
| 0 | — | — |
| * 1 | — | — |
| 2 | — | — |
| 3 | — | — |
| 4 | — | — |

**Figure A.14** Reversed NFA transitions and interchanged positions of initial and final states (a) After interchanging initial and final states

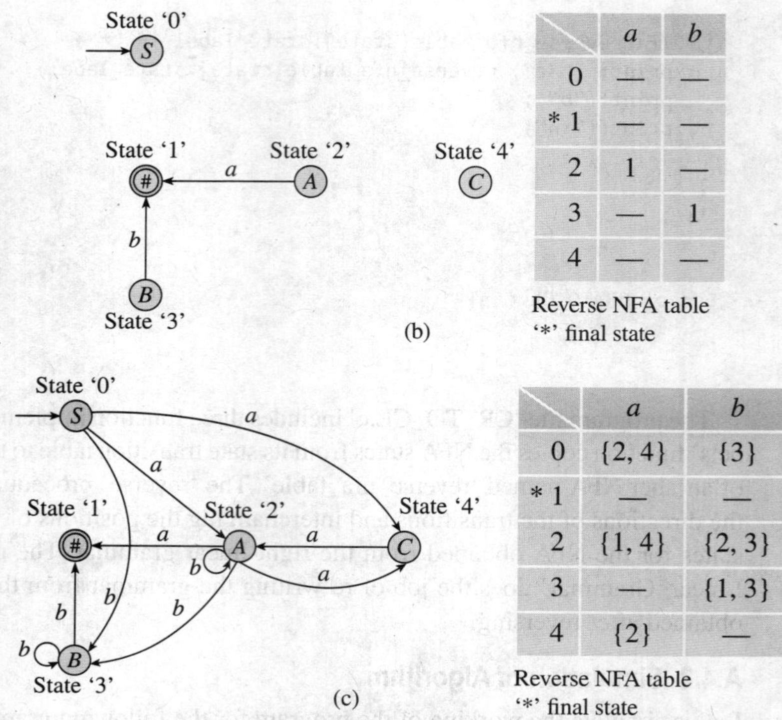


| | $a$ | $b$ |
|---|---|---|
| 0 | — | — |
| * 1 | — | — |
| 2 | 1 | — |
| 3 | — | 1 |
| 4 | — | — |

| | $a$ | $b$ |
|---|---|---|
| 0 | {2, 4} | {3} |
| * 1 | — | — |
| 2 | {1, 4} | {2, 3} |
| 3 | — | {1, 3} |
| 4 | {2} | — |

**Figure A.14** (*Continued*) (b) After reversing the transitions from state '1' (c) NFA after reversing all transitions

Initially, the program interchanges the positions of the initial and final states. It keeps the intermediate states in the same position and with the same labels. It records all these changes to a different structure, which is a state transition table for the reversed NFA that we require; this is shown in Fig. A.14(a).

The program now deals with the process of reversing all transitions, starting from state '1' of the original NFA. In the state transition table of the NFA in Fig. A.9(f), state '1' makes a transition to state '2' on symbol $a$. When reversed, state '2' would make a transition to state '1' on symbol $a$. Similarly, after reversing, state '3' makes a transition to state '1' on symbol $b$; this is shown in Fig. A.14(b).

Similarly, after reversing the directions all the remaining transitions, the new state transition table is as shown in Fig. A.14(c).

Using the NFA obtained in Fig. A.14(c), the program writes the equivalent left-linear grammar. For this, the program uses the following method:

If there exists a transition from the state labelled '$A$' to the state labelled '$B$' on symbol $a$, then the program writes the corresponding production as:

$$A \rightarrow B\,a$$

In case the second state is a final state, that is, a state labelled '#', and having 'state_type' = 'f', then there will be a transition from state $A$ to the final state on symbol $a$. The corresponding production is written as:

$$A \rightarrow a$$

Let us now use the state transition table of the NFA obtained in Fig. A.14(c) for writing the required left-linear grammar production.

From state '0', which is labelled '*S*', we see that there are transitions to states '2' (labelled '*A*') and '4' (labelled '*C*') on symbol *a*. The corresponding productions for the resultant left-linear grammar can be written as:

$$S \rightarrow A\ a$$
$$S \rightarrow C\ a$$

Similarly, the transition of state '0' to state '3' (labelled '*B*') on symbol *b* is written as the following production:

$$S \rightarrow B\ b$$

Likewise, the transitions from state '2' on symbol *a* are:

$$A \rightarrow a$$
$$A \rightarrow C\ a$$

Note that the production '$A \rightarrow a$' corresponds to the transition from state '2' to the final state on symbol *a*.

The remaining productions are similarly written and are as follows:

$$A \rightarrow A\ b$$
$$A \rightarrow B\ b$$
$$B \rightarrow b$$
$$B \rightarrow B\ b$$
$$C \rightarrow A\ a$$

Thus, the left-linear grammar equivalent to the given right-linear grammar is:

$$S \rightarrow A\ a$$
$$S \rightarrow C\ a$$
$$S \rightarrow B\ b$$
$$A \rightarrow a$$
$$A \rightarrow C\ a$$
$$A \rightarrow A\ b$$
$$A \rightarrow B\ b$$
$$B \rightarrow b$$
$$B \rightarrow B\ b$$
$$C \rightarrow A\ a$$

### A.4.3 Program Execution (Right-linear to Left-linear Conversion)

The main program that we should compile and execute for getting the required output is 'CR_TO_CL.c'. This program includes the header files 'GRAMMAR.h' and 'RG_NFA.h', which provide the required forms of the input right-linear grammar and construct an equivalent NFA respectively. We have already discussed these header files in Section A.3.5 and the main program in Section A.4.1.

The output of the program, for the input grammar that we have considered as an example in this section, will be as shown in Output A.3.

**Output A.3** Output left-linear grammar

```
Right-linear grammar to left-linear grammar conversion:
Enter the number of production rules: 10
Production rules:
                 S     ->     aA
                 S     ->     bB
                 A     ->     aC
                 A     ->     bA
                 A     ->     a
                 B     ->     bB
                 B     ->     bA
                 B     ->     b
                 C     ->     a
                 C     ->     aA
The equivalent left-linear grammar is:

                 S     ->     Aa
                 S     ->     Ca
                 S     ->     Bb
                 A     ->     a
                 A     ->     Ca
                 A     ->     Ab
                 A     ->     Bb
                 B     ->     b
                 B     ->     Bb
                 C     ->     Aa
```

In this appendix, we have discussed three major implementations:

1. Conversion of regular expressions to DFA
2. Conversion of right-linear grammar to DFA
3. Conversion of right-linear grammar to left-linear grammar

We have also discussed other allied algorithm implementations such as:

1. Conversion of NFA with $\epsilon$-moves to DFA
2. Conversion of NFA to DFA

We have also discussed many functions, procedures, and header files, such as stack implementation and infix to postfix conversion, which are required for these implementations.

This appendix aims to introduce the reader to sample codes and the process of implementing the theoretical concepts that we learned in the previous chapters. It is not necessary to always use the data structures mentioned in the sample code; the reader may select data structures and function implementations of his/her choice, and write different programs that do the same job. There are many other methods as mentioned in the text, but it is left to the reader to try and implement them.

# Model Question Papers

## B.1 INTRODUCTION

This appendix provides a few model question papers, which are designed in line with the pattern of some major universities in India. The aim of the appendix is to help the reader develop an in-depth understanding of the concepts and techniques discussed in the chapters.

Once the reader has worked out all the problems, he/she can check and compare the solutions provided on the companion website of the book using the following link: www.oupinheonline.com

## B.2 MODEL QUESTION PAPER 1

**Time:** 3 Hours **Max. Marks:** 100

***Instructions:***

1. Draw neat diagrams, wherever necessary.
2. The numbers on the right indicate the marks allotted to the respective question.
3. Assume suitable data, wherever required.

1. (a) Let $R = \{(1, 2), (2, 3), (1, 4), (4, 2), (3, 4)\}$. Find $R^+$ and $R^*$. (4)

   (b) Construct a Mealy machine that accepts the strings from $(0 + 1)^*$ and produces the following output: (6)

| String ends with | Output |
|---|---|
| 101 | $x$ |
| 110 | $y$ |
| Otherwise | $z$ |

   (c) Construct a deterministic finite automata (DFA) equivalent to the non-deterministic finite automata (NFA), $\{(p, q, r, s), (0, 1), \delta, p, (q, s)\}$, where '$\delta$' is given by: (8)

| $Q$ \ $\Sigma$ | 0 | 1 |
|---|---|---|
| $p$ | $q, r$ | $q$ |
| $q$ | $r$ | $q, r$ |
| $r$ | $s$ | $p$ |
| $s$ | – | $p$ |

2. (a) Using the principle of mathematical induction, show that $n^4 - 4n^2$ is divisible by 3 for all $n \geq 0$. (4)

   (b) Using pumping lemma, prove that the following language is not regular:

   $$L = \{a^n b^n \mid n > 0\}$$ (6)

   (c) Construct a reduced-state DFA $(Q, \Sigma, \delta, q_0, F)$ for the following regular expression:

   $$(01+10)^*11.$$ (6)

3. (a) Write a context-free grammar (CFG), which generates the language $L$ denoted by:

   $$(a + b)^* \, bbb \, (a + b)^*$$ (2)

   (b) Show that the following CFG is ambiguous. Remove the ambiguity and write an equivalent unambiguous CFG.

   $$S \to S + S \mid S * S \mid 4$$ (4)

   (c) Convert the following grammar into CNF:

   $$S \to a\,B \mid b\,A$$
   $$A \to a \mid a\,S \mid b\,A\,A$$
   $$B \to b \mid b\,S \mid a\,B\,B$$ (4)

   (d) Consider the grammar $G = \{(S, A), (0, 1), P, S\}$, where $P$ consists of:

   $$S \to 0\,A\,S \mid 0$$
   $$A \to S\,1\,A \mid S\,S \mid 1\,0$$

   Derive the input string '001100' using leftmost and rightmost derivations. (6)

4. (a) Construct a pushdown automata (PDA) that is equivalent to the following CFG:

   $$S \to 0A1 \mid 0BA,\ A \to S01 \mid 0,\ B \to 1B \mid 1$$ (6)

   (b) Construct a PDA for each of the following languages:
      (i) The set of palindromes over alphabet $\{a, b\}$
      (ii) The set of all strings over alphabet $\{a, b\}$ with exactly twice many $a$'s as $b$'s (10)

5. (a) Design a Turing machine (TM) that multiplies two unary numbers. Show the step-wise functioning of the TM for the following input sequences:
      (i) $111 \times 1111$ (ii) $111 \times 11$ (10)

   (b) Write a short note on:
      (i) Power of Turing machine over finite state machine
      (ii) Universal Turing machine (8)

6. (a) Write a short note on Post's correspondence problem (PCP). (6)

   (b) Prove that if a language $L$ and its complement $\overline{L}$ are recursively enumerable, then $L$ is a recursive language. (6)

   (c) Explain with the help of suitable examples: NP-hard and NP-complete problems. (4)

## B.3 MODEL QUESTION PAPER 2

**Time:** 3 Hours **Max. Marks:** 100

***Instructions:***

1. Draw neat diagrams, wherever necessary.
2. The numbers on the right indicate the marks allotted to the respective questions.
3. Assume suitable data, wherever required.

1. Attempt any three of the following:
   (a) Define the following and give suitable examples:
   (i) Alphabet
   (ii) Symbol
   (iii) Language
   (iv) Word
   (v) Closure of a set
   (vi) Reflexive and transitive closure of a relation (6)

   (b) Construct Mealy and Moore machines for the following:

   For the input from $\Sigma^*$, where $\Sigma = \{0, 1, 2\}$, print the residue-modulo-5 of the input treated as a ternary (base 3, and with digits 0, 1, and 2) number. (6)

   (c) Consider the following NFA with $\epsilon$-transitions, assuming that $p$ is the initial state and $r$ is the final state:

| | $\epsilon$ | $a$ | $b$ | $c$ |
|---|---|---|---|---|
| $p$ | $\phi$ | $\{p\}$ | $\{q\}$ | $\{r\}$ |
| $q$ | $\{p\}$ | $\{q\}$ | $\{r\}$ | $\phi$ |
| $r$ | $\{q\}$ | $\{r\}$ | $\phi$ | $\{p\}$ |

   (i) Compute the $\epsilon$-closure of each state.
   (ii) List all the strings, whose length is less than or equal to three, accepted by the automaton.
   (iii) Convert the automaton to its equivalent DFA. (6)

   (d) Convert the following Mealy machine to its equivalent Moore machine. (6)

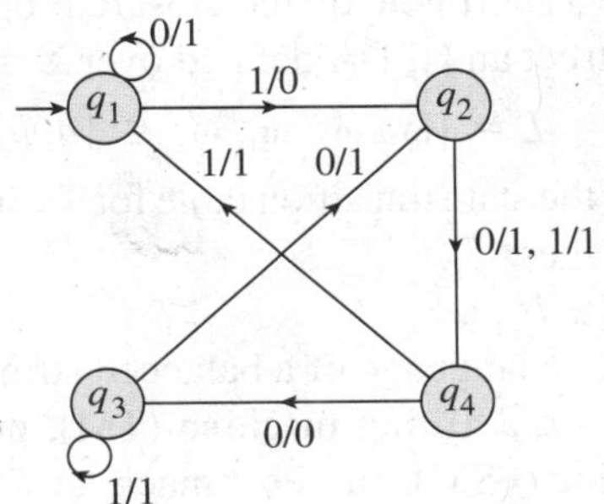

2. (a) Which of the following languages represent regular sets? Justify your answer.
   (i) $\{0^{2n} \mid n \geq 1\}$
   (ii) $\{0^m\ 1^n\ 0^{m+n} \mid m \geq 1 \text{ and } n \geq 1\}$ (4)
   (b) Is the following language regular? Justify your answer.
   $$L = \{0^p\ 1^p\ p^{p+q} \mid p \geq 1, q \geq 1\}$$ (6)
   (c) Construct a regular expression corresponding to the following transition diagram using Arden's theorem. (6)

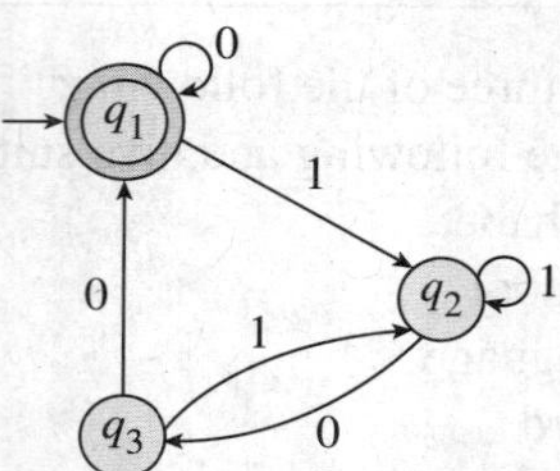


3. Attempt any four of the following.
   (a) Explain Greibach normal form with the help of suitable examples. (4)
   (b) Show that the following CFG is ambiguous. Remove the ambiguity and write an equivalent unambiguous CFG.
   $$E \rightarrow E + E \mid E * E \mid (E) \mid id$$ (4)
   (c) Convert the following right-linear grammar to its equivalent left-linear grammar:
   $$S \rightarrow a\,A \mid b\,B \mid a\,S \mid a$$
   $$A \rightarrow b\,A \mid \epsilon$$
   $$B \rightarrow a\,B \mid \epsilon$$ (4)
   (d) Write a CFG that generates the language:
   $$L = \{WCW^R \mid W \in \{a, b\}^* \text{ and } W^R \text{ is the reverse of } W\}.$$
   Use leftmost derivation, rightmost derivation, and derivation tree to derive the input string '*ababCbaba*'. (4)
   (e) Is the language $L = \{a^n\ b^m \mid n \neq m\}$ context-free? If yes, write the CFG that defines the language $L$. (4)
4. (a) Construct a PDA that accepts the following language:
   $$L = \{a^n\ b^n \mid n \geq 0\}$$ (6)
   (b) Write a short note on the closure properties of context-free languages (CFLs). (4)
   (c) Construct an NPDA defined over $\Sigma = \{a, b, c\}$ that accepts the language:
   $$L = \{\omega_1 c \omega_2 \colon \omega_1, \omega_2 \in \{a, b\}^*;\ \omega_1 \neq \omega_2\}$$ (6)
5. (a) Draw the state transition table for Turing machines that accept each of the following languages:
   (i) $\{a^i\ b^j \mid i < j\}$
   (ii) The language of a balanced string of parentheses (12)
   (b) Compare a Turing machine (TM), pushdown stack-memory (PDM), finite state machine (FSM), and Post machine (PM) (definitions are not required). (6)

6. (a) Define any three of the following:
   (i) Multi-track Turing machine
   (ii) Multi-tape Turing machine
   (iii) Recursively enumerable language
   (iv) Recursive language (6)

   (b) Describe the halting problem. Show that it is undecidable. (6)

   (c) What is a satisfiability problem? What role does it play in the complexity theory? Explain Cook's theorem. (4)

## B.4 MODEL QUESTION PAPER 3

**Time:** 3 Hours **Max. Marks:** 100

---

***Instructions:***

1. Draw neat diagrams, wherever necessary.
2. The numbers on the right indicate the marks allotted to the respective questions.
3. Assume suitable data, wherever required.

---

1. (a) Construct an NFA that accepts any positive number of occurrences of various strings from the following language:

$$L = \{x \mid x \text{ is made up of } \{a, b\}; \text{ and } x \text{ ends with '}aab\text{'}\}$$ (4)

   (b) Construct a 2DFA that accepts the following regular set:

$L = \{z \in (a, b)^* \mid$ number of $a$'s is a multiple of 3 and number of $b$'s is an even number$\}$ (8)

   (c) Convert the following NFA into NFA without $\epsilon$-moves. (6)

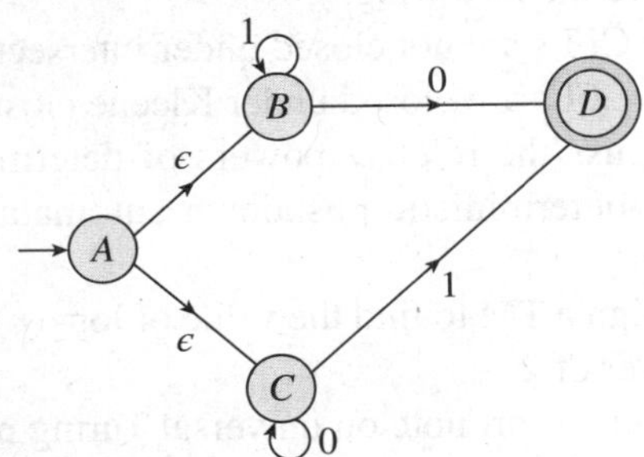


2. (a) Consider the following regular expressions:

$$R_1 = a^* + b^*$$
$$R_2 = ab^* + ba^* + b^*\,a + (a^*\,b)^*$$

   (i) Find a string corresponding to $R_1$ but not $R_2$.
   (ii) Find a string corresponding to $R_2$ but not $R_1$.
   (iii) Find a string corresponding to both $R_1$ and $R_2$. (4)

   (b) Let $L = \{0^n \mid n \text{ is a prime number}\}$; show that $L$ is not a regular language. (6)

(c) Construct an NFA with $\epsilon$-transitions, which accepts the language defined by:

$$(ab + ba)^* \, aa \, (ab + ba)^*.$$

Convert the derived NFA to its equivalent minimized DFA. (6)

3. Attempt any four of the following:

(a) Find the CFL associated with the CFG, $G$, Which is defined as follows:

$$S \rightarrow a\,B \mid b\,A$$
$$A \rightarrow a \mid a\,S \mid b\,A\,A$$
$$B \rightarrow b \mid b\,S \mid a\,B\,B$$ (4)

(b) Write a short note on derivation graphs (4)

(c) Construct a DFA that accepts the regular language generated by the following left-linear grammar

$$S \rightarrow C\,a \mid B\,b$$
$$C \rightarrow B\,a$$
$$B \rightarrow B\,a \mid b$$ (4)

(d) Convert the following grammar to Greibach normal form (GNF):

$$S \rightarrow A\,B\,A \mid A\,B \mid B\,A \mid A\,A \mid A \mid B$$
$$A \rightarrow a\,A \mid a$$
$$B \rightarrow b\,B \mid b$$ (4)

(e) Is the language $L = \{a^n\, b^m \mid n = m\}$ context-free? If yes, write the CFG that defines $L$. (4)

4. (a) Construct a PDA that recognizes the following language:

$$\{a^n\, x \mid n \geq 0,\, x \in (a, b)^* \text{ and } |\, x \,| \leq n\}$$ (6)

(b) Prove the following:

(i) CFLs are not closed under intersection.

(ii) CFLs are closed under Kleene closure. (4)

(c) Discuss the relative powers of deterministic pushdown automata (DPDA) and non-deterministic pushdown automata (NPDA) using appropriate examples of both. (6)

5. (a) Design a TM to find the value of $\log_2 (n)$, where $n$ is a binary number and a perfect power of 2. (8)

(b) Write a short note on universal Turing machine. (6)

(c) Discuss recursive and recursively enumerable languages giving suitable examples wherever necessary. (4)

6. Attempt any two of the following:

(a) Construct the look-ahead LR (LALR) parsing table for the following grammar:

$$D \rightarrow L : T$$
$$L \rightarrow L,\, id \mid id$$
$$T \rightarrow \text{int} \mid \text{real}$$

Simulate the LALR parser actions for the acceptance of the string '$a, b, c$ : int'. (8)

(b) Let $\Sigma = \{a, b, c\}$ be the input alphabet set, and $\Sigma' = \{\alpha, \beta\}$ be the auxiliary alphabet. Write Markov algorithm for duplicating the string in $\Sigma^*$. (8)

(c) Write a short note on:
   (i) Gödel numbering
   (ii) Diagonalization language (8)

(d) Prove the following: If $L$ is a recursive language, then $\overline{L}$ is also a recursive language. (8)

## B.5 MODEL QUESTION PAPER 4

**Time:** 3 Hours **Max. Marks:** 100

***Instructions:***

1. Draw neat diagrams, whenever necessary.
2. The numbers on the right indicate the marks allotted to the respective questions.
3. Assume suitable data, wherever required.

1. (a) Design a finite automaton that accepts the following formal language specification. Justify your design.

$$L = \{(a.\, b)^n \mid n \geq 1\} \quad (4)$$

(b) Design a Moore machine that reads sequences made up of the letters *A*, *E*, *I*, *O*, *U*, and returns the same sequence as output, except when an *I* directly follows an *E*; in this case, the *I* is changed to *U*. (8)

(c) Design an FSM that works as a divisibility-by-5 tester for decimal numbers. (6)

2. (a) Let $\Sigma = \{0, 1\}$. Construct regular expressions for each of the following:
   (i) $L_1 = \{W = \Sigma^* \mid W$ has at least one pair of consecutive zeros$\}$
   (ii) $L_2 = \{W \in \Sigma^* \mid W$ has no pair of consecutive zeros$\}$
   (iii) $L_3 = \{W \in \Sigma^* \mid W$ starts with either '01' or '10'$\}$
   (iv) $L_4 = \{W \in \Sigma^* \mid W$ consists of even number of 0's followed by odd number of 1's$\}$ (4)

(b) Explain the following applications of regular expressions:
   (i) 'grep' utility in UNIX
   (ii) Finding pattern in text (4)

(c) Which of the following are true? Explain.
   (i) $baa \in a^*b^*a^*b^*$
   (ii) $b^*a^* \cap a^*b^* = a^* \cup b^*$
   (iii) $a^*b^* \cap b^*c^* = \phi$
   (iv) $abcd \in [a\,(cd)^*\,b]^*$ (4)

(d) Write a short note on Moore's algorithm for FSM equivalence. (4)

OR

2. (a) Construct a transition graph that recognizes the following regular set:

$$R = [1 \cdot (00)^* \cdot 1 + 0 \cdot 1^* \cdot 0]^* \quad (6)$$

(b) Obtain the regular expression for the DFA described in the following figure: (6)

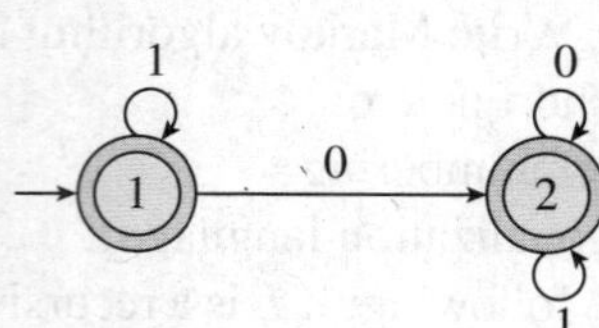


(c) Prove that the set $L = \{0^{i^2} \mid i \text{ is an integer}; i \geq 1\}$, which consists of all strings of 0's, whose length is a perfect square, is not regular. (4)

3. (a) Write a short note on Chomsky hierarchy. (4)
(b) Using pumping lemma, show that $L = \{a^n b^n c^n \mid n \geq 1\}$ is not a context-free language. (6)
(c) Discuss the applications of CFG. (6)

4. (a) Design a PDA that checks if a given set of parentheses is well-formed. (6)
(b) Discuss the relative powers of DPDA and DFA with the help of suitable examples. (4)
(c) Convert the following CFG into PDA:

$$S \rightarrow aB \mid bA$$
$$A \rightarrow a \mid aS \mid bAA$$
$$B \rightarrow b \mid bS \mid aBB$$ (6)

5. (a) Design a TM, which compares two positive integers $m$ and $n$ and returns output $G_t$ if

$$m > n,\ L_t \text{ if } m < n, \text{ and } E_q \text{ if } m = n.$$ (8)

(b) Write a short note on composite TM. (4)
(c) What is a linear bounded automaton? Compare it with a TM. (2)
(d) PCP is an unsolvable problem. Justify. (4)

6. Attempt any two of the following:
(a) Construct a PM that multiplies two unary numbers. (8)
(b) What is the halting problem? Show that it is an NP-hard problem. (8)
(c) Show that Hilbert's tenth problem is unsolvable. (8)
(d) Design a TM that divides one number by the other, and returns the result of division as well as the remainder, if any. (8)

## B.6 MODEL QUESTION PAPER 5

**Time:** 3 Hours **Max. Marks:** 100

***Instructions:***

1. Answer three questions from each section.
2. Draw neat diagrams, wherever necessary.
3. The numbers on the right indicate the marks allotted to the respective questions.
4. Assume suitable data, wherever required.

## SECTION I

1. (a) Define the following terms using suitable examples:
   (i) Basic machine (ii) Moore machine (iii) Mealy machine (6)
   (b) Convert the following NFA with $\epsilon$-transitions to:
   (i) NFA without $\epsilon$-moves (ii) DFA (10)

| $Q$ \ $\Sigma \cup \{\epsilon\}$ | 0 | 1 | 2 | $\epsilon$ |
|---|---|---|---|---|
| $q_0$ | $\{q_0\}$ | $\phi$ | $\phi$ | $\{q_0\}$ |
| $q_1$ | $\phi$ | $\{q_1\}$ | $\phi$ | $\{q_2\}$ |
| $q_2$ | $\phi$ | $\phi$ | $\{q_2\}$ | $\phi$ |

OR

1. (a) Construct Mealy and Moore machines for the following:
   For input from $\Sigma^*$, where $\Sigma = (0, 1)$, if the input ends in '101', the output should be $x$; if the input ends in '110', the output should be $y$; otherwise, the output should be $z$. (10)
   (b) Check the equivalence of the FSMs in the following figure, using Moore's algorithm. (6)

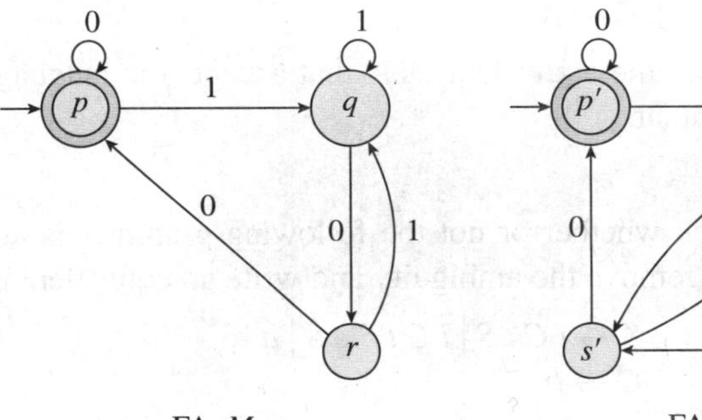


FA, $M$ FA, $M'$

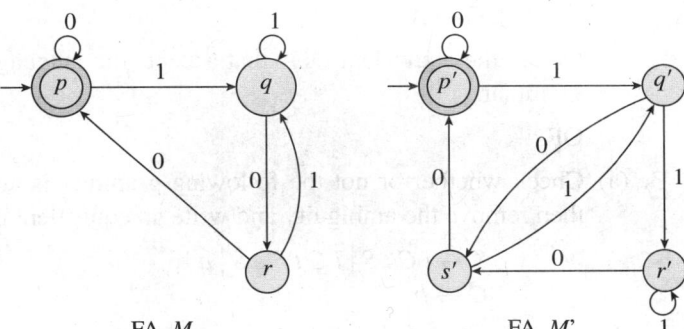

2. (a) State whether each of the following statements is true of false. Justify your answer. Assume that all languages are defined over the alphabet {0, 1}.
   (i) If ($L1 \subseteq L2$) and $L1$ is not regular, then $L2$ is not regular.
   (ii) If ($L1 \subseteq L2$) and $L2$ is not regular, then $L1$ is not regular.
   (iii) If $L1$ and $L2$ are not regular, then ($L1 \cup L2$) is not regular. (6)
   (b) Use pumping lemma to check whether or not the language $L = \{ww \mid (0, 1)^*\}$ is regular. (6)
   (c) Construct a regular expression for the following DFA: (6)

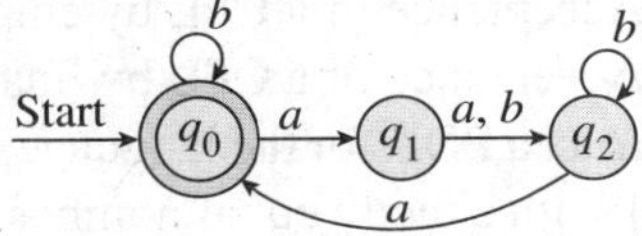


OR

2. (a) Construct a DFA that recognizes the regular set:

$$R = (a/b)^* \cdot a \cdot b \qquad (6)$$

(b) Construct the NFA and DFA for the following language:

$$L = \{x \in \{0, 1\}^* \mid x \text{ starts with 1; and } |x| \text{ is divisible by 3}\} \qquad (6)$$

(c) Discuss the limitations of the FSM. Give suitable examples. (6)

3. (a) Consider the following CFG:

$$G = \{(S, A), (a, b), P, S\},$$

where $P$ consists of

$$S \to a\,A\,S \mid a$$
$$A \to S\,b\,A \mid S\,S \mid b\,a$$

Derive the string '*aabbaa*' using leftmost and rightmost derivations. (4)

(b) Convert the following CFG to CNF:

$$S \to a\,S\,a \mid b\,S\,b \mid a \mid b \mid a\,a \mid b\,b \qquad (4)$$

(c) Convert the following left-linear grammar to its equivalent right-linear grammar.

$$S \to B\,1 \mid A\,0 \mid C\,0$$
$$A \to C\,0 \mid A\,1 \mid B\,1 \mid 0$$
$$B \to B\,1 \mid 1$$
$$C \to A\,0$$

Obtain the equivalent DFA that accepts the language described by the left-linear grammar. (8)

OR

3. (a) Check whether or not the following grammar is ambiguous; if it is ambiguous, then remove the ambiguity and write an equivalent unambiguous grammar. (4)

$$S \to i\,C\,t\,S \mid i\,C\,t\,S\,e\,S \mid a$$
$$C \to b$$

(b) What are the advantages of derivation graph over derivation tree? (2)

(c) Write a short note on:

(i) Backus–Naur form

(ii) Simplification of CFG

(iii) Leftmost and rightmost derivations

(iv) Context-sensitive grammar (10)

## SECTION II

4. (a) Explain the following using suitable examples:

(i) Acceptance of a CFL by empty stack by a PDA

(ii) Acceptance of a CFL by final state by a PDA (6)

(b) Construct a PDA for the language described as: 'The set of all strings over alphabet $\{a, b\}$ with exactly equal number of $a$'s and $b$'s'. (8)

(c) Give the formal definition of PDA. (2)

OR

4. (a) Construct a PDA (or NPDA) that accepts the language $L$ over $\Sigma = \{a, b\}$, where $L$ is defined as:

$$L = \{a^n b^n \mid n = 0, 1, 2, \ldots\}.$$

Simulate the working of this PDA (or NPDA) for the inputs:
(i) *aaabbb* (ii) *aab* (iii) *aaa* (10)

(b) Convert the following CFG into PDA.

$$S \to aB \mid bA$$
$$A \to a \mid aS \mid bAA$$
$$B \to b \mid bS \mid aBB$$
(6)

5. (a) Design a TM that finds the greatest common divisor (GCD) of two given numbers. (8)

(b) Explain the following terms in relation with TMs: (4)
(i) Solvability (ii) Semi-solvability (iii) Unsolvability

(c) Construct a PM that accepts the following language:

$$L_1 = \{a^n b^n a^n \mid n \geq 0\}$$
(6)

OR

5. (a) Design a TM that recognizes binary palindromes. (8)
(b) Design a PM that checks if a given set of parentheses is well-formed. (6)
(c) Write a short note on multi-track TM. (4)

6. (a) Construct an LALR parsing table for the following grammar: (8)

0: $S' \to S$
1: $S \to L = R$
2: $S \to R$
3: $L \to {*R}$
4: $L \to id$
5: $R \to L$

(b) Design an LMA that writes 2 at the right end of any word $w \subseteq \Sigma^*$, where $\Sigma = \{1, 2\}$. (8)

OR

6. (a) Prepare the following grammar for top-down parsing:

$$E \to E + E \mid E - E \mid E * E \mid E / E \mid E \wedge E \mid (E) \mid id$$

***Hint:*** Remove ambiguity, remove left recursion, and use left-factoring, if necessary. (6)

(b) Explain different mathematical notations for algorithm complexity measure. (4)
(c) Describe at least four undecidable problems in the case of CFGs. (4)
(d) Describe Ackermann's function. (2)

# Glossary

**Ackermann's function** Ackermann's function is a total computable function, which when evaluated on small inputs produces a very high value, with many decimal digits; it grows faster than the exponential function.

**Algorithm** An algorithm is a set of instructions that describes a computation, which, when executed, is a series of finite state transitions, starting from an initial state and initial input, and terminating at a final ending state, eventually producing an output.

**Ambiguous grammar** A context-free grammar (CFG) for a language is said to be ambiguous if there exists at least one string, which can be generated (or derived) in more than one way. One should remove the ambiguity from the grammar to make it usable for parsing.

**Backus–Naur form (BNF)** BNF is a notation used to express the syntax (or grammar) of most programming (or formal) languages.

**Basic machine** A basic machine is an abstract view of any program or machine. It can be viewed as a function which maps the input set $I$ to the output set $O$.

**Bottom-up parser** It constructs the parse tree from the leaves to the root (start symbol) of the grammar. It is also called a *shift-reduce* (SR) parser, as it consumes the statement to be parsed to reduce it to the start symbol. In this context, a 'shift' operation means pushing onto the stack, and reduction means replacing the right-hand side of the production by the left-hand side to reach the start symbol of the grammar.

**Cartesian product** The Cartesian product of two sets is defined as:

$$A \times B = \{(a, b) \mid a \in A \text{ and } b \in B, \forall a \;\&\; \forall b\}$$

It defines the association of every element of set $A$ with each element of set $B$.

**Chomsky hierarchy** The class of phrase structure grammars is very large; but by imposing certain constraints on the production rules, different classes of phrase structure grammar can be obtained, depending on the type of the restriction. It is more of a containment hierarchy of grammars. Chomsky has suggested four different classes of phrase structure grammars, which are known as Chomsky hierarchy, and are described as follows: Type-0 (unrestricted grammar), Type-1 (context-sensitive grammar), Type-2 (context-free grammar), Type-3 (regular grammar)

**Chomsky normal form (CNF)** A CNF is one of the normalization techniques used to simplify the CFG. In Chomsky normal form, the allowed type of production rules are either '$S \to A\ B$' or '$S \to a$', where $S$, $A$, and $B$ are non-terminals, and $a$ is a terminal symbol. Every grammar rule can either contain exactly two non-terminal symbols on the right-hand side of the production, or only a single terminal symbol.

**Compiler** A compiler is a program that takes any source language (for which it is written) program as input and transforms it into object (machine) code.

**Complexity of a Turing machine (TM)** The complexity of a TM depends on the number of symbols that are being used and the number of states of the TM.

$$\text{Complexity of a TM} = |\Gamma| \times |Q|,$$

where,
$|\Gamma|$ = Cardinality of a tape alphabet (i.e., number of tape symbols), and
$|Q|$ = Number of states of the TM.

**Composite TM** Two or more TMs can be combined to solve a complex problem, such that the output of one TM forms the input to the next TM, and so on. This is called *composition*.

**Context-free grammar (type-2)** It is a finite set of rules that represent a context-free language (CFL). Formally, it is denoted as $G = \{N, T, P, S\}$, where $N$ is a finite set of non-terminals, $T$ is a finite set of terminal symbols, $S$ is the start symbol of the grammar, and $P$ is the finite set of grammar rules of the form '$A \to \alpha$' such that $A$ is any non-terminal and $\alpha$ is a member of $(N \cup T)^*$. In this class of grammar:

1. The only allowed type of production is $A \rightarrow \alpha$, where, $A$ is a non-terminal and $\alpha$ is a sentential form, that is, $\alpha \subset (V \cup T)^*$; and $\alpha$ may be equal to $\epsilon$. The left-hand side of the production thus contains only one non-terminal.
2. The start symbol of the grammar can appear on the right-hand side as well.

**Context-free language (CFL)** A CFL is a language generated by a context-free grammar $G$. This can be described as $L(G) = \{w \mid w \subset T^*$, and is derivable from the start symbol $S\}$.

**Context-sensitive grammar (type-1)** The restrictions on this type of grammar are as follows:

1. For each production of the form '$\alpha \rightarrow \beta$', the length of $\beta$ is at least as much as the length of $\alpha$, except for '$S \rightarrow \epsilon$'.
2. The rule, '$S \rightarrow \epsilon$' is allowed only if the start symbol $S$ does not appear on the right-hand side of any production.
3. The term context sensitive is used because of the productions of the form:

$$\alpha_1 A \alpha_2 \rightarrow \alpha_1 \beta \alpha_2, (\beta \neq \epsilon),$$

where, the replacement of a non-terminal $A$ by $\beta$ is allowed only in the context of $\alpha_1$ that precedes $A$ and $\alpha_2$ that succeeds $A$. $\alpha_1$ and $\alpha_2$ can be empty if required.

**Derivation** It is the process of generating an input string by repeatedly applying the grammar rules from the set of rules defined by a CFG.

**Deterministic finite automata (DFA)** DFA is a finite automata (FA) that makes a transition to a unique next state based on the input symbol read.

**Deterministic pushdown automata (DPDA)** DPDA makes a transition to a unique next state and alters the stack in a unique way after reading a symbol from the input stream and the symbol on the top of the stack.

**Diagonalization language** Diagonalization language $L_d$ is the language defined as: $\{w_i \mid w_i \notin L(M_i)\}$, which means that it is the set of strings $w_i$ such that $w_i$ does not belong to the language accepted by any TM, $M_i$.

**Directed graph** (or **digraph**) In a directed graph, the edges are ordered pairs of vertices called *arcs*. An arc $(v_1, v_2)$ from vertex $v_1$ to vertex $v_2$ is denoted by, '$v_1 \rightarrow v_2$'; $v_1$ is called the *predecessor* of $v_2$, and $v_2$ is called the *successor* of $v_1$.

**Dyck language** It is the language consisting of well-formed parentheses. Dyck language is also called *parenthesis language* and is a CFL, as we can see. It is named after the mathematician Walther von Dyck.

**Entscheidungs problem** Entscheidungs problem is a German word for a 'decision problem' and was a challenge posed by David Hilbert in 1928. It can be viewed as asking for an algorithm to decide whether a given predicate is provable from the axioms using the rules of logic.

**Finite automaton (plural: finite automata; abbreviated as FA)** FA is the formalism of a finite state machine (FSM) that portrays the FSM as a language acceptor.

**Finite state machine (FSM)** A dynamic computational model with finite number of states that performs state transitions based on the input symbol read is a finite state machine.

**First** 'First ($X$)' is the set of terminal symbols with which the strings derivable from $X$ begin.

**Flowchart** A flowchart is a diagram that depicts an algorithm.

**Follow ($X$)** 'Follow ($X$)' is the set of all terminal symbols that immediately follow $X$ in any derivation for the given grammar.

**Graph** A graph can be defined as a relation over the set of vertices. It is not merely a diagram, but a visualization of the underlying relation among the vertices (or nodes).

**Greibach normal form (GNF)** GNF is a normalization technique used to simplify a CFG. In this form, the only allowed type of production rule (or grammar rule) is '$A \rightarrow a\alpha$', where $A$ is a non-terminal, $a$ is a terminal, and $\alpha$ is a (possibly empty) string containing only non-terminals.

**Greibach's theorem** Greibach's theorem is analogous to Rice's theorem in the case of CFLs. Greibach's theorem can be used to prove that many problems related to CFGs are undecidable.

**Halting problem** The problem of determining whether or not any given TM ever halts, is called the halting problem. The halting problem is unsolvable.

**Input alphabet (Σ)** A finite set of input symbols is known as an input alphabet. It is the set from which the input symbols (or characters) are chosen to formulate input strings.

**Instantaneous description (ID)** The ID of a TM $M$ is denoted by '$\alpha_1\ q\ \alpha_2$', where $q$ is the current state of the TM—$q \in Q$—and '$\alpha_1\ \alpha_2$' belongs to the string in $\Gamma^*$, that is, the contents of the tape bounded on both the ends by blank characters $b\!\!\!/$'s. Note that the blank character may occur within '$\alpha_1\ \alpha_2$' as well.

**Iterated TM** Another way of having a combination TM is by applying its own output as input repetitively. This is called *iteration* or *recursion*.

**Kuroda normal form** It is a normalization suggested for context-sensitive languages. A context-sensitive grammar is said to be in Kuroda normal form, if all the production rules are of the form:

$AB \to CD$, or $A \to BC$, or $A \to B$, or $A \to a$

where $A$, $B$, $C$, and $D$ are all non-terminal symbols and $a$ is a terminal symbol.

**Labelled Markov algorithm (LMA)** In LMA, it is possible to assign labels to different productions. These labels are normally their respective indices. Further, each production also specifies a go-to statement, indicating the next production rule to be applied. With the help of these labels and the go-to statements, the search required at each stage can be avoided, and the execution is comparatively much faster than the Markov algorithm.

**Language (*L*)** A language is defined as a set of strings from one alphabet. The null set $\phi$ and the set consisting of empty string, that is, $\{\phi\}$, are also languages. For any given alphabet Σ, any subset of $\Sigma^*$ is a language. Here, $\Sigma^*$ is considered as a universal language over Σ as it includes all possible strings over Σ.

**Left-linear grammar** This is a type of regular grammar. The allowed types of productions in left-linear grammar are: $A \to Bw$ and $A \to w$, where, $A$ and $B$ are non-terminals and $w$ is a string of terminals. The rule '$S \to \epsilon$' is allowed only if the start symbol $S$ does not appear on the right-hand side of any production.

**Leftmost derivation** If at each step in a derivation, a production is applied to the leftmost variable (or non-terminal), then the derivation is called leftmost derivation.

**Lexical analyser (or scanner)** A lexical analyser is a program that takes any source language program (considered as a text stream) as input and breaks it into valid words (or tokens) using the regular expression patterns. It is considered as the first phase of any compiler.

**Linear bounded automaton (LBA)** An LBA is a restricted form of a TM. While a TM has a tape, which is considered unbounded at both the ends, the LBA only has a finite contiguous portion of tape, whose length is a linear function of the length of the initial input. However, it is computationally equivalent to a TM.

**Markov algorithm** Markov algorithm is a Post Markov–Thue (PMT) system in which all the productions are indexed, or numbered. A production of the form '$\alpha\ x\ \beta \to \bullet$' is considered as a 'stop' indicator. No other production is applied after applying of this type of production. If more than one production can be applied to derive the string $w_2$ from a string $w_1$, then the production with the lowest number (or index) is applied. Further, if a production, whose left-hand side is '$\alpha\ x\ \beta$', is applicable to a word $w$ containing more than one occurrence of $x$, then the production is applied to the leftmost $x$ in the string $w$.

**Mathematical induction** It is a method of mathematical proof typically used to demonstrate that a given statement $S(n)$ is true for all values of $n$.

**Mealy machine** A Mealy machine is an FSM whose output depends on the current state as well as the input symbol read.

**Moore machine** A Moore machine is an FSM whose output depends only on the current state of the machine.

**Multi-stack TM** In a multi-stack TM, the symbols to the left of the head of the TM can be stored onto one stack, while the symbols on the right of the head can be placed on the other stack. On each stack, the symbols closer to the TM's head are placed closer to the top of the stack.

**Multi-tape TM** Multi-tape TMs are similar to single-tape machines, but have a constant *k* number of independent tapes with their own read/write heads. The TM has complete and independent control over all the heads; any of these can move and read/write their own tapes.

**Multi-track TM** A multi-track TM is a specific type of multi-tape TM. In a *k*-track TM, one head reads and writes on all tracks simultaneously. This is equivalent to the standard single-tape TM, except that it reads/writes *k* symbols at one go.

**Non-deterministic algorithm** If we allow an algorithm to contain operations, whose result is not uniquely determined but is limited to a finite set of possibilities, then such an algorithm is said to be non-deterministic. A deterministic interpretation of a non-deterministic algorithm can be made by allowing unbounded parallel operations. This means, many instances of the same operations execute at the same time (*multi-tasking*).

**Non-deterministic finite automata (NFA) with $\epsilon$-transitions** NFA with $\epsilon$-transitions is an FA that possibly performs transition to one of the multiple next states upon reading an input symbol or '$\epsilon$' (empty string). This is also a possibilistic machine.

**Non-deterministic pushdown automata (NPDA)** NPDA performs any of the multiple actions for the same input symbol read and same stack symbol that is on top of the stack. You cannot predict the behaviour of NPDA before execution. Hence, it is a possibilistic machine.

**Non-terminal symbols** These are symbols that can be replaced by any terminal symbol(s) and/or by other non-terminal symbol(s) in any derivation process.

**NP-complete problem** A problem *A* is said to be NP-complete if and only if *A* is NP-hard and $A \in [NP]$.

**NP-hard problem** A problem *A* is said to be NP-hard if and only if the satisfiability problem reduces to *A*.

**NP-type problem** If there is no polynomial time algorithm to solve a problem, then the problem can be classified as an *NP-type* problem. NP-type problems are also known as *intractable* problems.

**Ogden's lemma** It is a stronger version of pumping lemma for CFLs named after William F. Ogden. It differs from the pumping lemma by allowing us to focus on any *n* distinguished (or marked) positions of a string *z*, and guaranteeing that the strings to be pumped have distinguished (or marked) positions between 1 and *n*.

**Operator precedence parser** It is a type of shift-reduce parser, which handles a small class of parsers that use the precedence and associativity relations among operators for parsing.

**Output alphabet ($\Delta$)** Output alphabet is a finite set of output symbols. The FSM uses the symbols from the output alphabet to generate the output.

**P-type problem** A problem, whose solution can be given using a polynomial time algorithm, which means, the function $f(n)$ representing the computing time of a problem is a polynomial, then the problem is called a *P-type* problem. P-type problems are also known as efficiently solvable or *tractable* problems.

**Parser** A parser is a program that takes any list of tokens (generated by the lexical analyzer) as input and tries to formulate the sentences using CFG rules. If the sentence can be formulated using the CFG, it is considered to be syntactically correct; else, the parser generates specific error messages. A parser is one of phases of the compiler.

**Partial recursive function** If $f(i_1, i_2, \ldots, ik)$ is not defined for all values of arguments $i_1, \ldots, ik$, then *f* is said to be a partial recursive function. In other words, a function $f(i_1, \ldots, ik)$ computed by a TM, which may or may not halt on a given input, is said to be a partial recursive function. Partial recursive functions are analogous to recursively enumerable languages.

**Post–Markov–Thue (PMT) system** A PMT system is a symbol manipulation system, which does the same job as a TM and can be formalized as a finite set of productions termed as productions systems. Post, Markov, and Thue are the three scientists who devised the formalism of the PMT system; it defines an algorithm as a set of rules that transform a given initial string of symbols from a given alphabet set $\Sigma$ into another string of symbols over the same alphabet set. The initial string of symbols, which gets transformed into a new string, is called an axiom; it is analogous to the initial configuration of a TM.

**Post canonical system (PCS)** In a PMT system, if the productions in the rule set $P$ contains only constant strings over $\Sigma$, then that PMT system is called a post canonical system (PCS). In order to generate the class of rich and useful theorems or rich class of languages, the alphabet set $\Sigma$ is not sufficient and has to be extended to $\Sigma'$, which includes additional or auxiliary symbols.

**Post's correspondence problem** Let $A = w_1, w_2, \ldots, w_k$, and $B = x_1, x_2, \ldots, x_k$ be strings over some alphabet $\Sigma$. Post's correspondence problem (PCP) is to find the correspondence sequence of integers, $i_1$, $i_2$, …, $i_m$, for $m \geq 1$ such that: $w_{i1}, w_{i2}, \ldots, w_{im} = x_{i1}, x_{i2}, \ldots, x_{im}$. The sequence, '$i_1$, $i_2$, …, $i_m$' is considered as the solution for the PCP instance. Each PCP instance is constituted by some set of values for $A$ and $B$.

**Power set** The power set of a set $A$ is the set of all subsets of $A$, including $A$ itself and the empty set $\phi$. It is written as $2^A$.

**Propositional formula** A *formula* in propositional calculus is an expression that can be constructed using variables, their negations, and the operators $\bigwedge$ (and) and $\bigvee$ (or). For example, $(x_1 \bigvee x_2)$ and $(\bar{x}_2 \bigwedge x_3) \bigvee (x_4 \bigvee \bar{x}_1)$ are formulae.

**Pumping lemma** Pumping lemma for CFLs suggest finding some pattern near the middle of the string that can be pumped (or repeated) in order to describe the CFL. If such a property can be found for a given language $L$, then $L$ is considered as a CFL; otherwise $L$ is not a CFL. Pumping lemma can thus be used to check whether or not a given language is a CFL.

**Pushdown automata (PDA)** PDA is the mathematical model of PDM.

**Pushdown stack memory machine (PDM)** A PDM is a dynamic computational model with finite number of states and an external stack as an infinite memory. It performs transitions based on the symbol read and the topmost symbol on the stack.

**Recursive descent parser (RDP)** It is a type of top-down parser that needs no backtracking. This parser makes use of recursive procedures to validate the input for correctness.

**Recursive languages** This is a sub-class of recursively enumerable languages. Recursive languages are the languages that are accepted by at least one TM that halts on all inputs. A TM $M$ either reaches the 'accept halt' state if the input belongs to $L(M)$, or reaches the 'reject halt' state if the input does not belong to $L(M)$. Recursive languages belong to the solvable class of problems.

**Recursively enumerable language** The language that is accepted by a TM is called recursively enumerable language. If $L(M)$ is such a language, and if $w$ is any string in $L(M)$, then $M$ eventually halts on input $w$; but if the input string belongs to $\sim L(M)$—the complement of the set $L(M)$—then the TM $M$ might fail to halt on this input. Recursively enumerable languages belong to the semi-solvable class of problems.

**Reducibility** Let $A_1$ and $A_2$ be problems such that $A_1$ *reduces* to $A_2$ (written as $A_1 \propto A_2$) if and only if it is possible to solve $A_1$ using a deterministic polynomial time algorithm with the help of a deterministic algorithm that solves $A_2$ in polynomial time.

**Regular expression (RE)** The languages accepted by FA are described or represented by simple expressions called regular expressions.

**Regular grammar (type-3)** In this type of grammar, the following restrictions are imposed on the type of productions:

1. The left-hand side of each product should contain only one non-terminal.
2. The right-hand side can contain at the most one non-terminal symbol, which is allowed to appear as the rightmost or the leftmost symbol.

**Regular language (or regular set)** Regular language is the language that is accepted by any FA.

**Relation** A binary relation is defined as:

$$ {}_A R_B = \{(a, b) \mid a \in A \text{ and } b \in B\}, $$

where, set $A$ is the *domain* set and set $B$ is the *range* set.

**Rice's theorem** Rice's theorem states that every non-trivial property of the RE languages is undecidable. The essence of the theorem is that any problem that requires determining a property of the language recognized by a given TM is undecidable.

**Right-linear grammar** This is a type of regular grammar. The allowed forms of the productions are: '$A \to wB$' and '$A \to w$', where, $A$ and $B$ are non-terminals and $w$ is a string of terminals. The rule '$S \to \epsilon$' is allowed only if the start symbol $S$ does not appear on the right-hand side of any production.

**Rightmost derivation** If at each step in a derivation, a production is applied to the rightmost variable (or non-terminal), then the derivation is called rightmost derivation.

**Satisfiability problem** It is often written in capitals, or abbreviated as SAT. Satisfiability is the problem of determining if the variables of a given Boolean formula can be assigned in such a way as to make the formula evaluate to true.

**Semi-solvable problem** If there is a TM, which, when applied to any problem, always eventually terminates when the answer is 'yes', but may or may not terminate when the answer is 'no', we call the problem semi-solvable or partially solvable.

**Set closure** In terms of concatenation, closure of a set is defined as $S^* = S^0 \cup S^1 \cup S^2 \ldots$

Set closure always generates an infinite set.

**Set complement** The complement of any set $A$ is defined as $A' = U - A$.

**Set concatenation** Concatenation of two sets $A$ and $B$ is defined as:

$A \cdot B = \{x \mid x = ab, \forall a \in A \text{ and } \forall b \in B\}$

Every string of set $A$ is concatenated with each string in set $B$.

**Set difference** The difference of two sets is defined as

$$A - B = \{x \mid x \in A \text{ and } x \notin B\},$$

or $A - B = A - (A \cap B)$

It includes exactly those elements in $A$ that are not present in set $B$.

**Set intersection** The intersection of two sets is defined as

$A \cap B = \{x \mid x \in A \text{ and } x \in B)$

An intersection is essentially the list of elements that exist in both the sets.

**Set union** The union of two set sets is defined as

$A \cup B = \{x \mid x \in A \text{ or } x \in B)$

The union of two sets includes elements from both the sets.

**Set** A set is a collection of well-defined and distinct objects. These objects or entities in the set are called the *members* (or *elements*) of the set.

**Solvable problem** If there is a TM, which, when applied to any problem, always eventually terminates with a 'yes' or 'no' answer, we call the problem solvable.

**Stack alphabet (Γ)** A finite set of stack symbols. It is the set from where the symbols are chosen to be pushed onto the stack by the PDA. In case of a PDA, stack alphabet and input alphabet may be distinct sets.

**Stack** A stack is a data structure that operates on the principle of last-in-first-out (LIFO). Symbols are pushed onto the top of the stack and only those symbols that are on the top of the stack can be popped.

**State equivalence** Two or more states are said to be *equivalent states* if they have the same transitions on the same input symbol, and this is true for all the transitions; note that such states should be of the same type, that is, they should both be either final or non-final states.

**String (or word)** A string is defined as a finite sequence of symbols over a given alphabet.

**Subset** If every member of set $A$ is a member of set $B$, then $A$ is said to be a subset of $B$. We write this as $A \subseteq B$. Here, set $B$ is called the *superset* of set $A$.

**Symbol** A symbol is a user-defined entity, which is analogous to a point in geometry. A language designer can choose the symbols (or characters) he/she wishes. Strings are composed of symbols.

**Tape alphabet (Γ)** Tape alphabet is a finite set of tape symbols. It is the set from which the symbols are chosen to be written onto the tape by the TM. In case of a TM, the tape alphabet and input alphabet are the same, except for the blank character $\not{b}$; that is, $\Sigma = \{\Gamma - \not{b}\}$.

**Terminal symbols** Terminals are symbols that can appear in any of the input streams being parsed.

**Top-down parser** This type of parser begins with the start symbol of the grammar and reconstructs the statement that needs to be analyzed for correctness. In a way, it tries to derive the statement using the grammar. If it can derive the statement, the statement is considered to be syntactically correct; else, it is considered to be incorrect.

**Total recursive function** If $f(i_1, i_2, \ldots, i_k)$ is defined for all values of arguments $i_1, \ldots, i_k$, then $f$ is said to be a total recursive function. These total recursive functions correspond to the recursive languages, since they are computed by a TM that always halts.

**Tree** A tree is a digraph with the following properties:

- There exists one vertex called the *root* vertex, that has no predecessor, and from which, there is a path to every other vertex in the graph.
- Each vertex other than the root has exactly one predecessor.
- The successors of each vertex are ordered from the left.

**Turing machine (TM)** A TM is a computational model that can be used to solve any problem that has an algorithmic solution. Any problem for which we cannot build a TM is said to be unsolvable.

**Two-way finite automata (2FA)** 2FA is an FA that can read the input in either of the directions, that is, from left to right as well as from right to left.

**Unit production** Unit production is a production of the form '$A \to B$', where $A$ and $B$ are both non-terminals. These should be eliminated, as these unnecessarily add one insignificant step in any derivation process.

**Universal language** The language accepted by the universal Turing machine (UTM) is called universal language ($L_u$), and is defined as: $L_u = L(U)$, where $U$ is the UTM; $L_u$ is recursively enumerable, but not recursive.

**Universal set** A set that encompasses all possible sets that can exist is known as the universal set, and is denoted by $U$.

**Universal Turing machine (UTM)** A UTM is a TM, which is capable of simulating any TM $T$, given the following information in available onto its tape:

- The description of $T$ in terms of its SFM (in the *program area* of the tape).
- The initial configuration of $T$ with processing data (input string) to be fed to $T$ (in the *data area* of the tape).
- The UTM requires an *imitation algorithm* (simulating logic in the form of its SFM) in order to correctly interpret the rules of operation given in the SFM for $T$.

**Unrestricted grammar (type-0)** There are no restrictions on the productions of a grammar of this type. This type of grammar permits productions of the form '$\alpha \to \beta$', where $\alpha \neq \epsilon$; and $\alpha$ and $\beta$ are sentential forms, that is, any combinations of any number of terminals and non-terminals, that is, $\alpha$, $\beta \subset (V \cup T)^*$, but $\alpha \neq \epsilon$, because there must be something to be replaced by the right-hand side of the production.

**Unsolvable problem** If there is no TM, which, when applied to a problem, eventually terminates with the answer 'yes', we call the problem unsolvable.

**$\epsilon$-Production** $\epsilon$-productions have the form '$A \to \epsilon$'. One should avoid such productions unless the language contains the empty string, $\epsilon$.

# Bibliography

Hopcroft, John E., Rajeev Motwani, and Jeffrey D. Ullman, *Introduction to Automata Theory, Languages, and Computation*, Second edition, Addison-Wesley, Baltimore, 2001.

Hopcroft, John E., and Jeffrey D. Ullman, *Introduction to Automata Theory, Languages, and Computation*, Addison-Wesley Series in Computer Science. Addison-Wesley Publishing Company, Boston, 1979.

Cohen, Daniel E., *Computability and Logic (Mathematics and its Applications)*, Ellis Horwood Ltd, Chichester, 1987.

Cohen, Daniel I.A., *Introduction to Computer Theory*, Second edition, Volume 1997, John Wiley & Sons Inc., New York, 2003.

Martin, John C., *Introduction to Languages and the Theory of Computation*, McGraw-Hill Higher Education, Third edition, New York, 2003.

Aho, A.V., R. Sethi, J.D. Ullman, *Compilers: Principles, Techniques, and Tools*, Addison-Wesley, Massachusetts, 1986.

Aho, A.V. and J.D. Ullman, *Principles of Compiler Design*, Addison-Wesley, New South Wales, 1977.

Krishnamurthy, E.V., *Introductory Theory of Computer Science*, Affiliated East-West Press, New Delhi, 1984.

Gries, David, *The Science of Programming*, Narosa Publishing House, New Delhi, 1981.

Weizenbaum, Joseph, *Computer Power and Human Reason: From Judgement to Calculation*, W.H. Freeman & Co., New York, 1976.

Davis, M., *Computability and Unsolvability*, McGraw-Hill, reprinted Dover, New York, 1982.

Powers, Shelley, Jerry Peek, Tim O'Reilly, Mike Loukides, *UNIX Power Tools*, Third edition, O'Reilly Media Inc., California, 2002.

## WEB RESOURCES

A.M. Turing, 'On Computable Numbers, With an Application to the Entscheidungs Problem', http://www.cs.virginia.edu/~robins/Turing_Paper_1936.pdf, 1936, last accessed on 24 January 2013.

http://en.wikipedia.org/wiki/Main_Page, last accessed on 24 January 2013.

Barker-Plummer, David, 'Turing Machines', The Stanford Encyclopedia of Philosophy, http://plato.stanford.edu/archives/win2012/entries/turing-machine/, 2012 edition, last accessed on 24 January 2013.

Kulkarni, Vivek, Article on 'Looking Back: Alan Turing—The Father of Computer Science', CSI Communications, 2012, http://www.csi-india.org/c/document_library/get_file?uuid=43b1e947-fc82-4dc8-a385-f4834cc7f69a&groupId=10616, 2013, last accessed on 24 January 2013.

Kulkarni, Vivek, Lecture on 'Alan Turing's Theory of Computation', Persistent Systems Ltd., http://www.youtube.com/watch?v=5_p3DJcjDTc&list=UUcHUpqmNBz3lkTEbIVT_4mQ&index=1&feature=plcp, 2012, last accessed on 24 January 2013.

# Index

# Related Titles

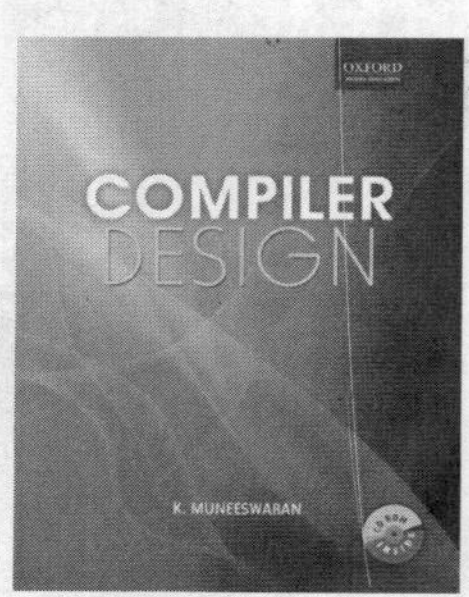


**Compiler Design**
9780198066644

**K. Muneeswaran,** Head of the Department, Computer Science and Engineering, Mepco Schlenk Engineering College, Sivakasi

*Compiler Design* is designed as a textbook for undergraduate and postgraduate students of engineering (computer science and information technology) and computer applications. It seeks to provide a thorough understanding of the design and implementation aspects of a compiler.

**Key Features**

- Contains a dedicated chapter on compiler writing tools, including Lex, Yacc, JavaCC, and ANTLR
- Provides numerous objective type questions with answers, review questions, and exercises at the end of every chapter, graded as per Bloom's Taxonomy principles
- Includes appendices on the parsing of C language using tools such as Lex, Yacc, and JavaCC, as well as additional solved problems and five model question papers

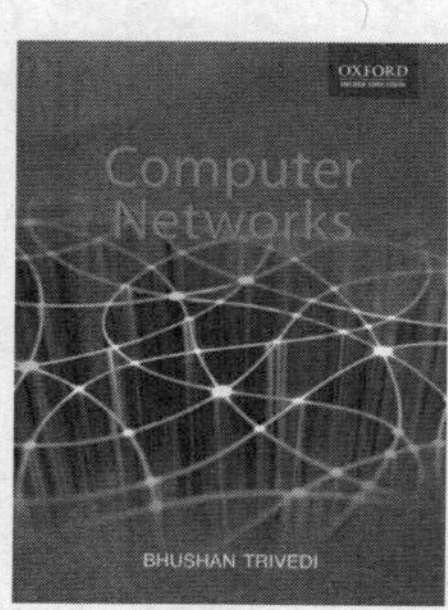


**Computer Networks**
9780198066774

**Bhushan Trivedi,** Director, MCA Programme, GLS Institute of Computer Technology, Ahmedabad

*Computer Networks* is designed to serve as a textbook for undergraduate students of computer science engineering as well as those pursuing MCA and IT. Following the tried-and-tested layered approach, it gives equal weight to all the network layers and their protocols.

**Key Features**

- Incorporates the layered approach with emphasis on TCP/IP model, Internet, and Ethernet technologies
- Explains several new topics such as Bluetooth, IPv6, QoS provided by WiMax, and the use of scalable OFDM in 802.16

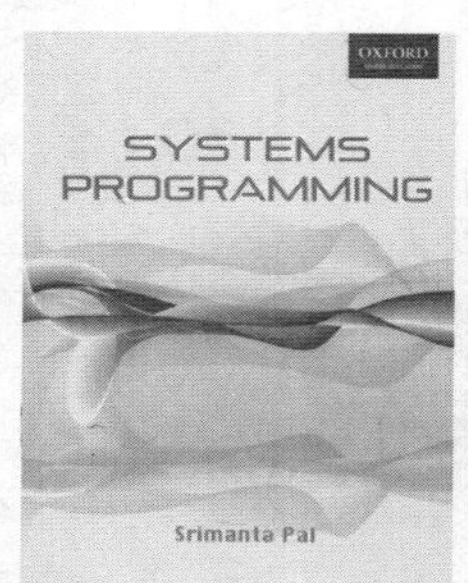


**Systems Programming**
9780198070887

**Srimanta Pal,** Professor, Electronics and Communication Sciences Unit, Indian Statistical Institute (ISI), Kolkata

*Systems Programming* is a textbook designed for undergraduate students of information technology and computer science engineering. Comprehensive in its coverage, the book aims to provide an understanding of the design of assemblers, loaders, linkers, and macro processors.

**Key Features**

- Presents real-life analogies to clarify the concepts discussed
- Includes separate chapters on debuggers, editors, system administration, and a detailed coverage of operating systems
- Contains plenty of programming examples, algorithms, and conceptual as well as analytical exercises
- Contains an appendix comprising instruction sets for SIC/XE machine, Intel 8086, and MIPS

**Other Related Titles**

9780195696561 Datta: *Software Engineering: Concepts and Applications*

9780195694840 Jain: *Software Engineering: Principles and Practices*

9780198079064 Senthil Kumar, Saravanan, Jeevananthan, and Shah: *Microprocessors and Interfacing*

9780198066477 Senthil Kumar, Saravanan, and Jeevananthan: *Microprocessors and Microcontrollers*

9780198061847 Chauhan: *Software Testing: Principles and Practices*

9780195671544 Padhy: *Artificial Intelligence and Intelligent Systems*

9780198068914 Raj Kamal: *Mobile Computing*, 2/e